THE
LONG HAUL
WEST

The Great Canal Era, 1817–1850

MADELINE SADLER WAGGONER

G. P. PUTNAM'S SONS

NEW YORK

To my beloved father and mother, children of pioneers. To E. C. W. for his kind and generous support. And to Bob and Bev, Jim and Pat, for their quiet faith.

CONTENTS

*Sixteen pages of illustrations
will be found following page 160.*

THE LONG HAUL WEST

CHAPTER ONE

A HANKERIN' FOR WESTERIN'

THE winds blew icy across the salt marshes of Cape Cod where two men stood huddled together, hugging their greatcoats close, each turning a defensive shoulder against the sleet. They were trying, in spite of the weather, to give their full attention to the narrow neck of land at the base of the Cape upon which they stood. The fact that an eight-mile waterway cut across the strip at this point would make the sea route from Boston to New Amsterdam materially shorter and safer was the subject under discussion—with due apologies to the good Lord for presuming to correct his oversight.

But the bitter winds grew more fierce, howling across the desolate waste. And the slanting sleet cut cruelly into their faces, soon forcing the two men to hustle rheumatic bones home to warm firesides where one of them, Sam Sewell, reached down a diary from his library shelf, flexed a chilled hand until it could hold a quill pen, then recorded the day's happenings.

"Mr. Smith of Sandwich rode with me and showed me the place some had thought to cut, for to make a passage from the south sea to the north."

The day was October 26, 1676. And this was one of the two earliest known suggestions for an American canal. But it would be 1914—another two hundred and thirty-eight years—before the dream of a waterway at this point could be realized. . . .

❖   ❖   ❖

The winds blew cold and the snows were knee-deep west of Cumberland when a young man named George Washington guided the British General Edward Braddock westward across the steep ridges and deep valleys of the Alleghenies, along a crude and primitive trace which he himself and the explorer Christopher Gist had hacked out of the wilderness two winters before. That earlier expedition had cost Gist a half-dozen frozen toes and ten frozen fingers during the thousand-mile trek through the forests. The present crossing was even more difficult, for this time the trace had to be widened sufficiently to allow passage of military supplies across Savage Mountain, Little Meadows, Negro Mountain, Great Crossing, Great Meadows—but here they were halted by advancing enemy troops, and the road making had to cease.

"Steep rugged Hills were to be clomb, headlong Declivities to be descended, down which Cannon and Wagons were lowered with Block and Tackles," wrote Washington. "We were 4 Days gett'g 12 Miles."

The year was 1755, early in the French and Indian War. It would be 1817—another sixty-two years before this mountain trace could be sufficiently improved to allow passage of a team and covered wagon, but this was the beginning of the first trail across the Alleghenies that could in any sense be called a road. . . .

The weather was warm for May when the Baltimore and Ohio opened her first section of railroad, a thirteen-mile strip that ran from Baltimore to Ellicott's Mills, Maryland. There was still some doubt as to what use these tracks would be put to. For they had been so long delayed in the laying, that the original plan had been concerned with nothing more than a new method of speeding horse-drawn carriages by the use of rails. But now with Robert Fulton's steam engine the center of experiment in half-a-dozen back yards, there seemed to be a possibility that locomotives could be made more powerful than the horse. Peter Cooper was one of the experimenters who believed this and was therefore willing to race his diminutive, steam-puffing Tom Thumb against any horse in the country.

Such a meet was arranged the following August, with a stagecoach company furnishing a powerful gray steed to support the negative side of the argument. Although the day chosen turned out to be the hottest of the summer, the entire thirteen-mile course from Baltimore to Ellicott's Mills was crowded with spectators by breakfast time. The excited throng eagerly placed bets while they speculatively eyed the new metal-capped, oaken rails and the queer, steam-puffing "tea-kettle-on-a-track," said to be powerful enough to haul twenty-four persons six miles in an hour and a half, before it must halt for additional wood and water.

The race is a matter of record. And the fact that railroading got a monstrous setback when the horse won, is due to the circumstance that almost no one believed that a slipping belt could be the cause of a locomotive slowing down to a stop—if the power of steam was all it had been cracked up to be.

The Tom Thumb was the first American-made locomotive. The year was 1830. It would be two decades before transportation by steam would be widely accepted. . . .

American trails. American canals. American railroads. Following one another down through the years, ever improving, expanding, multiplying; unconsciously making ready for that time when they must support the greatest migration in history, the so-called Big Push, a movement so mammoth as to transport people of many nations by the hundreds of thousands, across the Alleghenies into that vast American interior originally known as the Far West, later to be known as the Midlands, eventually to be called the Middle West.

The tremendous importance of this migration lay in the fact

that it was providentially so well timed in history, for it enabled this great territory to serve as a necessary springboard from which the United States as a nation could venture forth to fulfill her destiny. For if the young Republic had not yet conquered the Allegheny Mountains and found a way through the great wilderness of the Ohio Valley, certainly she could never have held unto herself, against Great Britain and Mexico, those vast regions between the Rocky Mountains and the Pacific Ocean known vaguely as the Oregon Country and the Mexican Territory.

It will be the object of this book to set forth some of the personal experiences of those pioneers who made up the push westward, some internationally famous, some quite unheard of, though all were vitally important in building and sustaining the mass movement through the years of decision. Their experiences are laid before the reader in order that he may better appreciate and enjoy his American heritage, understanding at what cost it has come down to him. Any story of the great migration and its ramifications must also include those factors that made travel possible—the pioneer's trails, his canals, his railroads. And the greatest of these by far were his canals, especially the beloved Old Erie because it provided the missing link of travel between the Atlantic Ocean and the Great Lakes, thereby helping to bring about the success of the Big Push. In fact, even the timing of the Canal Era was perfect. For it came into full existence during that critical though brief period after the Cumberland Road's seven-year heyday had passed, and before the pioneer railroads were sufficiently advanced to carry the load. As we shall see.

It was far from new—this notion that man might gash for himself a currentless ribbon of water across his land whereupon he could pole or tow his boat with equal ease in either direction. The Ancient Babylonians were using a crude type of artificial waterway hundreds of years before the birth of Christ, and many others had followed over the centuries.

The idea was not even new in the United States when the Erie Canal providentially was completed at the opportune moment to change the course of an empire. One hundred and fifty years earlier, the first two documented suggestions for American canals had been made, strangely enough, almost simultaneously although they came at opposite ends of this country. In 1673, a scant three years before Sam Sewell and his friend Mr. Smith braved the blizzard to examine the possibilities of a Cape Cod waterway, Louis Joliet, far out in the Western wilderness exploring the shores of Lake Michigan with Père Marquette, had offered a similar solution for Western transportation. It was recorded during the following year by another Jesuit priest, Father Dablon.

"According to the researches and explorations of Joliet, we can easily go to Florida in boats by a very good navigation with slight improvements. There will be but one canal to make, and that by cutting only one half-league of prairie from the lake of the Illinois (Lake Michigan) into the St. Louis River (the Illinois) which empties into the Mississippi."

LaSalle also mentioned this possibility. And as early as 1795, the Indians were wheedled into a deal whereby they ceded to the whites the necessary sections of land. But even after young America had the right-of-way in her pocket, she did little with it, for although this was one of the first canals to be suggested in the new country, it was one of the last to be built. Yet it had sounded so simple—"but one canal to make, and that by cutting only one-half league of prairie."

The excellent proposal for a Cape Cod Canal lay completely shelved, after Sewell's visit, to be revived in the deliberations of New Englanders only three times during the next two and a third centuries. The first of these occurred in 1697 and the second in 1776 when the General Court of Massachusetts twice revived the issue by appointing committees to view the ground in question, but nothing of consequence was accomplished on either occasion. A third attempt to do something about a Cape Cod Canal came in 1824 when an eight-mile survey was made here—even then by the National Government —which was also due to die of inertia except for brief reviews of it in the 1870's. During this first survey, however, the Bay State was admittedly trying to whip up a little local interest on the subject because of a letter signed "Shadrock" that had appeared in a newspaper called the *Universal Traveller*.

"Is old Massachusetts in her palsied dotage? Is her sun of prosperity . . . to rise no more? This sun with increasing splendor is now irradiating the hills of the Hudson and the fertile vales of New York. Where are the thousand ships of the Bay State, her accumulated wealth of two centuries? Has the building of a few roads and the cutting of one *ditch* of inconsiderable distance satisfied her ambition and put her 'at ease in her possessions'?"

The bitterness of the attack is understandable, for it was already evident that the Erie Canal had robbed New England of much of her shipping trade. But the letter accomplished little, as did that first Cape Cod survey. For it was 1914—long after the glorious Canal Era had come and gone and been quite forgotten—before ever a ship made its way across this narrow neck of land. Yet it must be acknowledged, in spite of all the delays, that here in the salt marshes men had dreamed of building an artificial waterway to solve a transportation problem when the canal idea was new and untried in America. There is even a strong chance that this plan may actually have lain in the minds of New Englanders before Joliet dreamed his dream on the shores of Lake Michigan.

During this same period, discussion about a third canal, a waterway between the Chesapeake and Delaware Bays, waxed loud enough to get itself recorded in 1679, although it was a full century later before so much as a survey of this project was attempted. Then the guns of the American Revolution halted the project, and the idea went the way of the wind for another thirty-five years before a second survey was started, only to drag along some sixty years in the making.

Meanwhile William Penn, in 1690, was first to suggest a fourth canal, "a union between the Delaware and the Susquehannagh . . . following the common course of the Indians with their skins and furrs." And at this spot in 1762—seventy-odd years later—an American canal for the first time came out of the dream stage and a survey was actually completed, thus preceding the Chesapeake survey by two years. But here too the Revolution intervened, and another thirty years whistled across the wilderness before anything more was done with it.

The next canal suggested in America was one which would connect Lake Erie with Lake Ontario, to avoid the great portage then necessary at Niagara Falls. Young America sanctioned it without benefit of funds, the French admired it, and eventually the British built it.

There were other plans, the most extensive being a proposition by George Washington "to connect the Atlantic Seaboard with the Mississippi Valley by way of either the Patowmack or Kanawha with the James River." It was the ambition of his entire life, and he actively campaigned for it from the time when he was a young and enthusiastic twenty-two-year-old surveyor trying to convince Governor Dinwiddie of the great need of opening up the West, until the very time of his death. For thirty years his efforts in its behalf were tireless and fruitless. Just before becoming President, he wrote to Edmund Randolph, almost sadly, "The great Object for which I wish to see the Navigation of the Rivers James and Patowmack extended is to connect the Western Territory with the Atlantic States; all Others with me are secondary."

To this end, as a result of his laying before Virginia's Governor Harrison that year the first general outline of a system of public improvements to appear in this country, two canal organizations were finally formed—the James River Company and the Patowmack Company. And during the following summer at roasting-ear time, the latter started its digging for a canal at Great Falls, just above the site chosen for the national capital. But this channel was not completed until 1802, following a desolate sixteen-year stretch of hardship and bankruptcy. Simultaneously, work on the James River project ran a similar gamut of troubles. It was ten years before the latter canal was able to carry freight down to Richmond, although parts of it were in use earlier.

However, during all of these heartbreaking delays on one waterway after another, there were three small American canals that were actually finished and put into full operation. There was the Carondelet, called Old Canal Basin, which edged away from New Orleans' iron-lace balconies for a two-mile run into the country. There was the little South Hadley, up in Massachusetts, another two-miler. And there was the Dismal Swamp Canal, bordering North Carolina and Virginia, which connected the lower end of Chesapeake Bay with the Pasquotank River. To one of these three goes the honor of being the first American canal to be put to practical use, although all three were open by 1794. Small as was this beginning, now at last—one hundred and twenty-one years after Joliet's dream—America's man-made waterways had passed out of the mists of imagination into the realm of reality.

There were others that followed shortly. Two on the Susquehanna—one on the Maryland side at Port Deposit and one on the Pennsylvania side at Conewago Falls. There was a third in New England on the Merrimac at Patopwick (Pawtucket) Falls. There was a fourth on the Connecticut at Montague Falls, and a fifth in Vermont at Bellows Falls. Although all of these were very short, less than a mile to three miles in length, all were important locally and tremendous morale builders nationally.

Meanwhile, by the beginning of the nineteenth century, there came two waterways of greater ambition and magnitude. In South Carolina near Charleston grew the Santee and Cooper Canal, named for the rivers it connected. It was built primarily to provide a better outlet to Charleston markets for South Carolina's rice, indigo, and cotton. It was eight years under construction and cost the good people of that state a cool three-quarters of a million dollars for a twenty-two mile ditch.

In New England the Middlesex Canal, stretching from Boston Harbor to a point on the Merrimac near present-day Lowell, was planned to replace the difficult and expensive wagon-trail route by which New Hampshire's timber and granite had to travel to reach Boston's markets. This twenty-seven-mile strip, even with diggers fighting one another for the chance to work from sunup to sundown for eight dollars a month, had soon cost more than a half-million dollars. This was a staggering sum in a sparsely settled territory, but who was worried? Certainly not the Bay State farmer as he filled his yard-of-clay pipe from his sheep's-bladder tobacco pouch, and in its smoke saw this canal extended to open a route by way of the St. Lawrence River all the way through to Montreal and Quebec. By holy dang, this was an exciting prospect.

But by the time the Middlesex had been maintained through fifteen years of operation, her cost had doubled. Stock which had originally sold at twenty-five dollars per share had risen —and with it the pulse of the people—to five hundred dollars per share in the first ten years. Then, as a quarter-century rolled past before a single dividend had been paid, while an even hundred extra assessments had struck as unpredictably as lightning, shareholders found that each single share had now cost $1,455.25. And Montreal and Quebec were as far away as ever.

Nor were her financial troubles the only problem for the Middlesex. "The science of engineering," wrote her manager, Caleb Eddy, "was almost unknown to anyone in this part of the country." This was a generous understatement of the facts, as was soon evident to all, for the project was first placed in the hands of a builder named Thompson, the best the district had to offer but admittedly no engineer. Considering the lack of technical knowledge in the entire country—let alone in this little neck of the woods—there should have been little surprise when his calculations resulted in some astounding figures. For instance, after many days of complicated computations, Thompson was ready to announce that the ascent from the Medford River to the Concord was 68½ feet, whereas it turned out to be 104 feet. He also concluded that the ascent from the Concord River at Billerica to the Merrimac at Chelmsford would require a 16½-foot climb, whereas it turned out to have a 25-foot drop.

After considerable more of his troubled fumbling, the canal commissioners called in an English engineer named Weston to correct the errors. Now the work proceeded on a more level keel, though not without difficulties, for the lack of proper machinery was also appalling. In fact, all channels still had to be dug the hard way—plow, pick and shovel, wheelbarrow, and horse-drawn wagon—a method which would not change for many decades.

Blasting was equally crude, there being no easier way than hand drilling to make the powder holes, and old-fashioned black powder to produce the blast—the "blowing," they called it. The procedure was simple. After a sizable hole had been drilled and stuffed with the powder, clay was tamped in, leaving a small opening for priming powder and a fuse, the latter being merely a twist of paper soaked in saltpeter. Many were the casualties therefrom. According to one engineer's report concerning the sudden disappearance of two blasters, "One run off, the other Blown up. We therefore was Obliged to have two new hands to Blowing and there was much attention gave to them least Axedents should happen."

The story of this Middlesex Canal, soon known as the "Middlesex Folly," furnished an example that might well have killed canal building in a less courageous nation, since it came as a climax to the heartbreaks that had ridden almost every waterway so far attempted. Instead, it seemed merely to inspire other builders. For they had courage, these people of young America. It was almost as if they could feel the pull of those early fighting words of Governor Bradford to the Pilgrim colonists: "Yea, though ye lose your lives in this action, ye might have comfort in the same. All great and honorable actions are accompanied with great difficulties and must therefore be overcome with answerable courages."

Courage they had, and comfort they found, a new comfort born of pride. Pride in their young nation, pride in themselves, pride even in this little Middlesex Canal, folly or otherwise. True, she did little toward opening the wilderness to the west or to the north. But what a grand sight she was, this thirty-foot strip of water, stretching like a silver ribbon for twenty-seven miles into the country, lifting herself by nineteen locks, fighting her way across the current of the roaring Concord while her tow mules crossed on a floating towpath, carrying boats large enough to haul twenty-five tons at a lick! True, she had cost them a pretty penny, but was she not worth it when you considered her great rafts floating down from New Hampshire with pine and maple and oak for a man's home and fireplace, fruits for his table, and granite for his tombstone? Surely there was not another like her in all the land.

Or to go a step further in this matter of national pride, were not all American canals now surpassing anything Europe had yet devised, thanks to a few elegant tricks of sheer Yankee genius? For instance, there was the so-called "Inclined Plane," over on the little South Hadley. Here was an arrangement whereby it was possible to portage an entire boat up a hillside —including passengers, crew, and cargo—taking her off a low canal and setting her upon a higher one or upon another low one on the other side of the mountain. The system was unique. First a specially constructed boxcar was backed into the lower channel, where its endgates were dropped so that a canalboat could be floated into it. Next the endgates were closed and part of the water was pumped out, leaving only enough to float the boat. Now the boxcar proceeded slowly, steadily, up the mountainside, borne on three sets of wheels which were graduated in size to enable the car to hold its burden so level that the canaller's wife could proceed with her potato frying— unless the breath-taking view from the hilltop wooed her away.

Power for this gigantic lift was produced by a combination of two sixteen-foot water wheels aided by a series of amazingly smooth planks forming the so-called inclined planes. A fine example of sheer Yankee ingenuity. But it worked! As did the same technique, in reverse, for a descending boat.

It was not without justification that the American of that day was proud of the many wonders he had been able to accomplish. And the additional fact that his canals from New England to New Orleans were struggling toward completion almost simultaneously was kindling an even greater fire in his breast. Poor beyond belief, unschooled for the most part, he was nevertheless beginning to expand with a mighty feeling of national ambition as he watched his horizons push farther back. For as long as there was a frontier, there was always the belief that beyond it lay the Promised Land. So it had always been. The children of Israel braving the wilderness for the land of milk and honey. Columbus venturing the Ocean Sea. The Pilgrims seeking out the new America.

And now, if there was any truth in the tall tales that were coming out of the Far West to make the rounds of taverns and oyster bars from one end of the eastern seaboard to the other, if there was any truth in what they said of the greatness and the richness and the wonder of the land out yonder, he wanted to be a part of it. His blood was hot with restlessness and the longing for new country, for he had inherited the pioneer spirit. It had driven his forefathers from continent to continent, from region to region. At last it had moved them to the very edge of the morning side of the mountains and left them there, wistfully yearning for the sunset side and a way through the wilderness beyond.

His yearning was groping toward an answer. A new light was beginning to dawn as the American turned a speculative eye toward his expanding canals, believing that here at last was the possibility of an answer to his cry for better transportation. Certainly he had no illusions about his roads and trails, for they were still so crude it was necessary to hold the Presidential inauguration four months after the election in order to be certain who had won.

By the turn of the century, the signs of a new era were already evident. Events of national importance were erupting more rapidly than ever before in the history of the young nation. Scarcely was the news of one soul-stirring event digested before another was in the making. Many of these happenings were concerned with the opening of a whole new world west of the Alleghenies, offering a strange but entrancing new kind of life for those who dared venture it. It was queer how often the most unlikely incident had a way of working around to add its own momentum to the great movement.

For instance, take the case of a young New Yorker who had

long been the laughingstock of his townsmen because of the crazy experiments he had been conducting on boats. Then came that day in August, 1807, when a few of his neighbors waited along the banks of the Hudson, primed for another field day of jeering at this young tinkerer who was so bound and determined to make his craft walk upstream against the current. The usual delay had become unusually wearisome, for most of the spectators had gone through this before. Many of them had already deserted to go back to their own pursuits, when suddenly the *Clermont* slipped her cables and began her frantic water-churning. Instantly she was greeted with the usual derisive shouts. But the blue smoke of her wood-fired engine floated gently skyward, and the white puff of her steam continued its strange whistling. And then abruptly she was off, moving out into the current, heading upstream for Albany, disappearing in the distance.

There were few among the watchers who believed that she was making history that day—one hundred and fifty miles in thirty-two hours. Their amazement that she could move at all was complete.

"Fulton's Folly!" they said to one another and shook their heads, wondering. "Fulton's Folly—she worked."

Four years later, out on the frontier at Pittsburgh, another steamboat worked—the first to walk western waters. A spark-shooting, steam-puffing monster churned along the Ohio, sending a frightened throng of spectators up into the trees for safety, a panicked crowd of them onto their knees in prayer, a courageous few into their own boats to follow along in a fine impressive parade, and a thoughtful group home to their farm clearings to ponder on the new way to market.

It was scarcely a year later when a greater happening further readied the path of the Big Push. The War of 1812 started an uphill, downhill fight that ended not only in clearing the seas for American commerce, but also in clearing the western frontier for expansion. It was definitely a matter of world-wide attention when the gallant young nation, not yet thirty years old, dared to set up her twelve little warships against Great Britain's thousand-ship navy. Europe was amazed. England was chagrined. And the United States was carried away with cocky young pride when twenty-eight-year-old Captain Oliver Perry with a handful of farmers turned the tide of war from losses to gain, after fashioning an additional five crude little warships from the green timber of the forests. Perry recorded the results of the ensuing battle on the back of an old envelope:

"We have met the enemy and they are ours . . ."

This Lake Erie encounter, together with William Henry Harrison's victory at the Thames and his Indian treaties, gave the United States what security she still lacked for her Western migration—freedom of the seas, complete control of the Great Lakes, and the undisputed possession of the Northwest Territory. The final encounter of this war, Andrew Jackson's tremendous victory at New Orleans, graphically pointed up the country's desperate need for better communication as well as better transportation, for the Battle of New Orleans was unknowingly fought two weeks after the peace treaty had been signed, making the slaughter of two thousand English lads regrettably unnecessary.

Four years later, a brief skirmish against the Spanish and Indians in the South subdued the red man in that area and paved the way for the purchase of the Floridas from Spain. There now remained no barrier to America's westward expansion from her entire eastern seaboard to the Rockies, except the natural barriers of the Allegheny Mountains and the wilderness—barriers which were still as tremendous as ever.

But equally tremendous was the general outcry for better transportation. Now, agriculture, commerce, and industry were adding their own demands for a better way to market.

Their reasons were excellent. Along the eastern seaboard, many of the new mills and factories that had sprung up to fill wartime needs had shown so much Yankee enterprise that they not only produced goods enough to replace those formerly imported from Europe, but they established a fine export trade as well. In the South, Eli Whitney's cotton gin had placed calico within the reach of every pocketbook, having increased cotton cloth production and decreased its cost. In Pennsylvania, the first arkful of something called anthracite had been loaded at Mauch Chunk and brought laboriously down out of the hills—though few believed there was much future in trying to burn rocks. And on the flatlands west of the Alleghenies, wheat stood a good chance of becoming a profitable commodity, now that England was willing to pay ten dollars a barrel for it—if only it could be exported by a cheaper route than the present long trek down the Ohio and the Mississippi and out through the Gulf. In fact, even the farmers of western York State, Pennsylvania, Maryland, and Virginia found little profit in agriculture, in spite of their shorter hauls, for they were currently paying ten dollars per ton for each hundred miles to market. Daily, from all of these branches of commerce, industry, and agriculture, the hue and cry for better transportation grew louder and more bitter.

But there were other, stronger reasons for the sudden enthusiasm for canal building. There was the pioneer himself, the depth of his desire, the longing of his soul, the sternness of his determination, and the urgency of his needs. Wrote John Randolph in 1813, "In a few years more, those of us who are alive will move to Kaintuck or the Mississippi, where corn can be had for six pence a bushel and pork for a penny a pound. I do not wonder at the rage for emigration. What do the bulk of the people get here that they cannot have there for one-fifth the labor in the Western country?"

He was not alone in his thinking. Hither and yon throughout

the East, underpaid clerks and mill hands were already staring thoughtfully at their meager pennies, gradually reaching the same conclusion. So was the coastal farmer, as he looked to his rocky land at time of plowing, bending his back to carry freshly loosened boulders to a stone-wall border that was already two feet thick. At such a time, poignant was his longing for soil that was rich and deep and black, like that along the Sangamon where, some said, wheat grew seven heads to the stalk. One hundred bushels to the acre. Where even the prairie grass grew so tall a traveler crossing on horseback could be lost to view with only the ripple of grasstops to mark his passing.

Nor was the traditional head of the household alone in his yearnings. His wife, too, was beginning to feel the pull of the West, as she raised weary eyes to the setting sun, wrapped her feverish chapped hands in the cool folds of her apron and remembered what some claimed it was like, yonder in the gentle paradise of the Wabash. Parakeets colored to shame the rainbow. Wild turkey and duck and pigeon so numerous as to dim the sun with their shadow. Rhododendrons that grew taller than a man could stand.

They all understood what hardships lay beyond the Appalachian Ridge, far from their well-built clapboard houses and barns, their well-cleared lands, their comfortably established villages with the white-spired meetinghouses and the crossroads schools. Why then, by the hundreds of thousands, should they now yearn to abandon all of this for a move into the unknown? What was this mysterious might that was engendering a migration so immense as to sweep an alarming portion of them, together with countless Europeans, into the wilderness of the Far West?

Whence, for that matter, had come the wind that blew Boone and Carver and Gist into the valley of the unknown? And whence came that power that drove the earliest settlers beyond the frontiers of Sudbury into the new lands of the Connecticut Valley? Or beyond the settled coast of New Hampshire into the backwoods of Vermont? Or out of the gentle Carolinas and Virginia into the wilderness of Kentucky and Tennessee? Who knew?

Certainly not the present pioneer, for he was seldom given to introspection. The hunger for new land was strong within him and would not be denied. Of that he was certain. He called it the Genesee Fever, or the Western Fever, or the Ohio Fever, or simply a hankerin' for wanderin'. Whatever its name, he knew it to be highly contagious, for when it struck a village it soon reached epidemic proportions, creating a widespread yearning for the Promised Land and a desperate determination to find a way to reach it. Abruptly life had become a thing of high hope and deep despair. At times it looked as if an inland waterway, gashed across the hundreds of miles of forest and through the difficult gaps, might well be the answer. But in the name of common sense, how remote that possibility was, when you considered that after a century and a half of effort, the most hopeful American canal to date was a bankrupt little twenty-seven miler!

Where, then, lay the way across?

CHAPTER TWO

EARLY THRUSTS AND FREQUENT SETBACKS

During these discouraging early years, there came, in 1802, the first bud of a promise for a way across the Alleghenies—not by canal after all, but by mountain trail. And although such a road—when it finally materialized—was destined to carry the burden of western expansion for only seven years, its importance was great, for during that brief span the Big Push at last got under way.

Strangely enough, considering how long a way across the mountain barrier had been sought, the solution came about almost accidentally. It started with a clause concerning a road to lead to the Buckeye Country, contained in the "Enacting Act" that admitted Ohio to the Union. From this beginning grew a movement for a national road, the only attempt to furnish public transportation ever supported by the federal government before modern times. It was to run from Cumberland, head of navigation on the Potomac, to Wheeling on the Ohio River—a scant ninety miles as the buzzard made it, but far enough to conquer the worst of the Alleghenies besides furnishing important water connection at each of its terminals.

The new highway would be officially known as the Cumberland Road, although Westerners were soon calling it the National Road or the United States Road, while over a mug of pumpkin flip in an Eastern taproom it was Uncle Sam's

Pike or simply the Road. There were those who took a dim view of its future under any name, remembering that along this same route at the beginning of the French and Indian War, Washington and all of Braddock's flashy redcoats had been forced by rough terrain to narrow their objective from a broad wagon road to a footpath, even before the Indians halted their progress—as well as the lives of most of them. But those who now favored Uncle Sam's Pike did so with all their hearts, believing that because of it life in America would be changed from a passive existence to a thing of vigorous hurry and glorious push into the Promised Land. Both factions were right. Uncle Sam's Pike was destined for success and doomed to failure.

The route that it would take was to follow faithfully the old trail across the Alleghenies—originally merely a buffalo trace, later blazed by an Indian named Nemacolin, and still later marked for the white man's use by Washington and Gist— except at its western end, where the new road would deviate to wind up at Wheeling in Old Virginia instead of at Fort Pitt (Pittsburgh) as had the wandering bison. Congress had chosen this more difficult pass because a ferry across the Ohio River at this settlement would place a man's feet directly upon Zane's Trace, a crude path gashed through the wilderness diagonally southwest across Ohio to Limestone, Kentucky (Maysville), a short cut that lessened the punishing western trek by a full hundred miles.

The Trace had been sanctioned by Congress in 1796 and completed two years later under the sole sponsorship of a lone, far-sighted, very determined backwoodsman named Ebenezer Zane. Never designed as a wagon road to begin with— although it was the only existing land route through the Northwest Territory—the completed trail was actually little more than a path through the forests, cut only wide enough to admit a man on horseback. Which was sufficient unto the day, the way Zane had it figured, and certainly a vast improvement over its previous existence as a half-lost, brush-choked trace, the width of a naked Indian.

Never surfaced to begin with, by the end of its fifteenth year it was already rated as "intolerable, shocking, wretched and devilish, in fact the worst in the world." Though somewhat widened by this time because of the constant march of west-bound livestock and vehicles, it was still so crude that horses expired on it, axles snapped, and it was said to possess "holes large enough to bury a team." When Bishop Asbury, riding the Methodist circuit, finally hobbled into Chillicothe, "much fatigued, feverish, and with the jaw-ache," he felt it his bounden duty to inform his elders by means of his blackberry-dipped quill pen that his own weakened condition was undoubtedly due to the fact that Zane's Trace was now "a mess of logs, stumps, ruts and bushes."

Yet as such, Zane's cowpath continued in use for another decade, to complete a full quarter-century as the only west-bound land route through the Buckeye Country—a circumstance that can hardly be overemphasized, for it actually influenced the direction of the western trek away from Kentucky and the South and into the old Northwest Territory. This was a fact vastly more important to the course of empire than could possibly have been suspected at the time, for the coming of Zane's Trace provided the first means of tying the West to the East—essential if the United States was to be able to extend her claims all the way to the Pacific. For it had long been feared that the accessibility of New Orleans via the Ohio and Mississippi Rivers could easily turn the western settler's heart and allegiance southward toward that Spanish-French colony —territory not yet a part of the United States at the turn of the century.

Throughout much of his adult life, Washington had feared this ever present threat, for loss of the West would have killed the young nation's chances of attaining world significance. But even as he feared it, he had also foreseen its solution. "The Western Settlers," he wrote, "from my Observation stand as it were a Pivot, the Touch of a Feather would almost incline them either Way . . . The Answer for us is easy. It is to open a wide Door and make a smooth Way for the Produce of the Country to pass to our Eastern Markets before the Trade may get into another Country." Zane's Trace formed the threshold of that open door, immediately admitting the beginnings of west-east trade from the southern parts of the Indiana Territory.

Moreover, such a large sprinkling of movers had somehow struggled down the rivers and along this land route that Congress had soon deemed it time to divide, then redivide the Northwest Territory—the great area bounded roughly by the Mississippi and Ohio Rivers, the western four of the Great Lakes, and a piece of Pennsylvania.

In 1800, the northwest four-fifths of this great expanse was hacked off, now to be known as the Indiana Territory, leaving in the original tract only a southeasterly chunk with practically the same boundaries it would retain upon entering the Union, three years later, as the state of Ohio. In 1805, a large section of the newly created Indiana Territory was detached and called the Michigan Territory. In 1809, another section was cut off to create the Illinois Territory, which at first included land that would eventually make two states, Illinois and Wisconsin. There now remained in the Indiana Territory only that area which it would possess when it became the state of Indiana in 1816. In 1818, the state of Illinois was created, and the remaining northern half of the Illinois Territory was temporarily added to the Michigan Territory, where it would remain until it eventually became Wisconsin—territory and state.

Thus, even at this early period in the history of the migration, the West was made ready for its influx—long before there was a tolerable way to reach it.

The Cumberland Road was fifteen years in the making, a period filled with heartbreaking delays and almost insurmountable obstacles that began with inadequate maps and confused information concerning the territory to be crossed. Next came the hurdle of inexperienced crews, facing the tasks of removing unbelievable tangles of virgin timber, roots, and underbrush, building bridges and culverts, filling in valleys, and leveling hills—all in spite of a doleful dearth of skilled engineers and adequate machinery. And never was there time enough or money enough for the task at hand.

When at long, long last the Pike slid down its final western hill into Wheeling, the eastern sections of the new highway— the first to be built—were already in sad need of repair. Moreover, malicious destruction was now painfully evident wherever disgruntled laborers could accomplish it undetected.

"Frequent abuses take place on the Road," Superintendent David Shriver reported to Congress in consternation, "such as throwing down walls, digging down the banks, felling trees, dragging over it with locked wagon wheels, placing fences within its sixty feet, and many other improper acts done."

Nor did the Pike's troubles end even during the seven golden years of its heyday, though the colorful stagecoaches and Conestoga wagons rolled westward the clock around, dodging the endless droves of animals and slow-moving foot travelers. For never was there a time when some legislative battle over the Road was not brewing in Congress. And although editors were joyously shouting, "A new era is at hand," the West was getting tired of begging for an extension of Uncle Sam's Pike through Ohio, and the East was getting tired of begging for repairs. But Congress was growing skin-and-

bones weary of the whole affair. It had expected that the first
appropriation of $30,000 would be sufficient for building the
entire Cumberland Road, but somehow the costs had risen to
nearly $7,000,000.

Moreover, while a legislative battle over the fate of the Pike
boiled for two years—with no appropriations whatever—much
of its surface had crumbled into a nearly impassable state. Besides which, settlers at the Wheeling terminus, maddened by
the Congressional delays, were gleefully building their cabins
on the right-of-way, moving their fences to include its cleared
land, planting their corn on its level shoulders, and dignifying
their dwellings with foundations of stone that had recently
supported Pike bridges. Congress was in a quandary, having
never appropriated funds for policing the Road, let alone repairing it or extending it on westward.

Then came the suggestion that was to ring the death knell
for the National Road. Build it on westward at Federal expense, build it all the way through to the Mississippi; then
give it to the states through which it ran, and let each be responsible for the improvement and upkeep of its own section!
This was the easy way out. And even President Monroe agreed
to this one, utterly disregarding the fact that all of the West
was poor and thinly settled, while the outer fringe states could
not have maintained a cowpath, let alone the National Road
within their borders.

And so a new appropriation was made, this time a meager
$10,000, which was hopefully dedicated to extending the Road
all the way from Wheeling to the Mississippi at a point halfway between St. Louis and the mouth of the Illinois River.

On October 5, 1825, Commissioners Knight and Johnson
summoned a gathering of contractors in Columbus, Ohio, the
"Wilderness Capital," to let bids for the first extension of the
Cumberland Road, into the Buckeye Country. And great was
the excitement among the assembled backwoods spectators

when a rap of the gavel started the bidding. Uncle Sam's Pike was about to cross the State of Ohio!

How could they know—gathering out there in Columbus on a quiet October morning—that at this very moment in history the National Road was doomed. That they of Ohio who had contributed so largely to its inception and waited so long for its coming, were now to be cheated out of it after all. That while the Road would eventually creep across their hills and plains, no more than a trickle of its former stream of traffic would ever brave its eastern hazards to reach their state. And how could they possibly know that before the first shovel of Ohio dirt could be lifted, the measured boom of cannon along the faraway Hudson would send echoing into the ears of every American the joyful news that there was now a far easier way to cross the Alleghenies than by the faulty Pike—a new way that would carry the Big Push far to the north. The Erie Canal was open!

Now for the story of the fabulous Old Erie, as she was called almost from her earliest days, a name used more as an expression of affection than to designate age—much as you might call the baby "Old Johnnie here." To understand the coming of this all-important canal, it is necessary to backtrack briefly through the years.

We have already seen with what favor many Americans had seized upon the notion of canal building, even from the time of Joliet and Sam Sewell, and how persistently they clung to it in spite of various disastrous attempts, still believing that this picturesque, comfortable, tranquil method of travel was a sweet answer to their vexing transportation problems.

The coming of the Cumberland Road had served to strengthen this determination. There were still many thousands who spent a deal of their time in dreaming about a new home beyond the rims of their respective worlds, yet had neither the desire nor the courage to face the hardships and loss of time inevitable in Pike travel. For scarcely was the building of the Road well under way before it became crystal-clear that a mover who chose this form of travel must walk most of the way west, constantly guarding his horses and wagon brakes, as well as his straggling livestock. Even his family must hoof it during the long and almost continuous mountain ascents and descents, in order to save the horses, since these were indispensable to both the trek and the new life in the West. This slowed progress to a point where a seven-mile day was considered excellent time. This meant that an Easterner, moving all of his effects into the fringe country, could be all summer at it, losing a full year's crops besides having to dip into his land-buying funds to purchase supplies as he went along. And his chances of making the trek without the loss of a horse or two and a goodly portion of his livestock were meager. Consequently, even after the Pike was open its existence was more or less ignored by those thousands who were willing to sit and let time run by, while they waited for the coming of the Old Erie.

Its coming had already taken an unconscionably long time. In fact, the idea dated back to Indian days—for the red man was the first to discover that the only practical break in the Appalachian Ridge from New England to Georgia was the line of the Hudson and Mohawk Rivers. Here, for untold generations, Iroquois moccasins had patted a trail from the Atlantic Ocean to Lake Ontario, following an ancient, half-lost buffalo trace, to which they had added fragmentary canoe short cuts by lake, river, and creek, as well as secret portages. The white man knew that this Old Iroquois Trail left the Hudson above Albany and tagged the Mohawk northwesterly to a spot the Indians had named Nun-da-da-sis, "around-the-hill" (Utica); there it crossed the river to head overland directly west to the Genesee River, which it followed north to Lake Ontario.

It was also known that an important branch ran northward from this trail, following the Oswego River to make a short cut to Lake Ontario at Swa-geh (Oswego). The whole of this vast territory was called the Long House of the Iroquois.

That it had possibilities for the white man's use was first mentioned by Jonathan Carver when he traveled these parts in 1766, reporting that soldiers of Fort Stanwix—backwoods military post on the future site of Rome—had crudely cut a way to join the Mohawk and the Oswego by way of Wood Creek, with sluices near their fort. Two years later, Sir Henry Moore, governor of this still British territory, suggested to the colonial Assembly the "advisability of making the Mohawk boatable around the falls of Canajoharie." And although this was early in the story of the Old Erie, the idea had caught on immediately. Many were convinced that this might well be the solution for an easy way West, the answer to man's ever-lasting yearning for new frontiers.

Six years later, Governor Tryon included in his Report of 1774 a recommendation for a system of locks and canals which he had worked out for the Mohawk and the upper Hudson River territory. Soon after that, Christopher Colles, a New York Irishman with a gift of golden gab, gave a series of lectures advocating a Western waterway, which so violently seized the public fancy as to force the Legislature to vote him the princely sum of $125 for a canal survey.

In 1777, while warming himself before an evening campfire during General Schuyler's slow and sullen retreat before Burgoyne's redcoats, Gouverneur Morris went a daring step further and proposed a waterway that would connect the Hudson River directly with the faraway Lake Erie instead of with Lake Ontario, which had until now seemed to be the logical

terminus. Quartermaster Morgan Lewis, a comrade at Fort
Edwards and later Governor of New York, was one of the
discouraged and foot-weary soldiers who listened to Morris'
quiet voice that memorable night. So intrigued was he with
the vision of a tranquil waterway cutting through hundreds
of miles of unopened wilderness that he never forgot the incident. Fifty years later, when the dream had become a reality
that opened the way for hundreds of thousands of emigrants
to enter the Promised Land, he penned a testimonial letter
dated May 26, 1828, giving full credit to Gouverneur Morris
for being the first to see this staggering possibility.

"One evening in particular," wrote Lewis, "while describing
in the most animated and glowing terms the rapid march of
the useful arts through our country—when once freed from a
foreign yoke—Morris announced in language highly poetic,
and to which I cannot do justice, that at no very distant day
the waters of the great western inland seas would, by the aid
of man, break through their barriers and mingle with those of
the Hudson."

As a matter of record, many of the Old Erie's chief protagonists such as Judge James Geddes, Surveyor-general Simeon
De Witt, and Engineer Elkanah Watson, also gave Morris full
credit for originating the plan, for they all had heard him discuss it many times before Congress. And to have heard that
eloquent statesman thundering forth on his favorite subject
was a thing you were not likely to forget. "Gentlemen! Some
day, ships will sail from London, bound for Buffalo via the
Hudson River!" Listening, it was easy to forget the hundreds
of miles of unbroken wilderness and to be convinced.

George Washington was another who believed in the Erie
Canal throughout the long years of her struggle toward existence. Ben Franklin, too, advocated her coming. But Thomas
Jefferson, though champion of the fringe country, consistently
opposed the Old Erie because he had hopes that his own be-

loved dream of a Potomac waterway west would yet come true.

Gradually, as newspapers became more common, they also took up the issue. *The Commonwealth,* out in frontier Pittsburgh, was first, carrying a series of letters written by Jesse Hawley, a New Yorker newly arrived in the West. To him goes credit for being the first to get the thing down in black and white. His letters were later carried to eastern readers by the *Genesee Messenger* of Canandaigua, New York, appearing from October, 1807, to March, 1808, under the signature, "Hercules."

Month by month now, sentiment for the Old Erie was gaining ground, until at last it had progressed to the point where a canal bill actually reached the New York Legislature. Although it was received by many members with what the press called "such expressions of surprise and ridicule as are due to a very wild or foolish project," there were also certain favorable omens. Something good might have come of it at this time if the War of 1812 had not been brewing. But the closer the war came, the colder grew man's desire for a waterway west. Times were hard and the people were discouraged. The song of the Promised Land no longer warmed their hearts. Certainly a 363-mile channel cut through a wilderness could be little more than a pipe dream, when you stopped to consider that the longest canal in the country to date—that little twenty-seven-mile Middlesex up near Boston—was finding that the only easy sledding in the canal business was into bankruptcy.

Meanwhile, Elkanah Watson, a New Yorker and one of the Old Erie's most dedicated backers, had spent five years in Europe studying canals, and had returned home to become the leaven that would at least sweeten the dough though he could not raise it very high. He toured the Mohawk Country, prepared a report on his findings, called on General Schuyler with an armful of canal maps, and succeeded in again creating an interest in the Big Ditch. In the end his efforts brought about grants for two semiprivate canal companies, in 1792, with the General serving as president of both. One was to be known as the Western Inland Lock Navigation, ambitiously expected to open a waterway from the Hudson to Lake Ontario and Seneca Lake by way of the Mohawk. The other, called the Northern Inland Lock Navigation, was expected to connect Lake Champlain with the Hudson.

To finance these two projects, $25,000 would be raised by public sale of one thousand shares of stock, upon the completion of which New York State would contribute an additional $12,500. As might have been expected, the sale of this stock was slow—discouragingly so, for of the hundreds of people who had cried most loudly for a westbound canal, few now felt called upon to step forward with loosened purse strings.

Wrote the saddened Watson, upon examining the subscription books that had been placed where prospective shareholders could readily sign, "They had been opened three days in New York City at the Old Coffee House, and not a share was subscribed. I considered the cause hopeless, called on my friend James Watson, Esquire, and induced him, with much persuasion, to subscribe twenty shares. From that moment, the subscriptions went on briskly. But on my arrival at Albany, where the commissioners had kept the books open several days at Lewis's old tavern in State Street, no mortal had yet signed to exceed *two shares.* I immediately subscribed seven."

After this public duty, the indomitable Elkanah set out on a second exploratory jaunt over some of the territory in question, this time taking along the entire canal committee and a few surveyors. For those who still needed to be convinced of the need for better transportation through this area, this trek should have provided proof enough, for it took twenty-nine

days for these men to force their way through the first fifty
miles of wilderness west of Schenectady.

In spite of initial difficulties, both canal companies now
tackled their separate undertakings with enthusiasm, though
with varying degrees of success. For although the two organizations were practically identical in personnel and faced
similar financial and construction problems, not a single waterway was ever completed by the northern division, while the
western group had improved their channel enough by 1795
to allow passage of ten-ton Durhams for a short distance. This
was considered quite an accomplishment, since it reduced
freight rates between Schenectady and Fort Schuyler (Utica)
from fourteen to five dollars a ton—a saving equal to top pay
for a man's work for eighteen days.

This western company also carved a crude waterway between the upper Mohawk and Wood Creek, to eliminate the
difficult portage at Rome. And while it was widely rumored
that this opening was scarcely large enough to swing a cat in,
it did furnish a certain crude access to the chain of lakes and
creeks that lace central and western York State. Moreover it
went a long way toward bolstering public confidence in the
canal movement. But it never paid a dividend, not a solitary
York shilling in its eighteen years of existence. "All receipts
have been absorbed in improvements and repairs," read the
recurring notices to irate stockholders.

And when the financially embarrassed Western Navigation
at last petitioned the state for more help, the legislators conceded that it was now high time that they assumed the entire
project themselves, laying out a new route that would follow
Gouverneur Morris' plan to feed to Lake Erie instead of to
Lake Ontario. After all, whose interior were they trying to
open—Canada's or their own? In this decision lay the birth of
the Erie Canal.

CHAPTER THREE

"THE IMPOSSIBLE TAKES LONGER"

Now at long last the Old Erie was free to start her lengthy, uphill, backsliding fight on her own. For in spite of the beginnings that the two navigation companies had made, it was soon evident that so gigantic was the task ahead, these small early thrusts were, in comparison, as ineffectual as nudging the ocean. In the first place, the territory in question was not only unbelievably rough, it was an uninhabited and in some places unexplored wilderness, in its western sections. A proposition today to span the Atlantic by bridge would hardly be more startling than was the undertaking that the Old Erie faced. And no one knew this better than did those few travelers who had somehow circled the wilderness to reach Buffalo, out on Lake Erie.

Although the locality was discovered early enough, Buffalo had made little progress so far. It was known that La Salle had visited here in 1679, pausing long enough to build the *Griffin* —first boat to navigate Lake Erie waters—but it was well over a century later before the first permanent inhabitant settled at this spot. This was a lone trader named Winney, and the year was 1792. Three years later, the French traveler Liancourt reported that "this beginning has now grown to a small collection of four or five houses." Between 1798 and 1803, Joseph Ellicott platted townships in this locality for the Holland Land Company. And during 1803 and 1804, a village officially named New Amsterdam was laid out here at the mouth of Buffalo Creek, soon to be known as Buffalo. In 1810, the Township of Buffalo was incorporated, possessing boundaries that it would eventually grow into, as a city.

But on December 29, 1813, the village was captured by a British and Indian force of 1,200, under the direction of General Riall. And on December 30 and January 1, it was almost completely wiped out by fire, set by the enemy. Two years later, when an attempt was made to rebuild this water-and-forest-surrounded village, progress was so slow and dismal that a French traveler, returning East, shook his head sadly at the thought of it, wearily fingered the pewter buttons on his turkey-red vest, and was forced to admit that it was "still a mere trading-post, struggling hopelessly to become a village."

This, then, was to be the western terminus of the Erie Canal. To reach it from New York City at this time involved the following: A four- or five-day delay to begin with, waiting for the correct combination of sailboat, tide, and favorable wind to carry you on the five-day jaunt up the Hudson to Albany. Once there, you dickered for a wagon lift and the privilege of being jostled for seventeen miles over the rutted trail between Albany and Schenectady where you took a boat up the Mohawk for the 104-mile run to Utica, now depending alternately upon sails, poles, and oars, with difficult portages at the rapids. For the next 114-mile trek to Oswego on Lake Ontario, you used both water and land. Once there, you were lucky if you caught a Lewiston boat within ten days, which then took you westward through Lake Ontario and southward into the Niagara River. At Lewiston you again took to wheels, overland to Buffalo.

With good luck and a tail wind, the trip took about fifty-two days, plus the hardship and worry of making arrangements and transferring yourself and your portmanteaus into and out of various boats and wagons—your burdens being gradually lightened by about one hundred and fifty dollars before you finally reached Buffalo. The reason for this circuitous water route through Lake Ontario was that a direct path overland would have included an impossible two-hundred-mile stretch through largely unconquered wilderness—the very land that the Big Ditch now proposed to subjugate.

In fact, most of the western two-thirds of the Old Erie's route would face difficulties of similar nature—along the strip between Rome and Buffalo, after the canal had cut away from the Mohawk River. For here the forests were great and the widely scattered villages were small. Chief among them along the proposed route in 1817 were Syracuse, Lyons, and Rochester. All were comparatively young. Lyons, the oldest of the three, was only twenty-two years old when the Big Ditch was started. Syracuse proper was a mere twelve years old, and she was still called "South Salina." She would require another three years to reach a population of 250. Rochester's first frame house had passed its fifth birthday and the village was still called "Rochesterville." In another three years her population would reach 1,500. Black Rock, a "beginning" near Buffalo, will be heard from later.

In fact, Canadaigua and Batavia were the largest villages in the entire central western area of York State at this time—neither one on the proposed canal route. By the time the Old Erie was five years old, Canandaigua would reach a population of 5,160, and Batavia would possess 4,264 souls—even without benefit of the canal's coming.

But perhaps a more graphic picture of the territory through which the Big Ditch now proposed to dig the western two-thirds of her path can be found in the diaries of two travelers who had recently made their way by foot through this wilderness.

Tilly Buttrick, a young Bostonian, traversed this country three times between 1814 and 1818. On his first expedition, bound for Kentucky, he was forced to circle back to Boston in the late autumn because he knew he could not survive the winter here, and the spring and summer months had not allowed him sufficient time to cross the wilderness of western York State. There had been days when his progress had approached zero, because of "very bad roads such as by many people would be considered no road at all." Most of his nights were spent in the open, although he had occasionally come upon a tavern—"so crude," Buttrick wrote, after entering one, "there is very little difference between my present condition and being out of doors." Bucking the heavy summer storms, alone in the deep woods with trees crashing all around him, had been a most terrifying experience for Buttrick. "Doubly terrible in giant forests," he wrote, "and seemingly nothing but death awaited in every moment."

His second expedition, undertaken the following year, was easier in one way for he was seldom alone, since more people were now venturing westward. But from another angle it was more difficult, because some of the settlements he had found in the deep woods a year ago were now abandoned. "What had been a considerable village, now remains naught but a few solitary huts," wrote Buttrick. The reason was twofold—starvation and the restlessness of those Indians who could not forget the War of 1812.

Estwick Evans was another New Englander who traveled these parts during this period. Sewed into a long-sleeved, long-legged union suit made of buffalo skins, and designed by himself, he was traveling without further luggage except a beltful of assorted firearms. His "Pedestrious Tour of Four Thousand Miles through the Western States . . ." probably gives as intimate a view of the times and conditions as does any pioneer's diary.

Evans made his trek across York State in the spring of 1818. The people, he found, were "more friendly than intelligent."

And he was "especially impressed by the general ignorance in Albany," claimed the New Englander. Like Buttrick, he was appalled at the poverty he found everywhere—the results of the War of 1812, he concluded. And while the beauty of the Finger Lake district—just south of the middle section of the Old Erie's route—was a thing he hoped to carry always in his mind, the poorness of the emigrant huts had touched his heart. Even the wealthy were without food, here in the forests. Ending his trek across New York State, he chose a more northerly route and found that "the twenty-four miles between Niagara and Buffalo were the bleakest of all, without a single habitation except a few scattered, deserted huts."

Crisscrossing the lonesome paths of these two pedestrious travelers, the Erie Canal now proposed to bring increased population, wealth, and contentment. It was quite an ambitious assignment, especially for its western two-thirds.

On the eastern third—from Rome to Albany—it was expected that conditions would be slightly more favorable for canal diggers. For although also somewhat lost in forests, here the Mohawk furnished a crude and limited access to the outer world by way of the Hudson—but only during those periods when the river was sufficiently in flood to carry a boat over certain shallows and cascades, yet not so greatly in flood as to sweep it out of control. Nor were the heavy spring freshets and summer shoals the only hazards of this outlet, for much of it was still labeled "unboatable" on all early maps because of its many falls and rapids, causing numerous difficult portages. And when all was said and done, the Mohawk was still its own boss, not yet having been conquered by man with his ubiquitous dredging and dam building.

Gazing at our subdued streams of today, it is difficult to realize that with the exception of the placid course of the Hudson from Albany to New York City, there was not a river in the eastern half of the country—including even the Ohio—

which was not beset with shoals and rapids and ledges and bars and sometimes even sheer falls, in its early days, to say nothing of the power of the spring freshets.

As to upstream travel, which could be accomplished only by oars or poling all the way, before the coming of steam, the Mohawk was rated with the Connecticut for its cruelty. And a poler's shoulder, where he rested the "button" end of his pole for his pushing, was bruised and lacerated after a few hours' toil through the rapids of either of these two rivers.

Little wonder, then, that the scattered villages along the Mohawk above Albany were still few and small and far apart, although they were river towns old and historically important. Although Albany, capital of the state of New York for two decades now, had reached a population of 10,744 souls in 1810, her neighbors along the Mohawk to the west were by no means a part of the plush life along the Hudson. Separated from Schenectady by a strip of Mohawk so hazardous as to cause the Old Erie to build twenty-seven locks to step down the last twenty-nine miles into Albany—and with no other connection to these upper towns than faulty pikes—it was no wonder that it had taken so long for them to grow.

Most often mentioned of these river towns on this eastern third of the proposed Erie Canal—the strip where she tagged the Mohawk from Albany to Rome—were Amsterdam, Little Falls, and Utica, in addition to Rome and Schenectady. Of these five, the oldest dated back to 1662 and the youngest to 1786. Two grew up on fort sites. Two were destroyed by fire during British and Indian raids at least once. And two still remained unincorporated at the time of the Old Erie's coming.

Official figures on the populations of these villages for that year of 1817 are unavailable. Even the United States Census for 1810 listed only counties in this district—not towns—as did also the dependable Chapin's *Complete Reference Gazetteer of the United States of North America* in 1839. And the

U. S. Census for 1820 avails us little because the building of
the Erie Canal had already affected populations by that time
—nor did it list these villages anyway. But of this we are certain, judging from the spotty information that is available. It
would take another four years after the canal building was
started before Utica could claim 3,000 souls. It would take
Schenectady thirteen years to possess 4,200. Amsterdam would
require eighteen additional years to tally 4,100. Little Falls
would need another thirteen years to reach 2,500. And Rome
would be eighteen years arriving at 4,800. Since all of these
increases would be achieved in the fabulous era of the Old
Erie's coming, it is probable that few if any of these villages
surpassed populations of a thousand at the beginning of canal
construction.

Take it all in all, from Albany to Buffalo, this was desolate
country, especially west of Rome, that region whose malaria-
laden swamplands would make the transportation of canal
materials possible only in winter when the ground was frozen,
at which time the blizzards made travel most hazardous. And
it was lonely country. For while the entire State of New
York boasted less than a million and a half souls in 1817, it
was still so thinly settled west of Albany that no stagecoach
had yet ventured an Albany-to-Buffalo run; there was not
even a first-class trace to follow. When an eminent historian
summed up the situation simply by stating that "The Erie
Canal lay chiefly through an uninhabited wilderness, so it
opened for settlement an immense territory," he was not noticeably stretching the truth.

Second to the hazards of rough terrain and lonely country
came the Old Erie's financial troubles, which were to badger
her progress throughout the long years of her building. At first
it had been halfway expected that the generous United States
that had financed the National Road might reasonably be ex-

pected to feel a similar impulse toward a west-bound canal. Consequently, when Secretary of the Treasury Albert Gallatin broke into print with his famous *Report on Roads, Harbors, and Rivers,* New York State—with an off-eye on her share of the proposed bonanza of twenty million dollars for internal improvements—had immediately packed off two of her high-powered legislators, William Kirkpatrick and Judge Forman, armed with a satchel of blueprints, to make a beaver-hat call on President Jefferson. They were received coldly.

"It is a splendid project and may be executed a century hence," Jefferson told them, still setting his own sights on a rival plan for his beloved though now somewhat weed-choked Potomac Navigation. "Why, sirs, right near here is a canal of a few miles, projected by General Washington, which, if completed, would render this a fine commercial city, which has languished many years because the small sum of $200,000 necessary to complete it, cannot be obtained from the general government or from individuals. *And you talk of making a canal three hundred and fifty miles long through a wilderness!*" The President's irritation was beginning to show now, for the Old Erie presented a real threat. He polished off the interview brusquely. "It is little short of madness to think of it at this day!"

Thus had New York's high hopes of federal aid died a-borning. So, for that matter, had Gallatin's twenty-million-dollar plan that had cost him a solid year of intensive study— a daring and extensive plan that would have opened all the territory east of the Mississippi.

From time to time there had been tall talk of borrowing canal money in Europe, or of soliciting financial aid from the various states that stood to gain by the coming of the Big Ditch. So far, nothing had come of either plan. And it was already beginning to be evident that if this canal was to be built, New York State had better get along with the job without looking too far afield for aid. With this thought in mind, they now called into the picture De Witt Clinton, the man who would eventually be known as Father of the Erie Canal.

This idea had come, strangely enough, from General Jonas Pratt, a Federalist senator—from the wrong side of the aisle— who had rashly stated that the canal measure would fail without Clinton's support, would probably succeed with it. This statement so flattered Clinton that it drew his attention to the problem for the first time. Although he had long been the Democratic leader of his state, he had so far shown little interest in the proposed Erie Canal. But now, having been dragged into the controversy for political reasons, he became its foremost advocate. His efforts in its behalf were eventually to lend more impetus to the Big Push than those of any other person.

De Witt Clinton was a born politician. As a young lawyer, he had received his first training for such a life as right-hand-man to his uncle, George Clinton, governor of New York State. By the time De Witt was twenty years old, he was already widely known as an Anti-Federalist; later he became the recognized leader of the opposition to President John Adams. By the time he was twenty-six, he was a member of the state Assembly, where his tactless and forthright speeches often got him into trouble—but not unknowingly. "The meekness of Quakerism will do in religion," he used to say, "but not in politics."

In 1802, at the age of thirty-three, he was appointed to fill John Armstrong's unfinished term in the United States Senate, where he continued to serve for two additional annual sessions. After that, although already nationally prominent, he withdrew to become mayor of New York City. While this removed him from the Washington scene, where he would undoubtedly have become a strong influence, it gave him his chance to concentrate his energies on affairs of his home state, and especially on the Old Erie.

As mayor, Clinton served his native city long and strenuously, and to as good a purpose as any. His office required much of him, and he always gave it full measure, pressed down and running over. A tall gangling figure of a man, he became well known in many phases of public life. He was the chief patron of the New York Orphan Asylum and the City Hospital, and visited both almost daily. He headed the City Fire Department, and his lathered horse could be expected to come steaming in at every fire, because there still existed an old ordinance that suggested that this was a mayor's duty. The ubiquitous De Witt even took it upon himself to quell personally any public disturbances that might arise, and to inspect religiously all markets and docks. Singlehanded he raised $100,000 for defense installations on Governor's Island, hoping therewith to stop the increasingly troublesome British practice of seizing American sailors in New York harbor.

In fact, there was little going on in civilized America with which De Witt Clinton was not concerned. In the field of education, he was a leading advocate of free public schools. As a naturalist, he discovered a new wheat and a new fish, and published papers on such far-from-political topics as the swallow, and rice. As a scientist, he was one of the foremost of his time. And in the field of art, he was once "widely extolled for the elegance of a discourse he delivered before the American Academy of Arts when acting as its president," according to the press. As a leader, he was president as well as founder of the New-York Historical Society, holding at the same time that same double distinction in numerous other organizations concerned with philosophy, human society, and the Bible. At the age of thirty-four—twice married by now, and the father of ten children—he was by all odds the most influencial political figure in the state.

By the year 1812, De Witt Clinton, aged forty-three, was being enthusiastically considered for the Presidency of the United States. Only Pennsylvania's negative vote, that stormy night of the caucus, kept him from being swept into office in place of Madison—with his Uncle George as his vice-president. This was the first of a chain of defeats that would bedevil the path of Clinton, for the pendulum of his success would soon change its direction. By 1815, his tactless consorting with Federalists would cause him to lose the renomination for lieutenant-governor. Later that same year he would be ousted as mayor, having served concurrently as both state senator and mayor, then concurrently as both lieutenant-governor and mayor. But these latter setbacks were still a part of the future, for De Witt Clinton came to the aid of the Old Erie in 1812.

Having been called to active duty on the Big Ditch at a time when Gouverneur Morris and his canal committee were again licking their wounds because a final desperate plea for federal support had just been blasted for good and all, Clinton now picked up the pieces, as was his wont, and boldly recommended that York State start off bravely by purchasing outright the Western Inland Lock Navigation. In spite of themselves, carried along by his boundless enthusiasm and forthrightness, New York's legislators now found themselves not only authorizing such a purchase, but also making plans for borrowing funds to finance it. They even sanctioned the buying of land for a 363-mile right-of-way for the Erie Canal, "providing the project still be deemed expedient after examination." With all this encouragement, Clinton now boldly approached the capitals of Europe for loans amounting to five million dollars to finance the digging.

While he waited for their response, the new chief pushed his surveyors and draftsmen into rapid action, hoping to get the thing rolling while the goose hung high. As a result, the first drawings included such impossible features as an inclined plane reaching from the Great Lakes halfway across the state to Utica, dropping six inches to the mile, so that Lake Erie could furnish the canal with water all the way east to a spot where the Mohawk River could take over. This mammoth inclined plane was to be carried over the mouth of Cayuga Lake on an embankment a mile long and 130 feet high. And at Schoharie Creek, it would follow the crest of another embankment 150 feet high. The cost of the novelty was expected to run between five and six million dollars. And it was what the committee now recommended.

Nothing could have brought them out of the clouds more rapidly than did a cold flat announcement arriving just then from Europe. Neither England nor France nor any other part of the Continent was interested in financing an American canal to the tune of five million dollars or any other sum.

Drastic economy now being the only way around this dilemma, such fancy notions as inclined planes were immediately abandoned in favor of the much cheaper lock system. This helped, but not enough. "Our canal troubles are still as thick as the trees of the wilderness," wrote Clinton, who, as a matter of fact, had not tasted real trouble as yet.

But the crosscurrents were beginning to run—jealousy, skepticism, selfish interests, disregard of practicability. Eastern New York was jealous of the attention suddenly showered on western New York. Certain politicians in New York City loudly and stupidly opposed the whole project. Citizens of the Lake Ontario counties wanted the canal to terminate at Oswego so that they could shop at Montreal. In Rochester they wanted it to turn north at their gatepost and follow the Genesee River to Lake Ontario. The southern counties along the Pennsylvania border objected to the whole affair because they would have to help pay for something they could never use, while they continued to float their products to market by way of the hazardous Pennsylvania rivers—a complaint Clinton was able to silence with the promise that he would run branch canals to carry their boats over to the Erie.

But to top all of his troubles, two years after Clinton had picked up the reins, the New York Legislature abruptly got cold feet on the whole matter and rescinded the authority previously given him to borrow money. Any lesser soul would have followed the course that Stephen Foster's minstrels were soon advocating—"lay down de fiddle and de bow." But not the indomitable Clinton. He chose to believe that this was a temporary halt and was the best thing that could happen to the project, since it would enable promoters to get a better start after the war was out of the way, using American engineers and American money.

But while the undefeatable De Witt may have found solace in the long view, few others had the same vision. The desire for immediate transportation into the West was now keener than ever, and certainly no longer a bauble to be tossed back and forth on the spears of sparring politicians. For now at long last, public opinion was beginning to stiffen in spite of canal difficulties, undoubtedly helped along by the tall tales drifting in from the West—tales of golden hoards of farm products, come by with little or no effort. It made the very thought of senseless delay in canal building quite intolerable.

There can be little doubt that the Baltimore editor Hezekiah Niles with his hand presses had no slightest intention of letting the western trek wait for more favorable times, for in edition after edition of his paper he offered some enticing bit of news about the New West, ranging from interesting tidbits to hearty, convincing arguments, until people everywhere were beginning to watch for these straws in the wind. For instance, there now appeared in his *Niles' Weekly Register* a letter written by Congressman Rufus Easton of the Missouri Territory to Senator William Hunter of Rhode Island.

"There neither is, nor ever can be anything like poverty here," wrote Easton. "All is ease, tranquility, and comfort. Every person, however poor, may with moderate industry, become in a very short time a landowner; his substance increases from year to year; his barns are filled with abundant harvest; his cattle multiply . . . And his children, active, vigorous, and enterprising, seem destined to sustain and extend the respectability of their parentage. Truly may it be said of this fortunate and highly favored country, a paradise of pleasure is open'd in the wild."

It was the sort of statement that left no hole large enough to let a weasel through, especially since it appeared under the banner of *Niles' Weekly Register,* the most widely read and thoroughly relied upon newspaper of the day. Because of the great influence that this periodical had on the westward trek, it might be well to give it a moment's attention.

The *Register* was published continuously from September 7, 1811, to June 27, 1848, a period nearly identical with that of the Big Push. It has been described as a "tabloid-sized newspaper without the pictures," and it consisted largely of extracts from other periodicals throughout the country, which were expected to make it what Niles called "a chronicle of passing events with a minimum of editorial opinion." Actually it contained everything from tables of weights and measures to Congressional reports and speeches, especially those of Clay and Randolph. To sweeten the dough, it occasionally tossed in a few mild anecdotes under the heading, "Amusing Scraps."

The paper customarily ran sixteen pages and was numbered from one to a possible five hundred during the course of a year, so arranged for the convenience of those who wished to have their copies bound for future reference. A year's subscription cost five dollars, which was equivalent to a month's wages for the average workman, or the price of four acres of Illinois prairie. Consequently, in fringe areas, a town's squire or minister was often its only subscriber, although any copy—no matter how ancient—went the rounds of all who could read, and was freely quoted to the rest.

For its first three years, this paper appeared as *"The Weekly Register* put forth by R. Mansfield with H. Niles, Editor." After that it came out as *Niles' Weekly Register* until 1837, when it was changed to *Niles' National Register*. Its first edition went to 1,500 subscribers, and in seven years its circulation reached 10,000.

As to the man himself, Hezekiah Niles started off as a printer, made a few other journalistic efforts, then settled down as the guiding light of the *Register*. They called him "the serene editor whose motto is the Past and Present for the Future." And for a quarter-century he strove to teach the country that "a newspaper may be useful for recording history as well as for fighting political battles." For most of his life he was a beloved, well-known figure on the streets of Baltimore, a short, squarely built man who stooped as he walked, spoke in a high voice, was addicted to snuff, and fixed you with a keen gray eye that lighted his plain face with a shrewd but kindly expression. He was a Quaker who married twice, fathering twelve children by his first wife and eight by his second. After his death he was succeeded in the newspaper business, though not too successfully, by one of his many sons.

From its beginning, Niles's little sixteen-page folder achieved character and an enviable reputation in every part of the civilized world. It carried the American story to the palaces of kings, to world-wide centers of commerce, and to cabins on the outer fringe. It was accepted as an authority in courts of justice and in legislative assemblies, and to this day it remains the truest chronicle of historical events of its time. And when Niles dedicated it to "Political, Historical, Geographical, Scientific, Astronomical, Statistical, and Biographical Documents," he was not noticeably stretching the truth.

With such a reputation, and with the background of the mass of material available to him in newspapers from all over the country, Niles's influence on the westward migration—to which he ardently devoted himself for a quarter-century—was far-reaching beyond calculation. Seldom did he put forth an issue that did not include some word about the West. And when he announced that a new land office had been opened in Uniontown or Terre Haute or Shawneetown, a great new wave of emigration to that locality could be expected—with an even greater wave of western sentiment sweeping through the hearts of those who still perched on eastern fences, growing thoughtful over the Promised Land.

Such was the influence of a single, simple man, wielding a gifted, honest pen, who had been providentially called to live out his days during the time of the Big Push.

Soon after Congressman Easton's letter to Senator Hunter appeared in the *Register,* Niles carefully hand-set a straight-talking editorial aimed at a certain English author who had gone to considerable trouble to explain to two continents the fallacy of seeking out American's Far West.

"He had heard that there were rich and fertile lands to be had on reasonable terms in our western country," reported Niles, "but he repeatedly claimed that these would prove of little use because they could never be thickly populated, from the impossibility of finding a vent." Now, after an irked quarter-century, Mr. Niles was in a position to point out just how wrong an Englishman could be in underestimating American speed and ingenuity.

"About twenty-seven years have elapsed since Lord Sheffield made his book," wrote Hezekiah. "The State of Ohio was then a mere wilderness, and indeed, most of the present thickly populated places on the western waters, not much better. The many powerful streams which intersect that delightful country bore on the bosoms of their waters only the solitary canoe of the Indian, stealing along their banks in quest of his game. But Ohio, by last census taken, was found to contain 230,949 inhabitants; its waters are enlivened by the appearance of majestic ships . . . holding their *adverse* courses. . . . About fifteen years ago, the writer of this article recollects to have heard that celebrated mechanic, Mr. Oliver Evans, give an opinion that the man was *then* living that might see the Mississippi covered with steam boats. The sentiment appeared extravagant at the time; but from what has happened, and is daily coming to pass, it assumes probability, and may be verified in its fullest extent, at a very early period. . . ."

Most especially, the subject of the western farmer's need for an outlet to market was uppermost in Niles's mind, and he never ceased to harp upon the fact that without it there was little chance for financial success in western agriculture. Many an item appearing in the *Register* was actually an arrow aimed at this target. "Wheat out there is scarcely worth two shillings a bushel, and corn and oats will not fetch more than eight or ten cents per bushel. Cider fetches more than it is worth, at fifty cents a barrel, but that includes the barrel." On the other hand Europe was hungry, and whereas America's eastern seaboard could not raise a surplus of grain, her New West certainly could—lacking only a way to ship it out. "American flour is selling from 18 to 20 dollars per barrel in Bordeaux," Niles reminded his readers, "and from 20 to 22 dollars a barrel in Liverpool . . . Remember the saying, 'There is no joking with the belly; it has no ears and will not be reasoned with.'"

In spite of his hands-off policy in all political matters, Niles often came out flatfooted for the Erie Canal, devoting more space to a government report on the subject than he had ever given to Uncle Sam's Pike. "In Great Britain more than a

hundred millions of dollars have been laid out in constructing about a thousand miles of canal navigation . . . and it
is considered of great national advantage . . . How much
stronger are the inducements in the United States to employ
a tenth part of that sum in effecting an object of ten times the
magnitude!"

Sometimes Niles kept the emigration ferment working by
simply including a report on the progress of the Big Push. "A
Mr. Bowman, a pilot in Jeffersonville, took 110 boats over the
falls of the Ohio during the period October 5 to May 5 . . .
During this period of high water, at least as many more passed
without assistance. The whole number from all pilots at that
point was estimated at 1200." Sometimes he turned to a little
daydreaming about the Erie. "Wafting the rich produce of the
western parts of Pennsylvania and Virginia with those of
Ohio and Kentucky to the markets on the seaboard! WHAT
A PROSPECT!"

But in spite of all favorable sentiment on the canal question
—public opinion as well as a friendly press—there came of
necessity a prolonged and discouraging lull in the affairs of the
Old Erie after the New York Legislature withdrew its permission to borrow canal money. This lasted a full year and a half
before two groups of prominent York Staters finally took it
upon themselves to hold identical meetings in Albany and in
New York in December, 1815. Object: to break the Old Erie's
deadlock.

At the New York gathering, a memorial was drawn up according to plan, petitioning the state of New York to sanction
the building of the Erie Canal under the direction of a new
committee to consist of De Witt Clinton, Cadwallader D.
Colden, John Swartwout, and Thomas Eddy. Actually the
plan as they presented it in this memorial laid the foundation
for our present system of waterways for this district, silencing

forever the noisy advocates of a circuitous Lake Ontario route.

Copies of it were now sent to every town and hamlet along the proposed canal, where its wide scope and forthrightness created such enthusiasm as to produce an immediate outbreak of mass meetings from New York to Buffalo. One hundred thousand citizens signed this memorial before Clinton bundled it up and carried it to the Legislature.

So stupendous was its impact on the people that *New York's Public Documents Relating to Canals* later recorded the event as a strong contributing factor. "The awakening courage of a brave people, recovering from the devastation and prostration of war, was somewhat stirred by Clinton's appeal . . . It was so comprehensive a view of the immense advantages that would be produced by the completion of the canal, that copies sent throughout the State were eagerly signed by thousands, and carried full conviction to every mind. The project immediately became popular, and it was the means of rousing laws in prosecuting this great work . . ."

The memorial was an extensive study of the entire canal situation, set forth in a scholarly, well-prepared, frank, and impressive 7,000-word document. So huge a petition was it, that it is doubtful if many of its signers actually read the entire thing—few of them could read. But this was not necessary anyway, for its substance was cried aloud from pulpit to kitchen, from stagecoach to plow. And many a New Yorker stood straighter and felt convinced, having just learned that he was "a citizen of a State that stood in exalted eminence, with power to prevent a train of the most extensive and afflicting calamities that ever visited the world—for such a train would inevitably dissolve the Union; a State that would be an enemy of all mankind if she failed in the golden opportunity which the Almighty now put in her hands." Namely, to build a canal that would join forever the East with the West in spite of the Alleghenies. It was a declaration that did not leave a man much choice.

During the following spring, when the farmers were dropping corn kernels into the warm soil, three to a hill—one for the worm, one for the crow, one to grow—it can be assumed that they glowed with inner satisfaction concerning the way they had handled that memorial. For up in Albany, the Legislature had just passed an "Act for Improving Navigation of the State of New York." And the following year during cherry blossom time, these same farmers completed the job by electing De Witt Clinton governor of New York in addition to his present roll as Canal Commissioner.

Meanwhile, gangs of engineers and chainmen were again dispatched to survey sections of the future Erie Canal and the contemplated Lake Champlain route. The passage of a final bill was still necessary to start the shovels flying—a measure to authorize once more the raising of needful coin. A last-minute, weak-kneed plea for aid from the neighboring states that stood to gain, plus Kentucky and Vermont, had just been repulsed as coldly as were the two earlier pleas to Jefferson and Madison and the appeal to Europe. There remained no alternative but for York State to shoulder the task alone.

Facing up to this fact, at long last, New York's Assembly now gave its full attention to a bill that had been dangling for some time, a measure concerned with ways and means of accomplishing this money raising. Many believed that it could be successfully done through direct taxation, and a dozen kinds were suggested—a tax on lotteries, or on auctions, or on salt, or a tax of a dollar a head on all persons taking a one-hundred-mile trip, or fifty cents apiece for those satisfied with a thirty-mile run. Others believed that a land tax alone could raise immediately a quarter-million dollars, which would turn the trick when added to the fine nest egg of land gifts already donated by certain individuals and companies who stood to gain most by the canal. There were still others who believed that a heavy toll system could easily finance the Big Ditch, once she was open, and also clear up all of her debts.

The bitter pros and cons over such an array of possibilities lasted a noisy discouraging month, with a growing opposition to any form of taxation coming, strangely enough, solidly and stupidly from New York City, that town about which historians would later agree, "She received her pre-eminence in America largely from the impetus generated by the Erie Canal during the first twenty years of its functioning."

Meanwhile, tension mounted, day by day, as the time grew short before the Assembly must adjourn for the year. For without passage of this bill before that fateful time, the Erie might yet die a-borning. Again it was the hour of decision, with America's destiny hanging in the balance.

In the end it was Martin Van Buren, that "offensive partisan" who had fought Clinton all the way—especially for the governorship of New York—who now, for once in his life, looked beyond his party and made the speech that led to victory during the last hour of the last day before the Legislature would adjourn. The success of the vote that followed was announced against a wall of wild cheering, and the resulting act of April 15, 1817, cleared away, with one exception, the last of the many obstacles that had long prevented the coming of the Erie Canal. That final exception lay in the fact that, according to New York's legislative rules, this bill could not become a law until it had the approval of the Council of Revisions. And here is where it had its closest squeak of all.

The situation was this. Two of the five council members opposed canal building, two favored it outright, and the fifth member rather favored it but insisted that the time was not ripe for undertaking so gigantic a project. There the matter hung. M. S. Hawley, friend of the Erie from her earliest days,

later retold the dramatic ending to this story as it had been
told to him on that memorable day by one of the five council
members:

"It was likely to be lost by the casting vote of the acting-
governor. Vice-President Tompkins, recently the governor,
entered the room at this stage of the proceedings, in an informal way, and joined in conversation upon the subject before the Council, in opposition to this bill. He said, 'The late
peace with Great Britain was a mere truce, and we will undoubtedly soon have a renewed War with that country. And
instead of wasting money and the resources of the State in this
chimerical project, we ought to employ all our revenue and
credit in preparing for War.'

" 'Do you really think so, sir?' said Chancellor Kent.

" 'Yes, sir!' replied the Vice-President. 'England will never
forgive us our victories. And, my word for it, we shall have
another War with her within two years!'

"The Chancellor, then rising from his seat, with great ani-
mation declared, 'If we must have War, I am in favor of the
canal and I vote for the bill!'

"With his vote the bill became a law!"

And the resulting cheers, when the joyful news reached the
crowds who waited outside in a drenching rain, fairly raised
the dead, we are told. At any rate, the Erie had won the day.
And so, by a frighteningly narrow margin, had America's
Manifest Destiny.

CHAPTER FOUR

TOIL AND TROUBLE

Now for the building of the Old Erie.

Rome had been chosen as the logical place to start the excavating because here the work could proceed in both directions at once. Also the going here would be comparatively easy since it presented neither the difficulties of the sharp descent around the Mohawk Falls to the east, nor of cutting through the sheer rock of the Niagara escarpment to the west. Moreover, since this district already possessed a nest-egg of locks and channels from the old Western Inland Lock Navigation, it was hoped that progress might here be aided a little thereby. There was a crude canal around Little Falls as we have already noted—less than a mile in length, containing five locks—which could detour a ten-ton Durham boat around the falls; an opening cut through a portage at Rome between the upper Mohawk and Wood Creek which opened a crude waterway from the Hudson into the chain of lakes in central New York; and another brief canal strip along the Mohawk. Also there was in existence a survey around the Cohoes or Great Falls which was never built, for lack of funds.

It was not a very impressive bonanza—all told—toward building a 363-mile canal. But it was the general consensus that it offered good propaganda for the voters back home.

The Fourth of July had been chosen as the most appropriate day to commence so patriotic a work. Thus was established a tradition that was to govern the entire canal era, for from this time forth no state ever seriously considered any other day for official sod-breaking, lest hard luck should dog the enterprise. It is even probable that the ceremonial digging of the first shovelful of dirt was performed with the left foot, a superstition that was religiously followed by every subsequent canaller, from captain to hoggee, who stepped off for a day's work on boat or towpath. Left foot first for luck.

The Glorious Fourth, that year of 1817, was a lazy summer day, too warm in the sun, too cool in the shade. And every last man in the wilderness village, dressed in his Sunday best, turned out for the spectacle, elbowing his way through the crowd and jockeying for a vantage point. An opening in the forest near the edge of the proposed channel had been cleared for the ceremony. Here huge trunks of giant trees, split in half lengthwise and placed in close rows, flat side up, puncheon style, formed the rough floor of a platform. Whale-oil torches in sconces, hung from the surrounding oaks to lessen the deep darkness of the forest, added a festive tone to the occasion as their pale smoke spiraled gently skyward through the chasm of trees.

Suddenly a growing tension swept through the group in the wake of a rumor that Clinton himself was going to be present —was, in fact, even now approaching. And then, above the confusion, there came a hearty cheer as the familiar gray horse appeared along the narrow trace, and its long-legged rider swung himself to the ground—De Witt Clinton, for these past three days governor of the state of New York.

Almost immediately there came the usual hushed silence, born of deep respect, as the Governor and a half-dozen notables took their places on the crude platform to deliver what one newspaper called "short graphic speeches, adapted to the occasion." Following these, the group moved to the rim of the proposed channel where the ceremonial shovel was passed

solemnly from Clinton to Judge Joshua Hathaway, president
of the village, to Canal Commissioner Young, to Judge Rich-
ardson, contractor, who promptly caused its shiny blade to
bite into the rich, black forest mold, two feet thick, while the
cannon boomed and the artillery popped.

"The contractor's example was immediately followed by his
own laborers and by all assembled citizens with shovels of their
own," wrote Mr. Hawley, who had arrived at daybreak to
pick up the news, "—all ambitious for the honor of participating in the labors of that memorable occasion."

And probably there was scarcely a person present at that
ceremony in the lonesome wilderness who had not dwelt in
his dreams upon what the coming of the canal would mean to
him personally—his first connection with the world beyond his
door. "A waterway that will spread civilization, wealth, and
refinement," Hawley called it. Nor was it surprising that many
wept, having waited so desperately long for the coming of the
Big Ditch, even as others gave vent to their emotions by shoot-
ing their guns at the sky, and huzzahing themselves hoarse.

Nor were there any present at that ceremony who could
possibly have guessed its greatest significance—that here in
the deep woods on that memorable Fourth of July, these pioneer backwoodsmen had just opened the fabulous Canal Era,
since the success of the Erie Canal was to create a unique
period in our history.

Before the close of that summer of 1817, the right-of-way for
the new canal was marked off by five rows of red surveyors'
stakes, marching over hill and vale in both directions from
Rome. The two outer rows, sixty feet apart, designated the
outer edges of the clearing while the inner two, forty feet
apart, marked the width of the channel, and the fifth row indicated the center of the proposed canal—and all lost in the
gloom of the forest before the chainmen could move a scant

twenty feet away. Yet so hopeful, so determined, so eager were the villagers and the canal builders that throughout that entire summer there was at no time any break in the intensity of the work so nobly started, that July afternoon. And though hundreds of workmen were already aware of the thickness of the thicket and the sickliness of the swamps, no one was ready to admit what tremendous odds were stacked against them, though all had begun to suspect. The truth of the matter was that while Uncle Sam's Pike had been almost humanly impossible to build, this would be worse. For where the road-maker had been hampered by tangled forest growth, the canal builder must also combat the tremendous underground labyrinth, a solid mass of intermingled roots that had been centuries in the tangling.

Second to the hazards of subduing a wilderness came the appalling lack of trained engineers necessary for the building of the 363-mile channel, for the country possessed not one worthy of the name. James Geddes and Benjamin Wright, two country lawyers, had been chosen to direct the work because each had done a little amateur surveying—nothing more. Yet Wright was expected to assume technical direction for the entire Erie Canal while Geddes was to assume direction of the Champlain Canal, which was a branch that was expected to open a way to the lake for which it was named. Since both men were believed to possess superior brains because both had managed to become lawyers, the Commissioners assumed that the science of engineering would also come to them, before the summer was over. And as a matter of fact, that was very nearly what happened, at least in one instance.

As a test of their skill and accuracy and to silence the scoffers, it had been decided that while Wright finished laying off certain sections along the proposed canal line west of Rome, Geddes would survey by a circuitous route through the deep forests between Rome and the east end of Oneida Lake, thence to Onondaga Lake, thence south 1¼ miles to the canal line where Wright was working. In due time these two separate surveys were completed and the report made public. "The Commissioners have the satisfaction to state that when the level of Mr. Wright had been carried along the canal line to the place where Mr. Geddes had terminated his line, the levels of these two engineers, which embraced a circuit of nearly one hundred miles, differed from each other less than 1½ inches." Which certainly furnished admirable ammunition to be shot at the scoffers.

Of course such astonishing accuracy could hardly be expected in all instances, but for the most part, these men of young America were learning to crochet the thing as they went along, eventually becoming even proficient enough to contribute suggestions more advanced than any yet offered by trained European engineers. Furthermore, while the scarcity of skilled help, plus the challenge the Erie presented, naturally attracted renowned Swedish and English engineers to this country, in the end it was an American youth of twenty-six with a smattering of academy mathematics who, after working on one of the labor crews, became the genius of the Erie Canal.

His name was Canvass White, soon synonymous with canal engineering in America. He was taking levels west of Rome when he first gained the eye of Wright and later that of Governor Clinton himself. At their suggestion, after he had spent two years in the Ditch, he was sent to Great Britain to get the hang of towpath construction. A year later he returned home, laden with new instruments, canal drawings, and a deal of firsthand information, having hoofed it, shanks' mare, along two thousand miles of European towpaths.

His first contribution after his return was the providential discovery of something he called "waterproof lime." Actually this was the first hydraulic cement in America, and an absolute necessity since the Erie's first locks, makeshift combinations of wood and field stone, were already beginning to show decay, and the cement that England was using was far too expensive to be shipped to this country. The new discovery came about quite accidentally, at a time when Canvass White and a few companions were doing some experimenting with a certain queer stone they had found along the canal near Chittenango. Testing its possibilities, they had burned it, pulverized it, mixed it with sand, and made it into a ball which they had set aside overnight in a bucket of water. In the morning, to their amazement, they found that the mass had "set into a ball of stone." This they joyfully seized as a new material for lock building. It also proved to be immediately helpful in the matter of keeping waves from destroying the banks, a problem that had been heretofore solved by including more and more curves, to discourage the speeding that was producing the waves. This method had already slowed travel down to a degree where a young blade could step ashore, shoot a brace of squab or pick a basket of strawberries for his lady-love, and be ready to hop aboard again when his packet came around the bend. In fact, as time went on, it became evident that many of the so-called wonders of the Old Erie's later days would have been impossible without Canvass White's "waterproof lime."

While the problem of securing enough engineers was to plague the Erie Canal all the days of her building, no one ever lost any sleep over the matter of hiring unskilled labor. From the beginning, thousands jumped at the chance of signing a workman's contract, since money was scarce and the means of snagging it proportionately few. The contractors themselves were usually local farmers with enough ready cash to build workmen's shacks, while three-fourths of their workers were native-born, thus avoiding the danger that had plagued the Cumberland Road when angry gangs of disgruntled foreign laborers menaced its early travelers. Most of the remaining workmen were the so-called "wild Irish bog-trotters," brought to this country from the west of Ireland because they had what Dr. C. F. Hubbard of Rome called "the ability to withstand sickness though they are set to work knee-deep in wet muck wearing naught but a flannel shirt and a slouch hat."

It was true that the Irish seemed to thrive on the life —mosquitoes notwithstanding. From the very day of their landing, to a man, they took to the new country. They liked its great forests and its wide, wide expanse. They liked their work and they liked the canal and they liked being free from the fear of starvation. They found it pleasant to see their names on contracts, though they could not read. Nor were any of them ever known to object to the visits of the jigger-man who warded off cholera with a swig of whiskey for each workman each hour —customary because Americans, like Daudet's Captain of *La Belle Nivernaisse,* believed that "when a man has to live with his feet in the water and his pate in the sun, it is quite necessary to quaff off a glass now and then."

The ubiquitous fist fighting on the Big Ditch was also lovingly embraced by the Irish bogtrotters, who soon established a reputation for going about hopefully with chips on their shoulders and doubled-up fists, never side-stepping a fight of any kind, though they preferred to mix it with their own people. The pay was another joyful adjunct of ditchdigging— eighty cents a day, plus warm sleeping space on the floor of a workman's shanty, plus "keep" that guaranteed roast beef twice daily instead of the everlasting roast turkey and duck that had formerly graced the long tables.

The contractor, too, was a satisfied individual. It cost him eighty dollars to erect a shanty that could accommodate forty laborers. It cost him the price of their equipment, their horses, their food, their whiskey, and their wages. But he received a shilling a yard for all canal dirt removed by his diggers, or $2,500 for each mile excavated. And so important was he to the forward march of the canal that the Commissioners were always ready to print up a little scrip for him when he ran out of cash—an IOU certificate that soon passed for currency. Often they even set him up in business with a two-thousand-dollar loan, plus the privilege of borrowing an additional two hundred to a thousand if he needed it to lay in supplies of beef, pork, and flour when the winter prices were low and the ground was frozen hard enough to support the wagons. Under this system, during the year of 1818 between two and three thousand laborers were at work on the Erie Canal—with a horse for every second man—digging and grubbing through what they called "the smiling country," the future Syracuse and Rochester districts.

That was the year when the Cumberland Road slid down its last weary hill into Wheeling. It was also the year when every canal builder, from Commissioner to hoggee, came to know for certain sure that fighting a way aboveground and beneath the sod through a practically tractless wilderness to construct a sixty-foot aisle from Lake Erie to the Hudson—with a forty-foot channel at its center and enough locks to take care of a nearly six-hundred-foot drop—was going to take a deal of doing. It meant that stone and lime and supplies must be hauled in, where there were no roads. Lumber must be cut, though there were few mills. Thousands of men and animals must be fed, in a territory that provided little but game. Illnesses must be cared for, though there were few doctors. And worst of all, great forests must be removed and great ditches must be dug, though there was no machinery adequate to either task.

It was in regard to this latter dilemma that the workmen of necessity learned most rapidly how to improve their condition, having discarded during their first year the slow English method of man-plus-spade-plus-wheelbarrow for the quicker horse-drawn plow and scraper, which also produced firmer embankments because of the constant treading of horses and men. By the second year, laborers on the Rome section had devised a cutting blade to be attached to the plow, which took care of stubborn tree roots. Next they discovered that a chain with one end fastened to the top of a tree and the other end wound around a wheel, worked by an endless screw, made it possible for a lone man to fell any forest giant, singlehanded.

Meanwhile, out near Syracuse—which was the midpoint of the hundreds of miles of black forest—workmen were tinkering with a thing they called a stump puller, which actually worked. This consisted of two immense wheels, sixteen feet high, connected by an axle thirty feet long, which bore at its middle a third wheel fourteen feet high. Upon the broad rim of this smaller wheel they wound a rope leading to a pair of husky horses, and a chain fastened to a tree stump. Next, the big wheels were firmly braced. Then to the tune of cracking whips and squeaking harness, the horses leaned into the traces, put their muscles into the task, and out came the largest and most stubborn stump, thanks to the rotary motion produced by the small wheel. With it, seven men and two horses could grub thirty to forty tree stumps per day. And the cost of this Yankee contraption was $250.

In the year of 1818, all but five of the ninety-four miles of the Erie's Middle Section were grubbed and cleared of forest giants by means of these powerful machines—a feat more fully appreciated when you consider what some of these trees were like. Wrote Hezekiah Niles, "A walnut tree in the New York wilderness fell to the ground, during a storm, about three years ago. A spectator possessed himself of the hollow trunk and converted it into a grocery store. Another spectator has since obtained it and it is to be sent to the City of New York and fitted up for a confectionery establishment. Its girth is about thirty feet."

By October of that same year, the first fifteen miles of the

Erie Canal, out near Rome, were completed, in spite of spring freshets that carried away new bridges, through a district that one engineer labeled "thirty-five solid miles of musquetoes." And while the Commissioners were well satisfied with this achievement—in view of the enormity of their task—the rocking-chair critics back home laughed merrily. "A scant fifteen miles finished out of more than three hundred and fifty miles, and a year and a half already gone! Well, hurrah for *Clinton's Ditch!*"

It was a name that stuck for years to come—used derisively at first, later proudly. As a matter of record, progress on the Old Erie to date had been considerably greater than the completed fifteen miles would indicate. An additional ninety-four miles of the middle section had been cleared, forty-eight miles of this had also been dug, and an eight-mile strip of it was actually boatable and waiting inspection—though admittedly at a cost of $578,549 already.

The year of 1819 was a tough one for the Erie Canal. At Montezuma, out near Syracuse, extensive swamps proved to be a double threat to the workmen. Here lay the hide-out of the Doanes and Tomblesons, a notorious gang of trigger-happy thieves whose guns continuously protested against any invasion of their marshy, traditional hangout, while their coffers increased in weight daily, thanks to the unwilling contributions extracted from Irish bogtrotters. Here, too, lay the breeding grounds of what one report called "such clouds of musquetoes as to hide the grubbers from view," each insect carrying its full quota of fevers besides the dreaded ague that laid low a thousand workers that terrible summer, some of them permanently—and there was not so much as a foot of dry ground for a decent burial. Even those who lived through that summer came out of it more dead than alive—weakened, retching, swept alternately by chills and fever for weeks to come.

This was the third year of grubbing and digging for most of

these weary workmen, and a growing ferment of discontent was at last beginning to surface. The strain of hard work had been bad enough. The plague of gnats and mosquitoes, and the eternal dampness, were worse. Brushing swarms of insects from every mouthful of food you attempted to eat, continuously wading through stagnant marshes, sleeping on drenched, moldy blankets, awakening to cold, weevily breakfasts, slapping the sides of the water barrel to send the wigglers to the bottom so that you could hastily scoop a drink off the top, all produced a life that was not worth living. Now you hated the whilom pal you joked with last spring. You both flashed fists whenever you met. And later you flashed knives. And when the "agur" struck you both down, you hoped to the high heavens that your friend would die, and he entertained the same love for you. And gradually as the burden of life and its strangeness grew into a heaviness that few could endure, you also longed for death for yourself. But most of all you wished it for the damned Old Erie. And when at long last you reached again for your shovel, it was only because you were as miserable idle as you were when working.

And yet, during that terrible third summer, considerably more of the middle section was made boatable, and the exploring and surveying of the eastern section and parts of the western section were well started. When the year of 1820 rolled in—much drier and more comfortable and more hopeful— rapid and important advances were made along much of the Big Ditch. A fifty-mile strip between Montezuma and the Genesee River was nearly completed, as was the entire middle section to the point of running boats in certain places, while the strip between Genesee Street in Utica and the Seneca River Lock was even polished off to the point of having its milestones already erected—ninety-six of them. On the eastern section, several parts were already let to contractors, and a survey of the Mohawk Valley by Canvass White was well under way.

By this time, canal building had progressed to a point where its problems were concerned mostly with the matter of water. It had been known from the moment when the first cannon signaled the breaking of sod at Rome, that one of the Old Erie's chief puzzlers was going to be how to keep her channel flooded throughout the boating season, especially on the western two-thirds, after she had cut away from the Mohawk River. From this need had sprung up an additional system of channels, called feeders, which brought water in from the neighboring lakes and creeks and from reservoirs built in the hills for this purpose. To increase the usefulness of these feeders, each was made wide enough to serve also as a branch canal, separated from the main channel by sluice gates so that an attendant could maintain the proper water level. In time this practice would produce hundreds of additional miles of channel, making the entire Erie Canal system into a thousand-mile waterway which would include the entire Finger Lakes district.

Soon it was evident that even so extensive a feeder system would not always be adequate to the task of supplying sufficient water. For it had already been discovered that in times of prolonged dry spells or extensive leakage, even the feeders went dry, making large sections of the Big Ditch useless. So now the spotlight of canal endeavor must be turned to the matter of water economy.

To begin with, the loss of a lockful of water each time a boat passed through was inevitable. A lock—often called a combine —consisted of a boxed-off section of the canal, ninety feet long and fifteen feet wide, built with gates at both ends. Upon approaching a lock from the west, a boat glided directly into the lock at her own level. Here she waited while the gates behind her were closed and the water was slowly drained out, lowering her to the level of the channel ahead. Now the huge wooden gates in front of her were opened to allow her to proceed eastward at the new level. The same process in reverse moved westbound traffic from the lower to the higher level. In either event—the law of gravity being what it is—the extra water must always be supplied from the upper channel, and the surplus run off through side gates in order to maintain the proper level in both upper and lower channels. This meant that the canal suffered the loss of a lockful of water each time the big gates were opened, which could happen a hundred times a day in a busy season. Also, the crude wooden lockgates always leaked.

It had long been recognized that a certain amount of evaporation would occur on all parts of the canal and nothing could be done about it, so that matter must be left in the lap of the gods. But the water lost through canal absorption was strictly man's affair. It was known that European canals suffered a total loss of two cubic feet per mile per minute, or one-tenth inch per day in canal depth. It was expected that the total loss would be slightly greater in the United States—not so much through absorption, since the nature of our soil was believed to be more favorable, but considerably more through evaporation because of our drier climate. That was the way the American engineers had it figured. But the staggering truth was much worse than they had feared. In York State it was found that along a twenty-three-mile stretch of completed channel, the drop in water depth was running two and a quarter inches per day—nearly sixteen inches per week, in addition to the loss at locks. Since the canal was only four feet deep to begin with, this was a matter of grave concern, with no solution in sight. But within a few months after this dilemma came to light, quite providentially along came the discovery of something called "the blue mud of the meadows," a muck that formed a nearly perfect seal as a canal lining, immediately cutting the water loss in half.

The problem of lock construction was next to cause concern. Although engineers sought level ground wherever it could be found, regardless of the meandering it might cause, sooner or later the canal must be stepped down from Lake Erie to the Hudson, the whole rise and fall of lockage to be 688 feet. And while a slight drop was necessary on the straightaways in order to feed water into the canal, it must never be so great as to produce a current which would hinder upbound boats, since the main advantage of canal travel over river travel was the absence of such a current. Countless calculations and endless days of careful construction finally produced some amazing results, notably along the Buffalo-to-Lockport strip, which wound up, some five years later, with a drop of only one inch to the mile. And this was accomplished without a single honest-to-goodness engineer on the job.

The locks themselves were difficult and expensive and numerous—there were twenty-seven of them between Albany and Schenectady alone. This caused so much delay, when the first boats went through, that it immediately became fashionable for passengers to abandon their packet at Albany and take off by ricocheting stagecoach along the handsomely shaded, seventeen-mile Mohawk and Hudson Turnpike. This allowed them time for a peaceful night's rest at Given's Hotel in Schenectady and a leisurely breakfast in the hotel's ordinary before their boat finally arrived, having been all night long going through the locks. This maneuver, however, was a long five years hence.

Meanwhile, in the matter of lock building, it was necessary to construct twenty-five of them between Schenectady and Utica—moving westward—in order to step the channel up to the strip known as the "Long Level" which ended at Syracuse. Beyond this, a series of two-step and three-step combines—up and down—would ease the channel into the long sixteen-lock climb between Montezuma and Rochester, where it crossed the Genesee Level to reach what was later to be known as the Famous Lockport Five, a group of combines that finally lifted the canal over the Niagara escarpment to level off for Buffalo. These latter five were expected to be the most difficult of all to build, for here was the only place on the line where separate locks would be installed for eastbound and westbound traffic —all to be cut from sheer rock walls, thirty feet high, with narrow towpaths chiseled in the solid rock high above the channel. Nathan Roberts, a thirty-third-degree engineer so far as experience was concerned, and due to be known as Father of the Lockport Five, was already losing sleep over the problem —though not in vain. For here, one day, he was to achieve what would eventually be listed as one of the wonders of young America.

In the course of a canal's run, sometimes it became necessary for her to cross another stream, perhaps to take advantage of level ground on the opposite bank of the river she was trailing as her feeder, or perhaps to traverse some angling creek that had got in her way. Each stream presented a separate problem, and all of them were tough. At times, the engineers erected a well-anchored towpath high over the offending stream, upon which horses and driver could cross, towing their canalboat directly through the current below. This method was very dangerous during a spring freshet, and many a flood swept boat, cargo, crew, and mules down some river to disaster. A simpler solution was to hire a professional tow by ferryboat, after horses and driver had been taken aboard to enjoy the

ride. But this practice was expensive, and almost unknown to
the Old Erie.

The safest and most satisfactory method for the Big Ditch—
and by all odds the most costly to install—was the aqueduct,
which was virtually a box-enclosed channel, built high above
a river or creek with its stone supports bearing aloft the combined weight of the water-filled aqueduct plus boat, cargo,
mules, passengers, and crew. It was built on a level with the
regular canal so that a tow horse walked into it as directly as
if he were entering a tunnel. There was also another kind of
aqueduct, less spectacular, which was built into the side of a
hill where there was no stream involved. This one simply kept
the canal at her proper level by circling a valley, without the
need of building locks to step her across it. In either case, while
stone was almost always used for the supporting arches, the
boxlike channels were usually made of wood—soon to become
rickety, rotting affairs that hung precariously for years high
above valley or stream. Yet, strangely enough, no serious collapse was ever known to occur on any of them.

Architecturally, the glory of Clinton's Ditch lay in these
aqueducts, even as they furnished her most difficult construction problem. Since her canal sections were parceled out to
various contractors, each being allowed considerable freedom
of design because each must build in accordance with his own
ability and the materials at hand, a growing competition
among contractors brought about some amazing engineering
feats. In later years, several of the Erie's aqueducts were included in lists of American wonders that all travelers should
strive to see.

The fact that the Mohawk and Genesee Rivers must be
crossed several times also contributed handsomely to the spectacular nature of these aqueducts. The one destined to attract
the most awe and admiration was now scheduled for Little

Falls, an immense 1,184-footer, rising forty to fifty feet above
the rushing Mohawk, supported by three huge arches—and
how was this to be accomplished without machinery! Twelve
miles below Schenectady, the longest aqueduct on the Erie
Canal would stretch 1,188 feet across the same valley, resting
on twenty-six stone piers set in Canvass White's waterproof
lime. Four miles northeast of that same village, the Mohawk
would again be spanned, this time by a 748-footer. To cross
the tumbling Genesee at Rochester would require an 804-
footer, so high it would need ten massive arches to support it.

In times of flood many creeks along the Erie's course were as
hazardous as the rivers. These, too, must be crossed by aqueduct. Through Herkimer County ran the Oriskany Creek,
known for her bad manners during spring freshets. It would
take a notably high 204-footer to conquer her whims. The
Skaneateles Outlet needed a 100-foot aqueduct. The Oak
Orchard Creek would require a 60-footer. And the Owasco
Outlet needed one 120 feet long. From lesser rivers and creeks
all along the line came dozens of pleas for similar structures,
most of them financially out of the question. To the harassed
Benjamin Wright, there must have been times when the Far
West looked very, very far west.

And to top it all, there was the matter of canal bridges, a
huge problem because it was necessary to build so many of
them—three hundred between Utica and Albany alone. With
the exception of the necessarily long spans—the one across the
Cayuga marshes was the longest in America—it was decided
to build exceedingly low bridges for the sake of economy.

This brought about some queer maneuvers when the lowest
ones were completed. For whenever a passenger missed his
canalboat, he could easily run ahead to the next bridge to drop
aboard when his packet passed under. The economy spans
also made it necessary for towpath drivers to be almost con-

stantly calling, "Low bridge!" so that deck passengers could duck down to avoid being beheaded.

Between the voyagers scampering to the floor in the name of safety, and those dropping aboard from bridges, a canalboat was somewhat lost in confusion at every bridge. It made an acrobat out of everyone.

CHAPTER FIVE

SNIPING AT CLINTON

MEANWHILE the wolves were howling. Almost from the Old Erie's earliest days, there had been organized carping against her. Much of this was due to a common misunderstanding about canals in general and what this one had to face in particular. To begin with, few people believed that a lock could actually overcome their oft-repeated objection based on the old saw that "You can't make water run uphill." Even fewer understood that Clinton's Ditch must require many years for her building because she was to be the longest canal in the world, to date, while her lockage at Waterford alone would double that of any other canal within the century —including Panama.

Irked by long delays, an increasing number of would-be pioneers had let their dissatisfaction come to the surface during the year of 1819, augmented, strangely enough, by a growing hatred for De Witt Clinton. Sensing the trouble that this might cause, the Commissioners then decided to discourage criticism by holding elaborate ceremonies from time to time in order to acquaint the people with the marvels that had already been accomplished on the Big Ditch. The first of these was to be held in October, 1819, two years and three months after the ceremonial sod-breaking at Rome. The occasion would be the official opening of the first completed canal section, the strip between Rome and Utica.

The boat honored on this occasion was a shiny new one, built especially for the event and named the *Chief Engineer of Rome*. She christened her flat bottom by being the first boat ever to spank the waters of the Erie Canal, taking two days for her ceremonial run between the two villages in question— down one day, and back the next. For once in their checkered careers, the Commissioners had guessed it right. The affair turned out to be a successful political maneuver, at least for the time being, and an occasion to be cherished forever in the memories of those lucky enough to be there.

Wrote a Rome reporter, who had stationed himself before daybreak on a canal bridge that commanded an excellent view, "The scene was extremely interesting and highly grateful. The embarkation took place amid the ringing of bells, the roaring of cannon, and the loud acclamations of thousands of exhilerated spectators, male and female, who lined the banks of the newly created river. The scene was truly sublime."

At Utica the next morning when the *Chief Engineer* started the return voyage, an appreciative spectator who had been following her all the way turned an appraising eye to the newly admitted canal waters wrinkling in the autumn breeze, to the quiet surrounding forest where the smoke of breakfast fires still clung thickly, to the excited throngs on berm and towpath, to the gaily festooned packet's catwalks, crowded with tall-hatted bigwigs. It put a pride in his heart and a lump in his throat, just to ponder on what these two days had been like. For here in the wilderness at this moment, history was in the making.

"I consider it the privilege of my life to have been present to witness it," he wrote as soon as he could get to quill and ink, "a sight that could not but exhilerate and elevate the mind. The waters were rushing in from the westward and coming down their untried channel towards the sea . . . The interest manifested by the whole country as this internal river rolled its first waves through the state, cannot be described. You might see people running across the fields and crowding the banks of the canal to gaze upon the welcome sight. A boat had been prepared at Rome, and as the waters came down the canal, this new Argo floated triumphantly along the Hellespont of the West."

The fact that an additional ninety-four-mile strip was nearly ready to be presented to the people at this same time should have completed the job of hushing the howling wolves. But for every one of the so-called "exhilerated thousands" who witnessed the canal opening, there were a half-dozen other New Yorkers who maintained a watchful, tongue-in-cheek attitude toward the whole matter. Some of these were irked because it was becoming evident that Clinton could never fulfill his campaign promise of 1817—that he would complete the Erie Canal by 1823 if he was elected governor. And since on the strength of that promise they had swept him into office with the greatest majority yet known in York State—43,310 to 1,479 votes—they now felt that they had been sold down the river. There were others who went a step further and spoke openly of their conviction that the Erie would never be completed, claiming that any plan to connect the Hudson with a lake 568 feet higher and 363 miles away was unadulterated nonsense.

By the following spring, the most widely discussed topic of the day centered around Clinton and his Big Ditch. Jefferson openly admitted that he personally "did not believe it would ever become a reality." And most of the eastern seaboard agreed with him. Even those New Yorkers who had most staunchly waved the flags for the canal now began to harbor secret misgivings. "Nearly two and a half years to complete so small a section," said one patriarch, wagging a twenty-eight-inch beard. "We will never see it finished—though our children may!" Among those who followed this train of thought—conceding that the canal might one day be completed, but certainly not within a quarter-century—were the officials of the Holland Land Company, who now stepped forward to donate 100,632 acres to help finance Clinton's Ditch—but only "providing it can be done by 1842."

1842! The idea disgusted Clinton. Boldly, disdainfully, without a single supporter, he answered the Holland Company and all other doubters. Whereas unforeseen difficulties had admittedly prevented his fulfillment of the 1823 date, he could now definitely promise that boats would freely run the full length of the Old Erie, Albany to Buffalo, by 1825.

This raised a derisive hoot and holler across the land—for two-thirds of the canal was barely started. Clinton was a "traitor who had opposed the prosecution of the recent war." And as for the Big Ditch, actually what had he done for her? Wasn't she pretty well jelled before he took over?

All that autumn and winter the indignation pots simmered, coming to a rolling boil the following spring when there developed a plan to bring Vice-President Daniel Tompkins home from Washington to oppose Clinton for governor in the next election. The trick failed. Although it had been widely believed that all New Yorkers were now dead set against this man, Clinton was re-elected in 1820—but by the skin of his teeth, with a majority of less than 2,000 of the 180,000 votes cast. Moreover he had lost his controlling support in both Houses, which later led to a change in the state constitution, so that his powers as canal commissioner could also be hamstrung.

To top it all, the Tammany Hall crowd now openly attacked the canal project, seeking to halt it on the grounds that it had already cost too many months and too many thousands of dollars. Secretly they sought help from Clinton's enemies in the Legislature, hoping to further their plans for halting the canal's westward path at the Genesee River and turning her north at Rochester on a short cut to Lake Ontario. This was the same old scheme that Clinton had been fighting every step of the way because it contributed nothing toward opening the Far West, since there was as yet no boatable route from Lake Ontario into Lake Erie without getting lost in Niagara Falls. Fortunately, this Tammany trick also failed.

Next they attempted to halt the Big Ditch by cutting her off at the Seneca River, suggesting that she continue her westward march after her eastern section and the Champlain Canal were completely finished. By this scheme it was expected that her western half would never be finished, due to lack of interest. This trick also failed. Next they induced the Legislature to appoint a "Block Clinton Committee," which accomplished little because there was still a huge block of public opinion to be reckoned with, an unknown quantity with a mercury-like tendency just now that made it doubtful which way it might run—toward Tammany, or home to Clinton.

Nor did the formidable De Witt take all of these maneuvers lying down. According to one editor, "His six-foot figure, of such proportions as to give him the sobriquet, 'Magnus Apollo,' is now seen everywhere." His golden tongue was likewise never quiet. For at no time did his faith in the Old Erie ever falter, much less his faith in himself. He had lost other skirmishes but, like England, "never the last battle." One of his greatest admirers, trying honestly to evaluate this human enigma, drew on his two-foot clay pipe for a thoughtful moment and decided, "Clinton is inept at intrigue, overbearing in manner, demanding support but indifferent to his supporters, cynical as to the virtues of others, and hence personally unpopular . . . His principles associate him with democrats, his taste with aristocrats . . . Yet he is generally admired and respected as a man of liberal ideas and administrative competence." But at this low ebb in the affairs of both man and canal, it is doubtful that even Clinton could have accepted such a conclusion. *Respected* and *admired* were hardly the words at this time.

Meanwhile the canal's commissioners, engineers, and laborers kept stolidly at the job. The Rome celebration had been happily received by all who attended. The sooner another section could be finished and presented to the public with another gala opening, the stronger were their chances of being allowed to complete the canal according to plan. Everyone on the job, from Clinton to the meanest mudslinger, now understood the situation and trotted double-quick from dawn to dark. Nine months after the *Chief* had made her lonely voyage from Rome to Utica, the village of Syracuse celebrated the opening of a large part of the middle section on the Glorious Fourth, with seventy-three brand-new boats floating on the Erie waters around her piers. Even some of the neighboring counties which had no connection whatever with the canal sent floats and delegates to the affair. Even Magnus Apollo Clinton doggedly showed his face.

Before the smoke of that Fourth of July had completely cleared away, parties with gangs of surveyors were set frantically to work on the wilderness of the other two sections, the extreme west and parts of the extreme east. This was a well-planned, strategic move, for even the newly opened middle third, unbeknownst to the average citizen, still had her mightiest hurdle to cross. This arose from a financial quarrel that had been blowing alternately hot and cold for three years, concerned with how much the Erie Canal owed the Western Inland Lock Navigation for having appropriated the remnants of its rotted, wooden combines and abandoned, crumbling channels.

Again it seemed probable that an unfriendly Legislature would seize upon this dispute as an excuse for eliminating in the name of economy the western third of the Big Ditch. So far, the matter had been successfully hushed, though it was far from settlement. But daily it was becoming more important nationally as well as locally, since halting the Erie at this time would also deal a wicked blow to the Big Push and therefore to the course of empire. And the time was growing short now —only a scant twenty-odd years during which America must conquer the Alleghenies and populate her Middle West in sufficient numbers to support her fling against Great Britain and Mexico for possession of the vast Oregon Country and the so-called Mexican Territory. This was indeed a time of decision.

Meanwhile, headed by Van Buren, those who opposed the canal, uniting with those who opposed Clinton, had banded themselves into a powerful ring known as the Albany Regency. So strong was this coalition, Clinton was not even nominated in the 1822 race for the governorship, nor would he seek it. To silence his followers, he was still allowed to retain his position as canal commissioner, but only because his opponents in the Legislature figured that they had him hamstrung enough to prevent much progress on the Big Ditch.

But here they had guessed it wrong, for the undefeatable Clinton was too much of a fighter and too much of a politician to believe that a single election spelled either success or defeat in the course of a man's career. In his own case, adversity had always served to double his efforts. And so it was now. From Albany to the wilderness hamlet of Buffalo, his tall stoop-shouldered figure became more and more familiar, shabby for the most part since he was nearly always poor—his ear was too sensitive to the cries of the needy, said his friends; no business sense whatever, said his enemies. Now, too, an old injury was beginning to take its toll, for a leg, shattered in an accident soon after the start of the digging, was already causing the increasingly frequent periods of invalidism that would end in his death six years hence. Perhaps some foreboding kept De Witt Clinton so determinedly at the tremendous job he seems to have been born to accomplish, seldom mindful of either excruciating pain or a world that had suddenly turned a cold back to him.

His chief concern at this time had to do with water. The entire western section must somehow be fed from Lake Erie with an additional leg-over occasionally from the Niagara River and a few doubtful creeks, although this meant carrying great quantities of water 140 miles through a channel that was not allowed enough drop to produce a current. Just how this was going to work out was anybody's guess. It was the kind of problem that could easily have halted a less determined crew than the De Witt Clinton-Canvass White combination. Instead it seemed merely to spur them on, both of them fully aware that here was the sort of circumstance that would hand the Old Erie's scoffers a tailor-made guffaw. A brand-new canal and no water!

Another staggering aspect of the Old Erie at this time was the fact that with so many separate contractors—each proceeding in accordance with his own ability—the completed sections, like blocks in a piece-quilt, were now so isolated from one another as to be almost useless until the canal could be finished. Take for instance the western end of the middle section, beyond which the Big Ditch was completed only in scattered patches. Let a westbound traveler of that day tell what it was like when you came to that spot.

"Changed to a small boat near Montezuma and there entered the Seneca River by a lock, passed into one of the inlets called the Clyde River, formed by confluence of the Canandaigua Outlet and Mud Creek at Lyons, distant fifteen miles by this route from Montezuma and twelve miles by canal when finished. At Clyde we entered the canal by a temporary wooden lock and took passage in a canal boat. At Lyons, nine miles, we changed to the *Myron Holley,* a boat of forty tons drawing eight inches of water and quite elegant. We lodged the night at Palmyra and next morning arrived at Heartwell's basin in Pittsford, eight miles from Rochester where navigation of all kinds now terminates."

Thirty-seven miles in a day and a half! By nobody's standards could this, after so many long and expensive years of canal construction, be considered satisfactory progress. Even the optimistic Clinton had to admit that, and he was therefore all the more determined to correct the situation before a hostile Legislature could further thwart his efforts.

Doggedly he pushed the work forward, both to the east and to the west, throughout that frustrating summer and fall of 1822, ending just before freeze-up time by admitting water to the eastern section from Little Falls to Schenectady. He also completed the huge aqueduct over the Genesee River at Rochester—connected at this time with nothing whatever at either end. The following March his pick-and-shovel crews beat the pussy willows to their respective jobs, so that by June the dauntless De Witt could present to the people of York State —with maybe a link temporarily missing here and there—220 miles of completed canal. From Schenectady clean out to Rochester, by holy dang! He flung it in their faces, along with a newly passed decree that was expected not only to protect berms and towpaths, but also to acquaint the entire country with what was going on, out where the Big Ditch was sufficiently completed to hit her stride.

"Henceforth, speeds of only four miles per hour will be permitted on the Erie Canal, necessary to discourage the breakneck velocity some are attempting, streaking along at what appears to be five miles per hour."

Once again friendly newspapers were filled with news of Clinton's Ditch, hoping to create a state-wide echo of the enthusiasm that now surged through every canal hamlet that found itself at long last on water. Joy to the bursting point had seized Rochester. For the records, she stationed a favorite son at a vantage point to observe and report on the elaborate ceremonies being conducted for the opening of so large a section.

This he did with admirable restraint, considering the importance of the occasion.

"On Wednesday last a boat was launched at Rochester, bound for Schenectady, and though we may not announce the event in as lofty language as is used in city prints on like occasions, yet perhaps it was an occurrence equally interesting as the launching of the proudest ship from a seaport. To behold a vessel committed to the water 400 miles inland, and in a place which ten years ago was a wilderness, excites emotions of no common kind."

At Utica, another reporter covered the same event, standing perhaps on the same bridge where we saw an earlier observer moved to oratory at the sight of water rushing into the Old Erie's first fourteen miles for the launching of her first canalboat, four years earlier. But times had changed mightily during those intervening years, for now there were boats enough and trade enough to warrant a regular travel schedule. Moreover, the packets of this latter day were hardly to be mentioned in the same breath with that early, crude little *Chief Engineer of Rome*.

"Our village on Friday, twenty-fifth inst., presented a scene of bustle and stir never before witnessed here," according to the Utica reporter. "Today the first packet boat to come from Rochester left here with eighty-four passengers on her return trip. A boat will leave this place every morning, Sundays excepted, during this season, and continue to the Genesee River . . . The new boats are built in the best manner and fitted up in a style of magnificence that could hardly be anticipated in the infancy of canal navigation in this country."

Clinton and his trotting crews, however, had little time for ceremonies, for there still remained a staggering amount of work to be done. His campaign promise that he would complete the job by 1825 still drew one-sided grins from the voters.

Now he turned his attention to the two farthermost parts of the canal. To the west, by October of that year, water lay sparkling in the 17-mile strip from Rochester to Brockport with the channel fully opened to traffic. Also the 45-mile stretch from there to Mountain Ridge was nearing completion as were the four gigantic embankments that would carry the canal across four wide valleys, including the 70-footer over Sandy Creek which would be the highest on the route.

To the east, during the same gold-spangled autumn, Junction Canal was also running boats. This channel, at the extreme eastern end of the Big Ditch, was formed by the union of the Erie and Champlain Canals, joining at Watervliet for the last eight miles into Albany. Following the opening of this doubly important section, boats from both the north and the west were free to glide down canal waters into the Hudson—once their respective channels had been finished—ready to be towed down to New York City or to be swept down with the current when the tide went out, God willing and wind blowing.

The grand opening for this Junction Canal set a record that was something for all future celebrations to shoot at, leading off with a military pageant that was followed by a parade, cannon salutes, fireworks, a grand ball, and finally a banquet that outdistanced all earlier attempts by offering thirty-nine stein-clicking toasts. This in some degree was common to all canal openings. It started off usually with a toast to the "Good old U.S.A." while the evening was young, progressing thereafter until nearly dawn when the imbibers finally got around to saluting "Womanhood." And so home to bed.

Surprisingly enough, considering how thin was the ice whereon De Witt Clinton was cutting figure eights, he now deliberately halted all building on the Erie and turned to the task of digging extension channels to three neighboring lakes —Seneca, Cayuga, and Onondaga. This was definitely a political move by the master politician, undertaken in a desperate attempt to silence the yapping opposition and jealousy in these outlying counties among those who felt hard put upon at being so heavily taxed for an improvement that had so narrowly passed them by. At best it was a daredevil move on Clinton's part, coming at a time when the cost of the Big Ditch had already taxed the patience of even his staunchest friends. There were many who doubted the wisdom of such a maneuver, even after a spectacular sixty-ton vessel had arrived at New York City with triumphant flags waving, having come from the farther end of Seneca Lake, seventy miles south of the Erie Canal—a 350-mile voyage by a still necessarily circuitous route.

"Flag-waving and back-slapping or not, De Witt Clinton will rue this day," claimed his enemies. "It may cost him the Old Erie." And it very nearly did.

For this was the very break that the Albany Regency had been watching for. This time he had gone too far. The Magnus Apollo was getting too magnus. Already they had deprived him of his majority support in both Houses and cheated him out of an election, but somehow they had failed to halt him. Obviously more drastic measures would have to be taken. They met in secret session and decided to shoot the moon. Controlling both branches of the Legislature, they now used their political power to strip De Witt Clinton of the only office that still remained to him of all his amazing earlier authority. By an overwhelming vote in both Houses he was deposed as Canal Commissioner. The news flashed across the land and across the ocean. The mighty De Witt Clinton, after all these years, was through.

And so, in all probability, was the Erie Canal. For now indeed did she come to a complete standstill, a sorry sight with her stacks of building materials and equipment abandoned hither and yon throughout the wilderness, while her desolate, half-completed aqueducts and bridges and yawning locks lay deserted and quiet. Helplessly now, travelers were forced to portage through knee-deep mud from one finished canal strip to another where an occasional boatman still offered service, or else abandon their westward trek. It was a situation that produced a baffled citizenry. Whereas they had formerly been angered by the slow progress of the canal's building, now they were completely frustrated because it had stopped altogether.

Furthermore, among those who had protested the loudest against the tardiness of the Old Erie's coming, there were many who had invested in canal land bordering on the proposed right-of-way, expecting to become village founders, or prosperous shopkeepers, or canalside farmers with a ready way to market. What now was to become of them—perched along deserted ditches like crows on a weather-beaten fence? And what about those others, the thousands in Europe and the eastern seaboard who had yearned so desperately for the Far West, and waited so long for a waterway to it? And the great migration—what was to become of it, with the Cumberland Road already crumbling and the Big Ditch bogged in despair? What possible leaven could there be, strong enough to keep the ferment of desire working in the pioneer's breast in spite of insurmountable circumstances, engendering the tenacity, determination, and dedication without which the Big Push would surely fail?

Again it was a critical moment in American history.

CHAPTER SIX

BLACKBERRY-DIPPED QUILL PENS AND SUCCESS

PROBABLY England was the last quarter in the world from which young America should have expected help in furthering her westward migration, since that powerful nation—her archenemy in two recent wars—was now her chief competitor in the race for possession of the vast Oregon Country. And yet by a queer quirk of fate, that was exactly where help did come from—quite unintentionally, as far as the British government was concerned.

At the end of the Napoleonic Wars, Great Britain found herself deep in a depression, with hunger and debt stalking her land and a dreary debtor's prison awaiting the man who could not make both ends meet. The farmers were especially hard hit, for even when the weather favored their crops it took thirty years to pay for a farm, partly because of the tremendous taxes that England demanded, partly because of the heavy tax the church demanded. During the wars it had been hoped that peace would correct these appalling conditions, but now, when peace had come, it was apparent that the reverse could be expected.

Pressed beyond endurance, the farmers were the first to give up the struggle, abandoning their meager acreages by the hundreds, lulled into forgetfulness by pied pipers who sang sweetly of a never-never land across the sea, a place where there were no taxes, where great open valleys offered the richest land in the world for ten shillings an acre, where a farm could pay for itself in a year or two. The place lay in America and it was called the Far West. The pipers were legion—Morris Birkbeck to begin with, followed closely by the two Flowers, Flagg, Fordham, Mason, Fearon, Thomas, Faux, Cobbett, Hulme, Woods, Flint, Derby, and many others.

Their songs were as varied as the men who sang them. The contribution of these men lay not only in the fact that great numbers of Europeans listened and took heed, but also because their blackberry-juiced quill pens brought into thousands of America's candlelit kitchens such floods of books and pamphlets concerning her own frontier as this country had never known.

Birkbeck and the two Flowers—Richard and son George—were the first of these visionary British authors who struggled to America's new Far West. During 1817 and 1818, they took up thousands of acres of raw Illinois land, later to be known as the English Prairies, hoping thereon to establish great estates similar to feudal holdings in England. Birkbeck alone took 26,400 acres to start off with, and would have purchased more except that the United States Congress, which smiled so sweetly upon the small homesteader, frowned upon extending credit for large domains. Nevertheless, his Wanborough Village grew in two years from empty prairie to a hamlet of 1,100 souls, including 700 Yankees—all lured thither by Birkbeck's sweet-talking quill pen.

All three of these pioneering landholders withstood the early hardships of frontier life—including an occasional quarrel among themselves—and stayed on to become Americanized. Eventually they even learned graciously to accept the fact that their hopes of establishing huge domains run by professional servants could never be fulfilled in this country because of a thing called democracy, wherein the hired man, too, invested every spare half-dollar as a down payment on an Illinois acre—thereby soon setting himself up as a landowner, a neighbor, and an equal of his British employers. To their credit, however, let it be said that they seemed to make the switch-over without too great a struggle, learning to clear land and plant crops without help whenever it was necessary. And at no time did their delight in the new country lessen.

Birkbeck's jubilant *Notes on a Journey in America in 1817,* which went into eleven editions, and his joyous *Letters from the Illinois Territory of North America in 1818,* which went into seven—including German and French translations—were providentially hitting their stride at the very time when the building of the Old Erie had come to a complete standstill. Added to the impact of these two books came a flood of pamphlets from the pen of Richard Flower, appearing in sufficient numbers to reach every second kitchen table in America. All of them dwelt on the glories of life in the fringe country, and their popularity was immediate and immense. To begin with, they cost only a shilling apiece which made them available to nearly everyone. In the second place, they held out a warm, comforting sort of hope to the anxiety-bitten mover, be he English or American who yearned to stake his all on the Western venture. And in the third place, no one could help loving the author.

Richard Flower was a gentle soul, already sixty-three years old before he left his native England to join son George in America. For two years now he had been splitting rails and infinitives out on the English Prairies—the former because immigrants were now flocking in and needed roofs over their heads, and the latter because a certain William Cobbett was currently in his finest and most sarcastic fettle, and needed to be taken down a peg.

Cobbett was another English author, recently removed to America. He was now raising rutabagas on Long Island while being subsidized by certain land speculators of Philadelphia and New York, in payment for his attempts to persuade well-to-do British immigrants to settle, with their pots of gold, in the East instead of going on to the fringe country. Almost immediately Cobbett became the idol of thousands, widely read and widely followed.

One of his earliest pamphlets, *A Year's Residency in the United States of America,* was an outright attack on Birkbeck's writings, bitterly deriding the entire Western fringe which, as a matter of fact, he had never seen. The subsequent verbal battle, in which the attack was answered largely by Richard Flower and son George, produced thousands of additional pamphlets, bringing the subject of the faraway Illinois prairies into unbelievable prominence on two continents. So bitter was this controversy, that soon the press of not-so-very-merry England seized Cobbett's accusations as a potent argument against all emigration to America. This succeeded only in advertising more widely than ever the English Prairies in the new land of Illinois.

The controversy lasted a full ten years, because the slowness of travel and the scarcity of American publishers caused a two-to-five-year delay between the writing and the publishing of any book or pamphlet. Also, throughout that full decade these Cobbett-Flower papers continued to appear, pouring countless shillings into the coffers of London publishers and quantities of detailed descriptions of the lush fringe country into the receptive minds of Americans and Europeans. Soon other writers were shoving their way into the free-for-all scrap. And each new British immigrant who possessed a pen and a passing knowledge of the mother tongue now also assumed the right to visit the Birkbeck-Flower settlements, review the situation, and add his own two bits' worth, pro or con, until the printed matter on this subject had run to many hundreds of thousands of copies. At no time was the controversy in itself very important. But its contribution was great, for it kept the desire for Westering eternally alive in the minds of the reading public.

Incidentally, these English-inspired books and pamphlets served the United States nobly in another capacity. Pros or cons, the British scribblers agreed on one issue with all the power of their split-quill pens—they hated and detested from the bottom of their souls what they called "the shocking circumstance of slavery in America." Faux and Woods denounced it roundly, as did the two Flowers and Birkbeck, the latter with such far-reaching results as to change the picture for the state of Illinois and perhaps for the entire country as well. For at this very early day, and in this unformed country, Morris Birkbeck, with the backing of other British writers, was able in 1824-25 to induce his English friend Edward Colles, governor of the six-year-old state of Illinois, to turn down a popular new constitution that would have admitted slavery to this territory.

Thus, in thrashing out problems of her own, did the unfriendly, faraway England contribute most handsomely to America's expansion and destiny. And the timing of this contribution—coming at the moment of the discouraging lull in the Old Erie's building and at the peak of the antagonism against Clinton—was little short of providential. Without it, there might have been no Canal Era.

By election time in 1824, the long pendulum that timed the progress of the Big Ditch had reached the turn of its swing. A determined change in public opinion plus a renewed and increased desire for the Promised Land were partly responsible. But so was the Old Erie herself. In spite of the hardships of innumerable portages and inconveniences on a canal that did not seem to be getting anywhere, her few operating sections were demanding the return of De Witt Clinton more loudly

and effectively than any human voice. The argument was ir-
refutable—$20,954 in tolls in six months from a mere forty-
five-mile strip, between the Genesee and Seneca Rivers, that
had managed to stay open in spite of all opposition and was
now handling 1,822 boats. Such a record seemed to indicate a
strong possibility of financial success for the first time in canal
history anywhere—which meant that the Old Erie could no
longer be cried down, since even her enemies had never found
anything objectionable about her except her tremendous cost.

Nor could there be any further doubt that the great migration would also weather the storm. Suddenly the seaports and
highways of the East were filled with emigrants and westbound
travelers, even before the spring freshets of 1824 had made
their way down the ice-choked brooks and rivers. Now all of
the completed canal units that had ever held water were reopened and put into full operation. Overnight they were
crowded with movers, adventurers, refugees, soldiers, missioners, hucksters, doctors, lawyers, teachers, merchants—
knee-deep in mud, maneuvering the many portages as best
they could.

Again the matter of better transportation became the most
widely discussed subject of the day, augmented by the restlessness that always arose when the sap ran free. "Ohio fever,"
they were calling it this year, even when they had in mind an
oak opening in Michigan, or a clearing among the sycamores
that edged the Wabash Paradise, or the Illinois prairie where
morning still lay young and fresh upon the land. And always,
come springtime, just as surely as pussy willows felt the stir
of March winds, the western editors felt the stir of destiny in
their souls and burst forth with enraptured effusions of their
own. Such a burst now appeared in the *National Intelligencer,*
copied from the *Chillicothe Supporter,* out on Zane's Trace.

"Looking only a few years hence through the vista of the
future, what a sublime spectacle presents itself! Wilderness,

once the chosen residence of solitude or savageness, converted into populous cities, smiling villages, beautiful farms and plantations! The happy multitudes, busy in their daily occupations, manifest contentment and peace, breathing their gratitude and their prayers only to the great King of Kings . . . The Mississippi rolls her proud waves as before, but her bosom is ploughed by thousands of keels, and her surface whitened by thousands of sails, bearing the produce of millions of industrious citizens, to its destined mart! What a scene—how beautiful, how grand! Another century will realize it. Yes, this fine country is destined to become the finest foothold of the Genius of American Liberty . . . which will endure when the stream of time shall have drained into the ocean of eternity!"

This was the sort of thing that always raised the pulse of the pioneer, giving him a noble and idealistic reason for doing what he hankered to do anyway. So now, in the spring of 1824, he was making up his collective mind that the western venture must be delayed no longer. It was not surprising, then, that the pendulum abruptly changed its swing, and De Witt Clinton found himself blessed with enough friends to nominate and elect him governor of York State with the gratifying plurality of 16,000 votes.

This was the turning point for the Erie Canal. Not complete victory, for there still remained the two most difficult problems of the entire project—the extreme eastern section with its twenty-seven locks in twenty-nine miles, and the extreme western with its twin sets of combines and double towpaths to be cut from sheer stone walls thirty feet high. With his tremendous energy, De Witt Clinton now announced, to the astonishment of all, that it was still his intention to present the fully completed canal to the state of New York by the end of the following year, 1825, just as he had originally promised, and this in spite of the loss of time that had been forced upon him.

He turned his attention first to the western terminus of the Big Ditch. Here, for three years, there had raged a fierce battle known as the Buffalo and Black Rock War, a classic example of the antagonism and jealousy that often sprang up between neighboring pioneer villages. In this case it was entirely understandable; the stakes were high, for the future of both hamlets was involved. The situation was this. To begin with, in all canal building, the first burning question was, "Which direction will the surveyors' red stakes take?" For it was well known that, magically, along that line lay riches. And if the issue included also the matter of a terminus, it had reached its ultimate in importance, for such a village was destined to become not only a great city, but also, willy-nilly, a great port.

Therein lay the cause of the Buffalo and Black Rock War. One of these two was destined to become the Erie's western terminus. It had been known from the time when the first cannon boomed at Rome that the east end of the canal would terminate in the great Albany Basin, where a thirty-two-acre reservoir would service a thousand canalboats and fifty vessels at a time. But an exact location for the west end had become so difficult to settle upon that the Big Ditch was running boats from Schenectady to Brockport before the western terminal had yet been named, let alone surveyed. The trouble lay in the fact that Black Rock and Buffalo were about equal in size, in harbor facilities, and in ambition. Yet one was destined to become rich and important while the other was doomed to obscurity. Moreover, the war was already well under way before the Commissioners had turned their attention to this faraway spot in the wilderness.

For three years now the bitterness had been growing, with each hamlet becoming more and more proficient in ways of insulting her neighbor while extolling her own virtues. In the latter months the whole matter had become too hot to handle. Locally there had been citizens' rallies, hectic and fierce, with speeches and fist fights that waxed hot and died down and flared up again. When it looked as if Black Rock might be the favored one, she dragged forth her rusty Revolutionary cannon, aimed it in the general direction of Buffalo, and let fly with a derisive blast which served only to start a riot in the other hamlet. Perhaps a month later when Buffalo seemed due for the royal nod, it was her turn to wheel out her own rusty relic. And so the matter had dragged along, growing more and more bitter until the Commissioners could no longer dodge the issue. Their belated decision in midsummer of that year waved the magic wand that was to make a great city of crude little Buffalo, even as it doomed Black Rock to the less glamorous existence of a mere canalside village, with nothing more important to do than to open and close her sluice gates when the Big Ditch called for Erie water.

This was a great day for Buffalo, celebrated on August 9 of that year with a huge sod-breaking ceremony, there in the wilderness, attended by the entire countryside including a few of the more curious from Black Rock. Let one who was there tell what it was like. "All people with oxen were invited to bring them. All met on a boggy flat and hitched the ten or twelve yoke of oxen to the largest plough in the world, then 'Go lang, Buck!' and the blade bit into the black mold and sod between the stakes that marked the new canal. Along the proposed route were placed barrels of rye whiskey at convenient spots, with part of the head cut off and a tin dipper lying by for all to help themselves free . . . Everybody worked that day."

And yet, so crude was this outpost village, not a single wheelbarrow nor scraper existed within her borders, although for three years she had been fighting to prove her readiness and desirability as a canal terminus. Now, faced with this lack, a few clever citizens turned their axes to the surrounding forests and fashioned something of their own invention, a contraption they called a "soul cart" because it was so difficult to manage. It consisted of two parallel poles, six to eight feet long, connected at their middles by a crude platform upon which great quantities of sod could be piled and hauled away, requiring the services of only two men. After the first example had been demonstrated, dozens more of these soul carts were immediately hewn from the forest and put to service. And according to the press, "Everyone from judges to urchins pitched in, that day."

Northeasterly from Buffalo, at the drop of the Niagara escarpment near Mountain Ridge, lay Lockport with her difficult task of hand-cutting five eastbound and five westbound locks through solid rock. To this project Clinton next turned his eager attention. For several years now Nathan Roberts, the so-called Father of the Lockport Five, had been puzzling over this particular problem. This was the only place on the canal where separate locks for separate lines of traffic would be attempted, which doubled the task. Here the work progressed slowly. The towpaths must be hand-chiseled from solid rock, which would later present the unusual spectacle of horses and driver creeping cautiously along a high, narrow mountain shelf, towing a canalboat far below. For that matter, the entire project was due to be tremendously spectacular, with it yellow lantern lights reflecting down the dark chasm onto ten water levels, a thing of star-spangled beauty in the night, at a place where so recently there had been nothing but black forest.

Simultaneously with this western project, Governor Clinton was pushing construction forward on the twenty-seven difficult locks between Albany and Schenectady. Luckily here, too, he was able to achieve his goal before freeze-up time that year, so that the joyful news could be shouted from both ends of the canal at once. Water was flooding the eastern section with all locks operating perfectly! And water was flooding the western section all the way to the Lockport Five! Moreover, both units were already besieged with westbound emigrants, jubilantly on their way.

The Old Erie could also report great financial gains for that year of 1824. By September it was announced that the season's tolls for the short strip between Mantz and Utica had already brought in a gratifying $77,493, while an additional $27,449 had come in from the far eastern section of the channel. But when the year's totals from all completed parts reached an astounding $294,546—not even including the amounts collected from mills for water rights where the locks produced waterfalls—the news came as a complete surprise to everyone, including De Witt Clinton. Nearly a third of a million dollars from a canal not yet finished! This was a staggering sum of money for such sparsely settled country, especially in view of the fact that no other canal anywhere had yet shown any profits whatsoever. Nor was any other passenger canal ever destined to. At this point in the history of the Old Erie many a scoffer doffed his Lafayette hat to the Big Ditch for the first time, wondering how on earth he could have been so mistaken about this man Clinton.

The following year, 1825, was one of triumphs. Now after seven weary years of struggle and heartbreak, success for the Erie Canal was at last in sight. Wide-eyed, the people of York State watched the rapid completion of the unfinished patches. Clinton's remarkable prediction during the early doubtful days—that he could complete the canal in five more years— was coming true! His success left them in an intoxication just short of frenzy.

Meanwhile, guided by the genius that had prompted him from the very beginning of this gigantic enterprise, and propelled by the knowledge that his present popularity could again be swept away as surely as it had now been restored to him, Governor Clinton directed his attention to the one factor that seemed most important to the taxpayer—toll collecting. It had already been decided that the rates could profitably be set in accordance with both value and weight of the cargo, as soon as a weighing method could be devised. Now three crude hydrostatic weighlocks were rigged up and installed for that purpose, the first of their kind in America. Immediately they were put to round-the-clock service, which soon produced a waiting line of sixty to seventy boats at each weighlock throughout every hour of the day and night.

There had been considerable lively discussion to determine the proper location for these three weighlocks. In the end, Troy, Utica, and Syracuse were chosen in hopes of catching all boats as soon as they entered the canal—the trend was definitely to the west—and of collecting the tolls due the Old Erie before the ubiquitous professional gamblers could step in to clean out the unwary. Gamblers were already doing a profitable business by setting themselves up with a stack of cards and a stack of money, topped with a loaded pistol to indicate that they meant business. From morning till night this practice made something of a battleground of every packet's so-called saloon, with gamblers plying their trade at one end of the long room while Methody missioners endeavored to ply theirs at the other end, the latter depending alternately upon argument and song to convince whomsoever they could corner that man had better tend to his knitting because life was brief and fleeting.

> "How feeble is our mortal frame,
>   What dying worms are we!
> What dying worms, what dying worms,
>   What dying worms are we!"

As to the weighlock itself, it was a crude contraption that worked amazingly well—another bit of Yankee ingenuity. It consisted of a ribbed cradle into which a boat could easily float upon entering the lock. Next the water was drained out, bringing the boat to rest on the cradle itself, whose fore and aft arms reached under the weighlock's shanty to record the weight of both boat and cargo. After this the lock was again filled with water, lifting the boat to proper canal level so that she could pay her toll and proceed on her way.

Passenger fare was estimated on the basis that the average adult weighed 150 pounds, the average child half as much. Full fare was a cent and a half per mile, which at first included all meals. This practice was soon abandoned, however, because it encouraged too many dead beats to hop aboard in time to gulp down a hearty dinner, then jump ashore, having paid the required cent and a half for a mile-long ride that had included a meal of four or five kinds of fowl and meat, half a dozen hot breads, great mounds of vegetables, and seven or eight kinds of pie and cake, all served family style, with the abundant variety lasting at least through what was known as "the first grab."

In June of that momentous year of 1825, the sluice gates at Black Rock were swung wide. At long last Lake Erie water was admitted for the first time, flooding those doubtful 140 miles of channel to the complete satisfaction of all. The official opening of this far western section was formally celebrated against a din out of all proportion to the size of either Black Rock or Buffalo hamlet, while Albany—363 miles away and now a town of 16,000—made jubilant announcement that as the eastern terminus of the Big Ditch she had quadrupled her wholesale business within two years, accomplishing the feat even before the canal was opened through to the Great Lakes.

At Lockport, there were equally elaborate ceremonies when Lake Erie water first flooded the ten great locks, with the hamlet's thriving young Masonic Lodge invited to do the honors because its members happened to be the owners of the only tall plumed hats in town. After this, however, although the five double levels of water lay fresh and inviting, no boats were admitted for another four months because Mountain Ridge, immediately west, was "in no condition for public use," nor would it be until late October, barely in time for the Grand Opening.

The announcement probably meant that this strip was unbelievably crude, for boats were usually admitted to any section as soon as they could possibily make their way through it in spite of mud and cluttering construction materials. Captain Basil Hall, a visiting Englishman, had already noted this and made comment in his writings.

"It was considered an object of primary importance to open the canal from end to end as soon as possible, even though some parts of it might not have been completed with the utmost degree of perfection. The results show the wisdom of this proceeding, as receipts from tolls have greatly exceeded the anticipated amount, and accordingly have furnished the canal Commissioners with adequate means for bringing the whole into proper condition."

Early maps and descriptions of the route of the Old Erie, before she was widened and deepened and slightly rerouted as the Erie Barge Canal of today, give us an exact picture of not only where her golden path lay in 1825, but also to what ends it was necessary to go in order to seek out level ground, no matter how many river crossings this might entail. One early writer was concerned largely with the complications between Albany and Schenectady.

"The canal from Albany proceeds north along the west bank of the Hudson to Troy. Then west to Green Island and Van Schaik Island to where the Mohawk comes in. Now she begins to veer northwest to follow the Mohawk on its south bank. Above Cohoes Falls she crosses the Mohawk to its north side, then crosses again to its south side before she comes to Schenectady." All of this, plus twenty-seven locks, in those first twenty-nine miles out of Albany!

John Fowler, who enjoyed both the voyage and seeing his *Journal* in print, left an accurate description of what the Old Erie's entire course looked like to him from where he stood ducking bridges, on a packet deck:

"The Erie Canal, beginning at Albany, passes up the Hudson nearly to the mouth of the Mohawk, thence along the bank to Schenectady, crossing the river twice by two aqueducts. From there she follows the south bank of the Mohawk to Rome. In some places she encroaches so near as to require embankments made up from the river to support her. An embankment of this kind at Amsterdam Village is 5 to 6 miles long. What is called the Long Level, a distance of 69½ miles without an intervening lock, commences in the town of Frankfort, 8 miles east of Utica, and terminates ¼ mile east from Syracuse. Thence the route proceeds 35 miles to Montezuma, situated on the east border of the Cayuga marshes, 3 miles in extent, over which to the great embankment—72 feet high and nearly 2 miles long—it is a distance of 52 miles; thence 8½ miles to the commencement of the Genesee Level, extending westward to Lockport, nearly parallel with the ridge road—65 miles. Seven miles from thence, to Pendleton Village, the canal enters Tonnewanta Creek which she follows 12 miles, and thence, following the east side of the Niagara River, communicates with Lake Erie at Buffalo.

"The whole line is 363 miles long, 40 feet wide at the top and 28 at the bottom and 4 feet deep, at moderate descent of ½ inch in a mile. The towpath is elevated 4 feet above the surface of the water and is ten feet wide. The whole length of the canal includes 83 locks and 18 aqueducts. The locks are nearly 90 feet long and 15 feet wide. The whole rise and fall of lockage is 688 feet and the height of Lake Erie above the Hudson is 568 feet . . . The whole workmanship evinces a degree of beauty and proportion consistant with the greatest strength. In many places, sides of the canal are either paved with small stones or covered with thick grass, designed to prevent crumbling of the soil by motion of the water."

Such an account of the Old Erie may have struck wonder in the minds of engineers the wide world around, but it did not do justice to the beauty and romance of this canal that lifted herself gradually, persistently over the hills, meandering gently ever westward, a mirror for the black forests she had conquered and the villages she had produced, a veritable pathway to the promised land. A pathway that profited greatly, but was tragically costly too, for although she brought wealth to everyone connected with her, she also carried tragedy. Along her berms and towpaths stretched the unmarked graves of hundreds of workmen who had deserted family and the comforts of home to lend her a hand with her digging, leaving little to mark their passing except row upon row of deserted workmen's shanties that would become shabby nest eggs for future canal towns.

By October, 1825, the Old Erie was completed and sparkling with water from end to end—Buffalo to Albany—with scarcely a scoffer in sight. Overnight, Clinton's Ditch had become the Grand Canal, by which name she was soon to be known around the world. Thus ended the gigantic work begun at Rome on the Fourth of July, 1817, the largest internal improvement yet tackled in the young United States. It was then, and still remains, the greatest and most successful of all American canals, and by all odds the boldest venture ever to be pushed through to successful accomplishment. Considering the times and conditions, the building of the Old Erie was even more of an undertaking and a greater achievement than was the laying of the first railroad, a few decades later, across the western mountains to the Pacific. The Erie's importance can never be overestimated, for all alone she directed the movement of entire populations, even European, fixing the destinies of countless cities, more than a half-dozen states, and entire sections of America.

Furthermore, she opened the Canal Era, that brief quarter-century of pure pioneering. Then alone did great masses of people move steadily, spontaneously, westward, motivated not by a desire for freedom of religion or state as had their predecessors, nor yet for gold as did the Forty-niners who followed them, nor even for free land, as did the homesteaders who came still later. Rather, these earliest westbound emigrants braved their barriers with a simple desire to occupy new land where a man could carve out his own destiny. Devoting their entire lives to the outer fringe, they chose to call themselves, not pilgrims, nor settlers, nor homesteaders, but movers. And that was what they were.

CHAPTER SEVEN

TOASTS AND TRANSPARENCIES

WORD that the Big Ditch was completed swept across the land with the speed and flare of a prairie fire. It was the greatest news in many a year, and the average man found little else to talk about. He knew that this affected him personally, whoever he was, because it pushed back America's barriers to double and triple her area. He mulled it over in his mind as he marched off to muster. He discussed it on his way home from meetinghouse. He pondered on it as he followed his plow or drove to town for sugar. Truly this was the day he had been waiting for. For now at long last it began to look as if anyone could find himself a place out yonder where there was still room enough to breathe, and yet avoid the gnaw of loneliness. A place with neighbors close enough so that he could count on them, knowing for certain sure that when they butchered of a morning, chances were strong that they would come calling, along toward evening, bearing the gift of a portion of the liver—because it would spoil in a day anyway—as was the pioneer custom.

It had been man's habit in America from his earliest days to celebrate each significant event or achievement in his life with a festivity of some kind. The Indians were past masters of the art, systematically devoting enough time to it to work themselves into the proper lather—even lifting an occasional scalp, if need be, to help spark the triumph. The pioneers did their own celebrating, sometimes following the customs that they had brought with them from the Old Country, but more often coming up with something as new and American as Yankee Doodle.

Such a one came to be known as the Grand Opening of the Grand Canal. It was planned not only to commemorate this most important pathway west, but also to do honor to the one person who had brought it about, for this seems to have been one of those moments in history when a man is born to fill the needs of the hour. There can be little doubt that without De Witt Clinton, the Erie Canal would never have reached completion. In that case, New York City might never have attained her present position of supremacy, because Baltimore, Philadelphia, Boston, and New Orleans were already vastly more important. And if the City of New York had failed to achieve prominence, so too would the state of New York, and this would undoubtedly have affected the history of the nation. And what was even more important, the Big Push might have faltered without the Old Erie, which definitely involved the course of empire. . . . They did well, those pioneers, to celebrate the opening of their Big Ditch.

Early in the summer of 1825 when York Staters first heard by the grapevine—they were now calling it "heard by the towpath"—that the Old Erie would reach completion by autumn, the village fathers, citizen committees, and trade guilds from one end of the line to the other, jumped headfirst into plans for creating the greatest jubilation America had ever witnessed. And it turned out to be exactly that.

The corporation of New York City, which from early to late had so largely and stupidly opposed the Old Erie, now moved from the scoffer's seat to the chief celebration committee. Elated by the 3,500 new buildings that had sprung up within her borders on the strength of the canal's success, she now felt justified in making this about-face, planning not only an extravaganza of her own, but urging every village and hamlet in the entire canal district to do likewise. To this end she dispatched hundreds of letters to various village bigwigs, hoping thereby to whip up a state-wide frenzy equal to her own. She even sent two of her aldermen, Esquires King and Davis, out to Buffalo to get the ball rolling properly from that end of the Ditch.

Jollifications, well-toasted banquets, and an abundance of artillery, bunting, and transparencies were to form the backbone of the festivities, with each canal town planning her separate celebration with an eye to putting her neighbors to as much shame as possible, even as the New York City letters had instructed. For many villages this was nothing new, for they had already engineered similar affairs of their own whenever a nearby canal section was opened.

That this must be vastly larger they well understood, and they kept the woods noisy all summer long with the whine and clatter of saw and hammer and ax, as the construction of countless transparencies got under way. These were long oblong boxes in which lighted whale-oil lanterns could be placed to illuminate phrases carved from their wooden sides. Some, comparatively small, were to be hung along piers and towpaths, or on homes and taverns. Others, forty to sixty feet long, were erected as huge arches to straddle the canal, so that the Clinton flotilla on its triumphant voyage could read as it passed under and bask in the various congratulatory messages. The effect of all this illumination at night was said to be magnificent. Letters of fire burned their messages down the black forest chasm for nearly four hundred miles—a chasm that was still not cleared beyond the required sixty-foot gash, except through the villages.

Weeks before the canal was ready for her opening, plans had progressed far enough to convince the eastern seaboard from Maine to Georgia that here would be a celebration the likes of which came but once in a lifetime. Even the Pike Boys, stumbling along the crumbling old Cumberland Road, stopped to pay it reluctant heed. Heretofore they had listened with amusement to the fabulous canal tales going the rounds, always ready with a guffaw and a stock phrase guaranteed to silence even the most rabid canaller—"What'll that Clinton-boy think up next, a bridge to Europe or a hole through to China?" But now, according to the towpath, they had turned quietly thoughtful over this mighty shindig up in York State and what it might mean—for it threatened their very bread and butter.

By the first of October, editorial eyes everywhere were turned toward what was shaping up to be the most important happening in America, for the press recognized at long last the real significance of the celebration—the opening of the West. In his *Weekly Register*, Hezekiah Niles returned to the subject again and again, even while his native Baltimore turned sick eyes on the project that was so surely stealing away her chances for supremacy. But Niles, never provincial, had long since accepted the whole world as his oyster. And nothing in it looked more important to him at this moment than the Big Push. Thoughtfully he hand-set his type that last summer to include every news item that might help engender greater interest in the Erie Canal as well as in the fringe country with its youth, beauty, and opportunities.

"It is stated that Mr. Plummer, one of the Pennsylvania delegation to Congress, who *is only about sixty years old, is the oldest white man now living who was born west of the Alleghenies*—a district of country now containing 2,225,000 persons," he reported in one issue. Later he wrote, "It is estimated that 2,000 boats, 8,000 horses, and 8,000 men are employed in the transportation of articles on the canal. If, then, the pay and subsistance of the men and horses be calculated at only fifty cents per day, including the interest on capital and depreciation of value in the last, it will appear that the *transport business* on this canal costs $8,000 daily, or $2,920,000 a year —say three millions—without allowing anything for wear and tear on boats and for the capital vested in them, or for the numerous persons employed to open and shut locks, or to keep the canal in repair!" Which by anybody's standards was definitely tall talk, in so sparsely settled a region.

Further encouragement came from the canal commissioners, whose financial reports continued to soar astronomically. The tolls collected during that last summer had reached a half-million dollars, money enough in six months to pay off nearly one-fifteenth of the entire cost of the canal—though she was not yet completed! Moreover, better than thirteen thousand boats had slid into or out of Albany's great basin that summer. And at Utica's long row of docks, from which she was sending forth forty-two boats a day, a total of forty thousand emigrants were counted as they drifted westward by luxury packet, freighter, lineboat, ark, timber raft, or an occasional battle-scarred Durham that had gloriously shot the wicked Mohawk rapids in the olden days and was now floating tamely at the far end of a mule-drawn towrope while her weather-beaten captain hung his head in shame.

By the time it was all added up, surely there could have been no more than a negligible number of adults in the entire country who were unaware of the fact that the Old Erie was Big Business, that she had finally hit her stride, and that she now planned to celebrate her achievements in a fitting and becoming manner.

The historic 26th of October fell on a Wednesday in 1825. And the *Farmers' and Mechanics' Almanack* for that year had predicted at press time—some ten months earlier—just what could be expected in the line of weather for the Grand Open-

ing. Under the heading, "Aspects of Planets and other Miscel-
lanies," the Almanack put forth this information in sign language—necessary for the thousands who tended crops but
could not read. Four tiny symbols did the job: a cross with
double cross-bars, the twin vessels of a doctor's cupping glass,
an O with a tail like the stem of an apple, and a thin sliver
of a moon. To any adult in York State the prediction was understandable—good bleeding, good cupping, conjunction, and
a cold, moist, changing moon.

To the citizens of Buffalo it was not surprising that the prediction was correct, for most October mornings were cold and
moist before daybreak, and that was when this hamlet's celebration got under way. Great numbers of people and horses
were now moving toward the canal docks, even before the first
pink of dawn had streaked the sky. By nine o'clock, so dense
were the throngs, it was necessary for squads of riflemen to
open a way for the beaver-hatted dignitaries to join the brass
band that would lead the lengthy procession from the
log-cabin courthouse to the Erie Canal, where the *Seneca
Chief* lay at her moorings.

Here Governor Clinton and Lieutenant-Governor Tallmadge
and their staffs, besides various local committees, were received aboard. And here the white-haired Jesse Hawley, who,
a generation earlier, was the youth in Pittsburgh who published the first articles in favor of this canal, now delivered
an address in behalf of the citizens of the neighboring Rochester who "wished to mingle and reciprocate their mutual con-
gratulations with the citizens of Buffalo on this grand effort."

The *Seneca Chief* herself had been rigged up for the occasion in a manner seldom recognized as proper boat decoration,
either before or since. Upon her deck stood two huge oil paint-
ings, facing the towpath. The first of these depicted the scene
now being enacted—Buffalo Creek and harbor in the foreground with the *Chief* starting her historic voyage. The

second pictured De Witt Clinton as Hercules, garbed in something believed to resemble a Greek costume, resting from his labors even as he was doing right now—standing relaxed and toga-clad before his own portrait while the boat left her moorings and the cheering throngs went wild.

Beside him stood two wooden kegs, gaily painted in patriotic design, which were attracting considerable attention because both were to be used in a ceremony called Wedding of the Waters which would take place at Sandy Hook, New Jersey, at the entrance of New York Harbor—the far eastern end of the voyage. The first keg, filled from Lake Erie, was to be emptied into the Atlantic to indicate a union of the Great Lakes and the ocean. And the second, symbolizing an even greater span of navigation, had been filled with waters from the Mississippi, Columbia, Thames, Seine, Rhine, Amazon, LaPlata, Orinoco, Ganges, Indus, Gambia, and Nile Rivers. The wonder of it, according to one canalside smart aleck, lay not in the fact that the old Erie had been completed in eight years, but that the props for her celebration could be amassed in so short a time.

Following the *Seneca Chief* as part of the official flotilla, came the *Superior,* the *Commodore Perry,* the *Buffalo,* and *Noah's Ark.* Aboard the latter were two Indian lads, a beaver, a bear, two eagles, two fawns, numerous wild birds, and a tank of fish, all typical of the Old West before the coming of the white man, carried along now to denote the subjection of the wilderness to man. Thus the tiny flotilla started its ceremonial voyage, well blessed with the cheers of hundreds of joyous people and the booming of countless cannon. Five quiet little boats, moving along quiet waters, with four handsomely matched gray horses and a driver plodding the towpath in advance of each small craft, while her sturdy steersman stood guiding the ponderous sweep that rose above the roof of her cabin. A nucleus of five small boats, to which would be added countless other craft of every possible type and hue —blue, green, yellow, white, lavender, magenta—which would fall in behind at every village and cross-stream until the colorful chain reached New York City.

Long-distance communication being at best no faster than a man carrying the message by horseback could travel, a new system had been devised for this occasion which would utilize in part the speed of sound. A string of cannon was placed within hearing distance of one another all the way down the canal and the Hudson from Buffalo to New York City. Each cannon was under the direction of a war veteran who would fire his own cannon the moment he heard that of his neighbor to the west. In telling the story of this experiment, Hezekiah Niles set something of a record himself by getting his *Register* onto the streets only four days after the event had become history.

"The first guns to announce the complete opening of the New York canal, were to be fired at Buffalo on Wednesday last at 10 o'clock precisely and it is probable that it was so. This was repeated by heavy cannon stationed along the line of canal and river, at convenient distances, and the glamorous sound reached the city of New York at 20 minutes past 11, when a grand salute was fired at Fort Lafayette, and reiterated back again to Buffalo. It passed up the river to Albany, 160 miles, in 18 minutes! The cannon that were used on this memorable occasion, on the line between Buffalo and Rochester, were some of those that Perry had used on Lake Erie, on that memorable September 11, 1814. . . . What an event are a joyous people called to celebrate!"

The parade from Buffalo to Sandy Hook covered 523 miles and took nine days in the doing, with a stopover at every place where local festivities had been planned. This included many towns along the Hudson, and every canal village except a few who were miffed for personal reasons and so preferred to sulk. But for the most part there was joyous hilarity everywhere along the Big Ditch, for many wilderness settlements owed their very existence to the coming of the canal.

On the local level, all festivities followed a general pattern of parades, illuminations, banquets, and speeches, though each hamlet strove mightily to add something unique or outstanding. Black Rock, generously willing to forget her own downfall when Buffalo was made a terminus, started the snowball rolling by contributing the handsome craft *Niagara,* which was the first addition to the flotilla. At Lockport, British guns captured by Commodore Perry at the Battle of Lake Erie were fired in salute by a gunner who had fought under Napoleon. The village of Holley served a collation which ended with an address said to be unusually elegant, while the flotilla rested there for a breather. At Brockport, the quiet of the wilderness was startled by tremendous artillery fire honoring the fleet. And at Newport, a parade of many floats led the officials to a bountiful banquet.

At Rochester, a more elaborate celebration was planned, leading off with what the officials chose to call a *feu de joie,* which was fired from the high aqueduct. Following this, a fine new boat, the *Young Lion of the West,* was sent to greet the approaching flotilla. The resulting pageant ran like this, according to the press:

" 'Who comes there?' cried the *Young Lion's* sentinel as the strangers drew near.

" 'Your brothers from the West, on the waters of the small and the Great Lakes.'

" 'By what means have they been diverted so far from their natural course?'

" 'By the channel of the Grand Canal.'

" 'By whose authority, and by whom, was a work of such magnitude accomplished?'

" 'By the authority and by the enterprise of the patriotic People of the State of New York.' "

Thus, having warmly patted their own and each other's backs, Rochester's share of the People of the State of New York gleefully proceeded to the Presbyterian Church to hear additional felicitations by Timothy Childs, before they moved on to a hotel banquet presided over by Jesse Hawley. Here in rye whiskey and rum-and-molasses blackstrap, they were free to drink themselves into forgetfulness about what a narrow squeak they had personally given the Erie Canal because they had objected strongly to what she was costing them, the route she chose to follow, and the haughty manners of the only man who was capable of handing them this golden gift—the indomitable Clinton. Having finally arrived at a sufficiently pleasant and well-buttered state, Rochester's citizenry moved their distinguished guests along to end the day with a lavish display of fireworks followed by a grand ball.

At Palmyra, their collective hammer and saw had produced an immense transparency, a large arch that straddled the canal and blazed forth, CLINTON AND THE ERIE, to dazzle the eyes of the eastbound, and INTERNAL IMPROVEMENTS for those who had already started west. Montezuma went a step further and erected a still larger arch so that the whole works could be crowded onto one side. DE WITT CLINTON AND INTERNAL IMPROVEMENTS, proclaimed her enclosed lanterns to those headed east, while the opposite side of the transparency was left blank—the theory being that those so badly stricken with Ohio fever as to be already westbound were more interested in the end than in the means of their Westering.

Buckville voted to celebrate by keeping every one of her

cabins "brightly illuminated until midnight"—or as bright as candles shining through greased-paper windowpanes could make it. Port Byron promised to make the same sacrifice, which was considered to be a fine gesture at a time when going to bed with the chickens was the way men lived, artificial light being what it was. At Weedsport, the village fathers commandeered a twenty-four-pounder to represent them with a mighty salute which was later reported to have been "both effective and highly successful, as only two were killed." On its fifth day out, the flotilla reached Syracuse. Here Joshua Forman, champion of the canal for the last ten years, gave an address to which Clinton made happy response before the little fleet moved on to Rome, where it ran into its first ill wind.

Here, because there was a wide divergence between the pro- and anti-Clinton factions, certain of the Governor's friends had planned to sneak in a fine celebration three days too early for the flotilla to attend—feeling that half a loaf was better, all things considered. But their noble scheme had to be abandoned in the name of peace because the antis came out even earlier with their own celebration. And the antis outnumbered the pros, three to one, for there were still many Romans who were angered by the fact that the Big Ditch had not followed the exact route of the old Western Inland Lock Navigation upon which the village had sprung up, thus leaving many an embarrassed, though prominent, homeowner or business concern facing the wrong waters. In consequence, at the very hour when the toga-clad Clinton was pulling out of Buffalo, a black-draped barrel filled with water from the old Inland Lock Canal was leading a solemn procession of Rome's foremost citizens, who marched out of town, to muffled drums, to dump the stagnant stuff into Clinton's brand-new ditch. After which they broke ranks and returned on the double to a local hotel to celebrate their rebellion in rye whiskey and fried oysters. Five days later, according to the press, "Clinton's flotilla arrived in Rome, felt the chill in the air, and remained only an hour."

Utica, reached by noon of the following day, was more friendly, for it had befriended the canal from its beginning. But Little Falls, reached by evening on that same Monday, was as hostile as Rome, because here, too, a change of canal route had displeased many. The old Lock Navigation had followed the north side of the Mohawk, but the new Erie Canal chose the south bank, again leaving many a disgruntled homeowner with his back to the music and no desire to turn around. Nevertheless, the stalwart few who stood to benefit sponsored a lavish banquet to honor the visitors, after which the flotilla was allowed to proceed in peace.

At three o'clock on Tuesday afternoon, Schenectady was reached by "the joyous voyageurs," as the newspapers were calling them before the week was over. And here they pulled into dock two hours ahead of schedule at a place where this was two hours too many, for here their reception was merely a staring cold front with no signs whatever of planned festivities. The local press had suggested "a funeral procession or some other demonstration of mourning" as a fitting expression of their true feelings. But even that was lacking. The new canal, said the village fathers, would be the ruination of Schenectady. Until now, as terminus of an old sixteen-mile overland portage from Albany—made necessary by the Mohawk's wicked rapids—she had grown admirably in both size and wealth because most river freight from the south had come by wagon to her docks to be loaded onto riverboats. This had made her a mecca for wagon routes as well as a terminus for Mohawk shipping. But now what? With the canal going straight through to Albany, what would become of Schenectady, or the nearby Cohoes Falls that was also nurtured by

Mohawk shipping? It looked as if Clinton's Ditch aimed to spoil everything.

Soreheads stood on every corner discussing the matter, and their lower lips hung loose. But the students of the local Union College, being youthful and less afraid of change, took matters into their own hands. And the College Guards did the honors of the gloomy, rainy afternoon, whipping up a hasty banquet at a local hotel, to which the visiting celebrities were invited. Clinton's complete party accepted, had an elegant time, and were again on their way by four o'clock that afternoon.

On the following morning as the flotilla drew near Albany, it was met by the village aldermen, bursting with enthusiasm over the news that their town had already doubled in size as the new gateway to the West. At 10:57 on that morning of November 2, the *Seneca Chief* and her escort passed through the last of the twenty-seven locks above Schenectady and found themselves at long last in Albany's huge thousand-boat basin. At once they were swept into an all-day celebration that started with an ode, a prayer, an address, and a tasty collation served at the pier, and ended in the wee hours with a grand ball at the Knickerbocker Hall, where all of the fashion and wealth of the city were gathered to do them honor.

Thus ended the canal voyage of the first boat ever to run the full length of the Old Erie, having endured a full week of bands and musketry, speeches and toasts, jollifications and illuminations wherever there were men to make them.

But once the flotilla had hit Albany, it had entered another world. Though still quaint enough to have cowherds and shepherds who passed along the cobblestone streets each morning, blowing their horns to collect the animals that they were to herd in the country all day, Albany was nevertheless a real city now, queen of the wild frontier. Her Tontine Coffee House, which had entertained the elite of many a day—Alex-

ander Hamilton, Aaron Burr, most of the early Presidents—
now offered the Old Erie's elite a cuisine second to none. Offered it with a special warning to the backwoods cousins who
had come along for the ride: "It is well to remember that pies,
pudding, and cider, formerly served for breakfast, are no
longer so served in genteel places, even though villages and
country sections may still continue the practice."

At nine o'clock in the morning of November 3, the ninth
day of her voyage, Clinton's *Seneca Chief* and her long string
of followers left the Old Erie and took to the broad Hudson.
Somewhere during the week's hubbub, unfortunately, the
Noah's Ark had been lost—complete with her painted Indian
lads and her menagerie of the wild West. No trace of her having yet been found, it was now considered advisable to sweep
along without her. From Albany on, the flotilla proceeded
without benefit of towpath or tow horse, for here on the Hudson all craft depended upon sails, poles, or oars, or riding the
tide and current, or hooking onto an occasional steamboat,
the strongest of which could tow fifty to seventy-five canalboats at once. Two such chugging monsters now assumed responsibility for getting Clinton's little fleet down to the ocean.

Here the wilderness had entirely disappeared, though the
hectic enthusiasm for the new way west certainly had not.
Soon the Hudson was covered from shore to shore with additional celebrators, joyfully determined to follow the procession down to the main show in any tub that would float.
Shoreside, all river towns—notably Catskill, West Point, and
Newburgh—were gay with bunting and noisy with artillery
salutes. Poughkeepsie, already old and established, with private academy, private wealth, and century-old churches, now
did her level best at shore line as well as in her famous Forbes
and Meyers Hotels to equal Albany's red-carpet spreading. Or
to surpass her own of a few weeks past when General
Lafayette had honored her with a visit, leaving her warm

with his memory and with a hankering to follow his twin fashions of a notably tall gray hat and what was known as "pantaloons so tight, if you can get into them, you needn't pay for them."

At daybreak on the 4th of November, against a wall of clanging bells and booming cannon, the tiny flotilla, now completely overshadowed by its immense following, pulled into New York City and anchored near the State Prison. Here it was met by the magnificently decorated steamship *Washington*, quite new and one of the first of her kind on the Hudson. Aboard she carried the officers and committees of the Governor's Guard, there to conduct certain ceremonies which were started immediately at sight of Clinton's approach.

"Where are you from and whither bound?" she signaled.

She was answered by the *Seneca Chief*. "From Lake Erie, bound for Sandy Hook."

Having got that settled, they proceeded together at the head of a sizable and ever increasing fleet, setting out for the open sea. The spectacle was one to attract much attention, we are told. There were military salutes from the Battery, from Forts Lafayette and Tompkins, and from installations on Governor's Island. Finally within the Hook, the great assembly paused and, to the tune of hundreds of tooting boat whistles, Governor Clinton aboard the *Seneca Chief* performed the Wedding of the Waters, first emptying the keg of Lake Erie water into the ocean to symbolize its union with the Great Lakes. Then he emptied the keg of waters from the world's greatest rivers, to indicate that commerce from all countries could now pass this way.

Moved by the color and significance of the scene, a youthful reporter fell to one knee and used the other as a support while he scribbled a description of what it looked like to him, there at sunrise on the quiet ocean.

"Never before was there such a fleet collected, and so

superbly decorated; and it is very possible that a display so grand, so beautiful, and we may add sublime, will never again be witnessed. We know of nothing with which it can be compared . . . The orb of day darted his genial rays upon the bosom of the waters where they played so tranquilly as upon the natural mirror of a secluded lake. Indeed the elements seemed to repose, as if to gaze upon each other, and participate in the beauty and grandeur of the sublime spectacle."

It was a great climax to a tremendous undertaking. And by the time Governor Clinton had reached his final "May the God of the Heavens and Earth smile propitiously on this work, and render it subservient to the best interests of the human race," he was leaning heavily upon his cane while tears streamed down his deeply lined face, so great had been his burdens during the thirteen years he had maintained his fight for the Old Erie while she repeatedly grazed failure.

But now the Captain of the *Young Lion of the West* was ready to salute the Governor "with a brave blast from a pair of brazen lungs which he had secured for himself at Rochester, against this day," we are told. After which, there on the quiet swell of the ocean, a collation was served to the entire flotilla.

Meanwhile, the greatest procession ever formed in America to date was lining up back in town. Throngs of visitors, estimated at anywhere between thirty and fifty thousand, had now joined the local citizenry, milling about in a fine confusion that gradually formed itself into units and columns, afoot and on horseback. The approach of De Witt Clinton and his followers was the signal for a mighty artillery blast that set the mammoth parade into motion—a solid mile and a half of bands, followed by the gaily festooned New York Fire Department, numerous clubs, trade guilds, military units, and civilian marchers. Two hundred elaborate banners and floats represented the butchers, bakers, tanners, cordwainers, and

candlestick makers, ending with a printers' unit that featured
a hand-powered press mounted on a high wagon, turning
off verse-bearing leaflets which were tossed to the hundreds
of celebrators as mementos to be cherished forever between
pages of the family Bible.

> " 'Tis done, 'tis done! The mighty chain
> Which joins bright Erie to the Main.
> For ages shall perpetuate
> The glories of our native State."

At the close of the giant parade came countless dinner
parties, both public and private. And when at long last the
day turned gray with twilight, the city-wide illuminations were
unbelievably brilliant—or as much so as yellow whale-oil lanterns within transparencies could manage. There was scarcely
a store or public building in town that did not feature either
a huge C or the word CANAL in blazing letters, while the private exhibits on inns and homes were limited only by the imagination and ingenuity of each exhibitor.

The day ended with a public display of fireworks, believed
to be the greatest in history. And on the following Monday
evening, the festivities were finally topped off by a grand ball
for which the Lafayette Amphitheatre in Laurens Street had
been enlarged by including two neighbors, a circus building
and a riding school, to produce the largest ballroom on this
continent, one hundred by two hundred feet, with a ceiling
covered with transparencies that blazed the names of the
canal commissioners for all to admire and dance under.

So ended New York's contribution to the Grand Opening
of the Grand Canal, a record of superlatives to do honor to
what Horace Greeley came to call "Old cent-and-half a mile,
mile-and-a-half an hour." To the thousands who had so long
waited and so fervently prayed for an easier way west, this

celebration had taken on the solemn importance of a high patriotic rite, manifesting itself in many symbolic features similar to ancient Roman pageantry in an endeavor to emphasize the significance of the event. It is difficult for us to fully appreciate the frenzy of the pioneer's joy at having the gates of the Promised Land open before him.

And when at last it was over, the celebrators departed quietly, the great and the small, whether they had come by elegantly printed invitation or through the dictates of an overflowing heart. Almost to a man, they departed carrying keepsakes—canal medals struck in brass and enclosed in cedar boxes to do honor to the statesmen who had attended: John Adams, Jefferson, Madison, Monroe, John Quincy Adams, and Andrew Jackson. There was also an immense assortment of specially decorated dishes, wallpaper, and dress goods, all bearing canal pictures, all easily obtained from the ubiquitous hawkers who cried their wares the loudest wherever the crowds were thickest.

The engineers were the first to depart, heading off to other projects even before the festivities were finished. Some went west to Louisville to lend a hand with the difficult channel that was expected to circle the wicked falls of the Ohio, at that point. Others headed for Baltimore to figure out how to go about building something called a railway. The canal committees were the last to leave, for there still remained a ceremonial voyage back to Buffalo in order to deliver a keg of salty ocean water to be dumped into Lake Erie for what was officially called Neptune's Return to Pan. Thus the month-long celebration would end much as it had started—brass bands, bursting rockets, and well-liquored toasts at the local Eagle Tavern.

All the world had watched the Old Erie's Grand Opening and paid it mind, albeit a few like Philadelphia reserved the right to express their own veiled views on the subject. "The completion of the Erie Canal has been celebrated with great éclat, pompous show, and parade, not unlike those triumphal games and processions that were given to some Roman Emperors!" But for the most part, it was widely hailed as a fitting recognition of a nationally important achievement. Young Ohio, already knee-deep in canal mud of her own, dedicated a night of revelry and high-toned speechifying in behalf of the Old Erie, to which Hezekiah Niles devoted generous space.

"At Cleveland on the 26th ult. (the day on which the Erie Canal was completed) there was observed a day of rejoicing and feasting. A large party dined at Merwin's Hotel. Many good toasts were drunk. To wit:

"1—*The Union of the Waters of Lake Erie and the Hudson,* a convention that will do more for the national constitution than all amendments in Congress for twenty years.

"2—*De Witt Clinton.* When his countrymen forget his services, it may emphatically be said that republics are ungrateful.

"3—*The Waters of Lake Erie.* The first time they ever went to New York by land.

"4—*The Big Ditch.* It has become the grave of canal opposition.

"5—*The Cannon Race.* Four years from now, to be tried over the Ohio course.

"6—*The Way to Make a Canal.* Stop talking, and like Ohio, start digging.

"7—*The New York and the Ohio Canals.* Like husband and wife, may their connection be known by frequent intercourse, and a progeny of young canals."

But probably the most significant of all who paid mind to the Grand Opening of the Grand Canal were the movers who had traveled many weary days so that their families might catch a glimpse of the greatness of the Old Erie. Now they turned home again through the black forest, knowing the swell of something fierce and glad in their chests as they boomed a final blast from berm and towpath, or breathed a quiet prayer, each in accordance with the set of his own personal sails. But either way they trudged along with thankful hearts. . . . Truly the voice of the Lord shaketh the wilderness. . . . For the Big Ditch had opened the way west.

CHAPTER EIGHT

RUNNING A CANAWL

BORN simultaneously with the Old Erie's opening, there came into American life a new type of workman and a new method of transportation. The workman called himself a canawler. And the thing that he traveled upon, or worked upon, or spent his life extending or repairing, was known to him as the canawl.

Even his canawlboat was something new, a forward step of an evolution in river craft that had been a long time coming. In the beginning he had managed his affairs well enough with a square-nosed, flat-bottomed, unmanageable, one-ton river scow which was in itself an improvement over a chained-logs raft. Next came the Durham, in which the river scow was modified by rounding its square ends at bow and stern so that it cut the water more easily, adding a slight rake fore and aft to make it more maneuverable, and enlarging its capacity from one to ten or twelve tons to make it more serviceable. Following this came the river ark and the keelboat, both of which were Durhams to which keels had been added to help balance and direct them.

Since all of these various kinds of craft had been designed to drift downstream only, next it became necessary to add wide, flat planks along the gunwales of a boat for the convenience of the so-called "polers" so that river craft could be propelled upstream against the current. This was at best a difficult and tedious method. Each poler settled the button end of a long pole into the curve of his shoulder, dug the pointed end into bank or river bottom, then walked his way aft with his back to the prow, pushing with all the might he could muster. With a crew of three to six such polers on each side of a boat, properly spaced, it was possible to form an endless chain of men, alternately pushing as they walked aft and resting as they walked forward to take a new position on the gunwale to push their way aft again. This method produced smooth, continuous progress. But it was a man-killer, as any exhausted crew would readily testify, especially those who had fought the current of the Mohawk or the Connecticut.

Imagine then how easy and luxurious canal travel must have seemed to the pioneer, with its well-equipped packets gliding smoothly, effortlessly forward. The canalboat had adopted all of the best features of the Durham, to which she had added a cabin for comfort, a huge rudder for better guidance, horsepower to replace manpower, and a currentless stream to replace river rapids. Little wonder that the Big Ditch became overnight the most popular, the most crowded, the most important water in America.

"It is not possible for me to convey any adequate idea of the pleasure and wealth which float upon this canal," wrote the astonished T. L. McKenny, making his first voyage, "—nor of the advantages which are experienced from it by the people who live upon its borders, and to those more remote settlements throughout the entire region of the Northwest. The truth is, the canal is in everybody's mouth."

The truth was even greater. The canal was in everybody's heart. For during that winter of 1825-26, everyone for miles around, from farmers and artisans to bankers and statesmen, found himself suddenly smitten with something called "canawl fever" which was manifesting itself in a deal of sawing and hammering and painting. For nearly everyone was mak-

ing himself a boat. It was a time to be cherished forever in the
memory of those who experienced it.

"A basin of canalboats is an unforgettable sight," wrote one
who was in the midst of it, "with not only the seven colors of
the spectrum, but symphonies in crimson, maroon, brown,
pink, lilac, magenta, yellowish green, and any other mongrel
shade an experimental mixer of paint might chance upon."

And he might well have added that the same gay abandon
was also extended to the style and size of these boats, for the
first ones were purely experimental, fashioned by amateurs,
and said to be so crude that most of them sank each night,
only to be raised and pumped out again the next morning. As
time went on, however, newer models became more reliable
and much more elaborate, destined eventually to reach an
unbelievable peak of elegance during the boom of the Thirties.
By then, many boats sported imported French china and Brus-
sels carpets, while their sleek, well-rounded horses tinkled
silver bells and harness rings as they plodded along the tree-
edged towpaths. Even by the end of the Old Erie's first year,
her boats had become more or less standardized, shaking
down roughly into five classes which differed in accordance
with their separate purposes.

By that time the canal packet, named for the fast sailboats
that plowed the Atlantic, had become the best equipped and
most elaborate of all craft. Considered strictly a passenger
boat, she allowed only hand luggage aboard. And because of
her importance, she held precedence over all other vessels at
points of contest, such as entering locks or passing midstream.
An average packet cost about $1,200, and consisted largely of
a cabin which was given over to what was elegantly known as
"the saloon," a long, narrow, low-ceilinged room, scarcely high
enough to stand up in, which served as both sleeping and dining quarters. If the boat strove to be considered genteel, it possessed a heavy velvet curtain that could be stretched across

the middle of this room at night, making a polite gesture toward offering separate sleeping space for men and women. On packets that furnished no such safety measure, it was considered good manners for the gentlemen to withdraw to the upper deck where they waited until the ladies had been given time to bed down and delicately pretend sleep. After this the men were free to return and curl up in their cloaks in whatever space they could find.

Aft from the packet's saloon lay the galley, a small cubbyhole which was the cook's living quarters as well as the place where he plied his art. Along either side of the cabin a row of small calico-curtained windows looked out upon the catwalk, a twelve-inch passageway along which crew and passengers could sidle between bow and stern whenever the saloon was too crowded to be crossed. Above the entire cabin stretched a cedar-floored upper deck, used for daytime travel. This offered a scattering of low-backed seats called "settles," from which passengers could comfortably enjoy the landscape and safely take to the floor at sight of a low bridge.

Fore on her hull the packet carried two large, whale-oil reflector lanterns whose feeble beams reached little beyond the gold-lettered names of boat and captain. Aft she carried a clumsy, carved tiller bar that guided her ponderous rudder. She was restricted to eleven feet in width because of the narrowness of the canal, and to eight in height because of low bridges. But her length was her own business, restricted only by the limits of her builder's fancy and purse. On the average she ran between eighty and ninety feet long.

A step lower than the packet on the canal's social ladder came the emigrant boat, sometimes called a lineboat. This was poorer and cheaper, and allowed a mover and his family to carry all of their possessions on board with them, even to the point of setting up housekeeping around their kitchen stove—preparing meals among their portmanteaus, stacked furniture, bundles of clothing, and crates of chickens. At night they slept on the floor wherever space allowed. An early engraving of this period pictured a lineboat upon whose deck a young girl held an umbrella above her mother's head while the latter cooked the family supper during a thunderstorm.

Emigrant boats possessed neither fine horses nor silver-mounted harness. And the poor skinny old nags were never replaced with fresh horses as long as life remained in their weary bones. Forty miles a day was considered a record for a lineboat, although a packet was expected to do eighty to ninety, by running the clock around and replacing horses and driver every fifteen miles.

Next below the lineboat came the freighter, which carried no passengers whatever, and was quite simply hell-bent on getting cargo from one spot to another, vigorously fighting for her rights at every lock. Sometimes she was built with a horse gangplank which was really a section of her hull that could be lowered to allow the hard-driven beasts to come aboard for food and rest. Often both owner and horses lived out their lives on a canal freighter, knowing no other home.

Fourth in importance of all Big Ditch craft came two types of very crude cabin boats. One was whacked together cheaply because it was expected merely to carry a family or two westward for the length of the canal. This furnished the most economical way of all to travel. With the exception of toll fees, it cost a man nothing but his time, since forest lumber was to be had for the chopping. Its sister craft, equally crude, was the shanty boat, a shiftless sort of stationary houseboat widely familiar on the Erie Canal. A shanty boat was little more than a flatboat to which a one-room hovel had been added, with a lean-to porch to the rear. It required neither horse nor driver for it was usually anchored at some wide spot in the channel for months or years at a time, and moved only when chance offered it a free haul to some spot beyond the horizon that suddenly seemed greener. Shanty boats were very numerous along the Erie and furnished a half-nomad existence for hundreds of canallers, who caused little trouble at the locks since they seldom used them. Many shanty boats remained on the Big Ditch long enough to rear a second, even a third, generation of canal-born boaters who had never lived on solid ground. The practice was widely frowned upon by all missioners and uplift societies, since canallers as a whole were considered a tough lot and the Old Erie was deemed hardly a fit place to rear children. The shantymen themselves, however, took a certain pride in the roughness of canal manners.

"Hain't never heard eleganter cussin' than what they is around a lock," was their common brag.

A timber raft, the crudest and clumsiest contraption on the canal, came lowest in her social scale. It consisted of from five to ten parts, called shots or cribs, which were required by law to pass separately through the locks, alternating with whatever other craft happened along. After that, they were again lashed together in order to travel as a unit. Each crib was merely a pile of logs chained together; a crude cabin for the crew balanced precariously upon the top of one of the cribs throughout the voyage. The timber raft was despised by everyone on the canal because its slow-moving clumsiness delayed every boat in its vicinity. And time was already a precious commodity.

Man and boy, it took a crew of twenty-five thousand to run the Erie Canal, once she had hit her stride. Most of these were drivers and steersmen, since every craft of any kind required at least one of each. Surprisingly enough, most of the drivers were young lads, hired at thirty dollars for the entire season—and lucky to collect that—although a man could demand and get ten to twenty dollars per month for performing the same service. The job required an ability to handle horses, an understanding of canal procedure, and complete control of the long towrope. This at times could be a tricky business, especially on upstream packets which took precedence over all other craft, for on a crowded section of channel this meant almost continuous passing and required great skill.

There were two ways of passing. If a packet captain wished to pass midstream, a double blast on his cow-horn signaled all neighboring drivers to halt and "trip" their towlines—which was done by holding back their horses while allowing their boats to glide to the far side of the canal, thus laying their lines flat along the towpath and the bottom of the channel. Meanwhile the captain's own driver was expected to maneuver his horses in such a manner as to allow no slack whatever in his seventy-five- to ninety-foot towrope, so that both line and horses could pass over all other towlines without entanglement. On the other hand, when a packet's captain wished to pass at a dock, his driver must maneuver his towline high over a standard in the ship's bow so as to clear all anchored boats. Failure in either case could so foul his towline as to cause a boat collision, or to drag a valuable horse or two into the canal. And since many a costly drowning was the result of such an accident, this was quite a heavy responsibility to place on the shoulders of a spindly twelve-year-old "hoggee," as the boy driver was usually called. But the practice was general.

Nor did a hoggee's troubles end here. With the larger boats he must at all times master from two to six horses walking tandem, or an equal number of stubborn mules, or a span or two of oxen, which always leaned stolidly into their traces, seldom got their heads above their knees, drooled silver threads to the ground, and were speeding if they walked at any pace above a mile an hour. Without proper care, many of these beasts could quickly develop lameness or open shoulder sores. Without proper attention, any of them might shy in sudden fright and land floundering in the canal. Then it was the hoggee's responsibility to detach the towrope and swim the panicky animal to the nearest horse ramp in order to get him back onto the towpath—all to be accomplished in jig time to the tune of an abundant and colorful vocal barrage from the boat's captain, who could ill afford such delay.

No matter how young, the boy driver was expected to walk two six-hour "tricks" a day, using his spare time to mend harness, care for his horses, and cook his meals. The hours left for sleeping in his tiny, cell-like cuddy were few and doubtful, with small chance of being augmented, except when a quick nap could be snatched behind some packing box while the boat was being loaded. His work was hard and his life was hard. Autumn and spring he walked the towpath through sleet no coat could turn, a forlorn, underfed, half-frozen waif, striving to keep awake during the long night tricks to save himself from a beating. Tuberculosis was common among hoggees. And those who escaped it were old men by the time they were fifteen, and were usually married, to boot—or living in what passed for marriage.

According to Deacon Mason, noted missioner, there were ten thousand boy drivers on the Erie at a time when her total working population was twenty-five thousand. From the year of 1826 on, the hoggee was the special target of the newly organized American Temperance Society, and a thorn in the flesh of every Methodist as well as the missioners sent out by the American Bethel Society and the Seaman's Friend to improve the prevailing order of too much whiskey, too much swearing, and too much fighting on the Big Ditch. But in spite of their eternal vigilance and their attempts to legislate the boy driver off the canal on grounds of his youth, they had little effect on him. For he knew himself to be where every red-blooded American boy longed to be—swinging a fifteen-foot bull whip over a span of high-steppers. And since any skinny-legged, canal-bitten hoggee could drive almost as soon as he could walk, and could outrun, outswear, and outspit his elders, he was not likely to be hampered by the notion that telling a whopper about his age was going to deprive him of heaven— Methody missioners notwithstanding.

Of all the lads working the Old Erie, those called redemptioners were the missioners' chief concern. And rightly so, for under most masters such a boy was little better than a slave. He might be Irish, or German, or Swiss. But most likely he was an English lad whose services for one, two, or three years had been signed away to a shipmaster to pay for his transportation across the Atlantic. In some cases, even though the practice was illegal, he was seized when hardly out of babyhood and held until he was old enough to work out the unfilled years of service pledged by a father or mother who had died at sea. Every redemptioner, man, woman or child, was subject upon landing in America to be put up for auction for a year's work at least, to reimburse the shipmaster for his passage fare. As in slavery, his services were widely advertised so that prospective employers could come to look him over, count teeth, and pinch limbs. Once bargained for, he was bound over to the master until he had worked out his redemption. An advertisement in a New York newspaper in 1829 read:

REDEMPTIONERS FROM THE BRIG BUBONA,
LIVERPOOL TO THE HUDSON.

Passengers at the sloop dock, April 15, at half after eleven. Willing to defray the expense of their passage by engaging themselves for a limited time. Persons of the following occupations, besides women and children, viz: 13 farmers, 1 baker, 1 whitesmith, 2 shoemakers, 1 brewer, 1 wheelwright, 2 barbers, 1 cabinetmaker, 1 stocking-weaver, 1 coal-burner, 2 coopers.

Apply ON BOARD HONEYMAN'S SLOOP, LADY. . . . HENRY FEARIN, MASTER OF BUBONA, PRESENT AT THAT TIME.

It was from the classification "children" that the best bargains in hoggees were to be found, since under most masters an orphan stood little chance of being set free even after his years of service were completed—until he was old enough to run away. Consequently, though his plight might be sad and the practice mighty shady, the contribution of these redemptioner hoggees to the furthering of the Big Push was undeniably great.

Besides its driver, every canalboat maintained at least one steersman whose duty it was to stand at the tiller bar to guide the ponderous rudder—a job requiring constant vigilance, for a clumsy craft, being necessarily towed at an off-angle, had a tendency to bump berms, bridge abutments, locks, or other craft, for which it was subject to stiff fines as well as damages. It was also his duty to be first ashore at all stops in order to snub-to with heavy ropes, both fore and aft.

A steersman rated no special uniform unless the boat was so small that he was also its owner. In that case he wore the proud, visored captain's cap, bearing the name of his craft in gold letters. Otherwise he dressed like any other canaller—voluminous pantaloons anchored by red or green galluses, a short box coat of homespun, a woolen shirt, and a pair of ear muffs. A steersman's pay averaged seven Oneida shillings per day (87½ cents) or fifty cents for a boy doing the same job. If he furnished a horse, another ten dollars per month was added to his salary. The boating season offered him work for about 210 days, except on southern canals, where it might run as much as 270 days.

Man or boy, like all other canallers, and many of their wives, he probably chewed tobacco, tucked a pinch of snuff under a shrunken upper lip, and smoked Old Warnick and Brown, Number One, Heavy. As a rule, he made it his business to

quarrel constantly with the canalside farmer, each disdaining
the work of the other, although as a matter of fact they were
mutually indebted for the better-than-average living both of
them were enjoying.

The problems of all canallers were numerous and difficult,
partly because the entire enterprise was too new to have been
worked out carefully, partly because of the crowded conditions everywhere. The packets and lineboats carried too many
passengers. The freighters were too heavily loaded—jammed
to the scuppers with boots, shoes, rope, furniture, stoves, mill-
stones, and farm machinery on their way west, and with
fruit, vegetables, meat, cordwood, ashes for the soap factories,
and unbelievable quantities of whiskey when they headed
back east.

It was the heavy shipments of the latter that caused most
of the trouble, according to the missioners, for whiskey was to
be had anywhere for a fip (6¼ cents) a quart, a bargain that
automatically converted the canal's entire working population
into a hard-drinking, hard-swearing, hard-fighting lot. To
counteract this evil influence, most uplift societies, hoping to
save the souls of canallers, issued numerous tracts. Two of
these, *The Swearer's Prayer* and *Esau or the Ruinous Bargain,*
were so widely distributed as to have reached every canaller
in York State, it was believed. But the drinking was in no wise
curbed thereby. Nor were the swearing and fighting.

The latter practice admittedly produced one of the greatest
of all Big Ditch problems, becoming so common that soon it
was a rare thing to happen upon any canal section where there
was not a fist fight in sight. Even the captains were guilty,
fighting for emigrant trade to the point of snatching passengers
from each other's boats, a practice which was naturally a
trouble breeder. In fact, the strip of canal between Albany and

Schenectady where most westbound movers embarked soon came to be known as Battleground, for there the skirmishing continued day and night with no holds barred. As a result of this state of affairs passengers could virtually name their own rates, while freight costs dropped from thirty-two dollars to one dollar per ton.

Even fiercer than the fist fights between captains were those that sprang up between toughened crewmen, especially at the locks. Admittedly there was an element of truth in the saying that "a well-hardened fist is both judge and jury on the Big Ditch," for certainly it was usually the bully who "locked through" first, rules or no rules. To restore peace in this respect, the commissioners hopefully installed a block system whereby a post was placed near each lock to mark the beginning of that particular block, and the boat that passed it first would be locked through first. Even this was not wholly successful, for upon approaching a combine the timid would make no race for it if there was a bully in sight. In fact, so important to the running of the Big Ditch was the successful fighter, that soon many of the big companies were frankly listing this talent as their top requirement when hiring help. With such a standard it was not surprising that most campfire legends were centered around such heroes as the Rochester Bully and Buffalo's Man-Mountain, two widely revered characters who upon one meeting were said to have "rassled, and fit each other up and down, and gouged, for a full half-a-day."

A later fight classic was concerned with a sixteen-year-old hoggee, one Jimmie Garfield, driver for the *Evening Star* on the Ohio and Erie Canal. Upon approaching the first of Akron's twenty-one locks, according to legend, Jim's packet raced that of a rival company, and the two boats came to a tie at the blockpost. There are two widely differing versions for the conclusion of this story as told by two canal captains, each willing to swear on a stack of Bibles as high as the pump handle that his alone was the God's truth. Captain Letcher claimed it happened like this:

"Young Jim had been advised by his own boss that the lock really belonged to the other packet but that they would take it anyway. To which young Jim cried, 'No, we will not!' Whereupon all hands aboard accused him of being afraid to fight, which bred considerable hard feelings until the captain stepped in. 'Boys, don't be too hard on Jim. I was mad but I've got over it. Jim may be a coward for aught I know, but if he is, he's the first of his name that I ever heard tell of. His father was no coward. He helped build this canal, weighed over two hundred pounds, and could take a barrel of whiskey by the chime and drink out of its bunghole. And no man dared call him a coward. You'll alter your mind about Jim before fall.'"

Captain Parkhurst's version of the same incident was shorter and more popular. "A taunting remark by a member of the crew caused a boy driver to take the blacksnake whip from around his neck and pitch into the fellow, knocking him down, with the result that the boy's boat entered the lock first. This boy afterwards became President James Garfield."

Another Erie Canal problem brought into the limelight by missionary attention was concerned with the matter of Sunday travel. At first it was customary for all boats except packets to "tie by" over the Sabbath. But soon, under the press of the times, all were running seven days a week. The first attempt at some type of blue law to curb this practice started off by forbidding horn blowing on Sundays, which was a sneaky way of forcing all traffic to slow down to a standstill since no craft was allowed to pass another or to be locked through without proper signal. As a counterirritant, the opposition further confused the issue by proposing a bill demanding complete silence for an hour each weekday evening. Although there seemed to be no special advantage to this latter proposition from any-one's angle, it soon had a following which included Canaller John Dows of Albany, who went a step further to suggest that all horn blowing be discontinued between the hours of seven and ten, every evening of the week. Without much thought on the subject, his home-town newspaper backed him in this with an editorial that claimed, "Those gondeliers do seem to be possessed with an unaccountable furore for bugles and French horns, and the whole country is seranaded by them to a pitiful extent."

Fully aware of the strategy behind these various proposals, the missioners were not to be so easily distracted from their original demands for Sabbath regulation, which was actually the only real issue involved. Daily the controversy, pro and con, grew greater and more bitter until both sides were holding frenzied mass meetings on the subject, ending in a half-loaf solution when the uplift groups decided to pool their assets and buy a line of packets which they were determined to run only six days a week. This, they hoped, would set a fine example to all. And so it did—until the new owners had lost $60,000 on the venture and so were forced to withdraw. But not in complete defeat, for their costly sincerity had actually aroused sympathy enough to bring about the so-called Sabbath Regulation, which was effective for a short time at least. The well-known Captain Parkhurst was one who had refused from start to finish to operate his boat seven days a week, bringing about the queer result that his craft was known far and wide for years to come as the Sunday Boat.

In later days, the Delaware and Hudson Canal handled this same problem effectively by the simple expedient of closing all locks on Sundays. This stopped traffic in a hurry, leaving a string of fifty to a hundred idle boats stranded at every combine with nothing better to offer their passengers than a day of hunting and fishing, with a fat purse of fips, York shillings,

Niagara fifty-cent bills, and Oneida dollars as prize money for the one who snared the biggest muskellunge or bagged the fattest buck. While this was not exactly the results the missioners had been striving for, it was an acceptable half-loaf.

"The practise at least causes no commotion," read one Methody report. Besides which, admittedly it gave the preachers an extra day in which to work on the flock.

The problems of canal operation and maintenance were never simple. A faulty lock always received first consideration because there was no possible way to detour around one. The resulting traffic jam when one failed to function sometimes presented as big a problem as did that of repair.

"Canal breach at Frankfort lock caused great loss to boat owners," stated the *Poughkeepsie Telegram* after a fierce spring freshet. "Coming up from Little Falls, the line of boats is ten miles long, extending from Herkimer to within four miles of that city. The breach repaired, it will take another fortnight to get boats cleared out."

Even aside from times of flood or drought, the lock-keep was a busy and important person, for it was his duty to open and close the ponderous wooden gates by walking the big sweeps around, seven days a week, catching whatever catnaps he could manage between boat bugles. From March until November he seldom got away from the lock shanty, which served as both home and office. Eventually it came to serve also as tavern, for it provided a place where canallers could gather on a sleet-ridden night to forget the bleakness of their jobs with a cheering nip of the ardent while doing a bit of rough harmonizing. Many were the canal chanteys that originated along some lock-keep's smoke-choked bar as various boatmen improvised songs to tell their tales of woe, the while they waited for repairs to channel or their own crude craft. One of the most important of these was named for the way it sounded—Ee-rye-ee Canal.

> We were forty miles from Albany.
> Forget it I never shall.
> What a terrible storm we had that night
> 　　On the Ee-rye-ee Canal.
>
> We were loaded down with barley,
> We were chuck up full of rye
> And the captain, he looked down at me
> 　　With his goddam wicked eye.
>
> Oh, the girls are in the *Police Gazette*,
> The crew are all in jail.
> I'm the only living sea-cook's son
> 　　That's left to tell the tale.
>
> O-o-oh, the Ee-rye-ee was a-rising,
> The gin was getting low,
> And I scarcely think
> I'll get a drink
> 　　Till I get to Buffalo-o-o,
> 　　Till I get to Buffalo.

Next in importance to the lock-keep in the canal's operation and maintenance came the towpath walker, who had a ten-mile section to patrol each day, seeking out erosion of banks or errors of water level due to leaks. In either case his common procedure was to stuff the offending hole with wisps of coiled straw, well trampled down by heavy boots and covered with a clay plaster called "puddle." Loose earth soon collected in such a trap and made it as good as new. Should the trouble occur in porous limestone, however, the matter was more serious, for here additional leaks could appear so rapidly as to ground all neighboring boats, and the entire section would then have to be closed off, drained, and lined with timber. Such a delay was one of the most unpopular aspects of canal travel.

Towpath walkers were also subject to duty the clock around, the week around. Often they were called from warm beds during severe storms or whenever an overloaded boat capsized, which usually entailed the gruesome task of hooking out the drowned. News of such a disaster eventually brought additional help, consisting of a special wrecking crew with a boatful of ropes, straw, picks, shovels, and pile planking; the planking was tongue-and-groove and became watertight upon swelling, making it possible to close off a canal section completely when the accident involved damaged floodgate or culvert.

But in spite of all precautionary measures, the loss of life and property on the Old Erie was tremendous, for in times of flood often hundreds of boats were swept over berm and towpath into fields or forest, where they were usually left to rot, for want of proper hoisting equipment to return them to the canal. The neighboring rivers were the worst offenders in this respect, overflowing into the feeders which in turn flooded the canals. Nearly every spring, the newspapers were full of accounts of such disasters. One of major proportions was reported by the *Poughkeepsie Telegram* in 1839.

"Many boats lost in the Erie canal after the ice broke and plunged in off the Hudson. Bridges piled with ice thirty feet high . . . The *Helen* broke loose while her ship-keeper was on shore and so he ran along side then hopped ice-cakes until he reached his boat and grabbed a hanging rope . . . At one place, twenty canalboats loaded with produce and lumber are lodged in ice. Bridges gone. Sometimes thirty-five boats are jumbled together, frozen in a lump. Barrels of pork float by. Warehouses are flooded and swept from their foundations, their contents floating away . . . This is the worst flood in eighty years."

It was such disasters as this that later spelled ruin to many of the small canals, for it took a gigantic financial surplus to put a flooded channel back into business. Part of the luck of the Old Erie lay in the fact that her tremendous profits kept her always ready with a pocketful of cash in times of freshet. A sudden autumn freezing, however, could sometimes catch her utterly unprepared, with countless boats frozen in for the winter because she had not drained her channels early enough.

Historian Caleb Atwater, out in the fringe country, later ran into this same sort of trouble when he received a request for a copy of his new *History of Ohio* and was obliged to reply, "The second edition is out, sir, but lying frozen up in a canalboat forty miles from here."

CHAPTER NINE

FOOT-LOOSE AND FANCY-FREE

Travel on the Big Ditch was whatever you chose to make it. To some a packet voyage was the adventure of a lifetime, something to be cherished forever. To others, it was definitely a hardship. To the roving Mrs. Trollop, who liked nothing whatever in America, canal travel held the honor of topping her black list. "I can hardly imagine any motive of convenience powerful enough to induce me again to imprison myself in a canalboat," she wrote in 1829.

And another visiting Britisher who managed to get around considerably, in spite of the fact that he carried in tow a wife and eleven children, was inclined to agree, mildly, with his countrywoman. "I never saw people packed so close as they were that night in the boat's saloon," wrote J. Richard Beste, in 1849. "Mattresses completely covered the floor, on which people lay as close as possible. The dinner table was covered with sleeping humanity, more thickly than Captain Davis ever strewed it with beefsteaks, and those who lay under the table thought themselves favored, inasmuch as they could not be trodden upon."

There is little doubt that there was some justification for such complaints. The so-called night accommodations on the Big Ditch were crude and uncomfortable, to say the least. The system was this. After supper was over and the missioners had taken their last crack at saving men's souls for that day, the boat's captain was wont to bustle into the cabin and settle down to desk or table, to make out his list of berth assignments. On some packets this should have included thirty-six to forty-two names, but even from the Old Erie's earliest days it was more likely to include seventy to a hundred. It was not difficult to believe the common rumor that one packet company was packing 150 emigrants into craft designed to carry only fifty, sardining in the extra hundred by arranging all sleepers edgewise on the cabin floor "spoon fashion; when one turns, all must turn."

Crowded or otherwise, the ceremony of bedding the voyagers down for the night was a thing to be remembered. After the captain had made his dramatic entrance, there usually came a parade of assistants bearing armloads of wilted sheets and blankets, skimpy pillows, and twelve-inch iron shelves that could be fastened to the walls to serve as berths. Since these hung three or four tiers deep, with the outer edges supported by the same heavy cord, it was considered a moment of high comedy when, as often happened, a rope gave way after the shelves had been filled with humanity. For the average fellow, the assigning of berths was a scene not to be missed. For others, it was an accepted matter of boat routine—important only because the captain chose to make a great to-do of the whole event, to the disgust of certain British visitors.

Wrote Captain Marryat of the English Navy, in 1839: "An American packet captain is in his own opinion no small affair, he puffs and swells until he looks larger than his boat. This personage, on our ship, as soon as we were under weigh, sat down in the narrow cabin before a small table, sent for his writing desk which was about the size of a street organ, and like himself, no small affair; ordered a bell to be rung in our ears to summon the passengers, then took down the names of four or five, locked his desk, ordered his steward to remove it, went on deck to walk just three feet, then returned again, set up the desk, and registered another four or five . . . After all, there is nothing like being a packet captain."

In any event, as soon as a passenger on one of the larger packets was assigned to a berth, he was expected to climb to his perch immediately, before the next assignment was made. And therein lay what constituted great fun for some and deep embarrassment for others. For the procedure was carried on in full view of the entire assembly, with most of the watchers waiting to guffaw mightily when some well-padded personage was requested to deposit himself on a top shelf, for the difficulty lay not so much in the climb as in his ability to stick there after he had negotiated the desirable edgewise position. At any level, it was completely unthinkable to attempt to turn over during the night.

Wrote Charles Dickens, who chose to accept his ledge assignment on a canal packet with a grin up his sleeve, "I have mentioned my having been in some uncertainty and doubt, at first, relative to the sleeping arrangements on board this boat. I remained in the same vague state of mind until ten o'clock or thereabouts, when, going below, I found suspended on either side of the cabin, three long tiers of hanging bookshelves, designed apparently for volumes of the small octavo size. Looking with greater attention at these contrivances (wondering to find such literary preparations in such a place) I descried on each shelf a sort of microscopic sheet and blanket; then I began dimly to comprehend that the passengers were the library, and that they were to be arranged edgewise on these shelves, till morning. I was at first in some uncertainty as to the best means of getting into it. But my shelf being a bottom one, I finally determined on lying upon the floor, rolling gently in, stopping immediately I touched the mattress, and remaining for the night with that side uppermost, whatever it might be. Luckily, I came upon my back at exactly the right moment."

Besides the difficulty of its location, the upper berth was further despised because it afforded little quiet, even after all shelves had been assigned and the captain had withdrawn for the night. For here the heads of the passengers rested a scant eight inches below the upper deck, with its constant tramping and banging of baggage at every stop. In addition, it was often unbearably hot, almost to the point of heat prostration during such summers as that of 1834 when even horses dropped dead on the towpath and scores of voyagers, crazed with the heat, jumped into the canal.

Nor did the packet sleeper's troubles end when he had been edged in for the night. The fear of suffocation was general, understandably augmented by a touch of claustrophobia, for by the time every available inch of floor space and table space had been assigned, a network of intertwined clotheslines was strung above the heads of all for the convenience of those few who felt the need of disrobing. Consequently, seldom did a half-hour pass without the necessity of clearing the way for some panicky passenger to stagger to the upper deck for a turn or two under the stars while he strove to build up courage enough to return below for another try.

There was one other annoyance of night travel on a luxury packet that many Easterners and most Englishmen found unbearable—even unbelievable. Mr. Dickens expressed himself audibly on this score. "One of two remarkable circumstances is undisputably a fact, with reference to the class of society who travel in these boats. Either they carry their restlessness to such a pitch that they never sleep at all, or they expectorate in dreams. All night long, and every night, on this canal, there was a perfect storm and tempest of spitting."

To all these irritations, the ubiquitous mosquitoes added little in the way of comfort. The elder Tyrone Power, noted

Irish actor, was so annoyed with the continuous necessity of slapping and scratching during his eastbound jaunt on the Big Ditch, that he appealed to a crewman for assurance that the condition would surely not prevail all the way to Albany.

"No, siree," he was told. " 'Twon't be like this all the way to Albany. Oncet we get into the fifty-mile Cedar Swamp, 'twill be considerable worser, but not nigh so bad as what 'twill be in the Long Swamp. Them's actual galinippers, yander—swum down from the Red and Balize Rivers." Mr. Power thought he detected a touch of pride in the crewman's answer.

Captain Marryat, also pest-infested when he was canal-bound, chose to laugh it off. "By the bye, the mosquitoes too have reaped benefit from the Erie Canal. Before the impervious forest retreats were thus pierced, they could not have tasted human blood, but if they tax all other boats as they have ours, a *canal share* with them must be considerably above par, and highly profitable."

Add to all of these annoyances the confusion of snoring men, crying children, women who babbled all night in Gaelic, German, Swedish, French, or Swiss, plus the racket coming from canalside taverns and oyster bars, the earthy medley at horse-exchange stations, the lusty cussing at every lock, the constant scraping and shuffling of passengers and baggage, the everlasting horn blowing and bell clanging, and you have what passed for luxury travel on the Old Erie Canal.

But no matter how rough the night may have been, the sheer freshness and beauty of a wilderness morning were breeders of courage and contentment for even the most obdurate, though the entire packet must be aroused at daybreak so that the cabin could be swept and the tables—still warm from sleepers—could be aired and set for breakfast. The world was sure to look promising now as the voyagers watched the Big Ditch come to life, while they took to the catwalks and lowered their buckets into the muddy canal for wash water, or waited in line for use of the public brush and comb chained nearby. Blue breakfast smoke from the shanty boats drifting down the canal. Wrapper-clad housewives astir on the lineboats, kindling fires and beating buckwheat batter. Chains of canalboats riding Erie waters like strings of bobbing beads, bright against the green of the forest gorge. Would-be hunters and fishermen, jumping ashore to try their luck where the wild game breakfasted and the lake bass leaped in the sunlight. Farmers in their clearings, sowing grain with long rhythmic sweeps of the right arm. Lamps and candles winking out in towpath shops and cabins as the dawn brightened and the villages came to life.

And all of it moving along against a wall of sound—the colorful noise of movers, cattle, pigs, horses, chickens, added to the song of hammer and ax, filling the air with the Old Erie's symphony. The gentle slap of water against the boats, the riffle of towropes, the swish of wind in the water grass, the splash and murmur of widening circles when a muskrat slid into the canal, the warning horns of craft coming in from the feeders, the roar of a neighboring river, rushing its gorge, the gentle tinkle of cowbells across open fields, the song of fiddle and jew's-harp, riding the wind, punctuated by the measured plop-plop of oxen hoofs as they plodded westward. All of it moving everlastingly westward. This was morning on the Erie Canal.

Even the disillusioned Dickens could not withstand the beauty of it as he poured a bucket of cold Big Ditch water over his head, and took off for a brisk walk along the towpath, reveling in the freshness of the wilderness and the quiet of the great woods. "It is pure heaven," he wrote in his *American Notes* before turning back in answer to his packet's breakfast bell. Breakfast would include fried ham, liver, sausage, salmon, beets, pickles, and pudding, besides great loaves of dark bread with freshly churned butter, and maple sugar aplenty to sweeten a man's tea.

Diversions for the day during canal travel were many and varied, for the towpath was the liveliest spot in America, and the most crowded. Popular were visits to the canal shops, the showboats, and the handy floating saloons where a man could step in for a drop of rum-and-molasses, still traveling westward while he imbibed. Aboard the packets between meals there was always the chance of a wildly exciting race between cockroaches, grasshoppers, bedbugs, or frogs. To take part in such a contest, it was only necessary that a man find a likely-looking beastie in the proper one of the above categories, which he placed in the middle of the dining table under an inverted cup. When all entries had been duly imprisoned and all bets had been placed, a large outer circle was drawn as the finish line. Now the cups were removed to allow the racers to wander about aimlessly until one happened to cross the chalked line. This was a hilarious affair that always drew a crowd—but it was deadly serious too, for many a fat purse changed owners by the time the course was run.

Along the towpath at every stop there were other contests to take part in or to bet upon. Spontaneous wrestling and foot races were soon in progress to entertain the men, while their wives examined the wares of the ubiquitous peddlers—bolts of calico, trays of ribbons, pins and needles, and square-lensed specs to be tried on if you suspected that there were things in this world that you did not see properly. At many ports there were also the sleight-of-hand artists—those thimble-rig experts of the pea-under-one-of-three-walnut-shells, which could cost you money if you guessed it wrong. At the large ports there were also gypsy fortune tellers and glass blowers, besides the self-styled "professors of astronomy," and those of the "hydrogen-oxygen gas," who displayed such wonders as slides

made from the blood of statesmen long since dead, or slides
made from your own blood that proved conclusively whether
or not you were married—always good for a horse laugh when
a young bachelor could be wheedled into submitting to the
test.

But the most important of all diversions for the traveler was
the opportunity it gave him to talk to others who were also
suffering from the Western Itch, always hoping to come upon
one who could tell him firsthand about the Illinois prairies,
or the Wabash country, or the lead mines along Galena's Fever
River; or what it was going to cost him for food out there; or
what were his chances for success; or how great was the likelihood of fatalities from runaway horses, or low canal bridges,
or exploding steamboats, before the western trek was finished.
And since the Old Erie's ports furnished the most abundant
sources for answers to these questions, scarcely did a packet
ever pull out without leaving behind a passenger or two, lost
in conversation. Even the canallers themselves were guilty of
this. News item: "Mrs. Captain Hawkins was so deep in con-
ference with Mrs. Captain Jones while their husbands' boats
lay in fleet at Syracuse, the Jones' towrope was picked up and
headed west without either woman noticing, causing the disgruntled Captain J. to proceed west a full month, wifeless."

During the summer of 1826, nineteen thousand boats and
rafts passed West Troy where the Junction Canal, coming
down from Lake Champlain, joined the Erie. Of freighters
alone, seven thousand left Albany that season, carrying unbelievable quantities of merchandise westward, while seven thousand packets toted untold numbers of emigrants into the
Promised Land. Syracuse, Rochester, Rome, Buffalo, and
Albany were rapidly becoming the great ports of the Big Ditch,
although even the smallest canal hamlet could expect a hundred boats a day at her docks. During July, one eastbound

freighter carried a $100,000 cargo of furs on which she had paid a $300 toll. In August, a boat carrying thousands of turkeys, ducks, and geese from Jordan, near Syracuse, passed into Lake Erie through Buffalo on her way to the West Indies. Europeans bound for New Orleans by way of the Erie were already common, paying seventy-three dollars apiece for the entire journey; this included fares for a sailboat up the Hudson, a canalboat to Buffalo, a Lake Erie steamer to Erie, Pennsylvania, a Conestoga wagon overland to Pittsburgh, and steamers down the Ohio and the Mississippi. It was so exciting a time and place in which to live that even the smallest hamlet on the Erie Canal considered herself to be at the crossroads of the world.

Already the quiet of the wilderness was a thing of the past, for eastbound or westbound, hustle had soon come to be the watchword of the day. Hustle, HUSTLE, HUSTLE. With time at such a premium, the racing at each lock became more and more hectic in the rush for the West, while the ten-dollar speeding fines rolled merrily into the canal's coffers, often several times from the same boat on a single trip. Since only freighters could afford such an extravagance, it soon became common for a packet's voyagers to make up a purse among themselves with which the captain would jump ashore at the collector's office, pay a few fines in advance, then hop aboard again, free to whip up a race with every boat that came his way, while his passengers cheered wildly and placed sizable bets among themselves. So great was the excitement during some of these contests that frenzied movers sometimes jumped ashore, ran to the opponent's boat to place bets there, then raced back to their own craft and seized the towrope to aid the hard-driven horses, which seldom showed much interest in a race.

Nor were the ship's crewmen idle during all of this confusion, for theirs was the duty and privilege of aiding the cause by cutting the opponent's towline, which could lead to bloodshed, and often did. Yet the whole affair was considered rare good fun and an important part of the business of getting West.

Soon even Europe was aware of this significant new trend in the United States, which they began to call the "American speed mania." In 1827, the editor of the *New York Advertiser* drew further attention to it with an editorial concerning the increased frenzy along the Big Ditch, ending with a yarn that became widely quoted.

"An old gentleman conveyed a just idea of those who are so fond of travelling at such a wondrous rate when he said he believed that his son John, if he was riding on a streak of lightning, would likely *whip up!*"

Soon the entire eastern seaboard had caught the spirit, according to a letter written in New England in the middle of the 1820's. "We were rattled from Providence to Boston by coach in four hours and fifty minutes. If anyone wants to go faster, he may send to Kentucky and charter a streak of lightning."

Actually the new trend was justifiable on the grounds that distances in America were already becoming so great that speed was the only answer whenever it was necessary for men to get together for business or political reasons, as well as for simple survival. Certainly when minutes became dollars in the rush for the West, patience was no longer a virtue. And the laurels naturally went to the captain who could somehow shorten the canal trip. This was a circumstance that brought about dangerous practices surpassing even the runaway speed of the Pike Boys down on the Cumberland Road, especially during the much detested delays caused by spring freshets and floods.

Perhaps the most dangerous of all time-saving risks occurred in those places where the Erie crossed directly through a stream instead of bridging it, depending solely on guard locks to protect her own channel from high or low water, while a floating towbridge carried her horses across. At such a place, during floods, traffic necessarily came to a complete standstill for days at a time because crossing was impossible, causing costly delay to hundreds of waiting canalboats. Sooner or later, at such a spot, some swaggering daredevil of a captain was sure to decide that he would wait no longer for the floods to subside. Since lives were at stake, there was always great excitement when word flashed from boat to boat that someone was going to force a crossing.

In a matter of minutes, berm, towpath, riverbanks, and surrounding trees would be crowded with awed but eager spectators—most of them placing bets. Now the venturesome craft entered the guard lock, the gates behind were closed and the channel's water level changed to equal that of the offending river or creek. Then with doubled team and doubled towrope, the boat moved cautiously out into the rolling stream, valiantly fighting to cross its boiling current broadside, with no more security than a couple of taut ropes leading to a span or two of straining horses, walking a tipsy towpath that bobbed precariously in the swollen waters like a lucky fisherman's cork. If it happened to be the wicked Schoharie Creek that was being crossed, this venture was folly of the purest kind, for here one slip of the horses or one frayed towline could immediately sweep the entire affair—boat, passengers, and cargo— over the dam into the roaring Mohawk, probably with devastating loss of life and property. After which, the boat must ride the rolling river all the way down to Schenectady before it could be returned to the canal.

There were other crossings, nearly as dangerous—and equally popular. The captain who could force his way through was the one who got the load, since strong was the general suspicion that there could not possibly be land enough in the Far

The Building of the Erie Canal, Lithograph by Catlin, 1825. *Courtesy of The Bettmann Archive.*

De Witt Clinton emptying the keg of water from Lake Erie into the Atlantic Ocean at the climax of the ceremony of the opening of the Erie Canal and the establishment of a connection between the Great Lakes and the Atlantic Ocean. *Courtesy of the New York Public Library.*

Erie Canal activities about 1830. Aquatint by John Hull. (1770–1850).
Courtesy of The Bettmann Archive.

View of Lockport, New York, with Erie Canal barge departing. Lithograph by J. H. Bufford after drawing by W. Wilson. *Courtesy of The
Bettmann Archive.*

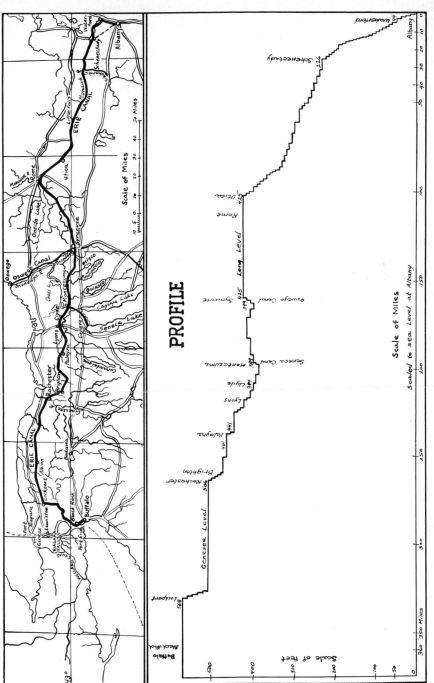

Map and Profile of the Erie Canal. From Poussin's *Travaux d'améliorations intérieures . . des États-Unis d'Amérique de 1824 à 1831* (Paris, 1834). Reprinted by permission of the publishers, The Arthur H. Clark Company, from *Historic Highways of America* by Archer Butler Hulbert, vol. 14, p. 133.

A scene along the Erie Canal, 1830. *Courtesy of the New York Public Library.*

New York Harbor: canal boats on the North River. *Courtesy of The Bettmann Archive.*

Looking down the Erie Canal from the Head of Locks at Lockport, from an engraving by W. H. Bartlett. *Courtesy of Illinois Historical Society.*

"Before the days of rapid transit," after a painting by Edward Lamson Henry. A canal packet of the early 19th century. *Courtesy of the Chicago Historical Society and The Bettmann Archive.*

Scene of the Erie Canal near Little Falls (1849). Painting by William R. Miller. *Courtesy of the New York Historical Society and The Bettmann Archive.*

View of the Erie Canal at Little Falls, New York, showing lock No. 37 in the distance and overhanging storage warehouse, from which grain could be lowered from canal boats. Used by permission of the publisher, Arthur H. Clark Company, from *Historical Highways of America,* by Archer Butler Hulbert. Vol. 14, p. 107.

"Rochester from the West," 1853, by D. W. Moody, after a drawing by J. W. Hill. Printed by F. Michelin and published by Smith Brothers and Company, probably in 1854. The Erie Canal is in the foreground and the Genesee River in the center. *Courtesy of the Chicago Historical Society.*

"Buffalo" by J. H. Colen, after a drawing by J. W. Hill, printed by F. Michelin and Shattuck and published by Smith Brothers and Company, 1843. The Erie Canal is in the foreground. *Courtesy of the Chicago Historical Society.*

Canal packet in sections being carried up the Allegheny portage railway. *Courtesy Commercial Museum Trade and Convention Center of Philadelphia and of the Illinois Historical Society.*

A weight lock on the Lehigh Canal. The woman in the foreground is cooking on her outdoor stove as the boat goes through the lock. From *Harper's Weekly. Courtesy of the Illinois Historical Society.*

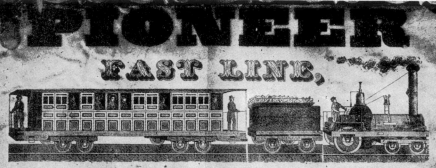

PIONEER
FAST LINE,

BY RAIL ROAD CARS AND CANAL PACKETS,

From Philadelphia to Pittsburgh,

THROUGH IN 3½ DAYS:

AND BY STEAM BOATS, CARRYING THE UNITED STATES' MAIL,

From PITTSBURGH to LOUISVILLE.

Starts every morning, from the corner of Broad & Race St.

In large and splendid eight wheel cars, via the *Lancaster and Harrisburg Rail Roads,* arriving at the latter place, at 4 o'clock, in the afternoon, where passengers will take the Packets, which have all been fitted up in a very superior manner, having been built *expressly for the accommodation of Passengers,* after the most approved models of Boats used on the Erie Canal, and are not surpassed by the Boats used upon any other Line.

These Boats are commanded by old and experienced Captains, several of whom have been connected with the Line for the two last seasons. For speed and comfort, this Line is not excelled by any other in the United States.

Passengers for Cincinnati, Louisville, Natchez, Nashville, St. Louis, &c.

Will always be certain of being taken on without delay, as this Line connects with the Boats at Pittsburgh, carrying the Mail.

OFFICE, N. E. CORNER OF FOURTH AND CHESNUT ST.

For seats apply as above; and at No. 200 Market Street; at the White Swan Hotel, Race Street; at the N. E. corner of Third and Willow Street; No. 31 South Third Street; and at the West Chester House, Broad Street.

Philadelphia, April, 1837.

A. B. CUMMINGS, Agent.

Young, Printer, Black Horse Alley, Philadelphia.

Poster of 1837, from Philadelphia. *Courtesy of the New York Public Library.*

The Miami Canal. *Courtesy of the New York Public Library.*

Collapse of this aqueduct on the Miami and Erie Canal near Dayton, in 1903, shows the Howe truss construction used on all early aqueducts, though it was usually enclosed to protect its timber framework from weather. *Courtesy of the Department of Public Works, State of Ohio, and Northwestern University.*

Log house built by Frances Slocum, about 1812, for her daughter Cut Finger. Frances Slocum, a white woman stolen by Indians from a Pennsylvania home when a baby, was discovered in Indiana many years later. She chose to remain with the Indians because she had already been a squaw to two chiefs. By an Act of Congress, she was allowed to remain on her large farm when all Indians, Potawatomis and Miamis, were ousted to make room for white settlement at the building of the Wabash and Erie Canals, between Fort Wayne and Logansport, Wabash County. *Courtesy of the Indiana State Library.*

Poster bearing the joyful news that the circus-boat on the Wabash and Erie Canal would soon make its appearance at Terre Haute, Indiana. *Courtesy of the Emeline Fairbanks Memorial Library, Terre Haute, Indiana, and Northwestern University.*

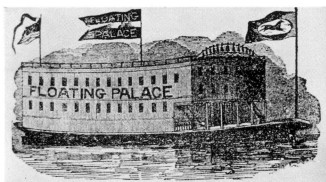

SPALDING & RODGERS CIRCUS CO
ON BOARD FLOATING PALACE,

WILL Exhibit in Terre Haute on **Saturday, April 23d**, at 2 and 7 o'clock, P. M.

PRICE OF ADMISSION.

Dress Circle, all armed Chairs..50 cen
Family Boxes, Cushioned Seats..25 "
Gallery...25 "
Gallery for Colored persons...50 "

The Company will perform at the following places:
Monday 18. Mt. Carmel at 2 & 7 p. m.
Tuesday 19, Vincennes at 2 & 7 p. m.
Wednesday 20. Russelville at 2 & 7 p. m.
Thursday 21. Hudsonville at 2 & 7 p. m.
Friday 22d at Darwin at 2 & 7 p. m.
April 9, '53 38 3t.

The famous packet, *St. Louis,* on the Miami and Erie Canal, with mules on the towpath in right background. *Courtesy of the National Cash Register Company of Dayton, Ohio.*

Repairing a canal whose banks had been destroyed by flood was an expensive and time-consuming procedure. *Courtesy of the Lehigh Coal and Navigation Company of Bethlehem, Pennsylvania, and Northwestern University.*

"Chicago, 1853" by D. W. Moody, after a drawing by George J. Robertson. Printed by Endicott & Company and published by Smith Brothers and Company in 1854. This was five years after the opening of the Illinois and Michigan Canal, which gave Chicago a waterway to the Illinois and Mississippi river basins. *Courtesy of the Chicago Historical Society.*

Wedding party on the Wabash and Erie Canal at Attica, Indiana, in 1872. *Courtesy of the Indiana Historical Society.*

Old wooden locks on the Illinois and Michigan Canal at Channahon, Illinois. These are still in existence, just fifty miles from Chicago's Loop. *Courtesy of Robert John Koch and Marshall Field and Company.*

Locks on the old Miami and Erie Canal. "The sadness of an empty ditch, with boats and horses and men and canawl . . . all run to their end together" (quote from W. C. Fox of Riley, Indiana). *Courtesy of the Anthony Wayne Parkway Board of Ohio.*

West for all of those who were now striving to get there—maps and reports notwithstanding.

Even Hezekiah Niles grew breathless in the sweep of this hot new westward rush. And his *Register* readily added to the conflagration whatever fuel came to hand. . . . The Indians in Michigan were now making great quantities of sugar, and the sailboat *Mariner* had arrived in Detroit from Green Bay with a rich cargo of thirty tons of it. . . . The population of Michigan Territory had increased unbelievably along the borders of Lake Michigan. In fact, the Erie Canal would soon help to make two more new states, and Michigan expected to be one of them. . . . Easterners arriving were currently averaging three hundred per week. There were already three swift steamboats that crossed Lake Erie regularly—the *Superior*, the *Pioneer*, and the *Henry Clay*—with more in the offing. . . .

Enthusiastic letters from the earliest movers and travelers to the fringe country were now beginning to flood the homes of those Easterners who still sat on the fence of indecision concerning the western trek. Some of these letters were so widely passed around as to become ragged scraps of paper, while many of them appeared in the newspapers of two continents. One that enjoyed wide circulation came from the pen of the British Samuel Crabtree.

"This is the country for a man to enjoy himself," he wrote, "the Ohio, Indiana, and Missouri territory, where you see prairie fifty miles long and ten broad, not a stick nor a stone in them, at two dollars an acre, that will produce from seventy to one hundred bushels of Indian corn per acre; too rich for wheat. I measured corn in Ohio State, more than fifteen feet, ears of from four to seven hundred grains . . . I saw more peaches and apples rotting on the ground than would sink the British fleet. I was at many plantations in Ohio where they no more knew the number of their hogs than myself. Apple and peach brandy, forty cents a gallon . . . The poorest families here adorn their table three times a day like a wedding feast. Say, is it so in England?"

Another letter that received wide attention was written by author Moses Langhum, fresh off the Trace, to the girl he had left behind. An excerpt from it set many an Easterner to pondering. "Lord, what a land of good this Ohio Country is! Would you believe, Anne, that here I can get a fine farm for $180? Say, where could I do that in Virginia?"

The enthusiasm contained in this deluge of letters and reports probably did more than any other single factor to induce the timid of two continents to make the plunge. The results were soon evident. Wrote a citizen of Philadelphia to the editor of Ohio's *Mount Pleasant Philanthropist*, "I can scarcely walk a city block without meeting Irish, Dutch, English, and Scotch emigrants whose destination is principally Ohio and Indiana Territory." And from a village near Pittsburgh came the report that two hundred and thirty-six westbound wagons and six hundred sheep had passed through there in a single week. From an editor in Maysville, Kentucky, across the Ohio from the western terminus of Mr. Zane's famous trail, came another breathless report. "We do not recollect of ever having seen so many families emigrating to the western country as are this fall."

Not only did they move to the new frontier, they continued to move, a fact that kept the British puzzled. "Easterners were going to Ohio, but when one gets to Ohio, people there are going on to the Indiana and Missouri Territory," wrote Morris Birkbeck back to England. "Old America seems to be breaking up and moving westward."

William Faux, another English traveler, was equally amazed to discover that settlers who had built along the Trace were already abandoning their new homes to seek greener pastures, deeper in the wilderness. "The American has always something better in his eye further west," wrote the disturbed Mr. Faux. "He therefore lives and dies on hope, a mere gypsy in this particular." This was a pioneer characteristic that would soon be accepted the world over.

At every canalside hamlet in York State now, taverns and boarding-houses were springing to life like mustard seed in a wet summer. And yet there was never enough of them. In fact, so crowded were they, it was said that certain landlords filled their beds to capacity, then eased onto the floor those sleepers who snored the loudest, in order to re-rent the beds to additional guests. Certainly, privacy had long since become a forgotten luxury. For here, as on the packets, men and women—utter strangers—were willing to spend the night on the same crowded tavern floor, demanding only that the men withdraw until the ladies had sacked in. For the very timid, a length or two of calico sometimes made a pass at dividing a room into separate quarters, "which does seem to give the ladies a sense of security," according to one *Traveller's Guide*.

Flotsam and jetsam of two continents included, there soon developed a certain common bond among all emigrants journeying to the fringe country that made them all Westerners together. Yet each group had national or sectional characteristics which distinguished it from the others.

"New Englanders may be known by the cheerful air of the women advancing in front of their vehicles, the Jersey people by their being fixed steadily within it, whilst the Pennsylvanians creep lingering behind, as though regretting the homes they had left," wrote the British Morris Birkbeck. Along the Big Ditch where the travelers were nearly as often European as American, the line of demarcation was even stronger. The Swiss were industrious but suspicious, was the general consensus. They arrived with their tongues in their cheeks and their wooden plows in their arms, lest the fabulous new country had been overtouted. The Germans were diligent but stolid, being accustomed to kicks and cuffs. The French were gay, with buoyant adaptability. The English suffered the change hardest, being the most prejudiced in favor of the customs and habits of their own country. The Scotch showed pliancy and patient endurance; they were the easiest of all to get along with. But the Irish came with laughter up their tattered sleeves, willing to forget the Ould Sod and eager to forget the poverty that had driven them across the ocean.

"As laughing a group as you'll find," Captain Marryat called them as he watched an Irish biddy juggle her five tin teapots onto a canalboat, "with but one spout to the lot of them," while a nearby urchin laughed merrily because his "pantaloons had their gap stopped by a patch made from a straw bonnet that furnished him forever with a straw-bottom chair to sit upon, which was more than his father before him ever had."

As to the Americans—it took an Englishman to sum them up. "They are great travellers," wrote Mr. Birkbeck, "and in general, better aquainted with their vast country spreading over eighteen States than are we English with our little island. They are also a migrating people, and even in prosperous circumstances contemplate a change which elsewhere only the most enterprising would venture upon when urged by adversity. To give an idea of the internal movements of this vast beehive, about 12,000 wagons passed westward through Baltimore and Philadelphia in the last year."

In other words, the American—traditionally a rolling stone —was now a man with a blaze in his eye. It was a combination that was responsible for bringing about the Big Push.

CHAPTER TEN

OLD ERIE WATERS

Just as our truest and clearest pictures of the unfolding New West during the nineteenth century's second decade came from the pens of journalists traveling overland, now in the third decade our most accurate and colorful accounts are concerned with the Big Ditch, coming from the pens of those who were riding her waters. One of the earliest of these, written during the first summer after the Grand Opening of the Grand Canal, was the diary of a nineteen-year-old youth who was making the voyage in the name of science. And while his botanical discoveries may have been big news to the young author, the Big Ditch itself certainly was not, for he was George W. Clinton, son of the world-famous De Witt, due one day to become the well-known Judge Clinton, a lifelong friend of the Old Erie.

He called his journal *A Tour from Albany to Lake Erie in 1826.* The boat he traveled on was the handsome packet *Lafayette,* chartered for this trip as a celebration to honor the first class ever to graduate from Rensselaer College at Troy. As was befitting so august a body, this expedition would be strictly scientific, searching out and classifying, in the interests of botany and zoology, the flora and fauna to be found in this unexplored western wilderness—with here and there a rock tossed in for the sake of geology. And oddly enough, the flower and rock classifications for this territory stand today much as the youthful Clinton's journal recorded them during that long-ago excursion.

It was early June when the young graduates set out, with "an assortment of carpetbags, some books, a barrel of beef, and a barrel of beer," wrote George Clinton, "and my blue camelot cloak which will serve as my bed." The entire trip was to cost them twenty dollars apiece, but young Clinton "agreed to take thirty" at the insistence of the illustrious De Witt, who was somewhat experienced in the matter of running short of cash on this Big Ditch. On their first day out, quite seriously the Class of 1826 drew up a set of rules to govern the enterprise, hoping thereby to induce both professors and students to keep the trip on a high, scientific level. Before the end of their third day out, young George, who in secret session with himself had "promised hereafter to keep the journal more faithfully," had already filled it in with Latin names that apparently poured forth from his split-quill pen with the vigor of a spring freshet: "Arrived at Flint Hill . . . here the calciferous sandstone makes its appearance . . . On the hill I observed a *trifolium erectum,* almost in flower, and picked up *helix albolabris.*"

Not that the expedition was at all times concerned only with scientific data. Before the boat had reached Buffalo, the diary was recording matters concerned with neither flora nor fauna: "After breakfast we walked a mile to examine some limestone thrown out in excavation. At Black Rock we were accosted by an officer and requested to take aboard a captain, his wife, mother, three girls, two boys, and a maid-servant, for six miles. We of course complied . . . The cabin was immediately in a bustle, and in less than a half-hour, dirty shirts were scarce, and disorder resigned the throne he had so long occupied."

It had been part of the original plan to include a sloop trip on Lake Erie, embarking in Buffalo Harbor. But by the time the group had arrived, heavy winds forbade it, so the Class of

'26 decided to take lodging in a local tavern instead. The village was teeming with life and already lost in the hustle-bustle of the western push, according to Clinton, "with every inn so crowded, for want of beds I and another were obliged to lie down before the inn's kitchen fire where we enjoyed the most refreshing slumber . . . In the morning on the beach, we noticed marly clay jutting out . . . Here we met Major Fraser, to whom I was before so much indebted, to use a vulgar expression—who now capped his kindness by this morning presenting me a fine *menobranchus laleralis* . . . Under a stone, I picked up two salamanders, one with a red back."

Before the end of the summer, the expedition had completed its return trip to Albany where young George surrendered his diary to posterity with the assurance, "N.B. I assert naught but what I have seen." This carefully accurate journal is especially interesting because it so strikingly points up the changes that the Big Ditch had wrought, especially upon Buffalo Village, during the sixteen years since De Witt Clinton made his exploratory trip through this same territory to determine the best course for the canal. For the thoroughly crowded, bustling, confused Buffalo of George's diary was the offspring of that forlorn little outpost about which Father Clinton had written, "There are five lawyers and no church here . . . And the whole place is supplied by a single hogshead in a stream of water, as it formerly was distributed in New York City."

During the Old Erie's fourth summer, Colonel William Leete Stone, editor, politician, and author, made a journey and wrote a book which he called *New York to Niagara, the Journal of a Tour in Part by the Erie Canal.* In high spirits he had set off in June of 1829 on the steamer *New Philadelphia,* which carried three hundred passengers when she left New York City. The voyage had started off auspiciously "with an

elegant run up the Hudson," we are told, "for the sky was blue,
the moon was nearly at her full, and the view glorious along
the beautiful and magnificent points, although there were too
many noses pealing forth nocturnal hymns to allow much sleep
to a nervous man." But at three o'clock in the morning, a loud
crash rolled every passenger from his berth, to learn that in a
sudden fog the river steamer had rammed a freighter, killing
two men and a boy—a happening amply balanced for Stone
by the fact that, to his great relief, "the ladies did not scream
and the gentlemen soon retired to berths and settles."

At Albany, the Colonel stopped at the Eagle Tavern, taking
time to attend a famous murder trial in which the victim's
wife, pleading for help because of the loss of support, was
awarded six cents—"equivalent to a defeat," Stone felt. On the
following morning he watched a highly controversial anti-
Masonic parade which had been organized to protest the abduction and death of one William Morgan, believed to have
been murdered by his lodge brothers for revealing secrets of
Freemasonry. "A shabby affair," wrote the Colonel, who royally despised the crudeness of the backwoodsmen, the while
he thoroughly enjoyed their back country.

On his third morning in Albany, Stone awakened to find
"a heavy frost covering the ground, spangling the meadows
with millions of gems, as the sunbeams glance over the landscape." By daybreak he was off for Cooperstown, taking a circuitous stage route for the purpose of enjoying more of the
hinterland. But the sort of people he was forced to ride with
spoiled the trip for him, "because all were ignorant and some
dissipated." A passenger who had lost an arm and a leg
claimed to have taught school in Ohio and Jamaica, "but the
odor of his breath sufficiently indicated the divinity he most
loved to worship." Another passenger swore to have learned
from the lips of the dying that the Royal Arch Masons actually drank from human skulls during their Royal Arch-de-

gree ceremony. And it was his private opinion that considerable murdering must have been necessary in order to equip the lodge rooms properly.

It was twenty-two days after the Colonel left New York City before he reached Rochester—"that far-famed city of the West which has sprung up like Jonah's gourd." This once crude little village now boasted two thousand homes, plus a promising range of stores, churches, public buildings, boats, bridges, and mills—"all standing where stood a frowning forest only seventeen years ago," wrote Stone. "Surely the march of improvement has chosen a herculean task."

Here at long last the Colonel climbed aboard an Erie Canal boat, "to glide smoothly, effortlessly on westward where the forests, yet standing in their native maturity and vigor, seem to defy the feeble arm of man, before which, however, so many myriads of trees have already fallen."

Since a strong head wind that day prevented the horses from beating ahead as fast as usual, it took six hours to cover the first fifteen miles. Brockport and Albion were hardly worth the effort when they were finally reached, Stone felt. They looked raw and naked and weary, with blackened brick and scorched paint due to the ubiquitous brush fires, "for every tree in both towns has been leveled and burned, since every backwoodsman seems to regard every tree as an enemy to be vanquished," according to the Colonel. Their attitude had recently changed, however, bringing about a queer state of affairs, for whereas "every townsman originally hated the wilderness, he now hates worse the bleakness of the clearings, and so all are busy planting saplings which will take a hundred years to equal their predecessors."

The youthfulness of the western scene astonished the Colonel more than any other aspect of the Old Erie, for rarely did he come upon an elderly person, "or even one slightly frosted with age." This, he concluded, was the result of emigration: the old ones remained at home to bury their bones with those of their ancestors, while the young ones swarmed forth to make their fortunes in the wilds of the West. "Thus the tide rolls on," wrote Stone, "wave succeeding wave, like the heaving ocean. When it will be checked or what barrier is to form the boundary of the West, time alone will determine."

Lockport was imposing and splendid, her famous Five now producing water power for enough mills to service all within a hundred miles. The village itself already supported four newspapers, which were at least three too many, observed the Colonel, the while he eyed a gang of boisterous Universal Suffragists coming aboard. "Jackson men, for the most part," he opined. "You can tell by the dirty state of their collars."

Like all travelers who could afford it, William Stone here side-stepped for a visit to Niagara, to see what he called "the place where God poured the water from His hollow hand." There he remained for three days, deeply impressed by the grandeur of the Falls, and thoroughly galled by his chance companions, notably the tailor who stood beside him and shouted above the roar of the waters, "What a fine place to sponge a coat!"

The return canal trip to Albany, like most of his journey, both pleased and irritated the Colonel. Syracuse, arising in the wilderness, was a thing of Aladdin's lamp, he decided, remembering that when he saw her nine years earlier "she had naught but five or six scattered tenements, the whole surrounded by a desolate, poverty-stricken country, enough to make an owl weep to fly over." Now she possessed eleven acres of wharf lots which had recently sold for a million dollars.

At Utica, a few hours later, the Colonel had to rub his eyes twice because he could hardly believe that this hustle-bustle village could have arisen from the desperately forlorn, underprivileged hamlet that he remembered. Herkimer, on the other

hand, turned out to be "still dull and third-rate." But Little
Falls was "the wildest and most romantic yet."

All the way to Albany, the countryside was fresh and beautiful, and the weather pleasingly cool. But Stone could
scarcely enjoy the landscape because the packet was so
crowded and he was so annoyed with his accommodations. "As
I have intimated, every berth and settle and all the space on
the floor was occupied by ten o'clock with horizontal exhibi-
tions of the human frame divine; and a squally child in the
ladies' cabin and a bull-necked, snoring man in the other, kept
up such a duet, refreshing sleep was banished. It was a sad
night for all, especially the ladies . . . N.B. Little children
and people who snore have no business on board of a canal
packet-boat."

During the following year, John Fowler, author and traveler, wrote his *Journal of a Tour in the State of New York in
1830*, a book famous for its wealth of rich detail concerning
the Old Erie Country, for nothing escaped his eye, from land
sales and election notices to quack medicine ads for "Antibil-
ious Pills and Specifics for Dyspepsia."

His was the sort of mind that seeks trends. At the Baggs
Hotel in Utica he observed that even the best-dressed men
wore cloaks which they could wrap about themselves when
they slept on tavern floors with their carpetbags serving as
pillows, "because the two shillings thus saved furnishes the
down-payment for a half-acre of Illinois prairie." Only thirty
years earlier, Fowler recalled, two shillings would have bought
a full acre of York State land at nearby Canandaigua, where it
was now selling for $45 per acre because the Big Ditch lay
only a scant twelve miles away. Let the wise take heed; this
was a straw in the wind.

Like Colonel Stone, Fowler found a bustling, newborn town
at every canal stop. But none, he decided, was more astonish-

ing than Rochester. For here, despite the rapidly sprouting
tree stumps left in the middle of every street, there was "progress to exceed anything ever heard of in this country or
maybe any other. And all of it due to the Grand Canal toward
which everyone is running and looking."

There were others who were stopped cold at the sight of
Rochester, nearly as many as there were visitors who docked
at her piers. For her mushroom growth did indeed surpass that
of any other canal town, even though this was a time when
mushrooming was everywhere evident. Already her achievements had earned for her the title of "Queen City," for her
population had reached eight thousand souls before the Erie
was two years old. Yet so new was she that not a single adult
of that entire eight thousand had been born in Rochester, nor
could have been.

But Queen or otherwise, this was a wild town whose confusion reached such huge proportions as to make her world-
famous. Few were the visiting journalists who did not attempt
to add some startling detail to the general picture of her bewildering, bewitching disorder. You walked her streets at your
own risk, they all agreed, for the whole village seethed with
bustling motion. Merchants doing business downstairs before
the roof was on. Painters finishing one half of the house before
the other half was built. Homes, churches, stores, breweries,
mills, distilleries, tanneries, factories, jail and courthouse, all
creeping simultaneously upward, plank by plank. Dozens of
city blocks lost in a maze of builders' stakes, construction
materials, mules, and men. Crisscrossing roads and lanes that
teemed with movers, wagons, horses, cattle, and pigs without
number, all lifting their voices in a fine confusion. Black forests
pressing in from every side, although countless woodsmen
labored therein the clock around and two huskies could now
fell a sixty-foot giant in three minutes. Land sharks on every
corner, selling lots on imaginary streets. Eleven flour mills

whose stones never stopped grinding, but which were still inadequate, though their four acres of floor space outdistanced that of any other town in the world. Newcomers doing a rushing business before they had a roof over their heads, still shaving in barrooms and washing at the public pump, where long benches with dozens of washbasins were lined up for that purpose. Shops selling French snuffboxes, silks, leghorn hats, and swallowtail coats to customers who had not yet cleared the tree stumps from their cellars. Factories installing help on the first floor before the second was built. Warehouses packed with valuable merchandise before their doors or windows were hung.

And all of it lost in mud. Mud to your ankles. Mud to your knees. Mud so deep no lady would venture to cross a street without masculine help. Mud on the side roads where hundreds of barrels of flour lay wallowing, because Rochester's 160 canalboats and 882 tow horses were in no wise adequate to the 150,000 barrels coming from the mills in a single summer. Mud and confusion. Confusion and rowdyism. Rowdyism that no law could control. Yet there was never a doubt in anyone's mind that Rochester was doing all right for herself. By the time the Big Ditch was three years old the town's population had jumped to thirteen thousand, while the tree stumps that still crowded the middle of her streets had become so thickly overgrown with alder bushes, it now took a stagecoach an hour to cover two miles through the heart of town. Yet her citizens purred in smug contentment. "Rochester is doing pretty considerably well," said her press.

Nor was little Buffalo very far behind. By 1830, when her population had reached six thousand, Fowler ranked her the sixth most important city in the state, following New York City, Brooklyn, Albany, Utica, and Rochester. Certainly as hub of an immense water wheel, she could hardly have escaped greatness—standing at the foot of Lake Erie, at the head of the Niagara River, and at the west end of the Big Ditch.

It was not surprising, then, that her important and picturesque frontier position should make her the apple of every writer's eye and keep her constantly in print. Soon even the stories of her meager beginnings had become important, notably those appearing in what came to be called the Hodge Papers. These were written by William Hodge, Junior, to honor the memory of his father. Their popularity was due to the fact that they carried the reading public back to Buffalo's outpost days, long before the Big Ditch was in anyone's mind.

Young Hodge, born in a dogtrot cabin soon after the turn of the century, had spent all of the days of his youth in this backwoods clearing, knowing the terrors of an unbroken wilderness as well as its beauty. "How plain is my remembrance of the road so lately cut through, full of stumps, logs, and brush. . . . The Fourth of July and election day were play-days for us boys," wrote Hodge, joyfully recalling how the fife and bugle corps used to let go for glory, on days like these. "And although we did not in those times have Thanksgiving days for family gatherings, our picnics and Sunday school excursions furnished great fun. . . . And then there were the apple-parings in the winter . . ."

By the time Hodge was seventeen, the Erie Canal was halfway built. And although it had by no means yet approached Buffalo, it was throwing its shadow long before. And something called culture had already arrived. This had manifested itself first in the form of a debating society that struggled nearly a year, trying to determine which had been of greater benefit to mankind—the printing press or the magnetic needle. And the fact that the ramifications of its research had lead through basket suppers, quilting bees, hog butcherings, and village sings was all to the good, Hodge felt, for without these the story of Buffalo would indeed have been a grim chronicle of hardships.

One of the more memorable aspects of life in this outpost hamlet came with the arrival of a young law student who planned to make his way by teaching school while he studied law, "boarding around" meanwhile to avoid starvation, since a teacher's salary was only $12.00 per month. This in due time brought him as a guest to the Hodge household, bringing about a deal of "frolicking," from time to time, since one of the Hodge girls was admittedly as pretty as sin. This "cutting of capers" seems to have manifested itself largely in snowball fights, but it was the beginning of a friendship that continued long after the young lawyer had entered the political arena and outgrown Buffalo.

"On the day of his funeral," wrote Hodge, many years later, "I was present amid a vast assembly, to take a farewell look at one of my old teachers; I was beholding all that was mortal of Millard Fillmore, once President of the United States."

With the coming of the Old Erie, the immediate improvement in Buffalo Village had been phenomenal. Only two years after the first canalboat touched in at her piers, Captain Frederick Marryat stepped ashore and caught his breath in amazement at his first glimpse of what he called "wider main streets and handsomer stores than the majority in New York City, besides five or six churches, a handsome theatre, a townhall, market, and three or four hotels, one of which is superior to most in America. And to all of these must be added a fine stone pier with a lighthouse and a harbour full of shipping and magnificent boats . . . It is almost incomprehensible that all this should be accomplished in so short a time. And what has occasioned this springing up of a city in such record time as to remind you of Aladdin's magic palace? *The Erie Canal!*"

As proof that this amazing improvement was no flash in the

pan, there came dozens of other chronicles singing the praises of Buffalo, including one called *The Social Life of Buffalo,* written a decade later by Martha Fitch Poole. "She was a first class town by now," wrote Mrs. Poole, "known for the elegance with which she was laid out . . . her magnificent trees bordering every street and lane . . . her full view of river and lake for uninterrupted miles . . . birds singing in the most populous sections, and such flowers! Yet Indians still walked the streets in blankets and moccasins. Cows grazed at the roadsides and pigs roamed at their own sweet will, only kept out of beautiful gardens by stout picket fences."

The knee-deep mud on Main Street was a thing of the past now, and the clatter of horses' hoofs on the new cobblestones formed a musical background day and night, augmented by the rattle of carriages, stagecoaches, carts, drays, and wagons, moving everlastingly between river, canal, and lake piers. For nine out of every ten transients bound for the West now passed through this portal.

Nor was this beehive activity confined to the village alone, according to Mrs. Poole. For "on Lake Erie's broad expanse one could scarcely count the white winged vessels as they quietly glided in and out, so numerous were they in those early days. It was quite the fashionable thing on the evenings when the steamboat went up the lake, to go down to the dock and 'see her off' . . . Hotels, taverns, inns, and boarding-houses were in every block, and turn where you would, the lumbering rattle of the stage, with its tooting horn, was apt to greet all passersby any hour of the day."

From the time of spring thaws until the Big Ditch was either drained or frozen solid for the winter, Buffalo kept her mind strictly on her bustling business. But the remainder of the year she devoted to her social life, while she waited for the season of boating to return. Throughout these gayer months "chivalry

held things in bound," Mrs. Poole believed, "although the flowing bowl often over-ran the limits of sobriety, in times of
frolic." Here, as in Philadelphia, the volunteer firemen led the
social whirl, mainly because they were organized early enough
to assume that privilege. Their flings were gay ones, "always
well attended by the fashionable and better class of citizens,"
we are assured.

On the whole, gay young Buffalo, still regarded by most
Easterners as a backwoods clearing in the western wilderness,
was actually having a glorious time of it, according to Mrs.
Poole, who recalled with relish a certain outstanding social
affair she had attended.

"A very gay sleigh-ride went to Niagara Falls and put up
for the night at Cataract Hotel where, the day before, a quantity of oysters, several cases of champaign, and other drink-
ables and eatables such as pioneers delight in after a twenty-
two mile ride, were sent down. This came between Christmas
and New Year's on a frosty cold day with plenty of glistening
snow. A hundred ladies and gentlemen, both married and
single, made the trip. There were thirty sleighs, from the slender cutter to the pretentious one that took the lead like an
ornate circus vehicle of the most bewildering style and color, a
bright scarlet with a yellow dashboard with golden swans on
either side, their long curving necks and slender heads standing out conspicuously in front. The cushions were red velvet.
There were six white horses, with the gayest of harness, and
tinkling tintinnabulating bells . . . And foot stoves and fur
rugs for comfort. Twenty couples took to the larger sleighs, but
the single ones preferred the cutters, as they so merrily went
forth for a winter's lark. Every Indian squaw had heard we
were coming and met us outside Cataract, selling beadwork,
maple sugar in birch boxes and skins of animals . . . Supper
was served before the great log-filled fireplaces, and the entire

company repaired to the ballroom where with dash and spring the dance proceeded . . . Considerable champaign disappeared that night . . . but none were the worse for it!"

As was common at most pioneer gatherings, the festive evening was finally polished off with a round of community singing, now featuring the three newest song hits of the day. First, appropriately enough, came "Some Love to Roam." Second, of all things, here in the deeps of the wilderness, came "Woodman, Spare that Tree." But along about daybreak, as Martha Poole recalled it, John Knott was rolling them in the aisles with his "killingly funny rendition of 'Being of the Livery, He was a Stable Man.'"

From the moment of the Old Erie's Grand Opening, there was never a trace of doubt about her complete success. Most surprising of all was her ever mounting financial achievement. This came as a shock to everyone, including the canal commissioners. For even they had entertained their secret doubts during the long years of her construction, because every estimate had run at least thirty per cent below the actual cost. Never in their wildest dreams had they expected her to pile up a cash surplus.

Now, at the end of her eighth year of operation, to their great bewilderment the commissioners found themselves with an extra two and a quarter million dollars on their hands. How completely baffled they would have been, could they have foreseen that in sixty years the Old Erie's net profits would exceed forty-two and a half million, a sum far exceeding the total cost of all packet canals of the Canal Era. In the entire commercial history of America, it would be difficult to find another success comparable to this one, especially in view of the times and territory involved. And the most astounding aspect of the entire enterprise lay in the fact that no one had been robbed to produce this utopia. For even by 1826, her freight rates had dropped lower than any politician would have dared promise. Flour was riding the entire 363-mile channel for a penny a ton, shingles for a mill a thousand, general merchandise for two cents per ton, and wood fuel for a penny a cord. Salt, still scarce enough to be one of the pioneer's most costly necessities, was now traveling from Albany to Buffalo for four mills per *ton,* while all the fuel necessary for its manufacturing rode free—a fact that was making ridiculous all who had pooh-poohed Robert Fulton's early prediction that if Congress would sanction the Big Ditch, the then current cost of $2.50 for hauling a mere *bushel* of salt for three hundred miles could be reduced to 7½ cents.

In addition to her own financial success, the Big Ditch was radically changing the picture of the entire country. She had helped to increase the population of New York City from 124,-000 in 1820 to 203,000 in 1830. She had helped to make New York State the largest in the Union. She had given the great migration a tremendous boost by providing an easier and cheaper way west. And she had increased the spending power of the entire nation because her cheap freight rates had radically reduced the price of eastern products to Westerners, and western products to Easterners.

It is hardly surprising that this unexpected success came as something of a shock to the canal's enemies, for it amazed even her staunchest friends. But who could have predicted the Big Push? And who could have foretold that by the time Clinton's Ditch had paid off only a million and a half of her $7,944,770 debt, without so much as the raising of an eyebrow the people of York State would vote an additional $12,500,000 to start the thirty-year task of doubling her single locks and lengthening them from ninety to a hundred feet, besides deepening her entire channel from four to seven feet and widening it from forty to seventy feet? All to be done with an eye toward admitting the longer, wider boats necessary to accommodate the tremendous and completely unpredicted shift of population that was now shaking the United States—and much of Europe as well. For while only 8,000 immigrants entered this country during the Old Erie's first year, by the time she had reached her fifth birthday, the entries had jumped to an astonishing 50,000 per year.

The great migration was beginning to fill up America's western territory. In 1810, seven years before work on the Erie Canal was started, the young state of Ohio ranked thirteenth in the Union in point of population. By the time the Big Ditch was fifteen years old, she would come very close to ranking third. Illinois, Indiana, and the Michigan Territory were already making comparable gains. And practically the entire burden of transporting this pilgrimage across the barrier of the Alleghenies was now being borne by the Erie alone, for Uncle Sam's Pike had deteriorated to the point of being almost useless.

"On the eastern side of Savage Mountain there cannot be found a handful of earth on the National Road for some distance, it being washed out, filling up culverts and drains, carrying with it all small stone on the surface," read a Congressional Report of 1826. "In fact, it is *distressing* to a traveler to see this great work in its present condition."

Although the average citizen was no more likely to make a habit of reading Congressional reports in 1826 than he is today, the news got around. And so did he. One of his number, one Lucius W. Stockton, a so-called "land admiral" by virtue of his owning a few mountain wagons and a couple of stagecoaches, made a trip out of Uniontown that year, to see how his mail and passenger stages were faring along Uncle Sam's Pike.

"I have been three times over the whole of it," he wrote, "and generally speaking, the surface is entirely destroyed, or sunk under the foundations, leaving the large stone on top. In one place the foundation itself has been carried away by the breaking up of winter, which with heavy rains leaves a broken link in the Road for twelve miles; the mail stage, carrying no passengers and with an excellent set of horses, was totally unable to make it in consequence of the delapidated state of the Road."

That was why the Old Erie found herself sitting alone in the driver's seat by 1826. And the importance of this fact to the future Middle West, to the claiming and settling of the Pacific seaboard, even to the outcome of the Civil War, cannot be overestimated. The Cumberland Road had been definitely leading the great migration in a southwesterly direction, as was now evident to all—for only the lower rims of Ohio, Indiana, and Illinois had yet been settled, while their vast northern stretches remained largely untouched. Even Ebenezer Zane's well-traveled Trace angled toward the south, leading traffic into Kentucky or lower Indiana and Illinois. But the tide of migration had now changed its direction, thanks to the Big Ditch, pouring movers by the thousands into northern Ohio, Indiana, Illinois, and the territories of Wisconsin and Michigan by way of Lake Erie, thus preparing the great Mississippi Valley to be ready to play its tremendous part when a panful of gold at Sutter's Creek should force the issue.

The Old Erie was not unaware of her importance. Even as early as her first year in business, she was already intent on making the most of it, for this was the beginning of the great Go-West-young-man-go-West movement. Her canalboats and way stations were plastered with advice to this effect. "Opportunity for all with the strength and will to grasp it," read her ubiquitous placards. *Niles' Register* and other newspapers of the day were quick to take up the cry, devoting wide coverage to an issue that involved hundreds of thousands of people, for the Old Erie was now the biggest news of its day, both at home and abroad. And by far the most impressive.

"These are a magnificent people," wrote a western editor, "working out with unexampled enterprise the first stern law of our human condition, in earning their bread by the sweat of their brow; the framework of a mighty power, an intelligent people; and scattered here and there among them are those who would be bright ornaments to any nation. The northwest will be the great granary of the republic, with the largest amount of arable soil capable of producing most bountiful returns from the least labor, and able now to reach a ready market. . . . The only present drawbacks are the crude and elemental character of its population, the hardships necessary to be encountered in the forest, and the unhappy nature of its climate. When these are overcome, it will be the most eligible place for settlement, and a most opulent part of the republic, wielding as it soon must, *the balance of power in this country.*"

By the glow of a winter's log fire, prospective movers by the tens of thousands continued to search out editorials like this one, sorting the chaff from the wheat and finally reaching the decision to join the great migration while yet the world was young. No longer were they frightened by either the crudeness of the West or its hardships. Abruptly they knew themselves for what they were—a sturdy people, able to conquer both disease and wilderness, and amply possessed with a glorious talent for perseverance. As for the "crude and elemental character of Western population" that was worrying that editor, perhaps they understood better than he that this was Democracy, a thing so tangible in the fringe country that men wore it like a shawl and were comforted by its warmth and dependability.

And so the exodus from the East grew in strength, some abandoning their old homes without so much as a backward glance, while others heard loneliness in the wind even before the first week was over. But either way, there were few among them who outwardly faltered as they pushed their way west,

day after day after weary day. Bound away, all of them, bound
for the Promised Land, come hell or high water. With youth in
their hearts, and with sad songs and glad songs to while away
the miles.

Come listen to my story, ye landsmen one and all.
And I'll sing to you the dangers of that raging canawl.
For I am one of many who expect a watery grave,
For I've been at the mercy of the winds and the waves.

It seemed as if the devil had work in hand that night,
For our oil it was all gone, and our lamps they gave no light.
The clouds began to gather and the rains began to fall,
And I wished myself off of that raging canawl.

Sad was the fate of our poor devoted bark,
For the rain kept pouring faster, and the night it grew more dark.
The horses gave a stumble and the driver gave a squall.
And they tumbled head and heels into that raging canawl.

CHAPTER ELEVEN

WHEN CANAWLING WAS IN FLOWER

THE success of the Big Ditch was the beginning of what later came to be known as the Canal Era, that fabulous period that brought about more changes in the American scene than any other double decade before or since. Almost overnight the question of artificial waterways was no longer a local issue, for not only was the ridiculed Old Erie now widely hailed as the answer to all who desired to head west, but canals in general had abruptly come back into favor. What the Big Ditch had done for York State, any canal system could do for any locality that possessed courage enough to start digging. Certainly this was the most satisfactory and economical method of travel yet invented. Besides which, one look at the pots of gold and the giant cities that Clinton's Ditch was amassing should be enough to clinch the argument.

It did—immediately galvanizing the entire country into action. The result was stupendous, with state assemblies called into special session everywhere—even in the middle of the night in some instances. Activity on the county level boiled with equal vigor, with seventeen inland sections in York State alone drawing up petitions for canals of their own. Early waterways, half-dug and long since abandoned, now again were objects of public interest. Half-forgotten canal blueprints were exhumed and dusted off. Rusty picks and shovels were scraped and sharpened. Wheelbarrows were greased. And the entire country buzzed with excitement—"lively as Dutch cheese in dog-days," Davy Crockett called it. Now for the first time, this wild frenzy for internal improvements knew no bounds, sweeping through the sparsely settled fringe country as well as the eastern seaboard.

Even before the Erie's Grand Opening, some of her closest neighbors, encouraged by reports of the success of her first completed sections, had already followed her example and so were now in a position to enjoy whatever head start their foresight had produced. Among these were certain courageous and enthusiastic Pennsylvanians who had cast speculative eyes across the hills toward Clinton's half-finished ditch, four years earlier. Immediately they had been inspired to resurrect their abandoned Schuylkill and Susquehanna as well as their forsaken Delaware and Susquehanna, hoping to sneak these two channels back into public favor as a new project under a new name—the Union Canal. During that same early summer the Cumberland and Oxford Canal was also planned and incorporated.

During the following year, the revival of an earlier attempt at a waterway to connect Providence with Worcester, tagging the Blackstone River, called forth New England's rusty picks and shovels. And before the cowslips had faded in the spring of 1823, the Chesapeake and Delaware project was dragged back to life. Later in that same year, two new canal companies blossomed into existence—the Hampshire and Hampden to connect Northampton to New Haven, and the Delaware and Hudson to create an outlet for Lackawanna anthracite coal.

In 1824, the Susquehanna and Tidewater was chartered to run a channel from Middletown to the mouth of the Susquehanna River. And the Morris Canal and Banking Company was granted permission to build a coal-barge channel across New Jersey from the Delaware River to New York Harbor.

The year of the Old Erie's Grand Opening saw the beginnings of the first two fringe-country canals. Both were in Ohio, and both were to be strictly north-south channels, forsaking the usual east-west trend in order to connect the Ohio River with Lake Erie in two widely separated paths, thereby opening thousands of acres of rich Ohio forest and farmland to new settlers. It was only a matter of time now until Illinois would cast a speculative eye at her own "half-league of prairie" where Joliet had dreamed, a century and a half earlier, that a short waterway could easily connect Lake Michigan to the Mississippi. Indiana was already turning lyric over a wild rumor that her Wabash was only about twenty-five miles from Lake Erie in certain of her unexplored northern regions.

Almost faster than hand-set type could record it, additional canal news was breaking all over the country, items that Hezekiah Niles eagerly gathered from newspapers everywhere for a new column called "Spirit of the Times." This was enjoying the widest possible attention, partly because the *Register* covered more of the globe than did any other American paper, and partly because this was the sort of news that kindled little bonfires wherever it was read and discussed, each flame adding its own heat to the fierceness of the great conflagration. Within a matter of months, Niles had made much of the civilized world aware that America had gone hog-wild over canal building.

"It is stated that 2500 men have been employed on the different sections of the Ohio Canal. The work goes on merrily and will probably be completed in much less time and for less money than originally was calculated. Cincinnati is already flourishing thereby. . . . According to the *Lancaster Gazette,* a Mr. Hamill, a gentleman experienced in the art of constructing canals, has contracted with the Conestoga Navigation for the whole work at a considerable less estimate than that of the engineers. That work will be commenced forthwith. . . .

A correspondence between Governor Troup of Georgia and Governor Carroll of Tennessee was concerned with opening communication by canal through Georgia, between the waters of the Tennessee River and the Atlantic Ocean. . . . Thirty miles of the Morris Canal, to connect the waters of the Delaware River with the Hudson, are under contract and 700 men are making excavations. The practicability of inclined planes in place of locks will be tested on this canal. . . . The Hudson and Delaware Canal, higher up the river than the Morris, also goes on merrily. A thousand men whose number is daily increasing, are now employed at twelve to fourteen dollars per month. It is supposed that the whole of this latter canal will be under contract by the first of November, ensuing. . . . The Delaware and Raritan is fighting over location, with people all along the line offering free land to get it to come their way. . . . The Blackstone Canal in Connecticut is already commenced. . . . A Champlain and Connecticut is contemplated. . . . The Delaware and Passaic is now being dug."

Before the year was over, even the northern sections of the country had got into the swing of the thing, in spite of the shortness of their boat season. These too made news for Niles's "Spirit of the Times" and were recorded as fast as the news broke.

"Public notice has been given in Vermont that application will be made to the General Assembly of the State at the session to be holden in October next, for a charter for a canal to unite the waters of Lake Champlain to the Connecticut River by the Valley of the Onion River. . . . Important canals are projected in Canada. The Welland plans to make a sloop navigation between Lakes Ontario and Erie, and probably another around the rapids of the Saint Lawrence between Lake Erie and Montreal. With these completed, a direct voyage may be made to the West Indies by vessels built one thousand miles in the interior of America. . . . The original 363 miles of the Old Erie, with its many projected branches into other districts will eventually reach a thousand miles of channel."

And although the average Johnny Pioneer was doing very well to spell out what Niles was saying in the first place— without trying to locate all the waterways mentioned—still the impact of such news in the aggregate was enormous, appearing as it did week after week, month after month. In fact, so great was it, he was ready and anxious to be swept along with the tide when the question of a canal for his own little bailiwick came up for a vote.

So the digging did everywhere indeed go on "merrily" as Niles was wont to describe it. Before the Big Ditch was a year old, her Seneca and Cayuga branch was moving along toward completion. And out at Louisville, a thousand workers were swapping sweat for scrip on the difficult little two-miler around the treacherous Ohio Falls, where the noted journalist John Woods once hired a professional fallsman to shoot his boat with all his earthly possessions over the rapids for him— a maneuver he later reported to be "entirely successful except that the rope broke and the craft was lost."

On the eastern seaboard, the so-called Schuylkill Navigation was already open, and the James and Kanawha had reached a point only twenty-seven miles from Richmond. Success was in the air all over America now, and great was the general excitement every time a news flash announced that another new channel somewhere was sparkling with water for the first time.

Not that every canal dream became a reality, for in spite of the great momentum that was sweeping the Canal Era into existence, many a dream-ditch never held water. Boston Town was one of the first to have her plans come crashing—to her own surprise. From her earliest days, she had expected to retain forever her position as the foremost city in the nation, only occasionally turning a halfway suspicious eye on the advances of Philadelphia, New Orleans, or Baltimore. The current boom in New York City therefore came as something of a shock to her—as, for that matter, had the success of the Erie. To put this upstart in its place, conservative old Boston now decided to build a canal of her own from her Charles River to the Hudson, thus giving her direct access to the fabulous Old Erie. This should put her back in the running, she believed. But such a channel, she soon learned, would have to include an almost impossible section containing two hundred locks within eighteen miles in order to cross the Hoosac Mountains. It would take two full days to lock a boat through. The only alternative was to tunnel under these mountains, a suggestion that was wildly embraced until bids for such a project were received. These ran as low as $370,000 and as high as $920,000; even the lowest bid would bring the cost of the canal up to a breath-taking $6,023,172. When this report was laid before the legislators, it took water to revive them. And the whole plan was thankfully abandoned.

Philadelphia, too, felt the menace of the Erie's success and was determined to do something about it in her own defense. She had for some time feared a Baltimore boom, since the Susquehanna River was a direct avenue for that city while she herself must send her goods by a circuitous wagon route to Middletown before she could take advantage of that stream. Furthermore, the abandoned Schuylkill and Susquehanna Canal, which had been expected to divert the Susquehanna River business to her own front door, had lain idle since 1794. Nor did the present plans to revive it as part of the new Union Canal seem to be making much progress. As matters now stood, her only connection with the West was a roundabout course by sloop to Albany, thence westward through Clinton's Ditch, a route too expensive to allow her products to compete favorably with those of New York City, Albany, Buffalo, or

Rochester. This situation was pointed up by a squib appearing in a Columbus, Ohio, newspaper:

"It takes thirty days and costs five dollars a hundred pounds to transport goods from Philadelphia to this city, but the same article may now be brought in twenty days from New York City via the Erie Canal for $2.50 per hundred. Suppose a merchant to import, on an average, five tons twice a year; this means a saving of $560.00 per merchant."

Nor was this the only fly in Philadelphia's ointment. The proposed Chesapeake and Ohio, which would connect the Potomac River with the Ohio Valley, would undoubtedly favor Washington City as well as Baltimore, adding another threat to the supremacy of the City of Brotherly Love. It was therefore now clear that Pennsylvania, too, must get into the canal business if she wished to save her chief city. Already her enthusiastic though slightly misinformed press had seen the handwriting on the wall, and started to boom up the issue.

"Geographically considered, no city is so favorably situated as Philadelphia, for commanding the whole inland trade of the continent," claimed one editor. "Seventy-five miles of canal are all that is needed to give full water communication with the Pacific Ocean via the mouth of the Columbia River."

He had arrived at this startling conclusion by mentally projecting a canal to connect the upper waters of the Susquehanna with Seneca Lake, from which a boat could progress by branch canal into the Old Erie, thence through the Great Lakes to Lake Superior; and—here most early maps were as hopeful and hazy as the editor—surely after you had reached Superior, an additional skip and a jump should land you somewhere along the Columbia River. After that there was nothing to it—straight out its mouth, and on to the East Indies. Or even to China.

This was a brave notion, carrying a magnificent wallop—an inland water route from Philadelphia all the way to the

Orient, with but seventy-five miles of canal-digging necessary! Its timing, too, was perfect, for when Clinton's report of
1826 disclosed a three-quarter-million-dollar profit for a mere
summer, Pennsylvanians figured that it was now high time to
come out of their pipe dreams and join up—whole hog or
none. "So that the entire territory of Pennsylvania will present
nothing but a congregation of islands," suggested one of her
Congressmen. Additional news, arriving at this time, disclosed
that the long-delayed Lehigh Canal was now actually under
way, and the long-contemplated Chesapeake and Ohio already
had eighteen hundred diggers on the job. These startling facts
furnished the final catalyst; Pennsylvania would immediately
start digging a huge canal westward, nearly the full width of
the state. And this she did. Within three years, she had five
thousand workers on steady pay, working this one ditch alone.

The extensive Pennsylvania canal system deserves special
attention because its problems were special, its sorrows were
deep, and its importance was great. Its entire construction
covered a period of fourteen years, from 1820 to 1834. And
although it eventually moved countless people into the Promised Land, financially it was a colossal failure. The largest and
most important of its waterways was the Pennsylvania Grand
Canal, which connected Pittsburgh with Philadelphia, though
the entire system included many lesser channels, of which
some were pioneers in new types of canal construction and
operation.

Such a one, the Schuylkill Navigation, was originally projected in 1821 and opened in 1825, connecting Philadelphia
with Mount Carbon near Pottsville. This canal won distinction as the possessor of the first tunnel in America, which entitled her to a certain amount of prestige in spite of the fact
that this big hole was entirely unnecessary—the offending hill
could have been avoided by moving the channel only a hun-

dred feet to the west. Still, there were those who felt that burrowing four hundred feet under a mountain was something of an achievement, especially in view of the fact that rival canals were threatening to pioneer with tunnels of their own.

This subterranean passage came to be considered one of the wonders of its time, and people traveled great distances to watch canalboats disappear into the bowels of the earth, only to come back into the sunshine on the other side of the mountain, little the worse for the experience. Catching a glimpse of its contractors was considered an additional bit of luck, for the famous Fudge brothers—Job, Samson, and Solomon—like Canvass White and Jim Geddes, were always off to greener pastures as soon as a job was finished, seldom waiting to receive their laurels.

This same canal won further distinction because her craft used neither tow horses nor drivers during the first two years of operation. Instead, each canalboat was drawn by two husky men teamed together as they walked the towpath, leaning into a breast board to which the towrope was fastened. It took them six weeks to walk the round trip from Philadelphia to Mount Carbon, two hundred and sixteen miles. And it cost them a new pair of boots, per man, per trip.

The Union Canal was also considered a part of the Pennsylvania waterways. From the time of her first survey until she ran her first boat—the *Fair Trader*—from Philadelphia to Middletown, it took sixty years to build her. Part of her channel, the old Delaware and Susquehanna, dated far enough back to have received the personal attention of President George Washington in 1793, when he traveled these parts by horseback on an inspection tour. And the following year, while accompanying troops bent on suppressing the Whiskey Insurrection, he again cantered off alone for a look at this waterway, later recording the incident in his diary.

"An Accident to one of my Horses occasioned my setting

out later than was intended. I got off however, to view the Canal from Myerstown towards Lebanon, and the Locks between the two Places; which, four adjoining each other in the Descent from the summit Ground along the Tulpehocken, built of Brick, appeared admirably constructed." Thirty-four years later, as part of the Union Canal, this channel admitted her first craft. By the end of that same year, 1828, she was running two hundred boats, all tailor-made for this channel because the locks were too narrow for the average canalboat.

Pennsylvania's most important waterway, her so-called Grand Canal, was nearly a decade behind the Old Erie in getting started. While this was unfortunate, it was also unavoidable, for in addition to her many difficult construction problems she was due throughout her existence to fight certain groups who strenuously objected to her being built in the first place. All of these were vociferous, but the most offensive of all were the wagoners, those knights of the road who had for some time enjoyed a lucrative living by hauling great loads of merchandise over dangerous and doubtful mountain trails. Now they feared that a waterway would sweep away their business, which of course was exactly what was due to happen. As a matter of record, once this canal was finished freight rates for the forty-three-mile strip from Pittsburgh to Blairsville would drop from 18½ to 3½ cents per ton per mile. And the usual run from the middle of York State to Blairsville would drop from a difficult twenty-one-day trip overland to a smooth and easy eight-day jaunt by water. Either one of these improvements could neatly eliminate the wagoner, just as he now suspected.

Sectional jealousy formed another obstacle to the building of this canal, for no inland county, with nothing to gain, intended to break its back paying for its neighbors' bonanza. A third group objected on the grounds that all canals were now obsolete because the coming of railroads was imminent.

This group had a point. Viewed from this angle as well as several others, Pennyslvania's Grand Canal was undoubtedly coming too late, and a keen eye could have foreseen her financial failure before a shovel was lifted.

But the most sensible objection of all came from the many who were convinced that the natural mountain barriers would eventually kill this project. The truth lay on their side, for here the lockage must be five times as great as that which had so long baffled the Erie. In fact, according to the original blueprints which would have carried the canal all the way west to the Great Lakes, her lockage in the final fifteen miles alone would have equaled the total lockage of Clinton's Big Ditch. Even in accordance with her later plans, which stopped her short at Pittsburgh, her problems were immense.

Nevertheless, on the Fourth of July, 1826, against a doubly noisy background—black powder explosions from the protagonists, plus bitter grumbling from the antagonists—Pennsylvania's bigwigs turned the official first shovelful of dirt to initiate digging on their Grand Canal. The canal's progress, once the initial plunge had been made, actually exceeded anything De Witt Clinton had been able to accomplish in point of time, partly because newer tools and methods were now available, partly because canal building was no longer a doubtful undertaking. Moreover, there was all of Clinton's experience to be leaned upon, plus most of his engineers. James Geddes and Nathan Roberts had been on hand from the beginning. By the time they had ascertained that lifting this canal over Pennsylvania's mountains by locks alone was completely out of the question, Canvass White had joined them to assume responsibility for building a portage railroad that could scale mountain peaks, conquering an elevation of 2,291 feet in less than 320 miles.

For the most part, this work proceeded smoothly and according to plan, and the eastern strip of railroad was actually authorized as early as 1828 and ready for operation by 1834. It was one of the earliest railroads in America, and the first in the world to be built by a government. Young and inexperienced and flushed with its own importance, this new form of transportation started off in business by furnishing only the tracks, inviting everyone to put his own horse and car on its crude tracks anywhere, running in whichever direction and at whatever hour pleased his fancy. The resulting confusion, brawling, and ill will when a determined westbound carriage met a stubborn eastbound one on a single track can easily be imagined. Almost at once the state was forced to double-track the entire strip besides assuming its full operation and furnishing the cars. Later, all horses were replaced with a crude type of steam locomotive.

From its beginning, the Grand Canal's construction followed the pattern set by the Old Erie and a few smaller waterways. First came a skyrocketing of prices wherever the surveyors' red stakes pointed the way. Next came an influx of contractors, subcontractors, foremen, and gang bosses, and armies of laborers, mostly Irish. Next appeared the shanty villages, springing up overnight, fully equipped with the necessary trios—blacksmith shops, boarding-houses, and dram shops. After that it was only a matter of hours until every country road for miles around was choked with farmers' Connie wagons, loaded with foodstuffs, gravel, sand, timber, and stone. By that time, life in Pennsylvania had become a thing of bustle and abundance. Money came easy and prosperity looked permanent. And who was worried about taxes, while the goose hung higher than a harvest moon?

In 1829, the western section of the Grand Canal—the strip between Pittsburgh and Johnstown—was partly opened, and by the next year it was in full operation. By 1832 the Juniata Division was practically completed, and by 1834 the Portage Railroad across the Divide was finished, following a bitter three-year struggle during which passengers were transported across the mountains by stagecoach or wagon. This troublesome delay had come about when politics entered the picture, demanding the building of four expensive branch canals before the main line was finished. But the delay had not been too costly; by the time the Portage was finally completed, it was generally conceded that it had been well worth waiting for, because it far outshone all other so-called wonders of the world.

The first emigrant's boat ever to make the crossing by portage was one that just happened along at the opportune moment, one golden day in 1834, and so was offered the privilege of being the guinea pig. This little keelboat had already floated its westbound owner and his family down the Lackawanna and the Susquehanna, proceeding thence by tow through Pennsylvania's Grand Canal to Hollidaysburg, where a transportation manager had made this startling offer. Here the emigrant had waited two days while the canal company whipped into shape a railroad car, calculated to be rugged enough to bear its novel burden. On the morning of the third day, this crude car was lowered into the canal beneath the emigrant's keelboat—appropriately named the *Hit-or-Miss*—and the ascent began.

"At twelve o'clock on the same day," reported the *Hollidaysburg Aurora,* "the delighted family began their passage over the rugged Allegheny. It was pleasing to see the comfort and convenience that the ingenuity of man had added to the journey of the emigrant. The whole family was comfortably located in the cabin of their boat, which appeared to glide up the heights of the Alleghenies, unconscious of its being a fish out of water, whilst some of the family were preparing the coming meals and others were lying on their downy pillows. . . . Soon you see her safely resting on the summit of the Allegheny mountains. Night has overtaken them, and there they wait the coming morn. . . . On Tuesday our boat and crew left the sunny summit and smoothly glided down her iron way to Johnstown, astonishing the natives. She was safely deposited in her own element on the same evening amidst the plaudits of the congregated citizens, and thence continued her unexpected journey 'to the wild Mis-sou-ree.' "

A Philadelphia editor, equally breathless over this historic event, also reported it as fast as scrabbled type could be lined up to tell the story. "It rested on top of the mountain at Blair's Gap like Noah's Ark on Ararat, and descended next morning into the valley of the Mississippi and sailed for St. Louis!"

Which was the truth, with certain reservations, as was also the brag of a third editor, covering another trial run over this section:

"The ten stationary engines that hauled the first load of freight ever to cross the crest of the Alleghenies by artificial means were made right here in the Young West in Pittsburgh!"

By the time Pennsylvania's Grand Canal was officially opened to the public in the mid-1830's, a journey over this route was considered something of an experience, valuable for bragging purposes in addition to its contribution to Westward-Ho. Fittingly enough, its service was presented with something of a fling. To begin with, a westbound passenger must call at the Philadelphia canal office on the night before his departure to sign up for passage, so that an omnibus could hunt out his boarding-house and tally-ho him out of bed at daybreak. When all passengers had been gathered from various parts of town and delivered to the canal's railroad station, each boosted his own carpetbag, portmanteau, valise, or hide-covered trunk onto the roof of one of the two crude railroad cars, then crawled inside.

Now the horses were whipped up to dash the carriages westward, making their first important stop at the foot of the first lift. This one required 2,800 feet to complete a 187-foot hoist.

An immense hawser with a stationary engine up top turned the trick, usually hauling up several cars at a time. Here on the crest of this first knob, fresh horses waited to trot the train on westward.

In later years when steam was adopted and open-topped carriages were in use, this same strip became a well-known race course where the young sports of the day were said to talk the engineers sometimes into speeding up to eight or nine miles an hour. Nor was this terrifying velocity the only excitement of the venture, for at this point it was always necessary to fire the engine to full capacity in order to produce the proper head of steam. This resulted in such a continuous shower of red-hot cinders from the puffing, wood-burning locomotive as to make it necessary for each passenger to sit with a pailful of sand in his lap, ready to extinguish fires as fast as they appeared in his own or his neighbor's clothing. This annoyance was still a part of the future, however.

Meanwhile our passengers had been trotted on westward by staid old horses to spend their second night at Lancaster, or at least that portion of it before two o'clock in the morning, when they were again tally-hoed out of bed for the run to Columbia, where the rails ended. Here the blue waters of the Grand Canal first greeted them. And a few blasts of a packet horn at 4 A.M. started the meandering canalboat northwesterly to follow the broad Susquehanna, said to be extremely beautiful at daybreak. On through Middletown and Harrisburg it now progressed to the point where the Juniata joins the Susquehanna. Here a nine-foot dam produced a reservoir across which a 2,231-foot bridge had been built. This bridge was famous for its two-story towpath, which was designed to avoid collision and confusion by providing one level for eastbound and another for westbound traffic.

Here at the junction of the two rivers the canal forked, the Susquehanna Division turning northward to tag what one guidebook called "that unusually elegant stream," while the main line continued westward, following the Juniata and at times even entering it for short distances. This canal section ended up near the headwaters of the Juniata at Hollidaysburg, 172 miles from Columbia, having reached the world-famous Allegheny Portage Railroad.

Here the crest was 1,398 feet above the village, and it required 10.1 miles for the climb. Its descent on the other side was 1,171 feet, to be accomplished in 26½ miles. This our travelers experienced at five o'clock the next morning, after spending their fourth night in one of the two scenic mountaintop inns. Since byway stations had been adding passengers all the way across the state, by now our train had probably reached its capacity, which was reckoned at one hundred people. During the Grand Canal's heyday, chances were strong that many other cars would also be in sight along this downgrade strip, most of them taking it at a smart clip, for the descent here was gradual enough so that westbound horses could trot most of the way down.

The scheme that Canvass White and other engineers had worked out for the inclined planes of the Allegheny Portage was similar to that used on the world's first inclined plane, the little South Hadley job up in New England that we saw constructed soon after the turn of the century. Here, however, the system must be much improved and much more elaborate, since vastly greater heights were involved. Also, this task was twice as difficult because it included descending as well as ascending cars, moving simultaneously to balance one another on each of the five separate planes, with a stationary engine at the top of each to furnish the necessary power. Between each two planes was a winding strip of railroad that required no hoist. On the opposite side of the mountain was a similar arrangement with an equal number of levels and planes—always with a descending and an ascending car moving simultaneously to balance one another, on each of the five planes. The hoists took care of the lifts and the horses took care of the levels, with a deal of time-consuming hitching and un-hitching necessary before the entire crossing had been made. The lifts averaged about 300 feet each, accomplished in less than a mile. The levels varied from a short 800-footer to one that was 16½ miles long.

Nor were our westbound voyagers through with the thrills of the trip by the time they had negotiated the ten ascending and descending lifts to cross the Divide, for soon thereafter they entered the third longest tunnel in the country, a 901-foot subterranean adventure four miles east of Johnstown. After that, they were again transferred to a canalboat for the final 104-mile run into Pittsburgh, tagging the Conemaugh, the Kiskiminetas, and the Allegheny Rivers into town. By then our travelers considered themselves to be 'way out West. With good luck, a prayer, and a tail wind, they had probably been able to cross the state of Pennsylvania in about seven days.

Many were the travelers who went west by this route, the great and the small, all of them being more impressed by the Portage than by any other part of the trip. One of the best known of all who ventured it was Charles Dickens. That gentleman, who had chosen to wax funny about numerous aspects of the American scene, including the crude facilities of night travel on the Erie Canal, now cautiously made the Pennsylvania crossing—more scared than amused—and gingerly entered his comments in his *American Notes:*

"Occasionally the rails are laid upon the extreme verge of a giddy precipice; and looking from the carriage window, the traveller gazes sheer down without a stone or a scrap of fence between, into the mountain depths below."

Perhaps he had reason to be frightened. Certainly the sys-

tem was purely experimental and its materials were crude, to
say the least, while its passengers were swung around precipi-
tous curves and suspended by a cable. To all outward appearances the lifts were especially preposterous. They floated a
canalboat into a submerged railroad car in a basin at the foot
of a mountain; then they hoisted the entire affair through
a narrow strip of clearing in a dense forest, plane by plane and
level by level until the crossing was accomplished, two thousand feet above sea level; then they lowered the contraption
in like manner until the boat rested in another canal on the
other side of the mountain. In the name of good sense, it certainly did seem that expecting such a series of doubtful maneuvers to be completed without mishap surely bordered on the
fantastic. Yet thousands of movers ventured it, without one
fatality.

There were plenty of reasons why Pennsylvania's Grand
Canal was a financial failure in spite of her successful engineering feats. In the first place, she came too late in the Canal Era,
for the Old Erie had already been skimming the cream off the
profits for a full decade—not to overlook the fact that railroading was now in sight. Furthermore, although there were still
hundreds of thousands of movers and unknown quantities
of cargo to be carried into the Promised Land, Pennsylvania
could at no time reap her full share of the profits because at
no time could she approach either the low passenger rates or
the high speed of Big Ditch transportation. Her locks were too
many and her portages too slow—two hundred locks and
twenty miles of portage between Pittsburgh and Harrisburg
alone. Furthermore, she had been forced to build, and now
maintain, thousands of miles of expensive feeder canals, since
her course ran largely through mountainous regions. Her
packets required special and costly construction because each

boat must be built in two or three sections that could be hauled in separate units over the portages. In consequence of all these complications, the cheapest passenger rate she was ever able to offer on her Philadelphia to Pittsburgh run was equivalent to the price of six acres of Illinois prairie; and the best speed she ever made was not even half as fast as that of the average Big Ditch craft.

But perhaps her most vexing problem of all lay in the fact that her navigation was necessarily so difficult that none but a master boatman would attempt it. Even her smallest canals were more complex than any other in the country—so complex, in fact, that her Schuylkill Navigation, one of her simplest channels, required separate guidebooks for eastbound and westbound traffic, of necessity offering detailed directions because of the shifting dangers caused by irregularities in current. From Reading to Philadelphia, navigation was especially tricky, notably below Manayunk, where directions ran as follows:

"Descending from Manayunk, direct from the locks after taking on the horse, veer to the opposite shore, that you might land at the lower wharf. Pass down near the other side by pushing with the poles. Pass to the left of the four bold rocks. Pass around them, keeping about twelve feet off to avoid the rocks on the left hand side. Pass down the middle till you come near the piers of the Falls Bridge. Keep to the right of the big rock over the middle pier. Land at Young's wharf and take on the horse that you unhitched at the wharf above the four bold rocks, then tow till you pass the island, keeping out about thirty feet. Unhitch the horse and row for the other side and keep down half a mile. Make for the towpath side again at the point. Hitch again, then tow to the locks, avoiding the stumps and rocks."

Obviously, such instructions required craft built with a horse gangplank so that the bewildered beast could be frequently taken aboard, lest he wind up on one side of the channel while his boat was on the other.

In the early Thirties, when the dancing had reached the "Home, Sweet Home" number and the fiddler must be paid, the state of Pennsylvania could think of only one way of accomplishing this without resorting to excessive taxes—lotteries. And in this effort, too, she was headed for dismal failure because again she came too late, although this form of gambling had been accepted for forty years as a legitimate way of raising money. Even the federal government had resorted to it for financing certain bridge building, while Harvard, Yale, Dartmouth, and Williams College had used it to raise capital for their various educational enterprises. Certain canals, too, had built up funds by this method, including Pennsylvania's own Union Canal, which with its predecessor had been running a profitable lottery for thirty years. This lottery had become nationally famous because its top prize was $25,000 with chances selling for $5.00 apiece, $2.50 for a half-chance, $1.25 for a quarter-chance, and 63 cents per eighth-chance.

The lotteries were widely patronized and competition between ticket brokers had long since become a running battle, with advertising that became nationwide. Known from border to border were Waites' Truly Fortunate Lottery and Exchange Office, Allen's Truly Lucky Office, and Carson's Old Gold Mint. Their handbills, designed to raise the public pulse, were plastered on every canalboat, every lock, every weigh-station, and most village halls. "Money made easy. . . . Try your luck and end hard times. . . . A speedy cure for broken fortunes. . . . Now is the time to fill your bags. . . . Nothing ventured, nothing have. . . . If once Dame Fortune lets you draw, you'll find her faithful ever; her only agent is Latshaw, and he'll forget you never."

Because of all the ballyhoo, great was the frenzy as the time drew near for the drawing at any major lottery. And scarcely was there a family anywhere—including the Methody missioners—who had not at some time taken a flyer on a lottery ticket, although the odds were increasingly heavy against the ticket holder because shady dealings were gradually becoming the rule rather than the exception.

As competition between the various lotteries grew more and more hectic, prize money, too, rose higher and higher until there came a time when a 63-cent square of cardboard might win as much as $36,000. On the rare occasions when such a killing was allowed to happen, the news of it traveled fast and far. The resulting excitement reached such a peak that it was an easy thing at subsequent ticket sales to rake in a third-million dollars for a single lottery. The newspapers were then filled with accounts of the throngs who had attended the drawing, the frenzy thereof, and the resulting suicides and insanity among those who had invested too deeply and lost beyond endurance.

Such a state of affairs was bound to explode. In the year 1832, it did just that in the state of Pennsylvania, where 420 lotteries had been held within a twelvemonth—most of them crooked. When investigation proved that the big profits from the bulk of these had gone to professional operators, the state closed the whole slippery business in 1833 by passing a law that banned further lotteries within her borders. A fine gesture —for but by virtue of this law, her own Grand Canal took a beating.

Surprisingly enough, though the extensive Pennsylvania canal system had never made a cent, and although it never offered serious competition to the Old Erie, still it managed to fill a certain destiny of its own, for, in a roundabout sort of way, it contributed greatly to the Big Push. In addition to carrying the thousands of movers who poured through its portals and floated down the Ohio River to Ohio State, Indiana, and Illinois, it played its most important role by bringing forth from previously inaccessible places great quantities of the newly discovered anthracite coal. This point can hardly be overemphasized, because within these shiny lumps lay the future of both railroad and steamboat travel, two vital necessities to the furthering of the Big Push.

CHAPTER TWELVE

BUCKEYE CANAWLS

ANOTHER canal system, coming into existence almost simultaneously with Pennsylvania's, was that of Ohio. Here was an outfit that never took its eye off the Old Erie, for between these two from the very beginning there had existed a strong mother-daughter relationship from which both stood to gain immeasurably, since each would complement the other to some degree when the east-west traffic reached its height.

As we have already observed, Ohio had celebrated the Old Erie's opening on October 26, 1825, with nearly as much vim and vigor as had York State herself. This was only natural, for on the previous Fourth of July when she broke ground for her own canal system, the busy De Witt Clinton had made the long trip to the Buckeye Country to do the honors from the top of Licking Summit with a flowery speech and a flag-bedecked shovel. What was more important, he had brought along James Geddes, thereby practically guaranteeing success for the new canal's engineering, although within a twelve-month this wizard of the waterways would also be directing the building of Pennsylvania's huge system.

During the six months prior to Ohio's official sod-breaking, while Big Ditch villages were busy buying bunting and building transparencies, out in the so-called "wilderness capital" the young Buckeye State was flinging forth her "Act of February Fourth to Authorize Canals." This was the bravest

gesture of all, coming as it did from a poor and sparsely settled
state that was only two decades old and was still without a
decent road. Besides being courageous, she was extremely
ambitious, for she was planning to build not only one but two
huge canals, both to run the full length of her territory from
Lake Erie on the north to the Ohio River on her southern border. The western channel was to be called the Miami and Erie,
and it would connect Toledo with Cincinnati, following the
great Miami Valley. The eastern channel, to be known as the
Ohio and Erie, would tag the old Scioto-Muskingum route,
connecting Cleveland with Portsmouth.

Like all decisions for waterways during the Canal Era, this
act had not sprung into being without birth pangs. To begin
with, a single canal through Ohio had been proposed for a
single purpose—to connect Lake Erie with the Ohio River in
order to open her wilderness interior from north to south.
Three possible routes had been suggested—a western channel
meandering through the Miami and Maumee Valleys, a central
waterway winding along the Scioto and Sandusky Rivers, or
an eastern canal sallying through the Muskingum and Cuya-
hoga Valleys. Each one offered advantages aplenty and each
had followers aplenty. And there the matter hung for many a
month.

It would be pleasant to report that the final decision satisfied everyone and was by all odds the best solution possible.
But such was never the case in the selection of any channel
site in the Canal Era. Like most of the others, this would end
in compromise, swayed by local interests. But there were
bitter battles to be fought first. The strongest argument of
all arose from the belief that any hamlet that did not border
on a river, Zane's Trace, or the still-hoped-for extension of the
National Road, must certainly die for want of transportation,
unless it could be provided with a canal outlet.

From this contention grew the final decision to build two

canals instead of one, each to meander as much as possible in order to include as many villages as possible. The result was a system of two pinchpenny, wandering channels instead of a single direct and adequate canal. It was not the easiest nor the cheapest way to build, for it even overlooked such natural advantages as the excellent reservoirs around the source of the Scioto River. But still it may have been the wisest way after all, for no compromise ever daunted a pioneer. In fact, he probably regarded a compromise as a clear victory, since his entire life was a matter of half-loaves, which he well understood were better than none. In this case, taking the middle ground actually worked out to advantage after all, since it provided work for so many men and helped to lull Ohio's economic as well as her political unrest.

But even after a workable compromise in canal building had been decided upon, the task was far from finished. For while double channels meant twice the victory, according to pioneer thinking, they also brought double trouble, though to what extent, no one was yet aware. Nevertheless, Ohio does well to include an ark on her official seal, for boating was to be the making of her, thanks to the courage and persistence of a man named Kelley, who was to the Buckeye canals what De Witt Clinton was to the Old Erie.

Alfred Kelley was born in Connecticut in 1789, but his earliest cradle was a jogging Connie wagon bound away for western York State, which was then Indian country. He grew up in a district where for a time there were only two other white families. Fortunately, when he was still a child a newly fledged attorney settled in this backwoods community and took upon himself the education of the likely-looking lad. By the time Al Kelley was twenty-one, he had passed the New York bar examinations and was outward bound for the newer fringe country.

Cleveland was a Lake Erie clearing with three frame houses

and a half-dozen log cabins when Kelley arrived there in 1810, to open a law office from which he would serve the surrounding territory as its newly appointed prosecuting attorney. In this capacity he was to succeed in building a large and lucrative practice in the next dozen years.

By the time he was thirty-four, Alfred Kelley was so badly bitten with the so-called canawl fever that he resigned his Cleveland appointment to become canal commissioner for an Ohio waterway that was not yet even a well-organized dream. When pressed to explain why he should sacrifice wealth and security for this maid-of-the-mist, he dug a stubby pencil from an overladen pantaloons pocket and listed his reasons on the back of a handwritten due bill. It looked like a grocer's list.

> "Oats—14¢ per bushel
> Potatoes—18½¢ per bushel
> Pork—2¢ per lb.
> Beef—3¢ per lb.
> Butter—6¢ per lb.
> Wool—4 shillings per lb.
> Chickens—5¢ each
> NB. ALL TO BE SOLD IN EXCHANGE FOR BARTER."

From a weskit pocket, Squire Kelley drew forth a second exhibit, a dog-eared newspaper clipping. "For those who are in arrears in the payment of their subscriptions, ye editor announces that poultry and eggs, fruit, canned or raw, and vegetables, especially potatoes, will be accepted in lieu of cash if settlement is prompt. This does not include turnips as we now have an over-supply."

Spreading Exhibit A and Exhibit B before his questioners and tapping the bits of paper significantly with an accusing forefinger, Kelley maintained that such poverty as this was a disgrace to the state of Ohio, especially since it was caused solely by a lack of adequate transportation, a condition that was correctible. And a fine howdy-do it was, when a territory that expected one day to lead the nation allowed herself to live thusly, down to her shoe thongs. It was high time that something was done about this, and he proposed to do it.

Having made public his decision, he closed his law office and his lakeside home, threw a long leg across the broad back of his sturdy gray horse, and headed for York State and the Big Ditch. Once there, he tarried only long enough to get the hang of canal construction, to make fast friends of De Witt Clinton and James Geddes, and to pocket for future reference a list of such canal errors as he could discover.

But not until after he had returned to Ohio and succeeded in promoting the Canal Act, and in amassing the quantities of materials necessary to start canal building, did Squire Kelley learn firsthand what real trouble was like. For after the digging was actually begun, something worse than financial and engineering problems dogged these Ohio canals every foot of the way, since both channels were eternally tormented by a mysterious scourge peculiar to raw new country—devastating, heart-breaking, uncontrollable epidemics of disease.

"Our general plan of operation was very much deranged by the extreme unhealthiness of the season," wrote one engineer, while another complained that "Few of the men employed to make up the necessary parties were able to preserve their health or continue their services for more than a week at a time."

Such comments became as common as canal reports, even before the first year was over, for life was like that for every laborer who slogged day after day through big-ditch mud, then dragged wearily home to a mosquito-infested workman's shack for a few hours of whatever sleep he could manage. Malaria took the heaviest toll, for here in Ohio most of the work must be done under water. To remedy this, it was soon deemed advisable to augment a man's pay of thirty cents per day with a free jigger of whiskey every five hours the clock around, plus suitable quarters to accommodate the sick when the shakes came on in spite of the jigger man. Akron originated from a cluster of shacks built for Ohio ditchdiggers.

In the beginning, Commissioner Kelley believed that this terror was a temporary visitation, due soon to pass. When it did, all other difficulties could be readily ironed out, for with the experienced James Geddes at his elbow, what more need he fear? This sounded to everyone like good reasoning, for the formidable Geddes was thoroughly skilled in making the best of conditions as he found them. In fact, in spite of a malaria-ridden summer that first year, he had two thousand men at work on the eastern channel by the first of November. And he had another two thousand on a waiting list begging to be taken on, even though pay had now been reduced to a flat six dollars per month.

On the western channel, he had already finished grubbing and clearing a thirty-mile strip by freeze-up time, besides completing three large reservoirs and excavating more than two million cubic yards of dirt—all without machinery. This was a stupendous showing for six months' work in an unbroken wilderness. The boundless enthusiasm of the man himself must have been contagious, for hundreds of movers along both routes now forgot their bitterness over early disappointments, and were swept into a frenzy of joyous excitement as they watched the progress of such wonders as a towpath that stepped its way across Summit Lake on a series of dikes and floating bridges. In the whole wide world there was not another like it.

Fortunately no one, during that successful first year, could foresee the rough days ahead for all of them—eight grilling years of alternating hope and despair before these two channels could be completed; years when even the strongest were laid low by every variety of frontier illness. "Work greatly delayed from exposure and sickliness," was a common report. "Only one hundred and forty miles completed in the twelve-month," reads one handwritten engineer's report, now yellowed with age. The wonder of the story lies in the fact that in spite of all this, apparently no one ever considered abandoning the enterprise. Instead, they simply plugged along as best they could, looking toward that day when they could again celebrate the opening of a canal channel somewhere. The ecstasy of watching water come at long last into a stretch of completed ditch—no matter how small a section—seemed always to be sufficient to keep the diggers digging and the taxpayers paying.

The pattern of their celebrations never varied—fluttering flags and bursting bombs and liquor enough to loosen tongues to the point where high-sounding oratory flowed freely, to the delight of all. The more difficult the task had been, the greater was the celebrating. When the thirty-eight-mile strip between Portage Summit and Cleveland was finally opened, the celebrants clicked pewter mugs through the night before they had finished toasting George Washington, the Present Administration, Domestic Manufacturies, Bunker Hill, Heroes of the Revolution, the Governor of Ohio, and finally—along about daybreak—Canals and Roads.

For the entire eight years of Ohio's ditchdigging, Alfred Kelley was the force that kept it moving, quietly sacrificing his own family life, his wealth, and the comforts of his lakeside home in order to spend his entire time in a cesspool of slogging mud alive with malaria-laden mosquitoes. Time and again, he braved untold privations and danger to health and even life in order to direct personally the work to which he was so fervently dedicated.

Upon his original appointment as canal commissioner, he had been voted the princely salary of three dollars per day, for which sum he then pledged the people of Ohio that he "would keep all appointments through storm, bog, and miasma." It was a promise that he kept religiously for the entire period of canal construction, even though it led him on one occasion to keep a wilderness rendezvous during a blizzard so fierce that no one else in the entire group made any effort to reach the isolated, snow-blocked, tree-choked spot.

So dedicated was he to the task to which he was devoting his life that for six long years he completely disregarded unbelievable fatigue and exposure, until an anxious Legislature passed resolutions to place him forcibly on leave of absence. The only attention he paid to these was to promise that he would try to take a little better care of himself. However, by 1832, when the heart-breaking task of building two canals simultaneously was nearing its end, Commissioner Kelley had become so feeble that all official business was necessarily conducted at his bedside in his new Columbus home. It was widely believed that he would never live to enjoy his success. But the fighting Irishman was far from through. Ten years later, he was elected to the Ohio State Senate—after he had completed a term in her Assembly and had supposedly retired from public life.

Meanwhile, on January 22, 1833, the reading of the eleventh annual report of the Board of Canal Commissioners before the General Assembly officially announced to the waiting people of Ohio that their twin canals were now open. The eastern ditch had wound up with a 308-mile channel, depending upon 146 locks and 14 aqueducts. The western canal, temporarily halted a little short of Lake Erie, was expected to reach Toledo directly to complete its tremendous length of 440 miles, with 184 locks and 22 aqueducts, making the total mileage for both

channels more than twice as long as that of the Old Erie. All
of this had been accomplished in a plague-ridden wilderness
in a raw young state barely three decades old. This was quite
a feather in Ohio's cap, especially as she then made the claim
—and no one has yet disputed it—that no other public work
of any such magnitude had ever been carried through with
less scandal or fewer accusations of fraud.

Be that as it may, Ohio's financial condition was nothing
to brag about. Like Pennsylvania, she had finished up a little
worse than broke. The cost of her eastern canal alone, originally estimated at $3,081,880 had amounted to $4,224,539,
which brought the total cost for both channels to a sum far
beyond the expected $5,800,000—which in itself was equal
to one tenth of the state's entire taxable wealth.

Sizing up this predicament, the United States Government
now decided to kill several birds with the same buckshot.
First, it would donate to Ohio, Indiana, and Illinois a total of
four and a half million acres of the now federally owned lands
lying within their various borders. And secondly, each state
could then open land offices of its own, offering acreage at
prices to attract the incoming movers. This double maneuver
was expected to serve three purposes. It would encourage
settlement in the fringe country. It would provide each of the
three states with working capital to finance its own internal
improvements. And in the third place, it would aid the federal
government most of all. For once a mover became a landlord,
he could be taxed forever from here to Kingdom Come.

In accordance with this plan, Ohio now received the gift
of one and one-tenth million acres of federal land, the sale
of which paid off one-seventh of her entire canal cost. This
was a sum not to be sneezed at—except for the fact that there
still remained six-sevenths of the total to be raised in a thinly
settled state that possessed only 700,000 souls, and not even

one sizable city. The only heartening aspect of the dilemma
was that the same waterways that had cost Ohio so dearly,
were now making amends by bringing in thousands of additional movers upon whom she could saddle the canal debt.

By the time Ohio's waterways had been in operation for six
years, her population had climbed to more than a million
and a half, thus reducing her debt to $12.13 per head for every
man, woman, and child within her borders, which certainly
sounded better. By the end of an additional ten years, another
half-million souls had drifted in, making her per capita canal
debt even sweeter-sounding—for the solace of those few who
were worried about it. And a very few it was, for Ohio was
made up entirely of movers, and they had not earned that
name by sitting still. With Hoosierland only a fortnight's walk
farther west and the Illinois prairies a scant fortnight beyond
that, what could be easier than tossing the husk-filled mattress,
the shotgun, the skillet, and the baby's cradle into the Connie
wagon—to be bound away again, should the canal debt become troublesome. Little wonder that it was a full generation
before Ohioans felt any great urge to go beyond paying the
interest on their debt, and to start whittling away at the principal. By that time Nature herself had obligingly stepped in
to reduce the per capita debt even further, by a method distinctly her own.

"No colony in history has shown a greater natural increase
in population; no country can show a greater number of children in proportion to the whole number of inhabitants," wrote
Timothy Flint as he floated down the Ohio, watching the
dozens of naked little Buckeyes cavorting along the river's
edge.

In spite of financial embarrassment, the twin Ohio canals
were well worth what they cost. Not that they contributed

greatly toward carrying settlers farther west, for their north-
south direction made them of little use to the westbound mover
and their great lockage and winding channels made them too
slow. The eastern ditch was often closed for weeks at a time
for lack of water, while the western canal actually never
reached her Lake Erie outlet until 1845, and by then the railroads had beaten her to it. When the canal tried to buck this
latter competition by repeatedly reducing her tolls, it proved
to be the death of her because her revenue was then insufficient to keep her in repairs. In the end she was to be sold in
small sections to various villages for local use, reaping only
$200,000 where she had sown millions.

Still, Ohio's two canals had reached their original objective,
which was to provide an easy way to market. Their benefits
were evident long before they were completed. The Ohio and
Erie had not yet crawled halfway across the state before the
price of wheat along its northern border rose from 25 cents
to 75 cents per bushel. In November, 1830, the *Scioto Gazette*
of Chillicothe announced that the canal "has reduced the price
of salt from 87 to 50 cents a bushel, and reduced carriage on
every article imported from abroad in a corresponding ratio.
It has advanced the price of flour from $3 to $4 per barrel, and
wheat from 40 to 65 cents per bushel. It has raised the price of
real estate and opened a ready market for it, and has increased
the business and hustle of the town fifty per cent."

And Hezekiah's *Register* announced the great new rush of
business in this frontier territory in 1831 by the following
report: "In March and April last, about 58,000 barrels of flour,
7,000 do. whiskey, 12,000 do. pork, 18,000 kegs of lard, 750
hhds. of hams and 1,800,000 lbs. bacon passed down the
Miami Canal." It was not too bad a roundup.

Moreover, regardless of the short period of their usefulness,
Ohio's two canals must be considered a magnificent success,

for they opened her interior for settlement, brought her cheap transportation, increased the value of her land, helped to develop her agriculture and industry, created new towns, and made possible vast enterprises.

The Grand Opening of Ohio's twin canals—when it finally came—was an occasion for world-wide attention because these were the first man-made channels in the fringe country. Newspapers from all corners of the globe hailed the New West for this great achievement, most of them turning pensive over the fact that a young state could come so far in a mere thirty years. Mr. Niles' *Register* recollected that "Less than fifty years ago, during the winter of 1784-5, at Clarksville on the north bank of the Ohio River, at the lower end of the Falls, the informant fired a salute in honor of the first white child born in Ohio Territory, whose mother was an American." And the *Poughkeepsie Telegram* remembered that "The land where flourishing Cincinnati now stands was swapped for a pony only fifty years ago, and its entire tract sold five years later for forty-nine dollars."

Even the work-warped, weather-beaten canawlers along the bar of every shiny new lock-keep's shanty on the entire line turned reminiscent, letting their talk run warm and pleasant as they helped themselves from the glass cruller jar, or mixed mugs of blackstrap from the pitcher of hot molasses and the barrel of Old Medford, marked "DRAW AT YOUR WILL." Remembering what it was like, here in Ohio, before the canals came through—corduroy roads where the logs floated in the springtime till a horse sank to his belly in the mud. Knowing what it was like now—the elegant sight of a lock in the moonlight, with her water wrinkling to the wind and her boats riding the swell. Cogitating on the fact that nary a one of them, sitting here in the dusk of this smelly, smoke-filled room, could pos-

sibly be sixty years old, if he was a white man born west of
the Alleghenies. . . . For certain sure, these were matters for
a man to ponder upon.

In the first five years after the Old Erie's Grand Opening,
the Canal Era had come far. During 1826, besides the hundreds of workmen finishing the Big Ditch, there had been
1,200 employed on the Delaware and Hudson, and another
3,500 on the two Ohio channels. During the following year,
the Morris Canal took on 1,100 workmen, the Chesapeake and
Delaware employed 1,500, and the little Portland and Louisville around the Falls of the Ohio was crowding 1,000 diggers
into her two-mile ditch. During 1828, there were 5,000 at work
on Pennsylvania's Grand Canal. And by the following year, the
Chesapeake and Ohio had started off royally with a crew of
1,800.

Between the years of 1820 and 1830, a total of more than
800 miles of canal were opened in New York, Pennsylvania,
Delaware, and Maryland, which included the Old Erie, the
Champlain, the Oswego, the Seneca, the Delaware and Hudson, the Chesapeake and Delaware, the Schuylkill, and the
Union, plus numerous smaller channels. During the year of
1830, construction on an additional 1,300 miles was well under
way and much of it was nearing completion, including the
Morris Canal, the Pennsylvania State Waterways, the Miami
and Erie, the James and Kanawha, the Chesapeake and Ohio,
and the Lehigh, besides a few lesser branches. By now, too,
the Delaware and Raritan channel as well as the canals of
Indiana and Illinois were at least in the wind if not on the
drawing boards. So the digging went merrily on, leaping from
state to state, working toward that day that Robert Fulton
had longed for, "when canals shall pass through every vale
and wind round every hill in this country."

By the time the Big Ditch reached her fifteenth birthday,

more than 4,000 miles of American channels were striving to equal her shining example. The network of artificial waterways reached as far north as the St. Mary's River Canal, built by the Hudson's Bay Company to connect Lake Superior to the other Great Lakes, and as far south as the Galveston and Brazos channel down in Texas; as far east as the Clubfoot and Harrow Creek Canal of North Carolina, and as far west as the Illinois and Michigan on the edge of the prairies. Some of these canals were of little importance to the Big Push and therefore not the concern of this narrative. Others, which later succeeded in furthering the western trek, will be considered in due time.

Meanwhile, by 1830 the canal movement was directing the destiny of the entire country and parts of Europe as well, for by then it was carrying most of the Big Push and was largely responsible for the fabulous boom of the Thirties, which began its steady ascent as soon as the Big Ditch started moving freight for four cents per ton per mile, tolls included. This low rate immediately revolutionized business because it enlarged the manufacturers' market to include the West as well as the East. Almost overnight, great transportation companies leaped into existence, fully organized to handle immense quantities of freight. These were followed in quick succession by new steamboat, pike, and canal companies, besides foundries, mills, insurance concerns, and factories for the making of all types of pioneer equipment. As a natural consequence, there was also a sudden blossoming everywhere of little banks eager to finance the great expansion.

Even the old ways of earning a livelihood were suddenly revolutionized. Men by the thousands deserted the ranks of unskilled labor to become movers, or to leap into higher paid jobs as mill hands and operators, machinists and mechanics, steamboat engineers and firemen, canallers and lock-keeps, printers, tailors, clerks, and bookkeepers for the hundreds of newly organized companies and stores, offices and banks. "The whole quiet course of life had changed into a thing of violent push and hurry," wrote one editor, almost regretfully.

Nor was the maelstrom confined to the canal areas. Soon the hustle-bustle was extended to such quiet waters as the Hudson, the Ohio, the Mississippi, New York's Finger Lakes, and the four eastern Great Lakes, bringing all of these into a fine new importance as integral parts of the Big Push transportation system. One of the most amazing outgrowths of this great network was an immense new business: towing large fleets of canalboats along rivers and lakes where there were no towpaths. This business developed rapidly, producing such bitter competition between various companies as to force rates down to a point where five dollars would secure tow for a canalboat—cargo and passengers included—all the way from New York City to Albany. On such rivers as the Hudson, which was now receiving boats from the Delaware and Hudson Canal at Randout as well as the Old Erie at Albany, it was soon common to see a fleet of sixty to eighty craft tagging a single steamer. Even a hundred canalboats in a single tow raised few eyebrows after that day when Captain Harvey Temple set an all-time record by proudly lugging a string of 108 boats into port behind his sturdily chugging *Connecticut*—a one-man parade, and a sight to see.

Soon many American newspapers were carrying listings for most of the larger boats, be they river, lake, or canal craft, making as great a to-do over the departure of one of these as they formerly had offered a European-bound ocean liner. Even the tramp tugboat came into a newfound importance. Wrote the optimistic editor of the *Poughkeepsie Telegram* in 1839, with something of a flair, "The *Emerald*, whose power for towing is too well known to need description, will henceforth leave New York for Kingston every Sunday morn at seven, touching Poughkeepsie on her way up, from twelve to one. She will leave

Kingston every Sunday at four, touching in at our fair city at six, to arrive in New York about midnight."

The skipper of a towboat that catered more to the carriage trade chose to run his own announcements. "Daily. Towboats for passengers, pulled behind a steamboat. Barges well equipped. No bustle and confusion of hundreds of passengers or the eternal clatter of machinery. Two spacious cabins; eight state-rooms upon the promenade deck, six of which contain two double berths each, and the other two, four. Families and friends can travel West together and pass the night in rooms carpeted and furnished in style equal to the best hotels as to comfortable chambers."

And so the Big Push moved into high speed, a queer mixture of rich and poor, sharing luxury and hardship together—more often the latter, because luxury travel was still to be had only east of Albany. To the west, no such extravagances existed nor should be expected, *Peck's New Guide to Emigrants* took pains to point out. But the thrill of participating in a thing called Democracy should provide an acceptable substitute, claimed its editor. For under this new influence, "every mover is as good as every other since all must share in the same fatigues and privations, partake of the same homely fare, and in many instances fight side by side in defense of their homes against the inroads of the savage. . . . Carpets may be scarce out there, but there are no qualifications for voters; loneliness may be more terrifying than the hustle-bustle of hundreds, but the judiciary has been made elective in the West, instead of appointed."

The missioners took a parallel point of view. "Count it all joy, my brethren, when ye meet divers troubles," they shouted to the jostling throngs who crowded up the gangplanks of hundreds of westbound canalboats. And dozens of off-key emigrants were likely to reply, singing as they shoved one another into the Promised Land:

"Then there's old Varmount. Well, what d'ye think of that?
To be sure the gals are handsome and the cattle very fat.
But who among the mountains, 'mid cloud and snow would stay,
When he can buy a prairie in Michigam-eye-aye?
    Yea, yea, yea, in Michigam-eye-aye.

Then there's the State of New York where some are very rich.
Themselves and a few others have dug a mighty ditch,
To render it more easy for us to find the way,
And sail upon the waters to Michigam-eye-aye.
    Yea, yea, yea, to Michigam-eye-aye."

CHAPTER THIRTEEN

FRINGE COUNTRY

ALL canals, from building to boating, were expensive beyond calculation not only in money, but also as to the lives they cost. For the same waters that brought wealth to the pioneer also brought him tragedies. The greatest of these arose from the Asiatic cholera, which chose a water path for most of its circuitous route to and throughout America during the terrible summer of 1832, and produced one of the greatest scourges in history. Even the time it chose for its coming was diabolical, for it struck when the Big Push was at its peak.

The Great Plague, as this cholera siege came to be called, appeared first in 1816 in India, whence it flamed through Asia and Africa in the next seven years. By 1830 it was raging across Russia and the Near East, and a year later it was making its way along the Caspian Sea and by boat and caravan to the Black Sea, thence along the Danube to southern and central Europe. During the summer of 1831 it appeared in London, by way of warships lately returned from the Baltic. Then it stole like a black thing in the night to Scotland, Wales, and Ireland, where it arrived just in time to join the Irish emigration to America.

During the spring of 1832, aboard four crude, filthy little boats, it crossed the Atlantic to the Promised Land via Quebec and Montreal, leaving 1,622 dead in the former city and 1,635 in the latter during the first eleven days of its terrible scourge in Canada. By the end of the summer, Quebec had buried 2,218 cholera victims and Montreal lacked only a half-dozen corpses to equal the same record.

Meanwhile, the Plague of '32 hit the Old Erie at Albany on June 13 of that dreadful summer, having ridden the waters of the St. Lawrence, Lake Champlain, and the Junction Canal. From Albany it took passage aboard a Buffalo-bound packet that carried fifty rosy-cheeked, rugged Irish, English, and Swiss passengers, according to *Niles' Register*, all of whom were cholera-stricken within the first six hours of their voyage.

Like prairie fire, it now raced the full length of the Old Erie and all of her feeders in a matter of hours, leaving a blackened path of death and such panic as this country had never before known. Soon every port had virtually become a hospital, and traffic everywhere had reached a dead standstill, partly because all lock-keeps had either died or deserted their posts, and partly because no village would allow the passage of boats within her borders.

"Cholera runs with Erie waters," was the terrifying conclusion that went winging throughout the country, sending chills along the spine of everyone who heard it.

Within a fortnight after the scourge reached Albany, the Big Ditch was a scene of terror, with funeral bells tolling day and night at Little Falls, Herkimer, Frankfort, and Utica, while Rotterdam reeked to the high heavens from the buckets of burning tar with which she expected to purify the miasma. You could smell Syracuse a mile away; rotting corpses were stacked at her every doorpost, awaiting the "dead-wagon," while vats of chloride of lime bubbled at half of her street corners as a preventive.

Local business in every village and hamlet along the entire Erie Canal had now stopped completely, with the exception of that concerned directly with the Great Plague. There were frantic calls for more doctors, more nurses, more bedside watchers, more gravediggers at two dollars per corpse. More medicine, more salt for stomach packs, more hartshorn to be sniffed as a preventive, more nitrous oxide machines to allay the miasma, more cotton for noseplugs and earplugs for the protection of bedside watchers. More opium for the cases in spasm, more iodine for the collapsed ones, more vinegar for bathing the sick. More prayers for the dying, more coffins for the dead—or, at least, more quicklime.

On the Fourth of July of that summer, the Plague hit New York City, joining her at her mammoth celebration of the Glorious Fourth, resulting in 800 deaths within three days among the 70,000 who fled the city in panic at news of the first cholera death in town, and an additional 300 dead and 800 new cases among those who refused to flee. And the peak had not even yet been reached here.

In late summer the Plague struck Washington and Baltimore. The Cumberland Road, too, was said to be riddled with it. Then came reports of the first cases in the fringe country. The disease had been carried into Illinois aboard the *Sheldon Thompson* and the *Henry Clay*, two troopships sent west during the Black Hawk War to protect pioneer holdings against Indian raids in the vicinity of a swamp-ridden nest of dilapidated cabins surrounding Fort Dearborn, a spot soon to be known as Chicago. Here the plague did its devilish worst, racing both north and south when it hit the Mississippi, mowing down red men and whites alike. Almost simultaneously, it was plowing through the wildernesses of Michigan and Ohio as well, because the troopships had put ashore their litter cases in Detroit and Cleveland.

From Ohio, it raced into Kentucky and went by water to New Orleans to break all records, killing off one sixth of that city's population within twelve days, and 10,000 before it moved on. From the Mississippi it branched up the Missouri, eventually reaching into territory that would one day become

Montana. And its only conquerors anywhere were the frosts that killed it off in one locality after another, as fast as the winter came on. So ended the Great Plague of '32.

Strangely enough, in spite of its diabolic power the Asiatic cholera was never able to halt the great westward migration. Onward they came, the patient movers—more slowly, more sadly, but forward nevertheless. When a family was stricken it halted only long enough to bury its dead, then silently took up the march again. There was nothing else to do, nowhere else to go. The East was as cholera-ridden as the West, the stay-at-home as sorely afflicted as the traveler. A man had best get along with his plans as well as he could, still walking the trails, riding the canals and rivers, eating what was to be had, and sleeping fifteen to the room.

He had been forewarned often enough to be forearmed, for scarcely had a western guidebook, journal, or diary yet appeared that did not devote space to the numerous illnesses to be encountered in the raw new country—seventy of them all told, of which the Asiatic cholera was only slightly worse in the fringe areas than were the milksick, the malaria, or the ague—usually known as the agur or the shakes. Already the trails west were dotted with small wooden grave markers and fresh mounds left behind by a bereaved people. It was part of the price you paid. That was understandable.

But if you were a true mover, so dedicated were you to the task at hand that you strove to be philosophical about the whole matter before long. Perhaps you even pushed into the Promised Land with a song on your lips. And if you could somehow add a laugh, so much the better. Four new chanteys were riding the canals and highways, almost before the Great Plague had left. The first was concerned with the Illinois Country, and it appeared originally in New York City's *Spirit of the Times.*

Great western waste of bottom land,
   Flat as a pancake, rich as grease,
Where gnats are full as big as toads
   And 'skeeters are as big as geese.
O, lonesome, windy, grassy place,
   Where buffaloes and snakes prevail—
The first with dreadful looking face,
   The last with dreadful sounding tail—
I'd rather live on Camel's Rump
   And be a Yankee-doodle beggar
Than where they never see a stump
   And shake to death of fever-n-agur.

And those who could not find a tune for it could at least recite it.

The second started out as a chantey, then turned into a saying, oft repeated to those heading for the Michigan Territory.

Don't go to Michigan, that land of ills.
The word means agur, fever, and chills.

The third to appear took a crack at Illinois again, choosing this time to sing her praises while admitting her faults.

Way down upon the Wabash
Such land was never known.
If Adam had passed over it,
The soil he'd surely own.
He'd think it was the garden
He'd played in when a boy.
And straight pronounce it Eden
   In the State of El-a-noy.

She's bounded by the Wabash,
The Ohio, and the Lakes.
She has crawfish in her swampy lands,
The milk-sick and the shakes.
But these are slight diversions,

And take not from the joy
Of living in this garden land,
    The State of El-a-noy.

Then move your family westward.
Good health you will enjoy.
And rise to wealth and honor
    In the State of El-a-noy.

The fourth of these ditties—sometimes running to fifteen or twenty verses—laughed at the plague itself. It was the most popular of all.

If Mr. A. or B. gets sick,
Send for the doctor, go be quick.
The doctor comes with a free good will
    And gives him a dose of calomel. . . .

The patient now grows worse indeed.
Send for the doctor, go with speed.
The doctor comes with a free good will
    And DOUBLES the dose of calomel.

The man in death begins to groan,
The fatal job for him is done.
His soul is wing'd for heaven or hell,
    A sacrifice to calomel.

O, when I must resign my breath,
Pray let me die a natural death,
And bid you all a long farewell
    Without one dose of calomel.

There was a fifth jingle, seldom sung, though it was repeated often enough during the dark days of the Great Plague. It was said to be a favorite with Johnny Appleseed when he paused to pick up the news at river cabins along the Wabash.

"From the time that you're born till you ride in a hearse,
    There's nothing that happens that couldn't be worse."

Not only were the pioneer's songs and jingles helping to lift him out of his slough of despair during times of epidemic, but his own determination to take all difficulties in stride soon led him to gauge his life in accordance with his lot. Take the matter of malaria, with its common pattern of chills-and-fever one day, followed by a well day, then a new chill on the third, followed by a free day on the fourth. Wrote a Mrs. Tillson of Pike County to her son during an Illinois epidemic, "On his last trip your paw had a shake of agy. Feelin that he was in fer a right smart grip of it, he rode seven mile towards Edwardsville where he stayed to have another shake. The next day bein intermedjet day, he rode twenty mile to Mr. Hoxie's where he waited for another shake which Mrs. Hoxie said beat all the shakes she ever see. He shuk the hull cabin."

And down in Shawneetown during a severe malaria siege, a carpenter posted a notice declaring that he would never again shingle a house whose inhabitants were in the shakes.

Over in the Michigan Territory—where cholera sieges followed upon one another so closely that it became a matter of pride to have lived through a record number of them, and a matter of distinction to have suffered the most severely—one Michigander claimed that he could shake the dishes off the shelves, once he had worked up a first-class chill. Not to be outdone, a neighboring Hoosier claimed that whenever he went into the shakes, his cows took to the woods on a dead run, while his little dog raced to the front gate where he could brace himself for the oncoming earthquake.

Indiana was still backwoods when the disastrous Plague of '32 finally drew to its weary end. And although New York and Pennsylvania were again operating their canals both day and night, and Ohio had completed her two channels, Indiana was still running along beside the band wagon, not yet having actually climbed aboard, although her mind by now was fully made up to attempt a big ditch or two of her own. Life was still simple and lazy in Hoosierland, and "responsibility for the universe had not yet been invented," wrote Lowell. Her people were poor and still sickly. Her wagon trails were few and faulty, and lay largely in the southern part of the state. Her clearings were choked with milkweed and Jimson. And her only commerce lay along her rivers, reaching a record high at Vincennes on the Wabash when thirty-six steamboats and seventeen hundred flatboats transported beeswax, venison hams, pork, and beef by the hundreds of thousands of pounds during a single summer in spite of epidemics.

But for the most part, the great forests of Hoosierdom still lay untouched, and her bluebirds, cardinals, and wild pigeons still formed flocks large enough to dim the sun with their shadow. In all the vast region of the upper Wabash Valley there were as yet only twelve thousand scattered settlers, though the lower valley was more densely settled. And it would be another decade before a boy on a pony would run the first mail into this Wabash paradise.

So dense were these forests, it was still common to see a mover burst into tears at first sight of the land he had purchased, as he measured his own puny strength against the hundreds of giant trees he must fell before he could raise corn enough to feed his family. "You cannot see two hundred yards into it," wrote a newly arrived mover, viewing his quarter-section in the Wabash Valley. "One oak is twenty-four feet around, and many are larger. Some are a hundred feet high. Everywhere here there is nothing but woods, woods, woods, as far as the world extends."

Further to the north in the great wilderness, Betsy Wade wrote the same sort of letter to her family back in Massachusetts, complaining that the trees up there grew so thick and so tall, she had to look straight up to see a patch of blue sky in the daytime. And at night, she could see no more stars than she could catch in her little apron.

But down along the Ohio River where the earliest Hoosiers had settled and where their land clearing was no longer a frightening task, numerous patches of wheat and corn were already beginning to create the need for a market, and an ever increasing demand for better transportation. That Ohio had just completed two of the nation's longest canals put a stone in the craw of every Hoosier. Not that the idea was entirely new in Indiana. There had been considerable talk about waterways six years earlier, but it had died a-borning because there were enough differing opinions on the subject to create a deadlock.

First there were those who believed it wiser to skip canal building altogether and go directly to railroad building, since they had already delayed so long—the state was ten years old. A second group felt that canals were preferable because they were more democratic—you could launch your own boat on them any time, any place. A third group held out for waterways, but only for a single channel to connect the Wabash with Lake Erie, in order to open Indiana's vast northern interior and catch the immigrants who were now coming west via the Old Erie and the Great Lakes. Another faction leaned toward an eastern channel only, tagging the Whitewater River which was the gateway into Indiana for those arriving via the Ohio River.

Favoring the latter suggestion, the state's General Assembly had gone so far in 1826 as to sanction the incorporation of the Whitewater Canal Company—capital, one million dollars. But the *Richmond Public Leger* labeled this "wind talk," and guessed it right, at least for the time being.

Meanwhile the so-called Wabash Men had been growing ever stronger. The canal they proposed would follow the early trade route northeast from Terre Haute to Lake Erie by way of Fort Wayne. It would tag the Wabash and Maumee Rivers, with a channel connecting the two and replacing a six-mile portage that led to the Little River. This land trail, known both as the Wabash Portage and the Maumee Portage, was famous even in Europe, partly because it was so difficult, partly because it was so important. Even General Washington had foreseen the advantage of a canal along this route. For the Wabash, lying west of the portage, ran nearly the full width of Indiana from east to west before turning southerly to run nearly the full length of the state. And the Maumee River, located east of the portage, flowed on eastward to open another large section of wilderness, completing an outlet to Lake Erie through Maumee Bay at Toledo.

European as well as American engineers had long considered a connection between these two great rivers to be a simple matter, completing an excellent new water route west. They could not have been more mistaken. Actual canal building would in time disclose that a considerable section of the Maumee, which they had expected to enter to avoid channel digging, was actually unnavigable for larger boats, so wicked were her rapids. This would eventually leave no recourse for Hoosier builders except to depend upon Ohio's Miami and Erie Canal from Maumee Bay west to Defiance—another matter that would take a deal of palaver before it was all settled.

As early as 1826, Colonel James Shriver, sent to run a surveyor's line along the Portage at Fort Wayne, had waded into the surrounding Hoosier swamps, fought a royal battle against millions of mosquitoes, and died in his tent in a matter of months. Asa Moore, delegated to finish the task, had also died on the job. But John Peter Paul, the third engineer sent into these marshes, had somehow managed to survive the ordeal, as did his diary—a thin little engineer's report, dignified with a title: *We Run the Canal Line.*

"Moschetoes troublesome . . . At Fort Wayne, many half-naked Indians and half-breeds . . . Today, saw a fine bevy of ladies at Fort Wayne. . . . Indians drunk and troublesome, inclined to steal . . . Killed seven rattlesnakes today, found one five-and-a-half footer in my tent . . . Saw a squaw in the last stages of consumption . . . My men are most damned tired . . ."

Before the task was finished most of these same weary men had also succumbed to the marshes. It had been an inauspicious beginning, but at least it satisfied the Wabash Men that their project was receiving some attention.

During the following year, news came from Washington City that Congress had now authorized financial aid for canal building in Indiana and Illinois through the sale of public lands in both states. Soon thereafter, offices for this purpose were opened at Logansport and Lafayette, supplementing land offices which had previously been established in half a dozen other Hoosier villages. Sales were immediately brisk, and 42,000 acres soon changed hands, though the total income was unbelievably small because the land was bringing only $1.78 per acre, of which little was cash and much was barter.

During the year of 1830, Indiana set up an Internal Improvements Commission, and debates immediately grew hot and bitter. There were a number of issues for Hoosiers to quarrel about. An exact location for their so-called Michigan Road, which would connect Madison, down on the Ohio River, to Michigan City, up on Lake Michigan, and pass through Indianapolis. A final decision on whether or not railroads and rivers together could provide sufficient transportation for all of Indiana's needs. And a final decision upon a route for a canal system, in case the railroads were voted down. It was an ambitious array, for a state only fourteen years old.

And it produced quite a bit of hectic debating before the summer was over. The greatest interest centered in the debates over a sanction for the building of the Wabash and Erie Canal, which reached an uproarious climax when the issue finally came to a vote.

The day of the showdown was unbearably hot, we are told, with the delegates completely exhausted and half-lost in the shimmering heat—until Johnny McNary, orator of the Wabash Men, leaped to his feet, raised himself on tiptoe, and shouted the words for which he was to become famous.

"Mr. Speaker! Our population on the Wabash am great. But our resources for salt am slim. *Salt they cannot emigrate up the Wabash!*"

There was no reply except the shouts of hilarious laughter. His Hoosier lingo and his Hoosier logic had won the day. And his beloved Wabash Canal was as good as built.

On Washington's birthday, 1832, Indiana's Board of Commissioners met at Fort Wayne to break ground for the first artificial waterway in the state. All of Hoosierdom went wild with celebrations that in some localities lasted for weeks. Soon contracts were let and the diggers' shanty towns began to appear, first in the Fort Wayne area, then throughout the Maumee-Wabash region.

By the end of the second year, a thousand laborers were at work. Their troubles were myriad, for illnesses here were the most varied and the most deadly yet encountered by any canal diggers anywhere. The situation was to grow steadily worse, until the time came when every six feet of completed channel had cost the life of one human being.

Even from the beginning, it had been necessary to distribute heavy doses of quinine, calomel, and blue mass to these Hoosiers, with the whiskey-bearing jigger-boss making the rounds three times daily and six on Sunday. But the deaths had increased in spite of everything, until at times the grave digging became more important than canal digging. By way of keeping count of the total dead, a system was set up whereby a cemetery was closed as soon as it had a thousand graves, whereupon a new one was opened. Then once again the ranks were filled with bog trotters, who were continuously lured from Pennsylvania by an extensive system of advertising that promised "roast beef with two dollars a day, guaranteed." Certainly a far cry from the six dollars per *month* that had kept Ohio's ditchdiggers digging. But here a man was betting his life.

Nor did the canallers' troubles end with the plagues. For when they were not burying their dead, they were fighting each other, since the Irish workmen in Indiana were about equally divided between men from Cork and men from Ulster —"Corkers" and "Far Downers." This meant a general skull-cracking on religious grounds whenever two of them chanced to meet. It was a serious business, with one fracas reaching such proportions as to require calling in the state militia to restore peace.

It was July 3, 1835, before the first three boats made their experimental run down Indiana's first completed canal section, from Fort Wayne to the forks of the Wabash. On the following day, the Glorious Fourth was celebrated by officially opening this thirty-two-mile summit strip with a shindig, complete with a speech by Hugh McNary that was long enough to fill seven newspaper columns. As a matter of cold fact, although wild rejoicing now raised the Hoosier pulse, the wooden aqueducts in this vicinity—the first to be built—were already rotting. Nevertheless, in a rosy glow over the canal's initial success, the Legislature now voted to extend the channel to Lafayette, where it planned also to build an important steamboat landing on the Wabash. This would be the canal's western terminus.

It was an ambitious operation that would require a river dam in one place, behind which the canal would cross the river, and a brush riprap barricade at another place where she must enter the river for a short distance. Often such problems had the engineers completely baffled for long periods of time, but occasionally help came from the most unexpected sources. For instance, at a spot where the task of uniting two streams had been long delayed while Hoosier engineers tried to figure out how it could be done, they found that beavers had meanwhile built a dam at this troublesome spot, actually accomplishing overnight exactly what they themselves had in mind, leaving nothing for the men to do except to run their lines across the beavers' dam.

So successful was this, the engineers immediately adopted the same type of construction for their own dams, one of which would now be built across the Wabash just above Lafayette. The finished product was later described as "a huge mass of forest trees, sand, and gravel, based on sand"—which in fact it was, starting with untrimmed trees, fifty to seventy feet long, felled and placed lengthwise upon a bed of solid sand with their tops pointing upstream to catch the sediment brought down by the current. To this mass, giant tree trunks were next added, with the chinks between filled with brush until the whole affair was seven feet high.

Against the butt ends of these tree trunks, a wooden bench was now built, furnishing a break for the falling water, to prevent the wearing away of the river bottom. On top of the entire mass, a crib was next constructed from smaller timber, forty feet wide at its base, sloping in on either side to a height of ten feet. This was filled with rocks and covered with huge planks six inches thick. Gravel and sand were now added liberally to cover the entire construction, which by this time was seventy feet wide at its base and forty-five at its top. More brush and stone were added to keep the gravel from washing away, large stones were placed below the dam to protect the river bed, and abutments were built to the riverbanks on both sides.

Upon completion, the massive construction rose 70 feet above the river bed and 15½ above low-water level. It was 230 feet long without its abutments, which consisted of huge gravel-filled cribs that added another 40 feet to the length of the dam. Its cost was $15,297. . . . And the beavers, examining it during the quiet night watches, doubtless had to admit that it had theirs beaten all hollow for size. But theirs was more expertly interwoven—and it had cost them only a sociable night or two.

In 1836, still in a comfortably rosy glow over their successes, Indiana's legislators went completely mad on the subject and passed their famous Mammoth Improvement Bill, authorizing completion of the earlier proposed Whitewater Canal, plus a Central Canal to run from Worthington to Peru, and an extension of the Wabash and Erie beyond Lafayette to Terre Haute. They also proposed a railroad between Madison and Lafayette, a turnpike from New Albany to Vincennes, either a railroad or a turnpike from Jeffersonville to Crawfordsville, and finally a canal to connect the Wabash and Erie channel with Lake Michigan. This was a tremendously ambitious program for a backwoods state still lost in the wilderness, for it would directly affect twenty-two thousand acres of Hoosier and Illinois land, including thirty-eight counties in the former and nine in the latter.

Scarcely had the applause for the passing of this bill ceased in the Capitol before the old bell in the Circle and the ancient cannons on the lawn set up a racket; and every hamlet in the state, once it heard the news, whooped it up with a giant parade of its own, ending with a lavish banquet that featured spread-eagle speeches and a few rousing rounds of a new song that had just hit the fringe country:

> We're diggin' a ditch through the gravel,
> Through the gravel and mud and slime, b'gawd,
> So the people and freight can travel,
>   And the packets can move on time, b'gawd.

And over on the eastern side of Indiana along the banks of the Ohio, Hoosiers were warming up their jew's-harps for another ditty, one written especially for them:

> There is not in the wide world a valley so sweet
> As that vale where the branches of Whitewater meet.
> O, the last picayune shall depart from my fob,
>   'Ere the east and the west forks relinquish their job.

Seven years hence, some of these same people would be celebrating the launching of the *Native*, the first packet to plow the waters of the new Whitewater Canal. Their plans would include a ceremonial run from Brookville to Laurel on the first day and a ceremonial return on the second. But since the canal was due to collapse during the intervening night, these jubilant celebrators were due for an embarrassing eight-mile hike home, to the utter delight of the catcalling few who had opposed the canal from the very start.

CHAPTER FOURTEEN

HOOSIER UPS AND DOWNS

WHEN the news first broke that Indiana had passed her $11,000,000 Mammoth Internal Improvement Bill, the entire country from Maine to New Orleans huzzahed her royally. "So young, so brave!"

But the Hoosiers, much too busy to accept their plaudits, were already reopening land offices to care for the great inrush of immigrants who were immediately fighting one another for possession of the precious lots along the proposed canals, railroads, and turnpikes. Fortunes were made overnight in such places as Evansville, where shrewd gamblers had quickly taken over. During that summer of 1836, sums as high as $25,000 were taken in at Fort Wayne in a single afternoon, while the total receipts for the season ran to a million and a half. It took a six-horse team and twenty-two soldiers to run the money down to Cincinnati each month.

So varied were the different kinds of exchange being offered in lieu of cash, that a note shaver soon established a fine business near the Fort Wayne office where for ten per cent he would exchange your barter—hens' eggs, turnip greens, canal scrip, or whatever—for gold or silver, which were the only media acceptable to the government, especially after Congress had issued the famous Specie Circular in hopes of curbing inflation. Similar land offices, each with its own note shavers, were prospering in eight other cities as well, with

Crawfordsville's log-cabin office leading the nation for several years.

Now certain Hoosier engineers, later known to history as the Eating Brigade, also got into the swing by maneuvering to collect for themselves salaries of fifty-five and sixty thousand dollars per year. Amazingly enough, considering Indiana's pinchpenny start, abruptly there was no limit, that first year, to her spending on any phase of her Improvement Plan, and $3,827,000 had soon melted away like snow in July. Nor was there any peace anywhere. Since the commission had parceled out various construction sections to the various board members —each to supervise the one in his own district—a royal battle for the lion's share of appropriations was soon flaring on every front.

Meanwhile, during that same hectic year, the Wabash and Erie had meandered westward across Wabash County, and . was there delayed for nearly a twelvemonth because no water was available until a feeder at Lagro could be tapped. Not that the Hoosiers were particularly disturbed about this. They were having a glorious time, using the dry canal bed for a driving course where they held their horse races. But by the end of 1837 this new section bore clay-yellow water all the way from Fort Wayne to Peru.

Next the canal passed through a district populated largely by Indians who had previously been induced to cede to the state the last of their lands at a dollar per acre; this included all territory northwest of the Wabash River. Now, so rapid was the advance of the canal and so slow was the red man's withdrawal, it was deemed necessary to order immediate evacuation.

A few Indians complied at once. Others, either ill or uncertain where to go, lingered on "twice through the moon of the blossoming elm," until the impatient white man—perhaps having not quite forgotten the terrible Fort Dearborn massacre at the hands of these same redskins twenty-five years earlier—gathered together the remaining 859 Potawatomis and Miamis at Grand Prairie, and started them on a forced march for the open lands beyond the Mississippi. It was said that the well-armed white men rode their fine wagons, herding the redskins on foot before them. Many Indians succumbed in the terrific heat before they even reached Logansport, and were left to die by the roadside. By the time the pitiful spectacle moved through Terre Haute, most of the children and all of the papooses were dead, their small stiff bodies still strapped to their mothers' backs.

When the tragic passing was completed, there remained only one Indian in all that northwest area that had once belonged to the red men. This was a squaw called Maconaquah, protected by an act of Congress and so allowed to abide on her large farm, eight miles from Peru, because she was known to be Frances Slocum, a white woman stolen by Indians when an infant and carried from her Pennsylvania home to Indiana. Here she was discovered by her brothers many years later. And here she chose to remain because she had already been the squaw of two chiefs.

During the following year, construction was begun on the eastern end of the Wabash and Erie. By early autumn what the Hoosiers called "a right smart chunk of it" had been completed toward its connection with Ohio's Miami and Erie Canal. So primitive was this northeast corner of Indiana that the channel again passed through a village of Indians—peaceful ones, this time; so peaceful, in fact, that a group of engineers obligingly took down the cabin of Cha-pine, orator of the tribe, moved it out of the canal's path, then carefully rebuilt it—all at the expense of the state, all in the name of maintaining peace.

During that same summer, rail-laying for the proposed Madison and Lafayette Railroad was begun in southern Indiana, and the "McAdamized" turnpike from New Albany to Vincennes was given a fine start. In addition to these, digging was started on a branch canal to be known as Cross Cut, which would run from Worthington to Terre Haute and connect the proposed Central Canal with the Wabash and Erie.

Construction problems were especially troublesome on this little Cross Cut, for here the spring and summer freshets from the Eel River near Clay City washed away what was known as Feeder Dam as often as it could be rebuilt. "But," reported Engineer Williams hopefully, "properly controlled and applied, it will drive 37 pairs of 4½-foot mill stones," which admittedly could crack a lot of Hoosier corn.

As fast as new sections were completed on these various projects—there were five thousand laborers at work that summer—Indianans flocked by the hundreds to view their new means of transportation. On the canals business was brisk, and shiny new packets were appearing faster than cowslips in a March meadow. But, contrary to the Eastern ways, here no regular time schedules had yet been attempted; no true Hoosier felt that life needed to be that obnoxiously regulated. It was the consensus that their present lackadaisical system was working well enough. At least it was simple. Whenever a captain considered that he had enough passengers to make the trip pay, he tooted his horn and they were off, gliding lazily through the enchanting tree chasms, fishing perhaps, or hopping ashore to shoot a brace of squabs for breakfast.

Soon luxury was added to all of this leisure, producing more elegance on Wabash canalboats than was ever known on the Old Erie or on the Pennsylvania waterways. In fact, Indiana was enjoying her heyday, since the Panic of 1837 had not yet reached the New West. Her packets were especially gaudy, for their colors knew no bounds and their furnishings were rich and extravagant, and often imported from Europe.

Most renowned of all was the *Silver Bell,* known the world around for her elegance. A visit to America that included a voyage on this Hoosier packet was considered an aristocratic achievement. Certainly she was distinctive, for from bow to stern, within and without, she was painted silver; she was decorated with musical silver bells that tinkled softly at the slightest jolt; and the gleam of the silver-mounted harness slapping the broad backs of her silver-gray mules announced her approach from afar. She traveled at the unheard-of-speed of eight miles an hour, which surpassed anything yet known on any canal.

The *Indiana* was another popular and successful luxury packet. Her arrival at Fort Wayne, day or night, was the signal for a hasty concert rendered by the enthusiastic Ed Parker and Will Patchen, who always dropped whatever they were doing at the sound of the captain's horn and raced to the dock to serenade the incoming voyagers with clarinet and fiddle.

On the other hand, the fabulous steam-propelled *Niagara* was a distinct financial failure because it had cost $10,000 to build her, while the price of the ordinary packet was about $1,200. But she was a joy to ride—a trip on her was good for a lifetime of bragging.

Wherever Indiana's canals were functioning, the world-famous Hoosier friendliness and hospitality were in evidence, with the gossip and news being bandied freely from canal to shore and from poorest shanty boat to richest packet. Many canalside settlers even went so far as to open their cabins to any traveler who jerked their latchstrings, often refusing pay for either meals or lodging. In fact, few Hoosier boats were equipped to offer either food or berths, and frankly expected the passengers to depend on the settlers for these services.

On the other hand, nothing could have elevated country life in Indiana more drastically than did the coming of the canals —especially for her young folk. Every mild evening, after the chores were done, the towpath parade began: Hoosier lasses pushing back sunbonnets, and Hoosier lads turning up cap visors, to insure a better view of the passing packets with their peau-de-soie-clad porkers' daughters from Cincinnati flaunting full skirts, bright spencer jackets, plumed bonnets, and tiny silken parasols.

It took eighty bushels of corn, shipped down to New Orleans, to pay for just one yard of such silk, as any Hoosier girl knew as she turned her envious eyes away. Away from the porkers' daughters to the porkers' sons, likely; they were much more lavishly dressed than their sisters, she would soon discover— with their hourglass figures, pointed boots, fawn-colored pantaloons, ruffled shirt fronts, buff-toned weskits, and claw-hammer coats. Their hats, which they were wont to sweep in mock greeting to any barefoot maid caught staring (or stooping to hide her brown ankles beneath homespun skirts), were likely to be bell-crowned beavers fashioned from white fur. Many of these lads sported camelot capes and carried gold-headed canes. And when they spoke, they b'gawded every statement for emphasis, a habit soon adopted by young Hoosiers, who were quick to see that their own drawled "I reckon" did lack something in potency.

But along with the introduction of luxury and elegance into the quiet Indiana wilderness came also the hustle-bustle of the East. Overnight, granaries mushroomed into existence at Lafayette, Huntington, Pittsburg, Lockport, Wabash, and Fort Wayne, all of them overflowing with flour-wheat and corn.

"The streets are daily more crowded with waggons loaded with grain," wrote editor Timothy Flint from a Wabash canal-boat. And from Lafayette came word that her courthouse square was now a confused mass of movers, horses, and camp-fires where hundreds of farmers waited week after week for boats to carry their products to Eastern markets.

Not that anyone objected to this new order. Prosperity was a refreshing novelty to most Hoosiers, as they watched the rising prices on their outgoing products and the drop in cost of the incoming goods from Eastern manufacturers, who were no longer burdened with heavy transportation charges. Even salt, that precious, hard-to-come-by commodity, had now become so cheap a farmer could present a barrel of it to his cattle for only four dollars instead of twelve.

With the increase in water power from the new locks and feeders came a fine upsurge in the number of mills available to these fringe movers—a real luxury, because many of them had formerly been required to drive three to five days to find a miller who could turn their wheat to flour. Now, too, their clearings were turning into small farms, making it possible to reap larger harvests. Their settlements were becoming villages. And the canaltowns that lay along completed sections were increasing as much as four hundredfold. In one such town, Huntington, lots cut from land that had so recently been purchased for $1.78 per acre were now selling for fifty to two hundred dollars apiece.

In the whole booming State of Indiana, there was only one fly in the ointment. Her canal debt had reached $17,000,000. This fact was now brought forcibly to her attention by the news that many another state, also floundering under too large an expansion program, had currently decided to shrug her shoulders and repudiate her obligations. The combined canal debts of twelve such states had recently passed $60,000,000.

All things considered, it is not surprising that this suggestion set well upon the shoulders of many a Hoosier. But the northern section of the state stood solidly against it. "Most of this debt was contracted in good faith," claimed the *Michigan City Gazette* sternly. "And we who are descendants of the old Pilgrim stock would hang our heads in shame at the thought of having our adopted state disgraced by repudiation."

But down in the poorer sections of Shelby and Washington Counties, it still looked like a good idea. Soon hectic mass meetings in this region were producing hot debates, which

ended finally in a declaration calling for repudiation, to be sent
as a written resolution to the state Legislature. "To place so
huge a debt on the shoulders of Indianans even though they
themselves may have fired cannon to encourage it, would be
to place a burden equal to those imposed on the serfs of Russia
and France," the Hoosiers declared stoutly in their resolution.

What was to become of this question, in a territory so bitterly
divided, and still so young and poor? "Try to forget the whole
affair until the issue is forced," agreed both factions. And so
for the time being, the canal debt was pushed far back in a
dark closet—out of sight, out of mind.

During 1837 and '38, because Indiana was admittedly tottering on the verge of bankruptcy, her various counties quietly
assumed the expense of all road improvements within their
respective borders, hoping thereby to ease the financial situation. But on August 18, 1839, when Commissioner Noah Noble
announced that all canal building must now be abandoned
because no more money could be borrowed, the shock was terrific throughout the state.

The decision immediately changed the entire picture. Everywhere now workmen remained idle, day after day, month after
month. Shovels and rails were left in the fields to rust, while
aqueducts and bridges and canal stations went to rot without
having ever seen water. Crops were abandoned in the fields
because the way to market had been closed when canal breaks
could no longer be mended nor lock-keeps paid. The golden
goose was dead. And Indiana's plush days had disappeared
as rapidly as they had come. Abruptly the Hoosiers were poor
again.

During 1840, by a hopeful scheme of issuing scrip instead of
money, the sum of one and a fifth million dollars was raised to
start the wheelbarrows feebly rolling again. The delay had
been costly to the canals, and the scrip was costly to the people,
for it was accepted almost from the beginning at only forty

cents on the dollar. But again the digging went on, and that was something. And the poor were salved by being allowed to turn a penny here and there, picking up bits of coal along the docks at loading time. Again hope ran high. . . .

On the 4th of July, 1843, the Wabash and Erie was officially opened all the way from Lafayette to Toledo, amid a hulla-baloo that outranked all previous Hoosier demonstrations. "LAFAYETTE TO NEW YORK CITY," proclaimed a thou-sand banners, fluttering the full length of the canal. Everyone was as jubilant as if the debt had been paid. At Fort Wayne, where the official ceremony was held, General Lewis Cass, speaker of the day, was adequately eloquent. And the first boat to glide down the entire 240-mile channel was a luxurious packet sent out by the Wabash and Erie Transportation Com-pany, and reported by the press to be "fit to take the shine off anything heretofore met in these diggin's."

Its ceremonial run from Toledo to Lafayette was a breath-taking affair that was accomplished in only two days and eight hours, setting an astonishing record—more than one hundred miles a day through a wilderness where five miles a day was formerly considered something of a feat. The cost for this trip would henceforth be $7.00 per passenger, it was now an-nounced, with the added warning that this initial breakneck speed should never again be expected.

With unbounded enthusiasm, excavation on the Wabash Canal was now optimistically pushed south out of Lafayette, heading for Terre Haute. More issues of scrip were soon in circulation, each issue named for the color of paper on which it was printed to designate the date of issue, and familiarly known throughout the fringe country as red-dog, white-dog, and blue-dog. Again it was accepted at only forty cents on the dollar, which caused considerable hardship since there was no other money in circulation.

Once more the digging moved into sparsely settled territory —only seventeen persons to the square mile, the engineers reported, but they were expecting the usual feverish influx as soon as canal water began to trickle.

Nor did the newborn enthusiasm end with ditchdigging. To the east of the Wabash Valley, fifty miles of track on the Lafayette and Madison Railroad were laid during 1844; upon them great quantities of corn and wheat from the southeast corner of the state were soon moving to the Ohio River and thence to eastern markets. In the northern section near Lake Michigan, a Hoosier plank road, patterned after the roads that had pulled Russia out of the mud, was now being put to full use by Michigan movers who brought a million bushels of their famed white wheat down this route to the canal at Fort Wayne that summer, creating a lively flurry of business for that village.

Farmers from western Indiana and eastern Illinois were doing a similar favor for Lafayette Village, which was again clogged with traffic—four hundred grain wagons arriving per day. And the Wabash Canal, moving all of these products eastward by the fastest transportation yet known in the world, was once again riding high. She had brought Indiana a long, long way.

By now the business of boatmaking had gone hog-wild. Even the farmers were sucked into it, diligently collecting L-shaped stumps (where tree trunk and large root meet) because these "knees" were essential for joining the ribs of a craft's hull to her deck timber. Down along the Ohio, Madison and Vevay and New Albany were now working day and night at the task, while naked boat skeletons lay in everybody's back yard.

New Albany took credit for the great *Eclipse*, built to ride the Ohio and Wabash Rivers. This was a mammoth steamboat whose hull was 365 feet long and whose water wheels were 42 feet high. Splendor was her aim and the sky was her limit, for the walls of her first-class passenger cabin were decorated with gold leaf that had cost $5,000, which was also the price of her imported Brussels carpets. The Haviland Potteries in Limoges had supplied her with china in a special pattern that flaunted a flying eagle and a gold E on every piece. Her table silverware was sterling. She carried a crew of 120 men. And she was destined to win a race against the famous *Shotwell*, steaming *upstream* from New Orleans to Louisville in a record four days, nine and a half hours. She was by all odds the loveliest craft yet to ride Hoosier waters. To view her against her home background of two-story houses, you might think that the East had now fully taken over here in southern Indiana.

But such was far from the truth, anywhere in the state. For even in the more densely settled sections, corn huskings, log rollings, backwoods politicking, open-hearth cooking, and Strictness of the Word still rulled Hoosierdom, while twenty miles inland from the Ohio or the Wabash, or the canals, or the plank road, or the railroad, the deep, silent wilderness, including the entire Wabash Valley below Terre Haute still remained largely untouched.

To remedy this, Indiana now decided to extend her canal all the way down to Evansville—458 miles, all told, which would make this channel the longest in the country, and nearly a third longer than the world-famous Old Erie. The very thought of it gave every Hoosier in the state a fine upsurge of faith. Evansville to New York City! Whee!

So, once more disregarding the ever rising canal debt, the overworked diggers went head over heels at the new section, beginning with the difficult feeder at Rawling's Mill and the dam at Splunge Creek, where a mile-long embankment was required.

It was another five years before the Wabash Canal ever reached Terre Haute, and an additional four before she moved down through Cross Cut to touch in at long, long last at Evansville. Tragic years, trouble-packed every mile of the way.

"Work held up, nearly suspended by billiousness and other diseases common to this country," wrote one engineer to Commissioner James Blair in 1842, "causing the death of two of our best contractors, Marshall Wines of Fort Wayne, and Robert Stewart, brought over from Cross Cut to do this job. . . . Forced to use oxen now. 2,000 men at work. More needed."

The 1843 report from Engineer Williams was equally distressing. "Work delayed by unprecedented severity of the winter, also its duration. Scrip depreciated. Laborers could be had at $12.00 per month, hard cash. . . . Trouble getting provisions. Prices of produce here have gone up 50 to 75%. Prices are about double cash value to workers. Scrip issued has thrown into circulation more than sales of land and tolls can absorb."

The 1846 report blamed the floods for the continued heartbreaking delays. "Worse by three feet than any freshet known to the oldest settlers." After that came two cholera epidemics that caused general panic, especially during that terrible week when 150 workmen dropped dead in the canal ditch.

As a result, a dearth of travelers on the completed sections reduced the 1846 toll receipts to $135,000, which was $11,000 less than that of the previous year. To top it all, during August of that summer there came a dry spell that grounded entire fleets of boats and caused tremendous damage and loss to canallers as well as shippers.

In an endeavor to create a new boom, Indiana now reduced the price of her public lands from $3.10 to $1.61 per acre. But even at this give-away figure there were few buyers, for once again Hoosier money was scarce and the canal debt was heavy —and due to grow heavier because nearly every channel in the state was now in need of repair.

What was a gallant young state to do when she had too much heart and too little cash? Even the most optimistic mover took a dim view of the whole affair—except when he paused to

take stock of what the Wabash and Erie had actually accomplished for all America. It had molded a chunk of wilderness
into a state, lifted a scattered, indolent population into an industrious people, doubled the Big Push through Lake Erie,
and insured that when the nation's time of crisis came, Indiana
like Illinois could be counted "free" instead of "slave."

Before the settling of the fringe country was two decades
along, Easterners had begun to look upon movers as a new
breed, with ideals and customs and even a language of their
own. Although all sections of the Far West were to follow this
new pattern, the Hoosiers were the first to show it. "A mixture
of old-fashioned cookery, decencies, virtues, bigotries, and
philosophies, overlaid with the smell of penny-rile and sassa-
frack," Irvin S. Cobb called it. Be that as it may, even from
her earliest days Indiana emerged from the melting pot as an
enthusiastic and eager individualist. The fact was noted by all
early travelers, and soon the term Hoosier came to have a special meaning, even in Europe.

A certain obscurity has long clouded the origin of this Indianan nickname, though the matter has sifted down through
the years to produce two schools of thought on the subject,
each with its own devotees. One camp claims that the word
Hoosier was originally used in England to denote a hod-carrier,
a rough fellow—which the early Indianan undoubtedly was.
The second group holds out for the theory that the term really
denotes hospitality, having originated from the fact that every
pioneer cabin in the state was open at all times to any stranger who jerked its latchstring, although in the middle of the
night, the master of the house was likely to demand cautiously,
"Who's yere?" Hence, Hoosier.

Whatever the origin of his nickname, a Hoosier was generally well liked and was noted for certain well-etched characteristics, for which he was admired or tolerated, as the case

might be, but respected nevertheless. For one thing, he was loyal to the point of clannishness toward his kinfolk, his village, and his state. From this trait arose many an early frontier quarrel, some of which grew serious enough to draw blood, and one of which made history. This was the so-called Attica War, and it came about in this manner:

Covington and Attica, neighboring river towns along the Wabash, had been rivals from the start. Both were laid out by pioneers who had come west by horseback at the time when the Old Erie was being conceived. Sixteen years later, when the Wabash and Erie Canal engineers were surveying the level valleys between Indiana's western hills, both of these villages were marked for canal ports.

This bonanza was thankfully accepted by Covington. But Attica was determined to undermine her neighbor's good fortune if possible, because she was still bitter over the fact that Covington had been chosen as county seat. The controversy over that earlier issue had been so strong that the Legislature had demanded from each of these hamlets a list of its inhabitants, promising that the larger settlement would get the official nod. In a matter of hours Attica had produced a fine, fat list that included her cemetery dwellers as well as those in town. And Covington's roster was made plump by the inclusion of her muster of 1812, which far outdistanced Attica's dead. Each hamlet felt that the other had acted in a distinctly shabby fashion in this affair, and promptly forwarded resolutions to that effect to the State Assembly.

The upshot of the entire squall was that an investigating committee arrived at Covington in due time and increased local tension by holding a secret meeting from which they emerged silently and galloped off to the town's public square, where they drove a wooden stake into the ground to mark the location of the new county courthouse. Then they betook themselves to a lavish banquet which the local ladies just happened to have hot and ready. The whole affair smacked of rank favoritism, according to Attica. For years she had been waiting for a chance to get even. And now there came a way.

It was the weather itself that gave Attica the whip handle, for the completion of this western canal section to the point of being ready for water came in the middle of Indiana's big drought of 1846. And when the clay-colored Wabash River water was finally admitted to the canal channel at this point, it was discovered that there was barely enough to flood the ditch as far as Attica, with not so much as a trickle left over for the Covington section.

This meant that the former village would enjoy the rare good fortune of acting as western terminus of the Wabash Canal for that entire summer. The monetary aspect of this coveted position—in addition to the honor of it—can hardly be overemphasized. Until now the cost of shipping a load of pork to market from this town had equaled four-fifths of its selling price, and the charge for transporting flour down the Wabash to New Orleans had been literally "cash on the barrel," since it was gauged by the number of silver dollars it took to cover the barrel head, which also amounted to about four-fifths of the value of the product. Under such conditions, making a profit was out of the question. But with the coming of the canal the entire picture had changed, and Attica was abruptly buzzing with shipping activity. Her dockside and warehouse business doubled overnight because her new canal rates to freighters were two-thirds cheaper than the old river rates.

This brought about a queer state of affairs that summer. The favored village, pausing in her money counting only long enough to send an occasional, derisive catcall down the hot, dry ditch to where the all-too-quiet county seat lay sweltering in the drought, basked in her prosperous ringside seat beside the cool waters of the brand-new Wabash Canal. All the way through to New York City from little, alder-choked, backwoods Attica!

The only cloud in the blue, blue sky lay in the fact that the autumn rains would undoubtedly ruin the picture, for the admittance of water to the Covington section would make that village the new western terminus, a position she would presumably hold for some time because the ditch south of her was far from completion. From Attica's point of view, this presented a revolting situation to which she had no slightest intention of submitting, as long as she could fight it off.

On the other hand Covington, foreseeing the same possibility, had no slightest intention of waiting for rain. At her continued insistence, canal officials were induced early in September to open the proper lock to admit whatever water might chance to seep in, which might in time be adequate since there was already a slight rise in the Shawnee Creek which served as a canal feeder. But when this important lock was at last opened and only the barest trickle came through, Covington suspected the worst. Attica was closing off the flow from above!

Covington's Senator Edward A. Hannegan—old "Fifty-four-forty or Fight"—who happened to be at home at this time to mend political fences, immediately offered the influence of his persuasive tongue if a local committee would care to accompany him to the upper river town in hopes of inducing that befuddled neighbor to see the light. The proposed visit was made. And while there is no report on their reception at Attica, we are told that the delegation returned home as mad as wet hens, and proceeded immediately to roll out a rusty cannon with which they set up such a mighty racket as to arouse the entire countryside. By nightfall, a sizable assembly had gathered on the village green, primed for a raid.

Fearing that the matter might get out of hand, a few persuaded the many to sleep on the idea first, then see how it looked in the morning. This was done. But by daylight, a raid looked even more advisable. So the Honorable Senator, together with three hundred townsmen and farmers and a fine array of clubs, started up River Road. Some rode horseback, some traveled shanks' mare, and some climbed aboard the wagons that carried the battle equipment. All were white-hot with excitement, and as stern in purpose as were the Minute Men of Concord and Lexington.

Meanwhile, old Jehu Wamsley, who lived on the bluff across the river, stepped casually out of his cabin for an early morning look at the weather, and discovered Covington's young army advancing along the opposite ridge. Without a moment's loss, he grabbed a couple of shotguns, an old yager, and a pistol or two, then leaped to his horse, galloped him down to the river, swam him across, raced him up the opposite shore and through the woods by a short cut to Attica, spreading the alarm as he went, a veritable Paul Revere.

The news was not altogether startling to most Atticans, who had guessed by the snide remarks of yesterday's visitors and the sound of their cannon fire that trouble was brewing. Already they had dispatched a well-armed wagonload of men down River Road to do a little scouting of their own. The two factions met midway, with the Atticans arriving too late with too little. In a matter of minutes they were surrounded, captured, disarmed, and held prisoner while the invaders continued their march to town and forced their way to the upper lock, which immediately earned the name it was to retain for years to come—Battleground.

Until now, most Atticans had considered the whole affair to be something of a lark. All business had been suspended and many townsmen had gathered along towpath and berm to enjoy a little excitement. But when the invaders had forced their way through the upriver hamlet and succeeded in opening the floodgates, letting the precious water rush into the thirsty lower section, it became evident to all that this was no longer a mock battle. Thirty expensive and heavily laden canalboats in the Attica section now stood in a fine position to be stranded —unless Covington's vigilantes could be stopped. Suddenly the stakes were very high.

Reinforced by additional villagers and the tough crews of the helpless boats, the home guard now attempted a rush attack, hoping to reclose the floodgates. Failing in this, they began moving haystacks and strawstacks into the channel above the lock, hoping thereby to plug it up. The idea was commendable, but a little late. In a matter of minutes, the thirty canalboats lay tipsily mired, dumping their precious cargoes into the mud.

Abruptly the battle was over, with the victory going to neither camp, since Covington's success had availed her little because her thirsty fourteen-mile canal section had absorbed most of the inrushing water, leaving scarcely enough to float a raft, let alone a canalboat. So now both towns were again lost in the wilderness, hundreds of miles plus two dry canal sections away from New York.

Hezekiah A. Martin, last known survivor of the Attica War, recorded the events during his youth, then helped produce an article on the subject at the age of ninety. "The scrap was bloody but no one was killed because Attica was never as serious as Covington," he wrote. "At the onslaught, William Wood of the aggressors struck Ezekial McDonald, Attica's captain, a blow on the head which tumbled him into the deep water of the lock, and was about to land him another blow when Hannegan called upon Wood to desist, thus saving the life of a very clever gentleman. The controversy involved two senators, Joseph E. Johnson, Esquire, brother of Zeke who lead Attica's forces, and the Honorable Mr. Hannegan of the invaders, prominent mainly through his eloquence."

Four years later, J. Richard Beste, that much traveled English journalist who had toted a wife and eleven children through most of the United States, exclaiming, "Is this not an everlasting great country!" finally got around to Indiana. His two-volume diary is one of the most colorful—and one of the rarest—of all accounts of the fringe country in its early days.

The Beste family's trail through Hoosierdom started off with a stage journey over an almost impassable strip of mired corduroy road that led into the great wilderness from Madison, where they had entered the state via the Ohio. This was followed by a breath-taking sprint on the Louisville, New Albany and Chicago Railway for the brief length of its tracks. They next rolled and jounced along the Central Plank Road to Indianapolis, in a new carryall that they had just purchased, a rickety, horse-drawn affair of the variety known as a "rough-and-ready" (when the roads get rough, you'd better be ready). From Indianapolis to Terre Haute they followed the trail that had been marked as part of the proposed National Road, but found it to be a mere wilderness pass of the crudest kind, stump-filled and at times barely traceable.

It was the evening of their third day out of Indianapolis when the Bestes reached Terre Haute in the famed Wabash Paradise. This village, recently made a canal port, was a beehive of confusion, having suddenly jumped to a population of four thousand souls, with a tangle of new stores, new homes, bustling mills, and mushrooming granaries—not to overlook the elegant new Prairie House, already famed for being what its handbills called "a hotel truly large enough to set a table worthy of so thriving a town."

Here the thirteen Bestes settled their belongings for the night, and were soon summoned to supper by a loud hand bell, vigorously rung through the corridors. With twenty-five others, they took their places at a long table and were immediately lost in the business of dish passing. For here all food was served family style, in great bowls and platters that made the rounds with unbelievable speed while each guest dipped into each dish in accordance with his own capacity and discretion.

In quick succession—as nearly as Beste could remember— came a land-turtle soup, roast mutton, boiled beef, roast lamb, veal pie, roast fowl, baked pigeon, hominy, potatoes, squash, corn, and what the British traveler called "elderly peas and beans." Then, with no pause whatsoever, abruptly the circu- lating dishes were offering desserts—cup custard, wedges of cherry, squash, and apple pie, stewed pears, roasted apples, cheese, and finally something Sir Richard called "that com- bination of iced water and watermelon known as 'cholera bomb shells,' believed by many to have produced the Plague of '32."

So abundant was the quantity, and so great was the variety of foods offered, the thought struck the Englishman that al- most everyone there must have got his money's worth—twenty- five cents. And when three of his family became violently ill during the night—including himself—it surprised no one. "I took blue pills and castor oil and laudanum, and tossed in my bed," wrote the British traveler. "The night was very long."

But when the morning found all of the other Bestes also stricken, one after another, a doctor was called, then a second —to confirm the diagnosis of the first. The Bestes had Asiatic cholera.

There followed a terror-stricken fortnight during which all thirteen of the English family approached death, ending with the burial of little Isabel, one of the youngest. They carried her to a country graveyard, with half the village following, out of deepest sympathy.

" 'Tis a great mercy to lose only one, from so large a family," the priest told them, stroking his beard thoughtfully.

"Here, we never *expect* to raise any of our children, until they have passed their eighth or ninth year," said their doctor, tucking a pinch of snuff under a shrunken upper lip.

The Bestes understood, for they had already observed the very high mortality in all fringe areas. It was the way of the frontier, the price you paid to become a part of the greatest migration on earth. And well worth it, they were told.

" 'Tis not for the purpose of detailing domestic sickness and trials that these pages are compiled," wrote the journalist upon leaving Terre Haute, "but that through much suffering and sorrow I may be enabled to exhibit a state of society in which and by which the greatest nation in the world is forming itself."

Now at long last, the Bestes turned again toward home and England. Boarding a luxury packet on the Wabash Canal they moved northward, gliding silently past the Attica-Covington Battleground. Here the giant oaks of the wilderness pressed to the very edge of berm and towpath, stretching to their towering heights without a branch or knot for their entire length to their tops, where they spread out like palms. "I never saw such magnificent timber!" wrote Beste.

Here, too, the wild rhododendrons grew unbelievably huge. And the colorful tortoises, lazily sunning themselves, took to the water at the packet's approach, while great flocks of frightened birds made a noisy whir of wings as they lifted to lose themselves in treetops and sky. The shrill croak of the cranes could be heard long after they had passed from view.

The brilliant coloring of the birds, the magnificence of the tangled vegetation, the beauty of the flowering shrubs and vines and creepers—all of these were balm to the saddened hearts of the Bestes, until at last they could lose their sorrow in the glory and bustling excitement of the magnificent frontier.

It set Richard Beste to pondering on the subject of the Hoosier backwoodsman in his isolated clearing, still hemmed in by timber so tall that it was like living in a cathedral. This was the state that was said to possess only three seasons—a summer of cholera and dysentery, an autumn of agur and fever, and a winter of consumption. Yet the Hoosier fringe farmer was the most contented and the most enterprising American that Beste had yet encountered.

He was primitive, but with a pristine simplicity of character and an independence of mind that were pleasing. He was free from fashion and foppery. Though he could never have managed a monocle, his aim with a rifle was deadly. He hated uniformity of dress and liked to swing independently along a country lane. He was afraid of neither work nor play. And he was willing to fight for liberty because he believed it necessary if his children were to enjoy the better life he craved to carve out for them. As for himself, it was enough that he could live in the woods that he loved, knowing the flash of a trout in a creek at dawning, listening to the song of the stars and the great silence of the wilderness. Or to the song of the katydid . . .

. . . Even as J. Richard Beste was listening to that song at this very moment. He took time from his reverie to make an entry in his journal, searching for the proper words to tell what it was like, here in the deep, deep woods, listening.

" 'Katy did,' says one. 'Katy didn't,' answer a thousand voices. And there is more poetry in the thought of this vast, untrodden, unmeasured wilderness of America than in all the reminiscences of the Old World."

CHAPTER FIFTEEN

BOOM AND BUST, AND THE IRON HORSE

THE Canal Era, one of the most colorful and significant periods in American history, was doomed from the day of its beginning, partly because its most successful channel, the Old Erie, was destined to create so great a boom as to produce a disastrous bust, and partly because the opening of the Big Ditch came at a time when George Stephenson, over in England, finally got the hang of harnessing steam to a locomotive that could pull cars. To trace the decay of this era, it is necessary to backtrack a few years to the Boom of 1836 and the resulting Bust of '37 which, though few suspected it at the time, formed the beginning of the end of the Canal Era.

As has already been seen, the boom was unavoidable, for times were so ripe for expansion that scarcely had the Old Erie opened her locks when the Big Push was on. And by the end of her first year, so remarkable was her success, almost any canal project anywhere could raise one or two million dollars within the hour after its subscription books were opened. There seemed to be no top to it, during the early Thirties, until a slight depression in '34 slowed matters down a bit, only to give way to a still greater boom that reached its astronomical peak in '36.

Considering the unbelievable numbers of emigrants who poured into the New West during the first decade of canalling—all of them expecting to grow rich in the Promised Land

—it is hardly surprising that a mammoth land craze developed. To meet the excessive demands for money to finance this wild spending, new banks had been popping into existence like stars on a moonfree night. At first, most of these were set up by sharpers merely to give themselves a chance to speculate with the public's money, but soon the older banks were swept into the maelstrom, tripling their capital by the simple expediency of printing more money. Thirty-five of these were state banks holding large government deposits formerly held by the Bank of the United States. These funds were now not only available to all, they were actually forced upon any borrower who was willing to sign a note, with no collateral whatever—a procedure that required little courage.

Moreover, since the bulk of these large sums had been made locally available through an outright gift when the United States government decided to divide up its surplus, the news soon went the rounds that verily this must be the millennium for which all good people had been taught to watch. Now that it had come, surely the sky was the limit, and spending could safely be wild and free.

For a time it began to look as if this belief were justified. For these abundant federal funds, together with the credit being extended by wildcat banking, more than doubled the nation's currency, making limitless sums available to everybody on terms to suit anybody.

By far the greatest part of the wild spending that resulted went for the purchase of western lands. The business hub of this mammoth land craze centered first in little ragtag, two-year-old Chicago, the newest and the fastest growing of all fringe villages. Since the subsequent growth of this hamlet was part and parcel of the so-called Speculative Craze of '35, which was to spell doom to the canals, it is well to digress a moment to consider Chicago.

Only six years earlier she had been a settlement of less than a hundred people, white and half-breed, huddled in the shadow of Fort Dearborn, a blockhouse situated at the foot of Lake Michigan in the unopened northeast section of Illinois. Within four years, this settlement had become an organized though unchartered village of twelve hundred, platted to include numerous imaginary streets which actually consisted of nothing more than rows of surveyors' stakes stretching across the prairie. By 1837, when the village was chartered by the state, she possessed by actual count a population of 4,170— which "included 104 sailors on vessels owned here." Two doctors, three lawyers, and a half-dozen innkeepers now graced the town, which also boasted fifty clapboard houses scattered among numerous dreary log cabins that faced the stump-choked paths known as Lake, Market, Canal, Franklin, and State streets.

The Speculative Craze, already going strong in early '35, found Chicago quite unprepared for her inrush of speculators and movers. According to one reporter, she was "a chaos of rubbish and a confusion of axes and hammers with lumber everywhere, everlastingly lost in a steady stream of emigrants unpacking or passing through, land sharkies as numerous as the grains of Lake Michigan sand, besides horse-dealers and horse-stealers and rogues of every kind."

So deeply was the village sunk in mud during all of this confusion, especially during spring freshets, that wagons were often abandoned wherever they happened to mire, sometimes leaving an entire block dotted with them for weeks at a time. Occasionally even the pedestrians were sucked into the black muck, from which they had to be pried out with long poles. Plank roads, laid in an attempt to remedy the situation, served only to produce other ills—for, since sewers and garbage collection were still undreamed of, and the cows that were pastured during the day were still allowed to roam the streets at night, all offal was wont to collect willy-nilly in the gutters, bringing about a dreadful state of affairs when a galloping coach hit the loose end of a plank while a pedestrian chanced to be passing.

Not that these untoward circumstances greatly bothered the game-for-anything movers. Rather, they chose to make a joke of the whole affair. Some even went so far as to erect signs on Chicago's fashionable Lake Street, especially in front of Mark Beaubien's famous Sauganash Hotel where the mud was particularly deep and slippery: "No Bottom Here" . . . "Shortest Road to China." And with a great deal of thigh-slapping and guffawing they gleefully told each other the one about the mover who had sunk to his chin in mud and was told to keep up his courage, help was on the way—to which he was reported to have answered, "Don't ye go to frettin' about me. I'm a-settin' on my wagon."

There were definite reasons why, in spite of her mud and crudeness, the infant Chicago should become the center of the western land boom. Her strategic location at the foot of Lake Michigan and at the head of the proposed Illinois and Michigan Canal, and the fact that she was about to become the hub of a half-dozen proposed railroads, were already attracting the attention of Eastern and European financiers. No one was quicker to observe this than were the land sharpies, who were already busy cutting her marshy lakefront into lots to be sold to European buyers. These 45-by-200-foot strips were bringing $7,000 apiece before Chicago Village had a population of four thousand. Land that would one day become part of her famous Loop—originally costing only $1.25 per acre and still to be had in 1832 for only $1.55 per acre—zoomed in the next four years to such heights that 375 lots cut from this parcel brought $1,335,755 at private sales.

So rapidly did these sought-after pieces of western property change hands—with every owner making fantastic profit before he would sell—that soon the land craze had become the most deadly of all types of gambling that went to make up the Boom of '36. And the worst thing about it all was that most of this fringe property, sold, pig-in-a-poke to Easterners and Europeans, was priced sky-high because of its location on some canal or railroad that did not yet exist.

Sometimes lots were sold for an entire town that was actually still an uncut western forest. Such came to be known as "paper towns" and "paper lots" since they existed only on promoters' maps. Part of the tragedy was that many of them never progressed beyond this stage before the crash came. In some instances these paper towns were even laid out around imaginary parks called "squares" or "places," where choice lots readily brought fabulous prices from rich Bostonians or New Yorkers who believed that they were buying fashionable locations—supposedly facing a fountain in a statue-bedecked park—where their families might dwell in style. To say that their subsequent awakening was rude would set something of a record for understatement.

By the end of 1835, the speculative game was sweeping the entire country. In St. Louis, store buildings were at such a premium that one owner, though admitting that he was raking in $1,800 per year in rent from buildings that had cost him only $1,400, was eager to sell because he "considered such meager profits hardly commensurate with the times." It was the same everywhere. A township up in Maine, purchased seven years earlier at 25 cents per acre, now sold at $12.00 per acre. A small plat near Louisville that had cost $675 in 1815 sold for $275,000 during the Craze of '35.

In the heart of Ohio's Covington, a 35-acre plat, purchased for $1,400 in '29, sold for $8,000 in the early Thirties, and was then cut into lots that brought a total of $200,000—though the original price had been laughed down as pure folly six years earlier.

Similarly, down in York State a Buffalo tract was bought at

$500 per acre and subdivided, then sold and resold until it brought $10,000 per lot. Another piece of land in Buffalo that had cost $7,500 yielded a harvest of a quarter million dollars within a year. Out in Ohio, Toledo land, bought from the government at $1.50 an acre, reached $100 per frontage foot within three years. In Cincinnati, land costing $25 per frontage foot brought $11,000 per fifty-foot lot within two years.

Even isolated Illinois prairie, still to be had from the government for $1.25 an acre, became immediately worth $200 a lot in eastern markets because a canal would supposedly run along its frontage within a few weeks—which made this look like quite a bargain when you considered the fact that eleven wharf lots at Utica had just brought a cool million dollars. In fact, the Old Erie's entire towpath property was now judged to have increased in value by fifty million within the past year, with plenty of additional profit in sight because new canal towns were still popping into existence with the vigor of weeds in June. For that matter, so were new canals, which were appearing hither and yon practically overnight.

By 1836 there was no part of the country that was not agog over the land craze. And little wonder. When a fortune could be made in the morning and doubled in the afternoon, it was everybody's business overnight. Guy Salisbury, author and traveler, was left breathless concerning the hysteria that he came upon in Buffalo. After a short scurry in the village streets, he hurried back to his hotel to tell his diary what a land craze actually looked like.

"In private parlors, in public bar-rooms, in places of business and on street corners, there are eager merchants and over-smart clerks; there are doctors, lawyers, editors, with now and then a divine to leaven the lump; there are scores of loitering mechanics and a few farmers, tarrying from their marketing—all occupied in the one great pursuit of getting suddenly rich—out of each other. The topic of conversation is the exhaustless theme of LAND. Passersby catch the same animated conversation from each knot of busy talkers—corner lot, water front, note at sixty days for the first payment and the balance in ten years, worth double in six months, make out your own papers. They chaffer, they negotiate, they mark out their lots with canes or umbrellas or their boot-toes upon the doorstep or sidewalk. 'Tis their dream of life from morn to night—land, land, still more land."

By the end of 1836, according to Mr. Salisbury, money was coming so fast and easy that no one bothered with the details of a transaction any more. " 'I'll give you a hundred and fifty thousand for all your property except your wife and babies and household furniture,' someone would offer. 'Done!' would bring possession of lands, tenements, mortgages, notes, etc.— it was too tedious to list everything, before the bubble burst."

By the beginning of 1837, all who had invested in canal bonds were either growing rich or going broke, depending on which channel they had chosen to sink their savings into. Those who had bought railroad stock found themselves in a similar fix. But all of those who were dealing in land were growing richer by the hour—with the exception of the federal government, which had never materially increased its land prices, and had often lowered them, because it desired the fringe country to be settled as quickly as possible to make it taxable.

This policy actually encouraged the sharpers who had by now webbed out from Chicago Village to open land offices in all eastern cities, where they were currently transferring millions of acres of government land to private ownership, almost entirely without cash. Never prior to 1834 had the sale of public lands reached four million acres in a single year. But in '36, twenty-four million acres were sold.

There can be little doubt that the main reason why the land craze of 1836 was now pitching headlong into the crash of '37 was largely because the thirty-five banks that held government deposits were childishly naïve in extending credit. The notes of buyers, which were acceptable as legal tender for government land, were riding a veritable merry-go-round, being loaned to sharpers, exchanged for more land, deposited as public revenue in one of the deposit banks, loaned again to speculators, used again to buy land, returned once more to a government bank, ready to be loaned again—whirling around and around, eventually transferring hundreds of thousands of acres from the government to land sharkies without adding one dollar to the nation's funds.

And one of the cruelest aspects of this dizzy whirligig lay in the fact that the speculator, with his pockets stuffed with inflated bank currency, could easily outbid the genuine settler, then hold the land for top prices and demand cash besides. Perhaps the most astounding feature of this entire land boom was that most of this wild speculation was concerned with fringe country which at this time possessed no railroads, few wagon roads, and no canals except those through Ohio and a small portion of Indiana.

Nevertheless, it was only natural that the land craze of '36 should give the Big Push its greatest impetus to date. The fear that choice locations would be gone, or that all of the $1.25 land would be gobbled up, soon produced the swiftest current yet in the stream of emigration. Even the crumbling old Cumberland Road was pressed feverishly back into faulty service, while canalboats on any westbound ditch in the country carried an everlasting chain of moving craft, often gliding so closely they touched one another.

"They pour West like an army of locusts to devour the broad acres," wrote Guy Salisbury from Detroit in July, 1836, having just witnessed firsthand the incredible eagerness of supposedly newly arrived movers, striving to make entries for public land. "The Receiver's office was literally beleaguered with applicants until the sidewalk and street had the appearance of the polls at a hotly contested election. Persons intent on locating the same tract, took fleet horses and ran races to the land offices as for a sweepstakes." So spake Salisbury before he had learned the truth—that chances were ten to one that the racers were sharkies, trying to beat out the settlers each time the government opened new territory.

Even as the land craze of '35 and the resulting boom of '36 were moving closer and closer to the crash of '37, the mad canal building and the skyrocketing canal debts throughout the country were also contributing handsomely toward bringing about disaster. With so many movers en route to homestead, each with his life's savings sewed into his money belt or hidden in the feather bed, there arose a certain competition among western states as to which could offer the sweeter bait as to transportation. By 1836, Ohio was smugly in the lead because her canal system was already attractive, though her canal debt was not.

Indiana, short of funds to begin with, was nevertheless now more determined than ever to hustle along with her Mammoth Internal Improvements in spite of the size of her mounting debt (she was already bonded for more than twenty dollars per Hoosier head). Illinois had embarked on an equally ambitious plan that would include not only her proposed Illinois and Michigan Canal and nine railroads, but river improvement or additional waterways for every possible county in the state and an outright gift of $200,000 to each of the others. She was already bonded for more than thirty-five dollars per person.

Luckily, Wisconsin—not yet even an independent territory —was still too young to undertake extensive internal improvements, though her *Milwaukee Journal* was beginning to ballyhoo ways and means to attempt such a program. But of all undertakings, those of Michigan—still a territory—were judged "the most insane" by most editors because, with only a

scant hundred thousand inhabitants, and without a single
dependable road in her entire expanse—even including Detroit—she now stepped into the whirlpool by appropriating
five million dollars as a starter for a program that would include sixty-odd turnpikes, a dozen railroads, and an impressive network of canals.

In the East, times were equally feverish. Maryland had just
voted eight million dollars toward improvements. Pennsylvania's canal spree had now put her twenty-four million in the
red—a debt upon which she could not even pay the interest.
And New York had just spread herself thin to the tune of another eight million for two additional channels—the Chenango
Canal and the Genesee Valley Canal, both due to fail.

By mid-1836 the spiral had hit its dizziest peak. Canal building and land buying now knew no limits—millions of dollars
going into doomed Big Ditches while millions of acres of public land went to buyers through sharkies, with seldom a cent
of cold cash reaching the government. What to do about it?
All Washington was wildly anxious. Then, one blistering day
in July, President Andrew Jackson believed he saw the light,
and came forth with his famous "Specie Circular." Henceforth,
the government of the United States would accept no payments for land except in gold or silver.

The news of it bewildered and shocked the entire nation
since it came so closely upon the heels of the government's
distribution of surplus funds, which had already caused a
dangerous shifting of deposits. From all directions and all
classes came hysterical vituperation against the President
and his drastic new ruling.

"It fell like a ponderous battle-ax through the paper helmets
of the Rag Barons and swept them down by the hundreds,"
wrote Salisbury. "The banks contracted like boa-constrictors
around their customers . . . and universal panic pervaded

the country. We tumbled from the zenith to the nadir, and it was a nine days' fall. The bubble had burst. Land that had sold for $125 a foot that morning would not bring $25 a lot by night."

Nor was the curtain of despair due to lift quickly. Land sales for that first year of the panic, in contrast to the 24 million dollars spent in the preceding year, barely reached $900,000. Immediately, building of all kinds, public as well as private, had come to a standstill, leaving long lines of rails to rust in the forests of three states. Half-completed depots, destined to wait many a day to smell locomotive smoke, were soon lost in a tangle of weeds and alder bushes, while laborers everywhere walked the village streets and country lanes in search of work. And there was no work.

Within three months, nine out of every ten factories had closed their doors. Poorhouses were overflowing. And while the starving of New York City and Philadelphia were breaking into warehouses to pitch barrels of foodstuffs out of the windows to their gaunt families, an angered farmer out on the western fringe stood slamming a bushel of eggs, one at a time, against his red barn to show what he thought of a situation so bad that no one in neighboring Springfield—capital of the great state of llinois—would give a measly two bits for an entire bushel of fresh eggs.

In Michigan Territory and what would become Wisconsin, the times were even worse, for here movers were subsisting almost entirely on what could be had from hunting and fishing, while many a $500-to-$1,000 lot was swapped gladly for a bushel of flour—because this was also the year when the Hessian fly chose to eat its way through the wheat fields of three western states.

Soon more than six hundred banks had closed their doors

forever; and the government of the United States, which had so recently shared its surplus, now found itself in the red by ten million dollars, and deeply embarrassed as well.

"Uncle Sam has run head and ears into debt, and John Bull wants his money," reported the *Cincinnati Gazette*.

And the *Western Courier and Piqua Gazette* stated flatly, "These are sad times, truly, and such as make the stones of Rome to rise in mutiny. Doubt, doom, and despair seem to have taken possession of all classes. Men of all parties are becoming alarmed at the state of things. One project after another is suggested to relieve the distress of the mercantile community but without avail. The notaries and lawyers are the only persons benefited by the universal loss. If the present is a foretaste of the golden age, God help our country!"

By 1839, the depression had hit rock bottom in the West as well as in the East, with Indiana suffering most severely because her canal debt was heaviest, though her neighbors suffered in direct proportion to how much each had actually spent in relation to its population. Illinois had accomplished very little so far, and Michigan—newly admitted to statehood —had not yet moved a single foot of canal dirt. Yet all three of these states had allowed large blocks of their bonds to get into the hands of brokers who now sneaked into bankruptcy without making any payments.

Indiana lost an additional two and a half million dollars by this particular shakedown, when she was already seventeen million in the red. Illinois, flat broke to begin with, now owed fourteen million, three of which arose from unpaid interest, actually leaving her without enough cash to buy postage for her official business. Michigan had lost her initial five-million-dollar investment to private concerns, but at least she had recovered from the canal fever before she was in any deeper, which should have been some solace. Wisconsin—still eleven years away from statehood—suffered nothing, because she had had only a daydream to begin with. She alone came out of the panic unscathed.

It was a long time before it was generally evident that the four disastrous years of the panic had spelled the beginning of the end of the Canal Era. Panic or no panic, no state had yet thought of defeat for its canals program. Indiana's artificial waterways, having actually struggled into existence during and immediately after the depression, continued to strive desperately toward completion. In Ohio, the panic was in its third year before the first section of the Pennsylvania and Ohio Canal was opened from Cleveland to Pittsburgh, "with a celebration second to none," according to the local press. And out in the Prairie State, no part of the Illinois and Michigan Canal was even started until after the Bust of '37 was gone and forgotten.

But as time went on, even the canal builders became aware that their various enterprises were living on borrowed time. The cancer was there. Soon everyone knew it, and hurried along with his own particular digging, in hopes of making as much progress as possible before the death pangs set in. The truth of the matter was that the four diastrous years of the panic, which had put a quietus on the American canal system, had given the railroads time to make necessary improvements. The Railroad Era was about to open.

The possibility of this catastrophe had actually been evident to canallers for some time, though the probability had seemed remote. Even before the depression, one of the most popular of parlor sports had been the ubiquitous debating over which was preferable, the Big Ditch or the Iron Horse. Apparently it was never conceded by either side that perhaps both were vitally important to America's great western migration. Rather it was the tendency of the times to condemn one and condone the other.

The canallers had held the upper hand for two decades now, mainly because their system was as old as civilization. Railroading, on the other hand, though born nearly simultaneously with the Old Erie, was nevertheless a new field of enterprise that had to perfect itself first in the uses of steam, then sell itself in the minds of men. Its setbacks had been numerous and heartbreaking for those who believed as ardently in it as had any canaller ever believed in the Big Ditch.

But after 1829, when George Stephenson's *Rocket* demonstrated in England that it was actually possible for a locomotive to pull a passenger car, the cause of railroading was given more favorable attention even in America, although there were many on both sides of the Atlantic who agreed with England's Parliament that "it was best not to damn the whole thing by talking about anything so ridiculous as speeds of twenty miles an hour."

In this country, railroads were at first looked upon as merely improved turnpikes whereon horse-drawn cars or trams could move more easily by rail than over rough roads. As such they had been useful around quarries and mills for thirty years before the *Rocket's* performance. But the possibility of substituting steam for the horse, and iron rails for canal channels was first introduced to the public in a series of articles written by John Stevens, a contemporary of England's Stephenson and sometimes called the Father of American Railroading.

Modestly entitled "Documents Tending to Prove the Superior Advantage of Rail-ways and Steam Carriages over Canal Navigation," these articles appeared first in Hezekiah Niles' *Register,* which in itself guaranteed them wide circulation. Further attention for the movement was gained by the colorful demonstrations that Stevens was conducting in his own back yard to prove that steam could be made even more powerful than was at first expected, simply by repeating the *Rocket's* initial performance over and over again—burning more wood, producing more steam, adding more mileage. By this system a railroad could run all the way across the continent, he claimed, simply by stopping every six miles to take on additional wood and water.

This was an amazing idea. It so seized the public fancy that Americans were soon rushing forth to purchase the new china, glassware, wallpaper, and sheet music that abruptly appeared on sale everywhere—even at ceremonial canal openings—all were decorated with pictures of squatty railroad cars and puffing, short-chimneyed locomotives.

Soon scores of editors, too, were allying themselves with the new movement, attempting to explain to their readers what a railroad was like, and what could be expected of it, though still a bit hazy on the subject themselves.

Timothy Flint of the *Western Monthly Review* was one of the first to catch afire over the prospect, foreseeing that "it could fill the noble forests and fertile prairies with new populations, all the way from New York Harbor to the Missouri Territory. . . . We suspect this to be the most magnificent project that was ever proposed in the sober conviction of practicability in any age or country," he went on. "It actually made our head ache . . . to stretch our thoughts from one extremity of this proposed chain to the other. We tried to imagine the thousands of loaded cars continually gliding along the iron track, speeding their everlasting course up the hills and down the valleys, swift as the roll of the rivers beneath them, or the lapse of time."

So frightening was this wildfire enthusiasm for railroads that irate canal stockholders quickly joined with a differing editor who foresaw naught but disaster if the Iron Horse was allowed to reach speeds that would encourage the whole world to go gadding.

"Twenty miles an hour, sir—why, you wouldn't be able to keep an apprentice boy at work! Every Saturday evening, he must make a trip to Ohio to spend Sunday with his sweetheart. Grave, plodding citizens will be flying about like comets. All local attachments will be at an end. It will encourage flightiness of intellect. Veracious people will turn into the most immeasurable liars. All conceptions will be exaggerated by the magnificent notions of distance. Only a hundred miles off— tut, nonsense, I'll step across, madam, and bring your fan!

"And then, sir, there will be barrels of pork, chaldrons of coal, and even lead and whiskey, and such like sober things that have always been used to slow travel, whisking away like a sky rocket. It will upset the gravity of the nation . . . a pestilential, topsy-turvy, harum-scarum whirligig. Give me the old solemn, straight-forward, regular canal—three miles an hour for express, with a yoke of oxen for heavy loads. I go for beasts of burden, it is more formative and scriptural, and suits a moral and religious people better—none of your hop, skip, and jump whimsies for me!"

Day by day, the controversy grew more bitter as additional facets came up for discussion. Some believed that the human body could never stand such terrific speeds as twenty miles per hour—the heart would stop or the blood would boil. Some felt that it would produce an immoral effect. Some feared that the danger to life and limb from the locomotive's flying sparks would be a serious matter—maiming and killing scores of people. Some believed that it was contrary to all democratic principles, giving the rich a chance to create a monopoly—it cost $4,000 to build a locomotive and eight carriages.

Further, it was widely believed that the farmers would destroy the tracks anyway, as soon as they discovered that their cows would no longer give milk nor would their hens let down eggs when the smoke-belching, ugly black monster came chugging through. And if the farmers did not split the rails, the winter frosts would.

"When you can run rivers backwards, 'twill be time enough for Rail Ways," concluded one editor.

The canal-versus-railroad debates produced their wildest oratory during the 1830's, and were widespread enough to include forensics at the plow, the church pulpit, the corn-cracker, and the parlor love seat. But conversation alone would never turn the trick. It would have been as easy to prevent the falling of morning dew as to outtalk the coming of the American railroad, once Bob Fulton had released steam and the English *Rocket* had led the way. Soon the desire for it had spread like an epidemic across the country, with little strips of crude rails appearing here and there and everywhere.

On the first railroad to be completed, a sixteen-mile Pennsylvania coal line called the Carbondale and Honesdale Railway, an English-built locomotive was used, known widely as the *Stourbridge Lion.* Soon thereafter, the Baltimore and Ohio completed its first section, a thirteen-mile strip of track running from Baltimore to Ellicott's Mills.

So early was this latter line started that it was designed for horse-drawn carriages. But, because it was a long time under construction, the use of steam had been introduced before its completion, causing the B & O to experiment with the first American-made locomotive. This was the Tom Thumb, owned by the inventor Peter Cooper. But the miniature engine had trouble on its first trial run, and it was allowed to travel only a few rods before it was removed to the Cooper back yard for further study.

During the year 1830, as we have already noted, the Tom Thumb was again hoisted to the B & O tracks to compete in a widely advertised race against a big gray horse belonging to a rival stagecoach company. The doleful results of this famous race served only to convince the B & O that her original plan to use horse-drawn carriages was the wiser after all. So the Tom Thumb was retired in disgrace behind the Cooper barn. And the "teakettle-on-a-track" movement conceded the issue to the large gray mares of the world.

But only for a twelvemonth. By that time, an Iron Horse had been induced to *push* a passenger car carrying twenty-four persons at four miles an hour for the full length of the thirteen-mile track between Baltimore and Ellicott's Mills.

Nor did the B & O's experimenting end with the use of steam. Once they mounted a horse upon a specially-built flat-car where he walked a treadmill to produce power enough to run the train. Another time they rigged up a basketlike car with sails, which glided along the tracks quite merrily until an unfriendly wind ditched the whole affair. In fact, for the first three years of this railroad's operation, there was considerable conjecture and widespread betting, whenever a train was due, as to whether it would come in by horsepower, steam, or sail—this depended completely upon which was workable at train time.

While the B & O was conducting experiments in these various media, down in Carolina the Charleston and Hamburg Railway was also tinkering with horsepower and sail cars. By the latter method fifteen passengers were once successfully propelled at the terrific speed of twelve miles an hour—until mast, sail, and passengers were blown overboard. Then this railroad adopted a locomotive called the Best Friend, which was the first full-sized American-made steam engine to be used in regular service. It was also the first to run off the track. And it was the first to explode—this being the first time an engineer ever sat on a safety valve to hush its hissing. After this incident, every railroad in the country carried a buffer car filled with cotton bales, placed between locomotive and passenger cars to protect patrons from engine explosions.

Before the Old Erie had worn the newness off her first

packets, the Mohawk and Hudson Railway Company had completed seventeen miles of track between Albany and Schenectady, hoping thereby to snatch off those impatient voyagers who were so irate over the many lock delays in this first section of the Big Ditch. They even impudently named their locomotive the De Witt Clinton. It made its first trip on the hottest day of summer—a memorable journey, for it carried three passenger cars and a half-dozen flatcars, a feat widely hailed by all except the spectators whose parasols caught fire when the train whizzed by, and the passengers whose clothing smoked constantly as they sat fighting the continuous shower of sparks from a wood-burning engine that had to be constantly fired to capacity to produce the proper head of steam. But the speed achieved by this flying locomotive was something to start tongues a-clacking; as was also its everlasting jolting, according to its dizzy, well-shaken passengers.

By the middle of the Thirties, even the fringe country was running railroads. A small Hoosier line, the Lawrenceburg and Indianapolis, was a mile and a quarter long when it was officially opened on the Fourth of July, 1834. It took in a total of $48 that first day, "and could have made more if the horse had not succumbed," reads the report. Four years later, the Madison and Indianapolis Railway had completed twenty-two miles of track and was running a steam locomotive that had been hauled in by oxen over a specially built trail with permission from the Indians through whose land it must pass.

During that same summer, a visiting Kentucky showman by the name of Joseph Bruen arrived in Indiana with a portable track, a small engine, and a passenger car which he set up in jig-time so that venturesome Hoosiers could ride briefly but importantly by steam for the price of two bits per family.

By 1836, Michigan—though still a territory—was running trains on the thirty-three mile strip of her Erie and Kalamazoo Railway between Toledo and Adrian. Then the Bust of

'37 brought all railroading everywhere to a dead standstill that lasted until each enterprise could figure out its own particular salvation. The comeback for a few was a comparatively simple matter, but for many it presented a nearly insurmountable task. Consequently more than a decade passed with little progress in the railroads' decidedly uphill climb.

The interim was not completely wasted, however, for even without funds enough for building, at least experimenting could still go on; and certainly there was plenty of room for improvement, for these early railroads were extremely crude. For instance, train travel was at first strictly a daytime activity. But as the momentum of the Big Push increased, night travel also became necessary, bringing about all kinds of adventuring in ways of lighting the tracks. One company tried engine reflectors that used candles, but the wind brought this experiment to a quick conclusion. A southern railroad used a bonfire of brightly burning pine knots, carried along in a small, sand-filled boxcar that was pushed ahead of the locomotive. This method succeeded at least to the extent of sending feeble, wavering rays down the tracks when the fire was at its height. But it was the general consensus that the problem of night travel was not yet completely solved.

Experiments in ways of bettering the roadbed were also under way, for until now this had usually consisted of little more than a crushed stone surface—named after its inventor, an engineer named McAdam. Now it was decided that all future tracks should be built two feet above the ground level, to avoid floods and snowdrifts. Other improvements followed rapidly. Small splint brooms were attached to the locomotive to sweep the tracks as it moved along, a gimmick that actually proved to be a blessing to Pennsylvania during the year of the grasshopper plague.

In order to furnish the great supplies of water and wood demanded by the Iron Horse, wood piles were now established every six miles along the right-of-way, with a nearby farmer hired to replenish each. New ditches paralleling the tracks were also added to bring water from neighboring creeks or rivers, so arranged that the engine's fireman could readily scoop it up in his leather bucket as the train rolled along— hence the expression "jerkwater railroads." These last two improvements were widely advertised as "luxury travel," since travelers would no longer be forced to alight and cut wood or carry water. But actually, both improvements were necessities if railroads expected to compete with the comfortable, lazy ease of canal travel.

Since all lines were at first one-tracked, collisions (called "concussions") were frequent enough to pose a serious problem. To prevent these, most railroads were now divided into sections with a pole erected in the middle of each division. When two locomotives entered the same section from opposite directions, the first to reach the pole had won the right to proceed while the loser must back up to the nearest "turnout" where it could be switched out of the way. This system served admirably to lessen the number of collisions, but it played hob with speed control and caused much fist fighting as well.

Another difficulty that occurred before the introduction of the telegraph system arose from the fact that there was no way of telling in advance when a train might be expected. To correct this, "lookout masts" were now set up at each depot so that the station agent could shinny up this pole to a little seat up top from which he could watch the horizon for smoke, then shout the news to the waiting passengers below. In fact, every possible angle for improvement was now being seriously studied in an effort to make train travel more popular than canalling.

Service was already the watchword of the day, even to the point where a certain conductor, upon learning at Utica that a sleepwalker had accidentally stepped off his train during the night, induced the engineer to backtrack all the way to Schenectady before the missing man was located.

By the late 1840's, the Bust of '37 was largely gone and forgotten, and the Railroad Era was fully upon us. Now it was making such rapid strides as to outdistance anything ever before accomplished in any field, including canalling. Before mid-century, by hook or crook, 7,400 miles of workable railroad had been laid in the United States, nearly nine-tenths of it along the eastern seaboard. To the west of the Alleghenies, Ohio already possessed 319 miles of the iron-capped wooden tracks, Michigan's system had been expanded to 270 miles, Indiana claimed 86 miles of railroad, and Kentucky boasted 54 miles of it. Only Tennessee and Wisconsin remained untraversed. Nor was there yet a single mile of track west of the Mississippi.

Illinois, so soon to spurt ahead of all other states in this respect, still lay in a coma among her rusting rails and orphaned depots, having been knocked out completely when her expansive plans for 1,341 miles of railroad, besides numerous plank roads and canals, had run her seven million dollars in debt before she had completed her first twenty-four miles of track. (She still had not lifted a shovel toward building her plank roads and canals.)

Admittedly, she had run into extraordinarily bad luck on this first railroad, the Northern Cross, which ran from Meredosia to Springfield—even losing the locomotive which had been shipped to her from the East by water but never seemed to arrive. Pocketing this loss, she had in due time been able to purchase another. This was the *Rogers*, which possessed no cab, no whistle, no spark arrester, no cowcatcher, and no bell. But it looked intriguing enough on its maiden trip to keep a string of movers trotting along beside it, peering beneath it every time it stopped, "because they could not understand what made its wheels go round, and believed it to be a supernatural power given to this smoking monster," explained one passenger.

By 1842, when 59 miles of this line had been completed, a local newspaper announced that the last 33½ miles of its trial run had been accomplished in two hours and eight minutes, "including stoppages." News of this kind traveled fast, and naturally stirred up as much excitement as had the first appearance of the Iron Horse itself. Eighteen miles an hour—whee!

This was indeed a fine start, but nothing more. For as the sparks fly upward, this line was doomed to failure—the victim of prairie grass! Its rails were always covered with the stuff, which grew faster than it could be cut, causing the wheels of the locomotive to slip and slide, and toppling the smoking monster into the ditch—often three times to a single trip. Moreover, certain sections of this line were impossibly slow because they depended on the passengers for help whenever the engine called for a bucket brigade to the nearest creek.

In 1847, the hard-pressed Northern Cross finally abandoned her Iron Horse and went back to her mules, selling the disgraced locomotive to a farmer who thought it might come in handy around the barnyard. The last the public saw of this puffing monster was when it deserted its tracks and took off across the prairie for the Alton farmhouse. Or at least it was believed at the time that this was the end of it. But certain curious settlers, later coming upon queer, unexplainable, deep ruts that disappeared in the distance, were mystified enough to track the Thing to its lair—a rusting, saddened old juggernaut, mired in a swamp, abandoned long since by its discouraged owner.

The Northern Cross Rail Way, which had cost Illinois a cool million dollars, was auctioned off for $21,500. This was a poor beginning for a state that had so greatly hankered for 1,341 miles of rails; it was now without a single track in operation. Illinois was back where she had started, depending on mules and mud-clabbered roads.

But the year of 1850 told a different story, for it marked the real beginning of railroading in Illinois. First, the old Northern Cross, now to be called the Sangamon and Morgan Line, was reclaimed and restored to steam. Secondly, a new "strap railroad," known as the Galena and Chicago Union, was completed for forty-two miles westward to Elgin, from which village the rattling little *Pioneer* chugged into Chicago that summer carrying the first shipment of grain ever to reach that thriving city by rail—though it would soon be known as the grain center of the world. And in the third place, an act of Congress that autumn provided for a land grant of more than two and a half million acres to help finance the construction of a much needed central railroad.

To the settling of Illinois, this would be as vitally important as were the elaborate canal systems in all other states involved in the great migration. For the Prairie State—due to her extreme western position in the Northwest Territory—naturally matured too late for the Canal Era. This fact alone gave this railroad a unique significance in the furthering of the Big Push. While all other early railroads either traversed well-settled territory or else ran parallel to already existing canal systems, the new rails would here open virgin prairie. For this reason, it might behoove us to tarry a moment, to consider the coming of the Illinois Central.

It would extend nearly the full length of the state, running from Chicago to the junction of the Ohio and the Mississippi at Cairo. It would also have a branch running from a spot to be known as Centralia to a point on the upper Mississippi opposite Dubuque, Iowa. Thus the mammoth spread of the proposed railroad would open nearly three million acres of wild land, a section which now included no settlement of more than a hundred souls along its entire 366-mile Chicago-to-Cairo division, while its 399-mile Centralia-to-Galena section would include only eight small hamlets. With the exception of these few "beginnings," as they were called, Illinois presented an unbroken prairie throughout this great expanse, fabulously plentiful in game, and fabulously lonesome; most movers' cabins, outside the villages, were a difficult day's drive apart.

Because this state was already buried under a seventeen-million-dollar debt, and therefore in no position to refuse help, she decided to allow this new enterprise to be privately owned and financed by a certain group of rich and prominent Easterners, chosen above other eager groups because they were willing to build their railroad exactly where the state wanted one built. Included in the new company were a shipowner from Boston, two railroad promoters of other lines, two successful bankers, a coffee importer, a noted fur trader and Indian guide, a locomotive manufacturer, a topflight New York merchant, three railroad presidents, and a United States senator.

Banded into a brand-new company, this group of courageous promoters now pledged to complete their proposed 765 miles of track within six years—more than twice the length of the longest railroad in America to date, to be built in a mere fraction of the time required for any other railway system anywhere.

Again it was like the beginnings of the Old Erie. Thousands of laborers pouring into the state. Dozens of shanty towns appearing in the wild lands. Hundreds of horses and ox teams making the cuts. Hundreds more transporting foodstuffs and the rails that were arriving from England by sailing vessels. Hundreds of lumberjacks trekking to Michigan and Wisconsin to log out the crossties and bridge timbers. Thousands of picks and shovels and sledge hammers and crossbars scattered hither and yon, with the usual appalling scarcity of the powerful machines needed for reducing hills and building up valleys.

Within five years, more than a hundred thousand men were at work on the Illinois Central at $1.25 per day, inadequately clothed, inadequately fed, fighting the cholera, drinking sick water, earning early graves.

Again came the great celebrations at the completion of each new section of track, now honoring the Iron Horse even as they had honored the Big Ditch a little more than thirty crowded years earlier. And when the great, puffing, black monster came into sight—even as when the first canalboat had once glided into view—"the people were struck dumb with amazement, as if they had just come out between the shakes of fever and ague," reported the press.

The day of the Illinois Central's greatest celebration, upon the occasion of her driving her last spike, was September 27, 1856, four months ahead of her deadline, and exactly three decades and eleven months from the day when the Old Erie's ceremonial cannons took ninety minutes to signal her big news from Albany to New York. The wonder of it now, as then, lies in the fact that the faith of the few had led the many. Neither wilderness nor depression, nor plague nor privation had been able to halt the canallers. Nor could anything now halt the railroaders. Even when the Illinois Central was completed— her crude tracks stretching far and away across the lonesome prairies—her task was but half finished, for the settling of this great wild territory still lay ahead.

Admittedly with its own interests uppermost in mind, the Illinois Central now launched one of the greatest advertising campaigns yet known to history. So widespread was this, it was believed that nearly every person in the United States, and hundreds in foreign countries, must have learned that Illinois was the land of plenty, heart of the Promised Land. The results were tremendous, once again giving the great migration a mighty boost, actually doubling the population of this state during a single decade, from 1850 to 1860.

The "civilized rails," many were calling them now, for they were bringing into the wilderness the teacher, the doctor, the lawyer, the merchant, the missioner—not to overlook the new wave of homemakers. For just as the Big Ditch was providentially ready when the Cumberland Road took to crumbling, so now the Iron Horse had come into existence just when the canals were failing for want of funds. But to the so-called Manifest Destiny of the nation, the coming of the railroads never possessed quite the importance and urgency that the canals could claim, for by this time the Mexican War had already secured the Far West to us, and a pan of gold at Sutter's Creek had provided an incentive for the great rush to California.

CHAPTER SIXTEEN

THE TOWPATH PASSES

THE passing of the Canal Era was a time of sorrow for the thousands of people who had staked their all in order to locate on some star-spangled waterfront, where the music of packet and oyster bar made the wilderness endurable by night, and the jingle of oxen harness and the tinkle of gold coin in the family coffers made it pleasant by day.

But when the combined canal debts of the country had passed the sixty-million-dollar mark with no relief in sight—while a new railroad popped into existence somewhere almost monthly—it came to be evident to all that the Iron Horse had come to stay, and the ditches were doomed. By now Indiana had defaulted on her canal debt. Maryland had defaulted on hers. Pennsylvania had also defaulted—because a troop of railroaders had the effrontery to parallel her Grand Canal from Philadelphia to Pittsburgh, even borrowing her Portage Canal until they could fill two ravines and cut away a mountain to give them a wide horseshoe ascent that would eventually cut travel time from 4½ days by canal to a 17-hour run by rail.

By now, too, foreign aid from private sources—which had been flourishing—was no longer available to canal builders. Too many Europeans had already been scorched by investing in American projects under the assumption that all states in that fabulous never-never land must be as rich as Croesus, since their federal government had divided its too-heavy surplus with them.

Forced to face these insurmountable circumstances, there were many who came to hate the ditches, even among those who had originally supported them. Feeling the weight of canal debts, admitting the inevitable growth in railroading, still believing that the plagues ran with Big Ditch waters, hundreds of thousands now became turncoats.

Irate farmers throughout the country were the first to hold hotheaded indignation meetings, which often ended with the malicious destruction of locks and aqueducts. In New England they cut the banks of one channel, dumped rocks into its locks, then sued the canal company because canal water overflowed into their fields. And although the *Democratic Herald* of East Hampton called these mischief-makers "mean, low spirited pappys, having nothing of manhood about them, nor intelligence enough to guide their malice," other indignation meetings in the East continued to perpetrate similar acts of violence.

Out in the fringe country, certain Hoosiers—living along the most important canal of the West and therefore heirs-apparent to one of the heaviest of all canal debts—had also decided to hold mass meetings. Here, aided by numerous journalistic sneers, these gatherings grew to huge proportions—as did their indignation. As a result, one dark night the huge, expensive Birch Creek Reservoir was completely destroyed.

This the state promptly rebuilt, at considerable expense. And when the new structure was also threatened by the same mob, state troopers were sent in to guard it. But so surprisingly friendly and peaceful did they find these hospitable farmers that they pitched their camps along the Eel River, where they spent the summer fishing and hunting. And when the weather was rough, they taught the natives some new card tricks. In return, the farmers showed them where the catfish lurked in

the quiet pools, and how to twist willow switches to snare the
raccoon—plying them the while with hard cider and corn
liquor. It made a merry summer for all of Clay County.

But when the lavender and purple haze of autumn had soft-
ened the bluffs along the river and the frosts had ripened the
persimmon, it was time for the troopers to break camp and
depart, disappearing one morning over the hills toward Indianapolis. Scarcely had they completed a half-day's march,
however, before they were startled at the sound of heavy explosions and the sight of billowing black smoke rolling along
the horizon, far to their rear—indicating beyond the shadow
of a doubt that once again dynamite had been put to the locks,
and torches to the bridges and aqueducts of a considerable
section of the fabulous Wabash Canal. It was even more difficult to believe the whole truth—that this dastardly, lawless
mischief had been accomplished by the very farmers with
whom they had so happily swapped yarns and tobacco twists
all summer.

There were others throughout this Hoosier countryside who
also watched the rolling smoke that morning, and knew the
truth beyond guessing. To the ones who still believed in the canals, it put a lonesome fright to the heart and a lump to the
throat, remembering whence came their deliverance from the
bleakness of a wilderness. But to the railroaders, the sight of
this dastardly act brought a surge of pure joy, for already they
were beginning to parallel Indiana's Big Ditch with their iron-
capped wooden rails.

It took many a long month before this expensive and expansive channel could be completed for the third time and
put back into operation; because of the delay, canal service
was halted all the way from Terre Haute to Evansville. Again
the thing completed was a thing of beauty, reflecting the syca-
more groves and the clay hills of southern Indiana. But it had
come too late, for the delay had been costly in time as well as

in money. The state of Indiana was to enjoy her fabulous Wabash and Erie Canal as a whole for only four years before it must close forever for lack of funds.

Nor were her allotted four years destined to be carefree, for Nature too seemed to have turned her back on this most important of all fringe canals. Spring freshets flooded the channels. Drought grounded the boats. Decay destroyed the wooden dams, bridges, aqueducts, and locks. And when the state legislators decided—in a last, desperate effort to salvage what they could—that the disgruntled bondholders should be presented with the tottering lower channel as an outright gift, it profited nothing, for the bondholders, too, were stony broke and could not finance repair. And so the canal debt— nine and a half million dollars on this many-times-rebuilt lower section alone—remained a millstone that was daily becoming heavier around every Hoosier neck. And the only way out of the dilemma was to abandon this Big Ditch, section by section, as it fell to rot.

" 'Twas a sad time when the scraper came along, fillin' in Old Cross Cut after the last boat pulled through on her last run," W. C. Fox of Riley recalled, even when he was approaching his ninetieth year. " 'Good bye, Jonathan!' 'So long, Cap'n!' Many wept, knowin' how soon the poplars and sycamores would take over, leavin' us back in the wilderness again. Wept for the sadness of an empty ditch. Wept for the boats and horses and men and canawl—all run to their end together."

There were thousands who agreed with this sentiment, Easterners and Westerners alike. But there was another school of thought on the subject, too. For over and above the rioters and the railroaders, there were those who in no way mourned the passing of the towpath, here or elsewhere. One who went on record in this respect was Horace Greeley, who had originally given the Old Erie her well-known nickname—"Old cent-and-a-half a mile, mile-and-a-half an hour." Now he came forth with a new statement that became a classic. "I say nothing against 'the good old times.' But if anyone would recall 'the good old lineboats,' I object!"

The upper part of the Wabash Canal still continued fitfully for a few additional years after Cross Cut and the lower channel had finally been abandoned. But this, too, ended ingloriously. For the last boat through—making a final ceremonial run before a large, saddened crowd—was abruptly swept down the roaring Deer Creek, drowning driver and mules, because a rotted aqueduct east of Lafayette had suddenly collapsed.

By 1875, there remained in use no smallest part of the fabulous Wabash and Erie. She had held the distinction of being not only America's longest canal, but also the most colossal, most tragic financial failure in all canal history. Nevertheless, with the exception of the Old Erie, she had made the most glorious contribution of all toward settling the frontier, including even Uncle Sam's Pike and the railroads. For her earliest sections had fostered the Big Push westward through Indiana, entirely alone, for two full decades, and had opened hundreds of thousands of acres of wild land in two fringe states and four territories.

Ohio's canals, though never completely trouble-free, enjoyed twelve good years before the railroads moved in to take over. Here, too, debt and decay and floods and drought played villainous roles, until gradually it became evident to all that the days of their waterways were numbered. Added to which, disgruntled farmers destroyed expensive dams, disabling two large aqueducts, "because they caused pestilence and fever," even as Kentuckians were currently tearing down their new telegraph poles "because the wires carried the agur."

The Miami Canal hung on longest because she was not completed until channels everywhere else were beginning to close. Still, though she had cost four and a half million to build and her lifeline was short, she too made a glorious contribution— as did all Ohio canals. For through forty years, from drawing board to decay, the Buckeye waterways had given their mother state her greatest impetus toward her future exalted position in the Union.

Moreover, within a quarter century, four canal towns had leaped to world fame. Cincinnati had grown from 2,600 to 200,000. Cleveland had expanded from 400 to 60,000. Dayton's 1,139 souls had become 25,000. And Toledo's 500 had zoomed to 14,000. These thriving cities had provided their parent state with one of her greatest attractions.

In Pennsylvania, during the narrow confines of a quarter-century, the Grand Canal had been dreamed up, built, and abandoned. Here at no time did profits ever catch up with expenses. The reasons were obvious. The Portage Railroad remained a bottleneck from start to finish, constantly clogged with freight. Also the number of locks this canal was forced to build and maintain doubled the number on the Old Erie, slowing travel to a point where even Pennsylvanians stepped across the state line to use New York's Big Ditch for their Westering. And when it was decided to unload by selling out, the only bids received for the Grand Canal came from her detested rivals, the railroads. Certainly this was an inglorious way to go down, but what choice was there? And so, with the exception of short sections suitable for coal hauling, all of her expensive and somewhat startlingly contrived channels had passed into the hands of railroad interests before 1860.

This brought to an end a waterway that had cost Pennsylvania dearly, but had served both her and the Big Push well. For during the lush days, it was reported that there was never a time, day or night, when less than forty boatloads of westbound movers could be sighted from any spot on this canal.

Moreover, her contribution to the mother state in bringing villages out of obscurity can hardly be overestimated.

The Chesapeake and Ohio, considered next in importance to the Old Erie and the Pennsylvania's Grand Canal among Eastern waterways, functioned a little longer than most because she was an autumn chick to begin with; early estimates had scared off her promoters for many a long year before she was even started. And so slowly did she progress that the period of her building nearly equaled that of the entire Canal Era.

Yet even as early as 1828 she was on her way, with John Quincy Adams starting her off hopefully by pressing the Presidential boot on the ceremonial shovel at Georgetown, "in the presence of a large concourse of people," we are told. In view of the importance of the occasion it was unfortunate that the President should run into a little trouble when his bunting-bedecked spade hit a tree root and failed of its purpose. A second attempt was also thwarted. At this point the President stripped down to his weskit, and with a brave show of strength plunged the shiny blade into the ground.

"At this turn of events, the multitude raised a loud and unanimous cheering," wrote one reporter, while John Quincy Adams went his weary way back to the White House to record the incident in his diary.

"Got through awkwardly, but without gross or palpable failure. The incident that chiefly relieved me was the obstacle of the stump which met and resisted the spade, and my casting off my coat to overcome the resistance. It struck the eye and fancy of my spectators more than all the flowers of rhetoric in my speech, and diverted their attention from the stammering and hesitation of a deficient memory."

Later, it seemed to many that this initial resistance actually presaged the type of existence this canal was doomed to endure. For even at the time when she was being initiated, the

B & O Rail Way—less than forty miles away—was also holding a ground-breaking. This was only the beginning of her troubles. Unbelievable expenses. Jealousy among wrangling property owners. Siege after siege of malaria and cholera. Financial embarrassment, time and again. Continual warring among the Irish laborers. Numerous legal battles with the railroad for possession of Point of Rocks, which was the only gap through the mountains, and too narrow for both, which finally ended with a decision that favored the canal. Whereupon, the railroad tunneled under, and the two rivals continued side by side.

It was thirty years before the *Cumberland Civilian* could announce, "After undergoing unparalleled vicissitudes of fortune, this great work had been at length consummated." At a cost of $60,000 per single mile, the Chesapeake and Ohio had arrived a quarter-century too late to aid either the Big Push or her own locality. But she was destined to serve nobly after all, though not as a canal. During the Civil War, her aqueduct across the Potomac was drained to serve as a wagon bridge, forming the only possible means of escape from Bull Run for the defeated Union Army.

In striking contrast to all other American canals, the Old Erie was a financial success from the very day of her opening, as was her tributary, the little Oswego. When it became evident in 1850 that packet boats were unprofitable on the Big Ditch and a nuisance as well, they were at once discontinued. And no passenger boat ever again moved through her quiet waters. Yet so extensive was her freight service that she continued to maintain her supremacy over all other American canals, although she did not reach her financial peak until 1869. By then most other canals had dried up and gone to grass.

In her later years, the little Oswego was to be incorporated as part of her system, and the Erie's entire channel would be widened and deepened and straightened, to make her the great barge canal which has been immeasurably helpful in all subsequent times of war and peace. She still functions in that capacity today.

Yet it is her early importance that must never be forgotten, for she formed the first wedge toward breaking the wilderness of the old Northwest Territory so that a thousand new cities might flourish. In addition, she transported the untold millions of tons of freight necessary to the building of five new states, and she contributed immeasurably to the growth and welfare of her country through a critical period in history.

One other notable exception to the general canal collapse was the fringe country's Illinois and Michigan Canal, a Johnny-come-lately that was so tardy in completion as to be more valuable to the opening of the Missouri Territory and points west than to the settling of her own state. As a packet canal she did little more than furnish excursions for Sunday School picnics and wedding parties. But as a barge canal she was largely responsible for the fabulous growth of Chicago.

The north end of her channel, later widened and deepened and revived as the Chicago Sanitary and Ship Canal, has served the nation well for more than a century. At the present time it is an important link in the so-called Illinois Waterway which connects Lake Michigan at Chicago with the Mississippi at Grafton, Illinois. This means that this relic of the old mule-towed Illinois and Michigan Canal now functions as a part of the fourth largest waterway in America today, surpassed in volume of shipping by only the Ohio River, the Mississippi, and the Monongahela. Already she forms a link in the nearly completed St. Lawrence Seaway which will carry ocean-going vessels to the Gulf of Mexico by an inland route.

The Canal Era, scarcely three decades long, had seen and helped produce the greatest changes ever known in America in so short a period. Largely alone, it had transformed the country from a narrow eastern seaboard, casting a desiring eye across the Alleghenies towards the deep soil of the Promised Land, into a great nation in which five new western states were firmly established, and four of them admitted to the Union. It had converted transportation from the pack horse and the floating raft through a series of ever improving conveyances, until men could move with ease and swiftness by water over territory that had recently been unbroken forests. It had altered America's concept of her own horizons, pushing her frontiers ever westward. No longer did movers gaze with awe at the Father of Waters, for now they could manage crossings without dying of fear, nor yet of drowning. There were even those who turned land-hungry eyes beyond the bottomless mud of Iowa and across the Big Sioux toward the new Far West, with no better reason for this hankering than the one that drove Dan'l Boone on westward from Missouri and "the last home I ever planned to have": because he heard the ring of an ax one morning, and knew that someone was settling within two miles of his cabin—an unbearable circumstance. For early or late, no true mover could abide life in a place where there was "no longer room to breathe."

The country had changed, and the frontier had changed, and even the people were changing as the West moved from its infancy into its adolescence. Now, halfway along in the process, life was still definitely homespun, though occasionally shot across with a yearning for something better. This was a queer combination that occasionally produced incongruous results that came in time to be considered typical of fringe country.

For instance, from New Albany, Indiana, came word from its *Daily Democrat* that a group of young gentlemen, appearing at a funeral in elegant swallowtail coats and moleskin hats, were abruptly involved in a free-for-all brawl that ended with a "lively and carelessly tossing about of the coffin because the bereft young widower was trying to bury his Catholic bride in a Protestant grave-yard." From Michigan came word that while movers there still considered it high sport to shoot forty to fifty rattlesnakes per day, there were now few among them who had not read Anderson's *Little Match Girl* and turned dewy-eyed when the waif froze to death while watching the stars fall, each one a soul going up to God.

Over in Ohio where whiskey flowed like water, and movers still staggered about the streets with the braggadocio air of not-so-very-darn-drunk-after-all, Peter Cartwright had abandoned this issue as a part of the nation's growing-up process, and was currently exhorting only against jewelry, gambling, cursing, pride, and fornication.

And out in windswept Illinois, a Chicago woman appeared at a concert so abundantly adorned that the local press called her "a walking jewelry store and a most valuable lady," because she was wearing nineteen rings, thirteen bracelets, a pair of earrings, a breast pin, and a fan fastened to her wrist by a gold chain. Yet in the entire state of Illinois, only one housewife out of five possessed a cookstove, while, less than thirty miles from the concert hall, the country folk still calculated the time of day by the number of hours it took to burn the "day log," a long sapling trunk, notched off in "hour lengths," gauged by the kind and thickness of the wood, that could be fed endwise into the fireplace.

Now, at long last, the first sharp edge of pioneering was a thing of the past, and the life of the mover was a little easier. Eli Whitney's cotton gin had made calico so cheap as to retire many a spinning wheel, and the sewing machine was coming into its own. Mr. Colt's automatic revolver was demanding open-mouthed respect. And for a dollar eighty-three, you could send word the breadth of the country about what things the Lord hath wrought, for the telegraph poles had again taken a firm stand over hill and dale, prairie and wilderness.

Now the minstrel show and the banjo possessed every town hall at some time during the winter, and the missioners' doleful "What dying worms are we" had given way to Susannah —when de buckwheat cake was in her mouf and de tear was in her eye. Dr. Townsend's Sarsaparilla, "wonder and blessing of the ages," was being freely swigged as a preventive for ague and the cholera. A dentist by the name of Bill Morton had removed a neck tumor through a three-and-a-half-inch buttonhole slit while the patient slept peacefully under an influence called anesthetic. And another influence, known as *Godey's Lady's Book,* had now put rustling bustles in a spot where homespun had hung limp and unmolested for so many years.

At long last the time had come when the farmer could laugh at the hardships of early pioneering, remembering how he used to tell the newcomers, "You'll get used to it—like an eel does to skinning!" He could laugh now because, at last, he had confidence in himself and in what he was doing. For when he looked about him he saw that it was good. For together with hundreds of thousands of others, who had also been bitten by the Western Fever, he had welded a nation from a pliable mass of sectionalism, ancestral differences, and diverse persuasions, into a forthright, courageous people with an energy hitherto unknown in any country.

Carolina Matilda Kirkland was thinking about all of these things as she lay on her three-by-six-foot space on a Detroit barroom floor, for which she had paid fifty cents for the night's lodging even though fifteen other sleepers already crowded it close.

It was a contagion that had seized them all—the Western Fever. More virulent than the Asiatic cholera or the milksick.

No one had yet been able to explain the power of it, although every mover had felt its pull.

Thoughtfully she turned her eyes to the dark windows between their bright folds of red calico. Black against the glass, the dense, endless forest pressed so close that its pine needles made a scratching sound against the panes when the wind blew. Even within this crowded room, you could feel its great solitude and the deepness of its stillness.

Caroline Matilda Kirkland was both thrilled and appalled by it. "To look into that deep woods and believe a town will soon be there is unbelievable," she thought, and turned her attention back to the warmth of the tavern, though still aware of the wolf-howl of the wind in the outer darkness.

In a dusky corner of the great room, near the fireplace, a carpenter worked quietly with hammer and saw and plane. He was fashioning a coffin by candlelight, for again the cholera ran rampant among them. She watched the yellow shavings fall away from his work. She watched the shadow of his massive figure move across the smoke-blackened rafters. She listened to the heavy breathing of her fifteen weary companions, and thought about the great freedom of this new life. Surely this was a far cry from the plush life that the *Emigrant's Guide* had led her to expect of this country, while she dog-eared its pages back in her sheltered Boston home. But now that she had come she knew that the Western Fever held her for keeps. For surely she would never be satisfied anywhere else on earth.

She listened to the crackle of the six-foot logs in the great fireplace as they fell to ashes. She inhaled the fragrance of pinewood smoke, and knew a deep contentment. The wilderness was in her blood. She believed in it as passionately as did the hundreds of others who were furthering the Big Push. Though they cut down every tree in the state of Michigan, she told herself, it would in no wise affect her. For the wilderness was abundantly in her blood.

The opening of the Canal Era had marked the real beginning of the Big Push, and now they had run to their end together, though not too soon for either of them, for the work of both was nearing completion. The canal had succeeded after the Cumberland Road had failed and before the railroad could arrive, because its coming had providentially coincided with that moment when a seaboard nation was ripe to spread out over a whole continent—a strip of time so narrow in years as to create a crisis. For the days were numbered wherein the young nation would be able to accomplish this before foreign forces could step in to take over.

While American canals in general may well have produced the greatest financial fiasco ever imposed upon this nation, they were also her savior, for they played an important role by providing the means by which she could fulfill her Manifest Destiny. And the supporting cast for this great drama of the old Northwest Territory included all of the people who produced the Big Push, a veritable product of the melting pot of many nations.

Their migration was great and of great momentum, because, from the bottom of their hearts, these people believed in pioneering—some even to the point of accepting it as a mission. "Go ye in and take possession of the land which the Lord swore unto your fathers."

This they had done. But at what a cost! It is well for us to remember. For a faith or a nation that forgets its roots in history loses its vision. And so must perish.

BIBLIOGRAPHY

PRIMARY SOURCES:

I—Manuscripts:

Ball, Engineer William J., "Report of 1843 on the Progress of the Wabash and Erie Canal." Indianapolis, 1843. Housed at the University of Michigan School of Engineering. Loose collection.

Blair, Engineer William, "Report on the Wabash and Erie Canal in the Lafayette District, 1843." Indianapolis, 1843. Housed at the University of Michigan School of Engineering. Loose collection.

Burr's Report of 1837, "Indiana's Internal Improvements." Indianapolis, 1843. Housed at the University of Michigan School of Engineering. Loose collection.

Congressional Globe, Records of the 25th Congress. Washington, D. C.

Cutler, William P. and Julia, "Life of Reverend Manasseh Cutler," vols. 1, 2. 1888. This collection contains the handwritten papers of Manasseh Cutler. Housed in Deering Library, Northwestern University.

Easton, Rufus, "Letters from Congressman Easton to Senator William Butler," *Niles Weekly Register.* Baltimore, 1816.

Emmeline Fairbanks Memorial Library Collection of loose pamphlets, clippings, handbills, scrapbooks, pertaining to early Indiana canal and river days. Terre Haute, Ind.

Gallatin, Albert, "Report on Roads, Canals, Harbors, and Rivers. . . ." Washington, D. C., 1808.

Knight, Jonathan, "Jonathan Knight's Plat Books of 1826-1827." 4 vols., handwritten. Housed in the Office of the Chief Engineers of the War Department, Washington, D. C. (Photostats at Indiana State Library, Indianapolis.)

"Laws of the State of New York, Relative to the Erie and Champlain Canal." Albany, 1825.

Paul, John Peter, "We Run the Canal Line." Fort Wayne, Ind., 1827. Housed at the University of Michigan School of Engineering. Loose collection of engineers' reports on early projects.

"Proceedings of the New York Convention for Rescuing the Canals from the Ruin with which they are Threatened by Exposing and Resisting the Railroad Conspiracy." New York, 1855.

"Public Documents Relating to New York Canals." Albany, 1820.

"Report on the Cumberland Road," *House Executive Documents*, 1826. Washington, D. C.

Wabash and Erie Canal, Documents Concerning. Collection at Defiance, Ohio.

Western Canal Company, "Proceedings of Special Canal Committee in 1834." Albany, N. Y., 1834.

Whitford, Noble Earl, "History of the Canal System of New York," United States Bureau of Statistics, vol. 2.

Williams, Engineer John, "The 1837 Report of the Progress of the Wabash and Erie Canal." Wabash, Ind. University of Michigan School of Engineering Collection.

II—*Books:*

Ackerman, William K., *Early Illinois Railroads*. Chicago, 1844.

Ashe, Thomas, *Travels in America in 1806*. London, 1808.

Baird, Robert, *View of the Valley of the Mississippi*." Philadelphia, 1834.

Barton, James, *Commerce on the Lakes in 1846*. Buffalo, 1847.

—————— *Northern and Western Lakes*, 1847. Buffalo, 1848.

Bernard, Karl, Duke of Saxe-Weimar-Eisenach, *Travels through America during the Years 1825 and 1826*, vols. 1, 2. Philadelphia, 1828.

Beste, J. Richard, *The Wabash: or Adventures of an Englishman's Family in the Interior of America*. 2 vols. London, 1855.

Birkbeck, Morris, *Letters from the Illinois—1818*. London, 1818.

—————— *Notes on a Journey in America from the Coast of Virginia to the Territory of Illinois*, 1817. London, 1818.

Bishop, Isabella Bird, *An Englishwoman in America*. London, 1856.

Bradford, Thomas Gamaliel, *A Comprehensive Atlas*. Boston, 1835.

Buck, Solon J., *Illinois in 1818*. Illinois Centennial Publications.

—————— *Travel and Description*, *1765 to 1865*. Springfield, 1914. Illinois Historical Collection, IX.

Butler, Frances Ann, *Journal*, edited by Fanny Kemble. London, 1835.

Buttrick, Tilly, Jr., *Voyages, Travels, and Discoveries of Tilly Buttrick*. Boston, 1831.

Chamberlain, E., *Indiana Gazetteer or Topographical Dictionary of the State of Indiana*. Indianapolis, 1850.

Chambers, John Sharp, M.D., *The Conquest of Cholera*. New York, 1838.

Chevalier, Michael, *Society, Manners, and Politics of the United States in 1839*. Boston, 1839.

Clapp, Asahel, M.D., *Diary of Asahel Clapp*. Philadelphia, 1852.

Cobbett, William, *A Year's Residence in the United States of America*. New York, 1818.

Colton, J. H., *Colton's Traveller and Tourist's Guide Book through the Northeast and Middle States*. New York, 1850.

———— *Sketches of the State of Indiana, accompanied by Colton's Maps.* New York, 1838.

———— *Colton's Guide through the States of Ohio, Michigan, Indiana, Illinois and Iowa.* New York, 1844

Corthell, E. L., *Canals and Railroads, Ship Canals and Ship Railroads.* New York, 1885.

Crevecoeur, St. John de, *Letters from an American Farmer.* London, 1782–1812. Twelve Letters.

Cuming, Fortescue, *Sketches of a Tour of the Western Country, a Voyage in 1810.* Pittsburgh, 1810.

Cummings, Samuel, *The Western Pilot containing Charts of the Ohio and Mississippi Rivers: a Gazetteer.* New York, 1839.

Dana, E., *Geographical Sketches on the Frontier Country, Designed for Emigrants and Settlers—1819.* New York, 1819.

Darby, William, *The Emigrants' Guide to the Western and Southwestern States and Territories.* New York, 1818.

———— *A Tour from the City of New York to Detroit in the Michigan Territory.* New York, 1819.

Darby and Dwight, *New Gazetteer of the United States.* Hartford, 1835.

Dickens, Charles, *American Notes.* London, 1842.

Disturnell, John, *Disturnell's Book: Railroad, Steamship, and Telegraph Guide.* New York, 1844.

———— *The Western Traveller's Guide through the State of New York, Canada, etc.* New York, 1836.

———— *The Western Traveller embracing Canal and Railroad Routes from Albany and Troy to Buffalo and Niagara Falls.* New York, 1844.

Drake, Daniel, M.D., *Principal Diseases of North America.* Cincinnati, 1850.

Eaton, N., *Five Years on the Erie Canal.* Utica, 1845.

Evans, Estwick, *A Pedestrious Tour of Four Thousand Miles through the Western States and Territories during the Winter and Spring of 1818.* Concord, N. H., 1819.

Faux, William, *Memorable Days in America, a Tour of the United States, 1818—1820.* London, 1823.

Finley, James Bradley, *Autobiography of an Ohio River Circuit Rider.* Cincinnati, 1853.

Flagg, Edmund, *The Far West, or a Tour Beyond the Mountains.* New York, 1838.

Flint, Timothy; *Geography and History of the Western States, or the Mississippi Valley,* vols. 1, 2. Cincinnati, 1828, 1832.

———— *Recollections of the Last Ten Years . . . in the Valley of the Mississippi.* Boston, 1826.

Flower, Richard, *Letters from Lexington and the Illinois: a Refutation of the Misrepresentations of Mr. Cobbett.* London, 1819.

Fowler, John, *Journal of a Tour in the State of New York in 1830*. London, 1831.

Greely, Horace, *Recollections of a Busy Life*. New York, 1868.

Gurney, Joseph, *A Journey in North America in 1841*. Published in New York for private circulation, 1841.

Haines, Glidden, *Considerations of the Great Western Canal from the Hudson to Lake Erie*. New York, 1818.

Haliburton, Thomas Chandler, *The American at Home: or Byeways, Backwoods, and Prairies*. London, 1854.

―――― *The Letter-bag of the Great Western Halifax*. Halifax, 1840.

Hall, Captain Basil, *Travels in North America in the years 1827 and 1828*, vols. 1, 2, 3. Philadelphia, 1829.

Hall, James, *The New Purchase*. Cincinnati, 1834.

―――― *The West: Its Commerce and Navigation*. Cincinnati, 1848.

Houston, Mrs. M. C. F., *Hesperos: or Travels in the West*. London, 1850.

Hulme, Thomas, *Journal of a Tour in the Western Countries of America, September 30, 1818 to August 8, 1819*. London, 1828.

Kingman, John, *Journal of a Tour in the West in 1838*. New York, 1839.

Kirkland, Caroline Matilda, *A New Home or Life in the Clearings, 1839*, edited by John Nerber. New York, 1953.

Langham, Moses, *Diary and Letterbook*. New York, 1842.

Latrobe, Charles Joseph, *The Rambler in America*, vols. 1. 2. New York, 1833.

Law, John, *A View of the Grand Canal from Lake Erie to the Hudson*. Albany, 1825.

McGuffey, William Homes, *McGuffey Eclectic Reader*, First through Fourth Grades. Cincinnati, 1848, 1857.

Marryat, Captain F. C. B., *A Diary in America*, vols. 1, 2, 3. London, 1839.

Martineau, Harriet, *Retrospect of Western Travel*, vols. 1, 2, 3. London, 1838.

Mitchell, Samuel Augustus, *Illinois in 1837*. Philadelphia, 1837.

―――― *Philadelphia in 1835*. Philadelphia, 1835.

―――― *Mitchell's Compendium of the Internal Improvements of the United States*. Philadelphia, 1835.

Monette, J. W., *History and Discovery and Settlement of the Valley of the Mississippi*, vols. 1, 2. New York, 1846.

Neville, Morgan, *The West, its Commerce and Navigation in 1829*. New York, 1834.

Oliver, William, *Eight Months in Illinois*. Newcastle-upon-Tyne, 1843.

Peck, John Mason, *Gazetteer of Illinois*. Philadelphia, 1834.

Peyton, John Lewis, *Over the Alleghenies and Across the Prairies*. London, 1870.

Poor, Henry, *History of Railroads and Canals of the United States of America*. New York, 1860.

Power, Tyrone, I., *Impressions of America during the Years of 1833, 1834, and 1835.* London, 1836.

Priest, Josiah, *American Antiquities and Discoveries of the West.* Albany, 1833.

Spafford, Horatio Gates, *A Pocket Guide for the Tourist and Traveller along the Line of Canals; and the Interior Commerce of the State of New York.* New York, 1824.

Sparks, Jared, *Life of Gouverneur Morris,* vol. 1. Boston, 1832.

Steele, Oliver G., *Steele's Western Guide Book and Emigrants' Directory,* vols. 1825—1849. Buffalo.

Stone, Colonel William Leete, *Holland Land Company and Canal Construction.* New York, 1819.

———— *Narratives of the Festivities in Honor of the Completion of the Grand Erie Canal.* New York, 1825.

Tanner, Henry S., *American Traveller, or Tourists' and Emigrants' Guide through the United States,* for 1839, 1844. Philadelphia.

———— *Canals.* Philadelphia, 1846.

————*Description of Canals and Railroads of the United States.* Philadelphia, 1840.

Trollope, Mrs. Frances, *Domestic Manners of the Americans in 1832.* London, 1836.

Turner, O., *Pioneer History of the Holland Purchase of Western New York.* Buffalo, 1850.

Vandewater, R. J., *The Tourist: or Pocket Manuel for Travellers on the Hudson River* for 1830, 1834, 1835, 1838. New York.

Watson, Elkanah, *History of the Western Canals in the State of New York.* Albany, 1820.

Welby, Adlard, *A Visit in North America and the English Settlements in Illinois in 1819.* London, 1821.

Woods, John, *Two Years' Residence in the Settlement on the English Prairie in the Illinois Country of the United States during 1818 and 1820.* London, 1822.

III—*Periodicals:*

Astronomical Calandar or Farmer's Almanack for Ithaca, intermingled with a few choice Tidbits. Ithaca, 1828.

Chillicothe Supporter for 1817, 1818. Chillicothe.

Cist's Weekly Advertiser for 1847, 1848. Cincinnati.

Cleveland Gazette for 1837. Cleveland.

Clinton, De Witt, "A Discourse Delivered before the New York Society of History," *Buffalo Historical Society Publications,* vol. 3. Buffalo.

Clinton, George W., "Journal of a Tour from Albany to Lake Erie in 1826," *Buffalo Historical Society Publications,* vol. 14. Buffalo.

Daily Democrat for 1849. New Albany, Ind.

Farmers' and Mechanics' Almanack for Cincinnati, 1856, 1857. New York.

Farmers' and Mechanics' Almanack for New York, for 1837. New York.

Free Labor Advocate and Anti-Slavery Chronicle for 1841. New Garden, Ind.

Gazetteer of the State of New York for 1824. New York.

Godey's Lady's Book for 1841. Philadelphia.

Haines, James, "Social Life and Scenes in the Early Settlement of Central Illinois before 1842," *Transactions of the Illinois State Historical Society,* 1905.

Hawley, Jesse and Merwin, "Origin of the Erie Canal." *Buffalo Historical Society, Publications,* vol. 2.

Hodge, William, "The William Hodge Papers," *Buffalo Historical Society Publications,* vol. 26. Buffalo, 1921.

"Holland Land Company and the Erie Canal." *Buffalo Harbor Papers, Buffalo Historical Society Publications,* vol. 14.

Hunt's Merchant Magazine, vol. 3. New York, 1840.

Illinois Monthly Magazine for 1830. Vandalia, Ill.

Indiana Journal, 1827–31. Bloomington, Ind.

Indiana State Sentinel for 1851. Terre Haute.

Lawrenceburg Palladium for 1840. Lawrenceburg, Ind.

Miami Herald for 1832. Hamilton, O.

New York Daily Advertiser for 1827. New York.

New York Enquirer for the Country for 1828. New York.

New York Evening Post for the Country for 1828. New York.

New York Spirit of the Times for 1847, 1850. New York.

Niles Weekly Register, 1811–48. Baltimore.

Oakland Gazette for 1844, 1845. Pontiac, Mich.

Ohio Republican for 1838. Columbus, O.

Ohio State Journal for 1833, 1837. Zanesville, O.

Parker, Benjamin, "Hesperian Tree," *Indiana Magazine of History*, 1907. Bloomington, Ind.

Phinney's Calendar or *Western Almanack, Calculated to Otsego* for 1830. New York.

Poole, Martha Fitch, "The Social Life of Buffalo in 1835," *Buffalo Historical Society Publications,* vol. 8.

Poughkeepsie Telegraph for 1839, 1840. Poughkeepsie, N. Y.

Public Leger for 1824. Richmond, Ind.

Salisbury, Guy, "The Speculative Craze of 1836," *Buffalo Historical Society Publications,* vol. 4.

Scioto Telegraph for 1820. Portsmouth, O.

Scott's Indiana Gazetteer (John Scott) for 1826. Bloomington, Ind.

Severance, Frank, "America: a Journal of a Tour in the United States." *Buffalo Historical Society Publications,* vol. 8.

Signal of Liberty for 1845. Ann Arbor, Mich.

"Some Elements of Indiana's Population: or Roads West and their Early Travellers." *Indiana Historical Society Publications,* vol. 4.

Spafford's Gazetteer for 1813. Albany.

Stone, Colonel William Leete, "From New York to Niagara, the Journal of a Journey in Part by the Erie Canal." Buffalo Historical Society Publications, vol. 14.

Stowe, Harriet Beecher, "The Canal Boat." *Godey's Lady's Book,* 1841. Philadelphia.

Temperance Advocate for 1834. (The first temperance paper issued in the West, included free with each copy of *The Plough Boy,* by John Osborne.) Greencastle, Ind.

United States Gazette for the Country for 1828. New York.

Wabash Enquirer for 1838–41. Terre Haute, Ind.

Western Emporium for 1825. Centreville, Ind.

"Epidemic Cholera," *Western Journal of Medical and Physical Sciences,* V. Cincinnati, 1832.

Western Monthly Review by Timothy Flint for 1827. Cincinnati.

Western Statesman for 1825–51. Marshall, Mich.

Western Travellers' Pocket Directory and Strangers' Guide for 1836. New York.

Zanesville Express for 1816. Zanesville, O.

SECONDARY SOURCES

I—*Manuscripts:*

Benton, Elbert J., "The Wabash Trade Route in the Development of the Old Northwest." *Johns Hopkins University Studies.* Baltimore, 1903.

"Maumee Valley through Fifty Years, 1763 to 1813," from documents prepared at the William Clements Library, University of Michigan, for the Maumee Valley International Historical Convention. Ann Arbor, Mich.

II—*Books:*

Alvord, Clarence, *The Illinois Country, 1673 to 1818.* Springfield, 1918–20.

Armstrong, Leroy, *The Wabash and Erie Canal.* Chicago, 1899.

Ball, Timothy Horton, *Northwestern Indiana, 1800 to 1900.* Chicago, 1900.

Beckwith, Hiram Williams, *History of Fountain County, Indiana.* Chicago, 1881.

———— *History of Montgomery County, Indiana.* Chicago, 1881.

Bradsby, Henry C., *History of Vigo County—Indiana*. Chicago, 1891.

Brigham, Albert Perry, *From Trail to Railway through the Appalachians.* Boston, 1907.

Buley, Roscoe Carlyle, *The Old Northwest, 1815–1840,"* vols. 1, 2. Bloomington, Ind., 1951.

De Voto, Bernard, *Across the Wide Missouri*. Cambridge, Mass. 1947.

―――― *The Course of Empire*. Boston, 1952.

―――― *The Year of Decision*. Boston, 1943.

Dillon, John B., *History of Indiana*. Indianapolis, 1859.

Dunbar, Seymour, *A History of Travel in America,"* vol. 3. Indianapolis, 1915.

Edgar, John F., *Frontier Life in Dayton, 1796–1840*. Dayton, O., 1896.

Esarey, Logan, *A History of Indiana*, vols. 1, 2. Fort Wayne, 1924.

―――― *History of Indiana from Exploration to 1850*. Indianapolis, 1915.

Ford, Henry A. and Kate B., *History of Cincinnati*. Cleveland, 1881.

Geddes, G., *Origin and History of the Measures that Led to the Construction of the Erie Canal*. Syracuse, 1866.

Greene, Nelson, *History of the Mohawk Valley*. Chicago, 1930.

―――― *The Old Mohawk Turnpike Book*. New York, 1924.

Griswold, Bert Joseph, *Fort Wayne, Gateway of the West, 1802 to 1813.* Indianapolis, 1927. (Historical Bureau of the Indiana Library and Historical Department.)

―――― *Picture History of Fort Wayne*. Chicago, 1917.

Harlow, Alvin Fay, *Old Towpaths*. New York and London, 1926.

―――― *The Road of the Century*. New York, 1947.

Hart, Val, *Story of American Roads*. New York, 1950.

Hulbert, Archer Butler, *Frontiers*. Boston, 1929.

―――― *Great American Canals*. Cleveland, 1904.

―――― *Cumberland Road*. Columbus, 1901.

―――― *Pilots of the Republic*. Chicago, 1906.

(All are from the *Historic Highways of America* series.)

Jordan, Philip D., *The National Road*. Indianapolis and New York, 1948.

Lee, Alfred, *History of the City of Columbus, Capital of Ohio*. New York, 1892.

Minnich, Harvey C., *William Holmes McGuffey and his Readers*. New York, 1936.

Paxson, Frederic Logan, *Paxson's Encyclopaedia, 1763–1893.*

―――― *History of American Frontiers*. Boston, 1924.

Pickard, Madge E., and Buley, R. Carlyle, *Midwest Pioneer, his Ills, Cures, and Doctors*. Crawfordsville, Ind., 1945.

Rawlings, Dr. Isaac D., *The Rise and Fall of Disease in Illinois*. Springfield, Ill., 1927.

Sandburg, Carl, *American Songbag*. New York, 1927.

Sparks, Edwin Earle, *English Settlements in the Illinois*. Cedar Rapids, Iowa, 1907.

Stuart, B. F., *History of the Wabash and Valley*. Delphi, Ind., 1925.

Sweet, William Warren, *Circuit-rider Days Along the Ohio*. New York and Cincinnati, 1923.

—— *Religion on the American Frontier*. Chicago, 1939.

Thwaites, Reuben Gold, *Early Western Travels, 1748–1846*, vols. 8, 10, 11, 12. Cleveland, 1905.

Weise, A. J., *History of Troy, New York*. Troy, N. Y. 1876.

Winsor, Justin, *Narrative Critical History in America*, vols. 4, 7. Boston, 1888.

Wright, Louis B., *Culture on the Moving Frontier*. Bloomington, Ind., 1955.

III—*Periodicals*:

Allen, Lewis, "The Cholera in Buffalo in 1832," *Buffalo Historical Society Publications*, vol. 4. Buffalo, 1896.

Beach, Richard H., "A Letter from Illinois, 1836." *Journal of the Illinois State Historical Society*, vol. 3. Springfield, 1910.

Comstock, Howard Payne, "History of Canals in Indiana," *Indiana Magazine of History*. Indianapolis, 1911.

Cottman, George S., "The Wabash and Erie Canal." *Indiana Magazine of History*, vol. 3. Indianapolis.

Esarey, Logan, "Early Indiana." *Indiana Historical Society Publications*, vol. 5. Indianapolis, 1912.

Grubb, Gerald G., "Dickens' Western Tour and the Cairo Legend," *Studies in Philology*, XLVIII, 1, January, 1951.

Hill, Henry Wayland, "Historical Review of Waterways and Canal Construction in New York State," *Buffalo Historical Society Publications*, vol. 12.

Hollister, F. N., "Some Early Buffalo Characters." *Buffalo Historical Society Publications*, vol. 17.

Huntington, C. C., "Ohio Canals." *State of Ohio's Archaeological and Historic Society Collection*. Columbus, 1905.

Indiana Magazine of History, 1907–34. Bloomington, Ind.

Indiana Quarterly Magazine of History, vol. 9 Bloomington, Ind., 1913.

Lansden, John M., "Cairo in 1841," *Journal of the Illinois State Historical Society*, vol. 5. Danville, Ill., 1912.

Leamon, Bertha Ruth, "Travel Notes on a 19th Century Frenchman," *Ohio State Archaeological and Historical Quarterly*, vol. 51. Columbus, 1942.

Mathews, Lois Kimball, "The Erie Canal and the Settlement of the West," *Buffalo Historical Society Publications*, vol. 14.

Ragan, W. H., "Indianapolis in 1843, a Henry Ward Beecher Letter." *Indiana Magazine of History*, vol. 3. 1908.

"Scenes and Songs of the Ohio–Erie Canal." *Ohio State Archaeological and Historical Society Collection*. Columbus, 1952.

ACKNOWLEDGMENTS

Any writer of history must inevitably find himself indebted to countless people. During the decade in which I have worked on this book, striving to capture the bigness and importance and color of the great Western migration in America, my research and study have been abundantly enriched by the many persons who have gone out of their way to provide me with information concerning this period.

This throng must include the hundreds of previous writers to whom I am indebted, many of whom are listed in my bibliography. Next it must include those armies of dedicated librarians who direct our public libraries, university libraries, and State Historical Societies. In the third place it must include the thinning ranks of senior citizens who know the past for what it was because they have lived through it, who are always eager to go the second mile, and beyond, in furnishing materials and information concerning the old days.

I am most deeply indebted to the fabulous Deering Library of Northwestern University without whose generosity this book could hardly have been written. There I was allowed to roam the stacks freely for three full years, and bring home such armfuls of books as I needed. I was further allowed the privilege of using hand-written documents so valuable that I had to be locked in the vault while using them. The facilities for study at Northwestern's Technological Library were also open to me. My deep gratitude goes to Librarians Mary Hilton, Alan R. Krull, and Mary Buckmaster. I am indebted to Librarians John P. MacGowan and Marjorie Carpenter for aid in obtaining photostats of certain old prints.

My second greatest indebtedness must go to the Illinois Historical Library and the Illinois State Library at Springfield, where I worked daily for a full year, and to Librarians Margaret Flint, Katherine Lindeman, and Mary Moyer.

Other Illinois libraries to which I am especially grateful are the four in Chicago—Newberry, Crerar, Chicago Public Library, and the Chicago Historical Library; the Rare Book Section of the University of Illinois Library at Champaign-Urbana; the W. L. Goble Library of Elgin; and, at the Gail Borden Public Library, to Librarian Ida Wilson, her aids, Mildred Lathrop and Ann Carlson, and staff.

In Indiana, I am indebted to Elfrieda Lang and Geneva Warner of Indiana University Libraries at Bloomington, to Caroline Dunn of the Indiana Historic Society at Indianapolis, and to the public library at New Albany and its files of early newspapers. In Ohio, I am grateful to the various branches of the Ohio State Archaeological and Historic Society, and the State Libraries at Columbus. I am particularly indebted to Mrs. Frank Peirano of the Ohioana Library. In Michigan, at Ann Arbor, I am beholden to the fabulous William Clemens Library, and to my brother Professor Walter C. Sadler, for the use of numerous valuable documents in the School of Engineering Collection. In Wisconsin, I am grateful to the staffs of the Wisconsin State Library, the State Historical Society of Wisconsin, the University of Wisconsin Library, and the Madison Public Library.

East of the Alleghenies, I am indebted to Frederick R. Goff, Chief of the Rare Books Division of the Library of Congress, Washington, D. C., for his ready answers to remote questions. And to all who are responsible for the pure gold ore to be found in such collections as the Buffalo Historical Society Publications or the Rochester Historical Society Publications, a special tribute is due.

I wish to thank abundantly, but with all humility for the time they have devoted to this task, the many people, most of whom I have never met, who helped me obtain prints for the illustrations. In addition to the prints being used through courtesy of The Bettman Archives and the New York Public Library, the following persons have either contributed from their own files or lead me to other sources: Leonard U. Hill, Piqua, Ohio; R. Max Gard and William H. Vodrey, Jr., Lisbon, Ohio; Eugene F. Kramer, University of the State of New York, Albany; P. W. Galleher of the A. H. Clark Publishing Co., Glendale, Calif.; Mary Frances Rhymer and Sybil H. Headland, Chicago Historic Society; K. B. Disher, Commercial Museum Trade and Convention Center, Philadelphia; Rose Daly, Harper's Magazine; Lee W. Blackburn, Dept. of Public Works, State of Columbus, Ohio; Stillman K. Taylor, Emeline Fairbanks Memorial Library, Terre Haute, Ind.; Charles Truax, National Cash Register Company, Dayton, Ohio; John M. Adams, Lehigh Coal and Navigation Company, Bethlehem, Pennsylvania; Robert John Koch of New York City and A. D. Bradbury of Marshall Field and Company's *Field Flyer,* Chicago; Milton C. Russell, Virginia State Library, Richmond, Virginia; Mrs. William Gurdian, Indiana Historical Library, Indianapolis; Mrs. Hazel Hopper, Indiana State Library, Indianapolis; Frances L. Goudy, Ohio Historical Society, Columbus; Walter Rumsey Marvin, Ohioana Library Association, Columbus; Richard Lawwill, Ohio State Historical Society, Columbus.

My deepest appreciation goes to a certain three, of all the persons interviewed along the various canals. The first was Mr. W. C. Fox of Riley, Indiana, whose forefathers donated land for the old Wabash and Erie Canal. Deep in an overgrown woods he searched out the crumbling, wooden gates of a forgotten canal-lock, for me to see. In Covington, Indiana, Mr. John Franklin, past ninety, recalled the old days for my benefit. In Joliet, Illinois, Mr. Ross Marshall, having lived out much of his life near the old Illinois and Michigan Canal, forced his car through long miles of overgrown, tree-lashed towpath, that I might see what the old trail had been like.

In conclusion I wish to do homage to a final three who have left their mark upon the book. To Professor Charles L. Peterson of Concord College, West Virginia, for his generous, talented, map-making pen. To Oliver Jensen of New York City for his valuable suggestions and encouragement. And to Lois Dwight Cole of G. P. Putnam's for her editorial guidance, kindness, and infinite patience.

MADELINE SADLER WAGGONER

Elgin, Illinois

INDEX

Law and Social Change in Zinacantan

JANE FISHBURNE COLLIER

Law and Social Change in Zinacantan

Stanford University Press, Stanford, California

1973

Stanford University Press
Stanford, California
© 1973 by the Board of Trustees of the
Leland Stanford Junior University
Printed in the United States of America
ISBN 0-8047-0821-5
LC 72-91678

To my parents

Preface

This study, like so many other first books, grew out of a doctoral dissertation, but it also represents several years of research and thinking. I began to collect records of Zinacanteco legal cases during the spring of 1963, and last visited the field in the summer of 1970 to study Mexican courts. During this time, my conception of "law" in general, and of Zinacanteco law in particular, underwent radical transformation. Having begun my research with the idea that law was a body of rules enforced by men with authority, I ended with the view adopted in this book: that law is a language used by individuals to interpret and manipulate their social environment. I also began my study with the idea that Zinacantan was a relatively autonomous, homogeneous community, preserving customs derived from its Maya past, but ended with a perception of Zinacantan as a particularly visible social field within a system of nested fields where seemingly traditional customs mark a realistic and ongoing adaptation to modern economic, political, and social conditions.

The evolution of my thinking can be traced through the series of working papers written to summarize portions of the collected data. My first summary of Zinacanteco law, put together in 1964, listed the duties of the civil officials and tried to show how different "types" of cases—theft, adultery, owning a talking saint, inflicting physical injury, murder, etc.—were handled at the town hall court. The aim of the paper was to discover the "laws" of Zinacantan: those rules whose violation led to sanctions imposed by men in

authority. But after spending a full year in the field, June 1966 to September 1967, and collecting data on Zinacanteco legal concepts and witchcraft beliefs, I realized that I would have to reconsider my theoretical framework. Zinacantecos were not concerned with crime and punishment. They cared about ending conflicts, to forestall supernatural vengeance. I finally understood why civil officials looked puzzled and gave inconsistent answers when asked "What do you do when someone commits . . . (type of crime)?" They didn't *do* anything. Their job was to wait for a plaintiff to state his wishes and then try to suggest a compromise solution acceptable to both sides.

Most anthropologists do fieldwork after completing graduate courses, taking exams, and writing detailed dissertation proposals, but I followed a reverse procedure. Most of my fieldwork was completed before I entered Tulane Graduate School in the fall of 1967. As a result, I had my own field data to use in evaluating the explanatory power of particular theoretical approaches. Not surprisingly, I found that studies of international law (Barkun 1968) or politics (Barth 1957, Swartz, Turner, and Tuden 1966) provided more insights into Zinacanteco processes of conflict management than did studies of African legal systems. My dissertation reflects this change of theoretical focus. It looks at Zinacanteco law "from the bottom up," explaining both legal procedures and outcomes in terms of choices made by litigants.

My dissertation focused on the static aspects of Zinacanteco law, conveying a sense of timelessness and stability. But the "bottom up" approach led me to think about legal change in terms of changes in litigants' choice of court. A two-year postdoctoral fellowship from the National Science Foundation allowed me to pursue this interest, and some of my findings have been incorporated in this book. I wrote an entirely new conclusion to my dissertation, reworked the introduction, added Chapter 2 on the organization of legal levels, split the witchcraft chapter into two parts, and added sections on change to each of the last seven chapters.

In reviewing the years I have spent working on Zinacanteco law, I find that I am indebted to many people: to my professors for guidance, to my colleagues and friends for ideas and criticism, to

various agencies for providing research funds, and to the Zinacan-tecos who told me of the cases that are the subject of this book.

I can never fully express my gratitude to Professor Evon Z. Vogt, who introduced me to Zinacantan in 1960 and who accepted me as a member of the Harvard Chiapas Project in the following years. Much of the research presented here was carried out under his direction and financed by Project funds. Working as a member of such a long-term project had many advantages. Not only was I able to profit from the work and insights of other researchers, but I was able to submit my own work to their informed criticism. Among those Chiapas Project members to whom I am most indebted for criticism, suggestions, and moral support are Victoria Bricker, B. N. and Lore Colby, Carol Greenhouse, John and Leslie Havi-land, Robert and Miriam Laughlin, Duane Metzger, Francesco Pellizzi, Renato Rosaldo, Daniel Silver, and Catherine Vogt.

I owe a particular debt of gratitude to Frank Cancian, whose photographs illustrate this book, and to Francesca Cancian, whose collected statements on Zinacanteco norms proved invaluable in my study of witchcraft beliefs. During my two years of postdoc-toral study, I profited from the guidance of James L. Gibbs, Jr., and from long discussions with Michelle Z. Rosaldo on the role of language in behavior. My husband, George A. Collier, provided helpful criticism and enduring moral support through the long years of research and writing.

This book owes a very special debt to Professor Munro S. Ed-monson, my dissertation adviser, whose provocative eloquence stimulated my thought and left me with a profound respect for the Maya and their civilization.

I would also like to acknowledge the following sources of funds that supported various stages of the field research and analysis: National Institute of Mental Health of the United States Public Health Service grant MH-2100, National Institute of Mental Health Predoctoral Research Fellowship 1-F1-MH-35,444, a National Sci-ence Foundation Graduate Fellowship, and a National Science Foundation Postdoctoral Fellowship.

Last, but certainly not least, I want to thank the many Zinacan-tecos who let me into their homes and answered my often naïve questions. Special thanks are due to José Hernández Pérez, Do-

mingo de la Torre Pérez, José and Guillermo Pérez Nuh, Pedro Pérez Condios, Juan de la Krus ʔAkov, and Antonio López Pérez, who collectively provided most of the case materials. Finally, I want to apologize to the Zinacantecos for the picture that I have presented of them. Although any study of conflict must focus on the evil that men do, often leaving the good unrecorded, I hope that this book also shows how effectively Zinacantecos handle the inevitable quarrels that arise in social life.

J.F.C.

Contents

Eight pages of photographs follow p. 118

Law and Social Change in
Zinacantan

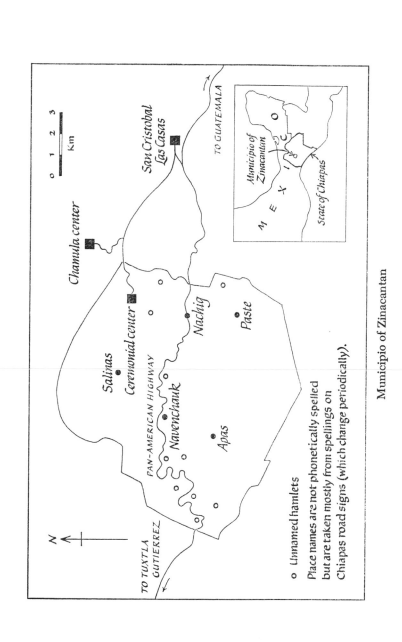

N

TO TUXTLA
GUTIERREZ

Chamula center

Salinas

Ceremonial center

PAN-AMERICAN HIGHWAY

Navenchauk

Apas

Nachig

Paste

San Cristobal
Las Casas

TO GUATEMALA

0 1 2 3
Km

Municipio of
Zinacantan

M E X I C O

State of Chiapas

o   Unnamed hamlets

Place names are not phonetically spelled
but are taken mostly from spellings on
Chiapas road signs (which change periodically).

Municipio of Zinacantan

Introduction

This book is a study of conflict management in a modern Maya community in the highlands of Chiapas, Mexico. It looks at the different ways in which the Tzotzil-speaking Indians of Zinacantan perceive, conduct, and resolve conflicts, and at the broad patterns of social action that are created by the sum of individual decisions on how to fight or to make peace with an opponent. The focus is on the individual and his options. What acts are recognized as crimes? What choices does the victim of a wrong have in seeking revenge or restitution? What recourse does an accused have? And how do the men who act as mediators work to resolve conflicts? Although its focus is on a specific community in an isolated part of Mexico, and although it takes the form of a detailed ethnographic description, this study is intended to shed light on the processes of conflict management everywhere.

I have used the word Law in the title despite the fact that common definitions of law might require an orientation toward "rules or modes of conduct made obligatory by some sanction which is imposed and enforced for their violation by a controlling authority."* But such definitions are too rigid for my purposes. They stress the certainty and power of the law, implying that rule violations are unmistakable and are inevitably followed by retribution, whereas I wish to stress the uncertainty of the law and the fallibility of the individuals who manipulate it. I am interested in

* *Webster's New International Dictionary*, 2d ed.

the gap between the violation and its sanction, in the multitude of decisions that must be made by living people between the time an act that may be considered a crime is committed and the time punishment is imposed or a settlement is reached. All along the route people face many choices that render individual outcomes uncertain but that create coherent patterns when seen in the larger context of many cases.

The definition of law that I have used is the one proposed by Barkun, who sees law as a language for conducting and resolving conflicts. Barkun's definition (1968: 92, 151) states that (1) "law is that system of manipulable symbols that functions as a representation, as a model, of social structure," (2) "legal symbols have some empirical referents," and (3) "law as a symbol system is a means of conceptualizing and managing the social environment." Barkun's definition is valuable for its separation of "the symbolic manifestations of law" from "the behavioral referents of law" (Moore 1970: 277), an important distinction because verbal categories for describing behavior can exhibit an ordered structure that is not an accurate reflection of the disordered events of the real world (Leach 1964: xiii). Separating the two allows room for inquiry into the relationship between them. One can ask how sequences of action are given the labels of legal language and how the fact of being labeled affects future behavior. As Moore notes (1970: 276), Barkun's definition leads the description of a legal system in full circle "from social relationships to ideas about social relationships and back again to empirical referents and management."

I have found Barkun's definition particularly useful because it allows for a discussion of change. His separation of law as a language from empirically observed behavior allows room for exploring the ways in which either can change without altering the other. New behaviors can be justified in terms of old categories, giving the legal system a timeless and static quality, or legal categories can change without affecting the behavior of most individuals. At the same time, Barkun's definition allows for a discussion of the ways in which changed behaviors have affected legal categories and vice versa. Important social changes can introduce new problems, leading to the creation of new rules; and

the introduction of new rules can open opportunities for litigation and for behavior that did not exist before.

And, finally, Barkun's definition is particularly appropriate for a description of Zinacanteco law because it mirrors the way in which Zinacantecos talk. When asked to tell about past trouble cases Zinacanteco informants supply a great deal of background information, discuss the motives of the participants, and imply that outcomes are due to the particular circumstances of the particular case. Outcomes seem to follow from the actions and desires of the litigants and not from the nature of the violation. Zinacantecos do not talk about crime and punishment but about quarrels and compromises. Although it would be possible to describe Zinacanteco trouble cases in terms of the violation of social rules and their just retribution—once the "crime" has been labeled and the relationship between the parties is known, the range of probable outcomes is quite small—such an exercise would distort the data by emphasizing facts that Zinacantecos consider irrelevant, and would ignore information that Zinacantecos consider of crucial importance. It is therefore easier to take the Zinacantecos at their word, to emphasize the ways in which individuals manipulate norms rather than the content of the norms, and to justify such an approach by appealing to Barkun's definition of law and to Barth's argument that ethnographers should seek explanations for cultural patterns by looking beyond moral injunctions to the wider set of constraints and incentives that channel individual choices (Barth 1966).

The Setting

Zinacantan, a township in the state of Chiapas, Mexico, is the home of approximately 9,000 Tzotzil-speaking Indians. The visitor from the north must reach the community by traveling through the state capital, Tuxtla Gutierrez, for Zinacantan straddles the Pan-American Highway between that city and the old capital of San Cristobal Las Casas. Tuxtla is a consciously modern city that has long been the home of the state's liberal politicians. It lies in the hot Grijalva valley and is the commercial center of that rich region. San Cristobal, by contrast, is a highland city. It is the home of the conservatives and is surrounded by Indian communities.

After leaving Tuxtla, the Pan-American Highway crosses the Grijalva River, runs through the old town of Chiapa de Corzo, and begins to climb the escarpment into the Chiapas highlands. At about 5,000 feet the *municipio* of Zinacantan begins. The motorist passes through the cornfields and scattered houses of the region known to Zinacantecos as *čobtik*, "the cornfields," better translated as "the sticks." Indians who live in the higher parts of the township look down on the hicks of the lower region, but envy them their better farming land.

The road continues to climb until it reaches Navenchauk, a densely settled valley at 8,000 feet with a lake in the bottom. A small plaza, with a miniature church and town hall, lies at the lake's edge, and the sides of the bowl-shaped valley are dotted with the houses of the 1,200 inhabitants. Leaving Navenchauc, the road winds around the side of the mountains and enters the valley of Nachig. Most motorists speed up to take advantage of the stretch of straight highway and gain only a blurred impression of tiny houses set back from the road in their cornfields. Climbing out of Nachig, the motorist leaves Zinacantan and, after winding around the southern flank of Huitepec volcano, drops down into the valley of San Cristobal.

The city of San Cristobal is traditionally known as the home of conservative politicians and a strong Catholic church. Its narrow central streets are lined with the little stores that cater to the Indians of the surrounding hinterland with their small purchases. There are candle shops and skyrocket makers to provide the materials for Indian rituals, and drugstores and drygoods stores to sell the necessities of everyday life. The market is full of activity each morning as Indians gather to sell their produce and buy the meat and hot-country fruits sold by Ladino* vendors. The market is a traditional tourist attraction because of the many Indian costumes to be seen. Each Indian township has a distinctive dress, making a crowd of Indians a colorful sight.

From San Cristobal a dirt road leads to the ceremonial center of Zinacantan over the north flank of Huitepec volcano. Coming down into the valley, the road passes the open fields of a ranch

---

* Ladino is a term used in the region to refer to persons who speak Spanish as a primary language.

before reaching the heavily populated Indian section of the valley. The ceremonial center, called Hteklum by the Indians, has a central dirt street with the large church of the patron saint, San Lorenzo, on one side and the *cabildo*, or town hall, on the other. A second, smaller church, San Sebastian, is located in an open field to the north. Hteklum, although predominantly Indian, has a few Ladino residents, who own most of the little stores and bars that line the main road across from the church of San Lorenzo and to the east of the town hall. The town center is laid out with streets in the traditional Spanish grid pattern, but the Indian houses are spaced somewhat haphazardly on the lots, and the grid pattern breaks down altogether about four blocks out from the center.

The town hall is a long adobe building with a covered porch supported by columns. The dark inner rooms house the town records and the desks of the Ladino secretary and the Indian municipal president. But most of the important activities take place outside on the porch, where the *Presidente* and the other Indian officials conduct business from their traditional places on the benches that line the inner wall. The porch is the official town court, and litigants engaged in a dispute argue their cases as they stand before the Presidente or lean against the columns, and bystanders and litigants awaiting their turn lounge on the unused benches. The setting is completely public, and anyone who wanders by can stop to listen. In front of the town hall, the main road widens into a small plaza. This is the area where public meetings are held when it is time to "elect" officials, or where unofficial crowds gather to hear a particularly exciting case.

Twice a year, in mid-January and early August, the ceremonial center is crowded with Indians who come to watch the two major *fiestas*. They come from all the outlying hamlets, dressed in new clothes, to drink together and watch the ritual. At these times the town hall is very active, with as many as five cases being heard at once, because people take the opportunity to bring up old disputes and fiesta drunkenness causes new fights among former friends.

Between the two major festivals, the ceremonial center is usually quiet. The smaller rituals that placate the community gods are carried out by the men in religious offices, *cargo* holders, who have moved to Hteklum for their year of service, while the town

hall probably averages only one court case a day. But because Sunday is the preferred day to bring up a dispute, several week-days may pass without the appearance of a single litigant.

Most of the Zinacantecos live in small, scattered houses sur-rounded by cornfields. For administrative purposes the township is divided into territorial units, or hamlets, which range in size from approximately 600 to 1,200 people. Some of the hamlets have a nucleus of dense population, whereas in others the houses are widely separated. Each hamlet has two minor officials, called *prin-cipales*, who act as messengers between the hamlet and the town hall, and a committee to handle the affairs of the local school or schools. Matters that concern an entire hamlet, such as the appoint-ment of principales or school committee members, are handled at meetings attended by all the men, but behind the scenes, hamlet politics are more variable. Some hamlets are run by a single strong man, others are controlled by several leaders who cooperate, and still others are split into bickering factions.

Zinacantecos are ideally patrilineal and patrilocal. Sons try to settle near their fathers but, given the haphazard nature of birth and death and the finite amount of land, the actual picture is one of local descent groups in the process of forming or disintegrating (G. Collier 1968). Zinacanteco houses are relatively easy to move, and through time the population shifts slowly over the landscape.

The smallest social unit is the domestic group: a nuclear or ex-tended family living in one or more houses around a common cleared area and sharing a single house cross. This wooden cross, typically three feet high, stands at one edge of the cleared area and is decorated with pine boughs and flowers for family rituals and major fiestas. The next larger social unit is the *sna* (Vogt 1969: 128), composed of two or more related domestic groups. These units can be seen as localized patrilineages, though they often in-clude men from other lineages who have married women from the dominant group. In densely settled hamlets only rich and powerful men can create such localized descent groups, but in more sparsely settled areas they evolve naturally from the patrilocal extended family. The largest social unit within the hamlet is the waterhole group, which is composed of the households that draw their water from a common source. There are few rivers in the limestone high-

lands, and Zinacantecos must depend on natural wells. All permanent waterholes are thus ritually important and are the focus of major ceremonies at least twice a year.

Individuals in Zinacantan appear to be closely tied to a single area. Few people move from one hamlet to another, and marriage partners are usually found among neighbors. Zinacanteco women know few people beyond their own kin and close neighbors, but men have opportunities to form a wider circle of acquaintances. Young boys, like the women, know few people, but as they grow older and serve in the religious hierarchy, they meet officeholders from other hamlets, and a politically active man can participate with other hamlet leaders in making community-wide decisions.

The only paved road in Zinacantan is the Pan-American Highway, which was built without consideration of Zinacanteco desires or communication needs. It has had a tremendous effect, of course, but primarily in the direction of allowing Zinacantecos easier access to the outside world rather than bringing outsiders, except anthropologists, into Zinacantan. From the point of view of this study, the highway is important because it has made the town hall more accessible to potential litigants from Čobtik and Navenchauk. They can now take a bus or truck to Nachig and hike over the ridge to the ceremonial center instead of walking for several hours. The most important communication routes within the community, however, are the trails, which form a network of major and minor paths linking every group of houses and the principal farming areas.

When traveling on the trails, Zinacantecos observe a definite etiquette. Mixed groups are led by the senior man, with the younger men in order by age behind him, and the women, also in descending order, bring up the rear. When two groups meet, the one led by the junior person stands aside to let the other group pass. Women in general, and particularly young girls, are supposed to step slightly off the path and keep their faces averted when being passed by men. Zinacantecos regard trails as dangerous places, frequented by drunks, strangers, and possibly demons. The ordinary person who must face these hazards meets them by observing the rules of trail etiquette.

When approaching a Zinacanteco house, the visitor must stand

in the cleared area outside and call to the woman within. She can easily hear because the houses are usually single-room structures of wattle and daub or adobe with a thatch or tile roof. If the woman answers, the visitor can either ask if the man of the house is at home or state his business. In many conversations, the visitor and the woman may never see each other, but if the visitor decides to wait, the woman may bring him a chair so that he can sit down in the cleared area outside. A visitor never enters a house until he is invited to do so.

The one room of a Zinacanteco house is conceptually divided into a women's area and a men's area. The women of the house sit on mats near the cooking table on one side of the fire, and the men occupy the opposite side of the open hearth and sit on tiny chairs. Visitors, both male and female, stay in the men's area. Because the corners are filled with family belongings and plank beds, there is little open space and the addition of a few people can make a small house very crowded. Most Zinacanteco houses are occupied by a single nuclear family, but there are many cases of a married son living with his father or an aged parent dependent on a child. Apart from these households, which occur normally in the domestic-group cycle, there are always households of unusual composition brought about by special circumstances.

Zinacanteco men are primarily corn farmers, and although each man has a small plot near his house, most of the corn is grown on rented fields in the more productive Grijalva valley. During the summer months, the men leave home for weeks at a time to weed their lowland fields. Women do not help with the farming, but do the household chores—cooking, washing, hauling water and wood —and care for the domesticated animals, the chickens and pigs. Several women own sheep, which produce wool, and every woman is supposed to know how to weave the family's clothes. Marriage is regarded as essential for every adult because men and women perform complementary economic roles. Men are needed to produce food, and the women turn the raw corn into cooked *tortillas*. But because the men tend to die younger, every hamlet includes a few single older women who support themselves by weaving or cooking for others.

Although Zinacantecos believe in several supernatural beings,

the principal deities are the Earth Lord, the Ancestral Gods, and the Catholic Saints. The Earth Lord controls the underworld and can be contacted through openings in the earth—caves, overhanging cliffs, and waterholes. The Ancestral Gods live inside specific mountains. The most important live inside the mountains that ring the ceremonial center and can be contacted through the crosses at the bottoms and tops of their mountain homes. The Catholic Saints, as expected, live in the churches. For some reason, the Sun, another major deity, has been confused with God the Father and has become more like a celestial saint than the earth-bound Maya deities. All of these gods are ambivalent in their treatment of men: although they provide health, wealth, and a bountiful world, they also send sickness and death.

The Earth Lord is pictured as a fat Ladino, wearing a wide-brimmed hat, who likes to acquire the souls of people and animals to work his underground estates. He is a particularly ambivalent god, for, although a clever man can induce him to part with some of his immense wealth, an ordinary mortal who falls into his clutches can die and spend a large share of his afterlife as a peon underground. The Earth Lord also controls water resources, and although he provides waterholes for people and gentle rain for the corn, he can cause droughts and send wind and hail to destroy the crops. The Ancestral Gods and the Catholic Saints are less self-centered than the Earth Lord. They take care of man and keep the world going, but they also send sickness and death to punish mortals who anger them by doing wrong.

There are two kinds of religious practitioners in Zinacantan, cargo holders in the religious hierarchy and shamans. The cargo holders care for the saints in the churches and perform the rituals for Catholic calendrical fiestas. They serve only a year at time, beginning with a position on the lowest of the four levels, and then wait a few years before serving another term at the next level (Cancian 1965). Wealthy men who have served on all four levels become honored elders, and are exempt from further community service. Shamans serve for life after making their debuts. In addition to officiating at curing ceremonies for individual patients, they handle all contact with the Maya deities—the Earth Lord and the Ancestral Gods.

To keep the Zinacanteco world going, certain ceremonies must be performed, and the visible sign of political cohesion is cooperation in staging a ritual. At the lowest level, persons who share a house cross affirm that they are still one household, though they may live in separate structures. On the next level are the local ancestral shrines and waterholes, which must be ritually visited at calendrical ceremonies. These rituals, performed by shamans, can be sponsored by a single descent group (which may be as small as one politically isolated family), by a set of descent groups who share a waterhole, or by an entire hamlet, depending on the size of the politically cohesive group. Descent-group fission and hamlet factionalism are clearly expressed when formerly cohesive groups conduct separate rituals. On the highest level are the ceremonies sponsored by the township. At the present time, there are no rituals that cross municipal lines, but the ceremonies held during the Tzotzil rebellion of the last century may have symbolized a larger political grouping.

Conflicts in Zinacantan are usually complex affairs because of the tightly knit web of relations that exists in small communities. Most Zinacantecos spend their lives in a single hamlet surrounded by neighbors and kinsmen they have known from childhood, and when a conflict arises it is usually seen in long-term perspective rather than as the product of a single isolated crime. Conflicts may flare up because of a single act, but Zinacantecos always seek the "cause" of the act by examining the past relations between the offender and his victim. When attempting to settle a dispute, Zinacanteco mediators also consider the wider network of relations. In such small communities people must go on living together, and it is more important to work out an agreement that will allow for future harmony than to punish an offender for an act committed in the past. When the parties at odds are closely related, the crime that precipitated the conflict is often forgotten in the search for the deeper cause of the dispute; settlements in such cases are more likely to be based on the type of relationship between the disputants than on the nature of the crime that caused the immediate quarrel. But when the disputants are only distantly related, the nature of the act that caused the conflict is generally more important in determining the terms of the settlement; in such cases the

lack of intensive contact between the parties minimizes the likelihood of an underlying quarrel, and there is no need to preserve an ongoing relationship.

Zinacantecos appear to commit the standard range of crimes that are found around the world: murder, assault, theft, adultery, witchcraft, rape, insult, abuse of public office, etc., although some wrongs have a distinctly Zinacanteco flavor. Kicking and stamping, for example, seem to be a common way of initiating fights between men, and Zinacantecos have a special form of insult, which is delivered by screaming outside an enemy's house at night. But most common by far are marital disputes, which are almost always discussed as instances of wife-beating. There are also many quarrels between kinsmen over rights to inherited property and disputes between the families of an engaged couple over the delicate bride-price transaction. Thus, although it is possible to study Zinacanteco legal procedures by looking at the kinds of wrongs that are committed, a better approach is to examine the relations between individuals.

Patrilineal kinsmen who live close together have frequent causes for conflict, but the ideal of family solidarity keeps many disputes from becoming public knowledge. When a dispute does break into the open, attempts to resolve it usually center on a discussion of property relations. Even if the immediate cause of the conflict is a fight between two brothers or a death presumed to be caused by witchcraft, the mediator will delve into the history of the family property and will try to offer solutions based on a redistribution of land instead of suggesting immediate punishment for the offender.

Relations between husbands and wives are typically strained, particularly in the early years of marriage. Young brides, after leaving the security of their homes to work under the supervision of a mother-in-law in a strange house, are often unhappy and want to leave. But even in the later years of marriage, men and women lead separate lives and tend to have their closest ties with members of their own sex. Marital disputes typically flare up when the husband comes home drunk and beats his wife. This is a common image that Zinacantecos have of marital disputes, and almost any type of marital discord will be attributed to wife-beating before deeper causes are sought.

Relations between the families of an engaged couple are also strained in Zinacantan. Courtships usually last about two years and involve the payment of a bride-price, which generally consists of fruit, bread, and coffee. Zinacanteco bride-prices are reported to be the highest in the Tzotzil area (J. Collier 1968a). During the time when the boy and his family bring the required "gifts" to the girl's parents, each side in the transaction is sensitive to any signs that the other is about to break the agreement: the boy's family fears that the marriage will never take place or that the girl will elope with another lover; and the girl's family fears that the boy's side will try to secure an early marriage or that they will have to break off the courtship because the boy will make a bad husband. In such a tense situation, any indication that either side is not living up to expectations will provoke a crisis that may lead to a series of hearings and attempts at settlement.

Disputes between people who are not related by blood or affinal ties tend to focus on a single issue and thus to be more straightforward. Long-term quarrels between close neighbors do occur, but most conflicts between unrelated persons are caused by a particular act such as theft, fights between drunken men, failure to repay a debt, failure of a religious practitioner to produce the promised results after he has been paid, or damage to property caused by an unwatched animal.

There are also cases in which hamlet and township authorities punish persons who have not fulfilled their civic obligations or who have committed acts that might harm an entire community. People are expected to pay taxes, to contribute labor for maintaining community trails, and to accept public office when asked to do so. They are also expected to refrain from practicing a particular type of witchcraft believed to cause epidemics, from using public office for private advantage, or from insulting officials or destroying public property.

The Research

The analysis of Zinacanteco law presented in this book is based on materials collected over the years 1960–70. The most important materials are a record of approximately 287 trouble cases collected by interviewing Zinacanteco informants, fifteen texts in

Tzotzil written by literate Indians, a series of notes taken during formal interviews, and some field observations. Most of the materials, as will be seen, were derived from verbal statements by informants, a procedure that has both advantages and disadvantages: a description based on such material lacks the immediacy and accuracy of directly observed behavior; however, informants' statements provide a structured version of events, edited by the persons who participated in the action. Informants' accounts of trouble cases stress the facts they consider important, the cues that even an observant ethnographer might overlook or might never have access to. This study, therefore, is primarily a description of the structure existing in verbal categories—an account of the ways in which Zinacantecos talk about motives for quarreling, types of wrongs, and means of seeking solutions—rather than a description, except by inference, of the ways in which they fight and make peace with each other.

I began collecting data on Zinacanteco law by asking informants who had served as civil officials about the cases they handled during their terms at the town hall. When I later realized that many disputes were being settled in the hamlets, I turned to interviewing politically powerful men about the cases they had settled at home. All these interviews were held in my office in San Cristobal. My informants included two past Presidentes, one former secretary, four hamlet elders, and one municipal judge, who was in office at the time. All of the interviews were conducted in Spanish, and the one hamlet elder who spoke only Tzotzil was interviewed through an interpreter. All of my informants were important men, community leaders who were describing primarily the cases in which they had served as mediators and not as litigants. But their case descriptions, and consequently this study, stress the motives and desires of the quarreling individuals—information that neither the informants nor I had access to. What the informants provided instead of the actual motives of real people were the cultural stereotypes of acceptable rationalizations for behavior. And, again, that is the focus of this study. It does not describe the decision-making processes of real people involved in a conflict, but analyzes the set of acceptable rationalizations for justifying behavior. This is a study of the culturally available motives for action and not a

study of what actually motivates people to behave in a particular way.

The fifteen Tzotzil texts were written by five literate Zinacantecos who helped in the translation. I asked them to write about disputes they had observed being settled and they produced accounts that were primarily records of conversations with brief narrative statements to clarify the action. I then picked out words and phrases that seemed to describe key actions during a hearing and explored their meanings through long interviews with two highly trained informants and with the help of the Tzotzil dictionary compiled by Robert Laughlin.

In addition to the interviews on legal terminology, I interviewed past and present civil officials about their duties and the structure of the town government. But anthropological myths about information from experts notwithstanding, their descriptions were never in complete agreement, and the account of the civil government organization in Chapter 2 had to be pieced together from a variety of sources.

In the summer of 1970 I interviewed some of the Mexican officials from San Cristobal, the center of the judicial district that includes Zinacantan, in order to find out what happened to cases that were taken outside of the Indian community. I spent several days going through the archives of the penal judge and talked briefly with the people in his office. Earlier I had been able to see the archives in the State Department of Indian Affairs, and these two records of cases, combined with a corpus of 109 cases collected by Daniel Silver from Zinacanteco informants, allowed me to explore the reasons given by Zinacantecos for wanting to take a case outside the Indian community and to understand the ways in which Zinacanteco cases were handled by Mexican officials.

Apart from my work on disputes, I interviewed Zinacantecos on two other subjects: marriage and witchcraft. Before beginning to work on law, I did a study of courtship practices (J. Collier 1968a), and while working on law, I took time out to concentrate on marital disputes and divorces. From a completed census of one hamlet, a trained informant from the area gave me an account of each divorce settlement he could remember. My study of witchcraft was

based on long interviews with four informants who described techniques for causing illness and misfortune. Despite their original reticence in discussing such a sensitive subject, all but one eventually warmed to the task and told of private complaints as well as cases that had become public knowledge.

The greatest gap in my knowledge of Zinacanteco law comes from a lack of direct field observation of disputes in the process of being heard. I spent three days at the house of an incumbent Presidente, accompanying him on his daily visits to the town hall, but I was personally uncomfortable as a woman in a setting that traditionally belonged to men. I also attended the hearing of one case that involved a Harvard Project informant. At these hearings I noted the demeanor and movements of the participants, but my Tzotzil was never good enough for me to catch more than the drift of the arguments presented. I have had to rely, therefore, on my own background knowledge about Zinacanteco life to flesh out the accounts of disputes given by informants in formal interviews. I spent about thirty days living with a Zinacanteco family over a two-month period in 1960, and since that time I have made many trips to Zinacantan to visit friends and attend rituals. I have also drawn upon materials gathered by the other members of the Harvard Chiapas Project.

The most exciting part of the research was putting it all together. At the beginning the materials lacked coherence because they had been collected in bits and pieces over the years as my interests changed. I had originally collected histories of trouble cases and their outcomes in order to discover the social rules that could be called laws in Zinacantan. But this proved to be a very frustrating exercise. With a given corpus of cases I could indeed pick out social rules that, if violated, brought a fairly specific outcome, but each new case I collected would turn out to be "anomalous" and would require me to rewrite my previous conclusions. The turning point came when I began to explore the meanings of Tzotzil terms. I soon found that Zinacantecos could speak of taking a case to the proper authorities with the same idiom used to describe the behavior of a belligerent drunk looking for a fight. Legal cases were treated as private quarrels between litigants and not as matters for public concern. The full implications of this

approach came to me only when, after observing a case where a mediator clearly favored one side, I realized that mediators were not expected to be impartial. They were not, like their African counterparts, "men of alleged impartiality, [who] sit on the evidence, and, through cross-examination, assess it in terms of social rules" (Gluckman, 1962: 442), because, at least in theory, it was not they who reached decisions. The outcome of a quarrel was as private as the quarrel itself, and the main requirement for a solution was that it be accepted by both sides.

Zinacanteco legal concepts were further illuminated by my exploration of witchcraft beliefs, which turned out to be far more important than I had imagined, because observable earthly conflict was seen merely as an overt manifestation of a far more important spiritual conflict. I began to realize that the language available to Zinacantecos for discussing trouble cases presupposed a world where conflict brought supernatural retribution, and that retribution could only be avoided by a reconciliation between the quarreling parties. Witchcraft beliefs thus explained "why" Zinacanteco mediators could not impose their own solutions but had rather to bring the litigants to some form of agreement.

By the end of my fieldwork I felt finally that I understood Zinacanteco law. New cases no longer required a change of framework and outcomes made sense. Most rewarding of all, I found that I could gossip with Zinacanteco informants over lunch without any sense of strangeness. I had mastered enough of the language of conflict to understand and share Zinacanteco reactions to descriptions of trouble cases.

The Plan of the Book

In broad outline the book moves from a concrete description of the legal institutions of Zinacantan—the ways available for settling disputes—to an abstract discussion of the concepts that underlie Zinacanteco dispute-settling procedures, and ends with a close analysis of particular cases in order to uncover the strategies available to persons who wish to quarrel or make peace. The first two parts set the stage and lay out the conceptual tools, and the last discusses the actors and the roles they play.

The two chapters on the structure and organization of legal

levels lay out the several alternatives open to Zinacantecos involved in a dispute. Chapter 1 gives a formal account of the various legal levels available, discussing the types of social groups in which legal procedures operate and describing the types of persons who appeal to a particular procedure. The legal levels range from procedures for settling conflicts between close kinsmen to Mexican government courts, but most Zinacanteco conflicts are handled within hamlets or by the civil authorities in the ceremonial center.

Chapter 2, on the organization of legal levels, discusses the broad patterns created by the ways in which legal procedures are used. Particular types of cases do not automatically go to particular courts; rather, the litigants choose the forum best suited to their purposes. Choices are far from random, and each legal level is characterized by a particular configuration of claims and litigants. Chapter 2 goes on to explore the interaction between social and legal change as affected by the choice of forum made by litigants.

Chapter 3, on the town hall court, provides a detailed description of a hearing. Using the metaphor of a stage production, it discusses the physical aspects of the setting, the immediate factors that affect the demeanor of the litigants, and the various components of social status that can be exposed or hidden by litigants attempting to present the appearance of someone worthy of respect.

The next four chapters describe Zinacanteco legal concepts. Chapter 4 explores the meanings of the Tzotzil words and phrases that indicate key actions during a hearing. Chapter 5 takes up witchcraft beliefs, summarizing the material derived from the intensive interviews I held on the subject, and discusses the relevance of these beliefs to Zinacanteco ideas of how conflict should be resolved. Chapters 6 and 7, on witchcraft cases and aggression, look at the symbolic meanings of overt physical acts. They explore the ways available to Zinacantecos for expressing direct hostility, and the ways in which hostile acts can be interpreted and handled by the victim.

Chapters 8–12 discuss different types of relationships between litigants and examine the kinds of cases brought by people so

related. Although detailed case descriptions show what Zinacan-tecos *do* fight about, the focus is on what it is *possible* to fight about. Using the case materials, I have explored the ways in which persons linked by a particular kind of tie are able to conduct the conflicts between them.

The Conclusion sets out the theoretical framework underlying the organization of the book. It discusses the relation between this study and other works on the anthropology of law and then reviews each chapter's contribution to the general argument. Readers with a background in anthropology may want to read this final chapter first in order to understand the wider theoretical implications of the ethnographic materials presented in the body of the book.

ONE

The Structure of Legal Levels

When involved in a dispute, a Zinacanteco has a choice of where to go to appeal for a settlement. His choice is limited to the set of available legal procedures; and within the set it is further limited by the content of his quarrel and the nature of the relationship between himself and his opponent. This chapter describes the formal structure of legal levels available to Zinacantecos and the various dispute-settling procedures in terms of the social fields within which they operate.

For the purpose of this description, I shall define a legal procedure as a recognized, recurring set of actions in which the parties to a dispute come together for the purpose of discussing their conflict and attempting to resolve it by settling on some plan of future action. The crucial points in this definition are (1) that the procedure be a recognized and recurring method of settling disputes, (2) that the two sides must have some form of confrontation, even if conducted through a go-between, (3) that the discussion take the form of a dispute, even if the overt issue is peripheral to the real interests of the parties, and (4) that at least suggestions for resolving the conflict be made, regardless of whether either side has any intention of following through. This definition allows me to discuss dispute-settling mechanisms as having a structure, while recognizing that the procedures themselves are often used for purposes other than settling disputes. It also frees me from having to consider all types of remedy agents. A one-sided appeal to a witch, god, or high official may result in the punishment of

an offender, but it is not a legal procedure by my definition because there is no confrontation between the disputing parties.

It has long been recognized that within a single society there may be various legal systems (Durkheim 1933) that correspond, more or less, to its functioning subgroups (Pospisil 1958, 1971). Rather than defining these subgroups in terms of the political authority wielded by leaders, I prefer to use Firth's concept of "fields of social relations" (1956: 28) and to look at the range of ways in which individuals can interact and can conduct the conflicts that arise between them. In broad terms there are three major legal levels in Zinacantan. Within a hamlet, disputes are resolved through "informal" procedures that are not recognized as valid by the Mexican government. The town hall, which handles disputes from the entire *municipio*, is the lowest recognized court. And beyond the borders of Zinacantan are the courts of the Mexican government. These three levels form a hierarchy of inclusiveness, and appeals travel up the system from the hamlet to the national courts.

But the picture I want to present is not quite so simple. There are alternate procedures within a single hamlet, and the Mexican government offers a variety of legal agencies. On closer analysis, the neat, nested system of levels breaks down. Different procedures involve different phrasings of a conflict, and a single dispute traveling up the appeal hierarchy may suffer many distortions, including that of having to pass from one cultural system to another.

Analytically, I have begun with a consideration of dispute-settling procedures, as abstracted from the cases described by Zinacantecos, and then linked these procedures to the social fields within which they operate. For each legal level so distinguished, I look at (1) the mechanisms for bringing up a dispute, (2) the roles that need to be filled, (3) the range of relationships between the litigants who use the method, (4) the usual types of disputes that are handled, (5) the expected sequence of actions, and (6) the kinds of pressures the litigants and the mediator can bring to bear on each other.

Curing Ceremonies

Curing ceremonies are marginal legal procedures. They are included in this description only because conflicts between close

kinsmen can be handled through ritual reconciliation, and because a description of curing ceremonies provides a convenient way to introduce the central behavior pattern that runs throughout all legal procedures in Zinacantan—begging pardon.

In Zinacanteco belief, certain diseases are seen as having been sent by the Ancestral Gods to punish persons who have deviated from community norms. According to Vogt, the Ancestral Gods are "especially quick to punish their living descendants for quarreling with kinsmen, failing to bathe and put on clean clothes regularly, mishandling maize, and failing to take ritual duties seriously" (1969: 301). Curing ceremonies held for the victims of the Ancestral Gods' wrath usually center on restoring relations with the offended deities, but if the patient has been guilty of quarreling with a kinsman the ceremony may include a separate sequence to reconcile the human parties involved. The crucial roles in such a sequence are the shaman, the patient, and the offended person. If the offended person is not present, the patient merely begs pardon of the gods and the ceremony cannot be considered a way of settling a dispute.

If the shaman who is conducting the ceremony announces that the patient is ill because of a quarrel with another family member who is also present, the shaman can investigate the nature of the dispute and suggest ways to resolve it. This is a legitimate part of the curing ceremony because a reconciliation between the quarreling kinsmen is one way to please the gods and cause them to remove the sickness. In attempting a reconciliation the shaman can pursue one of two courses. He can assume the role of a legal personage and discuss the quarrel, question the participants and the witnesses, and suggest acceptable solutions. Or he can avoid such a role and simply ask the members of the afflicted household to go through the motions of reconciliation without having decided on a course of future action.

The motions of reconciliation involve a sequence that I have called "begging pardon." The person who admits to being guilty of having wronged another presents the offended person with a bottle of the local rum and asks him to end the anger in his heart—to forgive the offense. If the offended person accepts the bottle, he indicates his willingness to forgive and forget, and the liquor is then shared by everyone present. This seemingly simple sequence

is in fact one variation of a wider behavior pattern that runs throughout Zinacanteco culture. Anyone making a formal request for anything from a loan of money to a petition for a bride presents a bottle of rum to the person who is being asked to grant the favor. To accept the proffered rum is to agree to the request, and the subsequent sharing of the bottle indicates that all the drinkers are in accord.

Drinking behavior is also highly patterned. The youngest man present at such a ceremony acts as a drink pourer and offers to each person in turn one full shot glass, beginning with the oldest man and ending with the youngest woman who is eligible to drink. As a person accepts the shot glass, he toasts each other person, in rank order, and says "I receive it." The person being toasted, if he is younger, comes up to the drinker, bows to him, saying "Drink it," and is released by a touch on the top of the head. If the drinker is the younger person, he goes to bow to each older person present before drinking. After toasting everyone of appropriate age in the room, the drinker downs the rum and returns the shot glass to the drink pourer, who refills it and gives it to the next-lower-ranking person (Vogt 1969: 396). This drinking ritual is carried out more or less rigidly depending on the formality of the occasion and the intoxication of the drinkers.

Begging-pardon sequences are open to ambiguity because it is not always clear just what has been requested, nor is it always clear just what has been granted when a bottle is accepted. In begging pardon, the offender formally requests the offended person to "end the anger in his heart." The offender does not have to admit that his behavior was the original cause of the anger. And in indicating agreement the offended person need not say anything at all. He has only to touch the bottle, or to tell the drink pourer to open it. Thus it is not necessarily clear just what everyone is agreeing to. The disputing parties are "reconciled" and everyone is "in accord," but the terms of the agreement can range from being highly specific to not being specified at all. The cordiality expressed through sharing rum may have a real foundation or may be entirely illusory.

In a curing ceremony, reconciliations indicate real agreements to the degree that the shaman acts as a legal personage. If he in-

vestigates the cause of the quarrel and suggests solutions, the drinking at the end of the sequence may express agreement on a concrete plan of action. But it need not. Symbolic reconciliation is all that is required to secure the favor of the gods, and the shaman may simply have the members of the quarreling household present rum to each other and drink it together without having discussed ways of avoiding future clashes.

Curing ceremonies can only be used for settling disputes between close kinsmen because nonrelatives are seldom invited to participate in them. Curing ceremonies, in fact, are usually limited to the members of a single domestic group. Within this unit, ritual reconciliations can be very important. The conflicts caused by the stresses and strains of extended family living are rarely amenable to rational settlements, and a ritual reconciliation, based on an appeal to the ideal of family harmony, may be the best way to patch things up sufficiently that the people involved can go on living together.

Begging Formal Pardon

The sequence of actions that I have called "begging pardon" is called *lahesel k*op*, "ending a dispute," by Zinacantecos. It is an acceptable conclusion to any legal procedure and can occur at any level. But begging formal pardon, which we shall take up now, is a very structured version of the basic pattern and occurs as a distinct sequence. It is a recognized and recurring way of resolving conflicts.

Begging formal pardon is a two-sided affair. The person who begs pardon *admits having committed the offense* that led to the conflict and takes the initiative in seeking a settlement. The offended person is usually treated *as if he were blameless* and only his pardon is sought. Because this sequence marks the end of a conflict, it is best seen as the last stage of a series of three actions. The first action is the offense, the second is some form of retaliation or threatened retaliation by the offended party, and the third is the request for pardon by the offender.

Unlike the pardon sequences embedded in a curing ceremony, begging formal pardon is a clearly demarcated affair. The guilty person initiates it by going to the house of the offended party, and

the ceremony is formally under way when the bottle has been presented and is standing unopened at the feet of the offended person. It is an expandable ceremony. In its simplest form the guilty person goes alone to present the bottle to the offended person in the patio of his house; the action may take only a few minutes, with the guilty person uttering the standard phrases for begging pardon and the offended party extracting promises of future good behavior before accepting the bottle. At the other extreme, the ceremony can be carefully planned, lasting a day or more and involving thirty or forty people who come to lend support to one side or the other.

Ceremonies for begging formal pardon usually end with a rational settlement. By admitting guilt, the offender acknowledges a concrete offense that is amenable to a concrete solution. Unlike curing ceremonies, begging formal pardon always involves a definite plan for future action rather than a mere appeal for better behavior. Between the time the bottle is placed at the feet of the offended person and the time it is accepted, the two sides discuss the issues and come to an agreement, which may be a simple statement that the guilty person will not commit the offense again, or an elaborate plan of future rights and obligations. When the bottle of rum is finally accepted, the offended party indicates his forgiveness and the general drinking that follows ratifies the agreement reached about future behavior.

Wife-beating is the most common offense settled by begging pardon. When a husband beats his wife, she can retaliate by leaving him. To get her back, the husband must admit his guilt and come to beg her pardon with bottle in hand. If the quarreling couple are mature, the husband will present the bottle directly to his wife, but if they are young, the ceremony of begging pardon may be taken out of their hands. Then the young husband will kneel mutely at the feet of his father-in-law while his own father, or an elder representing his family, discusses the issues with the senior man on the wife's side.

Although wife-beating is the typical offense behind a begging-pardon ceremony, any other type of offense can theoretically be handled this way if one person is willing to admit his guilt and take the initiative in seeking a solution. But, in fact, begging par-

don is restricted to people who know each other well: husband and wife, the families of a courting couple, kinsmen, or close neighbors.

The outcome of a ceremony to beg formal pardon is best regarded as a compromise. The final shape of the plan for future action is not determined by the nature of the offender's admitted fault but is a subject for negotiation. A wife's overt reason for leaving her husband may be that he beat her, but her real purpose could be to force her husband into building her a house of her own so that she will not have to live with her in-laws. When the husband begs his wife's pardon for having beaten her, he does not imply anything about his willingness or ability to build a new house. But between the time the bottle is presented and the time it is accepted, this is the issue that is talked around. The husband's family would "lose" if they had to agree to help build the couple a separate house, whereas the wife would "lose" if she had to accept the bottle without having extracted any concessions on future living arrangements.

In reaching a compromise, each side in a begging-pardon ceremony can bring strong pressures to bear on the other. The guilty offender may seem to argue from a weak position, but by initiating a settlement procedure he forces the offended person into discussing possible solutions and into choosing among them. It is very difficult for the offended person to adamantly refuse a settlement that could be interpreted by others as appropriate. He would risk being called a witch because witches are defined as people who cannot forgive, who do not know how to end the anger in their hearts (Greenhouse 1971: 61). The sanctions available to the offended person are more obvious. By the time the offender comes to beg pardon, the offended person has usually taken some measures of retaliation. The beaten wife has left her husband and can threaten to leave him for good, or an injured person can threaten to take his case to the ceremonial center in order to have the offender jailed at the town hall.

In spite of the strong pressures to produce a compromise, some ceremonies for begging formal pardon end without an agreement. The bottle remains untouched and the two sides go their separate ways. This is seldom the end of the affair, however. The guilty per-

son usually tries again to beg pardon, or the offended person carries the case to a higher authority. But formal sequences of begging pardon can never end with drinking over an empty agreement. Unlike the reconciliation sequences in a curing ceremony, which are invariably carried out if ordered by the shaman, shared drinking at the end of a ceremony for begging formal pardon always means that there has been some decision on a plan for future action.

Mediation by a Hamlet Elder

In almost every hamlet there are older men known for their wisdom in settling conflicts who can be approached by a person involved in a dispute. Such elders are usually leaders of their own descent groups, but affinal, *compadrazgo*, and political ties allow them to extend their range of influence. A plaintiff seeking an elder to mediate in a dispute will choose the one with whom he has the closest ties but who also commands enough authority to ensure the appearance of the defendant. In a few hamlets there is one paramount elder who handles most of the hamlet disputes. Such men are powerful political leaders, have extensive compadrazgo ties, and are known as men who look after their hamlets.

When an elder agrees to handle a case, he will conduct a three-party hearing in which he will listen to both sides and offer solutions. The elder is described as a mediator, not a judge, since he has no way of imposing his decision on a recalcitrant litigant; indeed, if the opposing sides cannot reach agreement, the hearing has failed and is closed.

A person who plans to take a dispute to a hamlet elder will go to the elder's house with a bottle of rum. After exchanging preliminary pleasantries with the elder, he will take out the bottle and place it at the elder's feet. The elder will eye the bottle and ask why it has been presented, and the person will state his case. If the elder decides the dispute is valid, he can have the other party called to his house by sending a child or minor hamlet official to notify him.

A person receiving notification that he is wanted at an elder's house will usually go, since refusal to appear would turn the elder against him. If he suspects why he is being called, and suspects further that he may need to make a request of the elder or to beg pardon of his opponent, he will take along a bottle of rum. It

often happens that the opposing sides in a conflict will arrive at an elder's house independently, each with his bottle of rum. They may also approach different elders; if this happens, the two elders may meet together and act as joint mediators. There are even cases in which one elder, when asked to hear a case, decides that he needs the help of other elders and sends a child to fetch them. I have called mediation by a hamlet elder a three-sided affair, as opposed to a two-sided begging-pardon ceremony, but the two types of hearings may merge. The elders who accompany a person going to beg pardon may end up acting as mediators, hearing arguments from both sides, or an elder who hears a case may end up helping the guilty party to beg pardon.

Hamlet elders, in their role as mediators, are supposed to hear both sides of the case. The elder can send a messenger to bring witnesses to help clarify disputed points, and he can cross-examine any of the people involved. Throughout the hearing, the elder has the job of bringing the case into focus and offering solutions. When both sides have been heard and the available solutions assessed, the hearing turns into a bargaining procedure in which the elder will side with the person most in need of help. If a compromise is reached, the hearing will end with everyone sharing the rum. The shared rum may be from the original bottle presented to the elder when he was asked to hear the case; from the bottle presented by the guilty person when he begged pardon of his opponent; from bottles presented to the elder at the end of the case to thank him for having reached a solution; or from all three sources.

To say that hamlet elders have no sanctions at their command is not entirely true. Though hamlet hearings are a failure if the litigants do not reach agreement, the elder can exert pressure to bring unwilling litigants into line. In addition to the inducements inherent in the power of his position and the weight of his friendship, his most obvious threat, and the one most frequently used, is to tell the litigants that the dispute will have to go to the ceremonial center if it is not settled in the hamlet. This would mean more lost time, the shame of a public hearing, and the possibility of a jail sentence or fine for the guilty person. This is no idle threat, since hamlet hearings are lower courts in a very real sense. If the case goes to the town hall in the ceremonial center, the Presidente always inquires into the solution previously proposed by the ham-

let elder, and he may even call the elder himself to testify. The powerful elder who handled the majority of the disputes that arose in the hamlet of Apas was in fact able to bring most litigants into agreement because of his reputation for suggesting settlements that would be upheld at the town hall.

Hamlet elders are able to mediate in almost any kind of dispute between persons who come under their sphere of influence. In practice, this means disputes between kinsmen, spouses, or neighbors. If a hamlet elder does not feel competent to handle a particular conflict, or if his attempts to resolve it have failed, he can advise the litigants to go to the town hall or to take their plea to the Mexican officials in San Cristobal. Some hamlet elders also act as local authorities: politically powerful men can order dangerous criminals or aggressive drunks captured and confined. Some hamlets have small jails where such an offender can be temporarily imprisoned until his case can be heard, whether on the local level or at the town hall. In hamlets without jails, prisoners can be locked in a room of the schoolhouse or tied with rope and bound to a post.

Meetings of Hamlet Elders

When the elders of a hamlet meet together, they form a powerful group, but they act as a body only in handling hamlet affairs and will seldom act together to hear an individual dispute. Most meetings of hamlet elders are held at calendrical festivals when all the men of the hamlet are gathered to perform a community task or ritual. Unplanned meetings may be called, however, on special occasions to handle an issue of hamlet-wide importance, such as a matter concerning the school, the installation of electricity or waterworks, or the discovery of a witch who may bring sickness to the entire group.

When the elders are gathered together, they act as a body to handle wrongs against the hamlet. People who have not paid festival taxes or contributed to community labor will be called in to make amends, and hamlet members who have endangered the welfare of the group will be pressured to change their ways. Such a hearing is a strictly two-sided affair: the elders make the accusation and decide what should be done. They will listen to the defendant's excuses, but though they can be swayed by the argu-

ments of an elder acting on behalf of the defendant, in the end it is the united elders, as representatives of the hamlet, who reach a decision and try to enforce it.

Hamlet elders, acting as a group, can threaten to banish an individual who refuses to bow to their demands. It is not clear, however, whether this threat can be carried out. I have never heard of anyone being forcibly ejected from a hamlet, but I have heard of people who left because their lives became intolerable. A survey of the recorded cases shows that most defendants bow to the demands of the assembled elders and pay their taxes or otherwise mend their ways. With a recalcitrant defendant, the elders have essentially three alternatives: they may drop the charges, saving as much face as that may allow; they may take the case to the ceremonial center; or, where feelings are running high over a case involving witchcraft, they may torture the defendant into submission. The action taken seems to depend more on the political situation of the moment than on any long-term authority of the elders to banish undesirables from their territory.

The threat of banishment, like all threatened sanctions in Zinacantan, is effective in producing compliance for two reasons: the defendant may fear that the sanction will actually be carried out; or, more practically, he may feel that it is not worth his while to put the elders to the test. Furthermore, the threatened sanction allows the defendant a face-saving reason for admitting his guilt and accepting a proposed solution. Even if he knows that a given threat can never be carried out, he can use it as an excuse for retreating from a position that has become untenable for other reasons. Later, he can claim to himself and to his supporters that he confessed, or gave in, only because he was forced to do so.

The Structure of Civil Government

The town hall houses the civil government of Zinacantan. As described earlier, it is a long, low building with a covered porch where the officials sit and an open area in front where political meetings are held. It is the highest court in Zinacantan. The disputes heard here come from everywhere in the township, and those that cannot be resolved at this level are insoluble in Zinacanteco terms.

The positions and duties of the officials who make up the civil government are prescribed by state law. The Ley del Municipio Libre requires that all first-class townships, a category that now includes Zinacantan, be administered by a *Presidente*, a *Sindico*, six *Regidores* and three alternate *Regidores*, and an *Alcalde Juez* (municipal judge) and his alternate (Cancian 1965: 17). These men are to be paid from community funds and serve three-year terms. Zinacantan outwardly conforms to the law, but closer examination reveals the existing civil government to be a compromise between legal requirements and Maya tradition.

The Presidente is the highest official. His prescribed duties are to oversee the functioning of the civil government and to handle official contacts with the outside world, but he spends a large part of his time hearing disputes and acting as the community's chief judge. Being Presidente is a full-time job. As chief civil official, he spends most of his days at his desk in the town hall's inner room or holding court from the bench outside. But because Zinacantecos view him as a "super hamlet elder," litigants feel free to visit him at home. Those desiring privacy and a chance to explain a case without contradictions will approach the Presidente at dawn before he makes his public appearance, or talk with him in the evening when he returns home. Even the night brings little peace, because the Presidente is frequently disturbed in order to lock a violent prisoner in jail.

The Sindico is legally in charge of social welfare and public works; he collects taxes, handles school affairs, and oversees the work done by prisoners on public projects. In addition to performing his own duties, the Sindico acts as the Presidente's right-hand man and occasional replacement. If the Presidente leaves the ceremonial center, the Sindico takes charge of the town hall and hears disputes. But although the Sindico is required to be on duty every day, he is much freer than the Presidente and can leave the ceremonial center from time to time to farm his fields.

Of the six civil Regidores and three alternates required by law, only six actually serve, and their duties are somewhat vague because the municipal subcommittees they are supposed to head in the eyes of the Mexican lawmakers do not exist in Zinacantan. As reported in Cancian (1965), the six civil Regidores were first ap-

pointed in 1962 when a political upheaval made it clear that the convenient fiction of the past, which had allowed the Regidores in the religious hierarchy to serve as civil officials, was no longer practical. Because the newly appointed Regidores were young men with unspecified duties, their perceived status was low, and most Zinacantecos now regard them as occupying a position somewhere between the lowly *Mayores* (about which more below) and the *Jueces*. The six Regidores, serving in groups of three that alternate in two-week shifts, have little to do: when they happen to be in the ceremonial center, they sit on the bench with the Presidente and listen to cases; they occasionally help the Jueces in the performance of their duties; and they may be sent to represent the municipal authority away from the ceremonial center.

Although the law requires only two Jueces—an Alcalde Juez and his alternate—the Zinacantecos appoint four, who serve in pairs and change off every two weeks. In contrast to the functionless Regidores, the Jueces have many duties, since their signatures are required on certain official documents. According to the law, Jueces are in charge of investigating serious crimes and altering the civil records, but in Zinacantan the Presidente makes all the important decisions. Jueces merely collect the physical evidence and sign the final report; the Presidente decides whether an official report is indeed needed and dictates its contents. In a murder case, for example, a Juez visits the scene of the crime, accompanies the witnesses and the most likely suspects to the ceremonial center, and then sits on the bench while the Presidente questions the parties. When the Presidente has arrived at what he considers to be a suitable version of the facts, the story is told to the Ladino secretary, who types up the required official documents—the report of the investigation for the Mexican authorities and the release to bury the body—for the Juez to sign. For his part in preparing these papers the Juez collects a fee from the murdered man's relatives. The amount charged varies according to the services rendered. An unfortunate man whose future son-in-law was murdered while visiting in his house was charged 150 pesos for an official document stating that there were no clues to the identity of the murderer. The Juez told me that the fee was so low because the man was clearly innocent. Had his innocence been in doubt,

it would have cost him much more to have the official report declare the murderer unknown.

Jueces also conduct other kinds of investigations. When the Presidente needs physical evidence assessed, he sends a Juez to estimate the damage to property or the extent of a bedridden victim's injuries. A Juez will supervise a property division or accompany a confessed witch who has been ordered to conduct a retraction ceremony—i.e. to return to the cave where he prayed that an enemy be struck by sickness and ask the Earth Lord to ignore the request. Jueces also handle warrants for arrest and accompany prisoners from Zinacantan to San Cristobal.

Although Jueces routinely sit beside the Presidente and listen to cases at the town hall, their closer attention is demanded when an elopement or divorce is being discussed, for such cases might lead to changes in the civil records. If the Presidente is busy, a Juez may in fact conduct such a hearing alone. Elopement cases more or less settle themselves, for everyone knows that the couple will have to get married, and divorce suits rarely lead to actual separations. If the hearing ends with a decision to change the civil records—either to record a new marriage or to erase an old one—the Ladino secretary performs the actual task of altering the books and the Juez merely adds his signature.

In their role as minor municipal officials, the Jueces act with the Regidores as representatives of civil authority. They may accompany a man having difficulty in his quest for a wife or provide moral support for a man who wishes to beg formal pardon. The role of the Juez or Regidor on such an expedition is to command respect and restrain abuse in word or action.

In the Zinacanteco view, Jueces rank below the Sindico and above the Regidores. When both the Presidente and the Sindico are away or occupied, the senior Juez present will hear a case. At busy festival times, when as many as five cases may be in progress at once, other Jueces also act as judges and conduct hearings. And at hamlet festivals, as well, when the Presidente and the Sindico are too busy to attend, the Jueces hear cases.

At the bottom of the hierarchy of civil officials are the Mayores, who sweep the town hall, run errands, and act as policemen. They are appointed jointly by the Presidente and the religious officials on

the advice of hamlet elders and are taken from the ranks of young troublemakers. In 1962 there were reported to be eight Mayores (Cancian 1965), and in 1965 there were twelve (Vogt 1969). Their number varies from year to year, and even within a year, as old ones run away and new ones are recruited from among trouble-makers who find themselves temporarily banished from home. The Mayores are the only civil officials holding positions that count for advancement in the religious hierarchy. Like the *Mayordomos*, who care for saints, they are considered to have passed a first-level cargo by virtue of their year of service to the community, and are accordingly in a position to apply for a second-level religious cargo at some time in the future. But unlike the Mayordomos, who spend a great deal of money and receive commensurate prestige, the Mayores spend no money and are considered to be at the bottom of the social ladder. Their religious duties are as low as their civil ones: they act as errand boys for the high religious officials. They are the only civil officials with one-year terms, and, like religious officials, they play a special role during the festival of San Sebastian after their year in office.

Mayores carry a small billy club as a sign of office. In their role of policemen they are sent to break up drunken fights, make arrests, notify witnesses and litigants to appear at the town hall, and guard prisoners. They receive no pay for their services, but do collect small fees from litigants for fetching a witness or an opponent. The economic burden of unpaid community service is lightened by alternating weeks of duty, as is the case with the Jueces and Regidores. On their free time Mayores can farm corn (Young 1965).

The Presidente in 1965 created a new position in the civil hierarchy by the appointment of two men as *Comandantes*. The position is that of "super-Mayor," since the incumbent on duty is authorized to carry a gun and accompany the Mayores when difficult arrests are to be made. Like other lower civil officials, the two Comandantes serve alternate weeks and thus have time to pursue other activities.

There are two other civil officials who do not serve at the town hall. These are the *Agente Municipal* of Navenchauk and his alternate. The Agentes have an office in the miniature town hall, with attached jail, near the chapel of the Virgen de Guadalupe in the

Navenchauk plaza. Although the Agentes are representatives of the civil government, they function as minor hamlet elders. They handle the routine disputes that occur in their hamlet—marital problems and drunken fights—and carry out the orders of local political leaders in more complex cases. The fact that they maintain an official jail allows them to act as minor Presidentes, but they have considerably less power.

The only Ladino official at the Zinacanteco town hall is the Secretary, or town clerk, who is appointed by the State Department of Indian Affairs. His job is to handle official records, prepare the census, and type papers needed by the Indian officials, but he also acts as the eyes and ears of the Ladino state government (Vogt 1969). The present Secretary appears to be a basically honest man who does not take advantage of his position, though he does wield considerable influence as the resident interpreter of Mexican law.

The law requires that civil officials be paid, but by Maya tradition community service should be undertaken as a duty without material reward. The present situation in Zinacantan is a compromise between the Mexican and Indian views of office-holding. The Presidente, who has a full-time job, does get paid from municipal funds: 100 pesos a month from liquor taxes and half of the fines he levies. The Sindico, who is able to leave the town hall to farm corn, has an irregular income made up of the one-peso-per-day fee charged to jail inmates and a cut of the fines. The Jueces, who farm during their off-duty weeks, get some additional income from the fees they charge for investigations, divided among the four of them. It is not clear how the Regidores make extra money, but their alternating service does give them time to farm.

Given the Maya ideal that officials should serve without pay, the Zinacanteco tendency to confuse fines and fees with extortion and bribes is understandable. Mexican law allows the town officials to levy moderate fines, but the wrongdoers who pay them see their money going into the pockets of the officials and not into the abstraction known as the town treasury. Presidentes state that all fines received are recorded by the town treasurer, but if this is indeed what happens, it is not immediately apparent to the community. Municipal officials thus tread a delicate line. They must exercise discretion in charging the fines and fees to which they are

legally entitled. But even the town officials confuse the issues. Some of the past Presidentes I have interviewed claimed that fines could not be levied in Zinacantan, whereas others claimed they could. They are not even certain what the fines and fees are for. The Juez mentioned above who investigated a murder obviously saw his fee as based on the content of his report rather than as a set sum for a specific type of document.

Before 1952 all civil officials served one-year terms. Between 1952 and 1962, the terms were lengthened to two years, and now they have been increased to three (Cancian 1965). Although the Mexicans who instituted the policy of lengthened terms saw it as a way to promote political stability in Indian communities, its effect in Zinacantan has been mixed. When the Presidente served a one-year term, the people who accused him of bribery and extortion had neither the time nor the incentive to coalesce into a united opposition. Tension increased noticeably when the term was lengthened to two years, but it is not clear whether the opposition was a response to the increased term or merely part of the general factionalism that prevailed at the time. The first Presidente to serve three years was the subject of bitter controversy. During his term the opposition party gained strength and power at the expense of his supporters. The next Presidente, an exceptional man with a great deal of personal charm, cut through factional lines and built a broad base of support. His somewhat weaker successor capitalized on this support and managed to survive without major political crises, but it may take only one ineffectual Presidente with a three-year term to revive factional conflicts and throw the community into turmoil.

The civil officials are "elected" at two open meetings held in the area in front of the town hall (Vogt 1969: 290–91), but as most of the election process occurs behind the scenes, the public meetings serve only to validate the candidates of the most powerful political faction (Cancian 1965: 24–25). The important civil offices are those of Presidente, Sindico, and first Alcalde Juez. The men who occupy these positions not only must be intelligent and able but must know Spanish in order to handle the required contacts with Mexican officials. The need to know Spanish has severely limited the supply of potential candidates for high civil office. The last

two Presidentes, who formerly worked for the National Indian Institute, both acquired a sense of Mexican values along with a facility in Spanish.

In Mexican eyes, the Indian officials in the civil hierarchy derive their legitimacy from the fact that they are duly elected and installed according to the laws of the state. Whereas this Mexican recognition gives the civil officials authority in Indian eyes, other lines of legitimacy have been slowly developing as the civil officials have assumed ritual duties. In Indian belief, the present civil government is an imperfect earthly replica of the supernatural government made up of Ancestral Gods. This connection has been emphasized by a recent Presidente, who instituted flower-changing ceremonies for his staff of office, thus converting a civil symbol into a sign of recognition from the gods.

The Town Hall as a Court

Although Mayores are always on duty at the town hall, they can hardly be said to police the community because they never seek out trouble. They leave the town hall only to run specific errands for the Presidente or other officials. Although they will intervene in a drunken fight in the ceremonial center or arrest a person causing trouble, most cases to reach the town hall are brought by private citizens.

The formal way to bring up a case is to approach the Presidente as he sits on the bench in front of the town hall and place a bottle of rum or beer at his feet. Although it is possible to approach the Presidente without the rum, as soon as a litigant asks a direct favor the bottle usually appears. It is the Presidente's duty to listen to the litigant and help him decide what action to take. On occasion, the Presidente may refuse to hear the case and advise the litigant to seek a hamlet settlement, but he will usually agree to a hearing and send a Mayor after the opposing party.

Many litigants prefer to approach the Presidente when he is at home. This procedure has the advantage of guaranteeing a private hearing, free of the many interruptions that occur at the town hall. And there is a secondary advantage: Presidentes and other civil officials save most of the rum that is given to them in the course of their duties and sell it later to derive additional income; the litigant finding the Presidente at home, then, simply buys a bottle

of his rum and presents it to him to open the proceedings. In Zina-canteco eyes, there is nothing curious about buying the rum from the Presidente and immediately returning it to him. Though the Presidente usually saves most of the rum to sell again, a portion of every bottle is always drunk to seal an agreement.

Although the Presidente will listen to complaints in private, the actual hearings are conducted in public at the town hall. Once a complaint is made, the case rests until the opposing side appears. If both sides arrive together, the case can be heard at once, but there is usually a delay of a day or more between the complaint and the hearing, depending on where the opposing party lives.

When the Mayores go to fetch someone, they try to arrive at the defendant's house at dawn (Young 1965). On such missions they carry their billy clubs as a sign they are on official business; but if they think the defendant may be dangerous, they are accompanied by a Commandante with a gun. They may even be accompanied by a Juez with a warrant; for according to Zinacanteco custom Mayores should not enter a house unless invited, and a Juez with a warrant is needed if a house is to be searched. A dangerous defendant or one who actively resists arrest is tied up and put in jail at the town hall until the hearing. But if the defendant is not considered dangerous, the Mayores may simply notify him that he is wanted and wait to accompany him or leave him to come by himself. If the case is not serious, the defendant has the option of refusing to come, in which case the Presidente can either order him brought in or advise the plaintiff to seek a hamlet settlement.

To conduct a hearing, the Presidente sits at the end of the bench with the other civil officials beside him. The plaintiff and defendant, either alone or surrounded by supporters and witnesses, stand separately or in separate groups before him. Bystanders, Mayores, or litigants waiting for another case sit on the remaining benches or stand against the columns supporting the porch roof. Women not playing principal roles usually sit on the floor to one side, but stand or kneel at the Presidente's feet when testifying. The children of participants cling to their mothers' skirts or play in the cleared area in front of the town hall.

In describing an idealized hearing, Zinacantecos say that the Presidente should ask the plaintiff to state his case and then allow

the defendant to reply to the accusation. When both sides have spoken, the Presidente should question the litigants and witnesses to arrive at a satisfactory version of the events. Actually, hearings are much less structured. The plaintiff may begin by stating his case, but be continually interrupted by the defendant's protests, the Presidente's questions, and the bystanders' comments, all talking angrily at once. The proceedings may in fact degenerate into confusion.

Cases end when an appropriate settlement has been found. In Zinacanteco eyes, an ideal settlement involves reconciliation: both sides agree to forget their differences and drink together, or the guilty person begs pardon and is forgiven through acceptance of a bottle of rum. Settlements often involve agreement to pay money or repair damages, though such agreements are seen as a part of the reconciliation process. A case that ends without reconciliation and drinking is considered less than satisfactory.

The formal sanctions at the Presidente's command are jail sentences and fines. According to the law, the Presidente may keep a suspect in jail for seventy-two hours while he conducts an investigation. If the accumulated evidence is then insufficient to warrant a formal charge, the prisoner must be released. A convicted criminal may be fined, or given a short jail sentence, usually not longer than six weeks. During this time the prisoner works days on community projects and spends the nights in jail. Zinacantecos call this *kučton*, "carrying stones," because the main community project of the last few years has been the reconstruction of the town hall. Prisoners were required to cut stones from the mountain and carry them to the town hall by tumpline. But one enterprising and prosperous prisoner cut his sentence short by hiring a truck to carry his quota of stones.

The Presidente's most effective sanction, however, is the threat of referral to a higher authority. For a litigant at the town hall this means the Mexican courts in San Cristobal, with the possibility of a long jail sentence or a large fine and where litigation is conducted in an alien language by lawyers who must be paid. Faced with this threat, many recalcitrant litigants cave in and bargain for a local settlement.

Many town hall settlements are recorded by the Ladino secretary. The documents, called *actas*, contain the signatures or thumb-

prints of the Presidente and all the litigants. One copy of the acta is given to each party, and the final carbon is filed at the town hall. A fee of about ten pesos is charged for the document, the fee split between the litigants if both are equally at fault, or paid entirely by the most guilty party. Actas tend to be short, seldom more than two typewritten pages, and they record only the final settlement. Cases that are long and involved may leave an official record of only half a page. But actas play a vital role in town hall settlements. For the litigants, the acta serves as a record of the agreement. If either party brings up the case again, the original agreement is usually upheld. Actas also protect the Presidente from future complaints. In his interstitial role as the lowest level of Mexican justice and the highest level of Zinacanteco justice, the Presidente often makes settlements unacceptable to one legal system or the other. If the Mexican authorities complain of a decision, the acta shows that both sides agreed to the settlement in Zinacantan, and if a Zinacanteco litigant complains, the Presidente can remind the litigant that he was not forced to sign the acta.

Other documents play a lesser role in the Zinacanteco legal system. A *diligencia* is a statement of charges against a prisoner being sent to the authorities in San Cristobal, where all serious crimes should be referred. On a charge of murder or other serious crime— causing severe injury, major theft, or possessing a talking saint— the prisoner is kept in jail for three days and interrogated three times a day. When all the evidence is in, the Presidente sums up the charges and the Secretary writes the formal diligencia. Persons accused of lesser crimes may be threatened by this recourse into making an appropriate settlement in Zinacantan. Two days of jail and interrogation are often enough to persuade criminals to make peace with their accusers and to repair the damage caused.

The Mexican Penal Authorities

San Cristobal is the center of a judicial district that embraces the surrounding Indian communities and includes Zinacantan. According to Mexican law, Zinacantecos who have committed serious crimes must be turned over to the state legal authorities for prosecution, and accusers in a criminal action have recourse to the same channels.

The Mexican legal system is in the civil law tradition, derived

from Spain and influenced by French legal scholarship. It is a complex system of federal and state courts and codes, but all that most Zinacantecos see of it is the small outpost of state criminal procedures maintained in San Cristobal. As far as I could ascertain, Zinacantecos seldom approach the federal judiciary or use the state civil procedures. A new jail has been built within the last ten years, and the front part of this building houses the offices of the *Agente del Ministerio Publico* (public prosecutor) and the *Juez Penal* (criminal judge). I spent about three weeks in the summer of 1970 visiting these offices, looking at records and observing procedures. The description given below is based on these observations and on statements by Zinacantecos.

Cases begin in the office of the public prosecutor. A Zinacanteco facing criminal charges is brought here with his diligencia. The charges are reviewed and an order is prepared for the prisoner to be detained in the jail below. Accusers also come here to file complaints. A complaint is easily lodged if it involves direct evidence, such as open wounds or destroyed property, but less clear-cut cases are more likely to be heeded if a lawyer is retained to file a formal complaint before approaching the public prosecutor.

Once a complaint has been formally lodged, the investigation proceeds along the lines laid down in the Codigo de Procedimientos Penales, the code of penal procedures. Each complaint is given a folder and a number and is entered on the records. The accused comes before the public prosecutor, who is the chief of the judicial police, to answer the charges. If the prosecutor and the judge believe that the evidence is too flimsy to warrant further prosecution, the case is dismissed. If the prosecutor is not able to find the accused but considers the charges worth investigating, he will pass the folder on to the office of the penal judge, to be held until the accused is taken into custody.

The assistants of the penal judge then hear the case. There is no public trial, as in common-law countries, but the case proceeds slowly through written documents. The public prosecutor now sheds his role as head of the judicial police and contributes to the prosecution, acting as the preserver of legal rights in the name of society and of the injured party (see Vance and Clagett 1945: 158). The accused may hire a lawyer to argue his case and to file

motions and petitions. If the accused is found guilty, the criminal judge pronounces the penalty according to the state penal code. Mexico does not have the death penalty, and most criminals are sentenced to a term in jail and/or a fine.

Considering the number of crimes that must occur in the vast Indian hinterland, remarkably few cases come to the attention of the criminal authorities. According to the records, the criminal judge handles around 160 cases a year, at least half of which involve only Ladinos. In searching through the cases of 1961, 1965, 1969, and the first half of 1970, I found only fifteen, three, seven, and four cases, respectively, containing accusations against Zinacantecos.

Communication between Zinacantecos and the Mexican legal authorities inevitably involves some degree of misunderstanding. Language alone is a major problem. Tzotzil and Spanish have no common roots, and even careful translating produces distortions. In the office of the criminal judge, a woman secretary did most of the translating. Although well-intentioned, she seemed to have little knowledge of Indian ways, and even I recognized some of her more obvious translation errors.

Cultural differences provide an even greater source of misunderstanding. In one case a Zinacanteco family who accused several men of having broken into their house one night stressed the fact that a child had died three days after the attack. Each time the testimony of the Indians was recorded and translated, this incident was brought out, but later versions of the case, prepared by the judicial authorities, contained no mention of the child's death. Zinacantecos believe that a severe fright can cause soul loss leading to death, and the parents of the child were essentially accusing the attackers of murder. The Mexicans, with different conceptions of causality, labeled the case *"daño en propiedad ajena,"* damage to another's property, and eventually released the suspects for lack of evidence. According to the records, the authorities did not ask why the Indians stressed the child's death; the question would have been irrelevant.

Another source of misunderstanding stems from the different naming patterns in the two cultures. The Mexicans follow the Spanish pattern of Christian name, father's surname, and mother's

surname. Zinacanteco naming patterns are just close enough to Mexican patterns that the discrepancy is not too obvious, but sufficiently different to provide a real source of confusion. Zinacantecos also have three names, a Christian name, a Spanish surname, and an Indian surname, but both surnames are inherited from the father. The Zinacantecos, however, have a very limited range of names, which means that at any one time there may be several persons named Mariano Lopez Chiku. Indians get around the ambiguities of this system by using nicknames (G. Collier and Bricker 1970). A person's proper name is rarely used and may be known only to his closest relatives. This system allows one person to be identified by several names and, conversely, a single "legal" name in the Spanish pattern can be applied to several persons. Zinacantecos appearing before the Mexican authorities have been known to make full use of the possibilities. One controversial political leader who had been accused of murder under three names (Christian name plus nickname, Christian name plus Tzotzil surname, Christian name plus Spanish and Indian surnames) "proved" that he was not the wanted man by producing a birth certificate giving his name in the Spanish fashion, with his mother's surname at the end. In another case a man accused of murder was freed when the corpse of his supposed victim could not be firmly linked to any single name.

But the greatest source of misunderstanding derives from the fact that Zinacantecos and Mexicans have different conceptions of what the legal process is about. For the Mexicans, criminal procedures are directed toward ascertaining whether the accused is guilty and, if so, applying the penalty laid down in the criminal code. For the Zinacantecos, legal procedures are designed to produce a compromise. The plaintiff makes an exaggerated accusation but expects to settle for less, while the accused declares his innocence but expects to confess to some form of the crime and then to beg pardon. Verifiable facts are vital to Mexican legal procedures and peripheral to Zinacanteco purposes; and a confrontation between the two cultures can be ludicrous. Zinacanteco litigants tell exaggerated, or completely false, stories, which the Mexican authorities are committed to verifying. Neither side gains respect for the other in the process. Zinacantecos are dismayed, and occa-

sionally amused, at observing Mexican officials searching for imaginary "facts," whereas the officials are annoyed at "those lying Indians."

The Mexican authorities are fully aware of the undesirable results produced by their legal system when applied to Indian affairs. The local explanation in San Cristobal for this phenomenon is that the Mexican legal system is the result of centuries of civilized thought, whereas the Indians, if not outright savages, are at least under the sway of primitive superstition. Thoughtful Mexicans phrase the problem in another way: "How does one prevent a miscarriage of justice when the penal code, which presumes that a crime was committed intentionally even if the criminal believed his aims to be legitimate (Codigo Penal 1968: 23), is applied to a person who, in committing murder, believes he is ridding the world of an evil witch?" It is not true justice to impose a harsh penalty on a superstitious Indian whose fault is primarily a lack of contact with civilizing Spanish influence.

Mexican answers to this problem are abstract. As in other civil-law systems, consistency within the law is more highly valued than real-world consequences (Merryman 1969: 71–72). The convenient fiction that allows Indians to be lumped with minorities and mental incompetents as people not responsible for their actions is not a viable alternative in a modern political context. A civilized nation like Mexico, with claims to moral leadership, cannot openly treat the adults of its ethnic minorities as children. But if Indians are to be full citizens, then they are liable for the legal consequences of their actions, and injustice results. A thesis by a graduate of the San Cristobal law school outlined two possible solutions to the problem (Robles 1968). One would create a separate set of penal laws for Indians, and the other would allow judges at their discretion to vary the legal penalty according to the education of the accused. The idea of a separate penal code was rejected as incompatible with the ideology of a unitary state, and the author ended by advocating judicial discretion in imposing penalties. Civil-law systems have been traditionally wary of the principle of judicial discretion, but given the problem as posed, it appears to be the least objectionable solution.

On a pragmatic level, the problem posed by the Mexicans seems

less acute. Witchcraft murders may capture the imagination, but the real-world situation is much more complex. In the first place, Zinacantecos, and probably most other Indians in the area, have only two "motives" for murder: the victim was a witch or the murderer was drunk, or both. This means that an Indian accused of murder will give a stock answer. The Mexican authorities inevitably conclude that liquor and witchcraft superstitions are the primary causes of violence in Indian communities. They are of course right, but they are also very wrong. Zinacanteco motives for violence are as complex as anyone's motives, but the language for describing them is simple. In seeking to understand the behavior of a murderer, the Indians go deeper for the explanation, whereas the Mexicans accept it at face value, since it reinforces their stereotype of the simple Indian—drunk and superstitious.

It is also important to ask how murder cases reach the authorities in San Cristobal. Here again the situation is complex. It is probable that the Mexican authorities do not see all of the "real" witchcraft assassinations that occur. If there is community consensus that the murder victim was a witch, it is most likely that the body will be buried quietly in the woods and no one will talk. But if the body is not buried quickly enough or if relatives of the victim wish to complain, the case goes to the officials in the municipal center, who will then send it to the Mexican authorities. Murderers, however, are rarely caught. They remain unidentified or they flee the area for two or three years. This means that the few murderers who are accused and caught are indeed a select minority. They are usually those who acted without premeditation and were too drunk to flee.

There is also an important difference between murders and murder accusations. In Zinacantan, murder accusations do not depend on the presence of a body but are leveled against a political opponent on the flimsiest evidence. In the judicial records of 1961, 1965, 1969, and 1970, I found seven murder accusations among the cases involving Zinacantecos. Five of these were from 1961, a year of violent political battles, and the other two were from 1970. Three of the five cases from 1961 were clearly political. The accused were prominent political leaders and the lists of opposing witnesses read like faction rosters. In all three cases the

charges were dismissed. Of the other two, one was declared an accidental death and the accused was freed, and the second case remained pending because the accused had fled. In none of the five cases did the Mexican authorities have to impose a penalty. Of the two cases from 1970, one appears to have been a genuine murder. A woman accused of murdering her co-wife while the latter was in childbirth was in jail at the time I read the records, but no penalty had yet been imposed. The second case had the aura of another political accusation and the accused had been released for lack of evidence.

For an understanding of the actual, as opposed to the theoretical, problems faced by the Mexican penal authorities, it is instructive to examine in the records the range of accusations against Zinacantecos. The most frequent cause, nine cases, was physical injury, *lesiones*. Next came seven accusations of murder, *homicidio*. There were five cases of property damage, *daño en propiedad ajena*, usually house-burning or breaking and entering. Four cases involved accusations of threatening behavior: two of being placed in danger, *peligro*; and one each of threats, *amenazas*, and attempted murder, *homicidio en grado tentativa*. Finally, there was one each of rape, *violacion*; robbery, *robo y golpes*; and a husband's desertion of wife and children, *delito contra la piedad social*, crime against social morality. All of these crimes except the last are crimes of violence.

In the disposition of these cases, the four from 1970 are not included, because most of them were still being processed when I saw the records. In nine of the cases sampled, the charges had been dismissed and the accused freed. In another six, the accused was never caught. Six cases ended with the accused found guilty and freed on paying a fine. In only one case did the accused go to prison, though the papers give no indication whether he was held or later released. In the three remaining cases I was unable to determine what the final disposition had been. From my small sample it appears that most of the accused never reached prison, or remained there only a short time.

The Zinacantecos' view of Mexican legal processes reflects the realities they see. From conversations, I have gathered that Zinacantecos think the Mexican authorities very gullible. They will

accept and investigate any charge that is phrased in legal language or backed by a minimum of evidence or sworn to by a few witnesses. And witnesses are easy to procure. Although the testimony of close relatives theoretically has less weight than that of a disinterested party, Zinacanteco full brothers can appear independent and disinterested simply by claiming different versions of their common surname.

Once the Mexican authorities begin to investigate a charge, the accused Zinacanteco is hopelessly entangled unless he runs away. He must counter the accusations against him, and this usually means he must hire a lawyer to conduct his defense. It is easy to see why the Zinacantecos view any entanglement with the public prosecutor or the penal judge primarily in terms of money. For them the question is not "Innocent or guilty?" but "How much?" Money goes for documents and lawyers as well as fines. The less sophisticated Zinacantecos tend to lump them together, for it is all money that must be paid to be free again.

At the beginning of my study I felt sorry for Indians caught in the web of Mexican justice, as poor people being judged under alien rules by powerful officials who spoke an unintelligible language. But since my visits to San Cristobal, I have come to have sympathy for the judicial authorities as public servants, maneuvered by crafty Indians into conducting impossible investigations. The formal legal contact between Zinacantecos and Mexican officials appears to parallel that reported from other areas of the world where a powerful, Western-style government maintains courts for an ethnically different people. The people usually have their own methods for settling disputes, if indeed they wish to settle them, and they use the alien courts only for revenge or to further their own interests (Bohannan 1965). Law becomes another weapon for furthering a conflict, and legal officials are invoked chiefly for the purpose of harassing an enemy (Cohn 1959).

Mexican Agencies Designed to Help Indians

Two agencies in San Cristobal are designed to integrate local Indians into the national Mexican culture: the federally sponsored Instituto Nacional Indigenista (INI) and the state-sponsored Departamento de Asuntos Indigenas (State Department of

Indian Affairs). The two agencies tend to handle different types of cases from Zinacantan: INI is asked to adjudicate the political battles, whereas individuals are more likely to take simple disputes to the Director of Indian Affairs. Zinacantecos complain that the INI lawyer demands too much proof before agreeing to sponsor an Indian's complaint to the penal authorities—it is easier, they say, to pay one of the local lawyers to do the job—but once an Indian is in the San Cristobal jail, the INI lawyer will come to his aid if asked.

INI officials do, however, intercede between warring political factions, because of their relations with Indian leaders. INI's program of economic and social development demands the cooperation of community political bosses, and INI officials have an understandable interest in supporting the Indian leaders who seem most likely to provide the type of stable and progressive governments necessary for successful growth. Many Indian leaders, moreover, including the two most recent Presidentes of Zinacantan, were formerly employed by INI as program promoters and schoolteachers.

Drawing the line between politics and law is always difficult, and it becomes particularly so in Zinacanteco factional fights, since a favorite ploy for removing an opponent from the political scene is to have him jailed in San Cristobal on a criminal charge. INI officials drawn into these battles find themselves caught between the formal demands of judicial procedure and the pragmatic demands of political expediency. Their difficult position is seldom made easier by the fact that they are usually aware of the issues and motives underlying actual events.

The State Department of Indian Affairs is the Mexican agency with the most noticeable effect on the Zinacanteco legal system, since (1) the Director can be approached easily by ordinary Indians, and (2) the agency is committed to working through Indian legal channels. The aim of the department is to Mexicanize, but not destroy, Indian political structures, and the Director tries to accomplish this task by instructing Indian Presidentes in correct procedures while upholding their authority. The unusual success of this agency can also be attributed to the personality of its recent Director. A deeply moral man, he has used persuasion instead of force and won the confidence of the Indians.

Individual Zinacantecos can approach the Director of Indian Affairs without elaborate preparation or fear of loss. The department, located in a house on a side street in San Cristobal, is open to all. When an Indian has a specific complaint, the Director will often give him a letter of instruction to take to his Presidente, in which he spells out the appropriate Mexican law to cover the situation described by the plaintiff: perhaps that legal interest rates on a loan cannot exceed 9 percent a year; or that no one can be forced to contribute to a religious festival against his will, since Mexico recognizes freedom of religion; or that a girl cannot be forced to marry without her consent regardless of any agreement between her father and her suitor. The plaintiff, armed with this letter, returns to his town hall, where he can argue his case from a much stronger position. The town hall outcome will still be a compromise, but the balance will be tipped decisively toward the plaintiff and the dictates of Mexican law.

The State Department of Indian Affairs handles a wide range of other matters affecting Indian communities. The agency was originally set up to handle labor relations, but the Director also looks into school attendance, public works projects, health programs, public property, and other matters. The office files, for example, contain a bulky folder of correspondence on some missing telephone wire, which was discovered as part of a Zinacanteco fence.

The Politicians in the State Government

The state government in Tuxtla Gutierrez is controlled by Mexican liberals, who outrank the conservative officials in San Cristobal. Although Zinacantecos may not understand the full meaning of the ideological differences, they understand enough to be able to take advantage of them. Indians seeking specific political advantages now bypass the San Cristobal authorities and take their cases directly to Tuxtla. Each political faction has men skilled in manipulating Ladino values who can phrase an argument in terms that will appeal to the heart of a liberal politician. Unlike the San Cristobal authorities, who live surrounded by Indians and whose very lives may depend on a realistic assessment of Indian politics, the Tuxtla officials need base their decisions only on the sometimes

extremely biased evidence presented to them. For example, I found a series of letters addressed to Tuxtla officials that obscured the real issues of a political power fight in pious platitudes. The author of the letters asked the Tuxtla officials to close some Zinacanteco *cantinas* that he claimed were a corrupting influence on the young children, who passed the drunks on their way to school. This sentiment is totally alien to Zinacantecos, who routinely send a young child with his father to a drinking session so he can lead the drunken father home. Zinacanteco children are continually exposed to drunken adults and quickly learn to avoid them. The "corruption of innocence" theme was simply a ploy designed to persuade liberal politicians to use their influence in closing down the lucrative *cantinas* owned by members of the opposing political faction.

Zinacantecos, as they become more skilled in Spanish and in political platitudes, have begun to make appeals to an ever wider range of Mexican officials. Health inspectors are asked to close down the "unsanitary" corn-grinding mills of enemies, school inspectors are asked to remove local school-board officers, and appeals are even directed to the President of Mexico on questions of land. But these appeals to high officials once again fall outside my definition of legal procedures: they are appeals to "remedy agents," but the remedies produced rarely involve the confrontations that my definition requires.

Conclusion

We have examined the formal structure of legal levels available to Zinacantecos and the range of litigants who appeal to them: the curing ceremonies concerning family members, the hamlet procedures involving neighbors, the town hall court settling disputes from the entire township, the San Cristobal authorities handling serious crimes, the State Department of Indian Affairs and INI working to integrate Zinacantan into national life, the Tuxtla politicians considering appeals from the entire state of Chiapas, and, finally, the President of Mexico representing the ultimate authority of the nation. But at either end of this spectrum there are procedures that I would hesitate to include in my definition of a legal procedure. Curing ceremonies need not involve any real discus-

sion of the conflict, and appeals to the Mexican agencies outside of Zinacantan are generally better seen as political maneuvers, since they are usually motivated by the desire for personal or group gain rather than to resolve conflict.

The most effective procedures for settling conflicts are those operating within Zinacantan: begging formal pardon, mediation by a hamlet elder, and arbitration before the town hall court. Though the following chapters focus on these three procedures, it was essential that the others be discussed, since it would be impossible to understand the core procedures without considering their place in the hierarchy of legal levels. A legal procedure must be described for what it is, but it must also be seen in terms of what it is not—i.e. in terms of its position within a set of available options.

The hierarchy presented in this chapter can be seen from two vantage points: authority flows from the Mexican national government down through the state authorities, the San Cristobal officials, the Presidente of Zinacantan, the hamlet elders, and the descent-group heads to men, women, and children; turning the hierarchy on its head, we see each Zinacanteco belonging to (and more or less supporting) a household, a descent group, a political faction, a hamlet, the township of Zinacantan, the district of San Cristobal, the State of Chiapas, and the Republic of Mexico. Although these levels are fairly fixed and static, the dynamic interaction between authority coming down and support moving up shapes the outcomes produced at each legal level.

TWO

The Organization of Legal Levels

Chapter 1 presented a theoretical set of legal levels and discussed the types of cases that can be handled by each procedure. This chapter introduces a dynamic element, for Zinacantan is a real community in historical time, and its people use their legal system for practical purposes. Taking Firth's concept of social organization (1956: 40), "the systematic ordering of social relations by acts of choice and decision," we look now at the cases handled at each level in terms of the patterns created by the cumulative choices of individuals. Chapter 2 outlined the options available to a Zinacanteco involved in a conflict; this chapter examines the way these options are used.

In a fundamental sense, the procedures followed on any legal level can be understood only in terms of the cases actually handled at that level. Patterns of court use and types of claims mold courtroom behavior and produce "styles" of court procedure (Nader 1969: 90). The apparently static quality of some legal levels— same old cases, same old outcomes—may result from the illusion created by a complex feedback process in which types of claims influence types of outcomes, which in turn influence types of future claims. With this more dynamic view, we can analyze some of the changes occurring in a legal system in terms of changes in patterns of court usage. Although a set of legal levels may be relatively invariant, the working of a legal system can change drastically as some levels become more popular and others decline through lack of use. I suggest that Zinacanteco law, although never static in the past, is presently undergoing a period of accelerated

change because litigants are more willing to appeal cases to the San Cristobal authorities. In this chapter, the analytically timeless structures described in Chapter 2 are seen as the momentary products of ongoing processes.

Zinacanteco law has an ephemeral quality. Legal systems have too often been described as the cornerstones of society, as preservers of order and the status quo. But such a view would only distort the Zinacanteco materials. Decisions reached at the town hall court cannot be taken as reliable guides to community norms. The town hall court is caught between two cultures and its decisions reflect pressures from both sides. I would argue that all legal procedures share this uncertainty. The effectiveness of the sanctions wielded by a legal personage depend in part on how they are perceived by the litigants. Even the "facts" of a case and the relevant norms can be shown to vary at different legal levels. In this situation it is imperative to look at the hierarchy of legal levels as a system and to ask how procedures, claims, and litigants are distributed through it.

This chapter is divided into three sections. The first presents a table offering a relatively static view of the interrelations between types of litigants, types of procedures, and types of claims at each major legal level. This description provides the base line from which ongoing changes can be analyzed. The second section discusses the factors mentioned by litigants as affecting their choice of court. Changes in the outside world—better roads, more liberal government policies, changing economic conditions—have been affecting these factors, and it is possible to create hypotheses linking outside changes to changes within the legal system through a consideration of the factors influencing a litigant's choice of court. The last section discusses the strategies of the political leaders who act as judges and mediators. These men manipulate the legal system to their own advantage, altering the kinds of solutions produced at different levels within Zinacantan, thereby affecting patterns of litigant choice and the kinds of cases coming before them.

Litigants, Claims, and Procedures

The factors interacting to produce a particular configuration of litigants and claims at any legal level are interdependent and

appear distorted if considered separately. Chapter 1 presented the legal procedures as a hierarchy of ever more inclusive levels: begging-pardon ceremonies can occur only among close neighbors in a hamlet; whereas Indians from the entire highland area can appeal to the Mexican judicial authorities. Such a scheme has immediate implications: cases go up the hierarchy far more easily than down; litigants who appeal to lower-level procedures necessarily have close ties, whereas those appealing higher up are less likely to have an ongoing relationship; and cases brought to lower courts tend to reflect the complex problems of people who must live together, whereas cases going to higher levels appear to be single-instance disputes. Obviously it is also more costly to appeal to a higher-level court. Transportation fees, loss of working time, and uncertainty of outcome all increase as a Zinacanteco appeals farther from his own hamlet. In general, then, lower-level legal procedures produce compromise solutions for the complex problems of closely related individuals, whereas higher-level courts produce zero-sum decisions for single-instance conflicts between individuals who have no lasting commitment to each other. This section of the chapter will attempt to chart these interrelationships, and to discuss the procedural style of a legal level as dependent on inherent assumptions about the types of litigants and types of claims to be expected at that level.

Table 1 presents a simplified outline of the various factors that interact to produce distinctive configurations of litigants, claims, and outcomes at various legel levels. For ease of discussion, only three legal levels are considered: hamlet procedures, the town hall court in the ceremonial center, and the Mexican authorities in San Cristobal. There is a broad gap between the Mexican and Zinacantecan levels, reflecting the different cultural contexts; the ceremonial center can be regarded as an extension of hamlet procedures, but San Cristobal is a world apart.

Ties between litigants. As we have observed, begging-pardon ceremonies and appeals to a hamlet elder are procedures that can be used only by persons with close kinship or neighborhood ties. The ceremonial center of Zinacantan handles litigants with no close ties as well as those closely related. Members of opposing factions within a hamlet or members of different hamlets can also appeal

TABLE 1

Litigants, Claims, and Determinants of Procedural Style at Each Legal Level

Ties between litigants	Types of claims	Cost of appeal	Sanctions	Shared knowledge of participants	Ideology	Assumptions underlying style of procedure
HAMLET						
Many-stranded ties, which at least one side wishes to preserve	Minor crimes and quarrels	Low costs and little risk of an undesired outcome	No formal sanctions but effective informal pressure	Intimate knowledge of the case, its background, and personalities of the litigants	Social harmony to be restored by placating the victim of the wrong; focus on the plaintiff and his wishes	Litigants seek compromise
CEREMONIAL CENTER						
Many-stranded and single-stranded ties	More serious crimes and disputes that hamlet elders have been unable to settle	Moderate costs and more risk of an undesired outcome	Minor formal sanctions and effective informal pressure	Shared cultural knowledge of expectable behavior patterns; litigants and officials known to each other by reputation	Same ideology as in hamlet	Compromise solution is desirable even if one of the litigants must be pressured into cooperating
SAN CRISTOBAL						
Many-stranded or single-stranded ties, which at least one side is willing to break	Major crimes and serious cases that have not been resolved in Zinacantan; political fights and violations of Mexican law	High costs and great risk of an undesired outcome	Primarily formal sanctions	Cultural misunderstandings between Mexican officials and Indian litigants; individuals seen in terms of stereotypes	Social harmony to be restored by punishing the person who committed a wrong; focus on the offender and his crime	Correct solution can be found for every case by applying abstract rules to the facts; wishes of the litigants are irrelevant

to the officials in the ceremonial center. San Cristobal, as would be expected of a more inclusive level, can handle all types of litigants but, in fact, receives a highly selected sample. The Mexican authorities tend to be left with the litigants who have no close ties or who wish to break the ones they have; they get the political faction fights, the husband or wife intent on divorce, the neighbor out for revenge, the kinsman who has broken with his relatives.

Types of claims. Hamlet procedures are invoked for most types of cases in which the litigants are closely related, but only minor disputes tend to be settled on that level. More serious cases, or cases in which one side refuses to compromise, usually end up at the town hall court. Hamlet elders, when asked for advice in difficult or violent cases, often urge litigants to appeal directly to the Presidente, since he has more power to force a reconciliation and can make an official record of the terms of the agreement. Some litigants go directly to the ceremonial center, bypassing hamlet procedures altogether—women intent on a divorce who want to avoid the reconciliation efforts of a hamlet elder, creditors wanting a debtor jailed until he pays, and angry plaintiffs wishing to invoke punishment for an offender.

According to Mexican law, all serious crimes must be referred to the penal authorities in San Cristobal, but as would be expected, relatively few cases actually get there. Murder is the only crime consistently reported, since the Zinacanteco authorities settle cases of major theft, serious bodily injury, and rape within the community if the offender agrees to make reparations and the victim seems satisfied with the settlement. But many cases are taken outside the community by private individuals. People who are in jail or who fear being jailed in Zinacantan or who might expect to pay heavy damages to a victim often appeal to the Mexican authorities in the hope of avoiding certain punishment. And in the cases where Zinacanteco custom and Mexican law conflict, such appeals can be very successful. As a result, the Presidente now hesitates to jail a person accused of witchcraft, a boy accused of eloping with a girl engaged to another suitor, a witness who refuses to tell what he knows, or a hostage who is held in order to force the real culprit to appear. And as discussed in Chapter 1, the Mexican penal authorities also receive imaginary, or exaggerated, reports of crimes that are brought up as part of ongoing political battles.

The Director of the State Department of Indian Affairs receives a different range of cases. He hears complaints against the Presidente's conduct, but he also adjudicates appeals from persons wishing to invoke Mexican laws instead of adhering to Zinacanteco custom. Women wanting more equal shares of inherited land, men wanting to avoid service in the religious cargo system, debtors trying to escape high interest rates, girls desiring to marry as they choose, and men refusing to contribute to religious fiestas, all may appeal to the Director for a letter to free them from customary obligations.

Cost of appeal. Both cost and risk are inherent in any appeal to a legal procedure, but at the hamlet level both are minimal. The cash outlay for the person invoking the procedures is the price of a bottle or two of the local rum—about three pesos a bottle—and he need lose no working time, since the appeal can be made at night or during a slack period. He also faces little risk, for he can be fairly certain of the outcome. The litigant on the hamlet level has the advantage of taking an active part in shaping the outcome, and he can take his case to the ceremonial center if he is dissatisfied.

Both cost and uncertainty rise in an appeal to the authorities at the ceremonial center. In addition to the cost of the liquor, a litigant faces transportation fees, depending on how far away he lives and how many people he asks to accompany him, and loss of working time owing to possible delays in assembling all the people needed for the hearing. The outcome is also more uncertain. The litigant knows he will be able to speak for himself and state his wishes, but he is less certain of being heeded, and he may fear the discomfort of being jailed overnight. Finally, if he is dissatisfied with the proposed settlement, he faces the difficulty of choosing between accepting an unsatisfactory solution and risking an appeal to the Mexican authorities.

Most Zinacantecos are reluctant to appeal to the Mexican penal authorities because they believe the outcome is unpredictable and likely to be costly. One Zinacanteco told me that taking a dispute to the San Cristobal officials was like putting it in the hands of the gods. In either case the litigants have little influence on the outcome. The lawyers and judges, like the gods, discuss the matter

among themselves in an unintelligible language and carry out their decision by force. In the opinion of this informant, the Zincanteco who approaches the penal authorities has little way of knowing whether he or his enemy will end up in jail. And if the plaintiff does become trapped in his own net, his neighbors will feel he deserved his fate. One angry Zinacanteco who disregarded all advice and took his case directly to the public prosecutor received little sympathy when he ended up paying large sums for lawyer's fees and received no compensation for the physical injuries he had suffered.

Appeal to the Mexican authorities also generates ill will, for Zinacantecos readily condemn the person who appeals to outside, arbitrary force. In Zinacanteco ideology, a satisfactory solution avoids future conflict, but an appeal to the Mexican authorities invites retaliation instead of reconciliation, and the Mexican officials find themselves plagued by Zinacanteco feuds waged with accusations and counteraccusations instead of killings and counter-killings.

Appeals to the Director of Indian Affairs are less costly and risky because the Director usually works through the town hall court rather than enforce his own decisions. This has both advantages and disadvantages: a Zinacanteco litigant can avoid some of the ill will generated by an appeal to the penal authorities, but he loses the possibility of decisive revenge. The process also takes time, bus fare, and someone with a knowledge of Spanish to appeal to the Director in San Cristobal, and there is always the possibility that the Director will investigate the matter for himself and enforce his own decision.

Sanctions. From the three legal levels shown in Table 1 it can be seen that overt, formal sanctions increase as informal means of persuasion decrease. A hamlet elder can persuade the litigants to comply with his decisions, whereas the decisions of the penal judge in San Cristobal are carried out by physical force. But this neat picture masks a much more complex reality, since it is far truer to say that the effectiveness of a sanction depends on how it is perceived by the person affected. Direct physical coercion tends to be effective because most people perceive it as something to be avoided, except of course for martyrs and fanatics, who will defy

earthly doom for a higher reward. Or, to put it in a Zinacanteco context, the informal sanctions of a hamlet elder may be far more feared than the Presidente's power to put someone in jail. Litigants usually realize that the hamlet elder can make life unpleasant for a person who defies him, but they know that a few days or weeks in the Presidente's jail need have no lasting consequences.

Shared knowledge of participants. Most Zinacantecos live in small hamlets surrounded by relatives and neighbors with whom they have long-term, face-to-face relations. As a result, most Zinacanteco conflicts are complex affairs of wrongs and counterwrongs, of little arguments and big fights, of deeds committed or omitted over a long period of time. When such a conflict is handled in the hamlet, all the participants have a fairly good knowledge of the real issues involved. The hamlet elder, when acting as a mediator, knows the individual litigants personally. He has some idea of the past history of the dispute and he probably understands the long-term goals of the antagonists.

At the town hall court the officials know less about the litigants and the history of their dispute, but they have a good idea of what to expect. Although some of the litigants may be friends of the officials or be known by reputation in the township, most people who come to the court are not seen as individuals with distinct personalities but are assessed through a system of complex categories, such as being a relative of a well-known person or a social nobody, or being marked by external characteristics such as male or female, old or young, rich or poor, well dressed or slovenly. The litigants themselves play up to these categories as they offer information to raise their status in the eyes of the officials and try to hide characteristics that will lower it. But since the participants in these proceedings share a single culture, they can usually see through each other's strategies and plots.

When cases come to the town hall court, the civil officials know that the events recounted by the litigants are but a small part of a more complex series of happenings. As Zinacantecos they expect the background of the events in question to be complicated and they wait for the details to unfold as the case proceeds. But the officials hear an edited version of the background; their cultural

heritage leads them to have definite expectations but they rarely have the firsthand knowledge available to hamlet elders. They know only what they are told, but they can, and do, ask searching questions. As a result, the version of events they get tends to be more standardized than the particularistic accounts heard at the hamlet level.

In San Cristobal the Mexican officials know almost nothing about individual Zinacanteco litigants and the history of their dispute, and they lack the cultural background to make informed inferences. The result is something of a vicious circle, for the Ladinos find their view of the Indian as "unreliable, irresponsible, mistrusting, superstitious and unchanging" (Colby 1966: 33) to be confirmed by the behavior of the Indian litigants who come to San Cristobal. As discussed in Chapter 1, Zinacantecos approaching the Mexican penal authorities do tend to be deceitful and mistrusting and to appear superstitious and irrational. The barriers of language, life-style, and social status combine to make Indian behavior unintelligible to all but a few, very sensitive, Mexican officials. Even when Mexican officials know enough about Indian life to inquire into the background of events or to suspect hidden motives, their efforts are frustrated by the lack of shared knowledge and by the structure of the Mexican legal system, which demands that accusations of wrongs be taken one by one at face value. As a result, complex Indian wrongs are put into categories that carry simple Spanish labels and then treated as if the labels were truly applicable.

Ideology. The ideology underlying the Zinacanteco settlement procedures differs from that of the Mexican legal system. The two cultures have different conceptual frameworks for justifying legal action. Though Zinacanteco legal concepts will be taken up in detail in Chapter 4, I shall outline them briefly here because they provide the rationale for compromise solutions and litigant participation.

In all legal systems the ultimate reason given for settling conflicts or righting wrongs is to restore social and cosmic order. For Zinacantecos this order is disturbed when a wrong is committed, not because of the wrong itself, but because the victim of the

wrong has anger in his heart and will seek vengeance. The rationale for settlement procedures, then, is to placate the victim and remove the anger from his heart. Simply righting the wrong, or punishing the wrongdoer, would not serve this purpose and might even leave the wrongdoer with anger in *his* heart and a desire for vengeance.

Ideologies are complex to discuss, but an examination of the Zinacanteco view of ultimate purposes does offer insights into the legal procedures that are aimed at reconciling the litigants. Such an examination makes clear why the Zinacantecos focus on the plaintiff and his wishes, and why the "facts" of the case are so unimportant. Facts and norms are both used as counters in the argument. There is no single set of facts and no single applicable norm, but all are used in the process of searching for a common ground on which to base the vital agreement. The final solution to a conflict may bear little relation to the "wrong" that initiated the settlement procedure, but it is considered satisfactory if plaintiff and defendant are reconciled.

Mexican legal procedures, on the other hand, are directed toward restoring social and cosmic order by righting the wrong. The focus is on the offender, who disturbed the order by breaking the rules, and not on his victim, who is seen simply as an unfortunate who happened to get in the way. Even when a victim receives compensation for injuries he has sustained, the compensation is justified as righting the original wrong, and not as a means of placating his anger. Given this ideology, the facts of the case are crucial, for how can a wrong be righted unless the specifics of the wrong are known? And the wishes of the litigants are completely irrelevant. Justice is blind to persons involved, and her scales balance only when the punishment is directly equal to the wrong committed, as determined by abstract rules. In Mexican ideology there is a "right" way of doing things, apart from the wishes of the individuals involved, whereas in Zinacanteco ideology the two are inseparable. Zinacanteco litigants speak for themselves, are cavalier about the facts, and expect and receive a compromise solution. Litigants before the Mexican authorities speak only when spoken to, and then answer questions designed by the officials to uncover the "facts" of the case. Solutions follow from

these "facts" and tend to place all the blame on one side, producing a zero-sum decision.

Assumptions underlying style of procedure. Hamlet procedures are informal, intimate, and particularistic. They exist to reconcile closely related individuals who have fought but must go on living together, and the tone of the proceedings is set by the assumption that the litigants want to settle their differences. If it becomes clear in the course of a hearing that one of the litigants does not want to settle, the procedure fails and the case must be dropped or taken to a higher authority. Participants in hamlet procedures can also take shortcuts not available to litigants in more formal proceedings. Because everyone knows each other well, much of the background of a case can be left unstated and the participants can concentrate on working out a compromise. The privacy of the hearing and the ease of invoking it add to its informal character. A lasting solution is desirable, but all concerned know that another hearing may be called if the one in progress proves unsuccessful. It make take several sessions of begging pardon, or a series of hearings in an elder's house to produce a settlement, but the procedures are inexpensive and private and can be scheduled for evenings and Sundays. The aim is to produce a lasting agreement and not compromise by coercion.

Proceedings in the ceremonial center are more formal, more constrained. The aim is still to produce a compromise, but force can be used if needed. As a result, the tone of the proceedings can be roughly characterized as "compromise or else. . . ." The Presidente will jail wrongdoers who refuse to admit guilt and beg pardon, and he will ridicule, and even threaten to jail, plaintiffs who refuse to lower their demands. It is hard to assess the reality of these threats but compromises are indeed produced. It may be that the town hall procedure is so effective because all parties realize it constitutes the last chance to settle their dispute in Zinacantan. And the threats may be effective primarily because they provide the litigants with a face-saving way of bowing to the inevitable.

Whereas hamlet procedures are based on the assumption that the litigants want to settle their quarrel and become reconciled, ceremonial center proceedings assume that each litigant is out for what

he can get but will agree to a compromise when all strategies are exhausted. The Presidente and the other civil officials are aware that only the more serious cases come to them—those not resolved on the hamlet level. Knowing that the litigants are reluctant to compromise, they begin by asking each antagonist to state his case and his wishes. Then they work toward compromise. Using their knowledge of general Zinacanteco behavior, the officials rephrase each litigant's statement to bring out points on which both agree. Hearings tend to be continuous once both sides are present; and the publicity of the town hall setting, combined with the tiring effects of steady argument, puts considerable pressure on the litigants to reach agreement.

The differences between hamlet and town hall hearings are emphasized in the following case, which shows litigants at the town hall being "forced" to agree to a settlement that was unacceptable when proposed by a hamlet elder.

Case 1. Two gossiping widows threaten a courtship transaction by questioning the reputation of an engaged girl. (The informant was the elder who handled the case.)

A boy called Andres was engaged to Maria, the daughter of Chep Vaskis. One night Chep and his *compadre* Mariano were drinking at Chep's house. Both men drank a great deal and were drunk when Mariano left to return to his home on the far side of the hamlet. Later, two widows living near Chep made known that they had seen the drunken compadre Mariano being escorted home by Chep's engaged daughter Maria and another woman. They told their story to a friend, who told it to her father, Miguel, who repeated it around the hamlet. Now that a man was spreading the story the affair became more serious, and Andres realized he would have to take action.

He therefore went to the house of his fiancée to question her father. Chep remembered nothing of the evening but questioned his wife and and daughter about their actions that night. Both women asserted that the drunken compadre had left the house alone. Andres and his future father-in-law discussed the matter and decided they would have to confront the issue of the gossip to protect their courtship transaction. Andres had invested a considerable amount in bride-price for Maria, and the girl's father had consumed all the gifts and did not want to repay in cash if Andres should decide against the marriage and demand his money back.

Andres bought a bottle of the local rum and called on the hamlet elder who had acted as one of his petitioners when he asked for Maria. The elder, Don Antonio, listened to the story and, upon being assured

that both Andres and his father-in-law wanted a hamlet solution, agreed to hear the case. Andres then went to fetch his future bride's family while the elder sent a minor hamlet official for the two gossiping widows and the man who had spread the story. Mariano, the drunken compadre, was not called because it was assumed he had been too drunk to remember his walk home.

When everyone was assembled at the elder's house, Don Antonio asked the two widows to describe what they had seen. The widows said they had seen Mariano pass their house at dusk, making a lot of noise and supported by two women, one being Chep Vaskis's engaged daughter. They claimed they had not recognized the other woman. Don Antonio questioned them closely for an admission that the other woman might have been the girl's mother, but they refused to cooperate, saying they had not seen her well enough to recognize her. The elder then turned to Miguel and reprimanded him for passing on the questionable story of two gossiping old widows. The elder's aim was to convince the engaged boy that such unsubstantiated gossip should be forgotten. But Andres was still unhappy. He had to decide whether to forget the gossip and continue the courtship or to believe the gossip and demand his money back.

Since Andres remained dissatisfied with the hamlet hearing, he determined to take the case to the ceremonial center. He asked the elder to accompany him, and all the participants agreed to meet the next morning at the town hall. Assembled before the Presidente, they repeated the story and the Presidente proceeded to question the widows. The Presidente's tactics were similar to the elder's—he also tried to undermine the widows' credibility in order to convince Andres to forget the gossip and continue the courtship. But the widows stuck to their story and refused to admit that the other woman supporting the drunken compadre had been the girl's mother. The Presidente then decreed that if their gossip caused Andres to break off his courtship, they, instead of the girl's father, would be responsible for returning the money Andres had spent. At this, the widows changed their story, admitting that perhaps the drunken man had not been Mariano and that the light had been so bad they were no longer sure they had even recognized the girl Maria. The Presidente scolded them for causing such trouble with their gossip and threatened to put them in jail if the girl's father requested it. But Chep Vaskis decided not to have the widows punished; one was the daughter-in-law of a good friend and he did not want to endanger the relationship. Finally, the two widows signed and paid for an acta stating that they would not repeat the story. Miguel was not even reprimanded.

This case provides a nice illustration of the contrast between hamlet and ceremonial center proceedings. On the hamlet level

the elder tried to persuade the widows to change their story and, failing that, then tried to convince Andres that the gossip did not matter. The entire emphasis was on smoothing over the conflict. At the ceremonial center, by contrast, everyone realized that more would be needed to produce a compromise. Persuasion alone had failed because the widows had refused to retract and Andres had refused to forget the matter. But a compromise was produced by referring to the heart of the matter, the bride-price. The Presidente's threat to force the widows to repay Andres, should he believe their gossip and break off the courtship, was effective because it promised trouble for both Andres and the widows. Though it is doubtful it could have been carried out, the threat was effective because it split the responsibility for the bride-price payments and warned all concerned that breaking the courtship off would lead to a whole series of problems. If Andres abandoned his fiancée, he would be hard pressed to recover his money from the girl's father or to force the widows to pay. And the widows were made to realize that they would be held responsible if the courtship was broken off, that they would be irrevocably drawn into the conflict over the money, with its resultant difficulties and ill will. And, indeed, the widows hedged on their story and Andres accepted their partial retraction. The result was not quite satisfactory to anyone, but it allowed them all to avoid the larger problems attendant on a broken courtship.

The tone of the procedures by which Indian cases are handled in San Cristobal is set by three factors: the ideology underlying the Mexican legal system, the lack of shared knowledge between Indians and Mexicans, and the fact that the Indians who reach the Mexican officials have passed the point of possible reconciliation. The Mexican officials, frustrated by the failure of the Indian litigants to cooperate and attributing the difficulty chiefly to the cultural gap, have developed two ways of handling Indian cases. The first method, used by the penal authorities, ignores the cultural differences and applies the letter, instead of the spirit, of the law. Hunt and Hunt (1969: 137) discuss an Indian region of northern Oaxaca where the district court judge applied the national standards more rigorously to Indians than to the non-Indians who came before him. The second approach to the cultural gap, taken by the Director of the State Department of Indian Affairs, recognizes the

cultural differences but tries to teach the Indians respect for Mexican law. Neither solution, however, recognizes the motivations of Indian litigants. Cultural blinders and the demands of the Mexican legal system prevent the officials from asking the crucial question why an Indian would want to appeal to Mexican justice. But even where officials realize that most Indian litigants come to them for reasons of personal aggrandizement or revenge, they are constrained to follow the legal codes of their own culture.

How Litigants Select a Legal Procedure

Litigants are not completely free to choose where they will take a case. If the litigants are not related and do not live in the same hamlet, they are unlikely to appeal to a hamlet elder; moreover, some types of cases can be heard at only one of the legal levels. But in most instances there is a choice. This section draws upon informants' statements to examine and test four hypotheses about why a particular case was taken to one level instead of another. In testing these hypotheses, I shall suggest that the distribution of litigants and claims across legal levels is the product of the cumulative choices of individuals. Legal levels appear static only because the factors influencing litigants to appeal particular types of cases to particular levels have not changed much. If these factors were to change, the cumulative patterns of choice and the procedural style of legal levels might also change.

The cases used in testing the hypotheses are a subset of the total number of cases I collected in the field. The sample does not include duplicate cases or case types that always went to one level. The assumption that the sample is random, necessary for statistical purposes, is open to question, since informants tend to remember the sensational cases, and witchcraft is undoubtedly overrepresented because of my interest in the subject. I also collected very few cases that went to the Mexican authorities because, at the time, I was primarily interested in dispute settlement within Zinacantan. But in spite of its deficiencies this sample of cases is the best available.

The first and most obvious reason the informants gave for taking a case to the hamlet instead of to the municipal authorities was the time involved. To take a dispute to the Presidente involves a trip to the ceremonial center, a wait of a day or two until the

TABLE 2

*Distance from the Ceremonial Center and Cases Settled for
Six Zinacanteco Hamlets*

Hamlet	Total cases settled at town hall	Population	Cases per capita	Distance from center
Center and Nachig	90	1,800	.05	Near
Salinas and Paste	30	1,450	.021	Middle
Navenchauk and Apas	30	1,850	.016	Far

other party appears, and finally the hearing. Traveling time and expense are also considerations. The hypothesis that the farther a disputant lives from the ceremonial center the less likely he is to take a dispute there was tested on 150 cases that were settled at the town hall. The six hamlets on which there were adequate population figures were ranked in terms of approximate distance from the ceremonial center and number of cases per capita that went to the town hall. The two rankings (Table 2) correspond exactly.

A second hypothesis was drawn from diverse statements of informants, all implying a common theme: relatives should settle disputes privately and reasonably to avoid a definitive break in the family. The public airing of family disputes is considered shameful for all involved, and to have a relative jailed or fined is to create an antagonism that will be hard to erase. The original hypothesis attempted to link degree of relationship to the level at which a case was settled, but the resulting data array contained many tiny cells and was not significant. This table did show, however, that all categories of relatives tended to settle their disputes in the hamlets, whereas nonrelatives went to the town hall. With the larger array condensed into the present Table 3, the relationship proved to be highly significant. In this table disputants are defined as related if they are close consanguines, husband and wife, or linked through the marriage of a close relative. Nonrelatives do not have close consanguineal or affinal links but may include the parents of a couple engaged to be married.

A third hypothesis was derived from statements made by infor-

TABLE 3

Distribution of Cases by Level of Settlement and Relationship of Disputants

Level	Disputants related	Disputants not related	Total
Hamlet	52 (+11.9)	18 (−11.9)	70
Ceremonial center	67 (−10.3)	68 (+10.3)	135
San Cristobal	7 (−1.6)	8 (+1.6)	15
Total	126	94	220

NOTE: The numbers in parentheses indicate deviations from the expected values as computed by the margins. Chi-square = 10.82; .01 > p > .001.

mants of two classes: those who took cases to the town hall because they felt they had been wronged and wanted the offender to be punished or forced to pay damages, and those who tried to settle in the hamlet because they felt themselves guilty and hoped to avoid punishment. Because the Presidente can put more pressure on an offender, it is clearly to the advantage of the person who has been wronged to take his case to the town hall, whereas the guilty one would more likely try to settle in the hamlet. In testing the hypothesis, a third group was added: those who brought up a case because they felt they were being accused of an offense they had not committed. Table 4 gives the distribution of cases by person initiating the settlement and the level at which it was carried out. The high value of chi-square allows the null hypothesis of no relationship to be rejected.

In Tables 3 and 4 the cells containing the few cases taken to San Cristobal show very little deviation from the expected values computed by the margins. Apparently the factors influencing where to take a case *within* Zinacantan are not operative on decisions to take cases *outside* the community; this leads to the hypothesis that only a person with little to lose and much to gain would go to the Mexican authorities. The evidence, such as it is, supports this interpretation. The only cells showing a deviation from expected values in a positive direction are those containing people who are not related and who therefore have no kin ties to

TABLE 4

Distribution of Cases by Person Initiating Settlement and the Level at Which It Was Carried Out

| Where settled | Angry plaintiffs | Initiators of settlement | | Total |
		Offenders who believed themselves guilty	Persons who felt falsely accused	
Hamlet	34	20	6	60
	(−12.7)	(+10.5)	(+2.2)	
Ceremonial	104	7	6	117
center	(+12.9)	(−11.5)	(−1.4)	
San Cristobal	10	3	0	13
	(−.1)	(+.9)	(−.8)	
Total	148	30	12	190

NOTE: The numbers in parentheses indicate deviations from the expected values as computed by the margins. Chi-square = 23.01; .001 > *p*.

break and those containing people who know they are guilty and perhaps feel the only way to avoid certain punishment is to take the case to San Cristobal.

Having examined some of the factors mentioned by Zinacantecos as affecting their choice of procedure against the actual distribution of cases, we shall do well to ask if some of these factors are being altered by changes occurring in Zinacantan and in the larger area. If indeed the time factor is important in deciding where to take a case, then the ever-growing network of roads should make the ceremonial center increasingly popular with litigants who live in outlying hamlets. Construction of the Pan-American Highway provided the first such impetus to change, and more recently a network of lesser roads has been spreading throughout the township. Increased traffic on the highway, which can be more or less counted on to afford a quick ride into town, and the fact that more and more Zinacantecos are sharing ownership of trucks, have made it far easier to get to the ceremonial center. Hearings, moreover, are expedited by the fact that the Mayores use trucks to pick up defendants. Increasing ease of transportation has clearly cut the time required to have a case heard at the town hall, and this change may well be reflected in an increased number of appeals from outlying hamlets.

The second hypothesis rests on the idea that closely related litigants would settle disputes in the hamlets, and nonrelatives would more likely go to the town hall. What seems to be happening, however, is that the pressures for preserving family ties are weakening because of economic changes, and increasingly personal gain comes before family solidarity. Men derive more profit by farming rented fields in the lowlands than by working inherited holdings in the highlands. It is also becoming easier for Indians to get credit from banks, which means less need to rely on relatives for loans and for support in times of crisis. Regression of the regional economic circumstance could of course be expected to reverse the trend and make Zinacantecos again more dependent on kin for economic survival.

The third hypothesis suggested that a plaintiff who expected a cash award or the satisfaction of seeing the defendant jailed would seek arbitration at a level higher than the hamlet, so that the strongest sanctions could be applied, whereas the guilty defendant would seek settlement at the hamlet level, where sanctions could not be enforced. But if defendants begin to decide that it is more profitable to await an outcome at a higher level, rather than admit guilt and initiate a settlement procedure, then the number of cases adjudicated at the hamlet level should decrease. As Zinacantecos become more knowledgeable about the tenets of Mexican law, they may become less willing to accept customary solutions without question.

The final hypothesis, which could not be tested, postulated that only a Zinacanteco with little to lose and much to gain would take a case to San Cristobal, where the outcome would be uncertain and the possibility of being fined or jailed would be great. As more and more Zinacantecos become willing to appeal to outside authorities, the officials of the town hall court will be under increased pressure to settle cases according to Mexican rules instead of traditional Zinacanteco rules.

All of the changes described seem to be pushing litigants toward appealing to higher-level courts and taking advantage of Mexican laws. Of course the situation is more complex than this. Hamlet procedures have not succumbed to change; nor have they even gone into decline. Rather, lower-level courts have retained popularity by adjusting their solutions: the substance of decisions is

approaching the standard of Mexican law, though the procedures used have remained wholly Zinacanteco. I would attribute this shift to the activities of the political leaders, who act as hamlet mediators and serve on the town hall court.

Political Leaders as Legal Brokers

The basic argument of this section is that political leaders, in their desire to attract and retain followers, have been manipulating information about the kinds of outcomes to be expected at various legal levels, and in the process have caused Zinacanteco-mediated outcomes to shift perceptibly toward the tenets of Mexican law. On the one hand, young men aspiring to political leadership help dissatisfied litigants refer their cases to the Mexican officials. Established leaders, on the other hand, have tried to retain their followers by offering mediated, and therefore less costly, settlements that provide some of the gains to be expected from an appeal to San Cristobal. But time passes and young leaders becoming old leaders change their tactics.

Political leaders have a vested interest in channeling a litigant's choice of legal procedure, since acting as mediator to a growing clientele of potential litigants is both a cause and a result of political power. If a leader becomes known as a good mediator, his following will grow. There is, of course, more to political leadership than settling disputes. Positions of high political power in Zinacantan have been, and still are, based on a leader's success in acquiring land for the community under the Mexican land-reform program. Thus the successful leader combines the ability to extract benefits for the community from the outside world with a capacity for engineering satisfactory compromises through hamlet mediation. Such a leader, with his reputation for expertise in handling Mexican officialdom, can threaten the opposition while offering his followers solutions to local quarrels based on "expert" knowledge of what would be gained or lost through appeal to San Cristobal.

The activities of political leaders and their influence on the substance of Zinacanteco law can only be understood within the context of recent political changes in Zinacantan. In the 1930's and 1940's Zinacantan was a fairly closed community run by a triumvirate of political bosses who controlled contact with the outside

world. By the 1950's two of the bosses had died, leaving the third with unchallenged political power as president of the committee administering the land granted to Zinacantan under the land-reform program. In the early 1960's the community split openly into two factions broadly reflecting the split between those with ejido land and those without. Factional confrontations were dramatic and often involved appeals to the Mexican penal authorities and other agencies for political advantage. At one time the leaders of both factions were in jail on criminal charges. Now Zinacanteco politics is in the hands of factional splinter groups. The Mexican authorities who must deal with the Indians justifiably complain that no coherent development program can be instituted in Zinacantan because there is always a new splinter group rising to oppose each innovation.

Against this background, would-be local leaders have competed for recognition as hamlet mediators by claiming expertise in producing low-cost settlements that approximate those reached by higher authorities. When the outside world was inhospitable to Indians and Zinacantan was a fairly closed community, the ceremonial center officials were the highest effective authorities. Hamlet mediators gained prestige by producing settlements that would be upheld at the town hall. But in the late 1950's an increased knowledge of Spanish, deriving from the government schools established during the 1930's, and a new openness on the part of national officialdom, as witness the establishment of agencies to help Indians and the success of the land-reform program, combined to produce a situation ripe for exploitation by political entrepreneurs. Aspiring young politicians launched their careers by acting as legal brokers between the two cultures.

At the time of my major fieldwork in Zinacantan in the mid-1960's, the political entrepreneurs of the late 1950's were becoming the established elders. The old hamlet bosses, whose fame as mediators had rested on their ability to predict ceremonial center decisions, were being replaced by younger men, who claimed a knowledge of Mexican law and friendship with Mexican officials. These legal brokers of the late 1950's, who had once urged litigants to appeal to San Cristobal, were now established hamlet mediators and had taken over the high positions in the civil gov-

ernment. It was now to their advantage to persuade litigants to stay within the community and to accept compromise solutions reached in the hamlet or at the ceremonial center. The new leaders used their knowledge of Mexican law to urge both sides to compromise. Though the new leaders communicated a great deal of information about the Mexican legal system in the process, they actually produced fairly conservative results.

Time has passed and the established leaders of the mid-1960's are now being challenged by the hopefuls of the 1970's. Again, beginning their careers as cultural brokers, these younger men are seeking out new Mexican officials to exploit. They are still at the stage of urging clients to appeal outside the community, and they seek to attract litigants by claiming contacts with an ever-growing range of Mexican officials, from the local sanitation inspector to high government dignitaries. The apparent political disintegration of Zinacantan can be fairly blamed on their activities, because they have tried to build reputations for expertise by capitalizing on minor discontent.

Thus the increasing salience of Mexican law in Zinacanteco decisions can be ascribed to the tactics of the political leaders, who have responded to pressures from aspiring politicians by adjusting the substance of mediated outcomes. The set of relevant norms at the local levels has shifted to include what Zinacantecos know of Mexican law as litigants become more willing to appeal to San Cristobal. If it is assumed that litigants appeal to procedures that offer the greatest potential gain with the least risk of loss, then it can be said that hamlet mediators have retained their followers by offering hamlet solutions that provide some of the benefits of San Cristobal but at a fraction of the cost. The apparently static distribution of litigants across procedure types, in the face of outside change, is actually a reflection of these shifts in hamlet and ceremonial center outcomes.

Conclusion

This chapter has presented a dynamic view of the Zinacanteco legal system by analyzing the procedures used at the various legal levels in terms of patterns created by individual acts of choice and decision. Zinacantecos use their legal system for practical pur-

poses. They are not slaves of tradition, and most Zinacantecos, most of the time, act rationally and pursue self-interest in deciding at which level to appeal. Using the concept of social organization developed by Firth (1956) and elaborated by Barth, I have described the pattern of legal-level usage as a reflection of the "constraints and incentives under which people act" (Barth 1966: 2). Zinacanteco choices are limited by the structure of the legal levels, and they are channeled by factors molding Zinacanteco perceptions of the gains and losses inherent in appealing a conflict to one or another type of procedure.

The legal procedures pursued in the hamlets, the ceremonial center, and San Cristobal are shown to be partly dependent on the assumptions people hold about the types of claims and litigants expected at each level. The first section of the chapter postulated a feedback effect in which types of claims influenced types of procedures, which influenced types of outcomes, which influenced types of future claims. In other words, hamlet procedures were for litigants seeking compromise, the ceremonial center forced compromises for those who wanted private gain but also sought a Zinacanteco settlement, and the Mexican penal authorities followed the letter of the law and satisfied Zinacanteco plaintiffs wanting an enemy to be temporarily removed from circulation.

Statements of informants were then examined to see why the informants took a case to one level instead of another, and the statements were then converted into hypotheses and tested against the actual distribution of a sample of cases across legal levels. The hypotheses were found to be generally valid and were assumed to reflect accurately some of the factors considered by Zinacanteco litigants. Then changes in the outside world affecting these factors were examined—better roads, economic development, more liberal government policies—all suggesting that recent changes have made it more possible and profitable for Zinacantecos to appeal to the ceremonial center and to the Mexican authorities.

But Zinacantecos have not begun to abandon hamlet procedures and flock to the San Cristobal courts. In fact, there seems to have been little change in the distribution of types of litigants and claims across procedures. What does appear to have changed

is the types of outcome. These changes are attributed to the activities of political leaders. Litigants may choose the court they wish, but the political leaders who run the courts and have a vested interest in maintaining a satisfied clientele of litigants manipulate information about probable outcomes in order to keep litigants appealing to ceremonial center and hamlet procedures. The result is that political leaders have offered themselves as experts on Mexican law in order to attract litigants and to keep followers who are now more willing to appeal cases to the authorities in San Cristobal. The tenets of Mexican law have become more accessible in arguments leading to a compromise decision in Zinacantan, but so long as Zinacantan remains an ethnic enclave, the necessity for compromise will assure the maintenance of a gap between Zinacanteco and Mexican outcomes.

THREE

The Town Hall Court

The town hall court can be seen as a stage on which the litigants and the officials act out their roles in the process of reaching a decision. The physical facts of the setting and the past history of the litigants provide the constraints on role-playing, but within these limits litigants and officials can, and do, manipulate the information they present about themselves and others as they bargain over the terms of a solution. This chapter examines the constraints on the actors, the roles and positions that can be assumed during a hearing. Three types of position are described: (1) those resulting from the structure of the court, (2) temporary positions, such as physical state on the day of the hearing, and (3) permanent positions, such as known reputation or past performance in acquiring recognized status symbols.

Zinacanteco legal decisions are compromises, and outcomes can be understood only by examining both the accepted norms and the relative statuses of the litigants and officials involved. The norms define the realm of possible outcomes, whereas the relative power of the litigants, as established during the bargaining, determines which specific solution will be chosen. We shall explore the resources available to litigants in attempting to raise their own status and to undermine that of their opponents. The relation between the statuses of the litigants plays an important role in another way, for it sets limits on the types of cases to reach the court. Litigants who feel they will inevitably lose simply do not bring cases. The Presidente's enemies understandably avoid the town

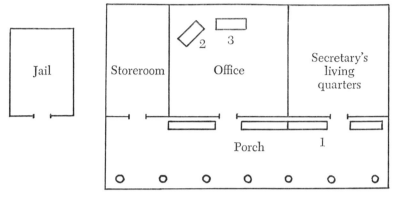

Fig. 1. The town hall. (1) The Presidente's position on the bench; (2) the Presidente's desk; (3) the Secretary's desk.

hall, and low-status persons seldom lodge complaints against high-status political leaders or powerful shamans. Disputes that remain dormant, of course, leave little record, and the discussion must therefore concentrate on disputes that *do* reach the town hall court.

Positions Inherent in the Court Structure

The following detailed description of one hearing provides an idea of what takes place. The town hall is a long, low building with a porch supported by columns. The diagram in Figure 1, though not to scale, does indicate the relative positions of the four benches occupied by the officials.

A marital dispute. This case was observed in July 1967, when I was staying with the incumbent Presidente. Before breakfast the Presidente was gone for an hour to let a prisoner out of jail. When I asked later why the man had been jailed, the Presidente said he had been drunk and abusive. He was an Indian from another Tzotzil community who had changed into Zinacanteco clothes and was now living in the hamlet of Nachig. He had arrived at the town hall the previous afternoon to demand that the Presidente, who had just returned from San Cristobal, settle a dispute with his wife then and there. The Presidente had tried to calm the drunken man by telling him to go home and rest until he was sober, but the man

refused and began haranguing a friend of the Presidente. When he became too abusive, the Presidente had him locked in jail for the night.

The Presidente and I arrived at the town hall around nine in the morning. After disposing of some preliminary business, he settled down on the bench to read his mail. A Juez sat down beside him. They were the only two civil officials present, though a few Mayores lounged on the benches at either end of the town hall porch when they were not needed for errands. An outsider would not have supposed a hearing was in the offing.

There were three main participants in the marital dispute. The husband, who will be called Juan, at first stood leaning against a column. His wife, Maria, sat on the ground just outside the eastern end of the building (at the righthand end, in Figure 1) with her little daughter. The three sons of Juan and Maria played in the open area in front of the town hall. The children, all of school age, played throughout the hearing and seemed not to be disturbed by their parents' public scrap. The third participant was an old man, Don Miguel, a relative of Maria, who sat in the middle of the eastern bench, surrounded by the lounging Mayores. Another young man remained leaning against one of the columns for the duration of the hearing. He offered a comment from time to time, but was not a major participant.

When the Presidente sat down to read his mail, Juan left his column and placed four beers in a row at his feet. The Presidente told him to wait, and Juan returned to his column, leaving the beers. The Presidente finished reading his letters and went into his office. While he was gone, the mood on the porch was easy and relaxed; the men joked together.

When the Presidente returned, he asked the woman, Maria, what she wanted. She rose and came to sit in front of him. As she talked, she pulled a bottle of rum and a large bottle of Coca-Cola out of her bag and set them down at the Presidente's feet beside the beers. In a high-pitched voice, for nearly half an hour, she set forth her complaint against her husband. Whenever Juan tried to interrupt, the Presidente waved him away. Another man then approached to ask the Presidente a question. The case was inter-

rupted while the question was answered. Taking advantage of the interruption to change the course of the case, the Presidente turned away from Maria and began to reprimand Juan. At this, Juan began talking and his wife soon interrupted. The two of them continued talking at once until Maria began to cry. Juan, then having the floor to himself, finally told his side of the story. Even when the Presidente was interrupted by still another man, Juan continued to talk. He did not break off until Maria, finally mastering her tears, interrupted him again, and accused him of not supporting her.

At this point the Mexican teacher came up to the Presidente to inquire why his son was not in school, and the two went inside the town hall to discuss the matter. Notwithstanding, the case continued outside. Juan produced another bottle of rum from his shoulder bag and knelt down to present it to his wife. Maria, for her part, leaped to her feet and turned her back on him. Juan remained on his knees while she addressed Don Miguel and the Juez. The Presidente, coming out of the door, was detained by a girl with a note, but Don Miguel and the Juez continued with the hearing. When Don Miguel began to scold Juan, he rose from his knees and went to bow to the older man. After bowing several times and being released with a touch, Juan retired to lean against a column and smoke a cigarette that had been given to him. Meanwhile, the Presidente again turned his attention to Maria. Juan, having finished his cigarette, soon left the column and knelt before the Presidente. The Presidente refused the gesture and told Juan to kneel to his wife. Juan turned to Maria, who was still standing, and knelt at her feet. It was obvious that Juan was prepared to remain in that position for some time, for he carefully knelt on his hat.

When Maria again refused to listen to Juan, the Presidente and Don Miguel began to scold her. But Maria continued making accusations against her husband, becoming more and more incoherent as she began to sob. The Presidente got up and walked around a little, while the Juez took over his role of scolding the woman. Shortly after the Presidente had returned to his place, his son, looking as indisposed as he was able, appeared, and the Presidente left to take him to school. While he was gone the situation calmed. Voices were lowered and the discussion slowed. When the

Presidente and his son returned from the school, the boy went home, and the Presidente sat down on the bench. At this point, Maria also sat down. Juan, still kneeling, pushed his bottle forward until it touched her knees. Although Maria did not touch the bottle with her hands, she did speak to her husband, telling him to give it to the Presidente. At this crucial moment, another man appeared. The discussion stopped while the stranger greeted all the men on the benches. When he finally left, Maria picked up the bottle and set it in front of the Presidente, beside the other six bottles. Maria remained kneeling, but Juan then stood up.

The Presidente, seeing that the case was over, ordered two Mayores to bring a shot glass. While the group was waiting, Juan passed around cigarettes. When the Mayores returned with the shot glass, one of them took the bottle that Juan had presented to Maria and served a round of drinks for everyone at the town hall. No one drank, but all accepted the rum and poured it into empty bottles they had brought with them. While the lower-ranking people were being served rum, the Presidente opened the four bottles of beer. He kept one, and gave the other three to Don Miguel, the Juez, and me. The beers were shared around until the bottles were empty, and the Juez then opened the Coca-Cola. Like the beers, the Coke bottle was passed around for each person to drink a little. Finally, the last bottle of rum was opened, served, and poured off like the first.

It was noon before the drinking had finished and the empty bottles were again lined up in front of the Presidente. Juan and Maria both thanked the Presidente and the Juez for hearing the case; then Juan took his four beer bottles and one rum bottle, and Maria picked up her rum bottle and the empty Coke, and the two, with Don Miguel, made a second round of farewells. After collecting their other belongings and their four children, Juan and Maria followed Don Miguel into the churchyard and over the ridge to their home in Nachig.

If my presentation of this case has overlooked the content of the dispute, it is because what I understood of the discussion appeared to be the usual stereotyped argument between husband and wife. Juan had come home drunk and had beaten Maria. In the course of the hearing, Maria accused Juan of mistreating her, and Juan

claimed that he was good to her and had bought her store-made bread to eat and provided her with a pig to raise for money. She accused him of not supporting her, and he claimed he was a hard worker. She accused him of trying to kill her, and he claimed that he had been drunk and pointed out that she was not visibly harmed. She claimed that he had said he wanted another woman, and he responded that liquor had made him say things he didn't mean. As the case resolved itself, Juan promised to drink less and not beat his wife, and Maria agreed to return to him.

This dispute had been resolved with little effort by the Presidente. He had been able to leave his seat and attend to other business while the arguments ran their course. But in more complex cases the Presidente must take an active role. In one political dispute that I observed, the Presidente sat in his place on the bench for at least seven hours, actively discussing the issues and suggesting possible solutions.

Many insights into court structure can be gained from an examination of such superficial elements as the arrangement of the furniture, the clothing worn by the participants, and the nature of the official record (Hazard 1962). These items set the stage and define the limits of possible action. Proceedings at the town hall court may appear to be haphazard, particularly in large disputes when several people are all talking at once, but there is always some degree of structure, some lines that are never transgressed.

The furniture of the Zinacanteco court consists of four wooden benches with their backs against the town hall wall and more or less identical columns supporting the roof of the porch. No physical marker sets off the Presidente's position on the bench from any of the other potential seats. The only apparent distinction is that the Presidente and the officials have seats, whereas the litigants must stand (male) or sit on the floor (female). But when the court is in session, the seemingly undifferentiated space is clearly divided. On the Presidente's right sit the other civil officials in rank order. If the Presidente leaves the town hall temporarily, the next ranking official conducts the hearing. On the Presidente's left is the break in the benches that is created by the doorway to the Secretary's living quarters, and beyond this space is another bench. This area is occupied by the prestigious people who act as friends

of the court. Such men either are entirely neutral or are there to help one of the litigants, as was Don Miguel. The area can also be occupied by bystanders. Particular cronies of the Presidente may stand in the doorway and hang over the back of the Presidente's bench to speak with him or interject comments into a discussion.

Directly in front of the bench occupied by the officials is a cleared area. The bottles of rum presented to the Presidente are placed in this partially open corridor where people not involved in a case pass through to speak with the officials. Between the bottles and the columns is the courtroom arena, occupied by the most active participants and the scene of all crucial moves. Here people stand to give testimony or kneel to beg pardon. The columns are on the periphery of the court. To lean against one is to indicate nonparticipation, temporary withdrawal, or supreme self-confidence. The supporters of the litigants form a semicircle around the central arena, where the active participants stand. In most cases, the two sides stand apart from each other.

All the participants in a case wear ordinary Zinacanteco clothing. The Presidente has a staff of office, but he does not carry it when sitting on the bench. The most significant thing about the clothing is that it is the Indian costume. A former employee of the National Indian Institute who became Presidente often wore a Ladino outfit, but he always wore Indian clothes when attending the town hall court. Indian dress is one way of affirming that Indian, not Mexican, law is being dispensed. The lack of differentiation in clothing also emphasizes the basic equality of the participants. There are no outward symbols of rank to suggest a controlling authority. Zinacanteco settlements are supposed to be compromises, agreeable to both sides, and the powers of coercion are hidden beneath an overt equality.

The action in a court hearing is two-sided. The officials and litigants face each other, unless a litigant is begging pardon. The friends of the court have an ambiguous position. When they side with the Presidente in proposing settlements they speak from the bench, but when arguing the cause of a litigant they move into the arena to face the Presidente. Speeches are never directed at the public, since town hall hearings are best understood as private

affairs that happen to take place in an open setting. Only the people actively concerned in a case are considered interested in the outcome. There is in fact no conception that the public should be present at a hearing. Cases are not viewed as public morality plays, nor do the Zinacantecos fear miscarriage of justice from a private hearing. They prefer private hearings simply because they suspect, quite correctly, that bystanders hang around solely to hear juicy stories that can be used to entertain future listeners.

Zinacanteco cases never leave an official record unless an *acta* is made out. But even then, all that may remain of a major political struggle is a short acta recording a peripheral settlement. In Zinacantan, the Ladino Secretary types out the acta, putting it in official terms, but I am not sure who dictates the content. In the only case I observed, the person with the most to lose by the agreement informed the Secretary of the terms to be included in the acta. Such a procedure seems logical, given the Zinacanteco emphasis on having the losing side indicate open agreement with a decision.

Temporary Positions

The demeanor of a person affects, and is affected by, the deference that others accord him (Goffman 1967). The temporary position of a Zinacanteco litigant on the day of his hearing can thus have a noticeable effect on the outcome of the litigation. If the litigant feels he is an object of ridicule, he will accept an otherwise unacceptable settlement. Given that Zinacanteco settlements are ideally compromises, anything that acts to put one litigant at a temporary disadvantage will necessarily affect the settlement terms.

Victoria Bricker (1968) notes that Zinacanteco humor usually centers on breaches of two types of norms, those having to do with the self-image that a Zinacanteco presents to others and those concerning the relations between men and women. The self-image norms have to do with cleanliness, proper clothing, and bodily control. When a person is seen as having departed from either or both types of norms, he becomes an object of ridicule.

Although Zinacantecos, like most other people, hesitate to ridicule someone to his face, a person up before the town court is an

ideal target. Not only do the bystanders indulge themselves, but the Presidente uses ridicule as a deliberate weapon to weaken the bargaining position of a litigant. Most persons, when subjected to ridicule, tend to express shame and embarrassment. Their opinion of themselves and therefore their demands on the world tend to be lowered in proportion to the low opinion expressed by others. It is a rare person who can stand up to ridicule and talk back to his detractors.

People are assessed on the evidence presented by their outward appearance, and a person in the role of defendant is often put in the position of having transgressed several self-image norms. If the defendant has been tied up and dragged to the town hall by Mayores, he is unable to move freely, and thus cannot control his body. Bystanders laugh as he struggles against the ropes, and they laugh even harder if he falls down. If his clothes are dirty, torn, or partly missing, the litigant will have no outward reason to command respect. In fact, his outward appearance—dirty clothes and restricted movement—leads onlookers to make inferences about his inward state. He will be seen as a drunk, or a person prone to violence, or both.

Bricker (1968) notes that court cases provide a constant fund of community humor because onlookers tell others of the indiscretions committed by the litigants. A person before the court will be ridiculed not only for his appearance but for his reported actions. If the norms he has transgressed are among those that define the relations between men and women, the onlookers listen with delight and the litigant is correspondingly embarrassed. At the town hall one afternoon, I saw two Mayores arrive with a man between them. The prisoner, looking shamefaced, was not tied up. The Mayores, barely able to contain their laughter, pushed the prisoner toward the Presidente. This man had been accused of attempting to rape his wife's sister while the sister's husband was away from home. All the civil officials gathered around to watch while the Presidente questioned the prisoner, and they snickered when he was led off to spend the night in jail.

Most people, when treated with open ridicule, react with lowered self-opinion, but some maintain an inner dignity despite outward circumstances. When such a person refuses to be intimidated

and talks back to the Presidente and his accusers, Zinacantecos acknowledge that he is p^*ih, "clever and lively." Although such a quality is an innate aspect of personality, it is treated here as temporary, because its manifestation is unpredictable. And although a few people are known throughout Zinacantan for being p^*ih, the quality may be manifested unexpectedly by a litigant with little else to recommend him. If he is fortunate, and clever, a downtrodden defendant can turn his detractors into admirers and win a more favorable settlement in the process.

Permanent Positions

A Zinacanteco who approaches the Ladino authorities is only an Indian, but the Zinacanteco who approaches the town hall has a much fuller identity. Age and sex are important, but a man is also classified through the roles he has played in Zinacanteco public life. The meaning of sex and age are now examined, as well as the public roles that serve as routes to personal power and prestige for men. It is obvious that the man who has led a full public life will command more respect at the town hall than a social nonentity.

Sex. The town hall is a male gathering place, a man's world. Men freely lean against the columns and pass the time of day, whereas women approach the town hall only for a specific purpose. A woman involved in a dispute sits outside until the hearing begins, and then gives her testimony in a high-pitched voice. When her case ends, she leaves immediately or retires to the background. A woman comes as an outsider, and if she has a complaint against a man, she must make it to other men. Women often act as plaintiffs in marital disputes, and in cases where women complain against their husbands at the town hall they try to phrase their accusations in terms that men will recognize. But when a woman demands a separation from her husband, the court officials take the male point of view and side with the guilty husband. Women involved in marital disputes usually try to get the support of an older male relative, but not even this guarantees male sympathy, because the elder acts as a friend of the court and sides with the other men against the woman unless the guilty husband has been so violent that the woman's life is in danger. Only a woman with

a strong mind or a strong case can get official approval for a divorce.

The fact that women are outsiders at the town hall not only influences their phrasing of a dispute but affects whether they will bring up a case at all. Women who have been sexually molested or raped rarely approach the town hall or even inform a male relative of the incident, for fear of being ridiculed and accused of having encouraged the attack.

Age. For a Zinacanteco man, increasing age brings increased power. Merely to have lived, while others have succumbed to sickness, is visible proof of a strong soul. And to have a strong soul is to be capable of harming as well as protecting others. But age does not always guarantee power, for respect gives way to ridicule when senility sets in.

Increasing age gives earthly as well as supernatural power. Young men are dependent on their fathers, but as they grow older they acquire land by inheritance or other mechanisms and come to have dependent sons of their own. When a man's sons are grown and able to work for him, he reaches a peak of power through the control of resources. His sons not only provide free labor but have the family interests at heart when they act as overseers of hired labor. A man with sons can run a more productive and profitable farming operation, and by using the surplus he can obtain prestige-giving positions in the religious hierarchy (Cancian 1965: 106). Sons and sons-in-law not only provide labor but act as reliable supporters in political crises affecting the father. An older man who actively heads his own descent group may thus become an important hamlet elder.

Age is important in making the distinction between senior and junior that runs throughout Zinacanteco life. Juniors bow to seniors upon greeting them, walk behind them on the trail, sit below them at the table, and are served rum after them (Vogt 1969: 238–45). A man, as he grows older, thus receives the outward marks of respect from an ever larger number of people. But unless he has exploited other mechanisms for gaining prestige, outward respect may only cloak an inward contempt. An older man who has made little use of his life may be ridiculed by the Presidente and other "modern" young men at the town hall even while they treat him

with the empty symbols of respect during drinking and greeting rituals.

Shamans. Shamans command respect because of their supernatural contacts. They are men singled out by the gods through three dreams to act as mediators between humans and supernaturals. They serve for life, conducting curing ceremonies for individual patients and calendrical rituals for descent groups, hamlets, and the township as a whole. In public emergencies, shamans within the threatened group gather to appeal to the gods for pardon and relief.

Shamans are ranked from most senior to most junior on the basis of time elapsed since a shaman's debut. Younger shamans may thus be more senior than their elders, because what is important is the length of their supernatural contact. Senior shamans occupy powerful positions. They may use their control over community ceremonies for political leverage, and they are feared as individuals for their demonstrated soul strength. Although shamans use their supernatural contacts for individual and community benefit, they are also able to bring sickness and death to their enemies. An ordinary Zinacanteco fears to anger a powerful shaman. Wrongs committed by shamans may be quietly forgotten, and if a shaman does take part in a court hearing, his words command respect.

Men known for violence. Although shamans are feared for their power to call forth supernatural evil, other persons are more directly feared for their earthly powers. Men who have committed murder usually leave the community immediately, but they may try to return later and resume their old life by carefully approaching hamlet elders and the relatives of the victim. But known murderers are always feared, and ordinary members of the community take care not to anger them or provoke them into murdering again.

Young men with reputations for violence are treated cautiously by persons in physically weak positions. A woman who lacks the protection of a man will go out of her way to avoid angering such a person. Older men known for their violent tempers are similarly avoided. But when an accusation is made against a person with a community-wide reputation for violence, the reaction against the accused is in proportion to the violence feared, and the Presidente

usually sends several Mayores and a Capitan to capture him and take him immediately to jail.

Men Who Mediate with the Outside World

Persons who have contacts with Mexican officials command respect and attention when they participate in a case at the town hall court, for they are assumed to have expert knowledge of Mexican laws and procedures. They are credited with being able to predict the outcome were the case to be taken to the Mexican authorities, and their pronouncements thus set limits on the kinds of solutions to be reached in Zinacantan. When such a man is acting as a litigant, or in support of a litigant, he can force others to meet his demands by threatening to take the case to the Mexican authorities, where his expertise in Spanish and his contacts would guarantee him a decisive advantage. This is a potent threat when used against someone with no knowledge of Spanish, who would be totally lost if the case were taken outside of Zinacantan. When acting as a friend of the court, or as one of the Presidente's cronies, a man with Mexican contacts can persuade both litigants to agree to a compromise solution by advising them of the outcome to be expected in San Cristobal.

Civil government officials. Former civil officials above the rank of Mayor command little direct respect, but their words carry weight when they participate in court hearings, because people credit them with having learned how to settle disputes during their terms of office. Civil officials, while actively serving, also command some measure of respect when away from the town hall. During their off-duty weeks their advice is sought by neighbors who see them as representatives of community authority. Civil officials who are successful at handling disputes within their own hamlets may build up a reputation as skillful mediators and rise to the role of hamlet elder with increasing age.

Ejido officials. For many years the most powerful political leaders in Zinacantan were the men who served on the *ejido* committee, the group controlling the lands given to Zinacantan under the Mexican land reform program (Edel 1962). The political boss of Zinacantan was the ejido committee president for many years, and

hamlet leaders in the past were consistently drawn from the ranks of local ejido representatives. Control of ejido land was an obvious basis for mustering political support. Just as a father could threaten to disinherit sons who refused to cooperate, ejido officials could implicitly threaten the receivers of ejido land with its loss. For many years, the political control of the ranking ejido leaders was seldom questioned, but factional fights in the 1960's between *ejidatarios* (those who received ejido land) and non-ejidatarios considerably weakened the position of the political boss and of the hamlet leaders dependent on him.

Ejido officials and powerful political leaders rarely appear at the town hall in the role of defendants. Not only do ordinary people fear to accuse such high-ranking persons, but the leaders themselves hesitate to appear at the town hall because of the public shame of having their behavior discussed. Political leaders who have beaten their wives make exceptional efforts to settle the dispute at home to avoid having their marital problems brought into the open. They know that Zinacanteco gossips will eagerly pass on any juicy stories about important men. When a powerful leader does appear before the court as a litigant, it is usually in the role of accuser, and the civil officials hasten to carry out his wishes.

Religious officials. The system of religious offices provides a rapid way of evaluating a person's social worth. As Cancian (1965: 135) states, "The cargo system ranks the members of the community into a single social structure. All sectors of the community accord prestige and respect to the incumbent and past cargoholder, and the public nature of cargo service makes it an effective way of ranking all Zinacantecos." Mayores, who hold the lowest office, are treated with disrespect, whereas men who pass the expensive first positions and go on to higher levels command a large measure of respect. But it is respect without fear. High performers in the religious hierarchy have no sanctions at their direct command unless they perform another role as well. Their service to the gods ensures supernatural favors for the community and the individual, but does not imply a knowledge of witchcraft. Their high prestige may earn them a respected position, but they are powerless to impose sanctions beyond their own descent group. Many men thus pass through the religious system into respected eldership

without wielding political power. But the men who have acquired political power through other activities can legitimize their claim to leadership by religious participation.

Men now or once high in the religious hierarchy are respected at the town hall because of their record of community service, their wealth, and a verbal facility derived from their years of service to the gods. Even if their legal knowledge is lacking, their dignity combined with the ability to inject the proper ritual phrase at the proper time lends weight to their words.

Conclusions

Hearings at the town hall court have been examined, in their superficial aspects, to contribute to our understanding of the resources that can be manipulated by litigants as they bargain over a solution. Zinacanteco legal decisions are compromises, and the specific terms of the agreement vary widely within the limits set by the norms that apply to particular kinds of conflicts. Knowing this, Zinacantecos work to present both themselves and their case in the most favorable light possible.

The physical aspects of the court as a stage set were taken up first. The participants in a hearing are assigned limited areas of the stage, but their movements within these areas carry definite messages to each other and to onlookers. The Presidente sits in a specific place on a specific bench, but he also moves around or turns his attention to other matters. This kind of behavior indicates the Presidente's lack of concern with the case at hand or his impatience with the stubbornness of the litigants. The plaintiff and defendant stand facing the Presidente, but they too move around. A litigant wishing to appear self-confident leans against one of the columns supporting the porch roof, and one wishing to humble himself and beg pardon kneels at the feet of his opponent or the Presidente.

Next, the temporary factors shaping a litigant's demeanor and his perception of himself on the day of the hearing were examined. Rumpled clothing from a night in jail or an untidy appearance from having been hastily summoned to the town hall flusters a litigant and makes it difficult for him to present himself as worthy of respect. Or a litigant's defenses may crumble during a hearing when

his past misdeeds are brought out and he is subjected to ridicule from an unsympathetic audience.

Finally, the ingredients that form reputation were shown. These are drawn upon by litigants as they seek to influence the terms of the compromise agreement. Older men strive to command the respect due to age, shamans may hint at supernatural retaliation, political leaders may make demands on the basis of their recognized power, and men who have served in the religious hierarchy may claim the respect due to exemplary, and rich, citizens. But men who are shown to have "wasted" their lives—who are poor or who have not performed effectively in public affairs—are at a disadvantage, for they can be shamed and ridiculed into accepting the terms demanded by a more prestigious opponent.

FOUR

Zinacanteco Legal Concepts

This chapter and Chapter 5, on witchcraft beliefs, explore the ideology behind Zinacanteco legal procedures. Zinacantecos have cultural explanations for the reasons people do wrong, for the consequences of a wrong, and for the nature of an appropriate settlement. These ideas are part of a native theory that relates man to god and man to man. But in explaining Zinacanteco cosmology my aim is not to suggest that ideology determines behavior, but rather to point out that ideology provides a language for justifying behavior, for explaining behavior, and for directing future behavior.

My road into Zinacanteco ideology was through Tzotzil terms that seemed to imply important legal concepts. Through dictionary glosses (Laughlin n.d.) and intuition, I picked out key words and phrases from texts written by literate informants and explored their meanings in long, unstructured interviews.* Such explorations of logical systems, despite their informality, carry their own rewards. The deeper one goes, the larger the vista, as more and more anomalous observations fall into place. Thus, I began with a

---

* Some of the people who read this book in manuscript have criticized me for not using the sophisticated interviewing techniques developed by other fieldworkers in the Chiapas highlands. I did in fact replicate in Tzotzil the Tzeltal-language system of legal terms elicited by Black and Metzger (1965) and found the two systems almost perfectly congruent. But I stopped formal elicitation because it was time-consuming and not as productive as less rigorous interviewing. In my opinion, formal eliciting techniques are useful for intensive exploration of a small domain but are impossibly time-consuming as a major research strategy for such a large and ill-defined domain as law.

naïve exploration of the Tzotzil word for crime, *mulil*, and ended up with a cosmological system in which crimes were related to highly abstract beliefs about the nature of witchcraft and political power.

In exploring the meanings of Tzotzil terms used in legal proceedings, I have concentrated on the consequences implied by their use. I have defined words not in terms of the attributes of the objects they refer to, but in terms of the assumptions that must underlie their use. For example, I have defined the word mulil as "an act that displeases the gods" instead of making a list of all the actions that could be called a mulil and proceeding to extract the semantic features shared by these actions. I have looked at terms in relation to their implicit assumptions, to explore their implications for future action. People rarely call an act a mulil for purposes of neutral observation, but rather to imply that something must be done about it. The gods must be placated. Mulil is a loaded term and its use spurs people into action.

We begin with a discussion of the Zinacanteco ideas of crime, and beliefs about why people do wrong. Then the consequences of an unresolved dispute are discussed in terms of the supernatural pressures on the disputants that cause them to seek a settlement. The heart of the chapter is the description of what actually occurs during a hearing as a compromise is sought. As we shall see, Zinacantecos do not simply hold bargaining sessions, nor do they assess all evidence rationally in order to derive proper outcomes; rather, they seek solutions through a complex amalgam of the two procedures. Three types of settlement are thus possible: one side begs pardon, both sides admit equal guilt, or both sides refuse to compromise. Each type of settlement is taken up in turn. After a short section on sanctions, the chapter concludes by comparing Zinacanteco legal procedures with those in other communities where reconciliation is stressed.

Committing a Crime

Zinacantecos use the single word *mulil* (noun *mul-* plus suffix *-il* indicating unpossessed form) to cover the concepts expressed in the English words "guilt," "crime," "sin," and "blame" (Tzotzil dictionary), but a mulil is best understood as any act that displeases the

gods and can provoke supernatural retaliation. The act may be as minor as an angry word spoken to a kinsman or as serious as murder. A person who has done no wrong is invulnerable, for Zinacantecos believe that not even a witch can harm a guiltless person; but when someone has committed a mulil, an explosive situation exists. Not only is the guilty person vulnerable to supernatural punishment, but there is a victim of the wrong who holds anger in his heart. Even if the victim does not express his anger openly, it still cries out to the gods for vengeance. The high rate of illness in Zinacantan offers visible proof of the fact that the gods are not slow to punish the guilty. For the protection of all those involved in a dispute, the wrong should be righted and the victim's anger placated.

The noun mulil can occur as the object of three verbs that indicate committing a crime. The verb -*pas*, "to do," when followed by -*mul* means to commit carnal crime, and the phrase ?*ispas smul* is most frequently used to refer to someone who has committed adultery. The other two verbs, -*ta*, "to find or encounter," and -*sa*?, "to search or look for," are the most commonly used forms and emphasize an important Zinacanteco distinction: -*ta* implies an accident, whereas -*sa*? implies intent to do evil. The noun mulil can also follow the nominal ?*oy*, "to be existent," so that the phrase ?*oy smul* means that someone has guilt, or is guilty.

In Zinacanteco ideology, people either commit wrongs without intention or carry out evil designs because they possess *manya*, a word derived from the local usage of the Spanish *maña*, which means "a defect or bad habit" and is applied principally to bad behavior in animals (Sandoval 1942). This distinction partly reflects the difference between drunken and sober acts. Most people who commit a wrong while sober are considered to have *manya*, whereas the acts of drunks are excused as having been motivated by liquor. But when a drunken man commits a greater wrong than can be attributed to his condition, he is felt to have been motivated by manya. The use of the verbs -*ta* and -*sa*? partly reflects the distinction between accident and manya. Someone who ?*ista smul*, "found his crime," accidentally happened to do wrong, whereas someone who ?*isa*? *smul*, "looked for his crime," was actively searching for something bad to do. But as actually used, -*ta* and

-sa? are best taken as indicators of the feelings of the speaker rather than as statements about the person who committed the wrong. Most people use ?*ista smul* when referring to someone who committed a crime, even if they are referring to a thief who deliberately stole while sober. When a person uses ?*isa? smul* instead, he is really saying he thinks the wrongdoer has manya and should be punished.

Mulil is talked about in terms of quantity, just as we talk about amount of blame. A serious crime is a ¢o¢ (very bad) *mulil* and a minor one is a *hutuk* (little) *mulil*. Hearings usually contain a discussion of *k*u yepal smul*, "the amount of someone's guilt," and many end with statements that the mulil of one side is greater than that of the other.

Bringing Up a Dispute

The Tzotzil word *k*op* means "dispute" as well as "word," "language," "war," and "curing ceremony" (Tzotzil dictionary). Its specific meaning must be derived from context because it is used with various verbs to form idioms. There are two verbs that take *k*op* as an object to imply settling a dispute: -*lahes k*op* means "to end a dispute" and -*mel¢an k*op* means "to conduct a hearing." To -*lahes k*op* is to "beg pardon," and the term applies to both the ceremony for begging formal pardon and for the begging-pardon sequences that take place in a hearing. It is thus concerned with two-party negotiations. But -*mel¢an k*op* is a three-sided affair. Literally "to settle a dispute," it refers to a hearing conducted by a *hmel¢aneh k*op*, "a mediator."

The words -*mel¢an* and -*lahes* also take mulil as an object. To -*mel¢an mulil* means to settle someone's crime. The mediator must try to achieve a settlement that will right the wrong and remove anger from the victim's heart. To -*lahes mulil* is to beg pardon, which can be done only by the person who actually committed the wrong. When someone goes to beg formal pardon, or to present a bottle and ask for forgiveness during a hearing, he can be said to *slahes smul*; he is ending his guilt and will no longer be vulnerable to supernatural retribution.

The words that Zinacantecos use to say that someone is bringing up a dispute provide an important clue to the wishes of the plaintiff and the probable outcome of the case. When it is said that

someone *xba ssaʔ kʷop*, the expression literally means "he is looking for a fight." The auxiliary verb *-ba* indicates intention. The phrase can refer to a belligerent drunk or to an angry plaintiff taking a case to the town hall. If it refers to a plaintiff, it means that he wants an offender jailed and does not care about a mediated settlement or a reconciliation until after the punishment has been meted out. Because hamlet elders cannot order persons jailed, a plaintiff who *xba ssaʔ kʷop* can go only to the town hall or to the Mexican authorities. Chapter 3 described the case of a young man, accused of attempting to rape his wife's sister, who was brought to the town hall and jailed. The complaint against him had been made by his father-in-law, the father of the two women, who had arrived in a rage at the Presidente's house early that morning. Anyone seeing the old man and knowing his errand would have said that he *xba ssaʔ kʷop.*

Pletu is a word borrowed from Spanish *pleito*, and when it is used in the context of *-saʔ pletu*, it carries the same meaning as kʷop. But *pletu*, in general use, has a narrower meaning because it can only refer to disputes likely to end up at the town hall. Both sides involved in a *pletu* are seen as interested in pursuing their own advantage and unwilling to compromise in the interest of continuing their relationship.

Xba skʷan parte is the usual way of saying that someone has deliberately gone to register a complaint with a hamlet elder or the Presidente. It means that the plaintiff has gone to tell the authorities of a wrong and ask their advice. This usually leads to a hearing in which the wrongdoer is questioned and a compromise sought.

When it is said that someone has gone to the Presidente or an elder to *-saʔbe skʷoplal*, it means that he is looking for a settlement. *Kʷoplal* means "a plan," and the plaintiff who goes to *-saʔbe skʷoplal* is literally "looking for a plan" agreeable to all parties to a dispute. The term usually refers to a person who is involved in a land dispute with kinsmen or to one who wishes to recover a debt. The emphasis is on a workable solution to a problem and not on punishment.

When both sides in a dispute approach an elder or the Presidente to have their case heard, it is said that *xba smelȼan sbaik*, "they intend to settle their differences." The term is also used to refer

to litigants while their case is being heard, but whereas the opponents who approach the town hall together can be assumed to desire a reconciliation, the term implies nothing about the feelings of parties to a dispute that is in process of being settled, who might indeed hate each other.

The most noncommittal way of saying that someone has gone to bring up a case is to say *ʔibat sk*opon preserente* if "he went to talk to the Presidente" or *ʔibat sk*opon mol*——if "he went to talk with old man ——." It literally means that someone went to talk, with no reference to what was said. The expression is more frequently used to refer to people who have gone to inform an elder or the Presidente of a dispute but do not wish the authorities to interfere. A rising political leader who informed the Presidente that his wife had left him was really asking the Presidente to refuse to hear the case and to send the woman back to the hamlet, where he would have a chance to beg pardon.

The Hearing

The aim of a hearing conducted by an elder or the Presidente is to reach a compromise solution satisfactory to both sides. Each litigant comes to the hearing with his own version of the dispute and tries to present the "facts" of the case in such a way that the logical outcome is the one he desires. Litigants know which outcomes are likely to follow from which facts, and they begin by presenting the most favorable version of the event. A litigant cannot be entirely free with the facts, however, for his version must have some relation to that presented by his opponent. But Zinacantecos do not limit themselves to the immediate issue at hand and may draw on ancient wrongs to justify recent behavior.

Zinacantecos do not have elaborate procedures for verifying the facts of a case, because the facts are not of crucial importance. Zinacanteco outcomes are compromises, and an important part of the procedure of a hearing is the compromising of the facts. Litigants begin with discrepant stories and the mediator's task is to rephrase the different accounts until the litigants agree on a single version of the events—a version that to the outsider might be puzzlingly skewed from reality. In the process of bargaining over the facts, litigants can use witnesses and physical evidence to sup-

port their version, but they expect to reach a compromise of some sort. This compromise can take various forms. The defendant may be persuaded to agree with the plaintiff on the immediate events of the conflict, but may try to justify his actions in terms of past quarrels. The compromise solution would then be based on the facts of the case, but would use past events to mitigate the harshness of the outcome. Frequently the facts are distorted beyond recognition. A case that begins with a complaint of assault may well end up being settled as an inheritance dispute, with the assault action forgotten altogether. Or compromise may be based on outright lies, which everyone knows are lies but which offer the only possible route to agreement. When both sides in a case have completely discrepant stories and refuse to give ground, the mediator can offer them a compromise solution based on a version of the events that neither side believes to be true. But they will accept it if they have been put in a position where reaching a compromise is more important than holding out. The case of the gossiping widows in Chapter 3 is a good example of this type of solution.

Zinacanteco ideas of truth also reflect their lack of concern with verifiable facts. The word used for truth, *melol*, means "the proper way." When a litigant is asked to -*albe melol*, "tell the truth," he is being asked to speak properly in addition to giving the facts. Regardless of the persuasiveness of his version of the events, if he gets angry, contradicts himself, or stumbles over his words, he will not be speaking *melol* and his case will suffer. It is obvious that a litigant who has lost his poise by being put in a position where he presents a contemptible front to the world will have far less chance of speaking *melol* and, therefore, of having his version of the facts prevail. Defendants who have spent the night in jail or who have been accused of committing shameful deeds have difficulty speaking *melol*, for they are already in the position of having behaved improperly. But plaintiffs can also suffer. People who are too angry to behave properly, or those with curious accents or boorish ways, also fail to speak "in the proper way," and suffer accordingly.

In a hearing the mediator must -*aʔibe melol*, "understand the truth." But such understanding requires active participation. The mediator must question both sides to bring out additional facts,

and then reinterpret the facts in such a way as to bring the litigants closer together. The mediator must be so persuasive that both sides accept his words. Ideally he should proceed "in the proper way," which means that he must not get angry, interrupt the speaker, or impose his will arbitrarily. But mediators often use ridicule, threats, and sharp accusations to encourage the litigants to change their stories or to accept a decision.

Zinacantecos have a wide concept of relevance. Their solutions are based on compromise, and any statement that causes one side to give in a little serves a useful purpose. Only the stupidest of Zinacanteco defendants at a hearing before a mediator would admit to being guilty without some effort to lower the plaintiff's demands. Even when his guilt is undeniable, he will plead drunkenness or dredge up stories from the past to show some justification for his actions. Part of the mediator's job, too, is to search for the roots of the trouble by delving into the past. Using his own knowledge of Zinacanteco life, or following the lead of the litigants, he searches for underlying issues that can be brought to bear on the case. In the process, the immediate wrong is often forgotten and the settlement is based on an agreement over another issue.

In a ceremony of begging formal pardon, the actual litigants may remain silent while their elders speak, but in a three-sided hearing the litigants must speak for themselves. Zinacantecos have a fundamental respect for the integrity of the individual, and every effort is made to get the disputing parties to agree to a course of action instead of putting them in a position where they feel compelled to accept something against their will. As he rephrases the facts, a Zinacanteco mediator will rely on persuasion and the legitimacy of his position to bring the litigants into agreement. Persuasion and appeals to reason will be tried first, but if the litigants refuse to compromise, the mediator can turn to threats or jailing. Hamlet elders can threaten to let a case go to the town hall, and the Presidente can jail a recalcitrant defendant on the theory that a night of chilly contemplation will cause him to see the advantages of begging pardon. Any defendant who can stand three days in jail and who does not fear being sent to the San Cristobal authorities can rest confident that no more serious steps will be taken to force him to compromise his position.

The Presidente is empowered to jail a person for seventy-two hours without formal charges. Though the Mexican lawmakers who instituted the seventy-two-hour jail sentence saw it as a means of securing a criminal while charges were being investigated, the Presidente of Zinacantan puts hostages and witnesses, as well as criminals, in jail in order to persuade them to cooperate. The archives of the State Department of Indian Affairs contain many letters from the Director to the Presidente instructing him that it is against Mexican law to hold hostages or to jail witnesses. Zinacantecos, however, regard the short jail sentence not as punishment but as a means of persuasion. And the Presidente will only jail someone who has committed a wrong or who can be expected to commit a wrong. Keeping hostages is justified by the expectation that such people would otherwise do wrong by hiding their wanted relatives; and witnesses are jailed because they have refused to talk. Plaintiffs who are innocent of wrongdoing cannot be jailed even if they refuse to lower their demands. Only a plaintiff who threatens to avoid court proceedings altogether and take his own revenge can be jailed by the Presidente.

In spite of the emphasis on having the loser indicate his acceptance of an outcome—drinking the rum, informing the Ladino Secretary of the terms of the settlement—Zinacantecos recognize that some solutions are basically unjust. A defendant forced into a compromise by being threatened or jailed may be deeply resentful of the mediator and the plaintiff who put him in such a position. In Zinacanteco ideology these decisions do not produce a lasting solution. The defendant is seen as having been left with anger in *his* heart, which cries out to the gods for vengeance on those who committed the injustice. Such a case is not "settled." The original mulil has been compounded by another wrong, and the gods are invoked in a continuing quarrel.

The Presidente and the elders who conduct hearings are not impartial mediators. *They do not have to be fair.* This is a crucial point, and a key to understanding the Zinacanteco legal system. Zinacanteco legal procedures are based on the premise that the litigants make their own decisions. The mediator's job is to produce a compromise, either by being impartial or by taking one side or even by shifting back and forth. This does not mean, however,

that Zinacantecos do not recognize bad mediators and bad solutions. Presidentes who are suspected of accepting bribes and hamlet elders who are too openly political are disliked and avoided. But Zinacantecos do not feel that the mediator must be impartial to produce a lasting solution. The two concepts are not mutually dependent. A satisfactory solution is one that is freely accepted by both litigants, and the role of the mediator is peripheral in theory though it may be crucial in fact.

Zinacanteco mediators usually side with the plaintiff in trying to force the defendant to make adequate reparations for his wrong, but the mediator can also side with the defendant in trying to get the plaintiff to lower his demands. In most hearings, the mediator will side with the plaintiff until an acceptable version of the facts is agreed upon, and then he will side with the defendant during the argument over the amount of the settlement. This description suggests that the mediator usually plays a role we would describe as impartial. But appearances are misleading, since Zinacantecos feel that a satisfactory solution can emerge from a hearing even when the mediator plays an obviously prejudiced role.

Because Zinacantecos do not demand impartiality from a mediator, their tendency to regard fines as bribes may appear inconsistent. But the tendency makes sense in the context of the total picture. Because settlements are ideally restitutive, and are reached by a bargaining procedure in which the plaintiff is persuaded to lower his demands, the plaintiff will agree to a settlement only when he sees no hope of extracting more money from the defendant. Once the plaintiff has agreed to accept a certain sum, if he then sees the defendant handing over money as a fine to the Presidente, he perceives the Presidente as appropriating money that might have come to him. It is then only a short step to claiming that the defendant bribed the Presidente to persuade the plaintiff to lower his demands.

When a Zinacanteco appears before the town hall, he may ask a respected elder to accompany him. The elder does not act as a lawyer, for litigants must argue their own positions, but is there to -ʔaʔi -mul, "understand the wrong" that was done. His most important function, however, is to provide respectability. The Tzotzil idiom for showing respect is -p*is ta vinik, literally "to measure a person as a man," to treat him properly. A litigant who might be

subjected to ridicule, therefore, partially protects himself by asso-
ciating with an elder and hiding under the aura of respect accorded to him. During a hearing, the elder usually acts as a friend of
the court. He sits or stands to the left of the Presidente and inter-
jects comments when needed. If he gives testimony in favor of his
protégé, he comes into the central arena to speak, but then retires
to a neutral position against the wall when finished. The elder's
role, like that of the Presidente, is to reach a compromise. He may
even scold his protégé in the interests of reaching an agreement.

Although I have spoken of the opposing litigants as individuals,
there are times when they consist of groups of men. If an elder is
participating in such a group, he does not act as a friend of the
court. His role is to argue vehemently for his side, not to explore
the possibilities of compromise. An elder in this position stands
with the litigants and behaves like one. Zinacantecos make a clear
distinction between an elder who argues a case and one who is
there to listen. An elder who comes to listen but ends up arguing
will find himself standing with the litigants instead of sitting on
the bench.

Settlements

A Zinacanteco dispute reaches settlement in one of three ways:
one side can admit to the largest share of guilt, both sides can
admit equal blame, or the two sides can refuse to compromise. If
one opponent admits guilt, he automatically assumes the responsibility of repairing the damage he has done, although he is still free
to argue over the actual terms of the settlement. When both sides
admit to equal guilt, they usually make up their differences and
agree on a solution. But if a compromise is not reached, though
one side may be punished for doing wrong the damage that was
done remains unrepaired and the plaintiff is believed to harbor
anger in his heart.

When a litigant admits to having committed a mulil, he must
beg pardon of the person he has wronged. He can do this in a
ceremony of begging formal pardon, or he can do it at a hearing
when it has become clear that his was the greater fault. The guilty
person begs pardon by putting a bottle of rum or several bottles
of beer at the offended person's feet and asking him to -*lah* -*oʔon*,
"end the anger in his heart." Depending on the degree of the

wrong, the guilty person presents the bottle and remains standing or kneels on the ground. The offended person never accepts the bottle at once, for the terms of the settlement have yet to be worked out. The rights of the offended person and the obligations of the guilty one remain to be discussed. Only when the exact terms of the settlement are decided does the offended person indicate his acceptance of the bottle by touching it. He either takes the bottle for himself or places it at the feet of the mediator as a gesture of thanks. At this point the guilty person is said to have ended his mulil and the offended person to have removed the anger from his heart.*

There are supernatural pressures on both the plaintiff and the defendant to give in. The defendant is vulnerable to sickness from the gods as long as his mulil is not ended, and the plaintiff who refuses to compromise is suspected of being a witch. Only witches do not know how to forgive and continue to harbor anger in their hearts, and a plaintiff who refuses to accept compensation that others regard as adequate is making a public announcement of his intent to resort to witchcraft. Although being known as a witch has a few advantages, it is not a role to be adopted lightly. Should the defendant later sicken and die, the plaintiff would be publicly branded as a successful witch and would be liable for retaliation from the defendant's angry relatives.

When both sides reach a compromise in which they admit equal blame, they usually indicate their agreement by drinking together. If both committed equal wrongs, they may present rum to each other to beg pardon, but if no mulil has occurred and the argument was over land division or how a debt should be paid, they need show only that they are in accord. When someone agrees to accept a mediator's advice, he usually says *tahč*un amantal*, "I will do as you say," and if he is younger than the mediator, he approaches and bows several times to show his respect. Although advice may be thus accepted many times during a hearing, an

---

* The acts of offering and accepting bottles of rum are external signs of inward states. Zinacantecos do not necessarily believe that such behavior is an accurate guide to personal feelings. If a "settled" quarrel flares up again, no one is surprised. Like people everywhere, Zinacantecos recognize the possible "contradiction between external behavior and secret emotions" and it is a "frequent source of anxiety and of expected misfortune" (Douglas 1966: 136).

acceptance marks the end of the proceedings only when the advice accepted constitutes a final settlement.

Hearings that produce acceptable solutions end with the drinking of the rum or beer. The liquor is shared among all participants, and to accept it means to accept the decision. There is always rum in cases that end with one or both sides begging pardon, but hearings that end simply with an agreement may lack bottles to share. Although both sides may just shake hands and leave, such a conclusion is not very satisfactory, and the party that is most pleased with the settlement usually presents the mediator with a bottle, or bottles, of rum to indicate thanks. But the liquor often serves quite another purpose. Because it must be shared, the party who is less pleased by the agreement is put into the uncomfortable position of having to choose between accepting the liquor, and therefore the terms, or refusing to drink and causing a scene. In an ideal ending, the two sides indicate their satisfaction by each presenting the mediator with a bottle.

Some cases end without a settlement that Zinacantecos regard as satisfactory. If a person considered guilty refuses to beg pardon and thus refuses to accept responsibility to pay for the damage he has caused, there is no way he can be forced to make restitution. He can be jailed and fined, but his victim remains without compensation and is believed to harbor anger in his heart. I have heard that the Presidente can threaten to confiscate a reluctant defendant's property—land and mules—in order to compensate the plaintiff, but in only one such case does the threat appear to have been carried out. A man who sold a piece of land that belonged to the hamlet as a whole had an equal share of his own property measured off and returned to the hamlet. But I have never heard of property being confiscated to repay a person. Confiscated property would be hard for the plaintiff to use because of the anger of the defendant and his kin, and it would be hard to sell for the same reason. Witchcraft is too real a threat in a community where sickness is prevalent and infant mortality high.

Sanctions

Most Zinacanteco sanctions provide restitution for the injured party in order to lift the anger from his heart. But Zinacantecos also have penal sanctions. In addition to having the guilty make

restitution, the Presidente is empowered to punish an offender by sentencing him to a term in jail if the plaintiff requests it.

Zinacantecos make a procedural, if not a verbal, distinction between jail as punishment and jail as persuasion: a person who is jailed before a settlement has been reached is being persuaded to come to a compromise, whereas a person who is jailed after a settlement is being punished. As mentioned earlier, the Presidente is permitted under Mexican law to jail a person for two reasons: as detention for up to seventy-two hours or as punishment for a longer period of hard labor. The Presidente never imposes the punishment of hard labor without a hearing and a formal charge, but he does occasionally use the seventy-two-hour detention period as punishment after a settlement has been reached. If a guilty person has been jailed before the hearing, the Presidente may consider that the pretrial term was sufficient to serve as the punishment and refuse to impose a longer sentence.

In Zinacanteco ideology, penal sanctions are imposed for the specific purpose of taking the manya out of a guilty offender. The phrase -lok*esbe smanya, "to take the manya out of someone," is used for both jail sentences and direct revenge. The idea of using a jail sentence as a punitive sanction thus hovers between the concepts of retaliation and of therapeutic treatment to remove evil tendencies. In some cases the Presidente will allow the plaintiff to choose between having the offender jailed and having him pay damages, a choice between revenge and restitution. And jail sentences are always subject to compromise; the defendant's pleas for mercy seldom go unheeded.

Zinacantecos justify imposing punishment only by saying that the offender has manya and is likely to commit the act again. A person who injures a nonrelative or does something that threatens the whole community may be jailed because the community and unrelated persons will always exist. But a man who beats his wife so brutally that she seeks and obtains a divorce will probably escape punishment because there is no danger of his beating her again. Only when the woman does not leave her husband do his evil tendencies need to be curbed.

Although the Presidente hesitates to impose fines because they are subject to misinterpretation, he is much freer to collect money

from someone in jail who wants his sentence shortened. Once the plaintiff has received his compensation and departed, the Presidente can negotiate with the jailed offender. In a few cases public pressure will be too great for the Presidente to allow the offender to be released, for if he has, say, stolen another man's wife he must be made a public example, but in most cases the Presidente is free to accept payment.

The punitive sanction of hard labor differs from the restitutive sanction in the respect that, in the former, jail sentences are imposed without the offender's agreement, whereas in the latter, his consent is required. When hearing fails to reach settlement and the guilty offender refuses to beg pardon, the plaintiff may ask the Presidente to sentence him to hard labor, but Zinacantecos regard revenge without reconciliation as an unsatisfactory solution that may lead to future reprisals.

Conciliatory Procedures in Other Communities

Zinacanteco hearings at the town hall are similar to those in other parts of the world where the litigants tend to be linked in enduring relationships, where the procedures are relatively informal, and where the overt aim of the hearing is to promote reconciliation between the contending parties (Gibbs 1963, Van Velsen 1969). Nader (1969: 88) has suggested the existence of a particular style of dispute settlement that occurs wherever "value is placed on the minimax principle, rather than on the zero-sum game." The invariant features of Zapotec procedural style that she abstracts from long-term observation of a Presidente's court in Oaxaca (1969: 87–88), even the patiently bored expression of the Presidente as he listens to the arguments of the litigants, could be said to apply equally well to Zinacanteco proceedings at the town hall:

1. The procedure is seen as a way of finding out what the trouble is. Instead of the assumption that the cause of the dispute is already known and that the proceedings function to settle, a variety of disputes may be discussed to mediate the basis of the dispute.
2. The goal is to have parties compromise their differences; the minimax principle (give a little, get a little) rather than the zero-sum game (win or lose) prevails.
3. The decisions of the court emanate from the characteristics of a

multiplex society. Regardless of who the litigants are, it is the wider network of relations that influence a decision. The greater social relevance is considered in solving a particular dispute. Utilitarian thinking is valued.

4. Norms and interests are recognized.
5. There is a legal expert.
6. It is not necessary to establish past facts or to establish guilt.
7. Conclusion is an agreement.
8. Compromise prevails even if the conclusion is either/or.
9. Agreement is backed by coercive force.
10. Reasoning is prospectively oriented.
11. The principals may exchange positions as ruling may be made on other than the original claim.

The only feature here that seems somewhat questionable in the Zinacanteco case is the ninth one: agreements in Zinacantan are spoken of as if they were backed by coercive force—the Presidente may warn a man that he will be jailed if he beats his wife again—but there is so little guarantee that force would, in fact, be applied that it is difficult to assess the power of the threat.

Nader suggests (1969: 90) that the style of dispute proceedings in the Zapotec situation is determined by three interrelated factors: the types of cases brought to the Presidente's court—that is, those that deal with human conduct; the facts of a multiplex, face-to-face society, which recognizes that litigants have to be able to continue to live together; and the Zapotec values and attitudes about dispute. These same three factors are operative in Zinacantan, although Zapotec and Zinacanteco ideologies appear to differ in their reasons for justifying conciliatory settlements. Zapotec ideology requires the officials to "make the balance," to restore relations between the litigants to a former condition of equilibrium, a condition when conflict was absent (Nader 1969: 85). Zinacanteco ideology, by contrast, demands that the victim of a wrong be placated in order to calm the anger in his heart. This ideological difference appears to be reflected in an important difference in court procedures. Among the Zapotec the Presidente himself "decides where the middle ground is" (Nader 1969: 85), whereas in Zinacantan the decision is supposed to come from the litigants. This suggests that courts in societies with multiplex, face-to-face relations where the majority of cases deal with human conduct

tend to develop legal procedures that produce compromise solutions, but that the means for arriving at such solutions—judge-imposed or litigant-agreement—are determined by ideological considerations.

Conclusions

This chapter has examined the Tzotzil words and phrases that describe key actions during a hearing in order to explore the wider conceptual framework in which Zinacanteco legal procedures are justified. Zinacantecos speak of wrongs by using the word *mulil*, a noun implying an act that angers the gods. When such an act is committed, the offender is left vulnerable to supernatural punishment, and the victim of the wrong is left with anger in his heart that cries out to the gods for vengeance. These ideas provide the justification for treating cases as private quarrels between individuals. The only way a case can be truly settled is to lift the anger from the victim's heart without arousing anger in the heart of the offender; both must accept the solution if the gods are not to be invoked in a continuing round of vengeance.

These ideas also explain the role of the mediator during a hearing. Zinacanteco mediators should not impose their own solutions, but should act as advisers to the litigants in helping them come to a mutually satisfactory agreement. Of course mediators have far more power than their overt stance might imply. They are invariably important men, and as legal experts they can manipulate information in order to produce desired outcomes. The Presidente also has more overt means of persuasion, for he can put recalcitrant litigants in jail until they become more pliable, more willing to accept a compromise. But mediators can push only so far. A forced solution leaves an unsettled case, because the dissatisfied litigant can cry out to the gods for vengeance both on his opponent and on the mediator who stepped beyond the bounds of his role.

Bargaining over a solution is not a free-for-all, but is strongly constrained by well-recognized norms. Plaintiff and defendant both agree that the person who has been injured should receive compensation from whoever has injured him. Guilty defendants expect to pay for the damage they caused, the only question being

how much. Zinacantecos also agree that people who have manya, the inner affliction that leads them to commit evil acts, should be punished to remove their evil tendencies. Plaintiffs who want a defendant jailed argue that the offender was motivated by manya, and defendants wishing to avoid a jail term plead that they were drunk. There is no doubting that people with manya should be jailed; there is only the question whether *this* defendant indeed *has* manya, and whether he is likely to commit the crime again unless curbed by punishment.

These are the ideas behind Zinacanteco settlement procedures that are reflected in the Tzotzil terms used to describe key actions during a hearing. A crime (*mulil*) is an act that angers the gods and leads to a fight (*k*op*) between individuals, which must be ended (*-lahes mulil, -lahes yoʔon*) by a mutually satisfactory solution. The mediator's job is to settle the dispute (*-melɕan k*op*) by searching for the truth (*-aʔibe melol*) and suggesting appropriate solutions to the litigants until they accept his advice (*-cun smantal*) and come to an agreement. Punishment imposed without the defendant's consent can only be justified by claiming that it is intended to relieve the offender of his tendency to commit evil acts (*-lok*esbe smanya*).

FIVE

Witchcraft Beliefs

Zinacanteco explanations for behavior presuppose a world where the most important interaction between individuals takes place in the realm of souls (Vogt 1969: 371). The language available for talking about conflict carries within it the idea that quarrels are simply an overt manifestation of a much deeper and more serious spiritual struggle. Overt quarrels are annoying, or even dangerous, but conflict between souls leads to sickness and death.

In Zinacantan, legal concepts and witchcraft beliefs belong to the same conceptual system and not to competing secular and sacred ideologies (Greenhouse 1971). Legal procedures and curing ceremonies both operate to end crimes and thus to spare the wrongdoer an onset of sickness. Begging pardon lies at the heart of both procedures. Chapter 4 explored specifically legal concepts; this chapter investigates the more abstract world of religious beliefs. But they are the same world, for legal concepts belong to the wider context of beliefs about relations between souls, both human and supernatural.

We start with a brief introduction to the world of souls, to set the stage for the more specific treatment of witchcraft beliefs, and follow this with a discussion of research methodology, which introduces the informants and shows how the beliefs were collected. The body of the chapter discusses the specific ways that witches are believed to cause sickness in a victim. These are the important beliefs, since by labeling the cause of a sickness, Zinacantecos imply the means for effecting a cure. The chapter concludes with a sum-

mary that relates witchcraft beliefs to legal concepts and legal procedures.

Witchcraft beliefs are of course difficult to describe, since they exist in people's minds and are not directly observable. Nor do they form a coherent system: Zinacantecos invoke witchcraft beliefs piecemeal, to explain events as they happen, and rarely do they feel the need to reconcile conflicting ideas. This lack of consistency is clearly illustrated in my material.

Souls

Most Zinacantecos believe that every person has two souls, an inner invisible one and an animal spirit companion who lives in the woods and is guarded by the Ancestral Gods on the mountains (Vogt 1965). Some people are born with strong inner souls and correspondingly powerful animal companions, and others are born with weak souls and insignificant animal companions. A Zinacanteco's self-image is largely based on, or reflected in, his conception of the strength of his two souls. If he feels that his souls are strong, he will have little to fear from the gods or from his fellow men, but if he feels that his souls are weak, he will walk in fear of angering more powerful beings. These beliefs also provide the language for talking about individual motivation. People who behave cautiously are described as fearing retaliation from stronger-souled persons, whereas impetuous or domineering behavior is often attributed to the actor's belief in his strong souls.

Zinacantecos talk as if the inner soul of every person can be ranked somewhere on a scale from weak to strong. As time passes, sickness and death attack the weak, leaving the strong to survive into old age. Age alone thus becomes an overt indication of soul strength, and this belief, common to many Maya communities, is used to justify the powerful roles played by older men. But a powerful soul is capable of evil as well as good. The strong-souled men who lead and protect their communities are also credited with the power to punish disobedient subordinates or political enemies with sickness. The line between justified and unjustified use of soul power is thin; the speaker's perspective determines whether a sickness is attributed to legitimate punishment or to evil witchcraft.

Guilt is the one thing that can alter the immutable power hierarchy of souls, because it makes the strong vulnerable to sickness

sent by the more powerful gods. When someone has committed a wrong (*mulil*), the injured person can cry out to the gods for vengeance and they will send punishment. This belief is at the foundation of all Zinacanteco procedures for settling conflicts. Zinacantecos describe the spiritual world they live in as a moral place, where the wicked sicken and die and the innocent, if they have relatively strong souls, flourish and remain healthy. This belief is constantly reinforced by happenings in the visible world. Sickness and death are everywhere, and no person has led such an innocent life that some wrong cannot be dredged from the past to account for present illness. But again, attributions of causality depend on the perspective of the viewer. The sick person may not want to admit guilt and may invoke counterexplanations for his condition. He may claim that he has been witched or that the gods were deceived into making him sick by the lies of his enemy. These counterexplanations, however, do not deny the basic validity of a moral universe. The person who uses such justifications also implies that the gods are right in every other case and that only in this particular instance has the evil power of an enemy brought sickness to the innocent.

By giving meaning to past events, the language of witchcraft beliefs directs future behavior. The person who attributes his sickness to witchcraft not only accounts for his condition but advises his relatives to hate the witch and to break off contact with him. At the other extreme, the person whose sickness is attributed to punishment from the gods must humble himself and beg their pardon. Witchcraft beliefs also provide shamans with an effective tool for managing the social environment. By using their expert knowledge to classify and cure existing illnesses, they can direct the future behavior of the patient and his family.

The Research Methodology

The discussion of witchcraft beliefs that follows is based on extended interviews with three informants who had long been associated with the Harvard Chiapas Project. A fourth informant was quite reticent and his brief answers were not very useful.

The interviews were conducted in my office in San Cristobal and were based on the information collected by Francesca Cancian as part of her study of the relation between norms and behavior. She

had employed three informants, two of whom participated in my witchcraft study, to complete four sentences, which, translated, began, "Mariano is good because . . . ," "Mariano is bad because . . . ," "Mariano is respected because . . . ," and "Mariano is not respected because . . ." The informants were instructed to go through the Tzotzil dictionary (Laughlin n.d.) and construct meaningful sentence endings from as many dictionary entries as possible. The result was a vast number of items on slips of paper, which were translated and sorted by Dr. Cancian. The preliminary sorting resulted in 192 slips apparently concerned with witchcraft, which she lent me. I then placed the sentence endings, still in Tzotzil, on separate cards and gave them to the informants with instructions to group together the cards that described similar actions. Then I asked each informant in separate interviews to explain the reasons for his groupings. All the interviews were very informal; I simply encouraged each informant to talk. They were all ill at ease discussing witchcraft beliefs, but the three who provided the best material gradually warmed to the task and became more open as the interview progressed. Their initial reticence, however, made me realize that without the slips to start with I would have learned very little about witchcraft beliefs.

These three informants had markedly differing personalities and perceptions of the spiritual world. The first was an extremely self-confident young man. He believed there are few witches or demons in the world and declared that witches cannot harm a person whose soul is stronger than theirs. He was convinced of the strength of his soul and in fact attributed the few illnesses he had suffered to occasions when he had been drunk and unable to defend himself from the malevolence of envious but less powerful people. He was sure that strong-souled people are invincible unless they commit some wrong or relax their guard.

The second informant, also a young man, saw a world full of evil beings, where even a strong soul can be overcome by more powerful witches. Not even the normally just Ancestor Gods can be trusted, for a persuasive witch can trick them into believing an innocent man guilty. This informant blamed his constant troubles not on his own lack of care but on the malevolence of witches and demons.

The third informant fell between the other two in outlook. He was an older man who believed that a strong soul and a blameless life provide immunity from sickness sent by the gods but not from sickness sent by powerful witches. This man enjoyed general good health, but he believed he had been made partly lame in one leg by a witch. The world, for this informant, was not such a fearful place as it was for the second informant, but it contained more witches and demons than the first recognized.

Some of the more glaring inconsistencies in this account of witchcraft beliefs can be attributed to the differences between the three informants. The spiritual worlds conceived by them can be ranked on a scale from basically benevolent to basically malevolent—from a world where the individual controls his own destiny to a world where the forces of evil are too great to overcome. But despite their differences, the informants did agree on the basic attributes of the spiritual world: souls are ranked and the strong can overcome the weak; leading a blameless life and exercising constant vigilance are the primary means of avoiding illness; and witches and demons do exist.

The following summary of witchcraft beliefs synthesizes the statements of the three principal informants. I have glossed over some of the inconsistencies in the raw materials and have stated the beliefs as positive facts. Of course no single Zinacanteco holds all these beliefs. The system of categories derives from the groupings made by the informants, but, again, I have imposed a neater order, with sharper distinctions between categories than actually occurred. The section relating witchcraft beliefs to legal concepts is also my synthesis of informants' statements, case materials, and informal observations. But I feel that both the synthesis and the catalog are basically accurate because the insights they provide serve to illuminate seeming anomalies in cases I had collected before doing the witchcraft study.

Witchcraft Beliefs

The general term for a witch is *hʔak*čamel*, a person who gives sickness. Though the central meaning of the term is quite clear, the boundaries are indistinct. At one extreme, human witches merge with demons, and at the other, ordinary people who pray

to the gods for vengeance can be labeled givers of sickness by an irate victim.

Witchcraft beliefs are best discussed in terms of somewhat fluid categories based on ideas of how witches cause sickness in a victim. Such categories coincide closely with Zinacanteco interests, since shamans base their curing practices on what they consider to be the cause of the sickness. The finding that Zinacanteco disease terms cannot be characterized by relatively exclusive sets of observable bodily symptoms (Fabrega 1970) can be understood in this context—pains and swellings are usually less important in determining the cause of a disease, and hence its cure, than is the past behavior of the victim and his associates. Most cures are aimed at placating the gods or reversing the witchcraft of an enemy, and only incidentally at removing a stomach ache or a pain in the ankle.

Witches who send sickness. Witches with the power to make people sick merely by coughing, spitting, blowing, or putting substances in food or drink are the most dangerous kind. The most fearful informant felt that the nature—and actual being—of such witches overlaps with that of completely supernatural demons, since they were born with their evil powers and the ability to send their inner souls out as disembodied spirits. The least fearful informant felt that such witchcraft could only be learned in caves from the Earth Lord, leaving the relatively weak witch dependent on the Earth Lord for renewal of his powers. What gives the category some integrity is the belief that the witch alone, with no help from other supernatural powers, causes sickness that is felt immediately. The victim develops a bad cough after drinking from a contaminated bottle, or a man who has been coughed at develops boils on his body. All the informants agreed that constant vigilance is the best protection from such witches, but only the most secure felt that vigilance is enough. The other two believed it impossible to avoid a powerful witch, who needs only to have his victim in sight in order to blow sickness at him.

A witch who can give sickness unaided may have the power to send his inner soul out at night to eat the inner soul of a victim. Instant death can result when the witch carries off the victim's soul to a conclave of witches, where it is devoured; or the victim can be made to suffer lingering agony, should the witch choose

to eat the soul little by little. A less final technique finds the witch going in person to pray outside the victim's house at night while he is sleeping. The victim suffers bad dreams and wakes up in the morning feeling sick, but there is little chance he will die. In both techniques the witch attacks the wandering inner soul of a sleeping victim, but the witch must take care not to choose a stronger-souled victim lest he be defeated himself.

X   *Witches who ask that sickness be sent.* In this form of witchcraft, believed to be the most common, the witch alone does not send the sickness but asks the Earth Lord to make an enemy sicken and die by taking his inner soul. Such witchcraft is called *čonel ta balamil*, "selling to the Earth," because the witch offers the victim's soul to the Earth Lord, who is always in need of workers on his underground estates. One informant believed that the Earth Lord repaid the witch by sending him better crops or good fortune in hunting, but the other two denied that the witch gained any benefits, except vengeance, from the sale. All did agree that selling souls was a dangerous business, since arousing the Earth Lord for any reason might cause him to take several souls, including that of the witch. The informants differed, however, on the qualifications required to address the Earth Lord. The oldest man said that anyone with a strong soul who knew how to pray well could sell souls, but the other two felt that the witch had to be born with his evil powers and to know the correct prayers.

Selling souls to the Earth Lord is quite different from giving sickness directly, although some witches are believed to practice both techniques. To sell a soul, the witch must bring a gift of candles, rum, or cigarettes to a cave, gully, or waterhole, where he recites the sins of his enemy to the Earth Lord. Although all three informants stated that the Earth Lord would take only the souls of persons who had committed a crime, the most fearful informant was convinced that the god could be tricked by a skillful witch into taking an innocent victim. Sickness sent by the Earth Lord is not immediate, as is sickness sent by an unaided witch through coughing, spitting, or blowing, but can take up to a year to strike. While the witch is waiting, he must return to the cave to pray again and again. Even after the victim becomes ill, the witch must keep praying to nullify the effects of curing ceremonies

held for the victim. Selling to the Earth can be a long and expensive process, made doubly dangerous by the risk of discovery and the belief that a skillful shaman can persuade the Earth Lord to return the sickness to the witch who asked that it be brought. Because of the uncertainties involved in selling a soul to the Earth Lord, the person who feels he has been witched need not despair. The most confident informant believed that a strong-souled person could fight the Earth Lord when he came to get him, and all three believed that a strong shaman could cure the victim by retrieving his soul from the underworld.

Souls can also be sold to other supernatural powers who desire Zinacantecos. The dead in the cemetery are always eager for company and are easily persuaded to take another soul, and witches from neighboring Indian towns so enjoy harming Zinacantecos that the sickness they send will spread from the original victim, bringing on an epidemic in which many will die. In these cases, as when a victim is sold to the Earth, there is a delay between the request and the time the sickness strikes; and the sickness can be prevented altogether if the witch is caught and forced to pray for its removal.

Witches who perform specific actions. Zinacantecos believe that each person has a quantity of luck, ?ora, which must run out before he dies. Luck is pictured as a burning candle; and a witch called *htuc* kantela,* "candle cutter," or *htuc* ?ora,* "luck cutter," slices candles into little pieces, thus cutting the victim's life span and leaving him open to attack by fatal illness. Although candle cutting can be practiced at home, most accounts indicate that it usually accompanies an attempt to sell a soul to the Earth Lord. Candle cutting does not cause sickness directly; it merely renders the victim vulnerable, and is one way of sufficiently weakening the soul of a strong victim that the Earth Lord will be able to carry him off. Some people seem to believe, however, that cutting candles will cause the victim to suffer sympathetic pain. Candles burned in kerosene bring a burning fever, and candles hung from the roof of a cave cause the victim to choke to death. In a related technique, the witch buries entrails, squashes, or meat, stuck with pins, in the cemetery or in a cave, causing the victim to rot away like the buried object until the dead claim his soul.

Witches who become supernatural animals. The three informants agreed that all people classifiable as witches have the ability to roll over three times on the ground at night and turn themselves into animals, usually goats. Since the only goats in Zinacantan are owned by one wealthy man and are confined at night,
any goats or goat-sized animals seen after dark are thought to be
witches. They are not dangerous, however, and only cause sickness
if the person seeing them suffers from fright, *ši?el*, in which case
the pieces of his inner soul dislodged by the shock are held cap-
tive by the Earth Lord. Witches are also believed to control birds
and butterflies, sending them to see how an intended victim is
faring. But beliefs vary, and the most fearful informant felt that
the witch was able to assume animal shape to do evil, whereas the
other two informants asserted that the animals only did the witch's
bidding.

Persons who can become or affect weather phenomena. Zinacantecos believe that some people can cause rain, frost, or hail,
and others can actually become such phenomena as rainbows, rolling balls of fire, or whirlwinds. People who can bring rain are considered useful to the community and are called on in times of
drought. But people who bring frost and hail are considered evil;
they use their powers to acquire wealth—their cornfields receive
the souls of all the corn they destroy. The oldest informant told
me a long story about a still-living woman who was believed to
hold ceremonies or orgies on mountaintops in order to bring frost.
According to the informant, the woman was brought before the
town hall court twice, and even confessed once to having caused
a recent, very destructive frost.

Some powerful men are also credited with having the ability
to become, or to control, rolling balls of fire, lightning, and whirlwinds. Stories tell of ancient leaders who defeated community
enemies; and living elders have been credited with driving the
Germans out of Mexico during World War II by sending rain,
lightning, and whirlwinds to block their way. These ideas seem to
parallel the more elaborate conceptions of the Tzeltal Indians of
a nearby town, where powerful elders are credited with having
whirlwinds and balls of fire for *naguales*, "spiritual counterparts"
(Hermitte 1964). In Zinacantan, the elders credited with such

exceptional abilities are believed to be capable of both good and evil, for power is always a two-edged sword. Elders who use their abilities to protect their fellow Zinacantecos from foreign witches are honored, but they are also liable for blame in time of community disasters.

Persons who can become rainbows are almost wholly bad, for Zinacantecos believe that rainbows scorch anything they touch, and cause people to get sick by chasing them and giving them *ši?el*, fright. But rainbows rarely seem to assume human shape. Unlike witches, who are primarily living Zinacantecos with the ability to turn into animals, rainbows that become human are usually strangers.

Persons who request money from the Earth Lord. The Earth Lord, as a wealthy Ladino, will lend money to people who agree to provide him with workers. Although he seldom pays the witch who sells a person's soul, fabulous sums are available to people brave enough to request money directly. Although asking for money is similar to selling a soul, it is far more elaborate. The petitioners usually go in a group with lavish gifts—huge candles, unopened bottles of fine rum, cartons of expensive cigarettes—to hold a ceremony inside a cave, complete with firecrackers and a ritual meal. The Earth Lord himself appears, to frighten the petitioners, but if they are brave he will soon talk terms. The Earth Lord is paid for his treasure in three ways: (1) the petitioners go to work right away and receive the money later, (2) the petitioners agree to return to the cave to work after a period of wealthy living, or (3) the petitioners give the Earth Lord a list of names of the people he can take. Since the third method is believed to be the most common, the rumor that someone has asked for treasure from the Earth Lord spreads terror through a hamlet.

Persons who own talking saints. Zinacantecos believe in the existence of saints that talk, *hk*ºopohel rioš*, but they often doubt the credibility of specific ones. The saints, which range from Catholic images to rocks, are kept by their owners in boxes that sit on the house altar. When asked appropriately, a saint answers questions about where to look for lost items or diagnoses the cause of an illness and suggests a cure. But talking saints are always suspect because most people believe they come from the Earth Lord. They

A marital dispute, aired at a hearing on the town hall porch. The Presidente (far right) listens to the woman's complaint and scolds her shamefaced husband. The lesser civil officials sit in descending rank order, from right to left. The doorway leads to the office of the Presidente and the township's Ladino secretary.

The same dispute, the officials beginning to doze as they and the litigants await the arrival of a witness. The Sindico, who has for the moment replaced the Presidente, talks with the woman while her husband indicates his detachment from the scene by leaning against a column.

Drunks in the town hall jail.
Jail sentences in Zinacantan rarely last more than seventy-two hours.

A litigant makes a point. In his left hand he holds the palm that he is weaving into strips for a new hat.

The town hall with a complicated case in progress. At the fringes are men who have stopped by to pass the time of day. The three seated women are litigants, as are the men near the center. On the far right, the lone man and the two women seated by the wall are waiting to bring up a different case.

The town hall at a slack period. It is a rainy Sunday, and the six highest religious officials (with the turbans) have joined the civil officials on the town hall porch. Across the muddy road is the Church of San Lorenzo, the patron saint, and behind it looms a mist-shrouded sacred mountain.

An important case in progress. The young man on the right speaks while
the others listen. At the feet of the civil officials stand three bottles,
one of the local rum, one of a soft drink, and one of beer.

A civil official makes a point while the litigants listen. The official acts as a
mediator, seeking a compromise acceptable to all.

A friend of the Presidente offers advice during a case. Such interruptions are routine; the crony may in fact be discussing the coming fiesta. The door leads to the secretary's living quarters.

While waiting for a case, the civil officials and their friends (all male) pass the time chatting and weaving hats.

The civil officials bow in traditional greeting to the senior religious officials, who have arrived to assume their Sunday places on the town hall porch.

A political meeting held in front of the town hall. The short pants are traditional; the jeans, imports from the national market.

One of the Mayores with his
billy club. These lowliest of
officials are recruited from the
troublemakers of the community.

A traditional Zinacanteco house.
Many houses, even in the outlying
hamlets, are now roofed with the
familiar Spanish tile.

A former Juez, now a hamlet elder, relaxes with his family at home. Neighbors who
prefer a settlement in the hamlet may ask him to hear their arguments at his home.

Members of a curing party pray to the gods at the crosses atop a sacred mountain. Persons wishing to avenge a wrong may lay their case before the gods in a similar ceremony. In either event a shaman is enlisted to perform the ceremony and speak to the gods.

The ceremonial center, from the top of a nearby sacred mountain. The main road runs along the far side of the Church of San Lorenzo. It is lined with little stores and cantinas, many of them owned by Ladinos. The town hall can be seen to the left of the church.

are usually found lying on the ground, and one informant stated that a person who wanted a saint should request one in a cave.

Talking saints derive both their powers and their liabilities from a close connection with the underworld. Saints are believed to be particularly good at diagnosing and curing cases of witchcraft in which the victim has been sold to the Earth, but people outside the victim's family fear that the saint may recover the soul of his patient by substituting an innocent victim to work the underground estates. Some people also fear that owners of talking saints practice outright witchcraft, accepting money to sell a soul to the Earth Lord.

Talking saints in general have a bad reputation because it is so difficult to distinguish the real ones from the fakes. Most Zinacantecos believe real saints exist, but they also believe there are unscrupulous persons who put ordinary rocks in boxes and claim extraordinary powers for them. Given this ambiguity over the credibility of particular talking saints, a person is free to accept or discredit the alleged accusations of a saint depending on whether he chooses to believe them or not. "Fake" saints are also feared and hated as ever-present troublemakers, since their false accusations of witchcraft instigate trouble between relatives or friends.

Persons who cause sickness by evil eye. All three informants felt that *k*ak*al sat*, evil eye, was not a serious form of witchcraft. It attacks only babies or convalescents and can be easily cured or prevented by simple, homely remedies. If the patient does not recover but sickens and dies, the original diagnosis of evil eye is discarded and a more serious illness is postulated.

People who exert evil eye are born with the power and often do not know they possess it. They may not even be aware that their angry or envious glances cause sickness in others. As unconscious givers of sickness, they can hardly be considered responsible for their actions and are seldom labeled witches. But there are indications that others may consider evil eye more serious than it appears from the statements of my informants. Zinacanteco mothers take elaborate precautions to protect their babies, and the most fearful informant talked of a more serious kind of evil eye in which the sender is a witch who deliberately uses his power to bring on sickness in an enemy.

Persons who cry for sickness. Sickness brought on by crying, ʔok*itabil čamel, is usually considered a just punishment because it is the result of a daylight appeal to the gods of the upper world —the sun, the saints, and the ancestral deities—who are protective beings and send sickness only to punish real offenses. There are three crying strategies, ranging from the purely legitimate to the borders of witchcraft. In the first and most legitimate technique, a person who has been deeply wronged by another may cry out in agony to the gods, asking them to punish his enemy. Such crying is spontaneous and sincere and is believed to be very effective because the gods are said to be like parents who hasten to comfort their crying child. It is also considered involuntary, the welling up anger from an overburdened heart.

The second, more elaborate technique of crying involves fasting and praying to the sun. This is a deliberate attempt to avenge a wrong, not the spontaneous crying out of a soul in agony. It involves planning, for the person who cries must refuse food and pray to the sun three times a day—at sunrise, noon, and sunset. Although the sun will send sickness only to the genuinely guilty, the offense can be relatively minor, such as angry words or a light beating. One informant stated that this was a favorite form of revenge between women and their mothers-in-law. A woman could hardly take a petty quarrel to an elder or to the ceremonial center, but if she stopped eating she might frighten her opponent into mending her ways.

The third crying technique is the most complex and expensive, since it involves special preparations and visits to sacred places. In its simplest form, the cryer burns candles and incense while he prays before his house cross. A more elaborate technique is to visit the saints in the churches and pray so loudly that all the humans within earshot, as well as the saints, hear of the enemy's misdeeds. And the most elaborate form of crying—one bordering on witchcraft—involves a major ceremony conducted by a shaman. Candles and incense are burned at the mountain crosses while the shaman prays to the Ancestral Gods of the enemy's sins. This technique is legitimate and effective if the enemy's sins are real, but the most fearful informant believed that skillful praying could trick even the upper-world gods into taking an innocent victim.

Witchcraft Beliefs and Legal Concepts

Zinacantan is not unique in its emphasis on the importance of spiritual interaction. Monographs on other Maya communities in the Chiapas highlands also stress the relation between soul power and political prestige, between earthly conflict and spiritual struggles, and between sickness and supernatural punishment (Guiteras Holmes 1961, Holland 1963, Nash 1970, Hermitte 1964, Villa Rojas 1947). All these Maya groups share a belief in a world where each soul must struggle for survival. It is a highly moral world, in the sense that the truly good survive and the wholly bad perish; but there are so many evil beings about, both witches and demons, that the good sometimes sicken and the evil receive treasure from the Earth Lord. These beliefs, in all the communities, provide a rich and flexible language through which a person may attribute the misfortunes of his enemies to the justice of the gods and claim that his own misfortunes are the work of evil beings.

The highly moralistic world of the Zinacantecos exists here and now on this earth. They are concerned not with retribution in an afterlife but with immediate earthly punishment. Zinacantecos state that the inner souls of people who die stay away only as many years as the person lived before being reincarnated in a body of the opposite sex. Legal procedures, therefore, are concerned not with preventing retribution in an eternal afterlife but with avoiding earthly misfortunes that are sure to strike the evildoer or some member of his family within the year. Zinacanteco offenders feel a far more pressing need to "end their guilt" than do people raised in the Judeo-Christian tradition, who can afford to put off repentance until the hour of death.

Witchcraft beliefs and legal concepts are not competing ideologies; rather, both rest on the same assumptions about the nature of the world. Legal procedures and legal concepts are invoked the moment an offense occurs or when a conflict breaks into the open; and curing ceremonies, with their attendant beliefs about witchcraft and supernatural vengeance, are staged when illness has struck. Mediators and shamans do not come into conflict—for they are invoked at different points in the offense-retribution sequence —but in fact reinforce each other. The mediator uses ideas about

the prevalence of witchcraft or the inevitability of supernatural punishment to persuade offenders to confess and beg pardon, and the shaman often tells the patient that if he had made amends at the time of the quarrel he would not have been struck by illness.

Individual Zinacanteco conflicts also alternate between legal and supernatural spheres. An old quarrel, long since settled at the town hall, may be invoked as the cause of an illness, which in turn leads to a new quarrel that goes to the town hall and provides a renewed fund of ill will, which can be invoked as the cause of the next illness, and so on. Most Zinacantecos live in small hamlets with little opportunity to move away when a conflict develops. In such closed communities old quarrels never die but are remembered with each new illness or aggressive act.

Witchcraft beliefs underlie all of the reasons given for actions during a hearing. They are invoked to justify everything from putting an offender in jail to persuading both sides to accept a mediator's advice. All the action discussed during a hearing is described as if supernatural vengeance were real and immediate. Indeed, Zinacanteco legal procedures can only be understood when seen against the background of witchcraft beliefs. The methods for reaching compromises can exist only in a world where some form of supernatural retribution, legitimate or illegitimate, is sure and immediate.

Someone who has clearly been wronged cannot afford to overlook the incident but must initiate some form of public legal proceedings if he wants to avoid being suspected of pursuing retribution through witchcraft. There is no conception that a wronged person can forgive and forget; even if his conscious mind might wish to ignore the wrong, his angry heart would still cry out to the gods for vengeance.

At the beginning of a hearing, the mediator often asks the plaintiff to state the solution he desires. The question is justified, since a hearing can end only when the plaintiff is satisfied and his anger is calmed. If the plaintiff declares that he wants no compensation, he is thought either a fool or a witch, and his answer is unacceptable. The mediator and the offender both press him to accept some form of compensation, if only a glass of liquor, to publicly proclaim that the anger is gone from his heart.

This stress on satisfying the plaintiff is a theme running throughout Zinacanteco legal procedures and explains why settlements are not based on abstract rules. Settlements serve to forestall future sickness, not to punish wrongdoers for past events. Anything that satisfies the plaintiff will produce the desired result. But Zinacanteco settlements are not as random as that statement might imply, since a plaintiff's demands are structured by the available ideas of what is appropriate. In the long run, Zinacanteco cases have fairly predictable outcomes, but if we are to understand the sequence of events of a trouble case as described by an informant, it is necessary to realize that the ultimate justification for a Zinacanteco settlement is that it calms the heart of the plaintiff and not that it satisfies some abstract notion of what is just.

People who have committed an offense are also expected to seek a hearing, where they can calm the anger of the wronged party in order to avoid supernatural vengeance. The obvious course is to go immediately and beg pardon. But even if the offender waits for the plaintiff to initiate proceedings, he is expected to appreciate the opportunity for reconciliation. At some point in the hearing he should confess, beg pardon, and offer restitution. Given Zinacanteco ideas of supernatural vengeance, it makes no sense for an offender to refuse to admit guilt, unless the reparations he would be expected to pay are impossibly high. There is nothing to be gained by escaping immediate sanction, since a more horrible punishment awaits. Even on purely rational grounds there is little advantage to defying the gods, for the next illness that occurs in the offender's family will almost certainly be attributed to his refusal to beg pardon, and even if the offender is a skeptic, his wife and elder relatives will blame him for the misfortune.

In the context of these ideas about supernatural vengeance, even a term in jail can be justified as having been ordered for the benefit of the offender. When someone has committed a particularly serious offense—flagrant adultery, fighting while sober, or performing witchcraft—thus provoking massive outrage in the heart of the victim, a stiff jail sentence is seen as protecting the offender. The suffering of the defendant is believed to assuage the plaintiff's anger and to calm his desire for revenge. Jail sentences are thus like other forms of restitution. The plaintiff is asked to suggest the

length of incarceration, and the defendant can plead for a shortened sentence.

Although Zinacantecos put more stress on abating the anger of the plaintiff, a mediator must be careful not to arouse the anger of the defendant, since it can also bring sickness. Defendants cannot, therefore, be pushed beyond the limits of what they regard as just solutions, whatever the desires of the plaintiff, and we have here another reason why outcomes coincide fairly well with community norms. In the long run, then, Zinacanteco compromise settlements are determined by the same factors that determine legal decisions the world around: the set of norms available for justifying a decision and the relative strengths of the plaintiff, defendant, and judge. Zinacantan appears to differ so markedly from Western legal systems, or from authoritarian African systems, only because Zinacantecos emphasize the role of relative power over the role of norms and because they speak of power in terms of soul strength.

Even mediators are not immune to the conflict of souls, and their role during a hearing must also be interpreted in terms of witchcraft beliefs. Mediators are thought to be men with strong souls, and they usually possess all the outward attributes of soul power, including age, service in a prestigious religious post, and political power. The mediator's soul power is believed to protect him from the wrath of dissatisfied litigants and to stand as a threat to any weaker-souled litigant who refuses to accept his advice. Though mediators have few overt means of coercion, they are often effective because of their power to inflict supernatural punishment.

Witchcraft beliefs also serve to explain the heavy emphasis on drinking at the close of a hearing. The liquor that is shared, and that must be consumed by all, is much more than an overt sign of reconciliation. It palpably calms the anger in the hearts of the participants and thus protects them all from supernatural vengeance. Zinacantecos say that drinking "revives the heart," and that in the reviving it erases the remnants of anger.

All of the actions that occur during a hearing must be interpreted on two levels. One is the overt level described in Chapter 3, where equality is stressed in direct interaction but where status differences are recognized; though there are few outward sym-

bols of rank, everyone is aware of differences in wealth and political power. The second is the spiritual level described in this chapter, where hierarchy is stressed, for souls are rigidly ranked and highly competitive, but where an essential equality is maintained before the justice of the gods. This perpetual tension between hierarchy and equality runs throughout Zinacanteco life (Colby 1966, R. Rosaldo 1968) and provides both litigants and mediators with a rich symbolic language for manipulating the social environment. Small wonder, then, that Zinacantecos place so high a premium on the ability to speak well in Tzotzil, for it is through adroit use of language that a person can force others to do his bidding without denying them the overt equality that is their due.

SIX

Witchcraft Cases

This chapter returns from the abstract realm of beliefs to undertake an analysis of the witchcraft cases described by informants. Sixty-three accounts of actual cases were examined to determine what kinds of people are accused of witchcraft, what types of relationships produce the most accusations, how witchcraft cases come before the authorities, and how settlements are produced. Chapter 5 presented Zinacanteco ideas of the ways one person can cause sickness to strike another; this chapter looks at the way these ideas are used by litigants and mediators in seeking solutions to conflicts.

There is little doubt that Zinacantecos actually practice witchcraft. Persons who believe they can cause sickness by blowing or spitting are probably rare, but there are clear indications that Zinacantecos try to sell souls to the Earth Lord. Mutilated candles have been found in caves and "witches" have been overheard praying in gullies (Laughlin, personal communication). It is easy to understand why selling souls is so attractive: the chances are excellent that any given Zinacanteco, or a member of his family, will become ill during the year's time in which the Earth Lord must do his work, and the rare failures to induce illness can be blamed on faulty praying or on the counter-witchcraft of a powerful shaman.

Very few cases of alleged witchcraft reach the town hall court or come before hamlet elders, since most of them are handled privately through counter-witchcraft ceremonies. This is so primarily

because the victim rarely "discovers" he has been witched until he becomes ill and consults a shaman. He is then already in the hands of a specialist and committed to a course of action, since most shamans recommend holding a ceremony that will simultaneously cure the victim and return the sickness to the witch who sent it. If the ceremony is successful and the patient recovers, the incident is forgotten until a new sickness or act of hostility recalls it to memory.

The few cases of witchcraft to reach the town hall become celebrated affairs, discussed throughout Zinacantan and remembered in differing versions for years afterward. Most of the cases I collected are of this type, for they are the ones that endure in an informant's memory. In at least two instances informants gave me differing versions of what was clearly the same case, but I have not tried to reconcile the differences or to seek out the "truth"; I have simply accepted both versions as equally valid accounts of what an informant thought happened.

The chapter is divided into four sections. The first examines the characteristics of accused witches through informants' descriptions and actual records. The second discusses the ways witchcraft cases become known, and examines the actions or events leading one Zinacanteco to accuse another of witchcraft. The third looks into the different solutions seen as appropriate to witchcraft cases settled at the town hall, whether brought as accusations of witchcraft or as pleas from an accused witch for protection. The last section examines the effects of the increasing availability of Mexican law on Zinacanteco procedures for handling witchcraft cases; minor changes have resulted from the fact that accused witches can now appeal to the San Cristobal authorities for protection.

Characteristics of Accused Witches

Although my informants described witches as lazy, worthless scalawags envious of their betters, most people actually accused of witchcraft turn out to possess demonstrated soul strength. In sixty-three cases I found fifty-two accusations against named persons, thirty-six of whom were older men. And well-known witches also tend to be shamans. Although the overlap is not complete,

most people with an established reputation for knowing how to send sickness are curers, and shamans renowned for their ability to retrieve souls from the Earth Lord are also suspected of knowing how to sell them (Francesco Pellizzi, personal communication).

The informants also said that most witches send sickness because they envy wealthier people and wish to see them suffer. This belief is used to explain the deaths of children of important men. However, in all cases where a living person was accused of witchcraft, he was described as having reasons other than envy for wishing his victim harm. The fear of envious witches has been seen as a mechanism for maintaining economic homogeneity within a small community by forcing wealthy persons to spend their surplus (Wolf 1955), but the companion fear of being accused of witchcraft is probably equally effective. Poor people often attribute the riches of the wealthy to pacts with the Earth Lord (Greenhouse 1971) and are ready to suspect any rich person of receiving treasure in return for the souls of his less fortunate neighbors.

My small sample of cases did not allow me to determine whether alleged knowledge of witchcraft ran in families. One informant stated that it did, and he further cited as example a family in his hamlet where father, son, and grandson were all believed to be witches.

Certainly, a large proportion of witchcraft charges are brought within families: of the thirty-seven cases where the identity of both witch and victim was given, fifteen involve people definitely not related but twenty-two involve relatives—eleven cases between patrilineally related consanguines and eleven between affines. The proportion of cases between relatives may be considerably higher than it appears from these figures, because my sample, which is based on cases that become public knowledge, is biased toward accusations between nonrelatives. The distribution of quarreling dyads within the set of cases between consanguineal relatives is just what would be predicted from a knowledge of the strains inherent in the Zinacanteco patrilineal family: seven cases are between siblings (four between brothers, three between brothers and sisters); three cases are between fathers and sons; and one is between mother and son. Quarrels over property

are endemic in the extended family, particularly among the adult men of the group, but also among adult women, who often advance their own claims to a share of the family inheritance.

The distribution of quarreling dyads among affinal relatives is harder to interpret. Three cases are between husbands and wives—a relationship always strained but usually marked by more overt forms of aggression. Two such cases are between men and their daughters' husbands, and two are between men and their sisters' husbands. The other affinal dyad types are represented by a single case apiece. It seems likely that quarrels between affinal relatives, other than those between husbands and wives, reflect tensions within the patrilineal family rather than tensions between affines, since Zinacanteco informants trace most witchcraft cases to irresolvable property disputes. My sample also includes three cases where groups of men were accused of having asked the Earth Lord for treasure; these cases do not involve strained relations between individuals, but they reflect the larger tension between rich and poor Zinacantecos.

How Witchcraft Cases Become Known

Witchcraft cases are brought up in three ways: (1) a person is discovered performing acts that can be interpreted as witchcraft, (2) a person brings up a complaint against someone he believes is witching him, or (3) an accused witch brings up a case to have his name cleared and to protect himself from the vengeance of an assumed victim.

The witch is discovered in the act. The actions taken when a person is discovered performing witchcraft depend on whether the identity of the intended victim is known. If it is, the witchcraft is seen to be his affair, and the discoverer usually informs him of it if he is a friend or relative. But if the intended victim is a stranger, the discoverer may simply forget the matter.

Case 2. A woman who eavesdrops to hear the name of a witch's victim is in no hurry to inform the victim. (The informant, who happened to be present when the case was heard, began his account by recounting what was told of the background of the quarrel between the witch and her victim.)

Two years before the case came to the town hall, some sheep left to wander after the harvest ate the roots of a *chayote* vine that belonged

to a widow. The widow, enraged, tried to beat the sheep off with a stick. When the woman who owned the sheep came running up to save her animals, the angry widow showed her the eaten vine. The sheep owner offered to pay for the damage but the widow unreasonably fixed her demand at 300 pesos. (The informant felt she should have asked only 10 or 20 pesos, since the vines were not permanently ruined.) The owner of the sheep said she could not pay that much money without consulting her husband, but offered to give the widow 20 or 30 pesos immediately. The widow refused to accept the money and began to beat the sheep again. A real fight then broke out when the sheep owner attempted to rescue her animals.

About a week after the fight the husband of the woman who owned the sheep returned from his fields in the Grijalva valley. When his wife told him about the quarrel, he took a bottle of rum to the widow's house to ask her pardon and to repeat the offer to pay for the damage. But the widow refused to let him into the house, saying it was too late to pay for the damage. The man had no choice but to leave with the quarrel unsettled. Some time later the little daughter of the sheep owner died. (It must be remembered that the informant did not witness any of these events. He first heard the story two years later when it was told at the hearing by the victim. The story, which portrays the witch as someone unable to forgive a wrong, is typical of a victim's attempt to account for an alleged witch's hostility. The sheep owner wished to imply that the witch had been praying for sickness since the time of the original quarrel and had been successful in causing the death of her child. The informant's account of the witchcraft case itself follows.)

One night the ten-year-old son of a woman living near the widow happened to wake up and go outside. He saw the widow in her patio, praying beside her house cross. She poured liquid from a bottle over the contents of a bowl and then set it on fire. The boy told his mother what he had seen, and the next night she sat up to observe. When the widow came out of the house just before midnight and again burned something beside her cross, the neighbor listened intently to the prayers uttered by the widow, but not hearing her own name mentioned as the intended victim she returned to bed and decided to forget the matter. It was not until she had been disturbed for five or six nights by the widow's praying that she finally informed the intended victim.

On hearing of the witchcraft, the sheep owner and her husband decided they should inform the hamlet *principales*. The principales told the husband to watch the widow's house and fetch them when he heard her praying. There would be plenty of time to catch her when she came outside to the cross after praying inside, and they were in any case not permitted to break into her house. So the husband watched the house. The first night nothing happened, but the second night he heard her start to pray. He ran to inform the principales and they all gathered outside the widow's house. When she came out, the men confronted

her, discovering her with a basket of little candles, all cut into one-inch pieces sharpened at the ends.

They took her immediately to the ceremonial center, arriving at the Presidente's house around four in the morning. The Presidente listened to the accusation, examined the evidence, and kept the woman in his house for the rest of the night.

The next morning they all gathered at the town hall, along with the victim and her husband and the woman and her son who had first observed the witch's ritual. The Presidente opened the case by asking the widow if she had been cutting candles. She admitted doing so only once. The boy's mother then told the Presidente she had seen the widow cutting candles and praying before her house cross at least five times and had listened in order to discover the name of the victim. The background of the quarrel, with the original argument over the sheep, was gone into. The sheep owner related how she and her husband had tried to pay for the damage to the chayote vine, and how the widow had demanded a ridiculously high sum and refused to accept any smaller payment. The widow claimed that her vine was worth a lot of money: by selling the chayotes she usually made around 400 or 500 pesos a year. But the Presidente reprimanded her for not having brought her complaint to the town hall two years before, when the vine was damaged. At that the widow began to cry, still insisting that she had cut candles only once. Finally she admitted having done so at least five times.

The sheep owner then told of her daughter's death, implying that it was due to the witchcraft of the widow. Upon the widow's denying having such powers, the Presidente sent for three respected shamans to feel her pulse, at both wrists and both elbows, to see if she was telling the truth. (Zinacantecos believe that the blood talks, telling a shaman who can interpret such messages the causes of a disease or whether the person being pulsed is a witch.) The shamans came, pulsed the woman, and said she was not able to send sickness but that she had prayed and cut candles (that is, she had cut the luck of her victims and made them open to sickness but had not herself actually sent the disease). Then the three shamans pulsed the sheep owner and her husband to see if they had begun to get sick. Since they were found to be somewhat affected, the Presidente and the assembled elders put pressure on the widow to confess so the couple might be cured. They asked her if she had cut candles and prayed in other places, and she finally admitted to having prayed in the church and on one of the sacred mountains.

A large party was formed, consisting of a shaman, several mayores, a juez, and various on-lookers, to go with the witch while she retracted her prayers, so that the sheep owner and her husband might recover. They went first to the stores, where the widow was made to buy the candles and liquor needed for the retraction ceremonies; and then they set out to visit the church, the sacred mountain, and the woman's house

in the hamlet. The entire retraction ceremony took twenty-four hours, at the end of which the woman was brought back to the town hall and sentenced to fifteen days of hard labor. She spent her nights in jail and her days pushing a wheelbarrow.

In this case the woman who discovered the witch listened to catch the name of the intended victim and then did nothing about it because the victim was not a relative. Moreover, at the hearing, nothing was made of the fact that she did not immediately report what she had heard. In spite of informants' statements that all witches are bad and should be punished, people who discover witches praying for illness will do nothing unless they or their relatives are likely to become sick. Witchcraft, like other wrongs in Zinacantan, is treated as a private affair between the two quarreling parties, and outsiders do not interfere.

When a witch is discovered and no victim can be identified, fear spreads among potential victims and actions are taken to force the witch to confess. If he refuses, he is either set free pending the appearance of a victim or forced to perform a ceremony to nullify the effect of the witchcraft. Such cases are usually handled on the hamlet level by the people most affected, and not sent to the town hall unless a victim is discovered to press the issue.

Case 3. Hamlet leaders force a witch to confess the name of his victim. (The informant was present when the "witch" was forced to confess. His father-in-law, Mol Petul, told him about the elements of the case that he missed seeing.)

When the hamlet church was built, a cross that had once stood on a hill was moved to a spot underneath the new altar. A few years later, on August 10, the fiesta of the patron saint of Zinacantan, it was noticed that the cross was missing and someone said he had seen Andres, a local shaman, take it. Some of the men who had remained home from the fiesta, in the hamlet, led by the acknowledged hamlet leader, Mol Petul, gathered to discuss the missing cross. Andres, called before the group for questioning, admitted having taken the cross, but justified his action by describing a dream in which a Ladino had come to him and told him to place the cross in a certain cave that was to become a sacred shrine. (Andres was in fact claiming that the Earth Lord had visited him and asked him to set up a shrine for use in curing and waterhole ceremonies.) Mol Petul then asked Andres why he had not told the other shamans of his dream so they could all participate in setting up the community shrine. Andres was silent. Mol Petul went on

to remind him that such secret actions could be interpreted as witchcraft, and suggested that Andres be left tied up and guarded by the principales. This was done and the meeting broke up.

The next morning a blast of the horn summoned all the hamlet men to a meeting in the church. When Andres was brought in, he repeated the same story before the larger audience. And since further questioning failed to elicit anything of interest, the group decided to visit the cave over the hill to find the cross. The cave was quite large and its entrance was marked by a small cross. In the middle of the cave was another cross, and at the far end stood the large cross missing from the church. Upon examining it the men found candle wax of many colors at its base. (Small candles of many colors are used only for selling souls to the Earth Lord or for recovering them.) Andres had been dragged to the cave with his hands tied behind his back, and now he trembled when Mol Petul questioned him about the candles. Since Andres did not answer, the men put a rope around his neck. Andres still refused to talk, so the men threatened to pull the rope until he strangled. Andres finally broke down and admitted burning candles to the Earth Lord to sell the soul of his enemy, an elder named Juan, who had fought with him in a *cantina* when drunk. After this admission, the men pulled the rope tight to see if he would confess to having sold other souls. But Andres protested that he had only one enemy, and they removed the rope, though his hands remained tied. He was later taken to the town hall by his intended victim and several other men.

But while the group was still at the cave, a woman approached, saying she had seen another shaman, the brother-in-law of Mol Petul, enter the cave with the confessed witch. Thereupon the men turned on the older shaman and put the rope around his neck. Tossing the end over a tree branch, they pulled the old shaman into the air to make him confess. However, he refused to admit anything and in fact flew into a rage. Finally they released him and returned to the hamlet.

The next morning the old shaman set out for the town hall with two relatives. Still so angry that he was crying, he was determined to see that Mol Petul and Juan, the victim of the other witch, were jailed— the former for authorizing the hanging and the latter for urging Mol Petul to carry it through. When the old shaman told the Presidente his complaint, mayores were sent to bring Mol Petul, Juan, and the woman who had made the accusation to the town hall.

Although Andres, the confessed witch, was already in jail, the two cases were heard together. Andres sided with the old shaman, the two agreeing they would complain of the torture to the Mexican authorities unless the Presidente agreed to keep Mol Petul and Juan in jail for as long as he kept the confessed witch. Thus all three stayed in jail, though Andres was taken to the cave to retract his witchcraft, and the expenses for the ceremony were split among the prisoners. Andres was

made to pay only half the transportation costs of the large group that accompanied him for the ceremony, but he did have to buy all his own candles. The candles used by the shaman who accompanied him were bought from hamlet funds and a meal was provided by the hamlet for all the participants. Mol Petul and Juan, still in jail, were unable to attend the retraction ceremony.

Within a year after these events, both Mol Petul and Juan died. My informant attributed both deaths to the witchcraft of the two men they had tortured, but added the qualification that the elders would not have died had they not tortured an innocent man. Strangling Andres was one thing, for he had confessed to stealing the cross, but hanging the old shaman on the flimsy evidence of the woman was wrong. The two elders had become vulnerable to witchcraft and had died.

This case is illustrative for the violent action taken by the assembled men of the hamlet when they suspected someone of witchcraft but were unable to identify the victim. Once the witch had confessed, however, the prosecution of the case became the victim's affair. Although several men of the hamlet helped to carry the witch off to jail, the victim was the plaintiff at the ceremonial center. But the case also embraces the incident of the second accused witch, who refused to confess and became angry at being hanged. The ultimate settlement of the combined cases was due to his vigorous threat to take the issue of the hanging to the Mexican authorities. He managed to have the two hamlet leaders jailed and to have the sentence of the confessed witch reduced, though the witch, to be sure, did perform a retraction ceremony.

Although some actions, such as cutting candles and praying at night in the cemetery, are clearly witchcraft, there are curing techniques for recovering souls from the Earth Lord that closely resemble witchcraft techniques for selling souls. It is never clear, therefore, whether a shaman found praying under suspicious circumstances has a legitimate or an evil purpose, and a clever shaman can generally talk his way out of difficulty.

Case 4. A shaman found praying in suspicious circumstances claims to be conducting a curing ceremony. (The informant lived in the hamlet where the case occurred.)

Andres was walking by an important shrine to the Earth Lord when he saw a well-known shaman praying with his face close to the ground. In front of the shaman were three large candles and beside him sat another man. Andres tried, unsuccessfully, to hear the words of the

shaman's prayer, and left quietly to get help. When he returned with his brother and two brothers-in-law, the shaman was still praying. To approach unnoticed was easy because the two were engrossed. The four men thus grabbed the shaman and questioned him. The shaman claimed to be conducting a curing ceremony for his companion's child, who had been frightened on that spot and had lost her soul to the Earth Lord. The shaman was trying to recover it. But he had not set up the usual paraphernalia that accompanies a legitimate ceremony for the recovery of a soul lost through fright; there were no flowers, no cross, no pine needles, no incense. Nor was the shaman dressed for the occasion. He wore his regular clothes and was not carrying his bamboo cane or wearing his black robe. Only the three large candles were before him. When questioned about his lack of accouterments, the shaman said he always prayed without the crosses of pine branches and flowers, because people who saw the discarded crosses the next day would laugh at them and vitiate the effects of the ceremony. With this answer the four men let the shaman go.

But the shaman had not gone very far when one of the men noticed that the ground beneath the three large candles looked disturbed. He called back the shaman and his companion and bade them wait. The four men dug up the earth and found a bundle of small colored candles tied with a rope, with a piece of pitch pine in the middle. Nearby was buried a bottle of bootleg rum. The shaman again had a ready answer: he had buried the candles and liquor as a substitute for the soul of the child. The Earth Lord did not want to give up the little girl, and the shaman hoped to persuade him to release her in exchange for the presents. The men accepted this explanation, and let the shaman and his companion go on their way. But later they took the candles and liquor to one of the hamlet elders and told him of the incident.

The next day, November 2, all the men of the hamlet gathered to work on the community trails. By this time all the important elders had heard of the suspicious actions of the shaman, and they came prepared to question him. But the shaman did not arrive. He was accordingly sent for, and when he arrived he repeated the same story. The most important elder took charge of the informal hearing and began to probe further. He reminded the shaman that it was not the custom to conduct such spare ceremonies and that he could be suspected of witchcraft. The shaman, for his part, claimed that the Ancestor Gods had taught him to bury candles and to pray with his mouth to the earth if he wanted to recover a lost soul. (All legitimate curing techniques are learned from the Ancestor Gods.) The elder was not satisfied, however, nor, he said, were the people of the hamlet. He and the other elders then decided to send a group of men to the house of the shaman's client to see the sick child. The investigators reported that there were no signs of sickness at the client's house. The child was outside playing

and the house cross was undecorated, a sure sign that there had been no curing ceremony there. But the shaman still had a ready answer: he had not burned candles at the house because it was impossible to keep a child in bed for the three-day taboo period following a ceremony. If a person gets out of bed right after the candles are burned, said the shaman, the Ancestor Gods are angered and send sickness.

This answer, like the others, failed to completely satisfy the assembled elders, and after some discussion the shaman was ordered to conduct three more ceremonies in the same place, accompanied by another shaman who would hear his prayers. The suspected witch's client paid for the candles and liquor. In the end the three ceremonies were held and the case never reached the ceremonial center.

This case points up once more the concern of the hamlet elders to investigate probable cases of witchcraft in order to abate the anxiety that spreads among potential victims. Since no single victim was identified in this case and the witch never confessed, a compromise solution was necessary, but the solution reached satisfied everyone. By praying again in the company of other shamans, the alleged witch was forced to offer legitimate prayers, which would either help the sick child further if the previous ceremony had been legitimate, or nullify the request for sickness if it had not.

The victim brings up a witchcraft case. Victims who take cases to the town hall usually have discovered direct evidence of witchcraft but are not yet sick. Few people fall into this category, since most victims either place themselves in the hands of shamans, who prescribe counter-witchcraft ceremonies, or recover unaided and decide to forget the matter. Most victims also lack the direct evidence needed for arguing successfully before the town hall. My cases show that plaintiffs who accuse an enemy of witchcraft without a prior confession, material evidence, or eyewitness reports are unlikely to succeed in having the witch confess. Confession, as we shall see, is a necessary prelude not only to the retraction ceremony, which protects the intended victim and his family from sickness, but also to having the witch jailed.

Cases 2 and 3 described the actions of victims who had definite proof of witchcraft and who were not yet sick or in the hands of a shaman. Both cases went to the town hall and resulted in retraction ceremonies and punishment for the witch. Two other cases

are now recounted, one of a victim taking direct action against a witch and the other of an unsuccessful plaintiff at the town hall.

Case 5. A shaman who turns into a witch during a ceremony is beaten. (This case involved the same elder as Case 3 and was related by the same informant, Mol Petul's son-in-law.)

When one of Mol Petul's children was sick, he asked a shaman named Miguel to hold a curing ceremony for the child. During the ceremony, Miguel became drunk and began cutting the candles in two, burying the top in the ground and lighting the bottom. In his drunkenness he told Mol Petul he had tried to make him sick but had found his blood too strong and so had caused the child's illness instead—perhaps the child's soul would be weak enough to kill. After taking in this performance for a time, Mol Petul became furious. He seized the drunken shaman, threw him out of the house, and beat him. The ceremony was left unfinished, but in spite of that the child recovered.

Because the victim handled this case himself, it never reached the town hall. It is perhaps more dramatic than most such incidents because of the direct confrontation between the witch and his victim, but it is fairly typical in portraying the victim as a strong-souled person who was able to deal with witchcraft directly, on a spiritual level. Similar cases were related by informants who had treated themselves with home or store-bought remedies and felt no need to take action against the witch after they had recovered.

Case 6. A victim accuses a relative of witchcraft because of statements by a talking saint. (The informant heard the case in his capacity as municipal secretary.)

When Juan's wife became ill, he visited the owner of a local talking saint to learn how he might cure her. The saint said the woman had been witched and that her brother, jealous of the fact that Juan was rich and had passed a high religious office, had caused her illness by praying to the Earth Lord to take her soul. Juan asked the saint if he could cure his wife and the saint prescribed medicine that made the woman recover. Later the saint's owner told Juan that he should take the case to the town hall to have his wife's brother punished so he would not send sickness again. Juan accepted this judgment and went to the town hall to accuse his brother-in-law, Mariano, of witchcraft. The Presidente listened to the complaint and sent for the accused. When Mariano arrived at the town hall, he vigorously denied having witched his little sister, saying he was not an animal to attack his own relatives. Mariano then asked the Presidente to send for the owner of the talking saint so that everyone could hear it accuse him of witchcraft.

The Presidente agreed and dispatched a group of mayores to bring the talking saint and its owner to the town hall.

When the owner arrived, his little box was placed in front of the town hall and asked if Mariano had witched his sister. The box said nothing. (Talking-saint boxes never seem to talk at the town hall, although this informant said he had heard that particular saint talk in its owner's house.) Since the box did not talk, Mariano asked that it be opened. The Presidente agreed. They forced open the box and found it empty. Mariano was now angry; he asked the Presidente to confiscate the saint's box and put the saint's owner in jail for having falsely accused him of witchcraft. At Mariano's request, the saint's owner was sentenced to three days in jail and made to carry stones for the bridge being built in the ceremonial center.

With the saint thus discredited, Juan and Mariano were reconciled and left the town hall together. The owner of the talking saint served his time in jail, but upon his release he returned to his hamlet and acquired another saint.

This case, told in bare outline, illustrates what happens when an accusation of witchcraft is based on evidence from a talking saint or from a shaman who can be discredited. It is unusual for the victim to appeal to the town hall to have a witch punished, but the informant offered no deeper reasons for the action than the advice of the owner of a talking saint.

The most direct action a victim can take, of course, is to murder the witch. This is also seen as an effective way of curing the victim, because it halts the witch's further appeals to the Earth Lord. But there seem to be relatively few witchcraft murders in Zinacantan. So many courses of action are open to a person who feels victimized that only the most desperate victim resorts to killing. It is also difficult to judge how many murders are actually due to fear of witchcraft. Most murders seem to have political overtones, which is not surprising given the intimate link between soul power and political power.

The accused witch seeks protection from the town hall. Many witchcraft cases are brought to the town hall by suspected witches, fearful of being killed, who ask the Presidente to call in the accusers and question their reasons for suspecting witchcraft. In most cases, such accusations are based on statements by talking saints and are forgotten after the saint is exposed and its owner punished. But some cases are not so easily handled. The following case tells

of an accused witch declared innocent at the town hall who eventually had to leave the hamlet to escape persistent rumors.

Case 7. An accused witch asks the Presidente to investigate charges against him. (The informant was the political leader who accompanied the accused witch to the town hall.)

Jose lived with his wife's father, Nicolas. One day Jose became ill and decided to return to live with his own father. When Jose's father also became ill, the two concluded, on the strength of the coincidence, that Nicolas and his wife must be witches. They repeated the accusation to many neighbors; and it finally reached the ears of Nicolas when Jose's older sister told Nicolas's brother-in-law that Jose and his father were thinking of murdering Nicolas and his wife at night. Frightened by the news, Nicolas resolved to move away. Since he was living on land belonging to a person in another hamlet, he went to tell the landlord he was leaving. The landlord, upon hearing the reason, advised Nicolas to seek help from a political leader of the landlord's hamlet. Following this advice, Nicolas consulted an elder he knew, Mol Romin, who said he should take his case to the town hall to resolve the matter.

Mol Romin accompanied Nicolas and his wife to consult the Presidente. By arriving at the Presidente's house just before dawn, they managed to explain their side of the case in private. The Presidente then sent a mayor and a juez to fetch Jose and his father and older sister. But when the mayor and the juez arrived in the hamlet, Jose persuaded them to give him time to assemble the many people who had accused Nicolas and his wife of witchcraft. The juez granted the request and returned to the town hall to have the case deferred for five days.

Jose spent the time gathering his supporters and even appealed to a leading political figure in the township. On the appointed day they all gathered at the town hall. Nicolas was there with his wife, the brother-in-law who had first warned him of the plot, and Mol Romin. Nicolas opened the case by saying that Jose had accused him of witchcraft. Jose denied it. Then Nicolas asked his brother-in-law to tell of the plot he had heard from Jose's sister. The sister was then questioned. After first denying it, she finally admitted having overheard her father and brother plotting to kill Nicolas. At this point the Presidente said they should call in some shamans to pulse Nicolas and his wife to see if they were indeed witches. Four senior shamans of the community came to the town hall and, after pulsing the accused, declared that Nicolas and his wife were innocent. Jose asked the shamans to reconsider—so many people in the hamlet were sick that Nicolas had to be a witch. But the shamans were adamant. At this, the Presidente scolded Jose and his sister for spreading dangerous gossip and had them confined to jail briefly to remove their evil tendencies. Jose stayed in jail overnight, but his sister was released as darkness fell.

When Jose was released, he presented a gift of liquor to Nicolas to ask his pardon. Then Jose and his sister signed an acta stating they would not speak against Nicolas again; if they persisted in spreading gossip, the penalty would be jail. After this the group dispersed.

But that was not the end of the affair, for Jose and his sister soon resumed speaking against Nicolas and again accused him of witchcraft. Once again Nicolas became frightened and went to ask Mol Romin's advice. They returned to the town hall, whereupon the Presidente immediately jailed Jose. He remained in jail for two nights and was then given a week of hard labor. But the Presidente also advised Nicolas to follow his previous plan and move away from the hamlet. Eventually Nicolas and his wife moved to Mol Romin's hamlet, where Nicolas's wife owned land. Their daughter, married to Jose, stayed with her husband throughout the affair and remained with him after her parents left the hamlet.

This case has definite political overtones. It involved a large number of men from the hamlet as well as important political leaders and produced only a temporary solution. In spite of the fact that the witches were declared innocent by respected shamans and that the accusers were jailed, rumors persisted and Nicolas was frightened into leaving his hamlet. It seems clear that the witchcraft accusation covered a deeper political cleavage that could not be healed by court action. But the case shows the steps taken by the witch between the time he heard that his enemies were plotting his murder and the time he arrived at the town hall accompanied by the political leader of another hamlet.

How Witchcraft Cases Are Settled

In the course of inquiring into the question of how witchcraft cases become known, we have seen that witchcraft cases reaching the town hall or the assembled hamlet authorities produce outcomes of three types: (1) the witch confesses and performs a retraction ceremony, Cases 2 and 3; (2) the witch refuses to confess and a compromise is reached, Case 4; and (3) the witch's accusers are discredited, Cases 6 and 7. Three further cases will illustrate variations in the basic patterns.

The witch admits guilt. From the record of cases I have examined it appears that witches usually confess when confronted with overwhelming evidence of guilt: candle stubs, buried meat, the report of an eyewitness, or being caught in the act. For a witch to

deny the accusation in the face of such direct proof would be to court murder by an angry victim, whereas a confession paves the way for eventual reconciliation. Witches who confess and perform a retraction ceremony are humiliated and punished, but they are no longer regarded as dangerous. Indeed, most confessed witches seem to lead fairly normal lives after they have gone through the ordeal at the town hall.

When a witch admits guilt before the authorities, the settlement always includes a retraction ceremony to remove the threat of sickness. In such ceremonies, the witch must revisit all the places where he prayed and ask the gods to ignore his request. If one place is missed, the victim remains vulnerable. For this reason the victim and the authorities seek assurance that the witch has confessed completely. Hearings continue until all possible evidence is heard; witnesses give testimony and shamans pulse the witch to see if his blood tells of actions not yet admitted. This necessity for a complete accounting of the witch's actions also explains the piecemeal character of witchcraft confessions. After the witch has made an original admission of guilt, he probably finds it difficult to deny the testimony of further witnesses and shamans. New admissions of guilt come out even during the retraction ceremony as further evidence is uncovered or as the terrified witch is beaten into submission. Because the confession of the witch is phrased in terms of the witchcraft techniques described in Chapter 5, the method for retracting each technique will be described in turn.

Witches who confess to having asked for sickness from the Earth Lord, from foreign witches, or from the dead in the cemetery must retract the request with a similar ceremony. Case 3 tells of a witch who returned to the cave where he had prayed, and Case 2 gives an example of a woman who revisited several mountain shrines and burned whole candles in place of the mutilated ones she had burned before. Witches or their clients are also made to pay costs of the retraction ceremony. They must buy the candles and liquor as well as pay transportation fees for the entire party. Some witches must even provide all the ritual food that is consumed and pay for the services of the accompanying shaman, juez, and mayores.

Men who confess to having requested money from the Earth Lord are also forced to retract, since it is believed that treasure is

given only in return for human souls. In each of three now famous cases in which men were believed to have asked for treasure, the accused were forced to return to the cave and hold a ceremony in the presence of shamans and civil officials, begging the Earth Lord not to take victims. A version of the most famous of these cases is given below to illustrate the town hall procedures for handling such explosive issues.

Case 8. Men who request money from the Earth Lord confess and hold retraction ceremonies. (This case occurred in the summer of 1960 and was related seven years later by the brother of the man who had handled it as Presidente.)

A young man named Marcos was told by his friend Chep that he should ask for money from the Earth Lord to avoid remaining poor all his life. Though Marcos objected that he would have to work as a peon underground after death, Chep convinced him the Earth Lord would be content with a few other souls instead. So Marcos agreed to go with Chep to ask for treasure. First they consulted a shaman from another hamlet with a reputation for knowing how to talk with the Earth Lord. He agreed to accompany them, telling them what candles to buy and setting a day to visit a famous cave. At the appointed time they went to burn candles, but no money appeared. Then they tried another famous cave, still with no results. Finally they visited a third cave, beyond the borders of Zinacantan, where the shaman laid his hat on the ground and talked through it with the Earth Lord. He then told Marcos and Chep they would have to visit all three caves three more times and then hold a big fiesta inside the most distant one.

Marcos and Chep began to assemble the necessities for all this ritual. They visited the caves three times and planned for the large fiesta inside the distant one. They bought 60 pesos worth of candles, much rum and food, and fireworks to set off inside the cave. They also procured the help of various acquaintances, including musicians to play the violin and guitar—the traditional harp could not be used because of the difficulty of getting it into the cave. When everything was ready, the group set off secretly. They stayed inside the cave for two days, eating ceremonial meals and praying to the Earth Lord. At one point the shaman went into a side passage to pray alone. When he returned he told Marcos and Chep he had spoken with the Earth Lord, who told him he was willing to send treasure in return for souls. Marcos and Chep would have to return to the cave later with small candles and a list of their neighbors whom the Earth Lord could take. Then they were to return home and prepare special boxes to receive the treasure. Candles and incense were to be burned in front of the boxes, and when people began to die the Earth Lord would send up their gold loaded on mules. Marcos, Chep,

and the shaman completed the required ritual and settled down to await the arrival of the treasure.

While they were waiting, one of the helpers, a boy in his late teens, told an older man about the ceremony in the cave. This man informed one of the hamlet elders, who had the boy brought to his house. At first the boy was afraid, but upon being convinced that the elder knew of the plot, he told all he knew. The elder then sent the hamlet principales to bring Marcos and Chep to his house. When Chep realized they had been found out, he fled from Zinacantan, but Marcos went with the principales. At the elder's house, Marcos was confronted with the story, which he denied. Marcos was known throughout the township for being *p°ih*, clever and lively, and he convinced the elder to let him go. But word had spread, and before long several men came to Marcos's house and took him off to the jail at the ceremonial center. At the same time, the shaman was picked up and jailed. All this took place at the time of the fiesta for the patron saint of Zinacantan, and the ceremonial center was crowded with people. News of the arrests spread through the crowds and caused panic among all the men from Marcos's hamlet. Soon they were milling angrily around the town hall, and the Presidente found it difficult to protect his prisoners.

After the initial furor had died down, the Presidente arranged a meeting between the senior shamans of the ceremonial center, the shamans of Marcos's hamlet, and the hamlet elders. Marcos and the shaman who had helped to ask for treasure were brought before the group and questioned. The shaman admitted everything but laid the primary blame on Marcos for having asked him to serve. Marcos was less cowardly: he admitted everything but said that no harm had been done; no one had died and he and Chep had received no money. After considering the evidence, the shamans and the elders decreed that three retraction ceremonies should be held in each cave. Between the ceremonies Marcos and the shaman were to be kept in jail, and several weeks of hard labor were to follow the last of the rituals. The first part of the sentence was carried out; Marcos and the shaman held the three retraction ceremonies, accompanied by three senior shamans, some jueces, and several mayores armed with machetes and rifles. But after the last ceremony, Marcos's relatives and friends appealed to the Mexican authorities, returning with a letter ordering Marcos to be turned over to the Ministerio Publico. The Mexican authorities then set Marcos free, on grounds that there was no law prohibiting people from holding fiestas in caves.

After being freed, Marcos remained away from his hamlet for several months to give people time to calm their anger; Chep returned only after six years had passed. To make their peace with the community the two men donated a belfry for the hamlet church. Marcos, who was now rich, paid for the materials, and Chep, who had learned masonry during his exile, built the belfry.

In this case, as in all cases where the Earth Lord is asked for treasure, an entire hamlet became involved in the settlement, since all its inhabitants were potential victims. The Presidente could not be expected to settle such an explosive issue on his own authority, and instead called a meeting of the hamlet elders and shamans. Moreover, three retraction ceremonies were required of the confessed treasure seekers; one would not have been enough to calm the anxiety raised by Marcos's admissions.

When a witch confesses to being solely responsible for giving a sickness through blowing, spitting, or coughing, it is felt that only he can remove it. But in most such cases the victim refuses to have anything more to do with the witch and prefers to engage a shaman. In only one instance known to me (see Case 19 in Chapter 9) did the victim allow the witch to attempt the cure, and when it was partially successful the witch's punishment was reduced.

Although crying to the gods of the upper world for vengeance is never punished, a person who cries may be asked to pray to forestall the sickness. Or the person who cries may be asked simply to cease his crying, so the victim may recover.

In almost every case where a person admits to having practiced witchcraft he is punished by being sentenced to a few weeks in jail with hard labor. He usually serves his sentence after taking appropriate measures to remove the sickness. The punishment is said to remove his evil tendencies, making him less prone to witch others in the future.

The witch refuses to confess and a compromise is sought. Cases that begin as accusations of witchcraft may end with compromise solutions in which the accused, while denying guilt, agrees to perform some sort of ritual that will protect the health of the supposed victim. Case 4 is a good example of this type of settlement. Two other short cases further illustrate such compromise solutions: the first tells of a witchcraft accusation that was settled as a land dispute; the second, a quarrel between drinking companions.

Case 9. A man accuses his sister's husband of witchcraft. (The informant was Presidente at the time.)

When Manuel's wife died, he consulted his son, who was a shaman, about the cause of her death. The son said she had died of witchcraft sent by Manuel's sister's husband, Andres. On hearing this, Manuel went

to the town hall to accuse his brother-in-law of witchcraft. The Presidente listened to his complaint and agreed to hear the case.

When Andres arrived at the town hall, the Presidente asked him if he knew how to send sickness. Andres, though himself a shaman, denied it. He told the Presidente that Manuel was accusing him of witchcraft only because of a quarrel over land. With that the background of the case came out. Andres, who had inherited no land because his father worked on a Ladino ranch, had married Manuel's sister and now wanted the land she was entitled to inherit from her father. But after his father's death, Manuel had kept all the land for himself, refusing to divide it.

When Andres explained the land situation, the Presidente advised Manuel to divide the inheritance and give Andres's wife her share. But Manuel refused. How could he divide the land now that his wife had died? The Presidente tried to reason with him, saying that if the land remained undivided it would continue to cause trouble. Even after Andres and Manuel were dead, the land question would lead to quarrels among their heirs. But Manuel angrily repeated that he could not divide the land now that his wife was dead. The Presidente persisted, arguing that since Manuel would have to give land to his sister some day why shouldn't he do it now and end the quarrel? Finally Manuel agreed to give his sister her share of the land if Andres would promise not to witch him any more. Andres was pleased with this solution and said he would be happy with his wife's share of her father's land. (The implication, of course, is that Andres's contented heart would no longer cry out for vengeance.) This ended the case; Andres never admitted to sending sickness, and Manuel was never charged with making a false accusation of witchcraft.

This case is typical of the many Zinacanteco quarrels that are settled in terms of an underlying dispute rather than on the merits of the initial accusation.

Case 10. A man accuses his drinking companion of having put supernatural worms in his liquor. (Same informant as Case 9.)

Domingo and Antonio were older men who shared a bottle of rum during the fiesta of San Sebastian. Domingo's nose later became infested with little worms, and he accused his drinking companion of causing his illness (that is, of witching him by putting supernatural animals in his drink). Domingo took his complaint to the town hall and the Presidente sent mayores after Antonio. They arrived late at night at Antonio's house. Antonio, already suffering a bad reputation as a shaman often suspected of witchcraft, had heard of Domingo's accusation and was terrified by the prospects of the case. Finally, however, he agreed to accompany the mayores to the town hall, where he spent the rest of the night in jail.

The next morning the case was heard. After listening to Domingo's side of the story, the Presidente questioned Antonio, who denied being able to cause worms and insisted he did not know how Domingo became ill. Then the underlying cause of the quarrel was revealed. Antonio had once tried to borrow money from Domingo but was refused, and thus had cause for wishing Domingo harm. At this, the Presidente scolded Antonio for trying to borrow from others and for allowing himself to become bitter when refused, when he should be working harder and earning his own money. Antonio agreed it was wrong to be bitter, but he would still not admit to causing Domingo's illness.

In the end the two compromised, signing an acta in which Domingo agreed not to accuse Antonio of witchcraft if Antonio would send no more worms. Antonio also agreed to contribute to Domingo's cure by purchasing the liquor for the curing ceremony.

Because this case was given in bare outline, the arguments leading to the compromise solution are a bit puzzling. The case was clearly not settled in terms of the underlying issue, for the accused was found to be in the wrong and had good cause for sending sickness. The wording of the acta, however, indicates a certain amount of bargaining. Thus the accused witch must have been able to muster good arguments. In the end neither side assumed full responsibility for the quarrel but both admitted a little guilt. Had there been no infestation of worms, one suspects, Domingo and Antonio would likely have found themselves at the town hall for another reason.

This case, then, may well have been a political battle. Both men were elders, which would help to explain the fact that the outcome seems unrelated to the issues. Politics in Zinacantan are fought through in many guises, and one of the most popular is to accuse an enemy of wrongdoing. When the accusations come to the town hall, despite everyone's understanding the political motivations, the real nature of the quarrel is never mentioned. Instead, the two sides argue over peripheral issues and finally settle for a compromise solution that reflects the prevailing power balance but bears little relation to most of the issues raised at the hearing.

The accuser is discredited. Many witchcraft cases, particularly those brought by accused witches, end with the accusers being discredited and jailed. In most instances, such accusations are based on statements made by a talking saint, and since saints never talk before the town hall authorities, the case ends with the "saint"

being confiscated and its owner jailed at the request of the accused witch. Less often, accusations are said to originate from shamans or gossips. Case 6 illustrates what happens when an accusation is based on statements of a talking saint, and Case 7 tells of gossips punished for spreading false rumors. The fact that accusers are often jailed may be another reason why relatively few accusations of witchcraft reach the town hall. Plaintiffs who lack sound evidence may rightly fear that they, or their friends, will be punished instead of the witch.

The Effect of Mexican Law on Zinacanteco Handling of Witchcraft Cases

Many Zinacantecos know that the Mexican authorities do not recognize witchcraft as a punishable offense, and some accused witches have taken advantage of this fact to escape long jail sentences imposed by angry plaintiffs and the Presidente (see Cases 3 and 8). As a result, methods formerly used for extracting confessions have been abandoned, and the Presidente often finds himself in the position of urging a plaintiff to settle for a shorter jail sentence, lest the witch appeal to San Cristobal. But the crucial element of the witch's punishment, the retraction ceremony, has been maintained. Several cases have shown that confessed witches appeal to the Mexican authorities for shorter jail sentences only after they have retracted their requests for sickness. Accordingly, Zinacanteco legal procedures remain effective in the handling of witchcraft cases.

Although there are indications that administrators in small Ladino communities believe in witchcraft and find ways to punish witches in spite of the law (Pitt-Rivers 1967), the San Cristobal officials are educated men who share the lawmakers' view that witchcraft beliefs are mere superstitions. But these men nonetheless recognize the power of witchcraft beliefs in Indian communities. Recognizing that most murders are attributed to witchcraft suspicions, the more conscientious officials investigate carefully the witchcraft cases that come before them. They can no longer jail people for witchcraft, but sympathetic officials often agree to detain an accused witch or to accuse him of practicing fraud on his fellows by false claims of supernatural power. More often, the

officials work from the opposite end by trying to calm the angry accusers. They visit the Indian communities, or call the accusers to their offices in town, and try to convince them that witchcraft beliefs are superstitions and that they should live in harmony with their fellows.

But cases where a witch has been tortured or injured are treated as ordinary instances of assault. The Mexican officials send out warrants for those responsible and may even jail an Indian Presidente if he is found guilty. Zinacanteco officials at one time seem to have extracted witchcraft confessions through torture, but to my knowledge the practice has been discontinued. An informant told me of a case long ago in which a man was accused of asking a witch in another community to make his brother die. Since foreign witches send epidemics rather than restricting their powers to a single soul, there was panic throughout Zinacantan as news of the accusation spread. Under considerable pressure, the Presidente finally extracted a confession by hanging the accused witch from a tree and lowering him every time he seemed about to lose consciousness. In the end the witch retracted his request for sickness and peace was restored. This case never reached the Mexican authorities.

Zinacanteco procedures for handling witchcraft cases have remained viable in the face of growing knowledge about Mexican law, probably because it is in the interests of the witch to have his case settled locally. Although he could escape immediate punishment by appealing to the Mexican authorities, such action would do little to calm the fears of the neighbors, who might murder him. An accused witch is much safer if he confesses and retracts, or if he is cleared by reputable shamans. The Mexican authorities are useful for avoiding jail sentences, but are totally inadequate for ensuring future protection.

Zinacanteco legal procedures are also effective in serving the interests of the supposed victim. The retraction ceremony protects him from future illness and makes further violence unnecessary. The relative rarity of killing may be an indication of the effectiveness of Zinacanteco procedures. The Juez that I interviewed could remember only three murders during his three-year term of office. But it may well be that if the Mexican authorities were to put more pressure on the Zinacantecos to release witches before they retract

—either because the witch's relatives appeal or because the government institutes a program to stamp out witchcraft—the results could prove disastrous to human life. Without confidence that an appeal to the Zinacanteco authorities will forestall sickness, victims of witchcraft may take to murder.

This prediction is in direct disagreement with that of Vogt, who believes witchcraft murders should decline. He predicts that "The patterns of institutionalized envy leading to witchcraft accusations will continue, but the incidence of assassinations will decrease under the influence of Ladino systems of law and order" (1969: 612). I disagree with this prediction because I believe that Mexican law is unable to cope with witchcraft in a meaningful way. Evidence supporting my position comes from the Tzeltal town studied by Nash (1967), where the decline of the traditional forms of social control exercised by elders and curers, coupled with the rise to power of Mexicanized town hall officials dominated by a Spanish-speaking Presidente, was followed by increasing resort to homicide.

SEVEN

Aggressive Acts

This chapter is about crime and punishment, for it discusses the overt acts of aggression that provide cause for legal action and then examines the norms invoked in the process of reaching a settlement. Zinacantecos, like all people, have many subtle ways of symbolizing hostile intent—sins of omission as well as acts of commission—but this chapter is concerned only with those acts of direct personal aggression that are accepted as just cause for lodging a complaint at the town hall court. Through an examination of the entire set of recorded cases, this chapter attempts to discover the categories of aggressive acts recognized as wrongs by Zinacantecos and then, by examining the demands of plaintiffs and the arguments of defendants, to identify the norms that are manipulated by litigants in seeking a solution.

Zinacanteco settlements are based on two types of norms: those concerning the rights and obligations of persons linked by kinship or community ties, and those describing the proper ways of righting specific wrongful acts. Almost all cases are settled with an eye primarily to the satisfying of obligations (such norms are described in Chapters 8–12), but this chapter focuses on the norms that describe ways of righting overt aggressive acts that can occur between persons linked by any kind of ties, from kinship to community. Both brothers and complete strangers can get involved in drunken fights; both affines and nosy neighbors can spread malicious gossip.

The categories of aggressive acts that are discussed derive from

my analysis of the case materials. They are not "native" categories. Although I did elicit a list of crimes, *muliletik*, in Tzotzil by asking an informant "What kinds of cases does the Presidente settle?" (see the Appendix, p. 266), I have not used the elicited categories, since the wrongs recounted in these cases were usually more complex than could be construed from the simple lexical labels given by the informant. I have constructed my categories, instead, on the basis of similarity of norms invoked in bargaining over a settlement. For this reason, some of my categories subsume several of the informant's categories, while in other instances mine separate wrongs that are included under a single Tzotzil label.

Although the categories I have isolated can be given simple English labels, the Zinacanteco acts that fall into these categories are often subtly different from what an English speaker might expect. All human conflict is expressed in terms of symbols, and even acts of direct physical aggression need to be interpreted within specific cultural contexts (Beals and Siegel 1966). An aggressive act brings on open conflict only when the victim's interpretation of the event causes him to take action. Though most cultures recognize similar broad categories of crime—e.g. murder, rape, arson, adultery, defamation of character—the specific acts leading one person to accuse another differ markedly from culture to culture. Adultery is perhaps the best example. In some African cultures an unrelated man and woman need only be seen talking together for an accusation of adultery to be made, whereas in others the couple must be caught *in flagrante delicto*.

Zinacanteco plaintiffs who charge an opponent with an act of aggression usually wish to make two claims on the court: that they be freed of the risk of future aggression and that they be repaid for damage to person or property. These claims reflect generally held Zinacanteco norms and lead to hearings that center on arguments over "facts." Because all the participants in such a hearing know what each admission of guilt implies, an agreement on the "facts" is tantamount to an agreement on the main points of the settlement.

A plaintiff can ask the court to free him from the risk of future aggression by (1) allowing him to move beyond the reach of the aggressor, (2) having the aggressor beg pardon and promise not

to repeat the act, (3) having the aggressor jailed to remove his evil tendencies, or (4) settling the underlying issue that caused the original act of aggression. Since Zinacantecos believe that the fourth method leads to more permanent solutions, most of the hearings concentrate on tracing the roots of the quarrel and then end with settlements reflecting obligations between kinsmen or neighbors.

Persons defending themselves against accusations of aggression usually plead drunkenness or try to bring up a past quarrel to justify the act. Outright denial is seldom a feasible alternative. It not only leaves the unrepentant offender vulnerable to supernaturally caused sickness, but is untenable when the accuser has competent witnesses or overwhelming material evidence. Most accused offenders, therefore, are willing to confess and offer restitution to calm the plaintiff's anger but, because of the lifelong stigma that attaches to people believed to possess *manya*—the inner quality that motivates evil acts—they concentrate on proving that their inner souls are free of deliberate malice. They plead drunkenness because it is believed that the soul leaves the body of a drunken person, or they argue that their inner soul was exacting revenge for a prior wrong. Once a person is believed to possess manya, he is more readily accused of further wrongs, and is often jailed on the basis of perfunctory hearings.

Threats of Witchcraft or Murder

Few cases are brought as a result of threats, but a threat of murder from a known murderer or a threat of witchcraft from an elderly shaman or a known witch may lead a person to appeal to the town hall for protection.

Case 11. A woman threatened by a past murderer seeks protection from the town hall. (Reported by the elder who accompanied the woman to the ceremonial center.)

Matal was a widow living with her grown children. One day when she was home alone with her youngest daughter and a small grandchild, a man named Marcos asked to talk with her. No sooner had he entered than he produced a bottle of liquor, which he set at her feet. When she asked why he had brought the bottle, he replied that he wanted to live with her (in common-law marriage). Matal refused; he was younger than she (most widows prefer not to remarry if they have stable homes with their grown children). Marcos then became

very angry and abusive and threatened to kill her. Matal was terrified, since Marcos's father was said to have killed many people and Marcos himself was rumored to have committed one murder. She warned Marcos that unless he withdrew the threat she would complain to an important local elder and take the case to the town hall. Marcos only became more abusive, declaring that the elder and the Presidente were stupid men and he would murder them, too.

When Marcos finally left, Matal went to tell her brother what had happened. The two then asked the elder to accompany them to the town hall. On arriving at the ceremonial center, they told the Presidente that Marcos had terrified Matal and threatened to kill her; and since Marcos had already murdered one person, they were afraid he would carry out his threat. The Presidente immediately sent mayores to fetch Marcos, and had him jailed for two days and two nights before holding a hearing. When he was released, Marcos said he remembered nothing of his visit to Matal's house, since he was drunk at the time; the liquor had uttered the threats. The Presidente scolded him, saying he should stop drinking and threatening women or he would be sent to the Mexican authorities. Marcos begged the Presidente not to send him to San Cristobal but to have the case settled in Zinacantan. With that he presented a bottle of liquor to Matal to ask her pardon. When she accepted the bottle, the Presidente sentenced Marcos to two weeks of hard labor in jail.

False Accusations

The few recorded cases I have that began as complaints of false accusations seem to have been initiated by plaintiffs who feared physical injury or loss of property. Chapter 6 treated cases brought by accused witches who were afraid of being murdered; we now consider other types of false accusations.

When an engaged or married woman is accused of having a lover, her father and fiancé or husband become alarmed that the bride-price transaction is in jeopardy. Marriage is an economic exchange, and a broken courtship or an early divorce may cause serious financial loss. Case 1 (p. 62) is a good example of what may happen when an engaged girl is accused of infidelity. Though the fiancé initiated the settlement process, the girl's father supported his claim. They both wanted the story of the gossiping widows disproved so the courtship could continue.

When a person is charged through gossip with damaging another's property, the accused may bring up the case to forestall being sued by the owner. I recorded only one such case and I

doubt that there are many, since most Zinacantecos simply wait to be sued and then defend themselves by trying to discredit their accusers.

Informants state that persons who spread false rumors should be jailed to remove their *manya*. To speak lying words (*nopbil k*op*) when sober is an act of unprovoked aggression and therefore an indication of evil tendencies that must be extirpated. The gossiping widows in Case 1 were spared jail only because the girl's father did not want to risk losing a friendship. The norm was clear and the issue was discussed, but other factors prevented its being applied. Lies are not considered particularly serious, however, and the offender's jail term is always short. One uncomfortable night in jail is considered enough to make a person think twice before repeating his offense.

Drunken Insults

Although both men and women spread false rumors, only men scream insults at night. After dark, women stay home or travel in groups, but men who have been drinking in the small hamlet stores or at the house of another man are often alone as they return home drunk and may stop along the way to shout insults outside the house of an enemy. Shouting insults is a characteristically Zinacanteco form of aggression—and not unlike its obverse, that of drunkenly crying outside a house to beg pardon. Because of the way houses are constructed, people inside (as well as the neighbors) can easily hear every word spoken outside, but they usually ignore the drunken man, whether he is shouting insults or begging pardon, until he finally wanders off. Shouting insults is not considered a serious act of aggression because the alcohol, and not the person, is felt to be doing the talking. But if the drunk repeats his shouting over the course of several nights, or makes a damaging accusation, or is a close relative, the people being insulted may feel that an underlying issue must be settled if they are to protect themselves from more serious forms of aggression.

Case 12. A drunken man claims that another's wife loves him. (The informant, Juan, was a participant in the hearing.)

Lucas, a boy engaged to be married, was drunk one night and called out in front of Jose's house that Jose's wife was his mistress, that he

wanted her, and that he intended to take her by force. He repeated his insults for several nights while Jose, his wife, an elderly aunt, and all the neighbors listened. Jose finally sought the advice of a relative who was an elder (the father of Juan, my informant). The elder had been away in the lowlands for several days and had not heard Lucas shouting, but his wife, who had heard everything, told him about it. The elder advised Jose to take his case to the town hall and agreed to accompany him after he transacted some business, which would take five days.

On the appointed day, Jose, his wife, his aunt, the elder, the elder's wife, and the elder's son Juan took the long journey to the ceremonial center. They arranged to stay the night after they told the Presidente their story and he had a mayor sent to fetch Lucas. The next day the mayor returned with Lucas, accompanied by a man who had helped Lucas ask for a bride, Lucas's fiancée, and the fiancée's father, mother, and brother. The fiancée's family had come to hear the outcome of the case; learning that Lucas had shouted that he intended to steal another man's wife, they were afraid he would make a bad husband. When all had gathered at the town hall, the Presidente began to inquire into the affair. Lucas, pale and trembling, denied having shouted, but there were too many witnesses to his drunken railings. He then sought to introduce other issues: he claimed he had met Juan one night on the trail; Juan had offered him a drink of liquor and, when he refused, had pulled a knife and wounded him. Juan denied the accusation and the issue was dropped for lack of witnesses. Then Lucas accused Juan of having talked with his fiancée. (Men are suspected of trying to steal another man's woman if they talk with girls who are engaged.) Both Juan and the girl denied the accusation.

The case was settled with an acta stating that Lucas agreed not to shout any more insults outside of Jose's house or threaten to steal Jose's wife. If he broke the agreement, he would be jailed. Lucas and Jose each received a copy of the acta, but Lucas paid for both.

(Shortly afterward, Lucas and his fiancée were married by the civil authorities. Juan told me that the girl's father was very angry with Lucas but could not afford to break off the courtship because most of the bride-price had been paid.)

Drunken men who shout insults at night are seldom jailed at the town hall, ample illustration of the Zinacanteco principle that drunkenness lessens guilt. Whereas the man who spreads false rumors when sober may be jailed to remove his evil tendencies, the drunk who shouts far worse accusations may be forgiven if he begs pardon and promises to desist from further shouting. But if the drunk goes beyond shouting and picks a fight or enters a house,

this indicates evil tendencies beyond those brought on simply by the liquor, and he is usually punished.

Fighting

Zinacantecos call a person who strikes another a *hmahvaneh*, "person who hits." They do not distinguish verbally between men who beat men and men who beat women, but the distinction is worth making here because the causes and the consequences of the two actions usually differ. For this reason, physical aggression between men is discussed under the rubric "fighting," and aggressive acts against women are discussed as "beating."

Cases in which men fight each other are handled in various ways, depending on where the fight occurs, the relationship between the fighters, the provocation, the physical injuries resulting, who brings up the case, and where the case is settled. The ceremonial center, with its several small taverns, is the scene of many drunken fights, which may be broken up by bystanders or by the mayores, who can be called to help. If after a fight is broken up the fighters remain belligerent or someone is found to be injured, the mayores may place the more active fighter in jail overnight to sober up. When the case is heard, the Presidente brings together all the fighters and asks what brought on the fight. If one of them is found to have provoked it, he may be jailed for a while, though any underlying conflict that is brought out is discussed in an effort to reconcile the fighters. But if there was no cause except drunkenness, and no one was hurt, the Presidente usually releases them with the admonition not to fight again. Similar drunken fights that occur in the hamlets never reach the town hall, or even the hamlet elders, unless one of the fighters pursues the matter.

When a party to a fight makes a case of the fight, before a hamlet elder or at the town hall, he wants either to be compensated for damages suffered or to protect himself from future aggression by settling an underlying issue. He may also be seeking to sever his relationship with the aggressor, to remove danger of future assault.

Case 13. A man who wants to end his daughter's courtship brings the girl's fiancé to the town hall. (This case was related by the Presidente who settled it.)

At the courtship ceremony in which the boy formally enters the girl's

house, Miguel became drunk and began fighting with his future father-in-law. The next day the man, who suffered a swollen face, complained at the town hall, telling the Presidente he wanted to end the courtship. He did not want a son-in-law who would beat him, and he no longer wanted his daughter to marry. Miguel was summoned to the town hall, where he pleaded for forgiveness, saying he had not meant to beat his father-in-law; he had been drunk. But the girl's father remained obdurate, and the engagement was ended. The girl's father agreed to recompense the boy for money spent on the courtship except for that spent on liquor and meals consumed by the boy's family and helpers. In addition, Miguel was jailed for half an hour at the request of the angry man.

When a person has been injured or had property damaged in a fight, he and his relatives sometimes choose to ask for a hearing, in the hope of forcing the other fighter to admit guilt and assume the responsibility for the cost of the cure or for the damaged property. Although the rule that the guilty should pay is generally recognized, the success of the plaintiff in collecting damages depends on his ability to deny the defendant's inevitable counterclaim that the plaintiff began the fight. Only if the injured man and his relatives are able to convince the authorities and the opposing side of their innocence, or that the beating was out of all proportion to the provocation, will they be assured of compensation.

Case 14. A drunken religious official beats his wife's seducer. (This case was related by the Presidente who handled it.)

Manuel, returning home drunk from a long religious ceremony, accompanied by a man named Dionicio, fell asleep on the floor. Manuel's wife, who had also attended the ritual, staggered into bed. During the night Dionicio, still somewhat drunk, got up and, forgetting he was not home, crawled into the plank bed with Manuel's wife. She screamed, waking Manuel. Still quite drunk and seeing another man in bed with his wife, Manuel picked up his staff of office and beat Dionicio over the head. When the staff broke in two, Manuel looked around for a rope. No doubt Dionicio was stunned by the blows, for Manuel proceeded to tie his feet together and, throwing the end of the rope over one of the roof beams, hoisted him, upside down, into the air. Then, with another stick, Manuel resumed beating Dionicio. Since Dionicio refused to die, Manuel, in his drunken stupor, began casting about for a rifle. At this point Manuel's daughter ran out of the house to fetch Dionicio's wife, who lived nearby. Manuel, who had by now begun to sober up, made no protest when Dionicio fell in a heap on the floor and did not move. Dionicio's wife spent the rest of the night tending her husband and the next morning she asked relatives to help carry him home.

After seeing Dionicio safely home, his wife went to the town hall. Upon hearing her story, the Presidente sent mayores to fetch Manuel and had him jailed, despite Manuel's holding an important religious post (religious officials are accorded special consideration because of the vital community services they perform). The Presidente then had the government nurse visit Dionicio's house. The nurse reported that Dionicio was badly beaten but would recover. His wife, however, was in a rage and demanded that the Presidente send Manuel to San Cristobal for punishment. The Presidente feared he would have to give in to her demands, since so serious a crime should be reported to the Mexican authorities by law. He would have preferred to handle the case in Zinacantan, both because Manuel was his friend and because vital community rituals would suffer if so important a religious official were confined in the San Cristobal jail. The Presidente talked to Manuel, telling him that he would have to send him to the Mexican authorities if Dionicio's wife persisted in her demands. The Presidente expressed the hope that Manuel would be able to talk his way out of the jail there, by virtue of his speaking such excellent Spanish and knowing many of the officials personally. Manuel was very upset at this turn and begged the Presidente to settle the case in Zinacantan, since in San Cristobal he would have to pay a large fine—and he was already in debt from the expenses of his religious office. The Presidente was sympathetic and agreed to wait three days (the seventy-two hours the Presidente is allowed to detain a suspect while investigating the crime) to see if Dionicio would recover enough to come to the town hall and settle the case.

At the end of the three days a hearing was held, attended by Dionicio, who was barely able to walk. The Presidente reminded Dionicio that he too had committed a crime—climbing in bed with another man's wife. Dionicio's excuse was that, being drunk, he had thought he was home. But the Presidente retorted that drunkenness was not a sufficient excuse, and that if the case where to go to the Mexican authorities Dionicio would be punished. If the case were settled in Zinacantan, by contrast, Dionicio would be neither jailed nor fined, since he had already been punished enough by Manuel's beating. Manuel, too, had received a punishment, three days in jail, and could be further fined 100 pesos, the Presidente continued. Dionicio finally acceded to the settlement, and an acta was drawn up stating that both sides had settled their differences and would forget the fight. Manuel paid for the acta but not for Dionicio's cure.

It was probably because Manuel was a rich and powerful man who had contacts with Mexican officials that Dionicio received no compensation for his wounds. Dionicio had little chance of making his demands prevail against the combined power of Man-

uel and the Presidente. This case, where no compensation was paid, can be contrasted with another case (not given here) in which an injured man, though guilty of provoking a fight by shouting insults in the night, was awarded money for his cure because the defendant was a less powerful person and agreed that the wounds suffered by the victim were more serious than his provocation warranted. If the injured party, whoever he may be, can convince everyone that he had not provoked the fight, he is almost certain to be compensated for his cure and the days lost from work.

Although the Presidente is supposed to refer cases involving serious injury to the authorities in San Cristobal, he often accedes to pleas for settling the case in Zinacantan if both sides can be brought to agree. But when the agreement is reached, the Presidente usually requires both sides to sign an acta stating their satisfaction with the terms. He is thus protected if one of the parties later becomes dissatisfied and takes the case to San Cristobal.

Beating

Although a man may fight with an unrelated drinking companion, he only beats a woman who is a close relative, since he has no access to unrelated women. For this reason, most cases in which men beat their wives or other female relatives are treated as family quarrels rather than socially aggressive acts. Wife beating is very common, and the beaten wife usually escapes to the house of her father or brother until her drunken husband sobers up and comes to beg pardon. But if a woman is attacked with a machete or is seriously injured, she and her relatives usually take steps to end the marriage, fearing that the woman's life may be in danger. In cases where the woman is able to prove serious injury and wants a divorce, the husband is usually made to pay for her cure and give her a share of the property. He is never jailed, however, unless the case is taken to San Cristobal. But if a seriously injured woman agrees to take back her husband, he is usually punished with jail to remove the evil desire to beat his wife. Zinacantecos feel that the evil desire needs to be lifted from his heart only if he has the opportunity of repeating the act; a man who no longer lives with his wife will have little opportunity to beat her again.

Occasionally a man may beat his grown daughter, causing the girl to elope with her fiancé or escape to the house of a relative. These beatings cannot be regarded as ordinary parental discipline, for Zinacantecos rarely use physical punishment, but must be seen as outbreaks of drunken aggression. In later hearings, the father always claims that he feared his daughter was being promiscuous, and these cases invariably end with the daughter's rapid marriage to her fiancé. As in cases of serious wife beating, an effort is made to remove the woman from the reach of a potentially aggressive man.

A man rarely beats his mother or sister unless she is trying to protect his wife, but occasionally a drunken man will hit any woman who gets in his way.

Case 15. A drunken man beats his brother-in-law's wife. (The informant was a neighbor of the family.)

Andres, who was living with his wife's family, got into a drunken fight with his father-in-law. The women of the family attempted to break up the fight, and in the confusion Andres hit Rosa, his wife's brother's wife, on the side of the face. Since Rosa's husband Marcos was away, Rosa fled to her mother's house and went to bed with a swollen jaw. The next day Marcos's parents went after her, but her mother refused to let her go. When Marcos returned from the lowlands, his parents told him what had happened and he went after his wife. Finding her still in bed suffering from pain, he determined to go to the town hall with his mother-in-law to have the Presidente summon Andres.

When Andres arrived at the town hall with his father-in-law, the father of Marcos, he said he remembered nothing of the fight, since he had been drunk. Then he added that, since he had hit Rosa with just the side of his hand, he could not have caused much injury. However, Rosa's face was still swollen, so the Presidente sent the government nurse to examine her. The nurse discovered two broken teeth; upon hearing this, Andres offered to take Rosa to San Cristobal to have the teeth replaced, even offering to pay for gold ones. But the frightened Rosa wanted only to leave her husband, saying that Marcos's mother and sisters did not like her, and now she had been beaten by Andres. Rosa's mother was also angry; she insisted that her daughter return to live with her and that the marriage could continue only if Marcos would live in her house. Marcos agreed to this. There remained only the question what to do about the teeth. Rosa was still afraid to go to a dentist and asked the Presidente to jail Andres. The Presidente replied that she must

make a choice: either have Andres jailed or have her teeth replaced, but not both. Rosa chose jail. But then a cousin of Rosa's urged her to have her teeth fixed instead. So, changing her mind, she asked the Presidente to release Andres if he would pay the dentist's bill. Andres agreed, and the next day they all went to San Cristobal to find a dentist. The Presidente even arranged to meet them in town to be sure that Rosa was satisfied. The dentist said he would have to replace the two broken teeth with gold ones. Andres paid the entire amount as well as the expenses of the group on their two visits to town. Rosa ended up happy with her new teeth, and she eventually returned to live in her husband's house.

In another case a drunken man, chasing his wife down a path, bumped into an old woman and left her with broken bones and bruises. The woman's son wanted to take the case to the town hall, but when the guilty man sobered up, he begged pardon and said he was willing to pay for the woman's cure. At a hearing in the house of a hamlet elder, the woman's son asked for 100 pesos, which was lowered to 50, about the charges of the local bonesetter. Since an agreement was reached in the hamlet, the case was never taken to the town hall. These two cases illustrate the usual solution, that a man who admits beating a woman without provocation assumes the responsibility of paying for her cure.

Causing Sickness

Zinacantecos believe that someone who has been badly frightened may lose parts of his inner soul to the Earth Lord and become sick. Since the relation of sickness to fright is believed to be as direct as that of injury to beating, the person who caused the fright is liable for the curing ceremony conducted to recover the lost parts of the soul. In one case, at a hamlet festival a child was badly frightened, but not physically injured, by a skyrocket that landed near him and blew up. Skyrockets are supposed to explode high in the air, but this one had traveled along the ground because it had been set off by an inexperienced teen-age boy. The town hall officials present at the hamlet ceremony heard the case and warned the parents of the teen-age boy that they would have to pay for a curing ceremony if the frightened child should fall ill. Another case is given at length below.

Case 16. A man pretending to be the *sombrerón*, a mythical demon who wears a wide hat and wanders about at night, agrees to pay for the cure of the man he has frightened. (The informant in the case attended the hearing.)

About ten years ago a man was caught impersonating the sombrerón by painting his face black, wearing a wide *charro* hat and flowing rubberized rain cape, and twirling a bull-roarer made from a tile on the end of a string. One night two men were passing a sacred cave when they were startled by a terrible noise. Suddenly the sombrerón jumped out, putting out their torch with his swirling cape. One of the men fell to the ground in terror and the sombrerón danced around him. The other man recovered his wits and tried to grab the apparition, and the first man then got to his feet; together they managed to subdue the sombrerón. They wanted to kill him then and there, but the sombrerón protested that he was just an ordinary person. So the two men carried him off to the house of the nearest *principal*, taking along his bull-roarer, hat, and cape. Then, with the help of the principal and four or five other men, they took the sombrerón to the ceremonial center and had him jailed.

The next day, news of the incident spread through the two hamlets bordering the cave. Large meetings were held in each hamlet, and delegations were appointed to attend the hearing scheduled at the town hall. When the groups arrived in the ceremonial center, they visited the sombrerón in jail. With his face washed, and his hat, cape, and bull-roarer nowhere to be seen, he was hardly a frightening sight. At the hearing the Presidente learned that the sombrerón was a man named Mariano. On being asked why he had impersonated the demon, Mariano replied that he had been drunk and was returning home from a distant hamlet, wearing his cape and wide hat because it was raining. Upon being asked who had taught him to scare people like that, Mariano answered that no one had. The Presidente asked how many times he had jumped out of caves; Mariano said only once. Then some men from the neighboring hamlet testified that many people had been frightened near that cave. But since there was no way of knowing if the other apparitions had been Mariano or the real sombrerón, the Presidente decided to adjourn the hearing for a while. Meanwhile Mariano would be jailed for four days to remove his *manya*.

The fifth day being a Sunday, many men could attend the resumption of the hearing at the town hall. The Presidente questioned Mariano again on his reasons for frightening people; did he have an enemy? (Was he trying to witch someone in particular?) Mariano still insisted he had just been drunk. But from one of the hamlets came a report that one of the men who had caught the sombrerón was now sick. The Presidente accused Mariano of being a witch. When Mariano denied it, the Presi-

dente summoned three senior shamans to pulse him. The shamans' conclusion was that Mariano was an ordinary person, neither witch nor shaman. But the rest were not satisfied, and it was decided that the shamans should pulse the sick man to determine the cause of his illness. Accordingly, a group was sent to the distant hamlet and the hearing was postponed again.

Upon returning, the shamans informed the Presidente at the reopened hearing that the sick man was suffering neither from fright nor from other witchcraft; he was merely being punished by the upper-world gods for another wrong, and a few herbs would cure him in a couple of days. But the assembled men began to murmur. Who could know if the shamans' diagnosis were accurate? Perhaps the sick man should have a more complete ceremony in any case, with candles and prayers. Mariano said he would pay for a ceremony, and still clinging to his statement that he had been drunk, he further offered to pay for the sick man's cure. After Mariano had given the money, the Presidente sentenced him to four weeks of carrying stones. But Mariano only worked for six days and then hired a truck to carry the stones from the mountain to the ceremonial center.

Some time later, a group of men from one of the hamlets asked the Presidente to call Mariano back in again because several more people had been frightened by appearances of the sombrerón. But the Presidente said they must catch him in the act to make sure it was indeed Mariano. He promised that when they did, he would send Mariano to San Cristobal for punishment.

Shamans Who Hasten the Death of a Patient

Zinacanteco shamans rarely administer powerful medicines, but rely on prayers to restore the patient's soul and return him to health. But a few illnesses cannot be cured by prayers; one of these is *sak ʔobal,* "white cough" (probably tuberculosis), in which the patient gradually coughs himself to death. Zinacantecos believe *sak ʔobal* is caused by witchcraft, and that the coughing is the result of hairs, spiders, or balls of mucus in the throat. The way to cure the disease is to vomit out the offending substance. In two recorded cases of advanced *sak ʔobal,* the shamans administered medicine bought in a San Cristobal drugstore to induce vomiting, and the patients died after vomiting blood. In one case, handled by a hamlet elder, the shaman agreed to pay for the patient's funeral, and in the other, handled at the town hall, the shaman was jailed and punished with hard labor. In both cases the shamans were

punished to prevent them from using strong medicines that might kill other patients.

Rape

Cases of rape in Zinacantan rarely come to public attention. Those that do usually result when a young man tires of waiting to marry his fiancée and decides to have sexual relations with her before the wedding. Because cases of rape usually involve a woman's bride-price rather than payment for injury, they are treated in Chapter 10, on courtship. In the rare cases where an older woman is raped, or a girl is raped by a boy who will not marry her, she remains silent out of fear and shame. Such cases go to the town hall only when the rapist is caught in the act or when gossip forces the incident into the open. Then the woman and her relatives may ask the Presidente to jail the rapist to remove his manya. They may also ask that the rapist pay them money as compensation for physical and psychic damages. Two other cases of rape, both referred eventually to San Cristobal, were viewed as unique and bizarre happenings. One concerned a man who took a child from school and raped her; the other involved a man known for his evil tendencies who had several of his cronies rape his wife.

Entering Another's House

Zinacanteco men, when drunk at night, have been known to enter another person's house if the door is unlocked. But if they are not aggressive and wander out as peacefully as they came in, the incident is forgotten. Although drunks are frequently aggressive in shouting insults outside a house, they rarely attempt to enter. If they do, the householder may go to the town hall to have the drunk punished, since forcefully entering a house may lead to property damage and physical injury. There are a few recorded instances of politically motivated encounters in which a group of men deliberately broke into the house of an enemy. These cases seem to involve much bitterness and cannot be settled by Zinacanteco conciliatory methods.

Incidents of theft and arson are not discussed here because they rarely involve direct confrontations between the aggressor and his

victim. One case, however, involved a thief who fell through a thatch roof while committing a robbery, and came face to face with his intended victim. Zinacantecos regarded the incident as a great joke, and the thief was jailed at the town hall.

Attempted Murder

Cases of attempted murder are hard to distinguish from cases of threatened murder or those where one person severely injures another in a fight or a beating. Invariably the plaintiff claims that the defendant is trying to kill him, and the defendant claims he was drunk and didn't know what he was doing. In the hearing, most of the arguments revolve around the question of future danger. Sometimes the murderer has shown the seriousness of his intent by carrying a gun when sober or has actually tried to shoot or knife his victim. If no one was injured, the Presidente may simply jail the attempted murderer (if he can be caught) to remove his manya and teach him a lesson, or the case may go to San Cristobal. A man who attacked his political enemies with a knife one morning was restrained and taken to the town hall. In spite of his pleas to have the case settled in Zinacantan, the Presidente sent him to San Cristobal, where he was jailed. (The guilty man did not belong to the Presidente's political faction but to the opposition.)

Murder

The Zinacanteco officials are required by Mexican law to report every murder to San Cristobal and to deliver the murderer if he can be caught. When someone dies unexpectedly, his relatives must report his death to the town hall, and if there is any hint of foul play, a juez, accompanied by mayores, is sent to investigate. A clearly accidental death requires no papers, but if doubt remains, the most likely murder suspect pays for the paper work.

A suspected murderer who is caught is jailed for three days at the town hall. Each day he is questioned by the Presidente, and if he is felt to be guilty he is sent to San Cristobal with a statement of the evidence against him. If the Mexican authorities then convict the prisoner, he is jailed. In cases of aggravated assault leading to serious injury the Presidente may detain the assaulter in jail as a potential murderer. Thus if the victim dies, the assaulter

is sent to San Cristobal, but if the victim lives and is willing to accept compensation, the case may be handled in Zinacantan.

The Effect of Mexican Law on Zinacanteco Handling of Aggression Cases

Although the effect of Mexican law in witchcraft cases is to strengthen the hand of the defendant and undermine traditional procedures, in cases of direct personal aggression Mexican law has the effect of preserving Zinacanteco compromise solutions because it strengthens the hand of the mediator. A mediator or the Presidente can persuade plaintiff and defendant to compromise by threatening to pass the case on to the Mexican authorities. If the case were taken out of Zinacantan both sides would lose: the defendant would face a harsh jail sentence or high lawyer's fees, and the plaintiff not only would be unlikely to receive compensation for damages but might have to pay a lawyer to see that his enemy is punished.

But Mexican law has not been an unmixed blessing to Presidentes, because Spanish-speaking litigants use it to their own advantage in cases that by law should go to the Ministerio Publico. Indian Presidentes are not empowered to handle cases of serious injury, major theft, murder, or talking saints, and they can be reprimanded if word of their actions reaches the Mexican authorities. When urging litigants to accept a compromise in such a case, the Presidente must take care to see that both sides are completely satisfied and that an acta is prepared; and he must be particularly attentive to the wishes of a litigant who speaks Spanish and has contact with Mexican lawyers (see Case 14, p. 157).

The Presidente has most authority in cases involving minor injuries or slight damage to property, for then he need not fear a reprimand from above if he handles the case himself. Because he controls the contents of all official documents, he can intimidate defendants by threatening to make out a *diligencia* stating a damning version of the crime, or he can persuade greedy plaintiffs to accept a compromise by threatening to refer the case to the Mexican authorities in a manner heavily favoring the defendant. Hamlet mediators who use their knowledge of Mexican law to produce compromise solutions do not have the same access to official docu-

mentation, but they can be almost as effective by threatening to accompany the wronged litigant to San Cristobal. Mediators can offer to help defendants whose offers of restitution have been rejected or to accompany a plaintiff if the defendant has refused to admit guilt. It is important to stress, however, that the net effect of all these threats to invoke the Mexican authorities is to keep cases within Zinacantan and to reinforce traditional compromise settlements.

Conclusion

This chapter has discussed generally recognized Zinacanteco wrongs: overt acts of physical or verbal aggression that initiate legal action, beginning with mild acts of verbal hostility and ending with murder. This ordering reflects, in a general sense, the probability that committing an aggressive act will lead to the lodging of a complaint. Charges of verbal aggression are rare and are usually initiated by plaintiffs who have reason to fear material damage, whereas more serious wrongs causing immediate damage or severe injury are taken directly to the town hall. The ordering reflects also the extent to which a case will be settled primarily in terms of the original complaint. If the wrong committed is a minor one, the mediator offers solutions based on underlying issues, whereas cases that involve severe physical injury or extensive property damage lead to arguments over the amount of compensation and length of jail sentence warranted. Zinacantecos justify jailing as a means of removing manya, an offender's inclination to commit evil acts, and it appears from the cases studied that there are three ways of inferring the presence of this quality: (1) the offender committed the wrong when sober, (2) the offender was drunk but committed a more serious wrong than could be attributed to liquor, and (3) the offender repeated an act after having been warned against it. These categories are, of course, quite elastic, but it is generally true that the more serious the wrong, in terms of physical injury or property damage inflicted, the more likely is the attribution of manya and jailing of the offender.

This chapter concludes the section on Zinacanteco legal concepts. Chapter 4 analyzed the meaning behind key actions during

a hearing, Chapter 5 explored the wider implications of conflict by looking at witchcraft beliefs, Chapter 6 described the overt indications of spiritual hostility, and this chapter examined direct acts of physical and verbal aggression. These four chapters, describing elements common to all types of Zinacanteco conflicts, prepare the ground for the next five chapters, which discuss in detail the strains inherent in particular types of social relationships. Following the format of a typical hearing, I discuss the overt manifestations of hostility before searching for the underlying causes of conflict.

EIGHT

Disputes Between Kinsmen

In the hamlets of Zinacantan, patrilineal kinsmen usually live close together and cooperate in ritual and economic activities. Their constant interaction inevitably leads to conflicts, some of which cannot be settled privately. Those that result in litigation, whatever their ostensible cause, are usually presented by both parties as disputes over land or other physical property. Thus persons wishing to make a complaint against a patrilineal relative advance a recognized claim to property, and kinsmen who have quarreled for more immediate reasons work with a mediator to search out some past inequity in land distribution. By this simple expedient Zinacantecos, like many other peoples, reduce the complex, subjective problems of kinsmen to straightforward disagreements over something tangible, something that can be objectively measured and divided. And indeed, given the material supplied by my informants, it has been impossible to separate "genuine" land disputes from deeper quarrels that have been conventionally formulated in terms of competing claims to property. By the time the two kinds of dispute are presented for settlement, they look alike and are argued in similar terms.

Zinacantecos have an effective method for handling potentially conflicting claims to land without an open quarrel. A person wishing to claim property presents the holder with a bottle of rum and makes a formal request. If the validity of the request is conceded, respected elders are invited to help work out the details and the agreement is sealed with rum and a formal meal. Such a

settlement is said to have been reached *ta lekil k*op*, "with frank or proper speech." Open fights between kinsmen occur only when one side refuses to concede the validity of the other's claim to property. Then a mediator is asked to hear the case or it is taken to the town hall. Such cases are said to be settled *ta ʔil pletu*, "with scolding or scornful speech."

Property Relations in an Ideal Family

Because of the central importance of land in disputes between kinsmen, we begin with a description of the ideal pattern of property division through the life cycle of a Zinacanteco family, taken from G. Collier's study (1968) of actual inheritance patterns and their effect on social structure. This description fits very well with the material from my cases. Almost all the accounts of family quarrels contain summaries of moral sermons delivered by mediators who use the technique of telling litigants how proper kinsmen should behave in order to persuade quarreling kinsmen to compromise.

Zinacantecos say that young children are an economic burden because the parents must pay for curing ceremonies and food. But older children are an asset. Boys help their fathers with farming and girls help their mothers in the house. When a girl marries, her fiancé takes her away but gives her parents a bride-price to repay their expenses in raising her. When a boy marries, his parents help him pay the bride-price, and he brings his wife home to help his mother. The boy continues working with his father as the family pays off the money borrowed for the bride-price. After two or three years, the boy and his wife formally request the boy's father to give them land to construct a separate house for themselves and their children. On a date arranged, elders are invited to help divide the property, both land and household goods, and are then given a formal meal for their help. A father may divide up his land little by little as his successive sons grow up and move out; or he may divide it all at once, saving land for himself and any sons not yet grown. Ideally, the youngest son cares for his aging parents and inherits his father's house on his death.

Property is not always divided equally. Sons who have displeased their father may receive smaller shares or be disinherited,

and daughters traditionally get less property. If a father is rich, he may leave plots of land suitable for houses to his daughters, but he will rarely leave a daughter farmland if there is a son to inherit it. The daughters keep the land they inherit to pass on to their children, thus transferring the land from one patrilineage to another.

The father's death brings the family together for a final property settlement. Sharing in funeral expenses affirms an heir's right to a portion of the deceased's property. Any land left undivided by the father is divided at this time. A portion is set aside for the widow, who lives with the youngest son and shares her property with him. When the land is completely divided and the parents are both dead, the heirs are obligated to light candles in the cemetery every Sunday and to provide a meal for the dead on All Saints' Day. These observances reaffirm an heir's right to the inherited property.

Problems Between a Boy and His Guardians or Parents

When a young boy's father dies and he is brought up by a relative, problems often arise over the property the boy would normally have inherited. The person who pays the expenses of raising the boy feels the inheritance is rightly his; the boy understandably disagrees. When such cases are heard, the elder or the Presidente tries to reach a compromise by which the boy gets the property but undertakes to pay the guardian a reasonable amount to cover the expenses of his upbringing. Such a solution recognizes both the son's claim to share in his father's property and the creditor's claim to have a debt repaid. The estimated expenses of raising the boy must of course be balanced against the value of his work.

Case 17. A boy brought up by his sister's husband asks for a share of his father's land. (The informant was a former town hall official.)

Miguel's father died when he was a child, leaving him with his older sister, Maria, and her husband. Since the father's property was left undivided, Maria's husband farmed it all and gradually began to speak of it as his own. But when Miguel grew up, one of his father's brothers, who lived in another hamlet, told him he had a right to a share of the land. The uncle advised him to present his brother-in-law with a bottle of rum and request half the property, adding that if the request was denied, he would accompany Miguel to the town hall and testify that

the land had belonged to Miguel's father. At first Maria's husband refused the request, but he finally agreed to give Miguel half of the land if he was paid back the expenses of Miguel's upbringing. Miguel again conferred with his uncle, and they decided to take the case to the town hall.

At the hearing, Maria and her husband argued that all the land should go to them because they had spent so much money on curing ceremonies and medicines for Miguel during his childhood. The Presidente replied that they had no right to deny Miguel his inheritance since he would soon marry and have children of his own, but that they should be recompensed for their expenses in bringing him up. An itemized list of expenses for Miguel's food and illnesses amounted to 500 pesos. When Miguel's uncle heard this sum he asked Maria's husband if Miguel had not helped him while he was growing up. Had the boy worked in the fields and run errands? Should not a worker be paid? In the end, Maria's husband agreed to cut the sum by half and Miguel agreed to pay the 250 pesos. Later some minor town hall officials were sent to Miguel's hamlet to measure and divide the land.

A relative who acts as a boy's guardian can demand, and receive, payment for childhood expenses if the boy leaves without working off his debt, but a father cannot. For this reason, it is hard to resolve disputes in which a father feels that his son has not repaid the expense of his upbringing and the boy disagrees. Neither party to such a dispute can make justified demands, and the tension may persist until the father dies. The unresolved conflict may erupt into fights when father and son are drunk, or lead to bitter accusations of witchcraft when family members die.

When a boy is brought up by an older member of his own generation, satisfactory property settlements can usually be worked out through exchanges of money and land, but a boy brought up by his parents or a member of their generation incurs a deeper obligation to care for them in their old age. Because this obligation can never be expressed in money terms, a parent or guardian who cannot persuade a son to live with him has no recourse. Zinacantecos assume that the bitterness of a neglected parent will be expressed through witchcraft, and they blame the misfortunes of an undutiful son on his parents.

Case 18. A boy who leaves his uncle's house becomes sick. (My informant was Presidente at the time.)

Jose lived with his mother in her brother's house and helped his uncle with the farming. When his mother died, he went to live with his fa-

ther-in-law. His uncle was angry at losing his labor. When Jose later became ill, his father-in-law consulted a talking saint in another town and learned that Jose's uncle—who was a shaman—had witched him. After consulting other shamans who agreed with the talking saint's accusation, the father-in-law went to the town hall to ask the Presidente for permission to shoot the uncle as a witch. The Presidente instead put him in jail to prevent him from carrying out his threat. The uncle, summoned to the town hall, denied the accusation.

The case was never settled. It was simply dropped after both sides refused to compromise. The shaman uncle refused to try to cure Jose; he did not care, he said, if the boy died. Jose's father-in-law, in turn, stated that he would not allow the uncle to enter his house. The Presidente finally stopped searching for a common ground on which to build an agreement and told both sides to go home. Two months later Jose recovered.

Disputes Between Siblings

Property disputes between siblings may occur when a parent dies leaving a tract of land undivided, or when one sibling is dissatisfied with his share of an already divided property. Although most such disputes are settled cooperatively with the help of hamlet elders, cases in which an older brother refuses to divide the land or a younger brother feels he is not receiving his just share may be taken to the town hall. These are difficult cases, since the complete history of the land and the relationship between the siblings must be explored; and even when a compromise is reached, resentment may linger.

Case 19. Property division between brothers leads to fighting and witchcraft accusations. (My informant was one of the men who arrested the accused witch.)

Andres and Mariano were married brothers living with their widowed mother and unmarried younger brother. Following a quarrel over money between the two older brothers, Mariano, the younger, decided to move out. A respected elder and his politically powerful son were asked to help the family divide the property. Land was not an issue in this case; the dispute was over ten mules that had belonged to the dead father and the sacks of corn recently harvested from the fields cultivated by all three brothers. Mariano, arguing that he had to set up a new household, asked for half of the mules and the corn; but the other family members and the elder disagreed. They argued that the corn should be divided equally among the four persons who had worked to produce it—Andres,

Mariano, the widowed mother, and the younger brother—and the mules divided four each to Andres and Mariano, who had worked with their father to buy the animals, and one each to the mother and the younger brother. Mariano argued that this division was unfair, because the household with three members kept a much larger share of the goods. The elder replied that he could complain to the Presidente if he thought he was being cheated. In the end Mariano gave in because he knew the Presidente would agree with the elder's decision. So Mariano took his share of the property and moved to a nearby house.

A few days later, Andres and Mariano had a drunken fight in which Andres broke Mariano's arm. The next day, when his wife told him what he had done, Andres went to beg Mariano's pardon. He offered to fetch the bonesetter and to pay for her services. He also offered to pay Mariano for the days he would lose from work. But Mariano refused to accept the money, although he did agree to have his brother pay the bonesetter.

Some time later Andres developed a large sore on his leg that prevented him from working in the fields. A shaman called in to cure it said it was caused by witchcraft. Later, some friends of Andres who had been working in hot country with Mariano informed Andres that Mariano had boasted of causing his sickness. With this evidence Andres went to the town hall, accompanied by the witnesses and the elder who had helped divide the property.

When Mariano was brought to the town hall by a large group of mayores and religious officials, the Presidente asked if he had made his brother sick. Mariano answered that he was not a witch, but that the sickness had come because one day, when his injured arm was particularly painful, he had cried out to the gods near a little cave in his cornfield. Two respected shamans, after pulsing him, reported that Mariano *was* a witch, but that he had also cried out to the gods. At that Mariano, who was a shaman, admitted knowing how to send sickness, but said that he would never use the power against his own brother. Then the shamans pulsed Andres to see if his sickness had indeed been sent by Mariano. But their verdict was uncertain: Andres had been witched, but they could not tell if the witch had been his brother. So the Presidente ordered Mariano to cure Andres by returning to the cave and asking the gods to remove the sickness.

Mariano returned to the hamlet accompanied by the mayores, jueces, and religious officials. Inside the cave they found a cross and candles. Mariano denied having conducted a ceremony and still insisted that his cry to the gods had been spontaneous. But the officials were doubtful and dug up the floor of the cave, where they found cigarettes, a bottle of rum, and some rope. Mariano still refused to admit that he had been practicing witchcraft. The officials accordingly had him ask the gods to remove the sickness and then took him back to the town hall.

When the hearing resumed, the Presidente produced the items from the cave and demanded the truth. This time Mariano admitted selling his brother to the Earth because of his dissatisfaction with the division of the family property. (This was probably the first mention of the property dispute.) The Presidente rebuked Mariano, saying that the elder had divided the corn and mules fairly. If the mother and younger brother had received nothing, he said, they would have been justified in crying out to the gods for revenge.

Eventually Mariano, who had admitted being a witch, knelt before his brother, presented him with a bottle of rum, and begged his pardon. Andres responded that he wanted only to recover from his illness, and asked if Mariano could cure him. Mariano doubted that he could, but agreed to hold a curing ceremony. The Presidente postponed Mariano's jail sentence until after the ceremony, and when Andres's health improved he sentenced Mariano to only a week of hard labor.

This event marked the beginning of a lifelong conflict between the two brothers, which led to further hearings at the town hall when Andres's health deteriorated and when a group of assassins tried to kill Mariano.

Problems of property division also arise when one person keeps an entire tract of land because other claimants to a share are too young to protest. In one case, a man kept all of his father's land after the death of his father and two brothers. He treated the land as his own and even sold portions of it. Many years later, the two sons of one of the dead brothers requested a share of the property. At a hearing in the hamlet, the man agreed to divide the land that was left among all legitimate claimants and everyone was satisfied.

Disputes between siblings over land that has already been divided often have to do with boundary lines.

Case 20. Two sisters disagree about a land boundary. (The elder who settled the case was the informant.)

Two sisters, one widowed and the other separated from her husband, quarreled over the boundary between their shares of a piece of land that had been divided between them by their dead father. One sister put up a fence that did not exactly follow the agreed-on boundary; the boundary curved, but the fence was straight. The other sister felt she was being cheated and ordered her sister to remove the fence. The sister refused. Both sisters then independently asked the advice of a respected elder. The elder went with the two women and their mother to measure the land, and concluded that the two pieces divided by the fence were still equal. Both sisters thanked the elder for his trouble, and each presented him with a bottle of rum.

Another cause for dispute lies in the division of purchased land. Though a father may divide the land equally, an older child may later claim a larger share on the ground that his labor contributed more toward the purchase than that of a younger sibling.

Case 21. A man claims a larger share of land for his wife. (My informants were the two elders who settled the case.)

A man who bought land from a former Ladino ranch divided the property equally between his two children before his death. Five years later, Nicolas, who was married to the daughter, told Manuel, the son, that he wanted a larger share of the property, and threatened to take the case to San Cristobal if Manuel refused. Manuel, afraid that his sister's fluent Spanish would unduly influence the Mexican authorities, appealed to two elders, one known for his contacts with Mexican lawyers. He gave them each several bottles of beer and a bottle of rum. The elders agreed to hear the case and went to Manuel's house, where Nicolas was asked to join them. Nicolas argued that that his wife deserved a larger share of her father's property because she was grown and doing a woman's work when the land was bought, whereas Manuel as a child had contributed nothing. The elders were not persuaded. They replied that the land had been properly divided; since Manuel and his sister were full siblings, they were entitled to equal shares. Moreover, the elders warned Nicolas that the authorities in San Cristobal would agree with them. Nicolas gave in, and all the men went to re-measure the land to make sure it was divided equally. Both Nicolas and Manuel presented the elders with rum, and Manuel provided a formal meal.

Problems over Property Held by Women

Women come to control land in two ways: as widows they manage a share of their husbands' property, or as daughters they inherit land from their fathers. A woman widowed when young and without sons keeps some of her husband's property only if he has no patrilineal relatives to contest her claim, but a widow with young sons keeps all of her husband's property to pass on to them. If a woman is widowed in later life, when her sons are grown and the property is divided, she receives a small share of her husband's estate to provide for her until her death. All land that a woman receives from her husband stays within his patrilineage and is held by the woman only in trust for her children. At her death, the children pay for the funeral and divide her property. Problems arise when a woman with sons is widowed before her husband

receives his property, or when a woman who is separated from her husband claims some of his property after his death.

Case 22. A widow asks the elders at her husband's funeral to help settle the future of his property; potentially conflicting claims are settled without conflict. (The informant was the son-in-law of an elder who attended the funeral.)

Maria, a childless widow, requested the elders who had been at her husband's funeral to ask her stepson and his family to move into her house to keep her company as she was now alone. Her stepson, who had paid for his father's funeral, was willing, but his wife refused. The elders agreed that the stepson should heed his wife's wishes and suggested instead that Maria ask her widowed sister to live with her. The sister agreed. Maria then asked that she be given her husband's mule, saying that she needed a source of income, since her stepson had refused to live with her. The elders and the stepson agreed that this was a just request. The stepson said that he wanted only his father's ejido land. Maria consented. These agreements marked the end of the discussion. Maria continued to live with her widowed sister in her husband's house and to rent out the mule for a small income. When Maria dies, her stepson will take over all of his dead father's property if he pays her burial expenses. A second son of the dead man by still a third wife did not participate in the settlement. He lived with his father-in-law and neither helped with the funeral expenses nor demanded a share of the property.

Land that a woman inherits from her father, unlike land she receives from her husband, passes to a different patrilineage and is thus more likely to cause problems. For example, when a woman marries and moves away, leaving an untended tract of land temptingly close to a brother's property, the brother may claim both shares on the ground that the land is not being used or that his sister has not fulfilled her obligation to burn candles for their father's soul.

Case 23. A man tries to take over property inherited by his sister. (The informant in this case was the Presidente who settled it.)

A man from a distant hamlet told the Presidente that he intended to take over a tract of land left to his sister by their father. She had married a man from another hamlet, he said, and did not look after the property; besides, a woman could not work the land. The Presidente urged the man to wait until his sister and her husband could be summoned to discuss the matter. When the case resumed several days later, the husband angrily maintained that the land belonged to his wife. The

brother declared that his sister had moved to a distant hamlet and no longer spoke with him, that she did not live near the land and could not farm it, and that she did not light candles for the soul of their father. The woman claimed that she had not lit candles because she had been moving; now that she had a house, she would again burn candles for her father. Her husband added that he would farm the land. At this the Presidente told the brother that as long as the land was properly farmed and candles were lit for the soul of its former owner, the land belonged to the sister. The brother was not satisfied but could do nothing. My informant heard that the case came up again later, but he did not know the outcome.

The Effect of Mexican Inheritance Laws

Another cause for land disputes between kinsmen is the conflict between Mexican laws of inheritance and Zinacanteco custom. Zinacanteco elders always award a larger share of the land to sons, whereas Mexican law decrees that all children shall inherit equally when no will is made. Therefore, a man may appeal to Mexican law in the name of his wife to increase their share of his father-in-law's property. This has happened so often of late that a recent Presidente, tired of having his decisions overturned in San Cristobal, decided to uphold the Mexican inheritance law if asked to do so by a litigant. Currently the conflicting principles exist side by side within Zinacantan but on separate legal levels: hamlet elders still advocate traditional inheritance patterns, but the Presidente upholds Mexican law when asked. As a result, persons who value continued cooperation with kin commonly appeal to an elder to solve inheritance problems, whereas those desiring economic gain appeal to the town hall.

Despite this recent development, most Zinacanteco land is still divided according to traditional precepts (G. Collier 1968), and such divisions are not challenged. Three reasons for not challenging them come immediately to mind. (1) Women need the support of their brothers in quarrels with their husbands; marital relations in Zinacantan are generally strained, and a wife must have the backing of her relatives if she is to make effective demands on her husband's family. (2) Most men need the good will of their brothers-in-law, who are a source of loans, of help when taking a religious office, and of support in political undertakings. (3) A person who flouts Zinacanteco tradition to take advantage of Mexi-

can law must fear that witchcraft, justified or unjustified, will be used against him by the people he has wronged.

Even when property is divided "equally," women tend to receive the less desirable portions. A study of actual landholdings in the hamlet of Apas (G. Collier 1968) showed women holding a higher proportion of worthless land: parcels subject to erosion by the growing canyon or so close to waterholes that they were marshy half the year.

Conclusion

This chapter has examined various justifications for claims to property that are used in arguments between kinsmen. Zinacanteco kinsmen who prefer to avoid disputes have an adequate mechanism for handling potentially conflicting claims, but those who wish to quarrel have a rich language of contradictory principles at their command. Thus we find it argued that all siblings should share equally in the parent's property; that sons should share equally, but should get more than daughters; that respectful sons deserve a larger share than disrespectful sons; that children who do not contribute to their parents' funeral expenses should receive no inheritance; and that children old enough to work for the family at the time land is bought ultimately deserve a larger share of that land. The list could go on to include equally contradictory statements about the rights of stepchildren, adopted children, and widows. The fact is that these principles do not govern Zinacanteco inheritance, but only serve as justifications for a claim to property. The actual distribution of inheritance is determined by a compromise between competing claims advanced at the time the land is being divided. A careful study of existing property holdings (G. Collier 1968) shows that some principles are honored far more than others, but such considerations will scarcely deter a litigant bent on taking land from a kinsman.

NINE

Marital Disputes

Marital disputes are the most frequent conflicts in Zinacantan. Although the great majority are settled in the hamlets, cases go to the town hall at an approximate rate of one every two days. Marital relations in Zinacantan are typically strained. Like many other societies with predominantly patrilocal residence, married women are the focus of conflict. Removed from their kinfolk to an alien environment, women tend to be fiercely loyal to their own children. In early marriage this means that the wife tries to detach her husband from his parents and brothers so his labor will benefit only his immediate family, but in later years it means that the mother will do her best to keep her sons together in the face of disruptive daughters-in-law. The strains created by the ambivalent position of women are manifested in marital disputes. Because husbands and wives have separate spheres of activity and little opportunity to talk over their problems, social realignments must be triggered by dramatic actions. In the typical sequence, the wife misbehaves, the husband beats her, the wife runs away, and reconciliation is obtained at a formal hearing where past disputes are revealed and future plans are made.

Zinacanteco men pay a high bride-price for a wife, from a couple of hundred pesos to a few thousand. Most marriages, however, go through several separations and reconciliations, and many end in divorce. Of 119 married men in the hamlet of Apas, thirty-eight had permanently separated from their wives and some had had several wives. The bride-price buys only the right to court

and marry a woman; it does not guarantee her presence after the wedding ceremony. The bride's father may feel morally obligated to urge his daughter to return to her husband, but if his efforts fail he will not refund the bride-price. Although courtship disputes can be put in economic terms and settled through the exchange of money between unrelated parties, marital disputes differ fundamentally in that the parties are deeply committed to a relationship that is impossible to express in economic terms. Reconciliation is the only satisfactory outcome of a marital dispute. Permanent separation leads to unsatisfactory property settlement or to no settlement at all.

The termination point of a marriage is difficult to determine. A Zinacanteco couple are married when they are living together, and the girl's relatives cannot be asked to return the bride-price; but once a husband and wife have separated, there is a long period when their relationship is uncertain. A true *divorcio* for couples married by Mexican law can be obtained at the town hall or in San Cristobal, but few people can afford such expense and trouble. Most marriages end through an explicit or tacit agreement between the couple and their relatives. The status of children is never an issue, although their support may be a problem. Any recognized child of a man can claim a share of his father's patrilineal property if he fulfills the obligations of a child and pays a portion of his father's funeral expenses. As discussed earlier, a person's rights to patrilineal property are determined more by his own actions in fulfilling the proper role of a child than by the actions of his parents. Funeral payments are critical, whereas the mother's bride-price is irrelevant.

The rate of permanent separations in Zinacantan reaches a peak in the first four years of marriage and drops off markedly after that. Out of fifty separations in the hamlet of Apas, thirty occurred in the first two years of marriage, only eleven in the next two years, and nine after four years of marriage. Although individual separations can only be explained in terms of the personal motivations of the people involved, it is permissible to ask what structural considerations bear on the divorce rate (Schneider 1953). In Zinacantan the answer can be found by examining the developmental cycle of domestic groups. This chapter begins with a description

of an average woman's life cycle, and then offers an analysis of marital disputes under the headings of wife beating, adultery, and divorce.

The Life Cycle of a Zinacanteco Woman

When a young girl marries, she leaves home for the first time to live with her husband's family, exchanging her role as a responsible older daughter for that of subordinate to her mother-in-law. Unhappiness is expected in this situation, and no one is surprised when a bride runs home to her mother. But as time passes, the bride is expected to work out a relationship with her mother-in-law as she begins to have children. Two reasons for the high rate of separation in the first four years are that (1) the woman has few ties to bind her to her husband's house, since she has few responsibilities and her small children are easily carried with her. and (2) the woman's natal home is likely to be still intact, allowing her to return to her role as daughter, where she can expect support and inherited property from her parents. Gluckman (1950), in contrasting Zulu and Lozi divorce rates, noted that the higher Lozi rate could be linked to their kinship system, which allowed a woman rights in her natal group as contrasted with the Zulu system, where a woman's only rights lay in her status as a wife in her husband's group. This same contrast can be applied in Zinacantan. For if a woman's parents are dead and the property is divided among her brothers, a divorcée has little chance of securing a house or land from her father's estate.

After a few years of marriage, a young couple usually build a house of their own on land provided by the husband's father. The wife now escapes her mother-in-law's domination and takes charge of her own house and her young children. Her labor no longer contributes to the larger household, but provides benefits for her husband and children alone. The woman now finds it more difficult to leave her husband because she has the responsibility of a house and several children, and chances are great that her natal household will have changed in composition. At this point, a woman's rights to property lie primarily in her role as wife and mother rather than as daughter to her own patrilineage, for, if her husband dies, she keeps his house and land in trust for his children. Even if a woman is the wife of a youngest son who remains in his

parent's house, her rights and responsibilities grow as her mother-in-law's power wanes. Clearly, a recently married woman with only a baby requires much less provocation to return to the warmth and sympathy of her parental home than it takes to tempt an older woman with several children to seek refuge with her less sympathetic brothers.

Wife Beating

Wife beating is common in Zinacantan, and when a woman leaves her husband, the assumption is that she has been beaten. Gossip is often correct, but a woman may leave because she is angry with her husband or his relatives. She may say she is ashamed of her husband, either for a physical defect or for his failures in the religious hierarchy, or she may resent the fact that he does not work harder or gets drunk too often. If a wife is living with her husband's relatives, she may leave him to dramatize a quarrel with the other women in the household, in this way provoking a hearing in which she is able to voice her complaints and perhaps force her in-laws to provide her husband with a separate house.

Although we shall concentrate on the patterned sequence of events that occurs when a wife's leaving her husband brings a marital dispute to public notice, the events leading to her departure are also highly patterned. Zinacanteco couples, like the South Indian villagers described by Beals, Spindler, and Spindler (1967: 195–99), employ a set of actions that convey easily understood messages. A wife may nag or be slow in catering to her husband's needs, and a husband may scold or beat his wife. As long as both sides stick to standard methods for indicating displeasure, there is little chance that the dispute will escalate into an irresolvable quarrel. The wife may run off, and the husband may have to make several attempts to beg her pardon, but reconciliation is likely. When a marital dispute involves accusations of adultery, however, or the wife is severely injured by being beaten, reconciliation is more difficult.

When a woman leaves her husband's house, she may return home if one or both of her parents are alive, but if they are dead, she must impose on a brother, compadre, or more distant relative. Such impositions are always uncomfortable because of the prob-

lem of securing food. Guests who move in for more than a day are expected to bring their own supplies. A woman who leaves her husband's house has no access to dried corn, and even her parents may tire of feeding her and her children if she stays too long. An adult woman acquires access to a food supply by working for it, either through buying corn with money she earns, or or through working for a man who grows it. As a daughter, a woman works for her father and brothers, who supply her with corn, and as a wife, she works for her husband. But a woman who has left her husband and not returned to her role as daughter must live off ever more unwilling charity.

A married woman living in a house that she owns is in the enviable position of being able to throw her husband out. Although a young girl marrying for the first time usually moves to her husband's house, an older woman who has inherited a house from her parents or a widow who lives with her children in a house left by her husband can insist that her new husband move in with her. If she later wants to separate from him, she has only to wait until he leaves the house and then lock the doors.

When a man realizes that his wife has left him, he must decide what should be done. Although a few men do nothing, most try to recover their wives so that the bride-price will not have been wasted. But before a man can persuade his wife to return he must first discover where she has gone and then decide how to approach her. If he is afraid he had beaten her while drunk, he must ask his neighbors to find out what happened. Then he must go to the various houses where his wife is likely to be and inquire after her. Although finding a missing wife would seem to be a simple task, it is made difficult by the fact that people sheltering a runaway woman may deny having seen her and refuse to let the husband enter the house. It often takes several visits before a woman's parents or relatives admit that she is there.

When he finds her, he may be allowed to enter the house if he has only scolded or threatened her and not beaten her. Once inside, he presents a bottle of rum to her and to her relatives to beg pardon. But usually more than one visit is required. And since her relatives will seldom allow the husband to enter by himself, he must enlist someone—hopefully someone with prestige—to ac-

company him on a formal visit. Although every attempt a man makes to beg his wife's pardon is called *lahesel k*op*, "ending a dispute," the actual events vary from a simple procedure where an unaccompanied man begs his wife's pardon to an elaborate affair involving several people and lasting a day. What makes all the actions *lahesel k*op* is the fact that the affair is two-sided, without a mediator between the two groups.

If the husband's fault is minor, he may simply request one of the minor authorities—a lesser civil government official or a hamlet *principal*—to accompany him as a representative of community authority. If the wife's status is high, more important officials may be asked to help. When the daughter of the highest religious official had left her husband after a beating, the Presidente himself participated in the expedition to calm her. But the men most frequently asked to help beg pardon are the husband's courtship petitioners, usually his father and older male relatives, and often a respected elder. One elder from Nachig known for his ability to calm angry wives was frequently asked to serve as a petitioner. The only person ineligible to help an abandoned husband beg pardon is the godfather of the wedding, because his role is to mediate between the husband and wife without taking sides.

Men in religious office whose wives have left them are able to muster powerful support to help beg pardon. Respected leaders accompany the husband when he presents his bottle, because the welfare of the community depends upon proper performance of the ceremonies, and proper performance requires the services of the religious official's wife. The work of the gods comes first, and rarely can a wife resist the pleas of the community's most respected leaders.

When Zinacanteco informants say that a husband asks an elder to accompany him so that his wife and her family will show *respeto*, the Spanish term implies two kinds of respect. The presence of an elder is expected to make the wife and her relatives show deference to the husband's side, *p*is ta vinik*, to treat them as men, as well as forcing the wife to listen to the elder's words and *c*un smantal*, to follow his advice. In a simple begging-pardon sequence, the role of the elder is to promote reason and harmony. The wife states her complaints, usually many and stereo-

typed. Wives accuse their husbands of getting drunk too often, being too aggressive, spending too much on drink, losing or ruining clothes when drunk, not providing money for necessities (such as thread for weaving), and occasionally sexual inadequacy. Specific instances of each fault are described in detail. Few wives accuse their husbands of not providing adequate food, however, since this can be easily checked by inspecting the corn supply in the house. This is also a serious accusation, for it reflects on the husband's role as provider and strikes at his manhood. The repentant husband, standing or kneeling at his wife's feet, occasionally argues with his wife, but usually concentrates on begging pardon and promising to drink less and work harder. The elder's role, as he sits in a chair, is to reason with the wife and her relatives, reminding them that all husbands drink and that nobody is perfect. He also chides the husband for his bad behavior and exhorts him to be better in the future. He may declare that he will be responsible for the husband's behavior and promise to aid the wife in getting a divorce if the husband should beat her again. After a suitable length of time, the angry wife should show signs of acquiescence. She may state that she is willing to return to her husband if he keeps his promises to drink less and work harder. At this point, the wife or her father will accept the proffered bottle of rum and pass it around. In later disputes, the elder who helped the husband can serve as witness by recalling the wife's conditions and the husband's promises of good behavior.

When a husband goes to beg pardon, it is important that the wife's father be present. One husband who persuaded his wife to return home while her father was away later had to beg his father-in-law's pardon. Because a woman usually leaves home when she marries, her father's one chance to give advice and commands to his son-in-law occurs when the younger man comes to beg pardon. The bride-price investment is at stake, and the younger man must heed his father-in-law's advice if he hopes to get his wife back.

The father who feels that his daughter's marital dispute is too serious to be settled quickly may tell the girl's husband to plan for a more formal hearing. On a prearranged day, the girl's father gathers all his relatives to await a visit from the husband and his petitioners, who must bring enough rum for the entire group.

During the hearing, the young husband kneels mutely at the feet of his father-in-law while the older relatives discuss the case. Both the husband and wife play minor roles while their fate is being decided, and when a decision is reached, they are expected to comply. One young wife who refused to drink the agreement-sealing rum had her relatives pour the drink down her throat by force.

Hearings mediated by a hamlet elder differ from two-sided begging-pardon ceremonies in the sense that the elder listens to both sides and may reprimand both husband and wife. But the two proceedings are alike in the sense that the elder's commitment to save the marriage puts him automatically on the husband's side. When a man asks an elder to mediate in a marital dispute, he usually feels that his wife shares the blame and he wants her faults explored. In the end, he may admit to having the greater guilt and beg pardon, but if his wife is also found guilty, she is apt to forgive him more readily and be more hesitant about running away in the future.

Accusations against women are of three types. The first fault is that of a woman leaving her husband for insufficient cause, as when she leaves the house on seeing her drunken husband approach, or when she is quick to believe rumors of adultery. A second type of fault occurs when a woman provokes her husband into beating her by nagging him or refusing to perform such wifely duties as serving a meal. The third type of fault, aggressive behavior, occurs when the woman fights back, taking advantage of her husband's drunken condition to beat him.

A woman with close relatives rarely takes a marital dispute to an elder, but if she lacks assured support she may ask an elder for help in separating from her husband. If the woman is badly beaten or the elder has already mediated in several disputes between the couple, he may agree to take the woman's side and help her present her case at the town hall, but he usually attempts first to settle the dispute at the hamlet level. The husband is called in to present his side, and the elder tries to reconcile the couple by scolding the husband for his delinquencies, at the same time persuading the wife to forgive him. Occasionally, the parents of a young wife abandoned by her husband may ask an elder's help

in persuading the husband to give his wife a share of the property as a divorce settlement or to help support the children. If the elder agrees to conduct the hearing, he uses the threat of a property settlement to persuade the husband to return to his wife.

When a man and woman have been through a long and expensive courtship ending in a church wedding, they have a godfather whose duty is to mediate between the couple in serious disputes. Minor marital rifts are settled by begging pardon, but if the marriage appears in danger of breaking up, the wedding godfather listens to the complaints and suggests solutions. If the case is later taken to the town hall, the godfather must be present to discuss his efforts to keep the marriage intact and his best guesses on why these efforts failed. Wedding godfathers are usually wealthy and important men, whose opinions carry weight at the town hall. For the godfather to side with the wife's family and advocate a divorce is to ensure the end of the marriage. When there has been no church wedding, and hence no wedding godfather, the parents of the husband and wife may come together and invite a respected elder to fulfill the function of godfather and suggest solutions.

There is a general feeling that marital disputes should be settled privately in the hamlets and not discussed in public hearings at the town hall. The Presidente may refuse to hear a woman who comes with a complaint against her husband—one woman was told to have an elder hear her case and return to the town hall only if he accompanied her—or an anxious husband may visit the Presidente in his house and ask him to send his runaway wife home if she should seek a public hearing. Nevertheless, many minor courtship or marital disputes brought by women do come to the town hall, where they more or less settle themselves (see pp. 76–79).

Marital disputes arising in the ceremonial center have a better chance of being taken to the town hall than do disputes occurring in the hamlets. When a drunken man is on the rampage there, his relatives may seek help from the Mayores, who will put him in jail until he sobers up. If the drunken man's wife agrees to take him back the next day, there need be no hearing, but if she complains, the Presidente will listen to her accusations and help the husband beg pardon.

Marital disputes that cannot be settled at the hamlet level are more serious and require the Presidente's full attention when they are heard at the town hall. A woman who has been badly beaten or who is accompanied by an elder who testifies he has attempted to settle former disputes in the hamlet has a good claim for a separation from her husband. If the Presidente can reconcile the couple by inducing the woman to forgive her husband, he usually puts the husband in jail to remove his evil tendencies.

The few men who bring marital disputes to the town hall do so because their wives have refused to return to them after attempts at hamlet settlements. Young husbands who have gone through an expensive courtship are particularly anxious to keep their wives because of the investment involved. If the couple have been married by Mexican law, the Presidente may try to preserve the marriage by threatening to make the girl's family pay a high price for a legal divorce. This threat may be enough to force the girl's father to send her back to her husband, but in some cases the girl's family will agree to pay a high price to be rid of an undesirable son-in-law.

In summary, cases of wife beating and minor marital disputes tend to follow a general pattern of actions and hearings. If there is no reconciliation on one level, the case may go to a more elaborate hearing. Figure 2 summarizes the steps in settling a minor marital dispute.

Adultery

Although gossip implies that many Zinacantecos indulge in extramarital affairs, a formal accusation of adultery, by either husband or wife, is a serious matter usually leading to divorce. Unless the accusation is dismissed as false at a hamlet hearing, the case goes to the town hall, where the aggrieved husband asks his wife's lover to recompense him for the bride-price and has the guilty pair jailed, or the aggrieved wife demands a divorce and a substantial share of her husband's property.

Married men in Zinacantan may have a single woman as mistress unless their wives complain. According to informants, only neighboring Chamulas have two wives and "live like dogs," but some Zinacantecos practice polygyny and manage to keep both

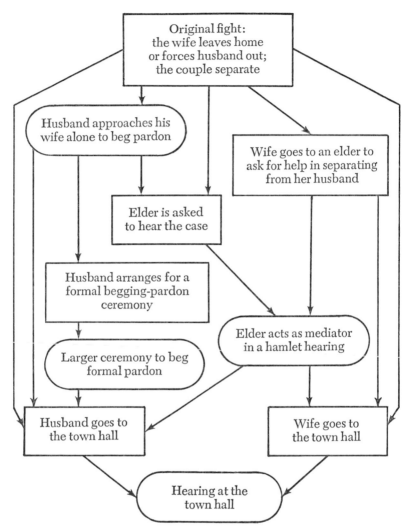

Fig. 2. Steps in settling a minor marital dispute. Actions in rectangular boxes indicate moves by husband or wife. Actions in ovals represent hearings where reconciliation may take place. Arrows leading from one box to another represent direction and time. If a reconciliation is not effected within one oval, the case may proceed to another level in the direction of the arrows.

wives content. Even when a man is accused of fathering an illegitimate child, the woman may take no action. But if a woman can prove that her husband has a lover and she wants to separate, she can claim some of his property.

Case 24. The wife of an adulterous man keeps part of his property. (The informant was from the hamlet where the case was heard.)

Jose and Maria eloped, although Jose later placated Maria's family and paid them a bride-price of 400 pesos. The couple had seven children. When the older children were grown enough to perform adult tasks, Jose began an affair with a widow who lived in her own house with her children. Upon hearing the rumors, Maria went to spy on the widow's house, and discovered her husband emerging from the door. She then went to her brother and aunt for advice. Jose, questioned by Maria's brother, admitted visiting the widow. However, he did not want to leave his wife and children, but wanted to support both women in separate houses. Maria refused, and went to the town hall to ask for a formal separation. Since the couple had not been married by civil law and Jose admitted having an affair with the widow, the major issue at the hearing became the division of property. Maria wanted her husband to give his sons a vacant house plot that he owned so she and the children could build themselves a new house. When the Presidente suggested she remain in the old house and have Jose move out, she refused, saying that he would come back if she remained, and she wanted a permanent separation. Maria was finally awarded both the existing house and the vacant house plot. The only land kept by Jose was his *ejido* farmland; he also received only a small portion of the corn and beans stored in the house, because it was argued that his sons had helped him farm and were entitled to equal shares. Maria kept his new woolen clothing and blankets, arguing that she had woven them and his new wife could weave more. Jose was left with his worn cotton shirts and tunics, a few pots, some tools, and a share of the raw sugar he had bought at harvest time to sell when prices rose.

After the separation Jose went to live in the widow's house, but when her brothers objected, the couple moved to a shack borrowed from a neighbor. After four months of desperate financial struggle the widow left, and Jose finally persuaded his wife to take him back.

There are also cases in which a man expressly separates from his wife so that he may take another woman. He may beat his wife until she runs away or he may return her to her father. But if she complains and is able to prove that he has already taken up with another woman, she may be in a position to demand a share of his property.

Cases in which a woman accuses her husband of having a lover but cannot prove it are likely to turn out badly for the woman. Even her own family may withdraw support, and her parents may scold her for believing false rumors.

It is a great crime, *¢o¢ mulil*, for a married woman to commit adultery, but men are seldom punished for having lovers. A married man who has an affair with a single woman faces the loss of property if his wife divorces him, whereas an adulterous wife and her lover are jailed and sentenced to hard labor. The harsh punishment is meted out specifically to preserve them from the anger of the gods. A husband who does not demand a stiff sentence for his adulterous wife is suspected of desiring her death by crying to the gods of the upper world for vengeance.

When a man finds his wife with a lover, or knows that she has run off with one, he may call on the Principales or Mayores to capture the guilty pair and put them in jail. At the town hall hearing, the Presidente asks the husband what he would like done. Most husbands refuse to take back an adulterous wife and try to convince the lover to take the woman and recompense them for the bride-price. Although the bride-price of a woman who returns to her relatives is forfeited, a man whose wife leaves him for a lover can make a legitimate claim to have his bride-price returned.

Case 25. A married woman elopes with another man. (This case was related by the Presidente who settled it.)
Rosa, a Chamula from the neighboring Indian community, had recently married Andres, a Zinacanteco. They lived with Andres's parents. One day, while her husband was away working in the lowlands, Rosa sat next to a young, unmarried man named Miguel on the bus returning from San Cristobal. Although she did not talk to him, her husband's brother, also on the bus, told his parents later that Rosa and Miguel had been nudging each other. When Rosa arrived home, her parents-in-law upbraided her so severely that she went to tell Miguel what had happened. Thereupon Miguel asked her to live with him, to which she agreed, only stealing back to gather her belongings.

When Rosa did not return that night, the parents-in-law asked the hamlet Principales to search for her at Miguel's house. Discovering the couple there together, the Principales tied them up and locked them in an empty room of the schoolhouse. The next morning the Presidente had Rosa and Miguel brought to the ceremonial center and put in jail

until a hearing could be arranged, and Andres's brother was sent to the lowlands to fetch him.

When all were assembled at the town hall, the Presidente asked Andres and his father what they wanted done. Andres's father replied that they wanted the courtship money back but that Miguel could keep Rosa. He claimed that the amount spent was 1,300 pesos, but Rosa countered that Andres had spent only 500 pesos. Being a Chamula, she had married for a much lower bride-price than a Zinacanteco. At this the Presidente asked Andres and his father to list all their expenses, which came to around 500 pesos. He declared this to be a fair sum, which Miguel paid. He also paid Andres's bus fare to attend the hearing. And he kept Rosa.

Miguel and Rosa were jailed for seventy-two hours and sentenced to four weeks of hard labor. At the end of this time, a delegation of men came to the Presidente to say that they did not want Miguel to return home, because he might have a devil inside him to attract other men's wives and they did not want him stealing their women. Since Miguel and Rosa had no place else to go, the Presidente appointed Miguel a Mayor at the ceremonial center for a year until things calmed down.

There is little a deserted husband can do to force his wife's lover to recompense him for the bride-price. If the lover is married, he may refuse to take the woman or pay the bride-price, preferring simply to let himself be jailed. When this happens, everyone loses: the husband loses his bride-price investment, the woman is turned out by her husband and her own family, and the lover serves a jail term. And although the lover does manage to avoid paying money, he puts himself in danger of retaliatory witchcraft.

A man suspecting that his wife has a lover but lacking proof may beat her to force her to confess. One man who strung his young wife from the roof beams to force her to name her lover was later severely scolded by all his relatives and affines, who held a large meeting to discuss the issue. Suspicions of adultery make wife beating a serious affair, and the beaten woman may refuse to return to her husband for fear of being beaten again.

If a married woman has sexual relations with a man other than her husband by being raped or through drunken behavior, the outcome of the case will depend on how it is presented and what the husband wants. If the woman is believed to have encouraged the assault, her husband may ask for a divorce and punishment,

but if he feels she is innocent he may be willing to keep her. These rare cases do not fit into any of the Zinacanteco categories, and the people involved are often unsure how to proceed.

Case 26. A drunken wife is seduced by another man. (The informant was the elder who accompanied the couple to the town hall.)

Nicolas, who lived with his wife and her mother, asked Marcos, a bonesetter, to set the mother's broken leg. After the curing ceremony, Nicolas, Marcos, and Nicolas's wife drank two liters of strong rum. Nicolas went to sleep on the floor, and his wife and Marcos began to embrace. When they went outside the house, the old woman tried, unsuccessfully, to rouse her son-in-law. At length the wife returned alone and fell into a drunken sleep.

The next morning the old woman told Nicolas what had happened. Nicolas was furious, but his wife claimed not to remember anything. After a fruitless argument, they decided to discuss the matter with a neighboring elder. By this time Nicolas was hinting that his wife might better leave him and go away with the bonesetter, while the woman was suggesting that her mother might have lied. The elder listened to their quarrel and suggested that they take the case to the town hall. He agreed to hear the mother's story and to act as witness.

At the town hall the hearing began after Marcos was fetched. Nicolas accused Marcos of seducing his wife and claimed, moreover, that he was in the habit of seducing women. Marcos denied everything, claiming that he remembered nothing of the night before; but if he had gone outside with Nicolas's wife, it was only because Nicolas had accused her of promiscuity earlier in the evening. Both men were angry, each wanting the other jailed for having brought on the seduction. After hearing both sides, the Sindico, who was substituting for the Presidente, expressed the opinion that all three seemed at fault, and that it was not in any case such a serious matter. After all, Marcos had visited Nicolas's house only once, and then at Nicolas's insistence; since he could hardly be having a prolonged affair with the woman, perhaps they should all forget the matter. He advised Nicolas to get another bonesetter and suggested that they draw up an *acta* stating that the argument was terminated. The litigants agreed. Nicolas and Marcos shared the cost of the *acta*, since both were at fault, and each then presented the Sindico with a bottle of rum to thank him for having settled the case.

Another type of case occurs when a woman goes to the town hall to demand support for an illegitimate child. Success in pressing the claim depends upon her ability to get the man to admit his guilt, and therefore his willingness to pay. As long as the man's wife does not become involved, cases like this can be considered

settled when the man makes payment for the child's expenses or takes the child himself.

Divorce

When a Zinacanteco and his wife separate, there is often a period when it is unclear whether the marriage will continue or not; and if it does not it can end either formally or informally. A man may be able to get his wife back by appeasing her anger, but some wives refuse to return. When the husband finally gives up and goes looking for another wife, the marriage is considered informally dissolved. In cases like this, the wife usually gets nothing unless she presses the issue and asks an elder to help her claim a share of her husband's property. But to make such a claim would afford her husband another opportunity to get her back, and women who are determined to separate usually let sleeping dogs lie.

A woman without the support of relatives who is determined to separate may run off to San Cristobal and work as a maid in the house of a Ladino family until her husband has given up searching for her. But marriages that end in this way can be a source of trouble later if the woman is without a guardian to receive bride-price payments should she marry again. For her to live with another Zinacanteco man would mean that her former husband could demand that the bride-price be refunded. Married women who have not returned to their relatives still belong to their husbands, and the wise man who courts a woman in San Cristobal will make an effort to seek out her relatives and negotiate a bride-price.

Most marriages end formally, however, with a decision made in the hamlet or at the town hall. The father of a bride who has returned home several times may conclude that the marriage is a failure and refuse to send her back when her husband and his relatives come to beg pardon. If the husband's family agrees that the marriage is doomed, they can decide to forfeit the bride-price and let the woman go.

A husband may ask an elder or the girl's family to have the wedding godfather or a respected relative mediate. But if the mediator is convinced that the marriage has no future, he will condone the bride's action and try to reconcile the groom's family to the loss of the bride-price. The elder or wedding godfather may

even supervise a property settlement. As a last resort, the husband who is determined to preserve his marriage may ask the Presidente for help in getting his wife back.

Occasionally a husband may end his marriage by returning his wife to her relatives. One man who had spent all his money on curing ceremonies for a wife who was constantly sick returned the woman to her parents and agreed not to make further claims on her or her family. But if no formal agreement is made, the woman's relatives may go to an elder or the town hall to seek a property settlement.

The Presidente always tries to reconcile a separated couple. But if all his attempts fail, he will acknowledge the separation and try to arrange a property settlement. Informants state that women who commit adultery or are otherwise bad wives deserve nothing, whereas innocent women who are the victims of vicious or adulterous husbands deserve a share of the property. But in most marital disputes both sides are at fault, and the accusations and counteraccusations are difficult to sort out. A look at fifty divorces in the hamlet of Apas, however, shows that certain factors help predict whether a woman will share her husband's property: length of marriage, existence of children, and where the case is settled. Table 5 shows significant chi-square differences in all three categories. Accordingly, it can be said that a woman who has been married more than four years, keeps the children, and obtains a divorce at the town hall is most likely to receive a share of her husband's property. This share can be small—some of the household goods and a portion of the stored food—or substantial—all of the man's property except his personal clothes and tools.

The Effect of Mexican Law on Marital Disputes

Although prestigious weddings in Zinacantan now include both a civil and a religious ceremony, neither Mexican law nor the Catholic Church seems to have had much effect on Zinacanteco patterns of divorce and remarriage. Most permanent separations are arranged through private agreements that return the woman to her natal home; second marriages are contracted like first ones, with payments to the bride's consanguineal kinsmen (J. Collier 1967). Former husbands are not consulted. The bride-price for a

TABLE 5

Property Settlements in Fifty Divorce Cases
from Apas According to Years of Marriage, Existence of Children,
and Place of Settlement

Category	Wife received property and goods	Wife did not receive property or goods	TOTAL
Years of marriage:[a]			
Less than 2	2	28	30
2 to 4	5	6	11
More than 4	8	1	9
Existence of children:[b]			
No children	2	29	31
Children	13	6	19
Where settled:[c]			
Apas	5	29	34
Town hall	10	6	16

[a] Chi-square, corrected, equals 19.5, with 2 degrees of freedom. Probability < .001.
[b] Chi-square, corrected, equals 18.7, with 1 degree of freedom. Probability < .001.
[c] Chi-square, corrected, equals 11.7, with 1 degree of freedom. Probability < .001.

divorcée is lower than for an unmarried girl, and the wedding ceremony is usually a private affair held at the bride's house, though the marriage is regarded as completely valid by Zinacantecos. A church wedding is easily arranged later if the husband is to take a religious office; even where some earlier marriage of one of the two has been recorded in the parish register, no difficulty arises—the couple simply use different versions of their proper names to deceive the priest.

Mexican law plays a role in Zinacanteco marital disputes only when invoked by a spouse who has been married in a civil ceremony. As we have seen, a man may ask the Presidente to preserve his marriage by demanding a high fee for a legal divorce, but this tactic has its limitations; an unwilling wife may well prove worse than no wife at all. A woman may appeal to the Presidente or the Mexican authorities for help in demanding support from a husband who has abandoned her. But this ploy may bring back the husband along with the property, for Zinacantecos feel that a man has a right to move in with his wife and children if they are living in his house, if they are eating corn produced by his labor, and if

the house is built on land inherited from his patrilineal ancestors. A woman who wishes to preserve her freedom must leave her husband's house and search for other means of support.

A Zinacanteco man who has been married by civil law may accuse his former wife's second husband of adultery in the hope of recovering some of his bride-price payments, but few men take this course. In the one case where such a claim was reportedly made, the first husband was regarded as a worthless person trying to justify a drunken attack he had made on his former wife. The tendency of men to remarry before women do may partly account for the few instances of this type of action.

Conclusion

Marital disputes are a normal and indeed necessary part of Zinacanteco life, since they lead to the reordering of social relationships crucial to maintaining cohesion in the developing patrilineal family. Consanguineal kinsmen are not supposed to exhibit open hostility; hence husbands and wives, who are expected to squabble, may provoke an open breach that forces all members of the extended family to reconsider their relationship. It is no coincidence that the early years of marriage are the most unstable, for all the strains inherent in extended family living come to a head in this period. Young brides are unhappy at leaving home and having to work for their mothers-in-law, and young husbands may wish to break away from working with the family group but fear the wrath of the father or the risks of farming alone. Wives, always viewed as selfishly looking out for their own interests, provide convenient scapegoats for husbands who wish to break away without quarreling openly with their patrilineal kinsmen. Marital disputes are thus outlets for the tensions of extended family living. The fact that they are frequent, highly patterned and seldom serious makes them efficient vehicles for dissipating the hostile feelings that develop between a man and a woman who must cooperate but who have few interests in common, spend most of their time apart, and cannot openly discuss the strains impinging on them by the nature of the patrilineal extended family.

Women are the volatile partners in Zinacanteco marriages. The reconciliation phase of a marital dispute is usually precipitated

by the wife's departure, and the husband is usually cast in the
role of wanting to preserve the marriage. In this, Zinacantan re-
sembles other predominantly patrilineal, patrilocal societies where
marital problems are blamed on the instability of women (see
Fallers 1969). In these societies men live surrounded by kinsmen
and beat their wives to keep them in line, but women have little
means of gaining their ends without running away in order to invoke outside help. Throughout the reconciliation process, women
are safe from further beatings and free to speak their minds in the
company of supportive kinsmen. But it is also true in Zinacantan
that women are able to live without husbands far more easily than
men are able to live without wives. Unlike some African societies
where there is no place for an unmarried adult woman, Zinacanteco widows, spinsters, and divorcées may live alone and support
themselves. A woman with a house of her own or living with relatives is able to work for her food, but a man needs a wife to cook
for him and wash his clothes. Zinacanteco women, in general, are
reluctant to remarry, and men in search of second wives often
have to approach several eligible widowed or divorced women
before finding one who will accept (J. Collier 1968a). A young
man whose mother is still active or an old man with an adult
daughter or daughter-in-law may manage without a wife, but a
middle-aged man who cannot persuade a woman to marry him
must leave the community.

Most Zinacanteco marital disputes follow a predictable sequence of events, both before and after the reconciliation process
is triggered by the wife's departure, and most are settled in the
hamlets. Even the permanent separations are usually arranged in
hamlet hearings. The only marital disputes that invariably reach
the town hall are those involving accusations of adultery that cannot be immediately dismissed as false. Adultery implies claims on
property as well as jailing, and such matters are usually carried to
the highest reasonable forum before the parties agree to a compromise.

TEN

Courtship Disputes

Courtship in Zinacantan is an economic transaction in which a boy, with his family's help, acquires the right to marry a girl by paying her parents for the expenses incurred in her childhood. It is a limited contract, considered complete when the bride is living with, and cooking for, the groom and when the girl's father has received the money. Bride-price payments do not continue after marriage, nor is the husband entitled to reimbursement if his wife leaves him. For this reason, the problems arising during courtship are settled in a fundamentally different way from those arising between husband and wife. Courtship cases, unlike marital disputes, can be couched in terms of money and settled by the exchange of cash between the two families.

Courtship disputes fall into three basic categories: (1) the problems incurred in breaking up a courtship, (2) the payments to be made when a couple elopes, and (3) the problems that arise when an outsider interferes in a courtship and threatens the completion of the contract. These categories point up the stress relationships in a courtship: (1) between the two families, (2) between the girl and her parents, and (3) between the principals and the outside world. We start with a brief description of courtship practices, taken from a study of several courtships (J. Collier 1968a).

Zinacanteco Courtship

Courtships begin dramatically when a boy and his petitioners force their way into the girl's house at night and kneel at the feet

of her parents until her father agrees to give his daughter in marriage. Careful preparations precede the actual petition, for after choosing the girl the boy must present a bottle of rum to his own father to tell him of the choice and ask his help in making the petition. Boys usually choose a girl by sight and reputation alone, since unrelated adolescents have no opportunities for casual conversation. Once the boy's parents have approved his choice, they invite at least four other men and their wives to serve as petitioners. The girl's family must know nothing of the boy's intentions, for men are believed to be reluctant to give up their daughters, and it is felt that the girl's father might foil the courtship by being away from home on the night of the intended petition. A father who is caught at home by the petitioners can seldom refuse to allow the boy to court his daughter. The only choice left to him is when to give in and accept the rum; if he is only mildly abusive and accepts the proffered rum after two or three hours, the courtship has a good chance of ending in marriage, but if he is truly angry and holds out for several hours, the outlook is gloomy and the boy's petitioners may simply give up. The girl has no say in the matter. While her parents confront the petitioners, she sits silently in a corner of the house. Even the boy plays a minor role in the opening drama of the courtship. He remains outside the girl's house until his petitioners have persuaded her father to accept the rum. Then he enters humbly and presents more rum to his future parents-in-law.

After this dramatic beginning, the courtship moves along quietly for about a year and a half. During this period, the boy or his mother visits the girl's family every two weeks with a small gift of food, and larger gifts of fruit are given on calendrical festivals. But even these informal visits do little to prepare the bride and groom for their future life together. They are seldom allowed to talk alone and can only observe each other silently across the room. Twice a year, on the feast days of the two major saints, the boy and his petitioners make a formal visit to the girl's house, where all of her relatives are gathered for the occasion. The adult members of the two groups drink together and discuss any problems affecting the courtship. This long, relatively quiet period is actually the most important part of the courtship, for it is during

this time that the bride-price is paid with each gift of fruit, offered in a net, and each bottle of rum that the boy gives his future father-in-law. If they are wise, both the boy and his father-in-law keep careful track of the money represented in the gifts, because as the amount invested by the boy grows larger, the girl's father becomes more and more committed.

This intermediate stage of the courtship ends when both sides consider that an adequate bride-price has been paid and everyone is content to let the marriage take place. Although the two ceremonies ending the courtship are likely to cost as much as has already been paid, they are not really part of the bride-price. The Zinacanteco bride-price buys the consent of the girl's father, and this consent is indicated when he formally accepts the boy into his family at a ceremony called *ʔočel ta na*, "entering the house." Many courtships simply end at this point, with the bride and groom starting their life together in the girl's house. Even if the marriage is not consummated after the house-entering ceremony, the boy is expected to stay and work for his father-in-law for a period of four weeks, but many young men now pay money to escape this service.

If the parents of the bride and groom have decided on a formal wedding, a procedure casting prestige on both families, the house-entering ceremony ends with the naming of a wedding godfather, who will accompany the bride and groom to the church and serve as mediator in later marital disputes. Weddings can be elaborate and expensive affairs. After the separate church and civil weddings, all the relatives of both bride and groom gather at the boy's house to celebrate with feasting and dancing. The heart of the marriage ceremony is the point at which the wedding godfather leads the bride into the groom's house and formally introduces her to her future home. At this point the girl's father has fulfilled his part of the courtship transaction. Should his daughter return home to him, he will feel morally obligated to send her back to her husband, but he will not return the bride-price if the marriage is a failure.

Because model courtships are long and expensive, many Zinacantecos cut the process short by giving cash payments instead of the traditional gifts. But all marriages, to be valid, require some

form of courtship payment. Finding someone to receive the bride-price may be a problem in some cases, especially if the girl is an orphan working for the family she is living with, for to receive a bride-price makes the recipient responsible for the woman. Older spinsters and widows who are effectively supporting themselves may receive their own bride-price, but relatives are always invited to share the goods and the responsibilities. Courtships for second marriages and cash courtships almost always end at a house-entering ceremony.

Breaking a Courtship

The economic aspect of a courtship is most obvious when it is broken off. Zinacantecos believe that a boy who does not receive his bride should be reimbursed because a young man must marry and will need the money for another courtship. But because courtship is rarely a cash transaction, problems arise. The girl's family eats well while the boy provides gifts of food, but if the courtship is broken off, the girl's father must reimburse in cash. This tends to promote courtship stability, for the girl's father must consider the cost of getting rid of an undesirable suitor. Courtship disputes often become bitter fights ending up at the town hall because of the large sums of money involved.

When a boy and his petitioners appeal to the town hall, it is usually because the girl and her family have indicated their reluctance to continue the courtship by refusing to accept the boy's gifts or by having the girl away from home when the boy or his mother calls. The boy then asks the advice of his petitioners, who may decide to seek an explanation by making a formal visit to the girl's father. If the meeting produces accord, the courtship continues, but if the father accuses the boy of having another girl or indicates a reluctance to continue the courtship, the boy and his petitioners usually go to the town hall.

Case 27. A boy asks that his fiancée's father be questioned. (The informant was one of the boy's petitioners.)
Pedro had been courting Lorenza for three years but had not yet formally entered her house when one day her father refused to accept a routine gift of corn. Pedro told his petitioners of the incident and the entire group visited Lorenza's family. Lorenza's father wanted to

end the courtship because he had heard that Pedro had another girl. Since discussion failed to resolve the matter, Pedro and his petitioners appealed to the town hall. At the hearing, Lorenza's father said that his daughter had told him about the girl. Upon being questioned, Lorenza replied that she had not seen anything herself but had learned about Pedro's girl from some people whose names she refused to divulge, even when questioned by her father. The Presidente then suggested that she had made up the story to avoid having to marry Pedro. She finally admitted this, saying that Pedro was too short. The Presidente responded that she did not have to marry against her wish; however, he said that her father must repay Pedro's courtship expenses so he could contract for another wife. Lorenza's father agreed to repay the bride-price within a certain period, and Pedro submitted a list of expenses amounting to just under 1,000 pesos for the three years.

When a girl's father wishes to break off a courtship because the boy has acted wrongly, the courtship can continue only if the boy begs forgiveness and the girl's father accepts. When a boy has misbehaved while drunk and reconciliation is not effected at the hamlet level, the case usually goes to the town hall. There the Presidente may try to help the boy beg pardon, but if he fails, the hearing concentrates on how much money should be returned. There is always disagreement over expenses because the boy must feed his petitioners and provide the rum to be drunk by everyone, and the girl's father counts only the value of the items he actually receives as gifts. Most arguments center on reconciling the disagreements between the two lists. If the boy is at fault, he rarely recovers more than the cost of the gifts the girl's father received, but if he is not at fault, he can demand that the entire amount be repaid. The girl's father rarely refuses to pay altogether, since returning the money marks the end of the courtship obligations. A rejected suitor who recovers his money can court another woman, but one who has been cheated can cause infinite trouble. If the unpaid suitor shouts insults outside the girl's house or attempts to rape her in the woods, public opinion sides with the boy and any mediator is most likely to advise the girl's father to pay if he wishes to avoid further trouble. Even if a rejected suitor takes no direct action, any illness or misfortune in the girl's family is attributed to his appeals for supernatural vengeance.

Case 28. A boy who behaves badly loses his fiancée. (The informant was the Presidente who helped settle the case.)
Jose was courting Maria, the daughter of a woman who lived in the

ceremonial center. When Maria became sick for a time, a curing ceremony was held at her home. Jose as official drink pourer at the ceremony became drunk and tried to carry off his sick fiancée. He tugged at her shawl, and when Maria resisted he cut it to pieces with his machete and threw her blankets into the fire. At this point other members of the curing party forced Jose out of the house. At the end of the ceremony Juana, the girl's mother, went to the town hall to ask the Presidente to send Mayores after Jose.

At a hearing the next morning the Presidente questioned Jose, who replied that he had been drunk and had become angry when a friend told him that Maria loved someone else. The girl denied the accusation, and Jose, upon being pressed, first refused to name his informant, then claimed he had forgotten who had told him. Juana demanded that Jose be punished for attacking her daughter; she wanted him jailed, or she would take the case to San Cristobal. The Presidente agreed to jail Jose for seventy-two hours, the maximum allowed, but urged Juana to forgive him and allow the courtship to continue. She promised to consult with her relatives and left.

When Jose was released from jail, he asked the Presidente how Juana might best be calmed down. The Presidente advised him to beg pardon. He went, but was turned down; he went again, this time with all his petitioners and more elaborate gifts. Maria insisted that she would not marry a man who attacked her in her own home—how would he treat her once they were married? The Presidente then advised Jose to submit a list of courtship expenses, which amounted to 300 pesos. Juana agreed to pay this amount and the courtship ended.

In the rare cases where a courtship ends neither in marriage nor in repayment, the boy can continue to make claims on his former fiancée. Should she find another suitor, for example, he can ask the new fiancé to pay him for his courtship expenses. His claims may be disputed or denied, but they cannot be dismissed without serious consideration.

Case 29. A boy who breaks off a courtship asks the girl's second suitor to repay him. (The informant was the elder who served as petitioner for both suitors.)

Five months after making a formal petition for Juana, Andres broke off the courtship. He had heard that she had a competing suitor. Andres's mother then went to tell the girl's family of his decision. When Juana's mother said she could not return the bride-price, Andres's mother agreed not to press the claim, since the boy had broken the contract. Andres later entered negotiations for another girl, but his petitioners had great trouble persuading the girl's father to accept a boy who had abandoned one fiancée. About a year later, another boy, Miguel, made a petition for Juana. Her mother was careful to tell the

petitioners, before she accepted their rum, that the first suitor had not been repaid. Miguel's petitioners acknowledged the complication, but went ahead with the petition. When Andres heard that another boy was courting Juana, he asked an elder, who had been his petitioner as well as Miguel's, for help in recovering his money. Andres furnished the elder with a list of expenses adding up to 500 pesos, and the elder, accompanied by Andres's other petitioners, went to visit the girl's mother. Her list of gifts received, however, came to only 200 pesos. Another meeting was held to compare the two accounts, and Miguel and his parents were invited to participate. After hearing both lists, Miguel's father offered to pay Andres the 200 pesos Juana's mother had totaled up. Andres objected and considered taking his case to the town hall, but finally agreed to accept the 200 pesos. When he was gone, Miguel's father presented a bottle of rum to Juana's mother and asked whether she preferred a traditional long courtship with gifts or would accept money to speed up the process. At first choosing gifts, she was persuaded by her son that money was more practical. She asked for 1,000 pesos, which was agreed to, but with the 200 pesos paid to Andres subtracted. The house-entering ceremony took place eight days after the money was paid and a small wedding was held within the month.

Courtship is a contractual relationship. When a courtship dispute is being heard, bad behavior may be given as a reason for breaking the contract, but it is never stressed—the boy may accuse the girl of having a lover, or the girl's father may claim that the boy is violent, but neither claim needs to be supported. What is crucial is whether the girl's father wants the courtship ended and will repay the bride-price.

Elopements

In a broken courtship, the girl and her parents side together against the boy. An elopement, by contrast, creates a new relationship: not only does the marriage have to be validated by a cash payment, but the kinship ties between the girl and her family have to be reestablished through begging pardon and reconciliation. Whereas courtship disputes end in either reconciliation or repayment, an elopement must end with both. Elopement settlements require a period of bargaining in which to set the bride-price and a period of reconciliation in which the girl's father is brought to recognize the marriage.

Unrelated boys and girls of marriageable age are not supposed

to talk to each other. Wise parents who wish to avoid a scandal take care that their daughters are always chaperoned, for young men are known to loiter around the stores, the corn-grinding mills, and the paths to waterholes in the hope of talking to a girl. If a girl agrees to marry a boy before a formal petition is made, the girl's father is robbed of his rightful role and is made to appear foolish. And indeed a father may precipitate an elopement by beating his daughter merely on suspicion that she is deceiving him.

Case 30. An angry father beats his daughter into running off with a boy. (My informant was the Presidente who settled the case.)

When Marcos and his parents made a petition for a twelve-year-old girl, her stepfather, Antonio, refused the gift of rum because the girl was too young. But Marcos said that, although she might look like a child, she had behaved like a woman in agreeing to marry him. The stepfather, now furious, asked if this were true, and when the girl did not answer directly, he beat her until she escaped into the woods. Marcos also took to the woods, in a different direction, but by morning the two were together.

Antonio then accused Marcos's parents of tricking him so that the two could run off together. They denied the accusation and asked how much money he wanted for his stepdaughter. The angry Antonio declared that he would accept nothing less than 2,500 pesos. At that the parents went to the town hall. The Presidente asked the Ladino secretary if Mexican law put a limit on the amount a man could ask for his daughter, but the secretary said there was no such law, since paying a girl's parents was an Indian custom, not a Ladino one.

At the hearing the following day, Antonio lowered his demand to 2,000 pesos. Marcos's parents countered that this was still too high, and that in fact their son had not stolen the girl, since she had given her consent to marry him. They had eloped; Marcos had not abducted her. Since the case hinged on whether the girl had given her consent, the hearing was postponed until the couple could be found.

Discovered hiding in the house of the boy's parents, the two were sent to the Presidente's house. Marcos was terrified that he would be punished for abducting the girl, but the Presidente assured him that he wanted simply to hear the girl's version of the story. She admitted that she had agreed to Marcos's courting but had not intended to elope, only running out of the house to escape her stepfather's beating. The Presidente told her to stick to her story because it would force Antonio to recognize the elopement and to ask for a more reasonable price. He then led the eloped couple to the town hall where their parents were waiting. After much discussion, Antonio finally accepted 500

pesos for the girl, and the Presidente had a civil wedding performed. But since Antonio had been so recalcitrant, the Presidente had everyone sign an *acta* recording the agreement.

When a couple elope, they usually seek protection with the boy's relatives. From this point, events may take one of several courses, depending on the actions of the couple and the girl's parents, but both sides must eventually come face to face and reach a reconciliation. The couple may hide with the boy's relatives or they may seek a civil marriage in San Cristobal or in the ceremonial center. The girl's parents may do nothing or they may go to the town hall. But the Presidente can take no action until the parents have found the girl.

At the town hall, once the Presidente has made sure that the couple can be married, he helps the boy beg pardon of his new father-in-law. When the girl's father agrees to recognize the marriage, the question of payment is discussed. The money represents the expenses incurred by the girl's family in raising her, including curing ceremonies, and is not the equivalent of the bride-price, with its nets of fruit, that would have been paid in a normal courtship. The case is settled when the girl's father accepts the proffered rum and payment is agreed upon. Even in the hearing at the town hall, however, the procedure is basically one of begging pardon.

Because elopements are settled by begging pardon, a town hall hearing may be avoided if the boy's family takes the initiative and visits the girl's father.

Case 31. The parents of an eloped boy visit the girl's father. (The informant accompanied the parents in their attempt to placate the girl's family.)

Mariano's job of running his father's corn-grinding mill gave him the opportunity to talk with the girls who patronized it, one of whom was the daughter of Domingo, one of the richest men in the hamlet. At the time of the fiesta of San Lorenzo, Domingo took his family to the ceremonial center. His daughter, who asked to stay home, was left in the care of an aunt, who was to spend the nights with her. One day the aunt's husband stopped by to see how the girl was doing and was surprised to find the house door locked. After he had pounded on it for a few minutes, the door opened and Mariano ran out. Knowing that

he had been recognized and must act quickly, Mariano returned later to persuade the girl to run away with him that night.

Mariano's mother discovered his absence the next morning. After looking for him at the corn mill, she finally woke her husband, Lucas. Just at that time Mariano arrived with the girl. Lucas was horrified, for the girl's father, Domingo, was not only rich but known for his bad temper, and Lucas was afraid they would all be jailed for abducting her. He quickly sent Mariano and the girl to the house of a relative while he called on his brothers for help. On the advice of a bilingual neighbor, they determined to have the couple married immediately in San Cristobal, not daring to approach the ceremonial center, since the girl's father, a close friend of the Presidente, was there. That afternoon, after a judge had married the couple, Lucas bought gifts for the girl's father. Ordinary bootleg rum would not do for such a wealthy man, so he bought several bottles of fine Bacardi to put in the traditional basket of bread. He also collected 1,000 pesos from his savings and from friends and debtors so as to have cash in hand for the girl's father when he relented.

On returning to Zinacantan, Lucas asked a compadre of the girl's father to accompany the group, which consisted entirely of men because the wives were afraid to go. They started out at three in the morning, wanting to give the girl's father a chance to sleep off the liquor he had consumed at the fiesta. However, the ploy was unsuccessful; when they arrived, he was waiting for them, still furious, and did not calm down until dawn. At last he began to discuss payment, first asking 3,000 pesos, on grounds that he had spent that much on curing ceremonies, but after bargaining he came down to 1,500 pesos. Lucas paid him 1,000 pesos right away, promising the rest as soon as he could sell a mule. The girl's father agreed, and the liquor was opened. Gradually the girl's father became more friendly, and finally he told Lucas not to sell the mule, but to wait and pay after the harvest.

In an elopement the girl's family, as the injured party, can claim payment for the girl's expenses, but the amount varies with circumstances and social class. A widow whose daughter eloped with a local tough was so afraid of future violence that she accepted the boy's rum without demanding payment. In another case, settlement was delayed for a month because the girl's father simply waited to see what would happen. The crisis came when the eloped girl was beaten by her husband and took refuge with an aunt. The boy tried to beg pardon, but the aunt refused to let him into her house, telling him to go to the girl's father instead.

The boy's parents then planned a formal petition. They prepared the traditional gifts and invited a respected elder to accompany them. At the girl's house, they begged her father to recognize the elopement and asked the girl to forgive her husband's beating. This time they succeeded in getting the girl back, but they had to pay her father a bride-price. In still another case, the girl's father was willing to recognize his daughter's elopement but the mother would have nothing to do with the couple. The boy's family finally gave up the attempt to beg pardon for fear of causing a quarrel between the girl's parents, and they then planned another visit after the harvest when they would have cash for the bride-price.

The father of a girl who elopes has the option of going to the town hall and demanding that the boy be jailed for flouting his authority. A boy who steals a girl at night instead of asking for her in the proper way shows ample evidence of *manya,* innate evil tendencies, in his lack of respect for his elders and for traditional customs. Many couples also fear that the girl's father might accuse the boy of abduction before the Mexican penal authorities. However, few boys actually end up in jail, either in Zinacantan or in San Cristobal. If the girl has consented to the elopement, the Presidente or an eloquent elder can usually persuade her parents to negotiate for a reasonable bride-price.

Because unmarried girls must not talk with boys, an adult catching a young couple flirting on the path will scold both of them. If a boy makes more serious advances, such as grabbing the girl's water jug or locking her in a store while she is making a purchase, the girl is expected to tell her father of the incident. Although Zinacantecos say that a father should protect his daughter by asking the Presidente to have the boy jailed, few men go to this trouble; the father may simply ignore the incident but take care to give his daughter better protection in the future, or he may admonish the boy or talk to his father. However, if rape is attempted, the girl's parents will usually go to the town hall.

Case 32. An unmarried boy attempts to rape a girl. (The informant was the Presidente who settled the case.)

Antonio attacked Rosa as she was tending sheep, but she escaped. When Rosa told her mother what had happened, they went to the town

hall, where the Presidente sent for the boy and asked him why he had attacked the girl. Antonio replied that she loved him and that he wanted to marry her. The Presidente then asked Antonio how he could expect the girl to love him if he attacked her and advised him to make a formal petition instead. But when Antonio begged pardon of Rosa's mother, she refused to listen to him, and the Presidente had Antonio jailed for two days. When he was released, Antonio went with his petitioners to make a formal petition for Rosa. This time her mother accepted the gifts, and after a normal two-year courtship Antonio and Rosa were married.

The outcome of a rape case depends on whether the attempt was judged successful. If not, the boy is punished for attacking the girl. There is a certain risk involved when the boy becomes impatient waiting for the wedding to take place and attempts to rape his fiancée, since if the attempt fails her family may end the courtship. But if the attempt is successful or there has been ample opportunity for sexual relations, Zinacantecos feel that they should marry, and the whole affair is treated as if they had eloped. A marriage is quickly performed, and the boy is expected to beg pardon and pay a bride-price.

Interference by a Third Person

Courtships are delicate and expensive transactions. When interference by an outsider breaks up a courtship, Zinacantecos argue that it is only right for the interloper to repay the boy's courtship expenses. But the stakes are high—several hundred pesos—and the interloper may prefer jail to paying such a sum. It is virtually impossible to force the intruder to pay if he refuses to marry the girl. The fiancé, however, can only lose, since he either gets a bride of questionable reputation or finds himself ridiculed by his peers for having lost his girl.

When a person who is highly unlikely to be able to marry the girl interferes in a courtship, the boy's chances of recovering his expenses are practically nonexistent, and the only thing to do is to put a good face on the matter. There are three recorded cases of outside interference by nonmarriageable interlopers, all of which ended by making the boy's impending marriage to a tarnished bride as attractive as possible. The first case, given in detail in Chapter 2, related how two gossiping women were threatened

with having to reimburse a boy for his courtship expenses if he believed their tale of the girl's misbehavior and broke off the engagement. This threat caused the old women to change their story, making it easy for everyone to believe they had lied. The fiancé could thus justifiably continue the courtship, while the women let themselves be known as liars to escape paying a large sum of money. In each of the other two cases, the girl was suspected of having sexual relations with a married man, which the man denied to escape repaying the fiancé's courtship expenses. In one of the cases, a man who had raped an engaged girl managed steadfastly to deny his guilt in spite of the girl's testimony and the Presidente's threats to send him to the Mexican authorities for punishment. Without an admission of guilt, a fiancé has no chance of recovering his money, and has little choice but to proceed with the transaction. In both cases, however, the boys were allowed to marry immediately, and thus escaped further courtship payments.

When an interloper is potentially marriageable, he may take the girl and repay the boy's courtship expenses. The problem lies in deciding whether the relations between the girl and the interloper are serious enough to warrant breaking the existing courtship, and the solution often depends on the statements of the girl. She may deny having had anything to do with the interloper, but if she admits to having had an affair with him or claims she wants to marry him, the interloper may find himself without grounds for refusing the woman and the accompanying payments. When a girl actually elopes with a boy not her fiancé, the outcome is more clear. The new husband then faces the prospect of paying his father-in-law as well as repaying the first suitor. Usually, however, the payments are combined, and the money given to the first suitor is subtracted from the bride-price paid to the girl's father.

Case 33. A girl wants to marry a boy not her fiancé. (The informant was a man from the same hamlet as the litigants. This case happened many years ago when boys could be jailed for fiancée stealing.)

While Maria was being courted by Jose, she talked with Martin. When she told her widowed mother that she wanted to marry Martin instead of Jose, her mother was angry, but at the insistence of Maria's older brother she sent for Martin to discuss the matter. Martin, afraid to come, sent his grandmother, who had raised him. When the girl's

mother heard that Martin did indeed want to marry her daughter, she became more enraged and went to the town hall to have the two punished. Martin brought all his older relatives to the ceremonial center to plead his case, but in spite of this he was immediately jailed for two days to take out his manya. At the hearing, following his release, Maria said that if Martin would not marry her she would work as a maid in San Cristobal. Martin's relatives insisted he was prepared to marry her and to repay Jose. Jose's accounting of expenses came to 1,200 pesos, partly because of giving expensive Bacardi rather than bootleg rum. The others did not believe him, and the Presidente sent a mayor to Maria's house to examine the empty bottles. There were Bacardi bottles, to be sure, but it was impossible to tell whether they had held the original rum or had been filled with bootleg at the time they were presented. Jose ultimately gave in to these arguments and reduced the sum to 1,000 pesos. Martin wanted to pay only the amount received in gifts by Maria's mother, but Jose's petitioners insisted that he pay the entire amount on grounds that breaking the courtship was entirely his fault. When he finally agreed, Maria's mother said that Martin could marry the girl immediately if he paid her 1,500 pesos. While Martin remained in jail, his grandmother raised 1,600 pesos, of which Jose received his 1,000 and Maria's mother 600. The mother then reduced her demands to 1,000 pesos at the request of Martin's relatives and the Presidente, providing that the remaining 400 was paid in eight days. She further demanded that Martin and her daughter be jailed for three weeks of hard labor as an example to other young people who thought of defying their parents. But the Presidente refused to jail the girl, and only agreed to jail Martin on condition that he could have until the end of the month to collect the other 400 pesos. When Maria's mother agreed to this, Martin was married to Maria by civil law and then jailed while the bride went home with his grandmother. Upon his release he followed the advice of a friend, and went with his relatives and an important elder to beg pardon of his mother-in-law and to persuade her to reduce her demands. She finally agreed to accept 100 pesos and then became reconciled to the marriage.

Zinacantecos feel that a boy who takes an engaged girl from her suitor should be severely punished to remove his *manya*. Fiancée stealers are equated with wife stealers because both knowingly seduce a woman away from the man who paid for her. Men who are caught speaking with an engaged girl, or who drunkenly claim to have enjoyed her favors, can be beaten by her suitor or her relatives. Although such self-help does not meet with direct approval, the Presidente will usually argue that the two sides share equally in the blame and should forget their differences.

The Effect of Mexican Law on Courtship Disputes

Because middle- and upper-class Mexican suitors do not pay a bride-price, the legal codes make no provision for recognizing the obligations inherent in Zinacanteco courtship payments. Under Mexican law, all such payments are seen as the boy's voluntary gifts to the girl he loves. A suitor is not obliged to pay the father of his bride, nor is a man who has received courtship gifts obliged to give his daughter in return. As a result, neither the boy who loses his girl nor the man whose daughter elopes is legally entitled to payment.

Among San Cristobal officials, Zinacantecos are notorious for their courtship disputes. The files of the State Department of Indian Affairs are filled with requests from persons seeking to avoid courtship obligations. What seems to be happening is that Zinacantecos, who have the highest bride-price and the longest courtships in the Chiapas highlands, have realized that for very little effort—a visit to the Director of the State Department of Indian Affairs—they can obtain a letter directing the Presidente to free them from all traditional obligations. Few Zinacantecos intend to escape all courtship commitments, but the letter is useful in bargaining over a traditional settlement. It is little wonder that an increasing number of Zinacantecos are taking courtship cases to San Cristobal, because the stakes are high—often several hundred pesos—and the costs of appeal are low, since complaints are directed to the Indian Affairs office instead of the penal authorities and the real settlement is reached in Zinacantan, where it is sealed with the traditional rum.

It is hard to assess what the long-term effect of this trend will be, but one of its more immediate consequences has been to stop the Presidente from using jail sentences to enforce traditional obligations. Boys who elope or who steal another's fiancée can no longer be jailed for violating the rights of a girl's father or suitor, for these rights are not recognized by Mexican law. The growing number of appeals to San Cristobal has also had the effect of lowering the amount of money repaid to a suitor when a courtship is broken off. The lack of Mexican courtship law has thus made Zinacanteco bride-price payments a more hazardous invest-

ment. But such payments were never without risk because of the instability of early marriages.

Most of the appeals that reach the State Department of Indian Affairs are from parents who wish to be rid of an unwanted suitor. They complain that a boy who has given them a few nets of fruit and baskets of bread now feels he has a right to marry the girl and has been harassing the family even though the girl refuses to marry him. The Director then writes a letter to the Presidente urging him to look into the affair and reminding him that a girl cannot be forced into marriage against her will. When the case comes to the town hall, the girl's father uses the letter to bargain down the boy's demands for money. The boy is warned that he will be jailed in San Cristobal if he continues to bother the girl's family, and he is advised to accept what money he can get and to look for another girl.

There are also a few appeals from girls who complain that their fathers are forcing them into marriage with boys they do not like. The Director writes his usual letter, saying that girls are free to choose their own husbands, but the outcome depends on the wishes of the girl's father: some fathers give in and agree to re-pay the rejected suitor, but others remain angry and refuse to speak to their daughters. When this happens, the girl has little choice but to become a maid in San Cristobal or to elope with someone else.

Increasingly, eloping couples now go to San Cristobal, where they try to obtain a civil wedding before returning home to con-front the girl's father. By invoking the Mexican authorities boys hope to avoid being jailed in Zinacantan, and the boy's parents hope to persuade the girl's father to be reasonable in his demands for money (see Case 31). The boy and his parents do not expect to avoid payment altogether, for cordial in-law relations can only be established through a proper reconciliation ceremony. Even the Mexican officials recognize the Indian custom and often advise the eloping couple to make their peace with the girl's father by paying him.

In Zinacantan the lack of Mexican courtship law has had its greatest impact on cases of fiancée stealing. Although Zinacan-tecos view this offense as equivalent to wife stealing, the Mexi-

can authorities consider the two to be very different and will order
the Presidente to release a boy who has been jailed and will tell
the interloper that he is under no obligation to repay the first
suitor. The Zinacanteco officials have responded to this situation
by dropping the punishment but trying to preserve the payment.
In true Zinacanteco fashion, restitution to the offended party is
placed above punishment for the offender: restitution leads to reconciliation and a lasting settlement, but punishment solves very
little. In fact, one informant stated that a recent Presidente deliberately dropped the four weeks of hard labor usually exacted for
fiancée stealing in order to reduce the likelihood that the boy's
family would appeal to the Mexican authorities and escape the
payment along with the punishment. A fiancée stealer now spends
only a couple of nights in jail, and every effort is made to talk the
boy into repaying the first suitor before he is allowed to marry the
girl.

Conclusion

Although courtship quarrels and marital disputes both involve
affinal ties, the two types of cases are handled quite differently.
Courtship disputes, except for elopements, are primarily money
matters, whereas marital disputes deal with past behavior and
future obligations. When a courtship is broken, money is paid to
dissolve former commitments, but marital disputes and elopements are settled by promises of good behavior in the future.
Courtship cases thus mark the transition between the complex
quarrels of people who have lived together in the past and who
must continue to cooperate in the future, and the simpler disputes
of nonkinsmen that center on a single issue and can be resolved
by converting obligations into cash payments.

If Zinacanteco role pairs are ranked on Metzger's (1960) continuum from lowly relational, in which the individual occupants
have few obligations to each other, to highly relational, in which
the occupants are bound together by extensive rights and duties,
the point (i.e. the marriage ceremony) between the role pair of
fiancé and fiancée and the role pair of husband and wife marks
the most definite break in the sequence. The role of fiancé is based
on a single tenuous contract that endures only while it is profit-

able to both sides, whereas that of spouse involves many obligations and constant interaction.

Courtship cases also mark the division between the disputes of
kinsmen, usually settled on the hamlet level, and those between
nonrelatives, most often taken to the town hall (see Table 3, p.
67). Patrilineal kinsmen, husbands and wives, and eloped couples
attempt private solutions in the hamlet, whereas persons wishing
to break off a courtship or those arguing with a nonkinsman are
more willing to invoke the town hall authorities. Courtship cases,
therefore, mark two types of transition in the natural continuum
between the quarrels of closely related people and the disputes of
strangers: the transition between settlements stressing future obligations and those dissolving past commitments; and the transition
between quarrels usually settled in the hamlets and those most
often taken to the town hall. This chapter on courtship disputes
thus marks the division between Chapters 9 and 10, quarrels between relatives, and Chapters 12 and 13, disputes between nonrelatives.

ELEVEN

Disputes Between Neighbors

Disputes between people who are not related by blood or affinal ties tend to be fairly straightforward, with the quarrels focusing on a single issue unhampered by past conflicts or future obligations. Neighbors who bicker for years over a common boundary are of course an obvious exception.

Most of the recorded cases of disputes between unrelated persons can be put into one of two large categories: damage to person or property and breach of contract. The nature of the settlement is determined by (1) whether the accused can be brought to admit guilt, (2) the amount of money involved, and (3) whether the accused is said to have shown evidence of *manya*.

Whereas marital disputes are usually settled in terms of requirements for future harmony, disputes between nonrelatives end with settlements that right past wrongs so that neither side will have cause to invoke supernatural vengeance. A man who begs pardon of his wife promises to behave better in the future, but a person who admits injuring a nonrelative begs pardon in the hope of having his punishment reduced. Between the time a man presents rum to the person he has offended and the time the bottle is accepted, the offender and the Presidente try to persuade the plaintiff to demand reasonable payment and punishment. When an agreement is reached, the rum is accepted and everyone drinks to show that no anger remains.

In cases where a person admits causing damage or breaking a contract, the cash settlement is computed with reference to the plaintiff's declared loss, but the question of whether the guilty per-

son should be jailed involves a determination of intent. Zinacantecos justify jail sentences by claiming that the offender exhibited *manya*, an inner quality prompting him to commit wrongful acts. Although some wrongs, such as stealing, are clear proof of manya, others are more doubtful and lead to long discussions in which the offender tries to show that he was drunk or that matters were otherwise beyond his control, and the plaintiff argues that the offender was sober and willfully did wrong. Although anyone may be jailed before a hearing or between sessions to persuade him to admit guilt, only a person believed to have manya will be jailed after the hearing to remove his evil tendencies.

Disputes between unrelated persons are far more likely to go to the town hall than cases between relatives. Close neighbors may settle competing claims peacefully in the hamlets, but because most conflicts between nonrelatives demand restitution, the plaintiff generally prefers the town hall, where he may receive more money and the defendant can be jailed or threatened with being sent to San Cristobal if he refuses to admit guilt and pay. The town hall is the most logical forum for such disputes because it is the last opportunity for a compromise settlement. If the case reaches San Cristobal, both sides might lose, for the plaintiff might not receive restitution and the defendant may be given a long jail sentence.

Most of this chapter focuses on Zinacanteco methods for handling single-instance conflicts between unrelated individuals. A closing section, however, explores complex disputes occurring over a long period of time: between individuals such disputes are the endless bickering between close neighbors that occasionally flares into open fighting; between groups, the long-term struggles between political factions that come to a head over particular issues. Complex long-term fights, in contrast to single-instance disputes, seldom end with a specific settlement, but are like family quarrels in that they end only when the two sides are reconciled or when one party dies or otherwise departs the arena.

Debt

Failure to repay a debt is the most frequent form of contract breaking in Zinacantan. Money is lent (1) as an interest-free loan to be repaid on a specified date or when the creditor needs it; (2)

as a loan with interest, usually a small loan for a short period at a prohibitive rate of interest—from 5 to 10 percent a month; and (3) as an investment in corn futures, in which the creditor lends money when the corn is green, with the understanding that he will receive bagged corn, worth approximately twice the amount of the original loan, after the harvest. Because few Zinacantecos have access to banks, loans of all types are vital to the community's economy, and there are heavy pressures on individuals to both give loans and to repay them. No one has enough money on hand to meet all of life's emergencies, but the man with surplus cash out in loans and a reputation for repaying borrowed money is able to raise large sums on short notice. On the other hand, failure to repay a loan on request damages a person's credit and makes future loans difficult.

To survive in Zinacantan, a person must maintain a minimum reputation for trustworthiness. Even a man known to have a bad repayment record may obtain a loan by having a trustworthy relative vouch for him and assume responsibility. But if his relatives refuse to support him, he has little choice but to leave Zinacantan. This fact was well illustrated in a hamlet hearing precipitated by a case of wife beating. The young husband had failed in all his responsibilities, and the last chance to reform offered by his relatives and affines was phrased in terms of repaying an old debt. Arrangements for paying the debt were made as easy as possible, but it was also made clear that if he should fail, he would lose his wife as well as the support he would need from relatives to ask for another woman. Without a wife, without the support of relatives, and without credit, he would have no future in Zinacantan.

Many Zinacantecos try to stall payment for as long as possible by presenting rum and requesting extensions. But when payment is long overdue or is needed to meet expenses, the creditor may go to his debtor and ask for the money. The debtor may take this opportunity to present the creditor with another bottle of rum to ask for more time. As long as the debtor follows the proper procedure of presenting rum and the creditor gives in to requests to delay payment by accepting the rum, there is no fault on either side and no case. Conflict does not exist openly until the creditor refuses to extend the loan again or the debtor defaults in present-

ing rum. Then, as a last resort, the creditor may take his case to the town hall and ask the Presidente to force the debtor to pay by threatening to sell his property to raise the cash.

At the town hall, discussion involves: (1) the amount of money loaned, (2) the terms of the agreement, (3) the ability of the debtor to pay, and (4) the history of the creditor's attempts to receive payment. If there is disagreement over the amount loaned or the terms of the agreement, both sides must produce witnesses. Only then does the Presidente investigate the debtor's ability to pay. If the debtor can prove hardship and show that he has regularly presented rum to his creditor, he may avoid paying interest. From a study of the recorded debt cases, it appears that only the original debtor can be held responsible for paying interest. If he should die and his heirs were not party to the agreement, either because they were too young or because they were farming separately, they need repay only the money received. The same is true for a man who agrees to make good the debt of a relative; should the debtor default, the creditor can collect only the principal.

The history of the creditor's attempts to receive payment becomes important in deciding whether the debtor has exhibited *manya*. If the debtor has played a proper role and requested extensions with bottles of rum, the Presidente will help him have the interest reduced or arrange easy payment terms. But if the debtor has lied about his assets, has run away to avoid payment, or has not paid after reaching an agreement at the town hall, he is considered to have shown proof of evil tendencies. Although debtors are seldom given hard labor as punishment, they may be charged interest and kept in jail until their relatives produce the money.

Case 34. A debtor who ran away to avoid payment was threatened with having his mule confiscated. (My informant was secretary at the time.)

Three years after lending money to a neighbor in the same hamlet, Lucas gave up trying to collect the debt himself and went to the town hall. Because both men were illiterate and the amount of the loan had never been put into writing, Lucas brought several members of his family to prove his statement that he had lent 250 pesos. The debtor at first claimed he had borrowed only 225 pesos, but finally agreed to pay 250 pesos if he could have a week to collect the money. An acta was drawn up recording this agreement. But after three weeks had passed and the

money was not paid, Lucas again went to the town hall. This time the Presidente sent Mayores to the lowlands to bring the debtor back from his cornfield. When the debtor arrived, he pleaded that he was working for a ranch owner in order to earn the money, and that when he was paid, in two weeks, he would repay the loan. Lucas asked the Presidente to draw up an acta stating that if the debtor had not paid within that time, Lucas could take his mule and sell it. The acta was executed, but eight days later the debtor paid back the money, saying that he had borrowed it from his employer.

Failure to Fulfill a Curing Contract

Most curing in Zinacantan is not done under contract, since the shaman does not guarantee the patient's recovery, and his fee, paid in food, is only a minor part of the total cost of the ceremony. But some practitioners claim to have special powers and demand high fees to be paid in cash. Because such curing is irregular, the relatives of a patient who dies may suspect that they have been tricked and try to recover their money by taking the shaman to the town hall.

Case 35. A shaman who claimed he could talk with the Earth Lord demanded a high fee for curing. (The informant was a man from the same hamlet.)

Because one of Miguel's mules and his mare had both died, when his remaining mule sickened, he consulted a shaman. The shaman pulsed the mule and said that it was dying because a witch had sold its soul to the Earth Lord. A ceremony was held on a nearby hill, at which the shaman knelt to talk with the Earth Lord. He claimed that the Earth Lord said there was no hope for the mule and that Miguel would go next; and further, the witch who was selling souls was a neighbor who had been burning candles beside a small waterhole. The shaman suggested that they hold another ceremony by the waterhole, and Miguel went to buy more candles. During the ceremony, word came that the mule was dead. The shaman then told the terrified Miguel that for 200 pesos he would try to prevent the Earth Lord from taking him too. At mention of this high fee, Miguel's younger brother, who was helping with the ceremony, became suspicious and accused the shaman of deceiving them. This precipitated a fight, and other members of the curing party suggested going to the town hall, which was nearby, to settle the issue.

There Miguel presented a bottle of rum and told the story. The Presidente asked if Miguel had heard the Earth Lord speak, and Miguel replied that he thought so. At this the younger brother said that it was just the voice of the shaman answering his own questions. The Presi-

dente then sent a group of Mayores and a Juez with the shaman to hear what the Earth Lord had to say. When the shaman prayed again, the Juez concluded that the shaman was answering his own questions and pretending to be the Earth Lord. He ordered the Mayores to seize the shaman and take him back to the town hall. The result was that the shaman agreed to pay for the mule he was supposed to cure, and at the insistence of the woman he had accused of witchcraft, he had to carry stones for three weeks to teach him not to deceive people or to accuse innocent persons of witchcraft.

Zinacanteco informants believe that a shaman or talking-saint owner who tricks people by claiming special powers should be punished to remove his deceit. But because they also believe that such phenomena are possible, they never know which claims are fraudulent. If the shaman or saint owner when brought to the town hall fails to demonstrate his abilities, he may retain his reputation for supernatural power by claiming that the real saint is hidden in the hills.

Most cases of fraud in Zinacantan involve talking saints, simply because of their number (see Chapter 5). Hearings in such cases are usually more complex than the original complaint would seem to warrant because of the political implications. And although a few cases brought by dissatisfied patients are dismissed when the saint's owner returns the money, most of the cases attract far more attention. Within a hamlet, saints have a following of believers and a group of doubters. If other issues reinforce this ideological split, a talking-saint case may well turn into a political crisis. And even more prominence is gained by the fact that the Mexican authorities are concerned to stamp out the phenomenon. Talking saints played major roles in both the Tzeltal and the Tzotzil rebellions, and the Mexicans may see saint owners as political agitators. San Cristobal authorities have put pressure on Indian Presidentes to confiscate saints and deliver the owners to them for punishment. Saint owners who come up before the Ministerio Publico and the Juez Penal are charged with fraud and fined. This policy of heavy punishment for talking-saint owners has had some effect: informants agree that there are probably fewer saints in Zinacantan today than there were fifty years ago and that the remaining saints are treated with less respect. Whereas saint owners used to hold large fiestas with fireworks, they now avoid public display.

Case 36. A man who paid a high fee to a talking-saint owner complained when its powers were unsuccessful. (The informant was the Presidente who settled the case.)

Nicolas asked the Presidente to call in a woman who owned a talking saint, whom he had gone to when his wife and child became ill. He had paid her two hundred pesos and she had assured him that both patients would recover, but they had died and Nicolas wanted his money returned. The Presidente sent for the woman and her saint, which turned out to be a box containing stones. When the saint did not talk, the Presidente put the woman in jail until she agreed to return Nicolas's money. Then he sent her to the Ministerio Publico in San Cristobal, where she was jailed for a day and a night and paid a fine of 400 pesos. When she returned home, she set up business with another talking saint. But she now has fewer customers.

Damage to Person

When injury is caused by a nonrelative, the hearing of the dispute is concerned simply with guilt and compensation, not future protection. The injured person must put a price on his injuries and offer enough proof of the incident to make the accused admit his guilt, whether the plaintiff has suffered direct physical aggression, feels himself the victim of witchcraft, or fears loss of money through false accusation. The defendant avoids payment by refusing to admit guilt or by showing that the plaintiff was equally at fault. The principles applying to such situations are straightforward and readily recognized: when a person admits damaging another, he must pay, unless the victim is guilty of provoking the attack.

Whether the guilty person has shown *manya* and should be jailed is a secondary issue. Witchcraft, making false accusations when sober, and unprovoked physical aggression are proof of evil tendencies, whereas drunken actions or clearly provoked aggression are usually excused.

Damage to Property

When property is damaged, whether intentionally or accidentally, Zinacantecos believe the owner should be compensated. If the damage is accidental—perhaps caused by an untended animal—the guilty person pays only for the actual loss, but if the damage is intentional, he is punished to remove his *manya*. There are three types of intentional property damage. The first is theft, a

clearly deliberate act, of which there are few recorded cases, because a thief is hard to catch. Drunken destructiveness is a second type, often occurring as part of a personal-injury case, since Zinacantecos rarely take out their aggressions solely on objects. The third type includes deliberate destruction, such as setting fire to an enemy's house. The only cases of arson I know of occurred during political fights and were taken to the Mexican authorities.

When an animal causes damage, the owner is asked to pay. If both sides agree on appropriate payment, the incident ends. But if unreasonable compensation is demanded or if the owner of the animal refuses to pay, the case may go to the town hall. When such a case is heard, the Presidente has a Juez estimate the damage and then tries to effect a compromise. But many cases of damage caused by animals are complicated by individual reprisals. The field owner may beat or kill an animal discovered eating his crops, while the owner of the animal may fight to rescue his property (see Case 2 in Chapter 6).

Case 37. The owner of a mule finds the animal dead in a field. (The informant was the Presidente who settled the case.)

One morning Antonio found his mule dead in a field of flowers (grown as a cash crop) belonging to Juan. Because the animal had a wound in its side, Antonio assumed that Juan had found it eating the flowers and shot it. But at the town hall he told the Presidente he had seen Juan shoot the mule. When Juan was summoned, he denied the charge, saying that he had not been near his field in several days and did not own a gun. The President did not believe him and told him that he should have asked Antonio to pay for the damaged flowers instead of taking matters into his own hands. The Presidente then jailed Juan to persuade him to admit his guilt.

Upon investigation, the Juez and several Mayores who cut up the mule could find no trace of a bullet in the animal or evidence of any flowers being eaten.

When the Presidente heard the report, he summoned Antonio back to the town hall and asked him if he had really seen Juan shoot the mule. Antonio then admitted that he had been lying. The Presidente scolded him and told him that now they would have a very hard time proving Juan guilty. If there were no witnesses, he could not be sent to San Cristobal because the Mexican authorities would merely let him go. The Presidente did what he could for Antonio. He kept Juan in jail for three days and questioned him every day, but since Juan always denied having killed the mule the Presidente finally had to let him go. Juan never

paid for the mule, and Antonio never paid for the flowers his dead mule had crushed.

While theft is not uncommon in Zinacantan, few cases lead to hearings unless the victim can identify the thief. If there are no immediate clues, he gives up and asks the saints for vengeance. The few cases that are heard involve a thief caught red-handed. Cases of theft are always heard at the town hall, since the guilty person not only must return the stolen property but must be punished to remove his manya so he will not steal again.

Unless a thief is caught in the act or with the stolen property in his possession, the hearing consists of attempts to persuade the accused to admit his guilt. The victim tells why he believes the accused is guilty and tries to produce witnesses to testify to the truth of his statements. But if the evidence is not conclusive and the accused steadfastly denies guilt the Presidente can only jail him for seventy-two hours.

If a thief is clearly guilty and admits guilt, he assumes the obligation to return the stolen property or pay for it and to repair any damage caused. A thief who entered a house by breaking through the roof later had to repair the thatch. A case of theft may become more complex, however, if victims of similar robberies come to complain. Once a person has admitted guilt in a robbery, he is presumed guilty of others, and the Presidente uses the threat of prosecution on the proved charge to persuade him to pay the other claims. After all the claims are settled, the Presidente decides how many weeks of hard labor to give the thief as punishment.

If a Zinacanteco drunkenly destroys another's property, the owner may ask for compensation, but the case is not taken to the town hall unless it is a side issue in a more important case involving a threat of aggression.

Long-Term Fights Between Neighbors

Most Zinacanteco houses are separated by cornfields, but in the more densely populated hamlets many houses have only a fence between them. If such neighbors begin to quarrel, mere proximity provides countless issues for dispute. Neighbors may argue over boundaries, over animals—especially chickens that go through

fences—and over trees that shade the neighbor's corn. Petty quarrels go on for years, and hearings that attempt to settle major issues only inflame the hard feelings.

Most land is inherited, but a person planning to buy land considers his future neighbors carefully. If they oppose the sale, the buyer may have difficulty getting along with them. Finding a buyer for confiscated land, accordingly, is always a problem. Although the Presidente may threaten to sell a debtor's land, it may be difficult to find a buyer.

Fights Between Political Factions

Political battles are hard to identify unless one is familiar with the background of the case. Although a charge of embezzling public funds is a traditional political ploy, almost any case assumes added significance when political opponents take sides. In one political fight I observed, the conservative shamans of Apas were opposing a Spanish-speaking man for leadership of the hamlet. Although the real issue was control of hamlet-wide ceremonies, the case ostensibly concerned a brief fight between two men and ended up treated as a case of debt. But the Presidente recognized the true issues and terminated the hearing by advising both sides to discuss their differences at a hamlet meeting scheduled for the following Sunday.

In another political battle of community-wide significance, a case of horse stealing was used to justify the removal of the Presidente.

Case 38. The Presidente is placed in an impossible situation as part of a political crisis. (This version of the case is that of the ousted Presidente.)

When two brothers with reputations as troublemakers were locked in jail at the town hall after a knife fight, several Chamulas arrived to accuse them of having murdered a Chamula eight years before. The Presidente told the Chamulas that he could not draw up the papers needed to send the brothers to San Cristobal until witnesses were found to sign the required *diligencia*.

The following day a man named Lucas arrived to enter a complaint that the two brothers had stolen his mule a year before. His witness, however, was a Ladino who refused to make a statement. The Presidente then told Lucas that it would be senseless to send the brothers to

San Cristobal without evidence—they would be immediately released—but that something might be gained by threatening to invoke the Mexican penal authorities. The brothers were brought before the Presidente and frightened with visions of large fines and lawyer's fees until they agreed to pay half the price of the mule. At this Lucas claimed that their willingness to pay was proof of guilt and demanded the entire cost of the mule. The Presidente ordered the brothers back to jail and again explained the issues to Lucas. At a later hearing, Lucas finally accepted the beers presented by the two brothers and agreed to their request for a two-month delay in paying half the cost of the mule. The two brothers were released, but Lucas then complained to the political boss of Zinacantan because he was not content with the solution. The boss ordered his own men to jail the brothers. The following day he instructed the Presidente to send them to San Cristobal, where they were promptly released for lack of official charges.

The Presidente's version stops at this point, but the rumor spread throughout the ceremonial center that he had kept the other half of the mule's price as a bribe to free the brothers—"murderers and thieves." The following Sunday a large group of men assembled in the cemetery above the ceremonial center to march down with the political boss to remove the Presidente from office. Again, according to rumor, the Presidente was rescued just in time from the clutches of a lynch mob by Mexican officials from the National Indian Institute who had been summoned by the Presidente's supporters.

The Effect of Mexican Law on Disputes Between Neighbors

Although the Mexican authorities recognize as punishable offenses most of the wrongs brought to the town hall court by Zinacanteco nonrelatives, few plaintiffs take their cases to San Cristobal because they prefer restitution and reconciliation to revenge and continuing hostility. But the availability of Mexican penal procedures has had an indirect effect on Zinacanteco handling of disputes between neighbors. Presidentes and plaintiffs now argue from a stronger position, since a defendant refusing to admit guilt can be threatened with San Cristobal.

Defendants in cases of debt, however, can profitably appeal to San Cristobal because the Mexican authorities do not always concede the validity of a plaintiff's claim. Few loans are recorded in writing, and Zinacanteco interest rates are often far above the legal ceiling. As a result, a debtor who is being charged exorbitant interest, and who does not anticipate needing another loan in the

near future, may ask the Director of the State Department of Indian Affairs for a letter to the Presidente stating the legal interest rates. Armed with this weapon, he then confronts his creditor and an agreement is worked out. There is little chance, however, that such tactics will force other creditors to set lower interest rates, because money is scarce and even Ladino moneylenders have been reported to charge up to 10 percent a month interest.

The effect of Mexican law on talking-saint cases has already been discussed. For what appear to be political reasons, the Mexican authorities have put pressure on Indian Presidentes to send saint owners to the penal authorities for punishment. Although there are no specific laws against owning miraculous images, the officials charge the saint owners with defrauding their neighbors and impose large fines. This policy has been partially successful, because saint owners now shun public display. But there are still a great many talking saints in Zinacantan; almost every hamlet has at least one, and several have more. Saint owners are also very hard to put out of business. When called before the authorities, if their saint does not talk, they pay their fines and return home to retrieve the "real saint" from its hiding place in the hills.

In cases of damage to person or property, the Presidente's hand has been strengthened, for he can invoke the Mexican authorities to force both plaintiff and defendant to accept a compromise. The defendant is persuaded to admit guilt by the threat of a long jail sentence and the plaintiff is urged to moderate his demands by the threat of losing all compensation. But if the plaintiff has little evidence and the defendant refuses to admit guilt, the case may end without a settlement. The Presidente may keep the defendant in jail for seventy-two hours to persuade him to confess, but if that produces no results the case is dismissed (see Case 37).

Fights between political factions often go to the Mexican authorities because the aim of the ostensible plaintiff is to inflict serious financial loss on his enemy. In these cases the plaintiff charges his opponent with a criminal offense, backed by witnesses loyal to his side, and then leaves the defendant to extricate himself from the web of Mexican justice. When political-faction fights come to the town hall court in Zinacantan, however, the Presidente avoids in-

flicting one-sided punishments if he wishes to stay out of the battle. As a result, hamlet faction fights that reach the ceremonial center usually end with partial settlements reflecting the prevailing power balance rather than the original charge.

Conclusion

This chapter ends the discussion of private disputes between individuals; the next chapter discusses the charges brought by community leaders and officials against individuals said to have brought harm to an entire hamlet or to have shirked public duty. A dispute between two individuals may be resolved by a compromise that ends the anger in the plaintiff's heart without leaving the defendant feeling wronged, but a case between the individual and the community may end only with the individual's submission, his flight, or his attempt to set up a rival political faction.

Most cases brought to the town hall by nonkinsmen involve accusations of specific wrongs in which the plaintiff hopes to recover compensation or to see an opponent jailed. Such plaintiffs rarely appeal to hamlet procedures, since they have no need to preserve enduring ties and want to recover as much money as possible from the defendant. Disputes between nonrelatives also tend to focus on a single issue and seldom mask a deeper conflict. As a result, such cases tend to be straightforward and are usually settled in terms of the original complaint. But political-faction fights and long-term disputes between neighbors, although superficially resembling single-instance disputes, are actually enduring struggles for power or advantage in which each new accusation marks only one episode.

TWELVE

Disputes Between Individual and Community

This chapter discusses the cases in which those who claim to represent a particular collectivity accuse an individual of wronging the group. The cases range from straightforward accusations lodged by recognized hamlet and township leaders against persons who have clearly shirked or outraged public obligation to the fighting within or among political factions in which, for example, a rising leader accuses an appointed official or an established elder of misusing his authority. The unifying theme in all these cases is that they are treated not as private quarrels between individuals but as wrongs against a larger group. Most of these cases also have political overtones. Persons who insult the Presidente or who refuse to pay taxes are challenging the authority of an established leader, and every time a leader takes action against an individual in the name of his group he is reaffirming his right to speak for others.

Most accusations made by community leaders against an individual fall into one of five categories: (1) failing to pay taxes or shirking a duty to contribute labor to community projects, (2) damaging or threatening community property, (3) insulting authority, (4) performing badly in public office, and (5) threatening the lives of community members by certain actions, usually witchcraft. In all of these cases, the political leaders claim that it is the group they represent that has been wronged and not themselves as individuals.

This chapter considers the kinds of cases handled in the hamlet

and then those taken by hamlet leaders to the town hall. Following that is a section on offenses handled at the town hall said to be against the township as a whole. Finally, we take a brief look into the complexities of political battles fought in the Mexican courts.

Wrongs Against the Community Handled in the Hamlet

Hamlets vary in organization: some are nucleated and hold one *k*in krus*, or waterhole ceremony, for the whole community; others are dispersed and hold only the year renewal ceremonies on a hamlet-wide basis, leaving *k*in krus* ceremonies to the individual family and waterhole groups. A community ceremony requires money to buy fireworks and candles, and the needed amount is raised by charging each head of household a small sum. Records are kept by the people who collect the money, and the names of those who fail to pay are noted for future action. Hamlet members also maintain the community's trails. Every year in November after All Saints' Day, the men gather to clear and repair the paths damaged during the rainy season. Those failing to show up are fined.

A list of those failing to pay fiesta taxes or contribute to road work is shown to the assembled elders at meetings. Principales fetch delinquents who do not show up, and a public rebuke by the assembled elders is usually enough to persuade a person to pay.

Case 39. A man who had not paid his fiesta taxes was called before the hamlet elders. (This case was related by the scribe.)

Most of the people from the hamlet were gathered to celebrate the New Year ceremony at the house of the mayordomo of the fiesta. The hamlet elders and shamans conducting the ritual were seated at a long table. The scribe, whose duty it was to keep the records, said that a man named Miguel had not paid his share of the present fiesta or of the two previous ones because he was always in the lowlands when the tax collector called. Miguel was sent for, and when the scribe informed him that he owed a total of seventeen pesos for the three fiestas, he insisted that he only owed eleven pesos because he had paid for one. After considerable argument, the scribe turned the matter over to the elders. The senior elder then asked Miguel to pay the amount on the books, and when Miguel continued to insist that he had paid for one fiesta, the elder asked him if he were a woman or a boy to shirk the obligations of an adult man. Miguel was deeply shamed at being reprimanded in front of everyone, and he agreed to pay; he borrowed the money from a relative and gave it immediately to the scribe.

The minor officials of a hamlet—Principales and school committee members—are appointed by the elders at community meetings.
Since their job performance affects only a single hamlet, the assembled elders may discipline or remove these officials without
appealing to the town hall. But school committee members may
pose special disciplinary problems because of their ties to the Mexican education authorities, and the elders must sometimes find a
way around the regulations. An overly aggressive Presidente of a
hamlet school committee who could not be replaced because his
name was on the Mexican records had his duties taken away from
him and given to the other members until a new election could be
held.

Politically unified hamlets or sections of hamlets may take steps
to get rid of talking saints. A group of neighbors may appeal to the
town hall to have a saint put out of business, or the hamlet elders,
if powerful enough and sufficiently united, may proceed against a
saint owner who lives within their territory.

Case 40. Hamlet elders force a woman to get rid of a talking saint.
(The informant was a member of the hamlet.)

Maria, having moved from another hamlet, was summoned by the
assembled elders to the schoolhouse for questioning about her talking
saint. She claimed the saint helped cure sick people by telling them the
cause of their disease, but refused to bring it to the school for them to
hear. When a Principal was sent to search her house, he could not find
it, said my informant, since Maria had hidden it. Maria insisted that she
had only the saints that were in the house—some saints' pictures and a
large cross—which the Principal took back with him.

In response to questioning, she said that the saints' pictures only
talked when a sick person asked a question, but when one of the elders
asked when he would die, Maria replied that the saint could not answer
with so many people present. They therefore concluded that she had
hidden the real saint in the hills, so they sent her to Tuxtla accompanied
by several men, to ask a diviner about the validity of her saint.

The diviner had the reputation of being able to close her eyes and
send her soul out to investigate. When the diviner returned from her
soul voyage, she said that Maria's saint was a bad thing. Upon this, the
elders gave Maria the choice of returning her saint to the Earth where
she had found it or of leaving the hamlet. Maria and her husband
wanted to stay, so they agreed to get rid of the saint and pay for all the
bus fares to the diviner. Maria still lives in the hamlet and is a practicing shaman, but she no longer has a saint.

Witchcraft cases in which a witch is discovered in the act but the victim is unknown are usually handled first on the hamlet level, as discussed in Chapter 6. An elder or a group of elders conducts an investigation to find out if the act was indeed witchcraft and to identify the victim. If a victim can be found, the case becomes his affair; otherwise, to protect the community the elders may ask the supposed witch to pray again before witnesses, retracting any witchcraft he might have performed (see Case 4, p. 134).

Wrongs Against the Community Taken to the Town Hall

When a hamlet investigation uncovers proof of a witchcraft ceremony that might bring sickness to many people, the case is taken to the town hall to ensure that the witch retracts properly and is punished. Although most witchcraft affects one victim or one family, the ceremonies of asking for treasure from the Earth or selling a soul to a foreign witch may cause epidemics. In such cases the hamlet leaders act as representatives of their communities and cooperate with the Presidente in seeing that the witch performs adequate retraction ceremonies and is punished to remove his *manya* (see Case 8, p. 142).

Every hamlet has public land used for roads and shrines. Minor infractions occurring when a man moves his fence a few feet to incorporate public land may be handled in the hamlet, but when a man boldly seizes a large piece of property, the hamlet elders take the case to the town hall. In one case a man who sold a piece of land set aside for school use to an unsuspecting buyer was made to forfeit a piece of his own land of equal size to the hamlet when the elders appealed to the town hall. This is the one recorded case of a person's land being confiscated on the Presidente's orders; it was done only after the offender had repeatedly failed to appear at the town hall when summoned, and the land was appropriated for school use, not given or sold to a private individual. In another case that was clearly a political battle, a leader accused his rival of fencing and planting the major ceremonial mountain belonging to the hamlet. The case went to the town hall and then to the Mexican authorities, and ended only when the rival leader conceded defeat by moving to another hamlet with his supporters.

When a person openly defies the authority of the assembled

elders by refusing to follow their orders, the elders usually take the case to the town hall. One man not only refused to do his share of road work but insulted the assembled elders when they fined him. He was jailed at the town hall for three days and given a week of hard labor at the request of the elders.

Although the assembled elders may remove a Principal from office or take away the duties of a school committee member, the Navenchauk elders were forced to get the Presidente's approval in order to remove an *Agente Municipal* because he was a township official. The Agente was accused of demanding large fines from hamlet wrongdoers, of pocketing the money left over from community projects, and of stealing food provided by the government for the men building a new school. The hamlet elders met at the house of the senior Juez, who was also from Navenchauk, and together they decided to remove the Agente; then they asked another man to fill the position. When their business was completed, they invited the Presidente to Navenchauk. At a mass meeting, the Agente was officially removed and the new man appointed according to plan. The former Agente was not jailed but was asked to return the 800 pesos that the elders said he had taken from the community. The Agente agreed to this and no one opposed the compromise solution. The new Agente took over immediately and used the money received from the former Agente for community projects that already had the approval of the elders.

Wrongs Against the Township Handled at the Town Hall

When the Presidente feels that his authority has suffered indignities from the actions of a litigant, he may send the man to jail to teach him respect. A man who was called to the town hall for failing to pay municipal taxes not only resisted the Mayores but made insulting remarks about the Presidente. When he was finally brought in by the federal policemen who were helping to maintain order during the fiesta of San Lorenzo, the Presidente had him jailed. The man protested, saying he would pay his taxes immediately, but he was held overnight to teach him respect.

The offense of failing to pay municipal taxes can be quite complicated because there are two kinds of taxes in the community: one, regarded as legitimate by the Mexican authorities, supports

the recognized civil government, and the other, used for religious fiestas, is legally a voluntary contribution because Mexican law recognizes the separation of Church and State. Zinacantecos, however, consider both taxes obligatory and believe that people should be jailed for not supporting major fiestas just as they are for not paying municipal taxes. Although an appeal may be made to the Director of the State Department of Indian Affairs for exemption from religious taxes—and it has been done—only a person who wishes to challenge the established political and religious leaders would take such action. As discussed in the Introduction, political cohesion in Zinacantan is symbolized by cooperation in staging a ritual, and refusing to contribute to a hamlet or township ceremony is a direct challenge to the political leadership of the elders and shamans who sponsor it.

A person damaging or destroying township property is expected to replace it. A young man attempting to escape from jail made a large hole in the wall, which he was made to repair by the threat of being sent to the Mexican authorities. He had to buy bags of cement, haul sand and rocks, and pay the wages of a mason, as well as pay a fine of 50 pesos for trying to escape. In a more complex and interesting case, two Principales from a hamlet were made to replace the tax money that had been stolen from the third, who had been murdered. The money had been collected in the hamlet to pay for the fiesta of San Lorenzo, and the three Principales were charged with delivering the money safely to the Presidente. But the three separated, and the one with the money was later found murdered. At a meeting of the civil officials and the members of the fiesta committee, it was decided that the remaining two Principales should replace the loss from their own pockets, since they had left the senior Principal alone with the money.

Formerly, when the top religious officials appointed men to fill the positions in the religious hierarchy, the Presidente would cooperate with them by threatening to jail those who refused to accept. But today, although he sits with the elders when they appoint people to the few positions not filled by requests, the Presidente is reluctant to jail people, since their relatives can easily appeal to the Mexican authorities to obtain a release. Failing to accept a religious position, like failing to pay fiesta taxes, is not a

crime in Mexican law. Although Zinacantecos still feel that it is
¢o¢ mulil, a serious crime, to refuse a religious position that one
is financially able to take, the punishment is now left to the gods.
Between the threats implicit in the stories of violent deaths inflicted by the angry gods and the inducements offered by the elders to make religious offices attractive, most appointees accept the
offered positions.

There are also cases of men refusing to accept low positions in
the civil government. The job of Mayor is particularly unpleasant
and many men would like to refuse it. In the past, those who refused would be jailed, but now they also can appeal to the Mexican authorities. The archives of recent years contain an increasing
number of letters from the Director of the State Department of
Indian Affairs to the Presidente asking that a person be excused
from serving as Mayor. So far, there have been a sufficient number
of young troublemakers willing to spend a year in the ceremonial
center, but it is not clear what will happen to the civil government
if such young men find other occupations.

Political Battles Phrased as Accusations Against High Officials

To accuse a high official of misusing community funds is to
attack the very basis of his legitimacy. Political support is traditionally expressed by contributing money to a cause, and men's
faith in their leaders is affirmed when they allow those leaders to
take charge of the collected funds. There are a great many small
causes in Zinacantan in which groups of individuals with a specific
project contribute money to stage a ritual or to send their leader
to Tuxtla or Mexico City to talk with Mexican officials, but the
major political turmoils that split the entire township are fought
over community-wide contributions. Zinacanteco informants claim
that the factional split of the early 1960's dates back to a fight in
the 1940's when the two political bosses in the community were
accused by a rival faction of appropriating public funds. Zinacanteco officials had just received word that all young men were to
be drafted into military service. The bosses responded to this threat
by collecting money from the whole community for three large
ceremonies to ask the gods to keep the recruiters out of Zinacantan. After the ceremonies, a group of men from the western end

of the community accused the political bosses of keeping the money that was left over. They took their complaint to the Mexican authorities, and soldiers came to search the house of the *ejido* committee treasurer. They apparently found a large sum of money, which they confiscated. The two bosses, knowing they would be jailed if they went to San Cristobal, made their supporters swear that the money had been collected for whitewashing the church rather than for ceremonies to avoid military service. Eventually the two bosses were jailed by the Mexican authorities and paid large fines and lawyers' fees. Factional fights continued to plague the community for the next twenty years, and the record of political crises can be traced in the archives through letters between the Mexican authorities and the town hall in Zinacantan.

There are two recorded cases in which a high civil official was removed from office. The first case is of a Ladinoized Indian, an acting municipal secretary, who was accused of charging exorbitant fees to make out civil records, and the second case, discussed in Chapter 11, is of a Presidente accused of accepting a bribe to let dangerous criminals go free (Case 38, p. 227). Each case was complicated by several minor accusations, and the Mexican authorities, hoping to understand the issues, called mass meetings in the ceremonial center. In both cases the Mexicans removed the official, not because they believed the accusations were true, but because they felt the official lacked the needed political support to remain in office.

Political battles are also waged by making criminal accusations against prominent, but unofficial, leaders before the Mexican authorities. These accusations, however, are usually phrased in terms of wrongs against specific individuals rather than as offenses against an entire group. For example, a political leader as an individual may hire a Ladino lawyer to accuse an enemy of breaking into his house or murdering a kinsman. The "witnesses" to the crime are, of course, faction allies, but they act as private individuals and make no claim to be representing a group. All the Zinacantecos involved, and often the Mexican officials as well, recognize that political power is the real issue at stake, but they all follow the Mexican procedures for handling criminal accusations. Both Zinacanteco factions hire lawyers, and the resulting web of

accusations and counteraccusations often becomes hopelessly tangled. In the most famous of these "murder" cases, the political boss was accused of murdering several people and dumping their bodies down a limestone cave in a hamlet. The Mexican officials had the cave searched and did find several human skeletons. Then the political boss's supporters produced "witnesses" who claimed to have seen the rival political leader dumping the bones in the cave one night. According to the Zinacanteco informant who told me one version of the case, the Mexican officials finally gave up their search for the "truth" and tried to promote a reconciliation between the two faction leaders. Since they were both in jail, the officials had them brought in to shake hands and drink together, and then gave them a lecture on the importance of harmony in the community. But by that time the political balance in Zinacantan had decisively shifted and the old boss never regained his former power.

Mexican Law and Accusations of Community
Leaders Against Individuals

Although the Mexican separation of Church and State theoretically makes it illegal for the Presidente to jail persons who fail to pay fiesta taxes or who refuse to accept a religious office, the increasing ease of appealing to the Director of the State Department of Indian Affairs has had little effect on Zinacantecos' willingness to perform traditional duties. Even though they know they will not be jailed for refusing to pay fiesta taxes, most persons are willing to contribute because they want to affirm their right to use a waterhole or to obtain the protection of the gods. Only those who wish to challenge the political authority of established leaders may try to avoid contributing to a fiesta. There is also little problem in persuading people to accept religious offices. There are long waiting lists for all but the least prestigious ones, and reluctant persons can usually be talked into serving without using the threat of jail.

The increasing awareness of Mexican regulations, however, has made it harder for Zinacanteco political leaders to remove undesirable officials who hold recognized positions. Although hamlet elders can discipline school officials, they cannot remove them from

office without becoming involved in Mexican red tape. Higher officials are even harder to challenge, since they have more power as
well as more stake in retaining the office. The removal of the Navenchauc Agente was effected by compromise and without Mexican interference, but the removal of the municipal secretary and
the Presidente had to be approved by Mexican officials and led to
controversial settlements. There was no need to prove the Agente
guilty of having appropriated community funds as long as he
agreed to pay 800 pesos into the hamlet treasury. In contrast, the
settlements arranged by the Mexican officials with reference to the
removal of the secretary and the Presidente left both sides feeling
bitter. Given the demands of Mexican law, the officials could not
ignore the "facts" in the cases of the secretary and Presidente to
seek a compromise. They needed proof of guilt and, failing that,
were forced to fall back on political expediency. As a result, the
removed officials' supporters felt that an injustice had been done,
and the opponents were angry that the officials had been allowed
to keep their illegally obtained money.

The growing awareness of Mexican law has had a pronounced
effect on Zinacanteco political battles, which during the time of
intense factionalism in the early 1960's were primarily waged by
lodging criminal accusations with the San Cristobal penal authorities. Zinacantecos found that opponents who were lodged in jail
were effectively removed from the political arena, at least temporarily, and political factions were able to provide an impressive
array of "witnesses" as well as the cash resources to hire lawyers
for the long battle.

Conclusion

This chapter has considered the kinds of accusations leveled by
community leaders against an individual and has examined the
handling of these cases on the hamlet level, at the town hall, and
by the Mexican authorities. All of the accusations have implied
that an individual has certain obligations toward his community—
toward his hamlet and toward the township as a whole. When a
person is accused of not contributing money to a hamlet ritual,
for example, the implicit assumption is that he has a duty to pay
his share and can be punished if he fails to comply. But the situ-

ation is not so simple, for the norms of community obligation are the language of political dispute. The person who fulfills his community obligations implies acceptance of the political situation, but the person who refuses to pay taxes shows defiance of the existing leaders. This chapter, then, has tried to show that the prosecution of individuals who have wronged the community depends on the pragmatic demands of political expediency. The lone man in Case 39 who was brought before the hamlet elders and shamed into paying his fiesta contributions could be prosecuted easily by the united elders, but in that same hamlet the members of one important patrilineage who not only had refused to help build the hamlet church but had not paid for any of its later ceremonies were not prosecuted. They were simply left alone in the hope that they would eventually return to the political fold.

The accusations leveled by leaders against individuals imply that Zinacantecos should (1) contribute labor to waterhole group, hamlet, and township work projects, (2) help pay for waterhole, hamlet, and township ceremonies, (3) pay taxes to the municipal government, and (4) take civil and religious offices when asked by the elders and if financially able to bear the burden of service. The accusations also imply that individuals should (1) not damage public property or try to treat it as their own, (2) refrain from insulting the existing authorities, both township officials and hamlet elders, (3) refrain from using public office for private gain, (4) avoid being either too lazy or too aggressive in performing official duties, and (5) refrain from endangering the lives of others by asking the Earth Lord for treasure or by hiring a foreign witch who would send an epidemic into Zinacantan.

Most of the cases concerned accusations made by established political leaders against persons who had committed some wrong against the group they represented, but there were a few cases in which rising political leaders accused established ones of misusing their authority or of appropriating community property. When established leaders disciplined a lone individual he usually had little choice but to submit or leave the community, but when both sides represented political factions the outcomes were far more complex. The accusations in the two types of situation could be the same but the outcomes tended to be very different.

The last five chapters have considered the kinds of cases brought by individuals in different types of relationships, beginning with disputes between kinsmen, which are usually phrased in terms of quarrels over land. The record of cases has been examined to find what Zinacantecos fight about, but the emphasis is on discovering the options available to individuals involved in a dispute. Kinsmen say they are fighting over land, wives usually claim that their husbands have beaten them, bride-price payments lie at the heart of courtship disputes, quarreling neighbors usually want money, and the accusations leveled by leaders against individuals or vice versa often have political overtones. These chapters have tried to show that Zinacanteco conflicts are two-sided affairs and not simple sequences where a person is punished for breaking a recognized law. Settlements reflect the defendant's motives for "committing the crime" as well as the plaintiff's reasons for appealing to a remedy agent.

Conclusion

My task in this last chapter is to place the rest of the book in perspective, to examine the questions implicit in the "facts" about Zinacanteco law. Any descriptive study like this one must follow a conceptual scheme that dictates which facts are to be stressed and which are to be ignored. Such a scheme has been implicit throughout the book; it is now time to set it out and examine it, to ask where it springs from and what insights it has provided. The chapter begins with a brief statement of the book's conceptual framework, then relates this framework to the questions asked by other anthropologists who have focused on legal systems. Finally, the Zinacanteco materials are reexamined, chapter by chapter, and the more important ideas identified. I shall hope, by the end, to have convinced the reader that the purpose of the book was not to describe the quaint customs and beliefs of an isolated, outlandishly dressed people, but rather, by laying bare the workings of a legal system, to allow Zinacanteco processes of conflict management to illuminate such processes everywhere.

The Conceptual Framework

"The classical task of legal anthropology has been to understand the relationship between law and society" (Moore 1970: 294). This study follows that tradition, but the nature of the understanding that is sought depends on how "law" and "society" are defined. In this study, I have defined law in Barkun's terms as a language for conducting and resolving conflicts (1968); and I have treated soci-

ety as a set of fields of social relations (Firth 1956). These definitions have led to the two primary emphases in the book: law is seen
as a more or less coherent language shaped by past usage and
affecting the future only as it is invoked by living persons; and
Zinacantan is but a small social field, embedded within a wider
system, allowing litigants to choose from a variety of possible legal
procedures.

In this view, "law" as a language comes to affect observable regularities in individual behavior through claims advanced by litigants
for reasons of self-interest. The role of legal concepts during periods of relative stability and in times of rapid change can be understood by looking at how potential litigants choose among their
various options. This study, therefore, has focused on defining the
range of options open to litigants and on analyzing the constraints
and incentives that channel the choices they make. The legal language through which claims must be advanced and decisions justified constrains both the types of claims and the range of possible
outcomes, while an individual's location, in terms of social fields,
structures the information available to him as he makes his choice
of legal procedure and affects his view of the desirability of various
outcomes. But instead of trying to understand the processes of *individual* decision-making, I have focused on broad patterns of
social action and tried to account for these in terms of factors that
structure the choices of many individuals. I have described the
relationship between law and society as a complex feedback process whereby types of claims influence legal procedures, which influence outcomes, which in turn influence the pattern of future
claims.

These ideas account for the three-part structure of the book. The
first part, Chapters 1–3, describes the "fields of social relations"
and their associated legal procedures. The idea is that such fields
are determined by historical and economic variables that structure
patterns of communication. The second part, Chapters 4–7, describes Zinacanteco legal language: the set of assumptions about
the nature of social order through which claims and decisions must
be justified. The first two chapters in this part describe the very
abstract assumptions used to justify legal procedures, and the last
two concentrate on the meanings attributed to particular aggres-

sive acts. The third part of the book explores the relationship between language and social structure by using the record of cases to see what claims are actually being made by litigants and to show how changing patterns of claims have been affected by and are affecting changes in Zinacanteco social life.

Other Studies in Legal Anthropology

The main elements of the conceptual framework used in this book derive from past studies of legal systems and political processes. The emphasis on law as a language comes from studies of judicial decision-making, whereas studies of the role of conflict in political processes have shown the importance of exploring the motives of individuals. This section attempts to place this study in the context of other studies in legal anthropology by briefly tracing the development of the two central themes that provide the conceptual backbone of the book.

Legal anthropology has always been concerned with the relationship between rules and social order—or between "law" and "society." But over time the focus has shifted from society viewed as an active force maintaining social order by punishing individuals who violate crucial rules (Hoebel 1954), to the individual seen as an actor using legal concepts to perceive and maintain order in his social world (Moore 1970). This shift in focus has come about as later anthropologists have sought answers to questions raised by earlier studies.

Llewellyn and Hoebel (1941) were the first to emphasize the advantages of basing an ethnographic account on a record of actual trouble cases. Almost every author since has followed their example, for cases contain a wealth of material and can be analyzed from a variety of angles to answer many kinds of questions. The earlier authors used cases primarily to discover the "laws" of a group. Law was commonly defined by anthropologists as a set of rules made obligatory through sanctions imposed on violators by men with recognized authority, and the ultimate aim of these studies was to relate laws to types of legal procedures and types of societies. The result was a series of studies focusing on the decisions made by men in authority (Pospisil 1958, Smith and Roberts 1954, Llewellyn and Hoebel 1941). The rationale for such a

focus was that actual decisions were the best available statement of the "laws" of a particular society, and the underlying assumption was that law served to maintain social order by defining the bounds of acceptable behavior and punishing those who stepped beyond them. Society was the main unit of analysis, and law was treated as a tool used by society to control individual behavior. But actual ethnographic studies of legal systems were always far richer than such a theoretical framework implies. Because every study contained records of cases, each author was forced to cope with instances of individual behavior. The result was a series of books that presented a dynamic view of the relation between law and society but had narrow concluding chapters. Llewellyn and Hoebel's *The Cheyenne Way* (1941), for example, shows a deep understanding of the complex interrelation between rules, politics, and social order in a rapidly changing group, but it ends with the unconvincing implication that it was the skill of the Cheyenne leaders in abstracting good rules from hard cases that maintained the integrity of the tribe during the tumultuous decades before the Cheyennes were confined to reservation life.

The idea that law was to be found in the decisions of men with authority led to a concern with how such decisions were made. If law affected social order through defining rules and providing sanctions against deviance, how did men in authority decide what the law was? This question led to a small number of excellent studies of judicial decision-making where there were courts (Gluckman 1955a, Bohannan 1957, Fallers 1969, Epstein 1954) and to studies of bargaining processes where there were no obvious courts or men with authority to pronounce decisions (Gulliver 1963). Out of these studies came the idea that law was a language—a set of rules or a set of ideas about the nature of social order—through which decisions had to be rationalized; and that there was another set of factors, to be located by studying social organization, that would account for the particular decisions chosen by judges from among the set of those that could be justified. But the second part of this idea emerged only gradually, for the earlier authors were primarily interested in the role of rules and abstract legal concepts. Gluckman, for example, was interested in the question of how "men of alleged impartiality sit on the evidence and through cross-examination assess it in terms of social rules" (1962: 442). Although he

ended his detailed study of Barotse judicial process with the statement that "the judges are able to come to a moral decision on the dispute and then select those statutes, precedents, etc., for attention which support this decision" (1955a: 362), he was clearly more interested in the role of statutes and precedents than in the way judges reached "moral decisions."

Bohannan also came to the conclusion that legal rules were primarily a language for talking about social order. His definition of law, for example, as "custom that has been restated in order to make it amenable to the activities of the legal institutions," (1965: 36) clearly implies that human behavior and the language for talking about behavior are very different things. With such a definition the unexamined assumption that behavioral acts directly violate legal rules and bring automatic sanctions down on the head of the offender has to give way to a much more complex view of the relation between "law" and "society," between "rules" and "social order."

Barkun (1968), in a primarily theoretical book, noted Bohannan's definition and took up the task of outlining the implications of viewing law as a language for describing behavior instead of as a set of obligatory rules for producing conformity. He set out to demolish the Austinian definition of law as the command of a sovereign, and in the process argued that law is made up of a shared set of action-guiding symbols that allows the members of a jural community to handle the conflicts arising between individuals.

Gulliver, working with an acephalous group where legal decisions were produced by bargaining, explored the political factors that influenced outcomes. In a book on the Arusha of Tanganyika (1963) he claimed that social norms played only a minor role in determining the outcomes of conflicts, that in fact decisions were usually based on the relative strength of the parties. But in a later article on another people, Gulliver (1969) rephrased his observations. He made the crucial distinction between decision-making and decision-rationalizing, and concluded with the idea—adopted here—that there is a set of "rules" through which decisions must be justified that limits the alternatives open to decision-makers, but that social factors must be explored to understand why particular decisions are chosen from among that set.

These studies were concerned primarily with how outcomes were

determined rather than with the claims advanced by litigants. This emphasis derived from the fact that "law" was considered to be embodied in the decisions that ended trouble cases. Although many studies treated records of actual disputes, and therefore had to deal with the motives of litigants, most authors never went beyond noting the fact that not all cases represented instances of legitimate grievance. But the question of litigant motives could not be avoided indefinitely because any serious attempt to understand how stated rules affect actual social relationships demands consideration of how trouble cases come to the attention of the authorities. Obviously, judges or other men in authority are able to make decisions only in the cases brought before them; it is equally true that individuals can indulge in highly "illegal" behavior if no one complains. Earlier studies based on the assumption that "law" affects social order by sanctioning deviants had focused on the actions of the judge, but studies of conflict and political process pointed out the importance of considering the motives of the offender and the plaintiff's reasons for invoking a legal procedure.

Many anthropological studies of conflict have stressed the existence of irresolvable tensions deriving from contradictory demands placed on individuals by social structure (Malinowski 1926, Turner 1957, Colson 1962, Gluckman 1965). These deep-seated conflicts lead to open quarrels, handled by recognized procedures, that provide relief for particular individuals but no lasting solutions. In fact, individual accommodations serve only to maintain and reaffirm the basic contradictions. These studies thus pointed up the complex relationship between legal decisions and social order: decisions may indeed reaffirm the basic tenets of social structure, but they also provide the basis for future "deviant" acts. Legal decisions in quarrels provoked by such irresolvable conflicts do not provide individuals with clear models to direct their future behavior, but leave them trapped in intolerable situations where relief can only be obtained by breaking some "law" that precipitates a crisis and a realignment of social relationships.

Studies of political processes that have focused on the competition between rival leaders (Turner 1957; Swartz, Turner, and Tuden 1966; Bailey 1969) have brought out the fact that legal cases are often used as the pretext for staging decisive confrontations.

By providing examples of leaders who consciously break a rule to precipitate a crisis or who invoke a legal procedure to defeat a political rival, these studies have shown that law is a flexible language used by persons for particular ends, and not just a set of rules universally applied by recognized authorities to control unambiguously deviant behavior. These studies have shown that the impact of "law" on "social order" is dependent on the intentional actions of motivated individuals.

Studies of political processes have also cast doubt on the desirability of assuming that persons playing judicial roles are necessarily and always impartial. Cultural norms may require impartiality, and theoretical formulations may be neater if persons in "umpire roles" are distinguished from political leaders—umpires work to preserve a political arena and are not in competition with umpires of other arenas, whereas leaders work to preserve their own teams in the face of competition from rival leaders (Bailey 1969: 135)—but such fine distinctions are not easily applied to observed events. Even Bailey admits that an umpire will behave like an embattled leader when the integrity of his arena is threatened, and that a leader will act like an impartial umpire when a dispute between his followers poses no threat to his position. This means that an umpire's impartiality in any given situation depends on the threat the particular case poses to the political structure that guarantees the umpire's privileged role.

And finally, studies of political competition have illustrated the difficulty of making fine distinctions between umpire roles on the basis of the sanctions at the umpire's command. Gluckman's (1962: 444) suggestion that the champion-at-law, intermediary, negotiator, mediator, conciliator, and arbitrator be distinguished by the ranges of social pressure they can apply may be useful in making broad cross-cultural comparisons, but such fine distinctions only obscure the dynamics of legal action within a political arena where the umpire's power in a particular case depends on the social status of the litigants and the nature of their quarrel.

Whereas earlier studies of conflict stressed the ultimately stabilizing effect of recurring quarrels (Gluckman 1955b, Turner 1957, Colson 1962), later studies began to emphasize the role of conflict in the process of change (Beals and Siegel 1966, Scheffler 1964).

The two views are not incompatible and are easily reconciled by realizing that both processes are at work in any social field. Recurring quarrels that develop from contradictory demands imposed by social structure usually lead to a reaffirmation of old values, whereas conflicts engendered by new or intensified pressures from the environment tend to produce cumulative, directional changes. But the stress on the role of conflict in promoting either stability or change has opened up new perspectives in the study of law. If "law" is to be seen as a language used in conflict management, then the role of law in promoting stability or change is to be understood by looking at how individuals use legal resources for conducting the conflicts that arise between them. It is no longer enough to realize that "law" is always out of phase with "society"; one must look at the interaction between them.

Several years ago Firth (1954) stated that the process of social change was best studied by looking at the options open to individuals, and Barth (1967) elaborated this theme by observing that cumulative, directional changes occurred when environmental pressures consistently made an originally unpopular option more desirable. Studies of legal systems have long stated that societies may have several legal levels (Durkheim 1933, Pospisil 1958, Nader and Metzger 1963), but such levels were usually discussed in terms of the authority wielded by leaders. These studies tried to explain why most cases of a certain type or between certain classes of individuals went to a particular level (Gulliver 1963) and tended to ignore the occasional cases that failed to fit established patterns. But with the growing interest in the role of law in the process of social change, legal levels are now being seen as alternative options available to litigants (Tanner 1970). By studying the constraints and incentives that channel a litigant's choice of legal procedure, it becomes possible to chart the interaction between legal change and social change in terms of patterns of court usage.

In conclusion, it is worth noting that most of these theoretical questions are raised by Moore in the final section of her excellent summary of legal anthropology (1970). In predicting future developments in the field, she states that "more emphasis will be placed on the development of legal rules and procedural practices through *time*" (292) and that cases will be seen as "microcosms of dynamic

interaction" that illuminate "both short- and long-term processes of institutional continuity and change" (292). She also notes a growing emphasis on legal concepts as "a manipulable, value-laden language" (294) and ends with the hope that as detailed, quantitative studies are produced anthropologists will come to "understand more about the way in which legal institutions, rules, and ideas function as part of the framework within which ongoing social life is carried on, and how the processes of social life affect that very framework" (295). Although Moore does not stress the need for studying the constraints and incentives that channel litigant choices, the questions she raises can only be answered by looking at the broad patterns of court usage created by the cumulative choices of individual actors.

Zinacanteco Law in Perspective

Throughout this book the "facts" of Zinacanteco conflict management have been presented as if their importance were self-evident. There has been a minimum of theoretical justification. But now that all the "facts" have been presented, it is time to reexamine the contribution of each chapter to the total picture. Although this book is a descriptive study of the legal system in one Mesoamerican Indian community, it is also an argument for a particular approach to the study of "law." Each chapter of the book, therefore, needs to be reexamined to show why it presents the facts it does and to see what insights it offers into the processes that link law as a language to patterns of social action. Following the conceptual scheme of the book, this discussion is divided into three parts: institutions, language, and claims.

Institutions. Chapters 1–3 point out that the social effects of the proceedings and decisions at one legal level, and even the proceedings and decisions themselves, can only be understood when that level is examined within the context of the other options open to litigants. These three chapters provide an argument against other ethnographic studies of legal systems that have focused on one legal level, usually a fairly high court, and have assumed that the cases before that tribunal derive directly from social trouble spots and that the decisions reached there accurately reflect community-wide values. By showing that the cases reaching the town hall court

represent only a selected sample of the total range of cases, I have suggested that court decisions affect only an equally selected range of social problems; and by arguing that the town hall court is caught between the demands of Mexican law and Zinacanteco custom, I have tried to show that its decisions often reflect political expedience rather than some mystic reaffirmation of society's integrative values.

While presenting an argument against studies that treat a single court in isolation, these chapters also try to show that similarly phrased cases can be handled quite differently at different legal levels. There are two main reasons for such differences. The first is that litigants have ideas about the types of outcome to be expected from each level and seek out the level that will most nearly satisfy their wants. Cases do not emerge directly from social trouble spots. They begin as a series of events that are given descriptive labels by litigants and are finally taken to a legal procedure selected on the basis of personal desires. This means that different legal levels tend to handle similar complaints in different ways because they represent different kinds of cases. A case of wife-beating taken to the town hall by a woman intent on getting a divorce is quite a different matter from a case of wife-beating brought to a hamlet elder by a woman who merely wants her husband scolded. Second, different legal levels must work with different types of information. Legal procedures operating in small neighborhoods where everyone knows everyone else operate with a much wider range of shared knowledge and commitment than do higher-level courts where the judge or mediator may have no personal acquaintance with the litigants. In the latter case officers of the court must depend on their general knowledge of the culture to assess the highly edited information presented to them by the litigants. This means, of course, that the more removed the officers of the court are in terms of social class or cultural background from the litigants in a case, the less likely they are to understand or care about the motives and desires of the people who will be most affected by the outcome.

These ideas suggest a method for understanding the process that so often sees compromise solutions produced in the small face-to-face societies where most individuals are linked by multiplex ties. The prevalence of such conciliatory settlements is often explained

in functional terms by the need of a small society to reintegrate deviant individuals in order to survive, but it is also possible to see conciliatory settlements as the logical outcome of a process in which individuals make decisions on the basis of self-interest. There is no need to postulate an abstract "society" that struggles to maintain itself, because in a small community where individuals must continue living together most litigants will find it advantageous to seek compromise solutions and most mediators or judges, who tend to be men of political influence, will be unwilling to alienate potential supporters by endorsing one-sided outcomes. As a result, the cumulative choices of litigants and mediators interact to ensure that legal procedures operating within a restricted social field will produce conciliatory outcomes and thus continue to attract compromise-seeking litigants.

In analyzing this process, however, it is crucial to explore the nature of the social field. If a small, face-to-face society is split into endogamous factions without cross-cutting ties, there will be no need for individuals to seek conciliatory settlements when quarreling with someone from another faction. In such a situation, the most obvious legal procedures may be distant courts where litigants appeal for vengeance, not justice, and conflicts that occur between faction members will be kept hidden, along with the conciliatory mechanisms used to handle them (Nader 1965).

But most "societies" are composed of several social fields, leading to complex interaction between courts, litigants, and outcomes. Legal procedures not tied to a single restricted social field, for example, usually handle a variety of litigants and produce outcomes varying from conciliatory to impersonal. In Zinacantan, the Presidente is reported to be more willing to seek compromise solutions in cases involving litigants from his own hamlet than in cases brought by unknown people from distant parts of the township. But it is also true that people from distant hamlets who want a conciliatory settlement tend to seek out a local elder. The situation in the court of the Juez Penal may be even more striking. Although I never investigated cases involving only Ladinos, it seems reasonable to assume that the judge in San Cristobal acts like his counterpart in Oaxaca who applies the letter of the law to cases involving Indians but helps his status equals find compromise solutions for their prob-

lems (Hunt and Hunt 1969). But it is again true that most of the Indians who reach such a court have passed beyond the point of possible reconciliation, whereas the judge's status equals come to him as friends for legal advice.

In the three chapters on legal institutions, I have tried to go beyond a mere description of the procedures available to Zinacantecos and the types of litigants and claims that are handled to lay bare the processes that generate the frequency patterns observed in the field (Barth 1966). Now in concluding, I have expanded the framework to argue that the processes at work in Zinacantan are relevant to understanding the working of legal institutions everywhere. All but the most restricted social fields offer potential litigants some range of choice in managing a conflict, and it is through an analysis of the constraints and incentives channeling individual choices that the patterns of claims, procedures, and outcomes observable on each legal level are to be understood. However stable the pattern of legal-level usage may seem, its stability is only momentary, and its continued existence depends on the stability of the conditions that produced it. Any sustained pressure from the environment leading to cumulative changes in the pattern of litigant choices or in the kinds of outcomes advocated by men in authority would set off a series of adjustments because of the feedback nature of the process that distributes litigants, claims, and procedures through a set of legal levels. The claims reaching a given level reflect the constraints and incentives channeling litigant choices; the procedures reflect the pattern of claims, the desires of the litigants, and the amount of shared knowledge that exists between the officers of the court and the people who come before it; the outcomes reflect the procedures used in reaching a decision, combined with the aims and perceptions of the mediator or judge; and the pattern of outcomes affects the decisions of future litigants on where to take a case.

Chapter 1, on the structure of legal levels, presents a static picture of the various procedures used by Zinacantecos, the social fields within which they operate, and the types of claims and litigants usually handled. The object of the chapter is to introduce the various options open to litigants and to show that Zinacantan is not a closed community but is embedded within the wider framework

of the Mexican state. Zinacantan cannot be seen as an autonomous society. It is only a restricted social field, able to appear so traditional and static because of its embedded position. Zinacanteco legal procedures seldom have to handle defendants who have no respect for the dominant values of the community or who are complete strangers to both plaintiff and mediator. True deviants leave Zinacantan and strangers rarely have cause to enter it. And since most offenders are easily reintegrated into social life, the legal procedures continue to produce conciliatory outcomes.

In discussing the structure of legal levels, I started with the most restricted social field and ended with the most inclusive. My purpose was to stress the options open to individuals. By charting the ever more inclusive fields to which a person belongs, I suggested that a litigant could go to almost any level, depending on how he cared to phrase the dispute between himself and his opponent. But this arrangement of the "facts" has the drawback of obscuring the degree to which social structure channels both type of claim and choice of procedure. Litigants linked by certain ties tend to fight over a very restricted range of issues and to seek solutions from particular legal levels. An approach that defines legal levels in terms of the authority wielded by leaders (Pospisil 1958, Nader and Metzger 1963) or that examines them in the wider context of social structure (Gulliver 1963) can illuminate much more successfully the dominant pattern of legal-level usage, but it pays the price of implying an unrealistic stability. Every legal system is characterized by aspects of continuity and possibilities for change, and an ethnographic account must choose which facet to emphasize. Most studies in the past have focused on continuity and have presented relatively neat pictures of legal systems tied to stable social structures; my study presents a deliberately fragmented picture of the relation between law and society in order to focus on the processes of social and legal change.

Chapter 2, on the organization of legal levels, is the theoretical heart of the book, for it sets out the central argument that "law" as a set of concepts for describing and managing the social environment only comes to affect observable patterns of behavior through the claims advanced by litigants. The first section charts the interaction between types of claims, style of procedure, and outcomes at

each legal level by looking at the factors that influence a litigant's choice of court, the shared knowledge of the participants in a hearing, and the ideology used to justify procedures. The second section examines the forces that have been weakening the traditional boundaries of social fields—better roads, more schools, increased pressure from government officials and national institutions—and suggests that increased communication across boundaries has altered Zinacanteco patterns of court usage. The final section of the chapter examines the nature of political competition in Zinacantan to show how legal institutions are used in the struggle for power and followers (Barnes 1969). The career patterns of politicians are examined (Eidheim 1963) to illuminate the process that has led Zinacanteco outcomes to approach the tenets of Mexican law while Zinacanteco procedures of dispute settlement have remained traditional and conciliatory.

Chapter 3, on the town hall court, uses the metaphor of a stage production to explore the strategies open to litigants seeking to influence the outcome of a case. Town hall procedures are discussed in this way to emphasize the fact that the terms of specific outcomes are best understood by looking at the relative status of the litigants as well as at the facts of the case and the applicable norms. In every legal system, however authoritative and overtly impartial its courts, high-status litigants tend to fare better than social nobodies. And this observation is particularly true in Zinacantan, where there is no pretense of impartiality and decisions are reached through bargaining. But the chapter also tries to show that relative status is not predetermined but is the result of "impression management" (Goffman 1959) on the day of the hearing. Normally high-status people can be brought low by exposing their shameful misdeeds, and low-status persons can win prestige through a ready tongue and a righteous cause.

By charting the effect of status differences on legal decisions, Chapter 3 elaborated the general theme of the section on institutions: the idea that the procedures and decisions of one legal level can be understood only when that level is seen in the context of other options open to litigants. The ingredients of status manipulated by litigants at the town hall court are peculiar to that level, for hamlet procedures rest on more intimate knowledge of individ-

ual personalities, and the Mexican officials relegate almost all Indians to the same low-status category. At the same time, the decisions reached at the town hall court have to be understood in terms of the court's dual position as the highest-level procedure in Zinacantan and the lowest court of the Mexican system. Town hall decisions are not simple reflections of Zinacanteco norms; they reflect the relative status and the desires of the particular litigants in each case. Persons with a reputation for expertise in Spanish can demand, and get, outcomes based on Mexican law, and senior shamans with direct access to native gods can be quite effective in demanding outcomes based on traditional practices.

Language. Throughout the book I have defined law in Barkun's terms as a "system of manipulable symbols that functions as a representation, as a model, of social structure" (1968: 92) that is used for "conceptualizing and managing the social environment" (1968: 151). Law as a conceptual system derives from the past and—to the extent it is invoked by the living—molds the future. Legal concepts do not have a direct effect on behavior; they provide a way of talking about behavior. In ordinary experience, legal concepts appear to structure observable social regularities, because behavior falling on the fringes may be assimilated into the norm through classification, and because individuals consciously planning to act think in terms of the labels that can be applied to their behavior. But there can never be a perfect correspondence between behavioral events and legal concepts: the one cannot be directly mapped onto the other. Behavioral events may be perceived as discrete units, easily fitted with a legal label, but all labeling involves some choice among possible alternatives.

Law as a language must be conceptually separated from observed behavior if we are to study the relationship between the two. The recognition that legal categories can never correspond directly to behavioral events makes it possible to explore the processes affecting the probability that particular acts will be treated as discrete units and given particular labels (Becker 1963, Scott and Douglas 1972). And this leads to a study of litigants and their motives, for they are the first to classify the "facts" of a case (Barkun 1968, Black and Reiss 1970). Judges and mediators can base their decisions only on verbal discriptions of events that cannot be

recreated. It is the litigants, then, as the first to decide if legal action is warranted, who ultimately determine the effect of "law" upon "society"—and vice versa—through the cumulative effect of their many individual choices.

Chapters 4–7 describe Zinacanteco legal concepts: the set of assumptions about the nature of social and cosmic order used to justify claims and decisions. Assumptions about the nature of cosmic order and man's place in the universe are highly abstract. Such concepts are relatively impervious to change because they are far removed from empirical testing. Zinacanteco ideas of soul strength, for example, can be used to "explain" almost any individual fate. Only drastically improved health conditions could conceivably undermine their utility. At the other extreme are ideas about specific rights and obligations inherent in particular relationships. Such ideas are closely tied to the realities of everyday life and are consequently more subject to change as ecological and economic changes lead to altered patterns of interaction. Most Zinacanteco complaints are phrased in terms of transgressions of such low-level rules of order.

Abstract assumptions about the nature of cosmic order are primarily used to justify legal procedures, whereas low-level ideas of social order are invoked to justify the substance (content) of particular decisions. This distinction between procedure and substance is mirrored in the organization of the book. Chapters 1–5 describe the more stable aspects of Zinacanteco law—the structure of legal levels and the abstract ideology justifying conciliatory outcomes—whereas the later chapters treat the substance of claims advanced by litigants. But this two-part division has been deliberately blurred in order to stress the inherent interrelatedness of claims and procedures.

The chapter on Zinacanteco legal concepts explores the ideology behind court procedures by focusing on the Tzotzil terms that refer to crucial elements in a hearing. The research methodology was deliberately informal, because the ultimate aim was to discover the abstract assumptions about the nature of universal order underlying the whole set of terms rather than to isolate the "meanings" of particular words. But this approach also derives from the view of "meaning" used throughout the book. I have always treated words

as labels for categories within an abstract system of classification rather than as names for natural categories existing in the real world. In spite of man's efforts to chop up experience and to define the boundaries between labeled categories, words remain inherently ambiguous; they can seldom be mapped directly onto objective experience (M. Rosaldo 1972). Language remains a flexible tool that offers each person a range of alternatives as he seeks to interpret and manipulate his environment. People are not confined to a sterile world where things have only "correct" names.

The chapter on witchcraft beliefs examines Zinacanteco ideas of soul power and ways of causing illness to provide a wider framework for understanding the assumptions underlying legal procedures. Once again there is no attempt to focus on the content of specific beliefs, but all beliefs, even those that are contradictory, are examined to discover implied assumptions about the nature of cosmic order. The chapter ends with the declaration that legal concepts and witchcraft beliefs are part of the same conceptual system: both rest on a single set of ideas about the universe and man's place in it. But these ideas are far removed from the realities of everyday life. Their utility lies in the fact that there are so few constraints on their use: they can be invoked to "explain" almost any noteworthy event, depending on the perspective of the viewer and what he wishes to accomplish. At the same time, these ideas are deeply coercive. They provide the "rules of the game" that every Zinacanteco must acknowledge if he wishes to remain within Indian society.

Throughout this book the coercive nature of legal concepts has been stressed, while physical force has been relegated to the background. This emphasis respects Barkun's (1968) definition of law, which deliberately rejects the concentration on force demanded by other definitions, but it also derives from my perceptions of Zinacanteco reality. In Zinacantan, satisfactory solutions to conflicts require the active participation of the offender. He must present a bottle of rum to beg pardon and agree to pay for any damage he caused. Although the offender's willingness to participate could be attributed to a desire to avoid physical sanctions, such a view is hard to justify. The Presidente has few such sanctions at his command and many of his threats are impossible to carry out. On an-

other level, it could be argued that offenders fear physical punishment from the gods as called down by a strong-souled mediator. But again such sanctions are relatively uncertain and cannot be directly observed. It is far more practical to attribute the cooperativeness of Zinacanteco offenders to the coercive nature of legal language. Zinacanteco offenders, like the Subanun compared by Frake (1963) to American poker players, confess and pay up so that they may play the game again. Banishment, whether enforced or voluntary, is the ultimate Zinacanteco sanction, although it is seldom openly acknowledged. Litigants who wish to remain community members in good standing must abide by the rules of community life. They must be active participants in the "legal" activity of applying descriptive labels to past acts, and they must acknowledge defeat when unable to uphold an alternative definition of events. In this context, the Presidente's exaggerated threats are best seen as face-saving devices that allow an offender to admit the defeat dictated by the rules of the game.

The chapters on witchcraft cases and aggression are the first to deal with actual case materials, and they reveal the two themes that underlie all subsequent case analysis: most cases involve an underlying conflict between plaintiff and defendant, and claims, far more than outcomes, reveal generally accepted social rules. The first theme leads to treating both the commission of a wrongful act and the lodging of a complaint as actions intended to convey messages. Within the restricted social field of Zinacantan, these behavioral messages are understood and influence the outcome of a case. The second theme leads to a stress on accusations. The basic question underlying all the case analyses presented is "What accusations can a person lodge against someone who stands in a particular relationship to him?" The chapters on witchcraft and aggression treat types of accusations that can be lodged against almost anyone, whereas Chapters 8–12 examine accusations specific to particular relationships.

The chapters on witchcraft and aggression conclude the section on Zinacanteco legal concepts by interpreting acts of overt aggression as a language for communicating hostile feelings. Although most of the acts considered are universally recognized as aggressive, the exact messages conveyed vary from culture to culture. This

means that Zinacanteco cases beginning as accusations of violence or witchcraft cannot be interpreted within the static framework of crime and punishment but must be seen from the wider perspective of continuing social interaction. The researcher must ask, along with the Zinacanteco mediators, what message the aggressor intended to convey, for in many cases the aggressor has deliberately escalated the conflict in order to provoke a hearing into deeper issues. For this reason I have focused throughout the book on litigants, not simply plaintiffs. People accused of wrongdoing are not passive objects victimized by society's need to identify and sanction deviants but are active manipulators of a rich symbolic system that includes acts of aggression as well as verbal concepts.

Claims. The five chapters on claims examine the kinds of accusations that are lodged by persons standing in particular relationships to those they accuse. Although many past studies have treated recorded cases as if they reflected actual incidences of "deviant" acts in a society or as if they arose directly out of stress points in the social fabric, my analysis is intended to cast doubt on both of these simplistic assumptions. The relationship between cases reaching a legal procedure and broad patterns of social action is very complex. Many obviously "deviant" acts are never reported and some extremely tense relationships seldom give rise to acts leading to legal hearings. My route for exploring the interaction between social structure and legal cases is to inquire into the motives of litigants, to ask why one person would break a "rule" and why someone else would decide to lodge a complaint.

The chapters on types of claims are arranged to reflect the closeness of the relationship between the litigants: from kinsmen through married and engaged couples to neighbors and political opponents. This progression from highly relational to lowly relational roles (Metzger 1960) points to other types of progressions: from the complex, subjective quarrels of people bound together by extensive obligations to the relatively straightforward, objective quarrels of people with few commitments to each other; from quarrels usually handled by intimate hamlet procedures to disputes normally taken to the town hall; and from outcomes phrased in terms of future obligations to outcomes justified as rectifying past wrongs. This arrangement also reveals the fact that closely related litigants

in Zinacantan have a far smaller range of legitimate causes for complaint than do nonrelatives. Almost all fights between kinsmen are reduced to questions of property distribution, whereas neighbors may fight over a variety of issues. This means that a record of cases cannot be used to discover all the tensions existing in particular dyadic relationships. Such a record merely shows the overt issues that people can fight about in a legal context. The low frequency of a particular type of accusation often testifies less to the virtue of individuals than to a lack of incentives for plaintiffs (see Frake 1969: 166–67).

At the end of each chapter on claims there is a brief section discussing the effect of Mexican law on particular types of customary relationships and cases. The overall impression conveyed by these sections is that Zinacantan has not changed much. Even an optimistic Mexican observer would have to admit that Zinacantan remains an ethnic enclave, that Zinacanteco customary law still "governs" most areas of life. Although the tenets of Mexican law are increasingly cited by Zinacanteco mediators and litigants while arguing cases, outcomes reflect bargains between the litigants rather than judge-imposed solutions based on an abstract legal code. As long as Zinacanteco outcomes are reached by bargaining, they may resemble, but never mirror, Mexican outcomes based on the application of rules to a set of facts.

Mexican efforts to engineer social change in Zinacantan have not gone entirely unrewarded, however. Road- and school-building programs have led to an increase in the number of bilingual men able to deal effectively with the wider society, and the government agencies designed to help Indians—INI and the State Department of Indian Affairs—have facilitated Indian contact with the basically hostile Ladino world. This dual attack on the problem of Indian isolation has produced some of the desired results: more Indians are willing to appeal to outside agencies for aid, and knowledge of Mexican customs and laws is more widespread within Zinacantan. For Zinacanteco law, this decreased isolation has meant that the Presidente and hamlet mediators have lost the power to impose sanctions on people who refuse to honor customary obligations not recognized by Mexican law: men who refuse to pay fiesta taxes or to accept imposed religious offices can no

longer be jailed; it has become a risky business to extract witch-craft confessions by torture; and a boy who elopes with an engaged girl cannot be given a long jail sentence to remove his *manya*. At the same time, persons seeking to claim rights granted by Mexican law—women wishing to claim inherited land or to choose their own husbands, and debtors trying to avoid payment of high interest rates—are more likely to have their arguments prevail.

Although decreased isolation has undermined the Presidente's power in cases where the two legal systems conflict, it has actually increased his power to impose traditional solutions in situations where Mexican law and Zinacanteco custom coincide in condemn-ing a particular behavior. The Presidente and hamlet mediators are now in a stronger position to extract confessions and promises of restitution from offenders who have cause to fear harsh punishment from the penal authorities.

But none of these changes is very dramatic. Most native prac-tices disliked by Mexican officials survive: some may have become less obvious, but others have actually been elaborated. Talking saints abound but are honored by less ostentatious rituals; many accused witches confess and perform retraction ceremonies; women rarely receive inheritances equal to their brothers; mar-riages have not become noticeably more stable; bride-prices are becoming increasingly expensive; interest rates on loans are still high; and the fiestas sponsored by religious officials seem more elaborate each year.

Why has Zinacantan remained so "traditional" in spite of govern-ment programs designed to break down ethnic boundaries? Why, in fact, has Zinacanteco ethnic behavior become increasingly elab-orate? Although adequate answers to these questions lie beyond the scope of this book, their outlines must be sketched to dispel the notion that Indians are inherently unimaginative and conservative, prisoners of an ancient and superstitious tradition.

Zinacantan remains an ethnic enclave, because it is located with-in a peripheral region of the Mexican state where the unequal rela-tionship between superordinate Ladinos and subordinate Indians is deeply entrenched and provides benefits for both groups (Aguirre Beltran 1967, G. Collier n.d.). Indians accept their in-ferior position in order to maintain control of the marginal lands

that are the focus of their social and religious organization. Local Ladino elites have a vested interest in promoting Indian ethnicity, for they rely on the exploitation of cheap Indian labor to maintain a standard of living appropriate to participation in the mainstream of national political life. In this situation, central-government programs aimed at breaking down ethnic barriers have necessarily come into conflict with the desires of the regional elite. Although national programs have succeeded in reducing the economic and cultural isolation of Indian communities, the intended homogenization of peoples has not occurred. Regional elites have maintained their economic domination through political control. They have consistently denied Indians access to local offices. As a result, Indians seeking to convert wealth and knowledge of the outside world into social prestige and political power have put their expanded resources into playing the old game of collecting Indian followers (see Chapter 2). But it would be wrong to imagine that Indians have been the passive victims of a Ladino conspiracy, for, over time, the "old game" has become far more profitable. Indian political leaders now compete with Ladino leaders for favors handed out by the central government. Efforts to promote national integration have paradoxically favored the development of ethnic-bloc politics (Geertz 1963).

Zinacanteco law will survive as a system apart from Mexican law only so long as Indians continue to use native ideas of cosmic order to justify procedures and outcomes. This book has described the Zinacanteco conception of the universe as if it had a reality of its own. But Berger and Luckmann (1966) remind us that conceptions of cosmic order are subject to change. They continue to exist only so long as there are concrete, living persons to reiterate their basic premises. Following Marx, Berger and Luckmann argue that "the success of particular conceptual machineries is related to the power possessed by those who operate them" (1966: 100). When those in power change, conceptual universes may change too. "Put a little crudely, it is essential to keep pushing questions about the historically available conceptualizations of reality from the abstract 'What?' to the sociologically concrete 'Says who?'" (Berger and Luckmann 1966: 107).

Most of this book has been devoted to describing the abstract "What?" of the Zinacanteco conceptual universe, but this concluding section is added to answer the question "Says who?" Zinacanteco ideas of cosmic order survive in the modern world because the present structure of the regional political system encourages ambitious Indians to convert wealth and expertise in handling Mexican officials into collecting Indian followers. And, having made such an investment, Indian leaders are committed to upholding the conceptual framework that legitimizes their authority. Zinacanteco law continues to flourish in a modern industrial state because able, articulate, and powerful advocates continually reiterate the ideas of social and cosmic order that guarantee its existence.

Case Types Handled at the Town Hall

The following responses were elicited from an informant in answer to the question "What kinds of cases does the Presidente settle?" It is the most complete of the several such lists collected and is included here for the benefit of those interested in native categories or Maya languages. Rough English translations are given for each response.

K°usi ti k°opal tasmel¢an li preserente?
What kinds of cases does the Presidente settle?

1. Tasmel¢an hmahbail.
   He settles (cases of) those who hit each other.
2. Tasmel¢an hmilbail.
   He settles (cases of) those who kill each other.
3. Tasmel¢anbe smul h?elek°.
   He settles crimes of thieves:
   h?elek° an¢ (thief who steals a woman, who elopes with her)
   h?elek° te? (thief who steals wood or cuts down another's trees)
   h?elek° k°a (horse thief)
   h?elek° čumte? (chayote thief)
   h?elek° vakaš (cattle thief)
   h?elek° tak°in (money thief)
   h?elek° turasnu (peach thief)
   h?elek° ?išim (corn thief)

(*At this point I asked the informant to stop listing kinds of thefts and go on to other types of crimes.*)

4. Tasmel¢anbe smul h¢ak?an¢.
   He settles the crime of a rapist.
5. Tasmel¢anbe smul h?ak°čamel.
   He settles the crime of a witch who independently sends sickness.

6. Tasmel¢anbe smul hčonvaneh ta balamil.
   He settles the crime of a witch who sells (souls) to the Earth.
7. Tasmel¢anbe smul h¢obvinik.
   He settles the crime of a woman who lies with many men.
8. Tasmel¢anbe smul yahval rioš.
   He settles the crime of a talking-saint owner.
9. Tasmel¢anbe smul hpoh'osil.
   He settles the crime of someone who takes another's land.
10. Tasmel¢anbe smul hyakubeltik.
    He settles the crimes of drunks.
11. Tasmel¢anbe sk*oplal hmilel.
    He settles what should be done about a murdered man's body.
12. Tasmel¢anbe sk*oplal hsa' k*opetik.
    He settles the problems of those who fight, who bring cases to court.
13. Tasmel¢anbe sk*oplal yil ka'.
    He settles quarrels over damage caused by a horse, the "debt" of a horse.
14. Tasmel¢anbe sk*oplal hvok*vaneh ta na.
    He settles quarrels caused by those who break into another's house.
15. Tasmel¢anbe sk*oplal hmahvaneh ta be.
    He settles quarrels that arise when one person hits another on a public path.
16. Tasmel¢anbe sk*oplal h¢ob'ol.
    He settles quarrels caused by a woman with many illegitimate children.
17. Tasmel¢anbe sk*oplal 'osil.
    He settles quarrels over land.
18. Tasmel¢anbe sk*oplal te'etik.
    He settles quarrels over wooded lands.
19. Tasmel¢anbe sk*oplal č*ivit.
    He plans the arrangement of the market for fiestas.
20. Tasmel¢anbe sk*oplal hčik*bail ta sibak.
    He settles what should be done when someone is burned by fireworks.

This list divides naturally into three parts: the first two responses with the form *tasmel¢an h——bail* (the initial *h-* transforms a verb into an agentive noun), responses 3 through 10 with the form *tasmel¢anbe smul h——* (except response 8), and responses 11 through 20 with the form *tasmel¢anbe sk*oplal ——*. The first two responses deal with the "crimes" that top every informant's list: *-mah*, to hit; and *-mil*, to kill. This particular informant used the reflexive form of the verb stem; other informants have begun their lists with the response "*tasmel¢anbe smul hmahvaneh / hmilvaneh*," "he settles the crime of someone who hits another / a murderer." Responses 3 through 10 deal with crimes commit-

ted by individuals. Several of the sentences end with an agentive noun in the form *h+verb stem+ object*. The last ten responses all contain the word *sk*oplal*, implying that the Presidente's job in these situations is to suggest a plan of action satisfactory to all rather than to help an offender "end his crime."

Although lists such as this are invaluable as research tools, their place in a finished report depends on the aims of the ethnographer. I did not use them as the basis for categorizing the "crimes" discussed in Chapter 7 because I wanted to analyze a body of cases and not a system of native categories. Although anyone who hits another person may be called a "*hmahvaneh*," the settlement of any particular instance of "hitting" depends on who hit whom where and whether either was drunk at the time. It is also true that lists such as this are heavily biased toward the sensational crimes. Murder, theft, rape, and witchcraft catch the imagination but do not occur very frequently.

Bibliography

Aguirre Beltran, Gonzalo. 1967. Regiones de refugio: El desarrollo de la comunidad y el proceso dominical en Mestizo América. Mexico, Instituto Indigenista Interamericano, Ediciones Especiales, 46.

Bailey, Frederick G. 1969. Stratagems and spoils: A social anthropology of politics. Oxford, Blackwell. 2d impression, 1970.

Barkun, Michael. 1968. Law without sanctions: Order in primitive societies and the world community. New Haven, Yale University Press.

Barnes, J. A. 1969. The politics of law. In Mary Douglas and Phyllis Karberry, eds., Man in Africa. London, Tavistock.

Barth, Fredrik. 1959. Political leadership among Swat Pathans. London, Athlone Press.

——— 1966. Models of social organization. Royal Anthropological Institute, Occasional Papers 23.

——— 1967. On the study of social change. American Anthropologist 69: 661–69.

Beals, Alan R., and Bernard J. Siegel. 1966. Divisiveness and social conflict: An anthropological approach. Stanford, Stanford University Press.

Beals, Alan R., with George Spindler and Louise Spindler. 1967. Culture in process. New York, Holt, Rinehart & Winston.

Becker, Howard S. 1963. Outsiders: Studies in the sociology of deviance. New York, Free Press of Glencoe.

Berger, Peter L., and Thomas Luckmann. 1966. The social construction of reality: A treatise in the sociology of knowledge. Garden City, N.Y., Doubleday.

Black, Donald J., and Albert J. Reiss, Jr. 1970. Police control of juveniles. American Sociological Review 35: 63–77.

Black, Mary, and Duane Metzger. 1965. Ethnographic description and the study of law. American Anthropologist 67 (6), pt. 2: 141–65.

Bohannan, Paul J. 1957. Justice and judgment among the Tiv. London, Oxford University Press, for the International African Institute.

―――― 1965. The differing realms of the law. *American Anthropologist* 67 (6), pt. 2: 33–42.

Bricker, Victoria R. 1968. The meaning of laughter in Zinacantan: An analysis of the humor of a highland Maya community. Unpublished Ph.D. dissertation in anthropology, Harvard University.

Calnek, Edward E. 1962. Highland Chiapas before the Spanish Conquest. Unpublished Ph.D. dissertation in anthropology, University of Chicago.

Cancian, Frank. 1965. Economics and prestige in a Maya community: The religious cargo system in Zinacantan. Stanford, Stanford University Press.

Códigos Penal y de Procedimientos Penales para el Estado L. y S. de Chiapas. 1968. Editorial Jose M. Cajica, Jr., S. A. Puebla, Mexico.

Cohn, Bernard S. 1959. Some notes on law and change in North India. *Economic Development and Cultural Change* 8: 79–93.

Colby, Benjamin N. 1966. Ethnic relations in the Chiapas Highlands of Mexico. Santa Fe, Museum of New Mexico Press.

Collier, George A. 1968. Land inheritance and land use in a modern Maya community. Unpublished Ph.D. dissertation in social relations, Harvard University.

―――― n.d. Man and land in highland Chiapas: The ecological bases of Tzotzil tradition. Unpublished ms., revised January 1973.

Collier, George A., and Victoria R. Bricker. 1970. Nicknames and social structure in Zinacantan. *American Anthropologist* 72 (2): 289–302.

Collier, Jane F. 1967. The economics of divorce and remarriage in Zinacantan. Presented at the American Anthropological Association Annual Meetings, November 1967 (unpublished).

―――― 1968*a*. Courtship and marriage in Zinacantan, Chiapas, Mexico. Middle American Research Institute Publication 25: 139–201.

―――― 1968*b*. The selection of legal procedure in Zinacantan. Presented at the American Anthropological Association Annual Meetings, November 1968 (unpublished).

Colson, Elizabeth. 1962. The Plateau Tonga of Northern Rhodesia. Manchester, Manchester University Press.

Douglas, Mary. 1966. Purity and danger: An analysis of concepts of pollution and taboo. New York, Praeger.

Durkheim, Emile. 1933. On the division of labor in society. New York, Macmillan. 2d ed., 1960.

Eidheim, Harald. 1963. Entrepreneurship in politics. *In* Fredrik Barth, ed., The role of the entrepreneur in social change in northern Norway. Bergen, Universiteloforlaget.

Edel, Matthew D. 1962. Zinacantan's ejido: The effects of Mexican land reform on an Indian community in Chiapas. Unpublished manuscript, Harvard Chiapas Project.

Epstein, A. L. 1954. Juridical techniques and the judicial process: A study in African customary law. The Rhodes-Livingstone Papers, no. 23. Manchester, Manchester University Press.

Fabrega, Horacio, Jr. 1970. On the specificity of folk illnesses. *Southwestern Journal of Anthropology* 26 (3): 305–14.

Fallers, Lloyd A. 1969. Law without precedent: Legal ideas in action in the courts of colonial Busoga. Chicago, University of Chicago Press.

Firth, Raymond. 1954. Social organization and social change. *Journal of the Royal Anthropological Institute* 84: 1–20.

———— 1956. Elements of social organization. London, Watts & Company. Original edition 1951.

Frake, Charles O. 1963. Litigation in Lipay: A study of Subanun law. Bangkok, Proceedings of the Ninth Pacific Science Congress, Vol. 3.

———— 1969. Struck by speech: The Yakan concept of litigation. *In* Laura Nader, ed., Law in culture and society. Chicago, Aldine.

Geertz, Clifford. 1963. The integrative revolution: Primordial sentiments and civil politics in the new states. *In* Clifford Geertz, ed., Old societies and new states. New York, Free Press of Glencoe, pp. 105–57.

Gibbs, James L., Jr. 1963. The Kpelle moot: A therapeutic model for the informal settlement of disputes. *Africa* 33: 1–11.

Gluckman, Max. 1950. Kinship and marriage among the Lozi of Northern Rhodesia and the Zulu of Natal. *In* A. R. Radcliffe-Brown and Daryll Forde, eds., African systems of kinship and marriage. London, Oxford University Press, for the International African Institute.

———— 1955*a*. The judicial process among the Barotse of Northern Rhodesia. Manchester, Manchester University Press, for the Rhodes-Livingstone Institute.

———— 1955*b*. Custom and conflict in Africa. Oxford, Blackwell.

———— 1962. African jurisprudence. *The Advancement of Science* 18 (75): 439–54.

———— 1965. Politics, law and ritual in tribal society. Chicago, Aldine.

Goffman, Erving. 1959. The presentation of self in everyday life. New York, Doubleday Anchor. First published in 1956 by Social Sciences Research Centre, University of Edinburgh.

———— 1967. Interaction ritual: Essays in face-to-face behavior. Chicago, Aldine.

Greenhouse, Carol J. 1971. Litigant choice: Non-secular and secular sanctions in Zinacanteco conflict resolution. B.A. honors thesis, Radcliffe College.

Guiteras Holmes, Calixta. 1961. Perils of the soul: The world view of a Tzotzil Indian. New York, Free Press of Glencoe.

Gulliver, Philip H. 1963. Social control in an African society: A study of the Arusha, agricultural Masai of Northern Tanganyika. Boston, Boston University Press.

———— 1969. Dispute settlement without courts: The Ndendeuli of

southern Tanzania. *In* Laura Nader, ed., Law in culture and society. Chicago, Aldine.

Hazard, John N. 1962. Furniture arrangement as a symbol of judicial roles. *Etcetera* 19 (2): 181–88.

Hermitte, Esther M. 1964. Supernatural power and social control in a modern Maya village. Unpublished Ph.D. dissertation in anthropology, University of Chicago.

Hoebel, E. Adamson. 1954. The law of primitive man: A study in comparative legal dynamics. Cambridge, Mass., Harvard University Press.

Holland, William. 1963. Medicina Maya en los altos de Chiapas. Mexico, D.F., Instituto Nacional Indigenista.

Hunt, Eva, and Robert Hunt. 1969. The role of courts in rural Mexico. *In* Phillip Bock, ed., Peasants in the modern world. Albuquerque, University of New Mexico Press.

Laughlin, Robert M. n.d. Tzotzil dictionary. Harvard Chiapas Project.

Leach, Edmund R. 1959. Social change and primitive law. *American Anthropologist* 61: 1096–97.

——— 1964. Political systems of highland Burma: A study of Kachin social structure. London, G. Bell & Sons (with a new Introductory Note). Original edition 1954: London School of Economics and Political Science.

Llewellyn, Karl, and E. Adamson Hoebel. 1941. The Cheyenne way. Norman, University of Oklahoma Press.

Malinowski, Bronislaw. 1926. Crime and custom in savage society. London, Kegan Paul, Trench & Trubner.

Mead, Margaret. 1961. Some anthropological considerations concerning natural law. *Natural Law Forum* 6: 51–64.

Merryman, John H. 1969. The civil law tradition. An introduction to the legal systems of Western Europe and Latin America. Stanford, Stanford University Press.

Metzger, Duane. 1960. Conflict in Chulsanto: A village in Chiapas. *Alpha Kappa Deltan* 30: 35–48.

Middleton, John, and David Tait, eds. 1958. Tribes without rulers: Studies in African segmentary systems. London, Routledge & Kegan Paul.

Moore, Sally Falk. 1970. Law and anthropology. *In* Bernard J. Siegel, ed., Biennial Review of Anthropology, 1969. Stanford, Stanford University Press.

Nader, Laura. 1965. Choices in legal procedure: Shia Moslem and Mexican Zapotec. *American Anthropologist* 67: 394–99.

——— 1966. To make the balance. Film on Zapotec courtroom procedures. Extension Media Center, University of California, Berkeley.

Nader, Laura, ed. 1969. Law in culture and society. Chicago, Aldine.

Nader, Laura, and Duane Metzger. 1963. Conflict resolution in two Mexican communities. *American Anthropologist* 65: 584–92.

Nash, June. 1967. Death as a way of life: The increasing resort to homicide in a Maya Indian community. *American Anthropologist* 69 (5): 455–70.

———— 1970. In the eyes of the ancestors: Belief and behavior in a Mayan community. New Haven, Yale University Press.

Pitt-Rivers, Julian. 1967. Words and deeds: The Ladinos of Chiapas. *Man* 2 (1): 71–86.

Pospisil, Leopold. 1958. Kapauku Papuans and their law. Yale University Publications in Anthropology 54.

———— 1971. Anthropology of law: A comparative theory. New York, Harper & Row.

Prokosch, Eric. 1964. Court procedure in the settlement of disputes in Chamula. Unpublished manuscript.

Radcliffe-Brown, A. R. 1933. Primitive law. *In* Encyclopedia of the social sciences 9: 202–6.

Robles Ramirez, Angel. 1968. La aplicación de la ley penal al indígena. Tesis. Escuela de derecho de Chiapas. San Cristobal Las Casas, Chiapas.

Rosaldo, Michelle Z. 1972. Metaphors and folk classification. *Southwestern Journal of Anthropology* 28: 83–99.

Rosaldo, Renato. 1968. Metaphors of hierarchy in a Mayan ritual. *American Anthropologist* 70: 524–36.

Sandoval, Lisandro. 1942. Semántica guatemalense o diccionario de guatemaltequismos. Guatemala, Tipografia Nacional.

Scheffler, Harold W. 1964. The genesis and repression of conflict: Choiseul Island. *American Anthropologist* 66: 789–804.

Schneider, David M. 1953. A note on bridewealth and the stability of marriage. *Man* (53): 55–57.

Scott, Robert A., and Jack D. Douglas, eds. 1972. Introduction. *In* Theoretical perspectives on deviance. New York, Basic Books.

Smith, Watson, and John M. Roberts. 1954. Zuni Law: A field of values. Papers of the Peabody Museum of American Archaeology and Ethnology, Harvard University, vol. 43, no. 1.

Swartz, Marc J., Victor W. Turner, and Arthur Tuden. 1966. Political anthropology. Chicago, Aldine.

Tanner, Nancy. 1970. Disputing and the genesis of legal principles: Examples from Minangkabau. *Southwestern Journal of Anthropology* 26: 375–401.

Tozzer, Alfred M. 1941. Landa's relación de las cosas de Yucatan. Papers of the Peabody Museum of American Archaeology and Ethnology, Harvard University, 18.

Turner, Victor W. 1957. Schism and continuity in an African society: A study of Ndembu village life. Manchester, Manchester University Press.

Vance, John T., and Helen L. Clagett. 1945. A guide to the law and legal literature of Mexico. Washington, D.C., Library of Congress.

Van Velsen, J. 1969. Procedural informality, reconciliation, and false comparisons. *In* M. Gluckman, ed., Ideas and procedures in African customary law. London, Oxford University Press.

Villa Rojas, Alfonso. 1947. Kinship and nagualism in a Tzeltal community, Southeastern Mexico. *American Anthropologist* 49: 578–87.

Vogt, Evon Z. 1965. Zinacanteco "souls." *Man* 29: 33–35.

———— 1969. Zinacantan: A Maya community in the highlands of Chiapas. Cambridge, Mass., Harvard University Press.

Wolf, Eric. 1955. Types of Latin American peasantry: A preliminary discussion. *American Anthropologist* 57: 452–71.

Young, Stephen B. 1965. Their people's servants: Political officials in a highland Maya community. Unpublished manuscript, Harvard Chiapas Project.

Index

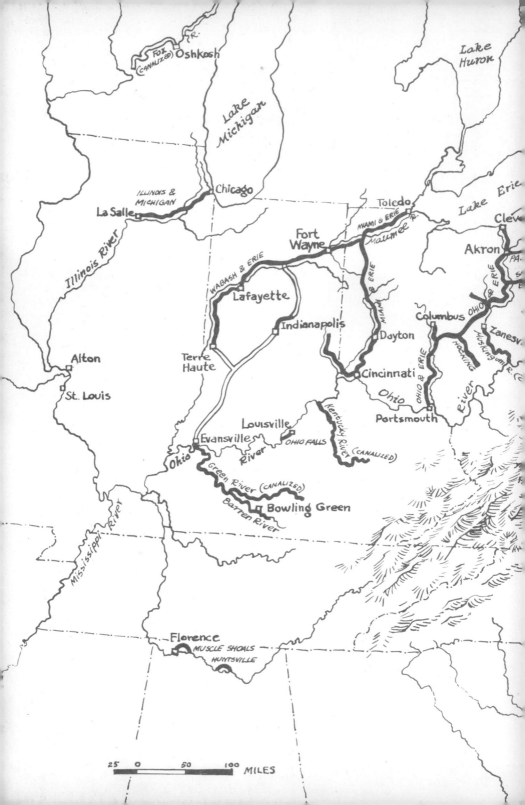